Advances in Psychological Assessment

Volume 3

Paul McReynolds

Editor

ADVANCES IN PSYCHOLOGICAL ASSESSMENT

Volume 3

Jossey-Bass Publishers

San Francisco · Washington · London · 1975

ADVANCES IN PSYCHOLOGICAL ASSESSMENT, VOLUME 3
Paul McReynolds, Editor

Copyright © 1975 by: Jossey-Bass, Inc., Publishers
615 Montgomery Street
San Francisco, California 94111
&
Jossey-Bass Limited
3 Henrietta Street
London WC2E 8LU

Library of Congress Catalogue Card Number LC 73-21077

International Standard Book Number ISBN 0-87589-242-6

Manufactured in the United States of America

JACKET DESIGN BY WILLI BAUM

FIRST EDITION

Code 7433

The Jossey-Bass
Behavioral Science Series

Preface

The field of psychological assessment is one of the most important and active areas in contemporary psychology. In addition it cuts across and impinges upon other important areas including personology, clinical and counseling psychology, developmental psychology, and educational psychology. It is fitting, therefore, to have a periodic examination of significant developments, procedures, and issues in a more detailed and critical fashion than is possible in textbooks. To provide this examination is the primary function of the present series, which is devoted to the description and evaluation of major techniques and trends in the field.

More specifically the series is intended to present information of three general types: chapters which describe and evaluate new tests, techniques, and innovative directions; chapters which review the literature and bring the reader up to date on standard, widely used assessment techniques; and chapters of a more diverse nature which provide helpful background material to assessment psychologists—this category includes chapters on philosophical and methodological bases, on historical background, and on relevant topics from related fields.

Advances in Psychological Assessment, Volume 3, includes chapters from all three of these categories. Thus, a number of the chapters describe new developments in assessment technology, including the application of both psychological tests, in the usual meaning of the term, and behavioral observation techniques. Several other chapters focus on conventional assessment devices, presenting evaluative reviews of recent advances in their use. Finally, two chapters provide relevant background—one from a physiological and the other from a historical perspective—for assessment psychology.

In editing this series I have been cognizant of the fact that psychological assessment, both in its theoretical bases and as currently practiced, involves more than merely the administration and interpretation of individual psychological tests. Properly conceived, the field of assessment encompasses the development and utilization of the full range of techniques—tests, interviews, experimental manipulations, and naturalistic observations—for gathering systematic information about persons, groups, and human institutions. I have attempted to keep this generalization in mind in developing *Advances in Psychological Assessment, Volume 3,* and I believe this orientation is evident in the diversity and scope of the topics included.

Each of the chapters in this book indicates an important direction in contemporary psychological assessment. Taken in their entirety, they reflect the vigor and innovative quality of the field. All the chapters are original and were solicited by me and prepared especially for this volume.

For the high quality of the book I am indebted to the contributing authors. I am additionally indebted to them for their enthusiasm and support throughout the course of this project. A number of persons, too many to list here, have been helpful in suggesting topics for inclusion in this series. Jacqueline Hutchins and Joann Hambacher were invaluable in coordinating the preparation of the manuscript.

Reno, Nevada   PAUL McREYNOLDS
September 1974

Contents

Contributors

RICHARD Q. BELL, *Department of Psychology, University of Virginia*

GISELA CHATELANAT, *Geneva, Switzerland*

CHARLES R. DICKSON, *Division of Mental Hygiene and Mental Retardation, State of Nevada*

JOHN W. FILLER, JR., *Arizona Training Program, Tucson*

H. CARL HAYWOOD, *Department of Psychology, George Peabody College for Teachers*

WAYNE H. HOLTZMAN, *Hogg Foundation for Mental Health, Department of Psychology and College of Education, University of Texas*

A. JACK JERNIGAN, *Psychology Service, Veterans Administration Hospital, Dallas*

RICHARD R. JONES, *Oregon Research Institute, Eugene*

BERT S. KOPELL, *Department of Psychiatry, School of Medicine, Stanford University, and Veterans Administration Hospital, Palo Alto, California*

PAUL McREYNOLDS, *Department of Psychology, University of Nevada*

SHARON MASTERSON, *Department of Psychology, Queens College, Charlotte, North Carolina*

JAMES K. MIKAWA, *Psychological Service Center, University of Nevada*

RUDOLF H. MOOS, *Social Ecology Laboratory, Department of Psychiatry, Stanford University, and Veterans Administration Hospital, Palo Alto, California*

GERALD R. PATTERSON, *Oregon Research Institute, Eugene, and Department of Education, University of Oregon*

JOHN B. REID, *Oregon Research Institute, Eugene*

RALPH M. REITAN, *Departments of Neurological Surgery and Psychology, University of Washington*

MARGARET J. ROSENBLOOM, *Department of Psychiatry, School of Medicine, Stanford University, and Veterans Administration Hospital, Palo Alto, California*

MARK A. SHIFMAN, *Department of Psychology, George Peabody College for Teachers*

RAYMOND K. YANG, *Child Research Branch, National Institute of Mental Health*

Advances in Psychological Assessment

Volume 3

For that we cannot enter into a mans heart, and view the passions or inclinations which there reside and lie hidden; therefore, as Philosophers by effects find out causes, by proprieties essences, by riuers fountaines, by boughes and floures the kore and rootes; euen so we must trace out passions and inclinations by some effects and externall operations. And these be no more than two, words and deeds, speech and action: of which two knowledge may be gathered of those affections we carie in our mindes.

Thomas Wright (1604)

Introduction

PAUL MCREYNOLDS

Contemporary psychological assessment is characterized by two seemingly opposite orientations: on the one hand there is a continued dependence, to an almost amazing degree, on evaluation devices, such as the Stanford-Binet, the Rorschach, the Strong, the TAT, and the MMPI, that were developed, at least in their original forms, several decades ago; and on the other hand there is an innovativeness, an openness to new departures, that is equaled in few if any other fields of psychology.

The explanation for this peculiar combination of conservatism and daring seems, in fact, simple enough. Assessment psychologists are conservative in the sense that professional practitioners, faced with the necessity of making real decisions about real people, are always conservative. They have an understandable tendency to depend on what they consider to be the tried and true, to count on techniques they are familiar with, and to be somewhat wary of banking too strongly on new approaches until these have been thoroughly tested. At the same time, assessment psychologists tend on the whole, I think, to be venturesome people, and—much more important—they are well aware of the striking limitations in the standard tests and techniques they conventionally employ and tend to be critical of them, sometimes harshly so. Consequently, they are characteristically, even eagerly, receptive to innovative ideas in assessment and to the appearance of new instruments, and they have supported the strong and continuing drive toward the development of new and improved assessment techniques.

Those who step back and look at the whole field of assessment, trying to see the forest rather than merely the trees, will be impressed, I believe, by the overall salutary effects of these two orientations—the conservative and the innovative. Further, they will become cognizant of certain broad currents that characterize the contemporary field of assessment and which reflect both advances in technology and changes in the needs of the modern society which assessment psychology serves. These broad movements, like all historical trends, are easier to identify in retrospect than they are in the present, but my examination of the current status of the field reveals three trends that appear to be particularly prominent. While I am aware that the following listing is neither definitive nor comprehensive, I do feel that the trends suggested are highly significant.

First, there is an increasing tendency to extend the coverage of assessment so that it includes not only individual persons, but also couples, families, and small groups. In accord with this trend toward broad applications, assessment procedures are also being used increasingly in the evaluation of organizations and agencies, such as hospital wards, classrooms, schools, factories, prisons, and even whole communities. These extensions of traditional assessment are not altogether new, but they seem each year to gain new strength. The impetus for them comes primarily from advances in clinical psychological and in sociological theory, which places great emphasis upon the roles of large social units in the determination and maintenance of given behaviors.

Second, there is a growing movement to provide for the assessment not only of persons, but also of the social and physical environments in which persons live and carry out the behaviors in which we are interested. Assessment of the social environment overlaps the trend toward group assessment in the sense that whether a given group is considered the object of assessment or part of the environment is solely a matter of perspective: a psychologist can evaluate a family either as an object of study in its own right or as a part of the significant environment of a child. Assessment of physical environments includes the evaluation of living spaces, working areas, and other physical settings as these affect people. This concern with environmental assessment reflects a mutual and overlapping interest among those who consider themselves assessment psychologists and those who identify themselves as environmental psychologists.

A third important contemporary trend in the field of assessment is an increasing emphasis upon naturalistic evaluation—upon the systematic observation of behaviors in the situations in which these behaviors characteristically occur. This approach to assessment can be contrasted with the more typical approach, in which the assessor makes inferences from the assessment situation as to how the subject is likely to behave in real-life situations.

In addition to these three rather broad trends, there are a number of specific areas in which important advances in assessment technology are currently being made. These include neuropsychological assessment, psychological evaluations of mentally retarded persons, assessment of infants, utilization of computers in assessment, and use of psychophysiological procedures in personality studies. Many of these areas are not within the range of applicability or competence of the typical, practicing assessment psychologist. They are, however, important areas of specialization and, as such, are significant subdivisions which all assessment practitioners should be informed about.

The present volume covers all three major trends referred to above, as well as several of the specific areas of progress. The twelve chapters each deal with a different topic, and each can be read as an up-to-date and authoritative contribution in the area it covers. I have, however, ordered the chapters in a sequence which seems to me to heighten their meaningfulness, with topics of a somewhat similar nature grouped together; consequently, those who wish to read straight through the book will, I trust, find the overall sequence helpful.

The first two chapters concern important new methods for assessing the relevant social climates in which important behaviors occur. The first, by Rudolph Moos, provides a general introduction to the assessment of social climates and then discusses in detail the Family Environment Scale (FES), which Moos has developed.

Moos has been one of the leaders in the relatively new field of environmental psychology, particularly with respect to the problem of dimensionalizing the social environment, and his authoritative chapter is an excellent statement of recent developments in this area.

The second chapter, by Richard Jones, John Reid, and Gerald Patterson, is a major contribution in the area of naturalistic assessment. For some years Patterson and his colleagues have been carrying on pioneering work in developing a reliable, systematic, and valid technique for observing and coding on-going behaviors in the natural—typically the family—environment. The material in this chapter makes it clear how immense their success has been. In addition to a discussion of their Behavioral Coding System (BCS), this chapter includes an examination of the methodological bases of naturalistic assessment.

The third chapter, by Carl Haywood, John Filler, Mark Shifman, and Gisela Chatelanat, is concerned with the assessment of mental retardation. Like the previous chapter, it includes, in its discussion of functional analysis, certain material based on an essentially behavioral orientation. However, it also espouses a cognitive orientation, and its integration of these two orientations is one of its strong points. The chapter includes an exciting review of important work going on in Europe and Israel, as well as of the trail-blazing work in Haywood's own laboratory; readers who may assume that there is nothing new in the theory and practice of the assessment of mental retardation will be surprised, as well as impressed.

The next chapter, by Raymond Yang and Richard Bell, is on the assessment of infants. Like the topic of Chapter Three, this is one of the oldest and most important areas in the entire field of assessment. Yang and Bell provide both an excellent historical survey of the area, focusing on the work of Arnold Gesell, Nancy Bayley, Psyche Cattell, and others, and a critical review of the current status of the field, including a discussion of recent trends, such as the increased emphasis on a cognitive development perspective in infant assessment. This outstanding chapter is scholarly and comprehensive, and covers a field for which no recent review is elsewhere available.

The next three chapters focus on particular test techniques, though they are otherwise quite diverse. The first of these, by Ralph Reitan, is on the assessment of brain injuries in both adults and children. This topic, like those of the two chapters which precede it, is an old one in assessment. In this case, however, only in recent years has the technology—primarily the test batteries inaugurated by Ward Halstead and developed by Reitan—reached a sufficient level for the assessment procedures to be highly valid, provided that the testing is carried out with proper care, cautions, and wisdom. This is one of the great success stories of modern clinical psychology and is due mostly to the skillful work of Reitan, who has earned an international reputation in this area.

Chapter Six, by Wayne Holtzman, summarizes the Holtzman Inkblot Technique (HIT) and discusses recent developments in the use of this instrument. The HIT is one of the most outstanding personality tests devised in the last several decades, and it is beginning to take its place as a standard instrument in many assessment batteries. It comes as close as any test we have to providing the ideal combination of the free structure of projective tests and the objectivity of structured instruments. Both psychologists already familiar with the HIT and those meeting it here for the first time will find this chapter extremely useful.

The next chapter, by Sharon Masterson, is a survey and critical review of adjective checklists. It will be exceedingly helpful to both research workers and clinicians. The adjective checklist method, though it has not usually been accorded the prestige of many standard personality tests, has in fact become one of the most widely used ways of assessing personality structure. Until now, however, there has been no overall review of this crucial area. Masterson's balanced and informative chapter effectively fills this gap in the literature.

Jack Jernigan's interesting contribution describes and explains the important and growing trend toward the use of group testing procedures in evaluating mentally disturbed patients. It had long been assumed that persons sufficiently disturbed to require psychiatric hospitalization could not take tests in a valid way in group settings, but Jernigan and his colleagues have demonstrated that this is not the case, provided appropriate care and cautions are exercised. This chapter, the first review about which I am aware on the use of group tests in clinical practice, will be important to psychologists working in hospital settings.

The next two chapters, by Charles Dickson and James Mikawa, examine and review the role of assessment in psychological intervention. The types of intervention considered in the two chapters are, however, quite different. Dickson's comprehensive chapter is a broad survey and critical examination of the techniques of assessment that have been developed in the behavior-modification movement. His excellent and balanced review indicates that these techniques are considerably more numerous than the rather skeptical attitude of many behaviorists toward assessment might have led one to expect. As Dickson makes clear, however, the techniques are based on quite different methodological assumptions than are the more classic trait-oriented tests.

Mikawa's interesting chapter surveys one of the newest, most complex, and currently most important areas of psychological assessment—the evaluation of the effectiveness of community mental health programs. The assessment of broad programs in community psychology requires a drastically different approach, in terms of both its underlying philosophical rationale and the specific techniques employed, than does the more traditional assessment of individuals or small groups. Mikawa's wide-ranging chapter is the first to bring the scattered material in this area together in one place and includes information from a number of studies not yet published.

Chapter Eleven, by Bert Kopell and Margaret Rosenbloom, is on the psychological correlates of evoked electrical potentials in the brain as recorded from the scalp. It continues the tradition started in earlier books in this series of bringing authoritative information to the readers on a topic in the forefront of assessment research about which most assessment psychologists are not likely to be otherwise well informed. This chapter is, I believe, the first general review of the area which focuses on the behavioral variables of evoked potentials, one of the most exciting areas in modern neuropsychology. The chapter will be extremely useful to many research workers, and it presents an approach which conceivably may eventually be of widespread practical use in assessment.

In the last chapter I survey the early, pre-Galton background of personality assessment. Although the material probably has little concrete utility in improving the everyday practice of assessment, I believe that most true experts in the art of assessment are interested not only in the immediate technology of their craft, but also in its background and wide social implications. I found, in tracking down the material included in Chapter Twelve, that the information gave me a new perspective upon and a deeper appreciation of the art of psychological assessment. I hope that those who read the chapter will share something of the experience of discovery that I had when writing it.

I

Assessment and Impact of Social Climate

RUDOLF H. MOOS

Environments have significant impacts on human functioning. It is therefore imperative that we understand the different methods by which environments can be described and by which these descriptions can be related to human behavior. Six major dimensions of the environment have been related to human functioning (Moos, 1973a): ecological dimensions, which include both geographical and meteorological and architectural and physical design variables; behavior settings, which are units characterized by both ecological and behavioral properties; dimensions of organizational structure; dimensions identifying the collective characteristics of the people in an environment; variables relevant to the functional or reinforcement analyses of environments; and dimensions related to the psychosocial characteristics and social climates of environments. It is the last of these methods with which we are concerned here. The primary focus is on our work in the Social

The work reported here was supported by NIMH Grant MH 16026, NIAAA Grant AA00498, and Veterans Administration Research Project MRIS 5817–01. Portions of this chapter have been adapted from Moos (1974b).

8

Ecology Laboratory (Stanford University), although relevant examples from the work of other investigators are included.

Social Climate Perspective

As I have pointed out elsewhere (Moos, 1974b), the social climate perspective assumes that environments have unique "personalities," just as people do. Social environments can be portrayed with a great deal of accuracy and detail. Some people are more supportive than others. In the same manner, some social environments are more supportive than others. Some people feel a strong need to control others. Similarly, some social environments are extremely rigid, autocratic, and controlling. Order, clarity, and structure are important to many people. Correspondingly, many social environments strongly emphasize order, clarity, and organization. People make detailed plans which regulate and direct their behavior. Environments, too, have overall programs which regulate and direct the behavior of the people within them.

Pace (1962) illustrates the importance of the social climate of a college or university. Colleges have their own special atmospheres and establish their own particular images. However, only certain information about a college is commonly available. It is easy to find out the size of a college, whether it is coeducational, where it is located, when it was founded, what degrees it offers, whether it is public or private, religious or nonsectarian, what it costs, and so on. Pace points out that having learned the answers to all these questions, one still knows little that is important about a given college.

"Suppose one asked the same kinds of questions about a prospective college student. What is his height and weight, sex, residence, age, vocational goal, religious affiliation, and his family income? Knowing all these things one is still left in ignorance about what kind of a person the prospective student really is. The important knowledge concerns his aptitudes and interests, his motivations and emotional and social maturity. In short the crucial knowledge concerns his personality. So, too, with a college the crucial knowledge concerns its overall atmosphere or characteristics, the kinds of things that are rewarded, encouraged, emphasized, the style of life which is valued in the community and is most visibly expressed and felt" (Pace, 1962, p. 45).

Popular and professional writers alike have tried to capture the "personalities" of different social environments. Almost every biography and autobiography attempts to identify the essential elements of the family environment which presumably was responsible for the outstanding achievements of its subject. For example, Mill (1873) describes how his father carefully controlled his education and helped him develop his intellectual interests. He remembers how he studied his Greek lessons in the same room with his father, who was then writing a history of India. His father patiently explained the meaning of each new Greek word even though the constant interruptions must have slowed down the completion of his own writing. Russell describes his grandmother's intense care for his welfare, which "gave me the feeling of safety that children need" (1967, p. 18). In describing his grandmother Russell states that she had an important impact on him, "her fearlessness, her public spirit, her contempt for convention, and her indifference to the opinion of the majority have always seemed good to me and have impressed themselves upon me as worthy of imitation" (p. 18). Russell also describes how his brother tutored him in Euclid, which was "one of the great events of my life, as dazzling as first love. I had not imagined that there was anything so delicious in the world" (pp. 37–38). Albert Einstein and Winston Churchill had similar recollections of academic and intellectual impact in their early lives.

Mahatma Gandhi was exposed to certain environmental pressure which must have been important in his later life. His father and grandfather were known to be men of principle. Gandhi described his father as "incorruptible, truthful, and brave" and as having a "reputation for strict impartiality" (quoted in Fischer, 1962, p. 21). Gandhi described his mother as deeply religious and saintly. She often made arduous vows and fasted for long periods of time. Once "she vowed not to eat unless the sun appeared." Gandhi and his sister and brothers would watch for the sun and when it showed through the clouds they would rush into the house and announce that she could eat. But her vow required her to see the sun for herself, and so she would go outdoors, but by then the sun was hidden again. "That does not matter" she would cheerfully comfort her children, "God does not want me to eat today" (quoted in Fischer, 1962, p. 22). These examples illustrate the potential importance of early family environment on later development.

Vivid and insightful case studies of the impact of positive and negative social environments have been compiled by many writers. Biographers, sociologists, anthropologists, physicians, and popular novelists have described social environments in exhaustive detail (for example, Greenberg, 1964; Kesey, 1962; Kozol, 1967; Riesman and Jencks, 1962; Ward, 1946). Their reasons for doing so have varied, as have their feelings about the impact of different social environments. However, they all agree on one central point: the social climate within which an individual functions has an important impact on his attitudes and moods, his behavior, his health and overall sense of well-being, and possibly even his ultimate fate.

But how can the "blooming, buzzing confusion" of a natural social environment be adequately assessed? Many procedures have been developed for this purpose. One of the earliest and most interesting experimental studies was carried out by Lewin and his associates (Lewin, Lippitt, and White, 1939). They were interested in the differential effects of authoritarian, democratic, and laissez-faire social climates on the behavior of ten-year-old boys in various activity groups. Clubs were organized on a voluntary basis. The boys in the autocratic groups were found to be either very aggressive or very apathetic. Aggression was usually directed toward scapegoats within the groups, none of it toward the autocratic leader. But the repressive influence of the autocratic leader often caused apathy and lack of aggression. For example, two groups changed radically in different leadership climates. Group 1 ("secret agents") showed moderate aggression in a democratic climate, decreased aggression in an autocratic climate, a "rebound" effect on the day of transition, and then a decrease in aggressive activity when the democratic climate was reinstituted. Group 4 ("law and order patrol") also showed low levels of aggressive behavior in the autocratic climate, a "rebound" effect on the day of transition, a moderate level of aggression under laissez-faire, and a relatively low level of aggression in a democratic climate. The results conclusively demonstrated that the behavior of the same boys changed markedly depending upon the social climate of their group.

Using a somewhat different approach, Withall (1949) developed a Social Emotional Climate Index which provided a method whereby teachers' statements could be placed into seven different categories, including commending or expressing approval of a student's behavior, helping a student organize his ideas and plans clearly, limiting or directing student behavior by advice or recommendation, and punishing or disapproving of the behavior of the student. Withall observed a group of seventh grade students in regular social science, English, science, and mathematics classes. The differences in classroom climate created by the different teachers were substantial, with some variation in the day-to-day climate in each classroom, but overall consistency in the atmosphere a teacher created in her classroom over a period of time. (For example, one teacher often punished or disapproved of student behavior (about 25 percent of her remarks were coded in this category), and she tended to limit students' choices of action and to control the classroom situation.) Withall concluded that the students had to cope with quite different psychological climates as they went from class to class.

In another interesting approach, Simpson (1963) defined the "social weather" as the overall social treatment given a particular individual. For example, some people may "give him the cold shoulder," whereas others may "treat him like a king." Simpson developed rating scales which measured nine different aspects of social weather: for example, acceptance-rejection, affectionateness-hostility, approval-criticism. This technique has not been extensively used, but Simpson did find that the social weather of six preschool children differed from that of six school children, even in similar behavior settings.

Much of the recent empirical work in this area derives directly or indirectly from the contributions of Murray (1938). Murray pointed out that the concept of personality need could describe the general course of individual behavior but that it "leaves out the *nature of the environment,* a serious omission" (p. 116). Murray decided to classify environments in terms of the benefits (satisfactions) and harms (obstructions, dissatisfactions) which they provide. He selected the term *press* to designate a directional tendency in an object or situation, and he concluded that "one can profitably analyze an environment, a social group, or an institution from the point of view of what press it applies or offers to the individuals that live within or belong to it. . . . Furthermore human beings in general or in particular can be studied from the standpoint of what beneficial press are available to them and what harmful press they customarily encounter" (p. 120).

Pace and Stern (1958) developed the concept of environmental press further by applying the logic of "perceived climate" to the study of the "atmosphere" at colleges and universities. They constructed the College Characteristics Index (CCI) to measure the global college environment by asking students to act as reporters about that environment. Specifically, the students' task was to answer true-or-false items covering a wide range of topics about the college such as student-faculty relationships, rules and regulations, classroom methods, and facilities. Similar approaches have been used by several other investigators (for example, Findikyan and Sells, 1966; Halpin and Croft, 1963; Peterson and others, 1970; Stern, 1970; Walberg, 1969).

Social Environment of the Family

My colleagues and I have been involved in work in nine social milieus which are representative of four categories of social environments: treatment environments—hospital-based and community-based psychiatric treatment programs (Moos, 1974b); total institutions—correctional institutions for adult and juvenile offenders (Moos, 1974a) and military training companies (Moos, 1973b); educational environments—university student living groups, such as dormitories, fraternities, and sororities (Moos and Gerst, 1974) and junior high and high school classrooms (Moos and Trickett, 1974); community settings—families (Moos, 1974c), industrial or work milieus (Insel and Moos, 1973), and social, task-oriented, and therapeutic groups (Moos and Humphrey, 1973).

An example of the construction and interpretation of the Family Environment Scale (FES) is presented here to illustrate the logic underlying the measurement of social climate. The FES focuses on the measurement and description of the interpersonal relationships among family members, on the directions of personal growth which are emphasized in the family, and on the basic organizational structure of the family. The rationale for the development of the FES was derived from the theoretical contributions of Murray (1938) and his conceptualization of environmental press. The logic of our approach is that the consensus of individuals characterizing their environment constitutes a measure of environmental climate, and this environmental climate exerts a directional influence on behavior. However, individual or highly deviant perceptions of the environment, particularly in families, also are of critical importance.

Several methods were used to gain a naturalistic understanding of family social environments and to obtain an initial pool of questionnaire items. Many individuals were interviewed regarding the characteristics of their families. Several people were involved in writing a large range of items. Possible press dimensions and additional items were adapted from our other Social Climate Scales (Moos, 1974d). These procedures resulted in an initial 200-item Form A of the FES which assessed twelve dimensions: Involvement-Cohesiveness, Support, Expressiveness, Conflict, Independence, Achievement Orientation, Intellectual-Cultural Orientation, Active Recreational Orientation, Moral-Religious Emphasis, Order and Organization, Clarity, and Control.

The exact choice and wording of items were guided by our formulation of environmental press. Each item had to identify characteristics of an environment which would exert a press toward Cohesiveness, Achievement Orientation, Moral-Religious Emphasis, and so on. For example, a press toward Cohesiveness is inferred from the following kinds of items: "Family members really help and support one another" and "There is a feeling of unity and cohesion in our family." A press toward Achievement Orientation is inferred from these items: "We feel it is important to be the best at whatever you do" and "Getting ahead in life is very important in our family." A press toward Moral-Religious Emphasis is inferred from items like these: "Family members attend church, synagogue, or Sunday School fairly often" and "The Bible is a very important book in our home."

Form A of the FES was administered to over 1000 individuals in a sample of 285 families. To ensure that the resulting scale would be widely applicable we sampled families from several diverse sources. First, families were recruited from three different church groups, from a newspaper advertisement, and through students at a local high school. Second, an ethnic minority sample was recruited in part from the above sources and in part by having black and Mexican-American research assistants obtain data from samples of black and Mexican-American families. Third, a disturbed, or "clinic," family sample was collected from two different sources, a psychiatrically oriented family clinic and a probation and parole department affiliated with a local correctional facility.

The data from these three samples were used to develop a revised ninety-item, ten-subscale Form R (real) of the FES. In brief, various psychometric test construction criteria were used to select items to be included in the final Form R. These criteria included the following: (1) The overall item split should be as close to 50–50 as possible in order to avoid items characteristic only of extreme families. (2) Items should correlate more highly with their own than with any other subscale (all of the final ninety items met this criterion, and only four of the items correlated below .40 with their own subscale). (3) Each of the subscales should have an approximately equal number of items scored true and scored false in order to control for acquiescence response set. (4) The final subscales had to show only low to moderate intercorrelations. (5) Each item (and each subscale) had to maximally discriminate among families. Using these criteria two pairs of subscales were collapsed (Cohesiveness and Support, and Order and Organization and Clarity) because their items were highly intercorrelated. Many items with relatively low item-to-subscale correlations or extreme item splits were eliminated. The final ninety-item Form R subscales are listed and briefly defined in Table 1. The complete Form R and its scoring key are given in Moos (1974c).

The ordering of the ten subscales reflects our formulation of the relationships among them. The Cohesiveness, Expressiveness, and Conflict subscales are conceptualized as Relationship dimensions. They assess the extent to which family members feel they belong to and are proud of their family, the extent to which there is

Table 1.

BRIEF FES SUBSCALE DESCRIPTIONS

RELATIONSHIP   *Cohesiveness*—Extent to which members are concerned and committed to family and degree to which members are helpful and supportive of each other

Expressiveness—Extent to which members are allowed and encouraged to act openly and to express their feelings directly

Conflict—Extent to which open expression of anger and aggression and generally conflictual interactions are characteristic of family

PERSONAL   *Independence*—Extent to which members are encour-
DEVELOPMENT   aged to be assertive, self-sufficient, to make their own decisions, and to think things out for themselves

Achievement Orientation—Extent to which different activities (e.g., school, work) are cast into an achievement-oriented or competitive framework

Intellectual-Cultural Orientation—Extent to which family is concerned about political, social, intellectual, and cultural activities

Active Recreational Orientation—Extent to which family participates actively in various recreational and sporting activities

Moral-Religious Emphasis—Extent to which family actively discusses and emphasizes ethical and religious issues and values

SYSTEM   *Organization*—Extent to which order and organization
MAINTENANCE   are important in family: structuring activities, financial planning, and explicitness and clarity in rules and responsibilities

Control—Extent to which family is organized in a hierarchical manner, rigidity of rules and procedures, and extent to which members order each other around

open expression within the family, and the degree to which conflictual interactions are characteristic of the family.

The second group of subscales is conceptualized as Personal Development, or Personal Growth, dimensions. This group measures the emphasis within the family on certain developmental processes which may be fostered by family living. The Independence scale measures the emphasis on autonomy and on family members doing things on their own. Achievement Orientation assesses emphasis on academic and competitive concerns. Intellectual-Cultural Orientation reflects the degree to which the family is concerned with a variety of intellectual and cultural activities. The Active Recreational Orientation and Moral-Religious Emphasis subscales measure other important dimensions of personal growth.

The last two subscales, Organization and Control, are conceptualized as assessing System Maintenance dimensions in that they obtain information about the structure or organization within the family and about the degree of control which is usually exerted by family members vis-à-vis each other. There is evidence that this conceptualization of the dimensions differentiating among family environments has direct relevance for a broad range of other social milieus (see Moos, 1974b, Chapter 14).

Clinical Interpretation of Family Profiles

Some primary uses for the FES are to derive detailed descriptions of the social environments of families, to compare parent and child perceptions, to assess changes in family environments over time, and to contrast different families with each other. Two illustrative profile interpretations taken from the FES manual (Moos, 1974c) are presented here. (Numbers beginning with 101 were arbitrarily assigned to the 285 families in the normative sample in chronological order of receipt of their forms.)

Family 142: High Relationship and Low Control. Figure 1 shows the FES profile for family 142, compared to the average score obtained by the 285 families in our overall normative group. This was one of the few families in our sample in which there were no children. The thirty-three-year-old husband was a student and the

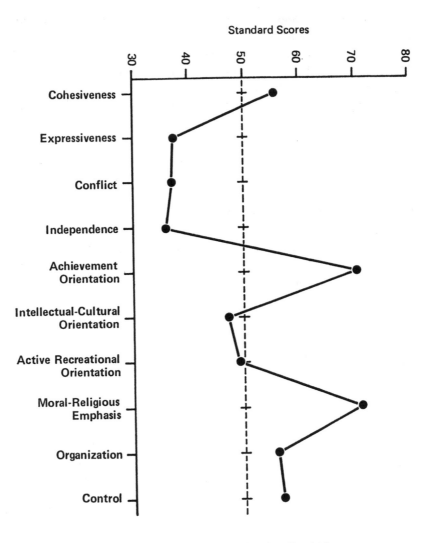

FIGURE 1.   FES profile for family 142.

twenty-six-year-old wife was working in a university community. This couple felt quite positive about the social environment they had established. They obtained substantially above average scores on the Relationship dimensions of Cohesiveness and Expressiveness and a substantially below-average score on Conflict. Both husband and wife agreed with items like the following: "We put a lot of energy into what we do at home," "There is a feeling of unity and cohesion in our family," "We really get along well with each other," "We say anything we want to around home," "We tell each other about our personal problems," and "Financial matters are openly discussed in our family."

There is moderately above-average emphasis on three of the Personal Growth dimensions in this family—that is, Independence, Intellectual Orientation, and Active Recreational Orientation. This husband and wife answered true to items like: "We think things out for ourselves in our family," "We come and go as we want to in our family," "We often talk about political and social issues," "Intellectual curiosity is very important in our family," "We often go to movies, sports events, camping, etc.," "Friends often come over for dinner or to visit." Degree of Achievement Orientation and Moral-Religious Emphasis was moderately below average. There was little emphasis on either Organization or Control. Importantly, the husband and wife in this family responded almost identically to the items on the three Relationship and the five Personal Growth dimensions. They showed slight disagreement on the System Maintenance dimensions (with the wife perceiving somewhat more Organization and Control than the husband), but basically their degree of agreement was extremely high.

Family 338: Achievement-Oriented. Figure 2 shows the profile for a somewhat different family. Family 338 was composed of four family members; the father, aged sixty, was born in a Central American country and had managed to obtain only a partial high school education. The mother, aged fifty-five, was born in the United States and had completed her high school education. The family was strongly upwardly mobile, as indicated by the fact that the twenty-four-year-old daughter and the twenty-three-year-old son had both finished their college educations. The family was relatively stable (they had lived in their current home for over five years) and quite well off—for example, their nine-room home had four bedrooms, a living room, and separate dining and laundry rooms. The family was Catholic and attended religious services about once a week.

Figure 2 indicates that the social environment of this family is quite different from that of our previous family. In family 338

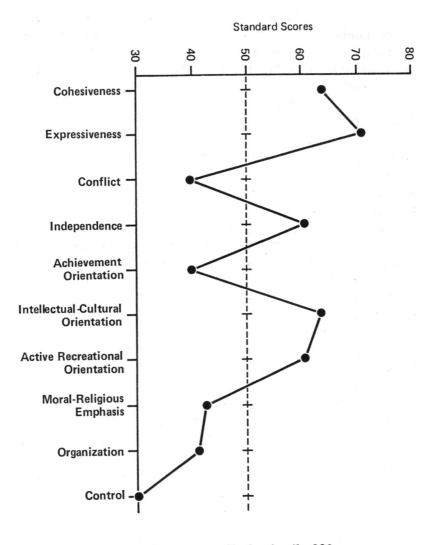

FIGURE 2.   FES profile for family 338.

the emphasis on Cohesiveness is only about average, whereas the emphasis on both Expressiveness and Conflict is moderately below average. The major Personal Growth Characteristics of the family are in the areas of Achievement Orientation and Moral-Religious Emphasis. For example, family members answered true to items like the following: "We feel it is important to be the best at whatever

you do," "Getting ahead in life is very important in our family,"
"We always strive to do things just a little better the next time,"
"We believe in competition and may the best man win." Items on
the Moral-Religious Emphasis scale on which the members in family
338 agreed include "Family members attend church, synagogue, or
Sunday School fairly often," "Family members have strict ideas
about what is right and wrong," "We believe there are some things
you just have to take on faith," and "The Bible is a very important
book in our home." On the System Maintenance dimensions, the
family members perceived their family as being slightly above average.

Thus families 142 and 338 represent two quite different
family social environments. Cohesiveness and Expressiveness are
fairly high in family 142, as are Independence, Intellectual-Cultural
Orientation, and Active Recreational Orientation. Family 338 does
not emphasize these dimensions but rates high on the Personal
Growth dimensions of Achievement Orientation and Moral-Religious Emphasis, which are both deemphasized in family 142. Further, family 338 is moderately high on Organization and Control,
whereas family 142 deemphasizes both these dimensions.

Underlying Patterns

Perhaps our most important finding is that vastly different
social environments can be characterized by common or similar
dimensions, conceptualized in three broad categories: Relationship,
Personal Development (Personal Growth), and System Maintenance (System Change). These categories are quite similar across
the nine environments we studied, although different settings do
impose unique variations within the general categories.

Relationship dimensions identify the nature and intensity of
personal relationships within the environment. They assess the extent to which people are involved in the environment, the extent
to which they support and help each other, and the extent to which
there is spontaneity and free and open expression among them. The
basic dimensions are very similar in all of the environments studied,
as shown in Table 2. Each of the environments has an Involvement
or Cohesiveness dimension. Involvement in a work milieu reflects

Advances in Psychological Assessment

Table 2.

COMMON SOCIAL CLIMATE DIMENSIONS ACROSS ENVIRONMENTS

Type of Environment	Relationship Dimensions	Personal Development Dimensions	System Maintenance and System Change Dimensions
Treatment (Hospital and Community Programs)	Involvement Support Spontaneity	Autonomy Practical Orientation Personal Problem Orientation Anger and Aggression	Order and Organization Clarity Control
Total Institutions Correctional Institutions	Involvement Support Expressiveness	Autonomy Practical Orientation Personal Problem Orientation	Order and Organization Clarity Control
Military Companies	Involvement Peer Cohesion Officer Support	Personal Status	Order and Organization Clarity Officer Control
Educational Environments University Student Living Groups	Involvement Emotional Support	Independence Traditional Social Orientation Competition Academic Achievement Intellectuality	Order and Organization Student Influence Innovation
Junior High and High School Classrooms	Involvement Affiliation Teacher Support	Task Orientation Competition	Order and Organization Rule Clarity Teacher Control Innovation
Community Settings Families	Cohesiveness Expressiveness Conflict	Independence Achievement Orientation	Organization Control

Table 2.   (cont.)

COMMON SOCIAL CLIMATE DIMENSIONS ACROSS ENVIRONMENTS

Type of Environment	Relationship Dimensions	Personal Development Dimensions	System Maintenance and System Change Dimensions
		Intellectual Cultural Orientation Recreational Orientation Moral-Religious Orientation	
Social, Task-Oriented and Therapeutic Groups	Cohesiveness Leader Support Expressiveness	Independence Task Orientation Self-Discovery Anger and Aggression	Order and Organization Leader Control Innovation
Work Milieus	Involvement Peer Cohesion Staff Support	Autonomy Task Orientation	Work Pressure Clarity Control Innovation Physical Comfort

the extent to which workers are concerned and committed to their jobs and how enthusiastic and constructive they are in the work setting. Involvement in a university living group reflects the degree of commitment to the house and residents and the amount of social interaction and feeling of friendship. Involvement in a classroom measures the extent to which students have attentive interest in class activities and participate in discussions. Involvement in a treatment environment measures how active and energetic patients are in the day-to-day functioning of the program, for example, expressing pride in the program, feeling group spirit, and displaying general enthusiasm.

The degree of Support present in an environment is particularly important. Emotional Support in student living groups re-

flects the extent of manifest concern for others in the group, efforts
to aid one another with academic and personal problems, and an
emphasis on honest and open communication. Support in a treatment program measures the extent to which patients are encouraged
to be helpful and supportive toward each other and the extent to
which staff are supportive toward patients. Staff Support in a work
milieu measures the extent to which management is supportive of
workers and encourages workers to be supportive of each other.
Officer Support in military companies assesses the degree of friendship and communication between officers and enlisted men and the
degree to which officers attempt to help and encourage them. Peer
Cohesion in military companies measures the social and interpersonal relationships that develop among the enlisted men and their
tendency to stick together and to help each other. Peer Cohesion in
a work milieu assesses the social and interpersonal relationships that
develop among workers and their tendency to support and help each
other.

A separate relationship dimension of Expressiveness or Spontaneity is identified in some environments. There are two reasons
why this dimension is not separately identified in all environments.
First, certain environments, military companies for example, differ
so little in Expressiveness that this dimension simply does not discriminate among them. Secondly, Expressiveness is sometimes very highly
related to one of the other Relationship dimensions, such as Emotional
Support in university living groups and to both Peer Cohesion and
Staff Support in work milieus. Thus there are basically three Relationship dimensions which characterize all environments: Involvement, Support, and Expressiveness.

Personal Development dimensions assess the basic directions
along which personal growth and self-enhancement tend to occur
in the particular environment. The exact nature of these dimensions
varies somewhat among the different environments studied, depending upon their underlying purposes and goals.

Personal growth goals of university student living groups are
different from those of families, and thus a different set of Personal
Development dimensions are identified in them. These include:
Independence (the extent of emphasis on independence of thoughts
and actions by individuals and on acting in diverse ways without

social sanction); Traditional Social Orientation (stress on dating, going to parties, and other "traditional" heterosexual interactions); Competition (emphasis on competing with one another for grades and dates and the casting of many activities into a competitive framework); Academic Achievement (extent to which strictly classroom achievement and concern are prominent in the house) and Intellectuality (extent to which scholarly, intellectual and cultural activities and interests are manifest).

Psychiatric and correctional programs emphasize still other, yet related areas of personal growth. In these environments the Personal Development dimensions essentially assess the overall treatment goals of the program, such as Autonomy (extent to which people are encouraged to be self-sufficient and independent); Practical Orientation (extent to which the program orients an individual toward training for new jobs, looking to the future, setting and working toward concrete goals, and so on); and Personal Problem Orientation (the extent to which individuals are encouraged to be concerned with their feelings and problems and to seek to understand them). Thus Personal Development dimensions differ across environments depending upon their basic purposes and goals.

System Maintenance and System Change dimensions are relatively similar across all the environments. These dimensions assess the extent to which the environment is orderly, clear in its expectations, maintains control, and is responsive to change. The basic dimensions are Order and Organization, Clarity, Control, and Innovation. For example, Clarity in a work milieu assesses the extent to which workers know what to expect in their daily routines and how explicitly rules and policies are communicated. Clarity in a classroom assesses the emphasis on following a clear set of rules and on students knowing what the consequences will be if they do not follow them.

The fact that it is possible to identify similar underlying dimensions along which very different social environments can be characterized is quite important, because these environments can be directly compared with each other, particularly in terms of Relationship and System Maintenance and System Change dimensions. This finding may eventually help us identify the reasons why an individual does well in one environment but poorly in another. For example, consider the important life transition when an adolescent boy or girl goes away to college. How similar will the dormitory environment be to the family environment of the student's? How similar will the college classroom be to the student's high school classrooms? Or consider the important transition when a psychiatric patient is released back into the community. How similar will his community living environment be to the social environment in the treatment program from which he was released? Will the social environment of his work setting be one to which he is capable of adapting?

In any case, social environments can be categorized along three common sets of dimensions. We have shown elsewhere that the overall conceptualization holds as well for scales developed by other investigators as it does for our own (see Moos, 1974b, Chapter 14). Now let us consider the evidence on the differential impact of social environments. The conceptualization of three categories of dimensions provides a convenient framework within which the relevant research can be reviewed.

Impact of Social Environments

As was pointed out earlier, environments have programs which organize and shape the behavior of their inhabitants. Social environments have differential impacts on the people who live and function in them. We will review some current evidence regarding this impact, drawing heavily on the work conducted in our Laboratory. We will consider three related categories of outcome criteria, subjective, objective, health-related. First, we cover criteria like satisfaction, morale, personal feelings (anxiety, anger). Second, we examine evidence relating to objective outcome criteria, such as achievement levels in high school and college and the outcome of psychiatric treatment. Third, we focus on health-related criteria, examining evidence that physical and/or mental symptoms may occur more frequently in certain social environments.

Treatment Settings. Relevant work in individual and group psychotherapy has focused almost exclusively on Relationship dimensions. The evidence indicates that there are certain important qualities in the therapist that are relevant to almost all types of psychotherapy (Truax and Mitchell, 1971). Three characteristics of an effective therapist have emerged from the divergent viewpoints: an effective therapist is nondefensive and authentic or genuine; he is able to provide a nonthreatening, safe, trusting, or secure atmosphere through his own acceptance or nonpossessive warmth for the client; and he is able to have a high degree of accurate, empathic understanding of the patient on a moment-by-moment basis. Truax and Mitchell state, "These ingredients of the psychotherapeutic relationship are aspects of human encounters that cut across the parochial theories of psychotherapy and appear to be common elements in a wide variety of psychoanalytic, client-centered, eclectic, or learning theory approaches to psychotherapy" (p. 302).

The evidence indicates that when these qualities are present in the therapist, positive personality change is likely to follow in the patient. Negative change or personality deterioration is likely to occur when these qualities are absent. The evidence that therapists or counselors who are accurately empathic, nonpossessively warm and genuine are effective with their clients seems to hold up regardless of training or theoretical orientation, and with a wide variety of clients varying from hospitalized schizophrenics to college underachievers and juvenile delinquents. These dimensions are clearly what we have termed Relationship dimensions. Empathy, warmth, and genuineness assess the overall quality of the relationship between the patient and therapist exactly as Involvement, Support, and Expressiveness assess the general quality of the relationships among individuals in a social milieu. Yalom (1970) has hypothesized that cohesiveness in group therapy is analogous to the concept of the "relationship" in individual therapy.

Charles Petty, Robert Shelton, and I have recently completed two studies linking treatment environment as perceived by patients and staff to treatment outcome as assessed by dropout rates, release (discharge) rates, and community tenure rates (Moos, Shelton, and Petty, 1973). We found that programs with high dropout rates tend to have few social activities, little emphasis on involving patients in the program, and somewhat poor planning of activities of the patients. Patients in these programs do not interact much with each other. They have a good deal of free time with little or no guidance. Staff discourage criticism from patients and are unwilling to act on patients' suggestions. Patients tend to criticize the staff probably because the program is seen (by both patients and staff) as poorly organized. Programs with high dropout rates are rather unfriendly, patients do not really feel comfortable or at ease, and staff seem somewhat unhappy with the environment and with one another.

Programs with high release rates typically emphasize making plans for getting out of the hospital, for training patients for new kinds of jobs, and for making concrete plans before leaving. There is a fair amount of Staff Control but staff are personally interested in the patients and tell them when they are making progress. There is relatively little emphasis on Expressiveness; patients rarely argue with each other and they keep their disagreements to themselves. Neither patients nor staff see much support in these programs. However, even though they are practical and "unexpressive" they do engender a certain kind of pride and involvement in their members.

Programs which keep patients out in the community the longest emphasize free and open expression of feelings, particularly angry feelings. Staff members think it is healthy to argue, are seen arguing among themselves and sometimes start arguments in group meetings. Patients are expected to share their personal problems and feelings with each other and with the staff. This emphasis on personal problems and the open expression of anger occurs within a context which also emphasizes Autonomy and Independence, a Practical Orientation, Order and Organization and a reasonable degree of Staff Control. For example, patients are transferred from the program if they do not obey the rules, but they are treated with respect by the staff and are encouraged to be independent.

In terms of the tripartite categorization of dimensions, programs with high dropout rates have little emphasis in either the Relationship or the System Maintenance areas. Programs with high release rates are seen as relatively strong in the System Maintenance areas and in the Personal Development area of Practical Orientation. In addition, they are seen as having moderate emphasis on the Relationship area of Involvement. Programs which keep patients out of the hospital longest are seen as having a high degree of emphasis on both the Relationship and System Maintenance dimensions, and also on the Personal Development dimensions, particularly Autonomy and Practical Orientation. Other studies of psychiatric treatment outcome show generally corroborative findings (Ellsworth and others, 1971; Spiegel and Younger, 1972; and see Moos, 1974b, Chapter 8, for more details).

Current evidence indicates that the qualities of the relationship in individual therapy and in group therapy (as conceptualized by cohesiveness) are strongly related to positive evaluation of treatment and to positive personality change. The results on the Relationship dimensions in our studies of treatment programs were strikingly similar to these findings. Thus positive relationship qualities appear to be essential in mediating positive personality change in all types of psychiatric treatment.

Total Institutions. We also conducted three studies in juvenile correctional institutions in an attempt to replicate the above findings in a different kind of environment (Moos, 1975, Chapter Seven). Our results were quite clearcut. As the emphasis on the three Relationship and the three Personal Development dimensions increases, residents like each other and the staff better and feel that they have greater opportunities for personal growth in the program. Exactly the reverse results were obtained for the System Maintenance dimension of Staff Control. As Staff Control increases, residents like each other and the staff less, and feel that they have less to gain from the program. Finally, there was a tendency for general satisfaction to increase as the emphasis on the Relationship and Personal Development dimensions increased, but this tendency was relatively weak. It seems reasonable that the social climate of a correctional unit (no matter how good) is not highly related to resident satisfaction, since the residents are being held against their will. However most correctional units emphasize learning vocational and job-related skills. Therefore, the climate of correctional units is highly related to residents' perception of the opportunities for personal development. These results indicate that the specific relationships between social climate dimensions and differential effects of living groups are mediated in part by the overall characteristics of these groups, for example, whether they are in treatment or in "total" institutions.

In an additional study in military basic training companies (Moos, 1975; Chapter 12) we found that enlisted men generally felt less anxious, depressed, and hostile in companies which emphasized the Relationship dimensions of Involvement, Peer Cohesion, Officer Support, and the Personal Development dimension of Personal Status. There was some suggestion of a specificity of relationships between certain dimensions of the social environment and certain moods. For example, enlisted men were most likely to feel hostile in companies in which Officer Support was low. The men were most likely to feel depressed in companies in which Peer Cohesion was low. They were also likely to feel hostile in companies in which there was a lack of clear expectations and rules. Finally, the dimension of Officer Control had a pervasive effect on the men's moods, that is, enlisted men felt significantly more anxious, depressed, and hostile in companies in which Officer Control was high. Dimensions of company environments were also related to objective indices of test performance at the end of basic training. Peer Cohesion, Officer Support, and clarity of expectations were the three most important characteristics of high performance companies.

Educational Settings. Pace (1969) presents a number of relationships between the College and University Environment Scale (cues) subscale scores and student attitudes and activities. Colleges high on cues Community and Awareness subscales (Relationship dimensions) have a high proportion of students who feel a strong emotional attachment to the college. In addition, it is rare for students to report not having participated in any extracurricular activities in college environments which are high on cues Community. Peterson, Centra, Hartnett, and Linn (1970) relate the subscales of the Institutional Functioning Inventory (ifi) to seven different factors of student protest in a sample of fifty institutions. A number of relationships are presented, but most interestingly, student radicalism as a protest factor was highly related to the ifi subscales of Human Diversity and Concern for Improvement of Society (Personal Development dimensions). The other relationships found were generally predictable ones, that is the absence of senior faculty and the quality of instruction were protest issues in institutions with a low emphasis on undergraduate learning. Classified research was a protest issue in institutions with a high emphasis on concern for advancing knowledge.

Edison Trickett and I have completed a study linking the satisfaction and moods of students to the social environments of their high school classrooms. Students expressed greater satisfaction in classrooms characterized by high student involvement, by a personal student-teacher relationship, by innovative teaching methods, and by a clarity of rules around classroom behavior (Trickett and Moos, 1974). Classroom social environment was also related to the moods of students. Students felt more secure and interested in classrooms emphasizing the Relationship dimensions of Involvement, Affiliation, and Teacher Support. Students reported feeling angrier in classrooms which were low in Teacher Support and in Order and Organization.

We also found that classrooms in which students felt that much material was learned were both similar to and different from "satisfying" classrooms. Involvement, Teacher Support, and Rule Clarity were highly emphasized. But this kind of classroom also emphasized Competition and Order and Organization. Thus the classroom in which students report a great deal of content learning combines an affective concern with students as people (Relationship dimensions), with an emphasis on students working hard for academic rewards (Competition) within a coherent organized context (Order and Organization and Rule Clarity).

Walberg (1969) has used his Learning Environment Inventory (LEI) to show that classroom social environment may mediate classroom learning. Data were collected from approximately 3700 students in 144 high school physics classes, measuring both cognitive and noncognitive learning criteria. The cognitive criteria included a test on understanding science, a test covering the assumptions, activities, products and ethics of science, and a test of general physics knowledge. The noncognitive criteria included measures of interest in physics. The results were extremely interesting. Students in classes characterized by high Satisfaction and low Friction, Cliqueness, and Apathy gained significantly more on all three noncognitive learning criteria. Students who were in classes characterized by high Difficulty gained significantly more on all three cognitive learning criteria. Thus classes seen as more difficult and competitive (Personal Development dimensions) gained more on physics achievement and science understanding, whereas classes seen as more satisfying and as having less friction, apathy, and cliqueness (Relationship dimensions) gained more on reported science interest and activities.

Walberg's study and ours are mutually supportive. Students

express greater satisfaction, show more interest in their course material, and actually engage in more course relevant activities in classes which are high on Relationship dimensions. Students feel they learn more, and actually do learn more in classrooms which are competitive and intellectually challenging. In some further unpublished work we found that teachers who establish socially cohesive classrooms (high on Relationship dimensions) tend to give higher average grades, whereas teachers in classrooms high on Teacher Control tend to give lower average grades. It is no wonder that students feel more secure, interested and satisfied in the first classrooms!

Physical Health and Well-Being. A physician advises a harried executive with high blood pressure to spend a week in the country. A pediatrician recommends that an underdeveloped, neglected child be sent to a foster home. An allergist encourages an asthmatic patient to find a job with more human contact. A heart specialist urges an overworked administrator to delegate some of his responsibilities to others. Each of these health professionals is in part responding to the belief that the social environment has an important impact on health. Space permits only brief examples here. Some of the relevant work has been reviewed elsewhere (Kiritz and Moos, 1974).

There is abundant evidence that one dimension of the social environment, namely, work pressure is related to health in an important way. Rosenman and Friedman have identified a behavior pattern which they believe is associated with high risk of coronary artery disease (Friedman, 1969). The coronary prone behavior pattern designated type A, as distinguished from the low risk type B, is characterized by extreme aggressiveness, competitiveness, and ambition along with feelings of restlessness and, in particular, a profound sense of time urgency. Rosenman and Friedman believe that the contemporary Western environment encourages development of this pattern. They also believe that the pattern represents the interaction of environmental influences and the susceptibilities of individuals and argue that it may not occur if a type A individual is removed to a type B setting.

Caffrey (1968) has shown that it is possible to rank environments according to the degree to which their "atmospheres" encourage type A behavior. He had three physicians rate fourteen Benedictine and eleven Trappist monasteries using paired comparison methods. The individual monks were also rated by their Abbots and peers. Caffrey then showed that groups of monks having a higher proportion of type As living in type A environments and taking a high fat diet had the highest prevalence rates of coronary disease.

The association of work pressure and coronary disease gains support elsewhere in the literature. For example, French and Caplan (1973) studied twenty-two white collar males over a three-day period. They telemetered heart rate, measured serum cholesterol, and had observers rate behavior. "Quantitative work overload" as indexed by the observers ratings was positively correlated with serum cholesterol. Subjective indices of work overload were correlated with both physiological measures. Other studies demonstrate relationships between work pressure and physiological changes. Froberg and his associates (1971) studied twelve young female invoicing clerks during four consecutive days doing their usual work in their usual environment. During the first experimental days, piece wages were added to the salaries of the subjects. Urine samples taken three times a day were assayed for adrenalin and noradrenalin. During the salaried control days the work output was very close to normal. On the piece work days, which the girls described as hurried and tiring, the mean adrenalin and noradrenalin excretion rose by 40 percent and 27 percent respectively. One additional finding supports the hypothesis that responsibility and work pressure may have accumulative noxious effects. Air traffic controllers who work under extreme time pressure and with the responsibility for hundreds of lives have higher risk and earlier onset of hypertension and peptic ulcers than a control group of second-class airmen (Cobb and Rose, 1973).

We have completed two relevant studies in this area, one of which related the social environments of eight military basic training companies to their sick-call rates (Moos, 1975; Chapter 12). We tested companies with the Military Company Environment Inventory (MCEI), a scale which measures the social environments of military companies, and found that fifteen of eighty-four items were highly related to the company sick-call rates. Men in high sick-call companies perceived the company to be very strict about following the daily schedule and about the men saying where they were going. The men felt that they were kept very busy and that the company was relatively well organized. Other items indicated that the men felt that they had particularly low personal status, were bored, that work was repetitious and boring, that they could not act differently if they felt like it, and that they were not encouraged to take leadership in the company. Additional items indicated that all of this occurred in the context of a company which placed high emphasis on Officer Control. For example, the men felt that the noncommissioned officers were constantly checking on them and closely supervising them. They felt that they were ridiculed in front of the other men, that the officers did not help them to get oriented, and that they never quite knew when an officer would ask to see them. Thus the characteristics of high sick-call companies include an emphasis on Order and Organization which borders on extreme restrictiveness; the men are kept busy, but with tasks they perceive to be repetitious and boring. Relatively strict officer control is emphasized and the enlisted man's own personal status is deemphasized. One obvious way to adapt to this kind of noxious social environment is to become ill.

These findings were supported in our unpublished study of nine high school classrooms. The social environment of these classrooms was assessed and careful absenteeism records were kept. Student absences were divided into those which occurred for medical and those which occurred for nonmedical reasons with striking results. Classrooms high in student medical absences were characterized by a lack of emphasis on the Relationship dimensions of Involvement and Teacher Support and the System Change dimension of Innovation, and also by a high degree of emphasis on the Personal Development dimensions of Task Orientation and Competition and the System Maintenance dimension of Teacher Control. The findings were basically similar for nonmedical absences. Thus, not surprisingly, students stay away from classes they perceive to be restrictive and difficult even if they feel that they learn more in these classes, and actually do learn more.

What all these studies tell us about the impacts of social environments is that people are more satisfied and tend to perform better when the relationship areas are emphasized. They are also less likely to drop out, be absent, and report that they are sick.

People also tend to do better in environments which emphasize the Personal Growth dimensions, but there may be some personal costs involved. Students learn more but are absent more often in classrooms emphasizing competition and difficulty. Patients do better in treatment programs which emphasize Autonomy and Practical Orientation. Students learn more in universities which emphasize independent study, high standards, criticism, and breadth of interests. But greater responsibility and greater work pressure may have certain negative physiological concomitants, such as greater arousal and increased probability of cardiac dysfunction. These kinds of effects probably also occur in patients who are pushed out of hospitals and in students who are pushed to the limits of their performance capacities.

Order and clarity generally appear to have a weak but positive impact on satisfaction, moods, and performance. Control generally has a negative impact; however this appears to depend in part on the rigidity of the control and in part on the age and developmental maturity of the people involved. Rigid control is less palatable with advancing maturity.

Future research is needed to assess the effects of relationship-oriented "benevolent" control on different individuals in different institutions. For example, there is evidence that autistic children tend to react more favorably to high structure situations (Shopler, Brehm, Kinsbourne and Reichler, 1971). In addition, autistic children functioning on a higher developmental level were better able to utilize relative lack of structure than were those functioning on a lower developmental level. Thus high control may be necessary and beneficial with certain individuals. The clearest conclusion is that satisfying human relationships in all social environments studied to date facilitate personal growth and development. However we know that "love is not enough," and that the effects of Personal Development and System Maintenance dimensions merit further study.

Practical Utility of Social Climate Concept

Information about the social climate can be fed back to the participants in a social environment. The logic is that this kind of feedback will often motivate people in the environment to seek to change it. Miles and his colleagues (1971) identified the basic processes that may result from this kind of feedback. Presentation of social climate data leads to a detailed inquiry of the reasons certain results were obtained and to a discussion of problems that were not originally the primary focus of the data collection. Individual involvement at this level promotes acceptance of the data and creates a positive atmosphere toward using it. Group meetings increase individual responsibility for making changes, can lead to positive interactions between members of social environments, to clarification of issues, and to increased discussion of values to the organization of specific strategies for change. As practical group problems are being worked on and change effected, groups also learn how to interact more effectively. This leads to basic changes in the relationships among the members of the social milieu, that is, to a change in the social climate.

We have conducted demonstrations in both hospital-based and community-based psychiatric treatment programs of how detailed feedback of Social Climate Scale results may be useful in facilitating social change (Moos, 1974b, Chapters 4 and 11). This change methodology represents an especially useful application of scales assessing perceived climate. Feedback and discussion sessions function in a manner which makes practical applications out of ongoing research. Individuals participating in a social system can help design and cooperate in research which is both acceptable and relevant to their own needs. Social change can probably best be facilitated by this method when dealing with relatively small groups, most of whose members interact directly with each other. The method utilizes and maximizes the involvement of each individual in the social setting, and thus in the definition and facilitation of change. The use of the method helps people to mold their social environments in desired directions, and at its best enables some individuals to achieve a new competence, that of being able to change and to control their own environments.

Selecting and Transcending Environments. The rapid proliferation of new types of institutional environments has increased the need and demand for more accurate and complete descriptions of them. Many people feel that different institutions know much more about the individuals they are attempting to recruit or place than those same individuals know about the institutions. For example, colleges know more about the characteristics of entering students than entering students know about the colleges they plan to enter. Social workers and other program staff generally know far more about the characteristics of the individual patient than they do about the program or programs into which they wish to place the patient. Further, the patient himself generally knows little or nothing about the important characteristics of the programs in which he may be placed.

Everyone seems to agree that currently available descriptions of social environments are woefully inadequate. These descriptions generally characterize the environment as it is seen by a very small and unrepresentative sample of the people in that environment, such as a company manager or administrator. In addition, they usually report on those characteristics of the environment that do not really give a "feel" of how that environment actually functions.

Some studies have been made on the extent to which published descriptions of environments give an adequate picture of the social climates of those environments. For example, Jansen (1970) reported that the descriptions of halfway houses for psychiatric patients did not seem to give an accurate picture of the programs she actually visited. As Jansen says, "on visiting such houses I was struck by the discrepancies between writeups and actual practices. This may well be caused by the complexity of community living where the real transactions are hard to put one's finger on." Speegle (1969) found that the college environment as described by eight college catalogs was not congruent with students' perceptions of that environment as measured by the College Characteristics Index. None of the catalogs he studied provided descriptions of the informal social atmosphere of the college.

We studied the published descriptions of a sample of community programs in order to evaluate the information about the treatment milieu which these descriptions presented (Otto and Moos, 1973). Descriptions were analyzed for five community programs for which Community-Oriented Program's Environment Scale (copes) test results of members and staff were also available. The copes assesses the social environments of community-oriented psychiatric treatment programs (Moos, 1974b; Chapter 10). Ten "naive" judges were given copies of these articles and were asked to complete a COPES questionnaire on the basis of the information therein. The comparison of the results of the judges to those of the actual members and staff in the program provided a measure of the extent to which the treatment milieu of the program could be inferred from the article. Two of the published descriptions were relatively accurate and complete; the other three tended to give judges an incorrect impression of the program. The accuracy of program descriptions would probably be enhanced if such descriptions systematically included information about the psychosocial characteristics and social climate of the program.

Social climate scales may be useful in helping to specify the psychosocial or perceived climate characteristics of a variety of social environments. At a minimum, program descriptions should attempt to systematically describe the various dimensions included in the Relationship, Personal Development and System Maintenance, and System Change areas. Information about the social climate of an environment should help individuals to more accurately select the specific social environments which might be most beneficial to them. Detailed and complete prior information about new social environments may enhance the accuracy of individuals' expectations and thus reduce the incidence of dissatisfaction, maladaptation, and dropout. In our view, these and other practical applications of the concept of social climate make it one of the most exciting and potentially useful ways of conceptualizing social environments.

References

CAFFREY, B. "Reliability and Validity of Personality and Behavioral Measures in a Study of Coronary Heart Disease." *Journal of Chronic Disease,* 1968, *21,* 191–204.

COBB, S., AND ROSE, R. "Hypertension, Peptic Ulcer and Diabetes in Air Traffic Controllers." *Journal of the American Medical Association,* 1973, *224,* 489–492.

ELLSWORTH, R., MARONEY, R., KLETT, W., GORDON, H., AND GUNN, R. "Milieu Characteristics of Successful Psychiatric Treatment Programs." *American Journal of Orthopsychiatry,* 1971, *41,* 427–441.

FINDIKYAN, N., AND SELLS, S. "Organizational Structure and Similarity of Campus Student Organizations." *Organizational Behavior and Human Performance,* 1966, *1,* 169–190.

FISCHER, L. *The Life of Mahatma Gandhi.* New York: Macmillan, 1962.

FRENCH, J., AND CAPLAN, R. "Organizational Stress and Individual Strain." In A. Marrow (Ed.), *The Failure of Success.* New York: AMACom, 1973.

FRIEDMAN, M. *Pathogenesis of Coronary Artery Disease.* New York: McGraw-Hill, 1969.

FROBERG, J., KARLSSON, C., LEVI, L., AND LIDBERG, L. "Physiological and Biochemical Stress Reactions Induced by Psychosocial Stimuli." In L. Levi (Ed.), *Society, Stress and Disease.* Vol. 1. London: Oxford University Press, 1971.

GREENBERG, J. *I Never Promised You a Rose Garden.* New York: Holt, Rinehart, and Winston, 1964.

HALPIN, A., AND CROFT, D. *The Organizational Climate of Schools.* Chicago: Mid-West Administration Center, University of Chicago, 1963.

INSEL, P., AND MOOS, R. *The Work Environment Scale.* Palo Alto, Calif.: Social Ecology Laboratory, Department of Psychiatry, Stanford University, 1973.

JANSEN, E. "The Role of the Halfway House in Community Mental Health Programs in the United Kingdom and America." *American Journal of Psychiatry,* 1970, *126,* 142–148.

KESEY, K. *One Flew Over the Cuckoo's Nest.* New York: Viking, 1962.

KIRITZ, S., AND MOOS, R. "Physiological Effects of Social Environments." *Psychosomatic Medicine,* 1974, *36*(2), 96–114.

KOZOL, J. *Death at an Early Age.* Boston: Houghton-Mifflin, 1967.

LEWIN, K., LIPPITT, R., AND WHITE, R. "Patterns of Aggressive Behavior in Experimentally Created 'Social Climates.'" *Journal of Social Psychology,* 1939, *10,* 271–299.

MILES, M., HORNSTEIN, H., CALDER, P., CALLAHAN, D., AND SCHIAVO, R. "Data Feedback: A Rationale." In H. Hornstein, B. Bunker, W. Burke, M. Gindes, and R. Lewicki (Eds.), *Social Intervention: A Behavioral Science Approach.* New York: Free Press, 1971.

MILL, J. S. *Autobiography.* New York: Columbia University Press, 1924 (original edition, 1873).

MOOS, R. "Conceptualizations of Human Environments." *American Psychologist,* 1973a, *28,* 652–665.

MOOS, R. *The Military Company Environment Scale Manual.* Palo Alto, Calif.: Social Ecology Laboratory, Department of Psychiatry, Stanford University, 1973b.

MOOS, R. *The Correctional Institutions Environment Scale Manual.* Palo Alto, Calif.: Consulting Psychologists Press, 1974a.

MOOS, R. *Evaluating Treatment Environments: A Social Ecological Approach.* New York: Wiley, 1974b.

MOOS, R. *The Family Environment Scale Preliminary Manual.* Palo Alto, Calif.: Social Ecology Laboratory, Department of Psychiatry, Stanford University, 1974c.

MOOS, R. *The Social Climate Scales: An Overview.* Palo Alto, Calif.: Consulting Psychologists Press, 1974d.

MOOS, R. *Evaluating Correctional and Community Settings.* New York: Wiley, 1975.

MOOS, R., AND GERST, M. *The University Residence Environment Scale Manual.* Palo Alto, Calif.: Consulting Psychologists Press, 1974.

MOOS, R., AND HUMPHREY, B. *The Group Environment Scale Technical Report.* Palo Alto, Calif.: Social Ecology Laboratory, Department of Psychiatry, Stanford University, 1973.

MOOS, R., SHELTON, R., AND PETTY, C. "Perceived Ward Climate and Treatment Outcome." *Journal of Abnormal Psychology,* 1973, *82,* 291–298.

MOOS, R., AND TRICKETT, E. *The Classroom Environment Scale Manual.* Palo Alto, Calif.: Consulting Psychologists Press, 1974.

MURRAY, H. *Explorations in Personality.* New York: Oxford University Press, 1938.

OTTO, J., AND MOOS, R. "Evaluating Descriptions of Psychiatric Treatment Programs." *American Journal of Orthopsychiatry,* 1973, *43,* 401–410.

PACE, R. "Implications of Differences in Campus Atmosphere for Evaluation and Planning of College Programs." In R. Sutherland, W. Holtzman, E. Koile, and B. Smith (Eds.), *Personality Factors on the College Campus.* Austin: University of Texas, 1962.

PACE, R. *College and University Environment Scales: Technical Manual.* (2nd ed.) Princeton, N.J.: Educational Testing Service, 1969.

PACE, R., AND STERN, G. "An Approach to the Measurement of Psychological Characteristics of College Environments." *Journal of Educational Psychology,* 1958, *49,* 269–277.

PETERSON, R., CENTRA, J., HARTNETT, R., AND LINN, R. *Institutional*

Functioning Inventory: Preliminary Technical Manual. Princeton, N.J.: Educational Testing Service, 1970.

RIESMAN, D., AND JENCKS, C. "The Viability of the American College." In N. Sanford (Ed.), *The American College: A Psychological and Social Interpretation of Higher Learning.* New York: Wiley, 1962.

RUSSELL, B. *The Autobiography of Bertrand Russell 1872–1914.* Boston: Little, Brown, 1967.

SHOPLER, E., BREHM, S., KINSBOURNE, M., AND REICHLER, R. "Effect of Treatment Structure on Development in Autistic Children." *Archives of General Psychiatry,* 1971, *24,* 415–421.

SIMPSON, J. "A Method of Measuring the Social Weather of Children." In R. Barker (Ed.), *The Stream of Behavior.* New York: Appleton-Century-Crofts, 1963.

SPEEGLE, J. "College Catalogs: An Investigation of the Congruence of Catalog Descriptions of College Environments with Student Perceptions of the Same Environments as Revealed by the College Characteristics Index." Doctoral dissertation, Syracuse University, 1969.

SPIEGEL, D., AND YOUNGER, J. "Ward Climate and Community Stay of Psychiatric Patients." *Journal of Consulting and Clinical Psychology,* 1972, *39,* 62–69.

STERN, G. *People in Context.* New York: Wiley, 1970.

TRICKETT, E., AND MOOS, R. "Personal Correlates of Contrasting Environments: Student Satisfaction in High School Classrooms." *American Journal of Community Psychology,* 1974.

TRUAX, C., AND MITCHELL, K. "Research on Certain Therapist Interpersonal Skills in Relation to Process and Outcome." In A. Bergin and A. Garfield (Eds.), *Handbook of Psychotherapy and Behavior Change: An Empirical Analysis.* New York: Wiley, 1971.

WALBERG, H. "Social Environment as a Mediator of Classroom Learning." *Journal of Educational Psychology,* 1969, *60,* 443–448.

WARD, M. *The Snake Pit.* New York: Random House, 1946.

WITHALL, J. "The Development of a Technique for the Measurement of Social Emotional Climate in Classrooms." *Journal of Experimental Education,* 1949, *17,* 347–361.

YALOM, I. *The Theory and Practice of Group Psychotherapy.* New York: Basic Books, 1970.

II

Naturalistic Observation in Clinical Assessment

RICHARD R. JONES, JOHN B. REID, GERALD R. PATTERSON

In this chapter we will describe a system for collecting behavioral interaction data in non-laboratory settings, and discuss some of the theoretical, psychometric, and practical matters attendant on the use of such data in clinical and research activities. The data collection system is the focal point for discussion of the following: some considerations in the decision to collect data in the natural environment rather than to use paper and pencil or laboratory techniques; some difficulties inherent in designing a single system to collect data for several, somewhat different research and clinical uses; and some possible problems in using existing psychometric techniques to support the reliability and validity of behavioral scores generated by the data collection system.

Historically, the data system to be discussed in this chapter

This study was supported in part by grants MH 10822, ROI MH 15985, and MH 12972 from the National Institute of Mental Health. Computing assistance was obtained from the Health Sciences Computing Facility, UCLA, and sponsored by NIH grant FR-3.

evolved in response to a clinical assessment task which had the following goals. First it was necessary to learn about the social interactions among family members in order to design treatment programs which would change these behaviors. Second, behavioral scores were needed for evaluating treatment outcomes. And third, information about family behavior in natural home settings was wanted which might contribute to the theoretical development of social behaviorism. To accomplish these assessment goals, it was decided to try direct or naturalistic observation of the behavior of family members in their homes.

The decision to use direct observation rather than interviews or questionnaires was dictated by the purposes of the clinical assessment problem. Interviews or questionnaires would certainly have been more economical than direct observation. But the clinical and theoretical focus was on the behavioral interactions among family members, and indirect assessment procedures such as interviews or questionnaires seemed unlikely to yield the kind of unbiased, highly detailed records of behavior judged necessary for the design of treatment programs, evaluation of treatment outcomes, and theoretical studies of social interaction.

While naturalistic observation seemed to be an appropriate assessment procedure for these purposes, there were serious concerns about the quality of data generated in this fashion. Observation of human behavior is certainly a ubiquitous phenomenon of everyday life, but when used as a data collection method in clinical research, measures based on observations might not meet scientific standards of precision and accuracy. Some investigators have assumed that because such observations are obtained under natural conditions, they possess inherent validity and that this is sufficient justification for their use (Barker, 1963). Alternatively, traditional psychometric techniques for evaluating the quality of observation measures could be used. Since use of these measurement procedures and conventional standards was anticipated, decisions were made during the design of the observation system, in part, to enhance the psychometric properties of the final instrument.

The foregoing overview describes the situation in the middle 1960s, when Patterson and his colleagues were developing behavioral intervention techniques for socially aggressive, preadolescent boys. Like other behaviorally oriented clinicians at that time, these workers were disenchanted with most available clinical assessment instruments. Parent ratings, structured personality inventories, and child self-report scales did not yield the kind of specific behavioral information deemed necessary for therapists who were interested primarily in changing behavior, and only secondarily interested in changing attitudes, underlying dynamic constructs, or global personality traits.

But then (and even now) naturalistic observation as an assessment procedure was neither well understood nor developed by psychologists. Interestingly, the terms *naturalistic* and *observation* do not appear in the subject index or table of contents in either of the two previous volumes in this series, *Advances in Psychological Assessment*. Naturalistic observation, however, is a fairly common method in other disciplines, notably ethology, zoology, and anthropology. But even in these disciplines, field observations are often conducted in highly idiosyncratic ways. Such individualistic methods of observation would not be suitable for psychological study, where it is desirable to assess all subjects under similar conditions so that statistical analyses of the resultant data can be used to compare subjects or groups of subjects. Thus, the problem was to design and implement an assessment procedure with little precedent in psychology, and to evaluate the naturalistic observation system using a psychometric and statistical methodology which had been developed for other kinds of assessment instruments, particularly tests or questionnaires.

In this chapter, we will chronicle the development of the Behavioral Coding System (BCS) now in use by the Social Learning Project at Oregon Research Institute. Particular attention will be given to the psychometric properties of the instrument and to aspects of this kind of measurement system which differentiate it from more conventional instruments, such as tests, inventories, and interviews. Our purpose, however, is more than historical. As noted by Johnson and Bolstad (1973), a major contribution to psychology from the behavior therapy boon of the 1960s and 1970s may well turn out to be the development of naturalistic observation assessment procedures as useful supplementary instruments to the more traditional assessment devices known to most psychologists.

Definition of Naturalistic Observation as an Assessment Procedure

Selected dictionary definitions of the terms *naturalistic* and *observation* serve to specify usage of naturalistic observation in psychological assessment research. *Webster's New World Dictionary* defines observation as ". . . 4. a) the act or practice of noting and recording facts and events, as for some scientific study; b) the data so noted and recorded." Naturalistic is defined as ". . . 3. in accordance with, or in imitation of, nature." And, nature is defined as ". . . 1. the essential character of a thing; quality or qualities that make something what it is; essence."

Combining these separate definitions, we define naturalistic observation as the practice of noting and recording facts and events in accordance with, or in imitation of, the essential character of a thing. Now, what in this definition makes naturalistic observation different from other kinds of assessment procedures such as interviews, maximum performance tests, or typical performance questionnaires? All kinds of assessment procedures involve noting and recording. The facts and events which are recorded in psychological studies range from inferred constructs, such as traits or attitudes, to overt behavior, such as eyeblinks, 100-yard dashes or punches-in-the-nose. Psychological facts or events such as these may vary in their accordance with, or imitation of, the essential character of a thing, depending on how the thing is defined. If a psychological thing is an inferred construct, it, by definition, is not overt or public. Hence, inferred constructs cannot be observed naturalistically; only their behavioral signs or indicants can be observed. And, the signs should be in accordance with the essential character of the construct. The targets of naturalistic observations are signs, indicants, or behaviors, and these data may or may not be used to make inferences about inferred constructs. For example, if a child is observed in a natural setting to hit another child, this datum can be noted and recorded as a behavioral fact or event. The user of this datum may wish to infer that the hitter is aggressive (a construct), or may simply treat the datum as a simple fact with no further extrapolation to broader characteristics of the observed child.

This matter of inference from naturalistically-observed behavioral events to broader constructs influences not only uses of data, but the design of assessment procedures as well. For the purposes of this chapter, a naturalistic observation assessment procedure is one in which little, if any, inference to unobservable or inferred constructs is inherent in the design of the procedure. For example, the assessment task for the observer is to record the occurrence of hits for each of several sequential time samples. And, a hit is defined for the observer in very specific behavioral terms, such that high agreement should be obtained when two or more coders record the behavior simultaneously but independently. Assessment procedures excluded by this definition of naturalistic observation are reports of behavior from interviewees (because the behavior typically is not recorded at the time it occurs, nor in its natural setting); self-reported questionnaire responses (because of the same reasons, plus the absence of a trained, impartial observer); and ratings by either the assessee or other assessors on broad construct dimensions (because of all the foregoing reasons, plus heavy reliance on inference from behavioral signs to constructs). The defining features of a naturalistic observation system include, therefore, the recording of behavioral events in their natural settings at the time they occur, not retrospectively; the use of trained impartial observer-coders; and descriptions of behaviors which require little if any inference by observers to code the events.

Historical Background of the Behavioral Coding System (BCS)

In 1963 a small group of colleagues began to develop social engineering procedures, first for acting-out children in the classroom (Patterson, 1965) and, later, for behaviorally deviant children in the home (Patterson, McNeal, Hawkins, and Phelps, 1967; Reid, 1967). The very first classroom observations of disruptive boys suggested a need for discrete categories of behaviors. For example, what teachers meant by hyperactivity turned out to be a set of behaviors which could be specifically defined and reliably observed. So, when the clinical focus shifted to children referred by parents for misbehaviors in the home, the researchers began by going to the home and looking for discrete behaviors which would identify the referral problems reported by parents. To start, several families were interviewed and then observed for several hours in their homes. Major discrepancies were discovered between the interview reports and the actual behavior of both parent and child during the home observations. The discrepancies were commensurate with a growing body of findings showing weak relationships between parent global reports and observations of the same behaviors made in the laboratory of the home observation (Honig, Tannenbaum, and Caldwell, 1968; Yarrow, 1963; Sears, 1965). The more positive findings generally showed correlation coefficients in the .30s or .40s (Antonovsky, 1959; Bing, 1963; Crandall and Preston, 1961; Smith, 1958).

The problem of eliciting satisfactory parent report data seemed to be twofold. First, when the parents were asked about the subtle relations between the behavior of parent or sibling and the problem child, it became obvious that they simply were not tracking and storing relevant information. And there was nothing in parents' implicit or explicit theories of child-rearing which would lead them to note and store such events as rate of sister tease, or rate of older brother's noncompliance, or rate of father's smiling, let alone the social contingencies controlling the occurrence of these events. But, the clinical and research requirements for such data quickly precipitated a shift away from traditional global interview data, and soon parental reports were abandoned as important sources of data. Recent developments in behavioral assessment techniques, however, suggest that such an extreme position may have been unnecessary (Campbell, Dunnette, Arvey, and Hellervik, 1973; Goldfried and Kent, 1972; Jones, 1973), since traditional assessment procedures can be constructed to measure specific behaviors, as well as broader constructs.

The second problem in eliciting good parent report data was that parents tended to underestimate rates of deviant child behavior in general, and to overestimate improvement in these behaviors (Clement and Milne, 1967; Collins, 1966; Walter and Gilmore, 1973). Early efforts by Lindsey suggested that by training parents to define behaviors carefully (pinpointing) and to record frequencies of occurrence, it was possible to obtain high quality data for categories of specific behavioral events. Douglas, Lawson, Cooper, and Cooper (1968) suggested that by using parent reports for relatively discrete categories and obtaining descriptions of these behaviors for only the previous twenty-four hours, these data could be significantly correlated with observed mother-child interactions. Peine (1970) demonstrated significant intrasubject mother-observer correlations by having the mother actually tabulate the occurrence of well-defined child behavior categories. However, it should be noted that mothers often underestimate the mean level of observers' data when tabulating deviant child behaviors. This suggests that even when mothers use specific behavioral definitions and tabulate actual occurrences of behavior, they may be biased when recording certain kinds of behavior in the same way that any relatively untrained observer may be biased (Kass and O'Leary, 1970; O'Leary and Kent, 1973). In the school setting, Wahler and Leske (1972) demonstrated that teachers' global ratings of behavior were little related to the ratings of, and changes in, observed child behavior. But the simple expedient of having the teachers tabulate actual occurrences of specific response categories as a basis for making their global ratings led to a closer match with changes in child behavior. This matter of behavioral specificity is of paramount importance early in the development of any behavioral observation coding system.

The initial task faced by the developer of any assessment instrument is to compile a preliminary item pool. The items in the present case were specific behaviors which were relevant to either the clinical or theoretical purposes of the assessment task. Clinical experience with the families of socially-aggressive children suggested some behaviors, but these had been observed via interviews with parents and their children, rather than in the natural setting. Alternatively, the researchers went into the natural home environment to observe the occurrence of behaviors which had been suggested by their clinical experience. As appointments to conduct these preliminary observations were being made, the first methodological or psychometric problem occurred to the researchers. What would be the effect of the observers' presence on the natural behavior of the family in their home? This is a specific instance of the general assessment issue about the influence of the measurement device on the psychological phenomenon being measured. We will return to this matter of observer-presence later in the chapter.

In comparison to contemporary observation procedures, these early excursions were chaotic. Various recording techniques were tried, including extensive note-writing immediately after the observation session, note-taking in longhand during the observation session, and even automatic recording during the session with a face mask device which concealed a microphone and battery-operated recorder. With this apparatus, the observer could inaudibly speak the stream of behavior onto permanent tape for later replay. All of these efforts served to sharpen the initial behavior categories and suggest others. A trial set of behavioral categories resulted, with working definitions of the specific behaviors admissible to each category. For example, the clinically-intuited category called aggression soon was refined into specific behavioral instances such as hitting, teasing, and destructiveness. It was found that the clinically meaningful construct, aggression, was too behaviorally nonspecific for reliable coding, and relied too greatly on observer inference. The specific component behaviors of the aggression construct, however, did not require inference and their definitions were sufficiently concise to provide satisfactory levels of interobserver agreement, at least in their preliminary form. The final product of this early work in developing an item pool for the bcs is the set of twenty-eight behavioral categories and abbreviated definitions shown in Table 1.

Note the six classes of behavioral categories.[1] The classification into First Order and Second Order behaviors represents a priority procedure for coding multiple behaviors, that is, to guide the observer as to which behavior to code when more than one behavior is exhibited by the target subject during a single time sample. First order behaviors are always recorded instead of second order behaviors when there is a choice. The division into verbal, nonverbal, or either verbal or nonverbal eases the observer's learning and cogni-

[1] The complete coding manual and extended definitions of the behavior categories are available as Document #01234. There are thirty-three pages of materials. Order from asis/naps, c/o Microfiche Publications, 305 East 46th Street, New York, N.Y. 10017. Remit in advance $5.45 for photocopies or $1.50 for microfiche. Make checks payable to Microfiche Publications.

Table 1.

SIX CLASSES OF TWENTY-EIGHT BEHAVIOR CATEGORIES
IN THE BEHAVIORAL CODING SYSTEM (BCS)

First Order	Second Order

VERBAL

CM (*Command*): This category is used when an immediate and clearly-stated request or command is made to another person.

CN* (*Command Negative*): A command which is very different in attitude from a reasonable command or request (CM).

(1) Immediate compliance is demanded.

(2) Aversive consequences are threatened if compliance is not immediate.

(3) a kind of sarcasm or humiliation directed to the receiver.

CR* (*Cry*): Whenever a person cries, with no exceptions.

HU* (*Humiliate*): Makes fun of, shames, or embarrasses the subject intentionally.

LA (*Laugh*): A person laughs in a non-humiliating way.

NE* (*Negativism*): A statement in which the verbal message is neutral, but which is delivered in a tone of voice that conveys an attitude of, "Don't bug me; don't bother me."

WH* (*Whine*): A person states something in a slurring, nasal, high-pitched, falsetto voice.

YE* (*Yell*): The person shouts, yells, or talks loudly.

TA (*Talk*): This code is used if none of the other verbal codes are applicable.

Table 1.   (cont.)

SIX CLASSES OF TWENTY-EIGHT BEHAVIOR CATEGORIES
IN THE BEHAVIORAL CODING SYSTEM (BCS)

First Order	*Second Order*

NONVERBAL

DS* (*Destructiveness*): The person destroys, damages, or attempts to damage any (non-human) object; the damage need not actually occur, but the potential for damage must exist.

HR* (*High Rate*): Any repetitive behavior not covered by other categories that if carried on for a long period of time would be aversive or annoying.

IG* (*Ignore*): When person A has directed behavior at person B and person B appears to have recognized that the behavior was directed at him, but does not respond in an active fashion.

PN* (*Physical Negative*): A subject physically attacks or attempts to attack another person with sufficient intensity to potentially inflict pain.

AT (*Attention*): When one person listens to or looks at another person, and the categories AP or DI are not appropriate.

NO (*Normative*): A person is behaving in an appropriate fashion and no other code is applicable.

NR (*No Response*): When a person does not respond to another person. Applicable when a behavior does not require a response, or when behavior is directed at another person, but the person to whom the behavior is directed fails to perceive the behavior.

RC (*Receive*): A person receives a physical object from another person and does not do anything as a result of the contact.

TH (*Touch*): When the subject touches other people or hands an object to another person.

EITHER VERBAL OR NONVERBAL

AP (*Approval*): A person gives clear gestural or verbal approval to another individual. Must include some clear indication of positive interest or involvement.

CO (*Compliance*): A person immediately does what is asked of him.

DI* (*Disapproval*): The person gives verbal or gestural disapproval of another person's behavior or characteristics.

SS (*Self-Stimulation*): Repetitive behaviors which the individual does to himself and cannot be coded by any other codes.

Table 1.   (cont.)

SIX CLASSES OF TWENTY-EIGHT BEHAVIOR CATEGORIES
IN THE BEHAVIORAL CODING SYSTEM (BCS)

First Order	Second Order

EITHER VERBAL OR
NONVERBAL

DP* (*Dependency*): When person A is requesting assistance in doing a task that he is capable of doing himself, and it is an imposition on the other person to fulfill the request.

NC* (*Noncompliance*): When a person does not do what is requested of him.

PL (*Play*): A person is playing either alone or with other persons.

TE* (*Tease*): Teasing another person in such a way that the other person is likely to show displeasure and disapproval or when the person being teased is trying to do some other behavior, but is unable to because of the teasing.

WK (*Work*): A person is working, either alone or with other people.
(1) the behavior is necessary for the smooth functioning of the household.
(2) the behavior is necessary for a child to perform in order to learn behavior which will help him assume an adult role.

tive cataloguing of the twenty-eight codes. From a procedural standpoint, the use of First and Second order classes is a useful technique when the goal is to record all behavior as it occurs, but to do so using a manageable number of behavioral categories.

In conjunction with developing this set of twenty-eight behavioral categories, other procedural and design decisions were made. The two most important decisions had to do with the behaver, or performer of the behaviors in the code, and the sampling of behaviors. Each individual behaver or person in the family was assigned a number, one for the target child, two for the mother, three for the father, and numbers four-on for the siblings. These numbers are used to identify the performer of a behavior which is coded according to the categories listed in Table 1. For example, if the father made a request of his son, and the child complied with the request, the code looks like this: 3 CM-1 CO, or in words, father commands, son complies. But to record this kind of interaction, and to do so sequentially over time so as to capture the flavor of ongoing interactions, a sampling procedure was needed. Should, for instance, the sampling procedure be designed to record all instances of the twenty-eight behaviors as performed by the different family members without regard to the timing or order of performances? Or alternatively, should there be an account of the behavior and the behavers as the stream of behavior unfolds, much as would be recorded by a movie camera? The first approach would be event sampling, where the observer looks for instances of the behaviors in the code and records them as simple tallies, disregarding them when they occurred in time. The second procedure would be time sampling, where the running emission of behavior by family members is recorded as it occurs in time.

Time sampling was the procedure chosen for the BCS. The goal was to produce a coded account of the behavioral interactions among family members, including the temporal arrangement of the behaviors as they unfolded. That is, if the younger sister teased (4 TE), and then the target child hit her (1 PN), the encoding should capture this sequence veridically. In coded form, this sequence would be recorded as 4 TE-1 PN, not 1 PN-4 TE. The order of the codes from left to right reflects the order of the behaviors in time. Long sequences of such dyadic interactions could be recorded continuously and written on paper as an unbroken string, where the left to right order of the recorded events reproduced their arrangement in time. While this procedure adequately covered the temporal or sequential order of the behavioral events, it did not represent the behavior in real time. This meant that the duration of events would not be captured by the coding system. And without the use of expensive electronic equipment, the behavioral data could not be recorded in real time.[2] Since a paper and pencil procedure was the only feasible method, real time, and hence precise durational measures, had to be forfeited. Compared to present-day observational coding systems (for example, Karafin, 1973; Sackett, Stephenson, & Ruppenthal, 1973), the BCS may seem rather primitive. But for the technology available then, and the purposes for which the BCS was intended, it represented a substantial improvement over other procedures for assessing family interactions.

But the time dimension could not be totally ignored, since rate-per-minute measures and the total span of time covered by the observations were needed. So, a bug-in-the-ear timing device was tried, which automatically signalled the observer at thirty-second intervals. One line or row of the data sheet represented thirty seconds, and experience showed that ten consecutive thirty-second intervals, or five minutes, was a reasonable time sample, given limits of observer endurance. Although the observer was free to record as many dyadic interactions as possible within each thirty-second interval, limitations of the system (including observer speed and the pacing of behavior) suggested that the thirty-second interval was usually divisible into five six-second sub-intervals. The rhythm of ongoing behavior, coupled with the cognitive and manual limitations of human observers, suggested this six-second subinterval, and in early experience with the system this pacing seemed to work well. Hence, the particular time sampling used in the BCS resulted largely from system limitations of the code as it developed, and well might differ for other kinds of behaviors or other recording procedures. There do not seem to be any set rules about appropriate time samples since, as in this case, the particular goals of the observational system probably define time sampling intervals more appropriately than any procedural rules of thumb.

A sample coding sheet is shown in Table 2. The six-second subintervals are shown within each row of the sheet, where each row represents a thirty-second interval. Since the goal of the ob-

[2] One could, of course, have used a device such as an Esterline recorder, but a more portable and less mechanically complicated system was needed.

servational system was to record dyadic interactions, each six-second interval contained what amounts to a stimulus behavior and a response behavior. If a behavior continues for more than six seconds, the code for that behavior is repeated in the adjacent and following subintervals for as long as the behavior continues. But in coded form, continuous behavior will appear to be interrupted by a response from the environment, simply because this is a requirement of the coding procedure. And, this points to a limitation or weakness of this particular approach to coding behavior, one which would be avoided if a real time electronic recording apparatus had been available and used in the development of the BCS.

The weakness is as follows: Looking at a completed sheet, it is not possible to determine if a behavior actually ran off continuously over a number of six-second subintervals, or whether the behavior actually occurred in on-off fashion. For example, if the target subject talked continuously for eighteen seconds, the record of this behavior would appear as follows: 1 TA-xxx/ 1 TA-xxx/ 1 TA-xxx. The xxx represents the response from the environment, which must be recorded because of the rules of the observational system. For scoring this behavioral record, it is unknown whether this is three distinct talks by subject 1, or whether this is only one talk which ran continuously for eighteen seconds. This difficulty of interpretation affects the scoring of the behavioral record, as, for example, in computing rates-per-minute, simple frequencies of occurrence, and probabilities of sequential interactions.

But this is not an uncommon problem with observational coding systems, since virtually all systems which use a time sampling technique rather than real time recording suffer the same difficulty. The basic rule in time sampling is to record whatever behavior is ongoing during the specified time sample. The fact that the time samples run consecutively and that a behavior may run across adjacent time samples is ignored by this rule. For example, if a thirty-second time sample is partitioned into three ten-second subintervals, and a behavior runs continuously for the thirty seconds, the record will indicate three occurrences of the behavior. If the same thirty-second behavior is recorded on a form partitioned into five six-second subintervals, the record will indicate five occurrences of the behavior. The point is that for modified frequency scoring, measures

Table 2.

BLANK SAMPLE CODING SHEET FOR THE BCS

Family Number ....

ID Number ....

BEHAVIOR CODING SHEET

Phase ....

Subject .... Observer .... Date .... No. ....

AP	Approval	HU	Humiliate	PP	Positive physical
AT	Attention	IG	Ignore		contact
CM	Command	LA	Laugh	RC	Receive
CN	Command	NC	Noncompliance	SS	Self-stimulation
	(negative)	NE	Negativism	TA	Talk
CO	Compliance	NO	Normative	TE	Tease
CR	Cry	NR	No response	TH	Touching,
DI	Disapproval	PL	Play		handling
DP	Dependency	PN	Negative physical	WH	Whine
DS	Destructiveness		contact	WK	Work
HR	High rate			YE	Yell

1					
2					
. . .					
10					

Description ....

will be partly determined by the size of the time sample. Continuous real time recording procedures do not have this problem, simply because behavior is logged as either off or on over time, and the frequency of behaviors in real time is directly and veridically tabulated by counting the number of times the behavior changes.

Reid and Patterson's (1973) description neatly summarizes the main characteristics of the code. The Behavioral Coding System (Patterson, Ray, Shaw, and Cobb, 1969; Reid, 1967) provides a running account of a subject's behavior in terms of the twenty-eight behavioral categories (Table 1) which are, by definition, mutually exclusive and exhaustive. Means and standard deviations for each code for samples of problem and normal boys are presented in Table 3. In using the code, a trained observer focuses on one family member as subject, and records a behavior for that subject each six seconds as well as behaviors directed at that subject by other family members, also coded in terms of the same twenty-eight categories. One observation for one subject lasts for five consecutive minutes. In any given observation session, each family member is the focus of two such five-minute periods. The observation sessions occur late in the afternoon, just prior to dinnertime. This time of day tends to highlight behavioral problems in a family's pattern of interactions.

From these observation data, the rate/minute for each of the individual behavior codes may be tabulated for each family member, as well as the rates at which other family members react to him. Since the behavior code permits sequential coding of the behavior of the subject and the reactions of others toward him, it has been possible to conduct a variety of functional analyses of the observation data (for example, Patterson, 1973; Patterson and Cobb, 1971). It is also possible to combine codes in any manner desired, to produce a frequency or rate at which a class of behaviors occurs. The best examples of this are Total Deviant Behavior, which combines the rate/minute of fourteen aversive, hostile, irritating behaviors (asterisks in Table 1), and Total Targeted Behaviors, which combines rate/minute of all behaviors being treated for each individual family. In the Social Learning Project, each family is observed for either six or ten baseline observation sessions, over a two-week period, providing from sixty to 100 minutes of observational data on every member of each family, prior to the start of treatment. The same format is used in collecting observation data during treatment, at treatment termination, and during the follow-up period for each of the treated families. A large and consistent effort has been made to refine the observation code and to evaluate its reliability (Reid, 1970; Reid and DeMaster, 1972;

Table 3.

NORMATIVE DATA FOR TWENTY-SIX AGGRESSIVE AND
NONAGGRESSIVE BOYS*

Code category	Rate per minute			
	Problem sample		Normal sample	
	Mean	SD	Mean	SD
AP	0.0165	0.0243	0.0276	0.0219
AT	1.3824	0.6448	1.3871	0.6325
CM	0.0478	0.0513	0.0392	0.0378
CN	0.0083	0.0147	0.0020	0.0051
CO	0.2263	0.1705	0.1811	0.1188
CR	0.0193	0.0586	0.0022	0.0115
DI	0.1339	0.1094	0.0841	0.0666
DP	0.0067	0.0217	0.0027	0.0076
DS	0.0306	0.0787	0.0064	0.0119
HR	0.0439	0.1356	0.0141	0.0403
HU	0.0202	0.0351	0.0010	0.0037
IG	0.0054	0.0090	0.0041	0.0091
LA	0.0808	0.0680	0.1100	0.1099
NC	0.0918	0.0931	0.0500	0.0555
NE	0.1153	0.1560	0.0245	0.0301
NO	2.7030	1.0809	2.5618	1.1552
NR	0.0714	0.0528	0.0547	0.0427
PL	2.0063	1.3699	2.5020	1.6972
PN	0.0422	0.0633	0.0093	0.0215
PP	0.0390	0.0900	0.0137	0.0386
RC	0.0541	0.0834	0.0310	0.0396
SS	0.2157	0.2358	0.1091	0.1336
TA	2.2377	0.6939	2.0274	0.7369
TE	0.0502	0.0612	0.0196	0.0361
TH	0.0173	0.0261	0.0107	0.0171
WH	0.0360	0.0545	0.0389	0.1163
WK	0.6222	0.7303	0.9709	1.0697
YE	0.0571	0.0835	0.0184	0.0786

* Based upon 6–10 observations sessions in the homes.

Taplin and Reid, 1973), stability over time (Jones, 1972; Reid, 1973), reactivity (Patterson and Harris, 1968; White, 1972), and validity.

Reliability of BCS

Reliability of measures can be appraised in numerous ways, depending on the assessment context within which measures are obtained and used. The reliability concept in psychological measurement has been broadened by the introduction of the Theory of Generalizability (Cronbach, Gleser, Nanda, and Rajaratnam, 1972). Classical psychometric theory (for example, Gulliksen, 1950) dealt with parallel forms, internal consistency, and test-retest reliabilities as conceptually distinct indices of measurement precision, and provided separate statistical procedures for the assessment of each. Users of observational data have traditionally been concerned with interobserver agreement as an index of reliability, which is conceptually close to parallel forms reliability in traditional psychometrics. Generalizability theory encompasses all of these forms, and provides a unified approach for assessing the influences on measurement precision due to similar instruments (parallel forms), temporal stability (test-retest), and different assessors (interobserver agreement). This section will emphasize the generalizability approach to reliability assessment, but will also provide some of the more conventional reliability results which may be more familiar to most readers.

One typically thinks of an instrument, such as a test, interview, or observation schedule, in terms of its reliability. More precisely, reliability is a concept which applies to particular scores derived from an instrument, and if a particular instrument can be scored in different ways, reliability could, and should be assessed for each kind of score. As a simple example, separate items or groups of items (that is, scales from a personality inventory) can be scored. Reliability of a scale score is different from reliability of an item. Many observation systems can be scored in numerous ways, and reliability indices should be specified for each different kind of score derived from the raw observations. This point is important when reporting research results for particular dependent variables. The variables used in a statistical analysis of results should also be the variables or scores for which reliability is appraised. That is, if daily frequencies of occurrence of deviant behaviors are analyzed in a treatment outcome study, reliability of the daily scores should be assessed, rather than reliabilities of scores based on separate time samples (for example, minutes) within each day. Since observation data of the sort obtained by the Behavior Coding System can be scored and analyzed in various ways, we will be careful to specify what kinds of scores are used in the various reliability analyses presented below.

Generalizability. Generalizability theory (Cronbach and others, 1972) provides an elegant and comprehensive set of procedures for assessing the reliability, or more correctly, the generalizability, of behavioral observations which are obtained under varying conditions. Subjects' scores derived from observations are classified according to conditions within facets, which are analogous to levels within factors in the analysis of variance. Estimates of variance components for each of the facets, and their interactions, are obtained via the appropriate ANOVA model, and these variance estimates are used to obtain generalizability coefficients. These results comprise the generalizability, or G study, and are used to estimate the reliability of observations collected in a decision, or D study, where the conditions within the facets of the G study may change. A familiar analogue would be to estimate the reliability of a fifty-item scale based on data from only twenty-five items, via the Spearman-Brown prophecy formula.

In assessing the reliability of observational data, a common facet is coders, classified into two conditions in this G study, a regular coder and a calibrating coder. The regular coder is the observer who normally collects the observational data, and the calibrating coder is the observer who is assigned to selected observation sessions for the purpose of collecting data simultaneously with the regular coder. For the generalizability analysis, we specify coders as a facet, with two conditions, regular and calibrating. Resultant observations may vary as a function of coders, hence this facet represents one possible source of variance in the observational data.

A second facet frequently used in the collection of observation data is occasions or trials. Observers typically collect data on more than one occasion, perhaps different days, weeks, or months. The different observation sessions are treated in generalizability theory as unordered conditions within the occasions facet. In our work, this occasions facet is crossed with the coder facet, since each of the two coders (regular and calibrating) observes on both occasions. This amounts to a replication of the simultaneous observations obtained by the two coders.

Subjects are treated as a third facet, where each individual is a separate condition within the subjects facet. Since each of the two coders observes each of n subjects on two occasions, we have a fully crossed experimental design, involving two conditions of the coder facet, two conditions of the occasions facet, and n conditions of the subjects facet. This 2x2xn facet design, in which a behavioral observation score is used as the dependent variable, is employed to obtain estimates of variance components by conventional ANOVA procedures. This analysis partitions the variance in the dependent variable among the facets of the experimental design. Variance components attributable to coders, occasions, subjects, and the interaction of these facets, are obtained.

The specific ingredients of the present generalizability analysis are as follows. During a ten-weekday baseline or pretreatment phase, each of thirteen referred deviant boys and seventeen normal control boys was observed by the regular observer and a calibrating observer for five-minute time segments, on two different days of the ten-day baseline period (Patterson and Reid, 1973). The two samples of boys will be analyzed separately, with each sample treated as a random sample of boys from populations of deviant and normal boys respectively. The two segments during which both observers coded behavior are treated as random segments from the population of occasions. The third facet, coders, is treated as a fixed facet, since the regular and calibrating observers exhaust the population of possible coder types used in our collection of observation data. Hence, we have a mixed ANOVA model, with random conditions for the occasions and subjects facets, and a fixed condition for the coder facet.

Numerous behavioral scores derived from the observations could be used as dependent variables in this generalizability analysis. But because of a measurement restriction imposed by the observation procedure, and to conserve space, only five dependent variables will be analyzed. The measurement restriction is caused by the fact that during any five-minute segment, a total of fifty observational frequencies are obtained by any one coder for any one subject. These fifty observations will be distributed among the twenty-eight behavioral categories according to their relative occurrence in the stream of behavior shown by the target boy during the five-minute time segment. If, for example, the boy played continuously during the five minutes, all fifty frequencies would be coded as PL (Play). Typically, of course, the subject's behavior changes during the five minutes, so the fifty frequencies are distributed among the twenty-eight code categories, but with a possible range of total frequency for any one category from zero to fifty. Total frequencies for the low-rate behavioral categories will tend to hover near the zero end of this score distribution, while higher-rate behavioral categories will have scores in the middle or upper range of the score distribution. Since there are only fifty observations to be distributed among the twenty-eight behavioral categories, and the base rates of occurrence among the twenty-eight categories vary substantially, choosing a low-rate category as the dependent variable in the generalizability analysis will result in a positive skew in the distribution of scores. And, choosing a higher-rate category will result in a negative skew in the scores. Such distributions of scores for infrequent versus very common events are distinctly nonnormal, and hence do not meet the normality assumption of the analysis of variance. Ideally, then, the dependent variable of choice would be one with a mean near the midpoint of the zero-to-fifty range, with an appropriate standard deviation given the fixed range of possible scores. Two of the dependent variables analyzed meet these specifications. The first is a combination of the frequencies for two high-rate behaviors, PL (Play) and NO (Normative), and the second is the frequency of Talking behavior (TA). The other three dependent variables, Total Deviant (sum of frequencies for fourteen deviant behaviors), CO (Comply), and NC (Noncomply) are of greater clinical interest than PL + NO or TA, but are comprised of low-rate behaviors and hence have definite positive skews. But ANOVA procedures are fairly robust for nonnormal data (for example, Box, 1953), and the generalizability of these low-rate behaviors is of particular importance for clinical intervention studies.

Components of Variance Analysis. The three facet design outlined above is shown schematically in Table 4. The coder and occasions facets are fully crossed. Not all coders observed each boy, hence the design would be displayed more appropriately as a nested arrangement in which some of the boys are crossed with some of the five different coders, and other boys are crossed with different pairs of the five coders. That is, some of the subject conditions (for example, boys)' are nested within the coder facet. But in our observational work, it is seldom feasible to have one coder observe all subjects. Thus, when behavioral scores are used in across-subjects analyses, all boys are grouped even though not all boys were observed by the same coder. Since our purpose here is to study the components of variance and generalizability of the behavioral scores as they are typically used in our clinical research, the nesting is ignored. The effect, however, should be noted. By treating subjects as crossed with coders, the variance due to subjects is probably increased compared to what it would be if the nested design was used. This point should be remembered when interpreting the magnitude of the variance component estimates.

Table 5 shows the variance component estimates, in percents, for the two samples of thirteen deviant boys and seventeen normal boys, for each of the five dependent variables. These estimates were obtained by standard analysis of variance procedures for this mixed model, with random conditions within occasions and subjects facets, and fixed conditions within the coder facet. Negative estimates were converted to zero, as suggested by Cronbach and others (1972). The percents show how much of the variance in the behavioral scores is accounted for by each of the facets or interactions between facets. For example, in the sample of thirteen deviant boys, the subjects facet accounted for about 45 percent of the variance in the PL + NO scores, and the interaction between Subjects and Occasions accounted for about 52 percent of the variance in PL + NO (Play + Normative). Zero or trivial amounts of the variance were accounted for by the other facets, and interactions between the facets. The residual component, or three-way interaction, accounted

Table 4.

Three Facet Design for Estimating Components of
Variance Due to Coders (Regular vs. Calibrating),
Occasions (Segment$_1$ vs. Segment$_2$), and Subjects
(Boy$_1$, Boy$_2$ . . . Boy$_n$)

	Regular		Calibrating	
	Segment$_1$	Segment$_2$	Segment$_1$	Segment$_2$
Boy$_1$				
Boy$_2$				
Boy$_n$				

for about 4 percent of the variance, a relatively small amount compared to the two main contributors, Subjects and Subjects × Occasions. Similar results were obtained for PL + NO in the sample of seventeen normal boys, but more of the variance was accounted for by the Subjects × Occasions interaction and less by the Subjects facet than in the sample of thirteen deviant boys. Again, zero or trivial amounts of variance were accounted for by the remaining facets and their interactions. So, for the PL + NO variable, the Subjects and Subjects × Occasions facets combined accounted for about 96 percent of the variance in the deviant sample and about 97 percent in the normal sample. Since virtually no variance in either sample was accounted for by the Coders or Occasions facets, or their interaction, it can be concluded that inter-coder agreement and across-occasions stability (over all subjects) were extremely high for this dependent variable.

The results for the Total Deviant scores were somewhat

Table 5.

Variance Component Estimates (Percents) for Two Samples Thirteen Deviant Boys and Seventeen Normal Boys and Five Dependent Variables in a Three-Facet Design

Behavioral score sample	PL + NO Dev.	PL + NO Nor.	Total Deviant Dev.	Total Deviant Nor.	CO Dev.	CO Nor.	TA Dev.	TA Nor.	NC Dev.	NC Nor.
Facets										
Subjects (S)	43.72	27.16	79.44	0.00	.36	37.56	7.96	0.00	81.17	0.00
Coders (C)	.07	0.00	0.00	0.00	2.14	0.00	.23	.04	0.00	0.00
Occasions (O)	0.00	0.00	0.00	0.00	0.00	0.00	0.00	0.00	0.00	0.00
S × C	0.00	1.13	2.84	0.00	0.00	.38	0.00	0.00	5.25	0.00
S × O	52.02	70.02	12.05	81.37	74.98	53.36	85.87	95.10	10.36	54.18
C × O	0.00	.24	0.00	0.00	0.00	.26	0.00	0.00	0.00	0.00
Residual (S×C×O)	4.17	1.25	5.64	18.62	23.53	8.44	5.93	4.72	3.23	45.82

N.B. Percents do not total precisely 100.0 due to rounding in calculations.

different, but predictably so. About 91 percent of the variance in the deviant sample was accounted for by the Subjects, plus Subjects × Occasions facets, but of this proportion, nearly 80 percent was due to the Subjects facet alone. Thus, variance in Total Deviant was largely attributable to differences among subjects. And this is precisely the expected finding since the BCS and the behavior categories comprising Total Deviant were designed to assess behavioral deviancy in samples of behaviorally deviant boys.

The construct validity of the Total Deviant score is supported by the results of the normal sample. Here, none of the variance in Total Deviant was due to Subjects. But interestingly, the Subjects × Occasions interaction accounted for about 81 percent of the variance. This suggests that variance in Total Deviant in this normal sample is mainly accounted for by subjects differing across occasions, but nonsystematically, since the Occasions facet alone did not account for any variance at all. Some subjects, therefore, increased their Total Deviant score over occasions, while others did not change or decreased. However, inspection of the raw data for the normal sample showed, visually, very little variation across any of the facets. Probably the most parsimonious conclusion is simply that Total Deviant is not a suitable measure for normal samples, or at least not so suitable as for deviant samples. Notably, the BCS and the Total Deviant categories were designed for use with deviant boys, not normal (that is, nondeviant) boys.

Of the remaining three scores shown in Table 5, none showed any important variance due to Coders or Occasions, further supporting the conclusion that over all subjects, agreement between observers and stability across time was substantial. Also, variance estimates for these other scores showed that most of the accountable variance was due to Subjects and/or the Subjects × Occasions interaction. As in the case of Total Deviant, differences between the Deviant and Normal samples were obtained. For instance, in the Deviant sample, about 81 percent of the variance in NC (Noncomply) was due to Subjects, while none of the variance in NC in the Normal sample was due to Subjects. And, in the Normal sample, about 38 percent of the variance in CO (Comply) was due to Subjects, while in the Deviant sample, less than one percent of the variance in CO was due to Subjects. But note that for both CO and

NC, in each sample, major portions of the variance were due to the Subjects × Occasions interaction.

The relatively large portions of variance due to the Subjects × Occasions interaction can be interpreted as follows (see Bowers, 1973, for a review on other findings on this topic). Imagine two kinds of measures from traditional assessment, a trait measure and a mood or state measure. Trait versus state measures would be expected to yield different components of variance if analyzed in a design like the three-facet model used here for observational data. The trait measure would probably show little variance due either to Occasions or to the Subjects × Occasions interaction, because traits are assumed to be stable over time and settings and are not greatly affected by situational influences. On the other hand, mood or state measures would show more variance due to the Subjects × Occasions interaction, since mood ratings specifically assess how the subject feels, thinks, reacts, and so forth, at the time the assessment is obtained. Mood or state ratings are seemingly analogous to the behavioral observations analyzed here. These observations record how the subject is behaving during a particular session. The observations (or mood ratings) are not intended to reflect general behavioral propensities across a variety of settings and time, as is true of trait ratings. They are, however, likely to reflect situational or setting specificity, as shown here by the variance due to the Subjects × Occasions interaction in the observational data. A similar variance component would be expected for mood ratings, which tend to shift from time to time and from setting to setting. Note that the absence of a significant portion of variance due to Occasions (main effect) is not contradictory to this conclusion, since important variance for this facet would be obtained only if all subjects changed systematically from one time to another. Typically, with both mood ratings and observations, some subjects will increase, some will decrease, and others will not change their scores. It is precisely this heterogeneity of change over time which produces the Subjects × Occasions interaction.

In brief, we can conclude from this components of variance analysis that variance due to Coders was trivial; hence, intercoder agreement was substantial; variance due to Occasions was trivial; hence, on the average, subjects did not change homogeneously over time; variance due to Subjects was large when the behavioral score was an appropriate or relevant measure for the sample; for example, Total Deviant accounted for substantial variance in the deviant sample, but not the normal sample; and variance due to the Subjects × Occasions interaction was typically large for all behavioral scores, indicating that behavior varies substantially over time for individual subjects, and that the nature of this intraindividual variation is highly idiosyncratic.

Generalizability Coefficients. The theory of generalizability allows the researcher to generalize over different facets of the assessment design. Typically, interest centers on how well a score represents an overall dimension or construct, across all facets of the design. In the present case, for example, the intention might be to interpret Total Deviant as a measure of overall deviance, which would generalize across the other facets of the design, namely codes, occasions, and the interactions. But this would ignore the relatively large influence of the Subjects × Occasions interaction shown in the variance components analysis.

Since the Subjects × Occasions interaction suggests occasions or situational specificity in these behavioral scores, it is more appropriate to generalize to both subjects and occasions. In fact, for some of the behavioral scores, there was no variance due to Subjects alone; hence, the only possible generalization is to the Subjects × Occasions interaction, that is, the situational specificity of the scores. Hence, we will report only the generalizability coefficients which indicate the reliability of behavioral scores for individual subjects behaving in different situations, that is, on different occasions.

Following the Cronbach and others (1972) procedures, generalizability coefficients were calculated for both samples and for each of the five behavioral scores discussed in the components of variance section. These coefficients are analogous to intraclass correlation coefficients, and represent the magnitude of the generalizability of these scores to an assessment situation where data would be collected for an individual subject, by one coder, during each week day of a two-week baseline period. For details of the computational procedures, see Cronbach and others (1972).

The results of the generalizability analysis are shown in Table 6. Since these are population estimates, they can be interpreted as squared intraclass correlations. Thus, the generalizability coefficients represent the proportion of the variance accounted for by Subjects and by the Subjects × Occasions (or situations) interaction. Situations in the present context are really a hidden facet (Cronbach and others, 1972), in that each subject is actually observed in a situation unique to that subject. Subjects were observed in their own home settings; hence, differences in home settings are totally confounded with subjects. In addition, home settings could be viewed as a hidden facet within the Occasions facet, as well, since each subject's home environment could be assumed to vary across occasions, although perhaps not so greatly as the variation in home settings across different subjects. Of course, these hidden facets or confounds are a true representation of the assessment conditions under which these kinds of observational data are normally obtained; thus, the generalization intended is veridical despite the existence of hidden facets.

Table 6.

GENERALIZABILITY COEFFICIENTS (INTRACLASS CORRELATIONS) FOR EACH OF FIVE BEHAVIORAL SCORES IN TWO SAMPLES, OVER BOTH SUBJECTS AND OCCASIONS

	Behavioral scores				
Sample	Total deviant	PL + NO	CO	TA	NC
13 deviant boys	.96	.99	.77	.98	.94
17 normal boys	.81	.96	.98	.95	.54

Of the ten generalizability coefficients shown in Table 6, only one is appreciably low, .54 for NC (Noncomply) in the normal sample. Inspection of the raw data for this score showed very little variance across any of the facets; hence, it could be argued that this measure is not particularly relevant for samples of normal boys, or that the base rate of this behavior in normal samples is so low that the amount of sampling in the G study was insufficient. The other behavioral scores in the two samples produced respectably high generalizability coefficients, allowing the conclusion that measurement of these behaviors for subjects in different situations is not greatly influenced by measurement error.

These findings, coupled with the absence of any appreciable variance due to coders, suggest that the data generated by the Behavior Coding System are substantially devoid of measurement error, and hence, meet the essential reliability requirements of any clinical assessment procedure. We turn now to other, more specific aspects of reliability assessment which serve to highlight other influences on the measurement precision of observational data.

Stability of Observed Behavior Scores. The temporal stability of observational data can be estimated either interindividually or intraindividually. Interindividual stabilities of behavioral observation scores are analogous to test-retest reliabilities in traditional assessment, and require the correlations (over subjects) between scores from two occasions, plus no significant changes in mean scores from occasion to occasion. Intraindividual stability can be assessed for a single subject's profile of behavioral scores, obtained on two occasions. The focus of the two kinds of stability analysis is different; in the first case the stability of single behavioral scores is estimated, and in the second case the stability of a single subject's behavioral repertoire is estimated. Note that when stability of single behavioral scores is estimated, some subjects in the sample could have relatively unstable behavioral scores, but this is masked by the across-subjects analysis. The interindividual analysis is an averaging procedure, where the stability estimate applies to the average subject in the sample. If one's focus is on individual subjects, as is often the case in clinical assessment, then an intraindividual method of analysis can be more illuminating than the interindividual analysis. Results from both types of analysis are presented in the following sections.

Stability of Behavior Scores across Subjects. During the early development of the bcs, various broad classes of behavior, for example, rates of social interaction or total deviant codes, yielded test-retest correlations from about .60 and .70 for observations separated by a week (Patterson and Reid, 1970, p. 146; Reid, 1967). For twelve families observed with an early version of the code, the test-retest reliabilities for individual code categories were determined for observations conducted during two consecutive weeks (Patterson and others, 1973, pp. 161–165). A median correlation of .71 was obtained for codes classified then as responses, and a median of .60 was obtained for other codes classified as consequences. A subsequent analysis in a larger sample (Patterson and Cobb, 1971, p. 103) was similarly reassuring.

More recent analyses are summarized in Table 7, showing the correlations between the first and second half of baseline for a combined sample of twenty-seven normal and twenty-seven problem families. Descriptions of these samples are in Patterson and Cobb (1973, pp. 165–169). Either six or ten baseline observation sessions were conducted, over two to three consecutive weeks. The stability correlations are shown separately for fifty-four target boys, fifty-four mothers, and forty-one fathers. Missing entries in Table 7 indicate insufficient observations of the behavior for calculation of the correlation coefficients; for example, Crying (CR) was never observed for either mothers or fathers; hence, no stability correlations could be calculated.

For the behaviors and samples where the correlations could be calculated, there is considerable variation in the magnitude of the stability coefficients both within codes across samples and within samples across codes. These results should be interpreted in light of the generalizability findings presented earlier. Recall that there was a substantial portion of the variance in those behavioral scores due to the subjects by occasions interaction, suggesting intraindividual changes in behavior from one time sample to another. Similarly, for some codes and samples, these stability correlations show poor temporal stability, which is expected if individual subject's behaviors are changing over time, but in nonsystematic ways, as shown in the components of variance analysis.

Overall, however, these stability correlations suggest moderate levels of behavioral stability for many of the codes in these three samples. Sixty-three percent of the coefficients in Table 7 were statistically significant at the .01 level (one-tailed), clearly suggesting

Table 7.

STABILITY CORRELATIONS (FIRST HALF VS. SECOND HALF OF
BASELINE) FOR 28 BEHAVIOR CATEGORIES IN SAMPLES OF 54
TARGET BOYS, 54 MOTHERS, AND 41 FATHERS

	First order				*Second order*		
	Boys	Mothers	Fathers		Boys	Mothers	Fathers
VERBAL							
CM	.23	.73	.44	TA	.26	.53	.38
CN*	.68	.80	.54				
CR*	.90	—	—				
HU*	.73	.54	.33				
LA	.23	.46	.35				
NE*	.54	.68	.39				
WH*	.63	—	—				
YE*	.74	.45	—				
NON-VERBAL							
DS*	.46	—	—	AT	.36	.38	.43
HR*	.16	—	—	NO	.44	.49	.15
IG*	.27	.63	—	NR	.21	.20	.12
PN*	.38	.63	.63	RC	.32	.21	.16
PP	—	.69	.19	TH	.31	.68	.38
EITHER VERBAL OR NON-VERBAL							
AP	.02	.48	.15	SS	.29	.05	.06
CO	.67	.37	.38				
DI*	.66	.62	.48				
DP*	.24	—	—				
NC*	.63	.34	.45				
PL	.51	.59	.48				
TE*	.35	.85	.43				
WK	.59	.50	.16				

* Deviant Behavior Categories. All other codes classified as Prosocial Behavior
Categories.

— Insufficient data for calculation of coefficients.

that most of the interindividual differences in these scores were at least moderately consistent from the first to the second half of the baseline period.

Stability of Behavioral Repertoires Within Subjects. As pointed out by Jones (1973), one might consider both intersubject and intrasubject frames of reference in evaluating questions of stability. Jones (1972) analyzed the behavioral scores for individual subjects by calculating profiles of scores for the first and second halves of baseline. The two profiles were compared for each of twenty-six problem children and their mothers, and for twenty normal boys and their mothers. The distributions of scores for each code category were standardized to provide a common scale of measurement across codes. A test-retest correlation was computed for each subject over the standardized scores between the profiles for the first and second halves of baseline. The average profile stability correlations were .42 and .37 for the problem and nonproblem boys, respectively, and .57 and .41 for mothers from those samples. Of the ninety-two profile stability correlations, 28 percent were nonsignificant. This suggests that for some subjects, six or ten baseline observation sessions may not be sufficient to obtain stable behavioral profiles. Jones (1972) suggested that behavioral stability should probably be estimated individually for each subject, particularly when the data are employed clinically, that is, subject by subject, rather than averaged across subjects.

Interobserver Reliability and Behavioral Complexity. The most common empirical estimate of the integrity of observation data is interobserver agreement or reliability. These empirical estimates are usually based on the ability of two or more observers to record the same information while simultaneously and independently watching the same stimulus situation. The estimate, as commonly used, is expressed in terms of a correlation coefficient or a percent agreement, and describes the general level of interobserver reliability over all categories in a code system.

Because of considerations such as expense and obtrusiveness, most observation data currently reported in the literature are not continuously monitored for interobserver reliability. Instead, reliability statistics are typically calculated from assessments carried out either before the collection of usable data, or at some point(s) during the course of a study. A number of recent studies have questioned the meaning or implications of such discontinuous reliability assessments of observation data (for example, Reid, 1970; Romanczyk, Kent, Diament, and O'Leary, 1971; Taplin and Reid, 1973). The finding common to these studies has been that observer performance is significantly less reliable after or between reliability assessments than while they are being conducted. The implication of these studies is that the quality of observation data is markedly overestimated by the discontinuous reliability assessments reported in much observational research. The problem of maintaining the level of observer reliability after or between reliability assessments has not yet been solved (DeMaster, 1971; Taplin and Reid, 1973).

If one examines closely the logic implicit in the use of a global reliability statistic to estimate data quality, some problems emerge. When an investigator supplies one set of reliability statistics, drawn from a subset of the actual observations, with no information given as to how the sessions, observed subjects, time of day, and so forth, were chosen for inclusion, it must be assumed that the investigator thinks of reliability as a characteristic of the skill level of the observers during training, or of the structure of a coding scheme, but not as a function of the ever-changing nature of the observational setting or the variable nature of ongoing behavior.

A number of recent analyses, performed on data collected via the BCS, suggest that interobserver reliability is not a stable characteristic of observational data, but changes as a function of the complexity of the behavior recorded. In this work, complexity has been found to vary systematically within subjects over time, between subjects, and between specific types of observational situations.

Let us now look at the relationship between complexity and observer agreement. Complexity as used here is some measure of the number of discriminations required of an observer during a data collection session.[3] The results of three studies have indicated that the relationship between complexity and observer reliability is quite strong. In a study by Taplin and Reid (1973) of the reliability of

[3] It also seems reasonable that the complexity of a given coding system will itself be predictive of the level of reliability attained by users of that system. Empirical support for this assumption has been reported recently by Mash and McElwee (1974, in press).

observers under conditions of overt and covert reliability assessment, the correlation between percent agreement and complexity of the criterion protocols was −.52 ($p < .001$) where complexity was defined as (n different entries/total entries for a five-minute observation segment). This result indicates a moderately strong tendency for reliability to drop as the complexity of the observed interaction increases. The correlation between the complexity of observers' own protocols and their agreement with criterion protocols was −.50 ($p < .001$).[4] Using two data sets, Skindrud (1972) obtained significant negative correlations of −.53 and −.65 (both $p < .001$) between observer agreement and the percent of unrepeated interactions within each observed behavior segment (a measure of complexity). Finally, Reid (1973a), using reliability assessment data from an ongoing observational research project, found a correlation of −.75 ($p < .01$) between percent agreement and complexity of the observers' protocols (as defined in Taplin and Reid, 1973).

This relationship between interobserver reliability and the complexity of observed interaction may turn out to be useful in two ways. First, complexity may be measured continuously without doubling up on observers. If the relationship between the two variables holds up in future research (or can be strengthened by more sophisticated formulae for measuring complexity), it may allow the investigator to anticipate observer drift in time to correct the problem. For example, suppose observers achieve 75 percent agreement during reliability assessment with an average complexity of .25. Later, during data collection, the average complexity of the protocols increases to .50. Given the relationship between reliability and complexity, it might be well for the investigator to institute another reliability assessment, using more complex observation episodes, and to give the observers further training if necessary.[5] If such an increase in complexity was discovered after all the data were collected, the investigator would still be in a position to qualify his estimate of the reliability of the data reported, and to give his cherished hy-

[4] Correlation between complexity as calculated from criterion protocols and as calculated from observers' protocols was $R_{xy} = .65$ ($p < .001$).

[5] Because of the strong correlation between complexity and reliability, it would be possible to use complexity as an estimator of reliability in a given observation project. The exact form of the estimate and its confidence limits could be worked out empirically during the development of the code.

pothesis another experimental chance if he fails to reject the null hypothesis on the grounds that lowered reliability increased the probability of a Type 2 error.

Second, the idea of complexity might be useful not only for monitoring and preventing observer decay as discussed above, but also for a partial understanding of the mechanism underlying the observer drift phenomenon. The research findings on observer drift may be summarized as follows. Observers are trained to some arbitrary level of intercoder agreement (usually between 70 and 90 percent, depending on the complexity of the coding system) for some observation period (for example, two consecutive sessions). After the observers reach the given criterion they are led to believe they are no longer being monitored for reliability (in fact, they are monitored covertly). Immediately following the transition from overt to covert reliability assessment conditions, there is an abrupt drop in observer agreement (for example, Reid, 1970; Reid and DeMaster, 1972; Taplin and Reid, 1973). After the initial drop, observer agreement appears to remain constant at that level.

To understand how complexity may fit into the observer drift phenomenon, consider the following example. Before data collection, an investigator trains two observers to use his code reliably. After the observers have memorized the code definitions and abbreviations and the rules for their use, the investigator collects data in the target classroom with the observers. The procedure is to compare his observations with those of each observer until the observers can agree with him at a level of 70 percent for two consecutive sessions. When the observers reach that criterion, they are considered adequately trained for independent data collection. During this training process the following events might occur. The coders may come across two consecutive sessions, purely by chance, during which the complexity of the observed interaction is minimal. The results would be two consecutive sessions of spuriously high reliability. In other words, because the observers chanced upon two simple (low complexity) sessions, they attained high agreement scores without attaining high proficiency. The point is this: if one assumes that complexity of observed behaviors varies across sessions, the reliability of observer performance gives incomplete or possibly misleading information about observer skill, and/or the degree to which the assessed reliability will generalize to posttraining data. The following example from Skindrud (1972) may serve to clarify the problem. He trained twenty-four observers over a three-week period. The average weekly performances during training in terms of interobserver percent agreement were 47 percent (beginning of week one), 55 percent (beginning of week two), 62 percent (beginning of week three), and 68 percent (end of week three).

These results indicate that the observers were becoming more proficient each week. These statistics are misleading, however, because the complexity was not equal across weeks. If we multiply the obtained percent agreement by the number of nonrepeated entries (a measure of complexity), we come up with a proficiency score similar to that used to judge diving competitions (that is, the difficulty level of the dive itself × the judge's ratings of its execution). Applying this formula to the Skindrud data, we find that proficiency as measured by agreement alone overestimates the observer skill when complexity is taken into account.

Inspection of Table 8 suggests that the steadily increasing percent agreement is overestimating the increase in skill because the sessions during the last two weeks happen to be less complex (lower percentage non-repeated segments). Note that the skill score in Week two was higher than in Week three, even though the percent agreement in Week three was higher than in Week two. Even though the skill score shows that observers are doing better at the end of Week three than in Week one, it does not yield the neat learning curve given by the percent agreement alone. For these observers we would predict a drop in percent agreement when they observed more difficult or complex sessions. The point is that if the only criterion for observer performance is some level of agreement over a couple of observation sessions, then in many cases criterion reliability will be achieved when observers by chance come across some simple observation sessions.

A similar problem exists when we consider the possibility of complexity differences between subjects. Just as it is possible for complexity to vary across sessions within subjects, it is reasonable for complexity to vary between subjects. Suppose, for example, we have subjects under investigation whose interaction patterns vary from extremely simple to extremely complex. Suppose further that

Table 8.

RELIABILITY, COMPLEXITY, AND OBSERVER SKILL ESTIMATES

	Week 1	*Week 2*	*Week 3*	*Week 4*
	Percent			
Mean percent agreement between observers (reliability)	47	55	62	68
Mean percent non-repeated entries (complexity)	76	84	72	73
Mean percent agreement X mean percent non-repeats (skill)	.36	.46	.44	.49

reliability is assessed using only the simple-behaving subjects. It might then be the case that the reliability figure obtained would significantly overestimate the mean reliability of data collected in the study. An example of this possibility is shown in Table 9, where the average complexity and percent agreement data for the baseline studies of two subjects are presented.

In this instance, it would be expected that an interobserver reliability assessment carried out only for S_1 would overestimate the

Table 9.

AGREEMENT AND COMPLEXITY ESTIMATES FOR TWO SUBJECTS

	S_1	S_2
	Percent	
Mean percent agreement	84.4	56.4
Mean complexity $\left(\dfrac{\text{number of different categories}}{\text{number of entries}}\right)$	.23	.49

reliability of data collected for S_2; and that an assessment carried out only on S_2 would underestimate the reliability of data collected for S_1.

Another example of between-subjects differences in observer agreement and complexity comes from the Taplin and Reid (1973) study on observer agreement. Although not discussed in that paper, a significant difference was found between average percent agreement for child versus adult subjects. The observations of child subjects were consistently less reliable ($\bar{x} = 55\%$ agreement) than for adult subjects ($\bar{x} = 74\%$ agreement) ($F = 272.47$, df 1, 9; $p <$ .01). It was also the case that the complexity of the protocols for child observations was more complex ($\bar{x} = .36$) than for adults ($\bar{x} = .19$) ($t = 2.11$, $df = 48$; $p < .025$).

The implication of these two examples is that reliability assessment data may not generalize across subjects whose behavior varies in complexity. This suggests that reliability data should be sampled for every subject observed. An estimate of the degree to which a discontinuous reliability analysis reflects the reliability of the entire data set would be derived by a comparison of the means and variances of the complexity for monitored and unmonitored data sets.

One commonly used procedure to reduce decay in observer reliability over time has been to assess observer agreement at points throughout the course of data collection (Berk, 1971; Hartup and Coates, 1967; Patterson and Reid, 1973; Walker and Buckley, 1968). The logic underlying this strategy is that any tendency for observer performance to decay over sessions becomes evident through intermittent spot checks. An analysis by Reid (1973b) is interesting in terms of this assumption. Twenty-two spot-check reliability assessments of observation data collected in the homes of aggressive boys were analyzed for both percent agreement and complexity (defined as number of different categories used $\div$ number of entries made for each five-minute segment). The mean agreement for these reliability checks was 72.6 percent (range $= 61.5$ percent to 85.5 percent) which was acceptable for our purposes. Thus, one would assume that data quality was holding up over time. The mean complexity for these reliability sessions was .28. Adjacent, unmonitored observation sessions were then analyzed for complexity. The mean complexity for these adjacent sessions was .32. A t-test for correlated measures revealed that the mean complexity for reliability sessions (.28) was significantly lower than that for adjacent observation sessions (.32). This difference was quite reliable ($t = 2.65$, $df = 21$; $p < .01$). The best guess, based upon the correlation between observer agreement and complexity, is that our spot-check reliability assessments overestimate the reliability of unmonitored data.[6]

There are at least two explanations for this finding, both of which make exclusive reliance on discontinuous observer agreement checks a questionable assessment of data quality. First, the observers may have an intuitive understanding of the relationship between complexity and reliability. If true, it is not inconceivable that they may simplify their recordings during reliability checks to insure higher levels of agreement. That is, they might have an implict agreement not to record subtle behavior changes during reliability assessment. Second, observation subjects may act differently (more simply) in the presence of two than in the presence of one observer (reactivity). Whatever the determinant of this effect, it is possible that spot-check assessments do not yield a veridical estimate of observer reliability.

Observer Effect. The effects of the instrument on the behavior to be measured is a problem of general concern to users of observational data. Sometimes parents have reported that observers did not see the family as it really was. Some said their children acted worse when the observers were present; others reported that the children and they themselves were better behaved when the observers were present. Our experience agrees with conclusions reached by reviewers of the research literature in this area (Heyns and Lippitt 1954; Weick 1968). The presence of the observer in the home is assumed to be a significant social stimulus which probably has some effect on family interaction. The question, however,

----

[6] This conclusion is supported by the analogue study of observer reliability conducted by Taplin and Reid (1973) in which observers were shown to agree at a significantly higher level during overt spot checks of observer agreement than during adjacent sessions when the assessments were covert.

concerns the magnitude, duration, and quality of the observer effect. The problems involved in the measurement of these effects have proven to be very complex.

There are at least two plausible biases that might enter observational data due to a general observer effect. First, subjects might behave in either socially-desirable or socially-undesirable ways, depending on the demand characteristics of the setting. For deviant families who are hoping to enter treatment, a socially-undesirable bias might occur to insure a place in treatment. For normal control families, who are participating as research subjects, socially-desirable bias might be expected because most people try to look good for the social scientist. A second kind of bias would be seen as an increase in the variability of behavior, particularly during the first several observation sessions when observers and observees are getting used to each other. These two effects, desirability and variability, could be associated, particularly in heterogeneous samples composed of both deviant and nondeviant families. Tendencies to respond desirably by normal subjects, and undesirably by deviant subjects would, of course, increase variability in the overall sample. Schalock's (1958) suggestion that variability would be increased in early sessions was not confirmed by Paul (1963) or by White (1972), who studied mother-child interaction.

But some studies have been supportive of the social desirability hypothesis, at least for some kinds of samples. Lobitz and Johnson (1972) showed that for normal families, parents could make their children behave in either socially-desirable or undesirable ways. Lobitz (1973) extended this study to samples of both normal and deviant families, and replicated the finding in the normal families, but found that deviant parents could make their children only look bad, not look good. These studies suggest that parental instructions can bias observations of their children in socially-desirable or undesirable ways, but that the direction of the bias in deviant families may be toward faking bad only.

Another set of studies manipulated the families' awareness of being observed. Harris (1969) and White (1972) showed that overall family deviancy did not differ under observation conditions when the families knew or did not know that they were being observed. White (1972), however, did show that older children, in a laboratory setting, did reduce their deviancy when they knew they were being observed, compared to their deviancy under covert observation. Both studies were characterized by serious methodological problems which necessarily limit the conclusions which can be drawn. However, as preliminary evaluations, they suggested that the effect of being observed did not produce as much distortion in family interaction as had been expected.

Another form of expectancy was represented in Walter and Gilmore's (1973) study which showed that although placebo treatment parents reported high expectations for change in their children, observations of the children actually showed increased deviancy during the placebo treatment period.

In summary, observed behavior in normal families may be biased under parental instructions to make their children look good or bad. Parental instructions in families of deviant children result in the children's looking bad, not good. Attempts to manipulate the awareness of family members being observed have been relatively unsuccessful in producing an observer presence effect. However, older (normal) children may be able to inhibit their deviancy when they know they are being watched. Parental expectations for behavioral change in treatment apparently do not influence actual, observed behavior of their children. But despite these few findings, it seems appropriate to conclude that although the notion of observer effects is ubiquitous, demonstrations of the effect are not so common.

Validation of BCS

The validity of the BCS is best appraised by asking the question, How valid are the behavioral observation scores for the decisions that the researcher or clinician wishes to make? The BCS was developed in a particular research and clinical context, focused on adequate description and measurement of aggressive behavior in children and social behaviors in the child's family setting. The validity issue therefore amounts to determining how well suited the behavioral scores are for their intended research and clinical uses. In this section, three types of validity analyses will be presented: content validity, concurrent validity, and construct validity (Cronbach, 1970, p. 122).

Content Validity. The validity question here is, How well does the BCS represent the behaviors that are important for the intended research and clinical purposes of the instrument? Usually, the content validity of observation systems is implicitly assumed to be high, because the behaviors typically included in such systems have considerable face validity. But this smacks of circular reasoning, so recourse to outside judgments of the content validity of the behavioral categories in the BCS was considered important. Recall that the behavioral categories were originally developed out of a clinical interest in developing treatment programs for the amelioration of aggressive behaviors in children. However, it is reasonable to check the clinical judgments of relevant behaviors for the coding system against others' perceptions of the aggressive or aversive quality of the behaviors.

In the development of the BCS, it was assumed that an aversive stimulus presented to another person constituted an aggressive act. *A priori*, fourteen different code categories (CN, CR, DI, DP, DS, HR, HU, IG, NC, NE, PN, TE, WH, YE)' were classed as noxious and labeled Total Deviant behaviors (see Table 1). In a study described in the Johnson and Bolstad (1973)' review, mothers rated descriptions of all behaviors for deviancy. The ratings for the fourteen noxious behaviors were consistently in the predicted direction, relative to the other, less noxious codes. Also, twenty mothers of preschool children were asked to rate descriptions of each of the twenty-eight behaviors on a nine-point scale ranging from (1)' very annoying to (9)' very pleasing. The mean ratings shown in Table 10 were used to rank order the codes in this aversiveness dimension. Note in Table 10 that all of the fourteen *a priori* deviant categories had mean ratings less than the midpoint of the scale (≤ 5), and with the exception of NR (No Response)', all of the nondeviant categories had mean ratings higher than the highest rated deviant category (DI)'.

Thus, these mothers' ratings confirm the *a priori* clinical judgments of the noxiousness or aversiveness of these deviant behaviors, and we interpret these findings as indirect support for the content validity of the code categories. Indirect in that only the aversiveness of the code categories has been confirmed, not the representativeness, adequacy, or relevance of these particular codes vis-à-

Table 10.

MEAN AVERSIVENESS RATINGS (9-POINT SCALE) FOR 20 MOTHERS
ON EACH OF 28 BEHAVIOR CATEGORIES

Code	Behavior	Rating	Code	Behavior	Rating
DS*	Destructiveness	1.5	CM	Command	5.4
IG*	Ignore	1.7	SS	Self-stimulation	5.7
NC*	Noncomply	1.9	NO	Normative	5.9
HU*	Humiliate	2.0	AT	Attention	6.0
TE*	Tease	2.1	TH	Touch	7.2
YE*	Yell	2.1	TA	Talk	7.3
WH*	Whine	2.2	RC	Receive	7.4
PN*	Physical Negative	2.3	PL	Play	7.9
HR*	High Rate	2.5	CO	Comply	8.1
CN*	Command Negative	2.8	LA	Laugh	8.1
DP*	Dependency	2.8	WK	Work	8.4
NE*	Negativism	2.8	AP	Approval	8.5
NR	No Response	3.8	PP	Physical Positive	8.6
CR*	Cry	4.2			
DI*	Disapproval	4.2			

* Deviant Behavior Categories

vis the population of possible categories. But, clearly, if the mother's ratings had shown these categories to be nonaversive, the content validity of the codes would be questionable.

Concurrent Validity. In clinical treatment of children, parents' reports of their child's difficulties are often taken as important clinical signs. If not the parents, some other significant adult in the child's environment usually provides referral information about the deviancy of the client. Hence, it is reasonable to ask about the concurrent validity of observational data with reports from significant adults, in this case the parents. A caution should be noted, however. Some behaviorally-oriented clinicians have come to suspect parent reports of their child's behavior, particularly when the required data are quite behaviorally specific. Parents may not be as good observers of their own children, without special training, as are professional coders. And because this is so often true, clinical intervention may involve teaching parents to be better trackers and recorders of their child's behavior. Hence, the convergence between observations of children and parent reports of the same child behaviors might be attenuated due to imperfect recording by parents. Nevertheless, since parents are key individuals in treatment, both as referral sources and as treatment agents themselves, it is important to assess the concurrent validity between observations and parents' reports.

Hendriks (1972) investigated the relationships between mothers' ratings of their children's behavior and behavioral scores derived from the BCS. The mothers rated their children on forty-seven bipolar adjectives, which were scored on five scales developed from Patterson and Fagot's (1967) refactoring of Becker's (1960) original checklist. Scores on each of the five factors were correlated with the baseline frequencies for each of the fourteen deviant behaviors (see Table 1). The correlations obtained for four of the five factors (*Relaxed disposition, Withdrawn/hostile, Intellectual efficiency,* and *Conduct problems*) were typically small and nonsignificant. But for the fifth factor, *Aggression,* seven of the fourteen deviant behaviors correlated significantly ($p < .05$ for $n = 15$). These correlations were .46 for Destructiveness, .51 for Humiliate, .54 for Noncompliance, .49 for Negativism, .50 for Tease, .46 for Whine, and .50 for Yell. Thus, mothers' ratings on adjectives which load an Aggression factor correlated significantly with half of the *a priori* aggression or noxious codes from the BCS, providing evidence of concurrent validity for these behavioral categories.

Two other studies have supported the concurrent validity of the BCS scores for the deviant behaviors. Devine (1971) obtained laboratory observations of the fourteen noxious codes comprising the Total Deviant score during a stress situation when mothers of preschool children were temporarily unavailable for social interaction with their children. The mothers rated their children on a dimension representing the extent to which their children became upset when left with a babysitter. The correlation between the two measures was .50 ($p < .05$). In addition, a correlation of .35 ($p < .05$) was obtained between the duration of deviant behavior in the laboratory setting and the mother's ratings of her child's tendency to get his way at home by coercion. In another study, Patterson (1974a) examined the relationship between the Total Deviant score from the

BCS and parents' daily reports of the occurrence of referral symptoms, some of which were among the fourteen noxious codes. The correlation of .69 ($p < .05$) between these two measures suggests that problem children who score high on observed deviant behaviors tend to display high rates of symptom behaviors as reported by their parents. All of these findings show moderate to high levels of concurrent validity between parent perceptions of their children's behavior and scores on the BCS.

Construct Validity. Construct validity is a particularly important type of validity for the BCS because of the theoretical and clinical orientation from which the observation system evolved. Aggression in children was posited as the result of social learning in the family setting, and the behavioral manifestations of this aggression were represented in the set of codes now included in the BCS. Clinical treatment of aggression in children was aimed at rearranging the social contingencies in the family constellation which in turn should change the levels or rates of deviant behavior exhibited by treated children and their families. Thus, construct validity should be evidenced by changes in child deviancy, as measured by the BCS, following treatment. Construct validity should also be evidenced by comparisons between samples of children treated as socially aggressive and samples of children from nonclinical or normal populations. Both forms of construct validity are presented below.

Reid and Hendriks (1973) compared samples of thirteen aggressive boys, fourteen nonaggressive boys who stole, and twenty-seven normal boys matched on relevant demographic variables. Baseline observations were scored on a measure called Negative-coercive behaviors, which is identical to the Total Deviant score mentioned above, with the exclusion of the HR (High Rate) behavior category. For ease of exposition here, however, we shall refer to this Negative-coercion score as Total Deviant. The mean rates per minute of Total Deviant in the three samples were .30 (normals), .57 (stealers), and .75 (aggressive boys). The F-ratio of 4.31 was significant at the .05 level, and individual comparisons revealed significant differences between the normals and the aggressive boys, but not the other two comparisons. Thus, the observational data, in the form of a Total Deviant score from baseline sessions, clearly differentiated normal from aggressive samples of boys, just as the BCS should if the behavioral categories are validly measuring the construct of aggression. Note that the rate per minute of Total Deviant in the aggressive sample was about 2.5 times the rate in the normal sample, .75 aggressive responses per minute for aggressive boys versus .30 aggressive responses per minute for normal boys. The preliminary normative data presented in Table 3 also show differences between problem and nonproblem samples for individual code categories.

The final set of evidence for the construct validity of the BCS is perhaps the most important, given the clinical and research purposes of the observation system. Here the intention was to demonstrate by direct observation of children's behavior that treatment programs designed to alter social aggression in fact were able to significantly reduce the rates of deviancy in treated families. A series of studies have dealt with this question (Patterson, 1974a, b, c; Patterson, Cobb, and Ray, 1973; Patterson and Reid, 1973). Only the main theme of these studies will be summarized here, but each of these separate investigations has supported the construct validity of the BCS by showing that significant changes in deviant behavior have occurred following treatment of socially aggressive boys.

Referrals come to the Social Learning Project from community agencies. The children are described as exhibiting high rates of social aggression. The BCS is used to collect from six to ten days of baseline data in the homes, for one hour each day. Then intervention and a follow-up period occur, during which the BCS is again used for a minimum of eight days spaced over these two phases of treatment. Thus, the behavioral observation scores are obtained for each family before, during, and after intervention.

For a sample of twenty-seven socially aggressive boys, the average Total Deviant score from the BCS for the baseline observations was .75 responses per minute. That is, on the average, these children were emitting about three deviant responses every four minutes. The responses could be any one or more of the fourteen deviant behavior categories noted in Table 1. At the end of four weeks into intervention, the mean rate per minute was .46, and at the end of treatment (length of treatment varied from case to case), the mean rate was .40. Thus, from baseline to treatment termination, there was a reduction in deviant behavior of almost one-half as measured by the Behavior Coding System. An analysis of variance for repeated measures showed the differences in these means to be statistically significant at less than the .01 level of confidence. The treatment programs used with these families were specifically intended to provide the parents with the child management skills necessary to reduce the boys' rates of deviant behavior. And, the BCS, which was designed to measure deviant behavior in aggressive boys, clearly reflected the impact of the treatment programs.

The behavioral observations during follow-up showed an initial rise in deviant behavior rate, requiring an average of about 1.9 hours of additional booster shot treatment in the sample of twenty-seven families. But over the full year follow-up period, the BCS continued to show reduced rates of deviant behavior compared to the baseline levels. Observations collected during the follow-up year yielded the following mean rates of deviant behavior: .34 at the fourth month, .36 at the sixth month, .30 at the eighth month, and finally, .40 at the end of the twelve-month follow-up. These findings provide substantial evidence for the effectiveness of the treatment programs, and for the purposes of establishing the construct validity of the code system, indicate that the BCS accomplished its clinical and research purposes by reflecting changes in the deviant behaviors of the treated children.

Summary

The development of the Behavioral Coding System (BCS) used by the Social Learning Project at ORI has encompassed approximately eight years of clinical and research experience with naturalistic observation as a clinical assessment tool. The BCS, while originally designed to accomplish certain broad purposes, also illustrates a solution to an assessment task that should be applicable to other research and clinical settings in which naturalistic observation of family interactions are needed.

A variety of reliability analyses, ranging from traditional interobserver agreement among coders to generalizability analyses, have supported the measurement precision of the BCS scores for their intended purposes. In conducting this series of investigations, certain problems in psychometric analysis of observational data have arisen and been documented. Most notably, the tradition of estimating re-liability via interobserver agreement has been questioned, mainly on the grounds that behavioral complexity intrudes into such analyses in ways that suggest current observer reliability estimates may be substantially biased. The usefulness of generalizability theory is argued, particularly for observational data collected under varying assessment conditions which may influence behavioral scores.

Three types of validity have been reported for BCS scores, content, concurrent, and construct validity. The BCS has favorably withstood these psychometric investigations, showing that the be-havioral measures are justified on content grounds, that outside re-ports of behavior coincide satisfactorily with the BCS scores, and that expected behavioral changes following treatment are readily indexed by the BCS scores.

References

ANTONOVSKY, H. F. "A Contribution to Research in the Area of the Mother-Child Relationship." *Child Development,* 1959, *30,* 37–51.

BARKER, R. G. "The Stream of Behavior as an Empirical Problem." In R. G. Barker (Ed.), *The Stream of Behavior.* New York: Ap-pleton-Century-Crofts, 1963. Pp. 1–22.

BECKER, W. C. "The Relationship of Factors in Parental Ratings of Self and Each Other to the Behavior of Kindergarten Children as Rated by Mothers, Fathers, and Teachers." *Journal of Con-sulting Psychology,* 1960, *24,* 507–527.

BERK, L. E. "Effects of Variations in the Nursery School Setting on En-vironmental Constraints and Children's Modes of Adaptation." *Child Development,* 1971, *42.*

BING, E. "Effect of Child-Rearing Practices on Development of Dif-ferential Cognitive Abilities." *Child Development,* 1963, *34,* 631–648.

BOWERS, K. S. "Situationalism in Psychology: An Analysis and a Cri-tique." *Psychological Review,* 1973, *80,* 307–336.

CAMPBELL, J. P., DUNNETTE, M. D., ARVEY, R. D., AND HELLERVIK, L. V. "The Development and Evaluation of Behaviorally Based Rating Scales." *Journal of Applied Psychology,* 1973, *57,* 15–22.

CLEMENT, P. W., AND MILNE, D. C. "Group Play Therapy and Tangible Reinforcers Used to Modify the Behavior of Eight-Year-Old Boys." *Behaviour Research and Therapy,* 1967, *5,* 301–312.

COLLINS, R. C. "The Treatment of Disruptive Classroom Behavior Problems by Employment of a Partial-Milieu Consistency Program." Unpublished doctoral dissertation, University of Oregon, 1966.

CRANDALL, V. J., AND PRESTON, A. "Verbally Expressed Needs and Overt Maternal Behaviors." *Child Development,* 1961, *32,* 261–270.

CRONBACH, L. J. *Essentials of Psychological Testing.* New York: Harper and Row, 1970.

CRONBACH, L. J., GLESER, G. C., NANDA, H., AND RAJARATNAM, N. *The Dependability of Behavioral Measurements: Theory of Generalizability for Scores and Profiles.* New York: John Wiley and Sons, 1972.

DE MASTER, B. L. "Effects of Differing Amounts of Feedback and Methods of Assessment on Reliability of Data Collected by Pairs of Observers." Unpublished master's thesis, University of Wisconsin, 1971.

DEVINE, V. T. "The Coercion Process: A Laboratory Analogue." Unpublished doctoral thesis, State University of New York at Stony Brook, 1971.

DOUGLAS, J. W. B., LAWSON, A., COOPER, J. E., AND COOPER, E. "Family Interaction and the Activities of Young Children." *Journal of Child Psychology and Psychiatry,* 1968, *9,* 157–171.

GOLDFRIED, M. R., AND KENT, R. N. "Traditional versus Behavioral Personality Assessment: A Comparison of Methodological and Theoretical Assumptions." *Psychological Bulletin,* 1972, *77,* 409–420.

GULLIKSEN, H. *Theory of Mental Tests.* New York: John Wiley and Sons, 1950.

HARRIS, A. M. "Observer Effects on Family Interaction." Unpublished doctoral dissertation, University of Oregon, 1969.

HARTUP, W. W. AND COATES, B. "Imitation of a Peer as a Function of Reinforcement from the Peer Group and Rewardingness of the Model." *Child Development,* 1967, *38,* 1003–1016.

HENDRIKS, A. F. C. J. "Reported versus Observed Deviancy." Unpublished manuscript, University of Nijmegen, Netherlands, 1972.

HEYNS, R. W. AND LIPPITT, R. "Systematic Observation Techniques." In G. Lindsey (Ed.), *Handbook of Social Psychology.* Vol. 1. Reading, Massachusetts: Addison-Wesley, 1954. Pp. 370–404.

HONIG, A. S., TANNENBAUM, J., AND CALDWELL, B. M. "Maternal Behavior in Verbal Report and in Laboratory Observation." Paper presented at the meeting of the American Psychological Association, September, 1968.

JOHNSON, S. M. AND BOLSTAD, O. D. "Methodological Issues in Naturalistic Observation: Some Problems and Solutions for Field Research." In L. A. Hamerlynck, L. C. Handy, and E. J. Mash (Eds.), *Behavior Change: Methodology Concepts and Practice*. Champaign, Illinois: Research Press, 1973. Pp. 7–68.

JONES, R. R. "Intraindividual Stability of Behavior Observations: Implications for Evaluating Behavior Modification Treatment Programs." Paper presented at the meetings of the Western Psychological Association, Portland, Oregon, April, 1972.

JONES, R. R. "Behavioral Observation Frequency Data: Problems in Scoring, Analysis, and Interpretation." In L. A. Hamerlynck, L. C. Handy, and E. J. Mash (Eds.), *Behavior Change: Methodology Concepts and Practice*. Champaign, Illinois: Research Press, 1973. Pp. 119–145.

JONES, R. R. AND COBB, J. A. "Teachers vs. Observers as Classroom Data Collectors." Paper presented at the meeting of the Western Psychological Association, Anaheim, California, April, 1973.

KARAFIN, G. R. "Discussion of Considerations for Selecting or Developing an Observational System." *Classroom Interaction Newsletter*, 1973, *8*, 13–32.

KASS, R. E. AND O'LEARY, K. D. "The Effects of Observer Bias in Field-Experimental Settings." Paper presented at a Symposium, "Behavior Analysis in Education," University of Kansas, Lawrence, April, 1970.

LOBITZ, G. AND JOHNSON, S. M. "Normal Versus Deviant: Fact or Fantasy." Paper presented at the meeting of the Western Psychological Association, Portland, Oregon, April, 1972.

LOBITZ, W. C. "Parental Response Sets and the Behavior of Deviant and Non-Deviant Children during Naturalistic Observation." Unpublished doctoral dissertation, University of Oregon, 1973.

MASH, E. J. AND MC ELWEE, J. D. "Situational Effects on Observer Accuracy: Behavioral Predictability, Prior Experience, and Number of Coding Categories." *Child Development*, 1974, in press.

O'LEARY, K. D. AND KENT, R. "Behavior Modification for Social Action: Research Tactics and Problems." In L. A. Hamerlynck, L. C. Handy, and E. J. Mash (Eds.), *Behavior Change: Methodology Concepts and Practice*. Champaign, Illinois: Research Press, 1973.

PATTERSON, G. R. "An Application of Conditioning Techniques to the

Control of a Hyperactive Child." In L. P. Ullmann and L. Krasner (Eds.), *Case Studies in Behavior Modification*. New York: Holt, Rinehart, and Winston, 1965. Pp. 370–375.

PATTERSON, G. R. "Stimulus Control in Natural Settings: 1. A Procedure for Identification of Facilitating Stimuli which occur in Social Interaction." Submitted to: *Child Development*, May, 1973.

PATTERSON, G. R. "Follow-up Evaluations of a Program for Parents' Retraining Their Aggressive Boys." In F. Lowy (Ed.), Symposium on the Seriously Disturbed Preschool Child, *Canadian Psychiatric Association Journal*, 1974a, in press.

PATTERSON, G. R. "Multiple Evaluations of a Parent Training Program." In T. Thompson (Ed.), *Proceedings of the First International Symposium on Behavior Modification*. New York: Appleton-Century-Crofts, 1974b, in press.

PATTERSON, G. R. "Interventions for Boys with Conduct Problems: Multiple Settings, Treatments, and Criteria." Submitted to: *Journal of Consulting and Clinical Psychology*, 1974c.

PATTERSON, G. R. AND COBB, J. A. "A Dyadic Analysis of 'Aggressive' Behaviors." In J. P. Hill (Ed.), *Minnesota Symposia on Child Psychology*. Vol. 5. Minneapolis: University of Minnesota, 1971. Pp. 72–129.

PATTERSON, G. R. AND COBB, J. A. "Stimulus Control for Classes of Noxious Behaviors." In J. F. Knutson (Ed.), *The Control of Aggression: Implications from Basic Research*. Chicago: Aldine, 1973. Pp. 144–199. See NAPS Document #02107 for 13 pages of supplementary material. Order from ASIS/NAPS, c/o Microfiche Publications, 305 E. 46th Street, New York, N.Y. 10017. Remit in advance for each NAPS accession number $1.50 for microfiche or $5.45 for photocopies. Make checks payable to Microfiche Publications.

PATTERSON, G. R., COBB, J. A., AND RAY, R. S. "A Social Engineering Technology for Retraining the Families of Aggressive Boys." In H. Adams and I. P. Unikel (Eds.), *Issues and Trends in Behavior Therapy*. Springfield, Illinois: Chas. C. Thomas, 1973. Pp. 139–224.

PATTERSON, G. R. AND FAGOT, B. I. "Selective Responsiveness to Social Reinforcers and Deviant Behavior in Children." *The Psychological Record*, 1967, *17*, 369–378.

PATTERSON, G. R. AND HARRIS, A. "Some Methodological Considerations for Observation Procedures." Paper presented at the meeting of the American Psychological Association, San Francisco, September, 1968.

PATTERSON, G. R., MCNEAL, S., HAWKINS, N., AND PHELPS, R. "Reprogramming the Social Environment." *Journal of Child Psychology and Psychiatry,* 1967, *8,* 181–195.

PATTERSON, G. R., RAY, R. S., SHAW, D. A., AND COBB, J. A. "A Manual for Coding of Family Interactions, 1969 Revision." Available as Document #01234, 33 pages of materials. Order from ASIS/ NAPS, c/o Microfiche Publications, 305 East 46th Street, New York, N.Y. 10017. Remit in advance $5.45 for photocopies or $1.50 for microfiche. Make checks payable to Microfiche Publications.

PATTERSON, G. R. AND REID, J. B. "Reciprocity and Coercion: Two Facets of Social Systems." In C. Neuringer and J. L. Michael (Eds.), *Behavior Modification in Clinical Psychology.* New York: Appleton-Century-Crofts, 1970. Pp. 133–177.

PATTERSON, G. R. AND REID, J. B. "Intervention for Families of Aggressive Boys: A Replication Study." *Behavior Research and Therapy,* 1973, *11,* 383–394.

PAUL, J. S. "Observer Influence on the Interactive Behavior of a Mother and a Single Child in the Home." Unpublished master's thesis, Oregon State University, 1963.

PEINE, H. A. "Behavioral Recording by Parents and Its Resultant Consequences." Unpublished master's thesis, University of Utah, 1970.

REID, J. B. "Reciprocity in Family Interaction." Unpublished doctoral dissertation, University of Oregon, 1967.

REID, J. B. "Reliability Assessment of Observation Data: A Possible Methodological Problem." *Child Development,* 1970, *41,* 1143–1150.

REID, J. B. "The Relationship between Complexity of Observer Protocols and Observer Agreement for Twenty-five Reliability Assessment Sessions." In preparation, 1973a.

REID, J. B. "Differences in Complexity of Reliability Assessment Versus Adjacent Nonreliability Assessment Sessions: A Technical Note." In preparation, 1973b.

REID, J. B. AND DEMASTER, B. "The Efficacy of the Spot-Check Procedure in Maintaining the Reliability of Data Collected by Observers in Quasinatural Settings: Two Pilot Studies." *Oregon Research Institute Research Bulletin,* 1972, *12* (8).

REID, J. B. AND HENDRIKS, A. F. C. J. "A Preliminary Analysis of the Effectiveness of Direct Home Intervention for Treatment of Predelinquent Boys Who Steal." In L. A. Hamerlynck, L. C. Handy, and E. J. Mash (Eds.), *Behavior Change: Methodology Concepts and Practice.* Champaign, Illinois: Research Press, 1973. Pp. 209–219.

REID, J. B. AND PATTERSON, G. R. "The Modification of Aggression and Stealing Behavior of Boys in the Home Setting." Paper presented at the Third International Symposium on Behavior Modification, Mexico City, Mexico, January, 1973.

ROMANCZYK, R. G., KENT, R. N., DIAMENT, C., AND O'LEARY, K. D. "Measuring the Reliability of Observational Data: A Reactive Process." Paper presented at the Second Annual Symposium on Behavior Analysis, Lawrence, Kansas, May, 1971.

SACKETT, G. P., STEPHENSON, E., AND RUPPENTHAL, G. C. "Digital Data Acquisition Systems for Observing Behavior in Laboratory and Field Settings." *Behavior Research Methods and Instrumentation,* 1973, *5,* 344–348.

SCHALOCK, H. D. "Observer Influence on Mother-Child Interaction in the Home: A Preliminary Report." Paper presented at the meeting of the Western Psychological Association, Carmel, California, 1958.

SEARS, R. R. "Comparison of Interviews with Questionnaires for Measuring Mothers' Attitudes toward Sex and Aggression." *Journal of Personality and Social Psychology,* 1965, *2,* 37–44.

SKINDRUD, K. D. "An Evaluation of Observer Bias in Experimental-Field Studies of Social Interaction." Unpublished doctoral dissertation, University of Oregon, 1972.

SMITH, H. T. "A Comparison of Interview and Observation Measures of Mother Behavior." *Journal of Abnormal and Social Psychology,* 1958, *57,* 278–282.

TAPLIN, P. S. AND REID, J. B. "Effects of Instructional Set and Experimenter Influence on Observer Reliability." *Child Development,* 1973, *44,* 547–554.

WAHLER, R. G. AND LESKE, G. "Accurate and Inaccurate Observer Summary Reports." Unpublished manuscript, Department of Psychology, University of Tennessee, 1972.

WALKER, H. M. AND BUCKLEY, N. K. "The Use of Positive Reinforcement in Conditioning Attending Behavior." *Journal of Applied Behavior Analysis,* 1968, *1,* 245–250.

WALTER, H. I. AND GILMORE, S. K. "Placebo Versus Social Learning Effect in Parent Training Procedures Designed to Alter the Behavior of Aggressive Boys. *Behavior Therapy,* 1973, *4,* 361–377.

WEICK, K. E. "Systematic Observational Methods." In G. Lindsey and E. Aransen (Eds.), *The Handbook of Social Psychology.* Vol. 2, 2nd Ed. Reading, Massachusetts: Addison-Wesley, 1968. Pp. 357–451.

WHITE, G. "The Effects of Observer Presence on Mother and Child Behavior." Unpublished doctoral dissertation, University of Oregon, 1972.

YARROW, M. R. "Problems of Methods in Parent Child Research." *Child Development,* 1963, *34,* 215–226.

III

Behavioral Assessment in Mental Retardation

H. Carl Haywood, John W. Filler, Jr.,
Mark A. Shifman, Gisela Chatelanat

In most cases the diagnosis of mental retardation is not difficult. In fact, if assignment to a diagnostic category were the only purpose of psychological assessment, or even its major purpose, most psychological testing of suspected mentally retarded persons would be not only unnecessary but certainly superfluous and perhaps unjustified. By the time psychological tests are given to persons thought to be mentally retarded those individuals have already demonstrated some degree of failure in school-related tasks. Such failure represents criterion information, while scores on intelligence tests are predictor information. In any assessment situation, criterion information, when available, always is preferable to predictor information. One might well ask, then, why psychological testing is done with persons thought to be mentally retarded. As with any other group, there are three goals: classification, selection, and intervention. The procedures examiners use

The authors gratefully acknowledge the support of the Joseph P. Kennedy Jr. Foundation through the first author's Kennedy Professorship.

depend upon which of these goals instigates the examination; in other words, the purpose demands the strategy.

In this chapter, focusing upon the goal of educational intervention, we will examine two somewhat new strategies for the psychological assessment of mentally retarded persons, contrasting them with what has been the major traditional approach to psychological assessment. The two strategies are assessment of learning potential and direct behavioral assessment by functional analysis of behavior. The latter strategy is generally familiar to operant behaviorists, while the former is less generally familiar, especially to American psychologists. At this point it will be useful to characterize the dominant approach to psychological assessment (the measurement of the products of prior learning) and to contrast that approach with one that we call the measurement of learning processes.

Process Versus Products

The traditional method by which psychometrists estimate the intelligence of individuals is to measure achievement relative to age norms; that is, individuals are compared with respect to their relative mastery of the products of prior learning. Such an approach assumes that the individuals being compared have had equal opportunity to learn. In addition, adherents of this method are forced to assume, at least implicitly, either that long-term memory is an essential component of intelligence or that all persons are equal in their retention of learned information or skills. The first assumption is patently untenable (Haywood, 1970). Differential opportunity to learn clearly is associated with social-class variables, one's geographic access to educational opportunity, race, the intelligence and education of one's parents, and the relative excellence of one's teachers. Extensive research on memory has enabled us to call seriously into question both parts of the second assumption. For example, Haywood and Heal (1968) have shown that substantial individual differences in long-term memory occur across intelligence levels, and Haywood, Heal, Lucker, Mankinen, and N. Haywood (1970) demonstrated that, when appropriate controls are applied to equalize the strength of learned associations, mentally retarded persons retain learned associations with no less efficiency than is demonstrated by nonretarded persons. The critical variable in long-term memory is the efficiency of learning itself, which is in turn related to individual differences in the kind of ability expressed by the results of traditional psychometric techniques, that is, the products of prior learning. In both the studies of Haywood and Heal (1968) and of Haywood and others (1970) there was considerable overlap among IQ levels in the efficiency of learning and subsequently in the long-term retention of learned associations, but the individual differences in retention were primarily related to differences in learning efficiency rather than to differences in psychometric intelligence. These general conclusions have been supported by other investigators (Belmont, 1966).

Standard tests such as the Stanford-Binet Intelligence Scale, the various Wechsler scales, and the Peabody Picture Vocabulary Test (all quite commonly used to estimate the intelligence of mentally retarded persons) depend rather heavily for their validity upon assumptions that can be shown empirically to be not entirely tenable. For that reason, it is necessary to examine carefully which of the various goals of psychometrics can be reached through the use of these tests, which depend upon measurement of the products of prior learning, and which of those goals will require alternative strategies of measurement.

The principal goals of the measurement of products of prior learning include prediction, selection and classification, and group planning. Such tests as the Binet-Simon scales were designed primarily for selection purposes, but rather quickly were used toward the achievement of all these goals.

Prediction may refer to a relatively narrow band of events, such as prediction of relative success in a standard academic situation, or it may refer to prediction in a much broader sense, such as prediction of vocational adjustment and attainment or even success in life. Obviously, the narrower the band of predicted events the greater the success of the predictive instrument. When used to predict relative standing on academic achievement, traditional intelligence tests are moderately successful, their scores being associated with as much as 50 percent of the variance in subsequent achievement measures. Such a success rate is of considerable academic interest, unless one is concerned about the other 50 percent of the variance. When such tests are used for selection, the error variance becomes vitally important. Selection refers, of course, to the use of tests to choose individuals who may and who may not participate in criterion activities such as special training programs, regular school classes, special classes for mentally retarded persons or other handicapped children, training courses in the military services, or graduate education. If one's goal is to conduct such criterion activities in the most efficient manner possible, that is, with the least effort expended on behalf of those who in fact will not succeed, then these tests as predictors and selectors are reasonably successful. If, however, one's goal is to match opportunities most efficiently to each individual, with the primary emphasis upon the individual, these tests do not do such a good job, and frequently do great harm, particularly in the educational system with its emphasis upon tracking (Mercer, 1971).

Individuals may make poor scores on product-oriented tests not necessarily because they lack aptitude for academic pursuits but frequently for two other reasons: opportunities to learn the associations and skills demanded by the tests have not been uniformly present; the tests do not measure adequately the fine grained skills and strategies required even for academic learning. There is, however, sufficient commonality between the tasks demanded on these predictive instruments and subsequent school-related tasks to enable the tests' predictive use to become a succession of self-fulfilling prophecies. Their use for selection and classification can also become person-defeating. Finally, their use for group planning has great potential for becoming system-failing. For example, when product-oriented tests are used to plan the number of classes for educable and trainable mentally retarded children that will be needed in a school system, the number of children who should be in such classes is almost always overestimated (Mercer, 1971), if one's criterion is who can benefit from special classes rather than who should be out of regular classes.

A cardinal principle of the psychological testing movement always has been that the best test of any event is a sample of that very event. For example, if one wants to know whether an individual will be a good drill press operator, the best test is a situation in which he must operate a drill press. If one wants to know whether a person will be a good guard on the basketball team, one would be well-advised to observe him playing guard with a basketball team. Rather than taking this direct approach, psychologists seem to be particularly fond of devious measurement, that is, measuring a set of presumably correlated events and then inferring probable performance on the criterion events. Clinicians have learned that asking a psychiatric patient if he hears voices is at least as valid a diagnostic procedure as giving him a projective test from which one might then infer that the patient has auditory hallucinations. Admissions officers in colleges and universities have learned that academic performance in high school is one of the best predictors of subsequent academic performance in college, and that undergraduate grades, combined with other indices of undergraduate academic performance, constitute the best predictors of academic success in graduate school. The following discussion of the measurement of process variables is based on the following assumptions: the goal of behavioral assessment for diagnostic purposes is not to establish the subject's relative standing on some inferred latent variable such as intelligence, but to find out what the individual may need in the way of treatment and/or education and how to meet those needs best; the best way to predict the learning efficiency of an individual is to measure his efficiency in an actual learning task or series of tasks; it is possible to identify and to measure characteristic processes by which individuals learn, and to generalize these processes to subsequent learning situations; and the processes through which individuals learn are modifiable.

The ultimate goal of the measurement of learning processes is the prescription of intervention procedures designed specifically to modify these processes in order to enhance the efficiency of learning. In pursuit of this ultimate goal, measurement of the products of prior learning can play an important initial role, provided one does not stop the diagnostic process at this point. One should first gain a comprehensive picture of the strengths and weaknesses of the individual's learning strategies and processes across a wide variety of qualities of learning situations. It is important to know that the individual has been relatively successful or unsuccessful in learning different kinds of materials or associations in the past. The next goal is to try to discover the degree of modifiability that is possible, or in a more direct sense to ascertain how much teaching is required for the individual to reach a particular standard of performance. Finally, process measurement will be involved constantly in educational treatment in a repeating diagnosis-prescription-treatment chain. In this last characteristic, this approach is similar to the functional analysis of behavior, to be treated later in this chapter.

The Dynamic Assessment of Learning Potential

The following discussion of the assessment of learning potential is based heavily upon the developmental concepts of Jean Piaget (Flavell, 1963), psychometric procedures developed by Piaget's colleague, the late Swiss clinical psychologist André Rey (1952), and elaborated upon by Rey's students (Feuerstein, 1970), and upon contemporary research being conducted in three laboratories: Budoff's in Cambridge, Massachusetts, Feuerstein's in Jerusalem, and Haywood's in Nashville. Of these, clearly the most important as to its scope and its clear relationship to the theoretical work of Rey and Piaget is Feuerstein's work in Israel.

During more than fifty years of research in child psychology, Jean Piaget and his coworkers in Geneva provided a detailed description of cognitive skills as they develop from birth to adolescence. In addition to describing behavior patterns as they are applied by the child to various domains of mental activity such as perception, sensorimotor intelligence, memory, and logic (Inhelder and Piaget, 1958, 1964; Piaget, 1954, 1963, 1969; Piaget and Inhelder, 1972), Piaget has attempted to provide an explanation of the changes those forms of behavior undergo with increasing chronological age. Since excellent summaries of his findings and his interpretations, provided by Flavell (1963), Hunt (1961), and others, are familiar to most readers of this volume, we shall mention only briefly a few key notions of Piaget's theory as the possible origin and foundation of what we have called process measurement.

Piaget has divided intellectual development into three major stages. Each stage is characterized by a different structure or organizational framework in which the child integrates environmental data and which allows him to respond in a consistent manner to a variety of situations and stimuli in different content areas. The structure of one stage integrates the structure of the previous stage rather than simply replacing it. Thus the sequence of developmental stages is invariant and not subject to variations associated with individual differences. Even so, the pace with which an individual progresses from one stage to the next can vary, and chronological age is at best an approximate indication of an individual's level of functioning.

Continuity of development across the succession of qualitatively different structures is assured by what Piaget calls the functional invariants that are operating throughout the entire developmental sequence. These invariants are the two complementary mechanisms of assimilation and accommodation, necessary components of the process of adaptation. According to Piaget, adaptation is an inherent tendency of each organism that is achieved through assimilation of environmental inputs to the existing system of the organism and the adjustment of the system to specific demands of a situation or stimulus. The general process of adaptation with the assimilatory and accommodatory activities accounts for the construction of more and more complex forms of behavior (never isolated but always organized in a coherent system), and in the final analysis defines the nature of intelligence itself. In the Piagetian perspective, intelligence appears to be the ultimate extension of biological adaptation whose function is "to structure the universe just as the organism structures the immediate environment" (Piaget, 1963, p. 4). Obviously, intelligence in this theory is considered to be a process and not a static entity measurable as such. In the Piagetian framework, the evaluation of an individual's intellectual development can be made only through a series of inferences about the complexity, stability, and appropriate functioning of the underlying cognitive structure.

Learning Potential and the Concept of Modifiability

Rey (1934) observed that psychometrists seem to be more interested in the already-existing adaptive responses than in the process of adaptation itself and the development of the responses. As a result of this focus, a given global score on an intelligence test may be earned by persons of quite different abilities and by persons who attained those abilities by quite different processes. For some, the psychometric rank may well express the level of functioning that they attained under favorable circumstances. Others who occupy the same rank may be functioning far below their potential because of destructive influences or the absence of developmentally facilitating situations. Regardless of these differences, a static assessment technique will lead to a similar prognosis for all. Vygotsky (1962) suggested that since we know that the higher mental processes have a history of developmental interaction between child and adult, it makes little sense to rely on a static, product-oriented assessment for prognosis or intervention. Further, what is needed is an assessment of the degree to which a child can benefit from the help of an adult and a comparison of this with his independent performance. In this way assessment can lead directly to an intervention program and a more realistic prognosis.

E. W. Gordon (1965) also suggested that we develop means to assess potential for learning as well as a description of an individual's pattern of strengths and weaknesses. This would result in a qualitative analysis, rather than a quantitative one, and could lead to a prescription for intervention.

Several investigators have begun work in this direction and have found some interesting results when learning tasks have been used as the assessment technique.

Empirical Observations Leading to a Learning Potential Hypothesis

Haeussermann (1958) described her process of educational evaluation as a technique to assess how a child solves problems similar to those found in the Stanford-Binet. She then carefully analysed successes and failures in terms of the processes used and developed an appropriate educational program based on individual needs. Schucman (1968) developed an index of educability for use with children classified as trainable mentally retarded. She uses a test-teach-test model to assess a child's ability to profit from instruction. A child's ability to retain the content and to transfer the principles learned to new tasks is the index of potential.

The Nashville Laboratory. The concept of *modifiability* refers to the alteration of cognitive structures in a more or less permanent way. Research on the modifiability of retarded persons requires evidence that experimenters have been able to change certain aspects of thought-dependent behavior believed to be mediated by the inferred cognitive structures. Haywood and his associates at George Peabody College have undertaken the study of a small aspect of this problem; specifically, they have attempted to enhance the ability of mildly retarded persons to form verbal abstractions.

The ability to form verbal abstractions is an essential characteristic of social interaction in human society. The concept of verbal abstracting refers here to the activity of grouping and classifying isolated events and placing abstract labels on the resultant categories. Thus, the events *orange, apple, plum, banana,* and *grape* can be grouped into a common category and assigned the abstract label: Fruit. In a sense, the individual performs a factor analysis on the data that impinge upon his senses; that is, he uses a central process to reduce a large number of isolated events to a smaller number of abstract categories. Events that come later into the individual's experience can be compared with his store of abstract categories to determine whether a new event can be assimilated into an existing category. If so, the new event can be understood more easily.

The basic phenomenon discovered in the Nashville laboratory is that mildly retarded persons, especially those whose retardation is associated with cultural deprivation, appear to have significantly more ability to form verbal abstractions than is characteristically revealed on standard intelligence tests. The apparent deficiency of such persons in organizing verbal events into abstract categories appears to be the result of a secondary deficiency in information-input capacity, rather than a deficiency in the ability to form abstractions given adequate information input. The notion of information-input deficits was derived from earlier work by Blaufarb (1962) and Hamlin, Haywood, and Folsom (1965), who applied the idea to schizophrenic patients, using interpretation of proverbs as a test of verbal abstracting ability. Using a verbal similarities test in subsequent studies, the notion of information-input deficit has been tested in several configurations and applied to mildly retarded persons. For a discussion of conceptual similarities in these two populations, the reader should see Haywood and Switzky (1974).

In the earliest study in the current series, Gordon and Haywood (1969) gave twenty-item similarities tests under two conditions to organically retarded and cultural-familially retarded persons in a residential institution. In the regular procedure, items in the similarities test were given just as they are in the Wechsler scales: "In what way are an orange and a banana alike?" In the enriched procedure, each item had five exemplars: "In what way are an orange, a banana, a peach, a plum, and a pear alike?" These same procedures were used subsequently with a group of nonretarded children matched with the retarded children on mental age (MA). Retarded children in both groups scored significantly lower than did MA-matched nonretarded children on the similarities test using two exemplars with each item. Under the five-exemplars procedure, the verbal abstracting scores of the cultural-familially retarded group were significantly higher than were their scores on the two-exemplars test, significantly higher than the five-exemplars scores of the organically retarded group, and not different from the five-exemplars scores of the nonretarded group. In other words, giving verbal enrichment in the form of an increased number of exemplars of each concept improved the abstracting performances of cultural-familially retarded subjects, but not those of organically retarded subjects, and not those of nonretarded subjects. The authors concluded that cultural-familially retarded persons are not necessarily deficient in the ability to form verbal abstractions, but do have an information-input deficit, which can be overcome by enriching the amount of information available to the subject. In the case of the nonretarded subjects, since one does not assume that an information-input deficit exists, there is nothing to overcome by the enrichment procedure; consequently, one should not expect the enrichment procedure to improve their abstracting performance. With respect to the organically retarded group, the defining brain damage might actually have brought about impairment of the central abstracting processes; an alternative explanation is that the enrichment procedure was simply not sufficient to overcome the deficit that might have been present in this group.

These basic phenomena have been replicated several times with different samples by the Nashville group (Call, 1973; Foster,

1970; Tymchuk, 1973). Foster's data indicate that, under some conditions, three exemplars may actually be sufficient to produce the maximum enrichment effect in children of subnormal intelligence and low social class.

If increasing the number of exemplars of a concept can bring the verbal abstracting performance of mildly retarded persons up to that of their MA-matched peers, one might ask whether, with further intervention, it is possible to overcome the apparent retardation altogether and bring their performance up to that of their CA-matched peers. Call (1973) has compared the effects of verbal enrichment and verbal-pictorial enrichment on the verbal-abstracting performance of eight-year-old children of both high and low general intelligence, all of lower social class families. Children were tested on the twenty-item verbal-similarities task twice, under nonenriched (two exemplars) and enriched (four exemplars) conditions. For one-half of the subjects the verbal-similarities task was presented aurally, while for the other half of the subjects, pictures were combined with the aurally-presented items. An analysis of difference scores revealed greater gain as a result of stimulus enrichment for the low-ability group than for the high-ability group. Presenting the materials under the aural-plus-picture condition significantly increased the mean abstracting scores of the low-ability group as compared to the aural condition alone. In addition, the mean abstracting scores of the low-ability group were increased under the aural-plus-picture condition to a level equal to the abstracting performance of the high-ability group. There was no difference in the verbal-abstracting performance of the high-ability group as a result of enrichment conditions or of mode of presenting the items. The appropriate generalization appears to be that the more enriched is the information provided as input (increasing the number of exemplars and adding pictorial cues), the more readily can the information deficit be overcome.

In the most recent study in this series, Haywood and Switzky (1974) gave the verbal similarities test to intellectually average and mildly subnormal children in school grades one, four, and six. One-half of the twenty items in the test were administered under a nonenriched (two exemplars) condition and the remaining items under one of three enriched (three, four, or five exemplars) conditions,

There was also a baseline control condition in which all items were presented under the nonenriched procedure. Order of presentation was arranged in such a way that the design permitted assessment of the extent to which experience with enriched verbal input would generalize to subsequent nonenriched items. The intellectually subnormal children demonstrated higher verbal abstracting scores under the enriched conditions as compared to their baseline control group. These children also showed evidence of a learning-set-like phenomenon: experience with the enriched items raised their verbal abstracting scores on subsequent nonenriched items. These effects were not present with the intellectually average children.

These studies have provided some experimental specification of a simple mechanism by which one can infer the modifiability of cognitive structures in retarded children. Further, there is rather convincing evidence that mild mental retardation that is associated with cultural deprivation is characterized not so much by deficiency in the ability to form verbal abstractions as by deficiency in the intake of information. When the supply of information is enriched, thus allowing the verbal message to gain access to the processing system, such mildly retarded individuals are able to perform verbal abstracting tasks at a normal level.

These simple procedures may also help to explicate Jensen's (1970) theory of mental retardation based on his two-level theory of intelligence. Jensen has distinguished between Level I abilities (based on associative learning) and Level II abilities (based on transformations or complex operations performed on the stimulus input). Mental retardation can be of two types: primary and secondary. Primary retardation refers to a deficiency in Level I abilities. Jensen further distinguished between two types of primary retardation. Individuals may have low Level I abilities that mask and depress the expression of normal Level II abilities (Type A) or individuals may have low amounts of both Level I and Level II abilities (Type B). Secondary retardation refers to a deficiency in Level II abilities (though Level I abilities may be normal). Individuals with Type A primary retardation have an information-input deficiency which can be remedied by enriching the information on the input side of an abstracting operation. It may be possible to distinguish between Type A and Type B primary retardation by enriching the stimulus input. If that is so, the procedure presented here will be useful in exploring further the ramifications of Jensen's intriguing notion of the division of retarded persons into these types.

The Cambridge Laboratory. Budoff (1967) has used a nonverbal task to assess learning potential. He presented Kohs' Block Design Test three times to a group of educable mentally retarded (EMR) adolescents. The first time the examiner assessed a child's initial level of functioning. A coaching procedure was then instituted, stressing an analysis of each design into simple elements, systematic comparison with the standard design, and the concept of two-color blocks as the components of more complex designs. The designs were then presented a day later and again one month after the coaching. The results of the later tests revealed three patterns of responses by EMR children. Some EMR children solved difficult problems during the initial testing and benefited little from the coaching, and thus were called high scorers. Other children did poorly on the initial test but made significant gains after the coaching sessions (gainers), while a third group did poorly on all three administrations (nongainers). Budoff (1969) found that there were also significant differences between gainers and nongainers on Wechsler Performance IQ, on Raven's Progressive Matrices, and on concept shift tasks. In general, gainers were superior to nongainers in speed and efficiency of learning. Budoff interpreted these findings as support for the notion that there are two types of EMR-labeled children: those whose verbal deficiencies caused them to be labeled EMR, and those who may be "more truly intrinsically mentally retarded" (Budoff, 1969, p. 286). The implication of this research for educational practices is that with a suitably designed curriculum gainers should benefit from schooling at least as much as their regular-class, low-achieving CA peers. In addition, a learning potential assessment at an early age might identify able children who are at risk of academic failure, and thus permit the provision of suitable intervention programs in order to remedy their deficiencies in the verbal conceptual areas. An alternate suggestion is that these children are less able "to handle verbal conceptual material" and therefore "require very different educational goals" (Budoff, 1969, p. 290). An additional unresolved problem is what to do with the nongainers.

Budoff and Corman (1972) found that a learning potential

test based on Kohs' Block Designs yielded lower scores for females and black students. The authors suggested that the task did not motivate these two groups sufficiently and was particularly biased against black females who were overrepresented in the experimental sample. The Kohs test was also inappropriate for children under twelve years of age in that it could not discriminate among them. In addition, Budoff (1973) felt that using only one test might bias the results and that adding an additional task might reduce these biases.

More recently, Budoff (1973) and his associates have made substantial changes in their original work on learning potential. Since beginning his work on learning potential, Budoff has incorporated into his program a modification of Feuerstein's (1968) Learning Potential Assessment Device (LPAD), which will be discussed in detail later in the chapter. The purposes of Feuerstein's procedures, however, are rather different from those that characterize Budoff's program at the Research Institute for Educational Problems (RIEP). Investigators at RIEP found Feuerstein's procedure unsuitable for their purposes, and therefore decided to develop a modification of the LPAD matrices technique, using Raven's Progressive Matrices (A, AB, B, C, D, E). This modification, called the Raven Learning Potential Test (Budoff and Hutten, 1971), had two major goals: to discriminate among primary-grade, low-functioning children and assess learning potential among them; and to develop a second learning potential procedure for use with individuals in the adolescent age range.

Budoff and his associates (Budoff and Hutten, 1971) developed a training procedure for use with the Progressive Matrices. They used tasks similar but not identical to the matrices developed by Raven (1956, 1958), and training procedures relevant to problems in all the series (A, AB, B, C, D, E).

These training techniques were interposed between a pretest and posttest on Raven's Progressive Matrices (Sets A, AB, B, C, D, E), and this entire procedure is called the Raven Learning Potential Test. The training was quite successful in improving the scores of all trained subjects, both regular-class and EMR. The EMR trained group had a mean posttest score equal to that of the regular-class pretest mean.

These results indicated that the Raven Learning Potential

Test developed at RIEP is a useful technique for assessing learning potential among psychometrically EMR children. In addition, the Raven tasks show good reliability, are interesting to children, are a good test of general reasoning, and can be successfully administered to groups. Budoff (1973) has said that these characteristics make it potentially the best instrument for assessing learning potential.

Another instrument developed at RIEP, by Babad (Corman, 1973), is the Series Learning Potential Test. This instrument is a nonverbal reasoning task consisting of a horizontal row of cells, each of which contains a stimulus figure. The row of figures constitutes a series representing a reasoning task, with one blank cell that the subject must fill in using one of four available choices. The blank space may appear at any point in the series and the subject must determine the existing pattern and complete it. Four dimensions (semantic content, size, color, and orientation) appear in the series tasks, with a maximum of three dimensions being used in any one series. The child is trained to "sing the tune" that describes the series, one dimension at a time (for example, large, large, small; large, large, small; _____, large, small), and successively eliminate those choices that cannot complete the pattern until all the concepts used have been examined and only the correct choice remains.

There are seventeen coaching items and two distinct sixty-five-item test forms. The items are both pictorial-meaningful and abstract-geometric in nature. Budoff (1973) has considered the test suitable for children from seven to sixteen years of age.

In initial work with this instrument, most children reached "a de facto ceiling on the test by eight years of age" (Budoff, 1973, p. 29), thus limiting the present usefulness of this test. Corman (1973) found that "the Series test forms are reliable and equivalent, and training is effective for first through third grade students; however, because of the ceiling of scores at the fourth grade, and because of the relationship of the Series scores to race and social class, the Series test appears to be less useful as a measure of learning potential than other measures" (Budoff, 1973, p. 29).

Although results from this test would present a more optimistic view of a child's potential to educators, significant reorganization of school programming would be necessary for this potential to be realized. Babad, now at Hebrew University, is continuing work on this measure and adapting it for use with older children.

Most of the work discussed above has been concerned with a child's ability to extract abstract principles and rules after having experienced a number of concrete instances of a concept. Some researchers have suggested the possibility of teaching the abstract principles and rules directly rather than by expecting them to occur by inductive process. Clarke, Clarke, and Cooper (1970) have proposed that there should be a shift in education from element teaching to rule teaching. Rohwer (1971) has taken issue with Jensen's (1969) contention that elaborative abilities cannot be taught. In a paired-associates learning task, Rohwer (1971) found that a major difference between children of low and high socioeconomic status was in their ability to benefit by direct exposure to the stimulus materials. The high-SES children improved with practice while the low-SES children did not improve until they were given training in elaborative skills such as imagery, verbal mediation, and rehearsal techniques. Rohwer (1971) concluded that tests must be developed to measure learning proficiency and learning style. These tests should lay the foundation for the training of elaborative learning skills in the early school years.

Budoff's current work is going in this direction. Recent efforts have been focused upon organizing and interpreting the data obtained from the learning potential assessment. These efforts have been motivated by the need to identify individuals who are classified as EMR by standard intelligence tests (which are biased toward individuals with high verbal-conceptual skills) but who, on the basis of the learning potential assessment, demonstrate an ability to profit from experience.

A recent modification in the classification system used by RIEP has eliminated the previous trichotomous definition of learning potential status in favor of a linear continuum of learning potential. Now three scores are used to define three types of performance derived from the learning potential assessment.

Pretraining scores reflect the present level of functioning and correlate moderately to highly with scores on standard intelligence tests as well as with social class variables. The posttraining scores represent "the child's optimal level of performance following an optimizing procedure" (Budoff, 1973, p. 33). Finally, the posttraining score adjusted for pretest level is said to indicate a child's capacity to benefit from training given suitable curricula and school experiences.

The Cambridge researchers have examined the implications of a learning potential assessment strategy and have concluded that this strategy can differentiate among psychometrically EMR children in terms of academic potential as well as various areas of personal and social adjustment. The details of these studies are presented in in-house publications available from RIEP entitled "Studies in Learning Potential." The gainer and high-scorer groups are significantly more competent in all aspects of social functioning than are the nongainers.

The unresolved question of the problems of nongainers has begun to be addressed by the RIEP group. Although nongainers demonstrate much of the behavior often ascribed to mentally retarded children, evidence is beginning to accumulate that suggests that the problems of these children can be resolved. It appears that the current trend of thought in the RIEP group parallels closely the ideas described by Clarke and others (1970) and Rohwer (1971). The more detailed work of Feuerstein (1970) will be described later.

Frank (1970) has found that some of the children who failed to learn Kohs' Block Designs with the coaching of the examiner performed much more adequately when the children had some control and initiative in the process. In the subject-controlled condition, the child is told the restrictions or rules for making designs with the blocks (for example, all blocks must touch and designs must be square) and then he is asked to make as many designs as he can. After each design the child makes, either he or the examiner draws the design on grid paper. Later the child is asked to reconstruct the designs he has made, using the two-dimensional representations of them as models. This procedure has enabled some nongainers to grasp the requirements of the task to the extent that they could then solve difficult nine- or sixteen-block designs, whereas they had been unable to solve simple four-block designs under examiner-controlled conditions.

The Frank (1970) study, together with other evidence, suggests that the classification approach to assessment, even by a process technique, is not the appropriate strategy. The more useful and beneficial application of assessment must be in planning an individualized set of educational experiences for every child that will be consonant with his particular needs and learning style.

The curricula of most school systems are based on some prior assumptions about the information-processing strategies that the children in the classroom use and that are required in order to benefit from the educational process. A problem arises when there are children who do not use these strategies because the schools are not prepared to teach them. This is not the fault of the schools since there is little information available to educators concerning what these skills are and how they can be taught.

Budoff and his colleagues are beginning to realize the need for "a taxonomy of necessary or appropriate skills that facilitate educability" (Budoff, 1973, p. 67). Given such a taxonomy, the task of assessment would be to describe an individual's pattern of strengths and weaknesses on these information-processing skills, and to design appropriate intervention strategies to develop these skills. Thus the task of the psychologist would change from classification and prediction to a concern "with the child's present status in some finite area(s) of functioning, and his amenability to training on that function(s). The psychologist's contribution would be more closely related to the educational situation of the child, and might involve quite specific recommendations regarding how he might be taught, whether the teaching is done by the classroom teacher or remedial personnel" (Budoff, 1973, p. 68).

The Israeli Experiment. All of the investigators referred to so far have made significant contributions to the notion of a dynamic, process-oriented approach to intellectual assessment. None, however, has developed a full model and procedure for assessing learning potential in such a way as to lead directly to a description of the specific deficiencies that an intervention program could remedy. A program has been developed and presented by Feuerstein, Hoffman, Shalom, Kiram, Narrol, Schachter, Katz, and Rand (1972) that employs and extends the ideas discussed thus far. In addition to the concepts shared by some other researchers, the work of Feuerstein and others (1972) represents more than twenty years of direct clinical experience with disadvantaged adolescents in Israel. The result is a comprehensive system of assessments and intervention strategies that together have improved the functioning of thousands of immigrants who arrived in Israel functioning academically at a retarded level. Feuerstein's description of his original disadvantaged population is remarkably similar to the descriptions of the cultural-familially mentally retarded persons so often found in American literature (Gordon, 1965; Riessman, 1962). However, the term cultural disadvantage is not only applicable to persons of low socioeconomic status, but also applies to individuals whose social circumstances have interfered with their intellectual development.

Feuerstein's program, unlike the work described thus far, has been based on a theory of the nature and development of intelligent functioning. Although related to the work of other theorists in the area of cognitive development (for example, Bernstein, 1960; Bruner, 1966) Feuerstein's conceptual orientation leads to some direct implications for intervention. These features of his approach will be discussed briefly.

The definition of intelligence in Feuerstein's system is quite similar to Budoff's. Intelligence is the capacity of an individual to use previously acquired experience to adjust to new situations. The ability of an individual to acquire information that can be used in novel situations is referred to as modifiability. The concept of modifiability is central to Feuerstein's program; it corresponds in some degree to the notions of learning sets and concept formation, but the development of modifiability is a unique version of these constructs.

Feuerstein (1970) distinguishes between two basic types of learning that can occur simultaneously in an individual but that have different importance at different developmental stages. Direct-exposure learning refers to the spontaneous, chance encounters between the organism and the environment. For most individuals, direct exposure to stimulation results in some modification of the existing cognitive schemes through a process such as assimilation and accommodation (Piaget, 1963). Mediated learning is a prerequisite to effective, independent, direct exposure learning. It is defined as "the interactional process between the developing human organism and an experienced adult who, by interposing himself between the child and external sources of stimulation, mediates the world to him by framing, selecting, focusing, and feeding back environmental experience in such a way as to create appropriate learning sets" (Feuerstein, 1970, pp. 358–359).

This process of mediated learning probably begins at birth and its effects appear at a preverbal level. It is not limited to particular content or mode of communication. The most important aspect of the process is its intentional nature; a child is made aware that he is learning something that is of value in the adult-infant interaction.

The combination of sufficient mediated learning plus opportunities for direct exposure learning is the key to the development of the information-processing strategies valued in our culture and collectively termed intelligence.

In Feuerstein's approach, the cause of retarded intellectual development among cultural-familially retarded children is seen as insufficient mediated learning (1970). In the United States, this is complicated by insufficient opportunity for direct exposure learning for many underprivileged persons. Thus, two major causes for cultural-familial mental retardation are postulated: for lower class minority subcultures, racial and ethnic discrimination has resulted in a lack of opportunity for direct exposure learning; these same factors of discrimination have resulted in the perpetuation of cultural-familial mental retardation due to insufficient mediated learning. If a child's parents do not possess adequate cognitive skills, they cannot transmit them to the child.

Most of the intervention research with cultural-familially retarded children has focused on the first deficiency. Feuerstein (1970) contends that we must focus initially on the second deficiency and develop appropriate learning sets in the child. The deficient learning sets can be seen as affecting three phases of cognitive operations: an input phase (I), an elaborational or processing phase (E), and the output of the processed data (O). Feuerstein and others (1972) listed twenty-eight different skills that may be lacking or deficient in the child with a deficit in mediated learning experience. For the present purpose only a few are listed: exploratory (input) behavior that is limited in scope and unsystematic; a lack of spontaneous comparative behavior; impulsive motor responding coupled with a lack of internalization; an episodic grasp of reality; an approximate qualitative rather than exact quantitative approach to data manipulation.

The remainder of the observed deficits, a more detailed explanation, and a more complete discussion of mediated learning can be found in the original source (Feuerstein and others, 1972, pp. 28–49).

In order to facilitate development of appropriate learning sets, we must be able to assess the specific deficiencies to be modified for the child to be able to benefit from direct-exposure learning. The Learning Potential Assessment Device (LPAD) (Feuerstein, 1968) is designed for this purpose.

The Learning Potential Assessment Device (LPAD). In a sense, the LPAD is a model of mediated learning. It is not designed to induce lasting modification, but rather to indicate the type and amount of training or mediated learning that is necessary to induce permanent change to the extent that the individual can benefit from direct, spontaneous interactions with the environment.

Existing psychometric instruments were not designed for use as a measure of modifiability. Their product orientation promotes the use of a wide range of tasks as a sample of intellectual functioning. In order to analyze the process used in solving these tasks, one must use tasks in which the method of successful solution remains the same, while changing the specific stimuli. The tasks used both by Budoff (1973) and in the LPAD are of this type. They allow the examiner to assess the ability of a child to use knowledge acquired in a focused learning situation to solve progressively more complex and novel problems. In addition, use of the LPAD enables the examiner to assess the amount and type of teaching necessary for a given amount and type of modification. This assessment includes the degree of modification of various cognitive operations, the extent to which the new skills are used in novel situations, and the individual's preferred modalities for learning and responding.

To accomplish these goals, the structure of the LPAD is based on three dimensions: degree of novelty and complexity of the task; the language or modality of presentation (for example, figural, pictorial-concrete, verbal, numerical); and the variety of cognitive operations the task represents (for example, classification, analogy, syllogism, permutation).

The way the LPAD instruments are used is somewhat analogous to a functional analysis of behavior. The quality of the response is the dependent variable. The degree of novelty and complexity of the task, the mode of presentation, and the cognitive operations necessary for successful solution are the independent variables. The independent variables can be manipulated systematically, either singly or together, and the effect of the manipulations on modifiability can be assessed. This does not imply that a standardized procedure is used. On the contrary, the procedure is a highly individualized, clinical approach that requires a revision of the test situation itself, parallel to the development of new instruments.

Two major changes in the test situation have been introduced as part of the LPAD: the examiner-examinee relationship, and the introduction of the training process.

A problem often encountered in work with cultural-familially mentally retarded persons is the low level of motivation generated by the test materials. Cognitive deficiencies themselves make it difficult for a child to perceive that there is even a novel problem to be solved. In addition, a history of academic failure is often reflected in low need for achievement and generalized avoidance of intellectual tasks. The neutral attitude that examiners adopt traditionally in the standardized test situation contributes to this low level of motivation. The subject often interprets this attitude of careful neutrality as an apathetic or even hostile response to himself (Feuerstein and others, 1972). Even some active encouragement by the examiner is usually insufficient because of the incongruity between the examiner's confidence and the subject's actual level of competence. During administration of the LPAD, the relationship becomes one of teacher and pupil working actively together to achieve success. There is constant interaction between examiner and subject in the form of remarks, explanations, and most of all, concern.

The initial result of this demonstration of interest by the examiner is often that of inducing a desire on the part of the subject to please the examiner. While this task-extrinsic type of motivation (Haywood, 1971; Switzky and Haywood, 1974) is a useful mechanism for beginning the assessment process, it results in a rather artificial means of developing motivation for intellectual work.

Often, at the slightest interruption of the interaction, the child quickly loses interest and does not perform efficiently, but as the LPAD process continues, a shift to a more task-intrinsic type of motivation appears. This shift is produced by two factors related to the initial problems described above. As the child begins to learn the requirements of the task, the mass of stimuli becomes a problem to be solved. Simultaneously, the child's increased competence and the positive attitude present in the process promote a reinforcement process or circular reaction (Piaget, 1963) that consolidates the novel schemes produced by the problem-solving behavior. As a result of these two changes, the task, rather than the examiner, becomes the motivating factor.

An important dimension of the feedback process from the examiner to the subject is the information that will make future success and progress more likely. This is not possible in a static, product-oriented approach in which the nature of the items keeps changing. In the LPAD, when a child fails to solve a problem, any negative feedback is structured to point out areas of successful processing plus an analysis and explanation of the errors such that they may be corrected and lead to future success. All of the positive feedback should be sincere and intense.

The major goal of these changes in the examiner-subject relationship is to increase motivation by conveying to the child the meaning of the task, the importance of mastering it, and the child's capacity to solve the problem. In addition, the feedback process helps to shape the behavior that will be appropriate to successful problem-solving. As a result of inducing task-intrinsic motivation the child becomes easier to teach, more independent and reality oriented, and more modifiable by direct-exposure learning (Feuerstein and others, 1972).

The training process used in the LPAD is somewhat similar to that used by Budoff (1973). The difference between the two techniques lies in the reasoning behind the development of the training procedures. In the RIEP procedure, training is, to a large extent, specific to the task. The RIEP system is to analyze a complex task into less complex components, and teach the child to do the same. The LPAD technique, growing out of a rich body of theory, proceeds from the other end. The components of a task actually are a subgroup of the cognitive skills that Feuerstein, Rey, and others have found to be deficient among cultural-familially mentally retarded children. Thus, a task is chosen because of the particular variety of cognitive operations it requires. Training is oriented toward improving the child's capacity to use those operations, while simultaneously assessing the strength and weaknesses of the individual.

The LPAD is a process approach to assessment, as were the techniques described earlier. Feuerstein, however, uses the term process measurement in a more restrictive way. The question to be answered by a process measurement for Feuerstein and others is "to what extent and by what means can we modify the level of an individual's functioning" (1972, p. 109)? An answer to this question can be found only by an analysis of the way in which an individual copes with a novel task. By using an individualized clinical interaction, the examiner can find areas of strength, describe and analyze deficiencies, and pinpoint the phase of cognitive processing (I, E, O) responsible for the performance. The approach is similar in many respects to Piaget's *méthode clinique* (Piaget, 1960) in which the examiner asks the child for clarification about how the problem was solved. This information is then used to isolate and focus upon areas of deficient functioning and to build upon the more adequately functioning areas of cognitive processing.

One of the most radical changes in technique reflected by the LPAD is its approach to interpretation of a child's performance. In standardized product-oriented assessment techniques, the examiner generally attempts to describe an individual's usual or typical way of functioning. There is no emphasis on eliciting an individual's best performance and, consequently, occasional high-level responses are usually discounted as some kind of measurement error. Feuerstein sees these occasionally excellent responses as indicative of the child's ability to learn. The area of higher functioning may indicate a rare instance in which a lower class child has had an opportunity to learn something typically found only in the middle class majority culture. Therefore, this rare response may predict modifiability more efficiently than the usual test responses predict ability.

Thus, the LPAD practitioner not only takes notice of unusual responses, but actively attempts to elicit them as well by arranging the test situation in the most conducive way. It is only through means such as these that a useful estimate of an individual's ability to profit from the most optimal situation available can be obtained. Differences between individuals can only be inferred when each individual has had the maximum opportunity to develop his potential.

The LPAD is a battery of four types of tasks used to obtain the information needed for planning an intervention program. The four tasks are nonverbal in nature and, with the exception of Raven's Progressive Matrices and its LPAD variations, are largely unknown in the United States.

The first two instruments were developed by Rey (1934; Rey and Dupont, 1953) but modified for use in the LPAD. The first is Organization of Dots (Rey and Dupont, 1953). The basic task is to recognize in an apparently amorphous cloud of dots the geometric structures suggested by the organization of the dots and to construct these structures by connecting the dots with straight lines. The ability to solve these problems is not achieved by means of a sudden, insightful process elicited by a correspondence between the perceptual field and innate neutral structures. Rather, it is a developed skill in which both maturational and cognitive developmental variables interact to create the necessary schemes. Due to the insufficient developmental opportunity (mediated learning) that characterizes cultural-familially mentally retarded children, only the discrete dots are apparent at first. Through the LPAD interactive process, the child is taught the functions necessary to recognize the implicit structures that the dots suggest.

The Organization of Dots task is used to analyze and measure modifiability of particular cognitive skills, the first of which is the ability of the child to conserve the structure of the geometric forms when their orientation in space is changed. Another skill tapped by the Organization of Dots test is the ability to analyze and segregate the relevant dimensions from the various irrelevant ones. Of great importance in this task is the ability to delay responding and plan ahead before attempting a solution. Finally, there is a need for a high level of precision in thinking since there is only one correct solution.

The task of the child becomes progressively more difficult as the number of geometric structures to be discovered among one group of dots increases and the space between the dots decreases. Training begins with tasks in which the component dots of each structure are separated and the dots are far apart. As the individual learns to construct the forms by connecting the dots, the structures progressively change orientation with respect to the base and in relation to each other. Thus each figure changes orientation and the separate figures begin to overlap while the distance between the dots comprising them decreases.

As the cloud of dots becomes more ambiguous, the cues for organizing the dots begin to fade and the child must learn new ways of perceiving the structures. Cognitive strategies begin to develop, the rate and degree of this development being one index of modifiability. The result of developing these skills is a change from associative, rote learning of the geometric forms to an ability to perform transformations on the stimuli in order to perceive the known structure in a novel context.

The Plateaux Test, the second instrument in the LPAD battery, was developed by Rey (1934) for use in evaluating educability. It is designed as a task that initially requires simple associative learning and subsequently requires the use of more and more elaborative transformations for solution of the problem.

The test instrument consists of four plates, each with nine buttons arranged in three parallel rows of three buttons each. One (and later, two) of the buttons on each plate are fixed in place, while the remainder may be removed. The plates are stacked one upon the other and presented to the child, whose task it is to discover where the fixed buttons are. In the initial task, there is one fixed button on each plate and the child is instructed to explore all the buttons by removing them in order to find the fixed one. The plates are then stacked again, in the same order, and the child is told to remember where each fixed button is and indicate this without touching the plates. If he must touch the buttons, each touch is counted as an error and the process is continued to a criterion of three errorless trials. This phase of the test can be completed successfully using associative types of processing mediated by some simple higher-order concepts (left-right, top-bottom). Necessary abilities are a systematic approach to exploratory (input) behavior and the capacity to deal with several aspects of a problem simultaneously.

After successful performance on the initial phase of the Plateaux Test, the task is made more difficult. The child must transform the knowledge about the position of the buttons in three-dimensional space to a two-dimensional representation of the configuration of all the buttons. A single sheet of paper is provided, with the nine-button arrangement represented by circles. The child is instructed to mark each fixed button with the number of the corresponding plate (the "number" having been established earlier by the order of stacking). This requires the child to use or develop some simple symbol manipulation skills in addition to the associative learning. The task is made even more difficult by increasing the number of fixed buttons to two on each plate.

Upon mastery of this second phase, a third variation of the task is presented. The plates are rotated in the presence of the child through 90 degrees and 180 degrees, and the child must again represent the positions of the fixed buttons on a sheet of paper. Thus the test progresses from simple associative learning through to an elaborational type of process requiring increasingly complex cognitive transformations on the original stimuli.

The use of Raven's Progressive Matrices as a test of learning potential has been described in relation to the work of RIEP. It appears that the work of Budoff (1973) derives, in part, from information about Feuerstein's (1968) description of the LPAD. However, as noted above, the goals, and therefore the application, of the LPAD variation on the Progressive Matrices is quite different in the two approaches.

Feuerstein and others (1972) have made it clear that Raven's Progressive Matrices is not considered to be a culture-free IQ test, a measure of nonverbal intelligence, or in any way a test of innate ability. The Progressive Matrices is seen as a useful instrument in analyzing the processes used by an individual on problems that require a broad range of cognitive operations.

The LPAD Matrices Test consists of some of the problems from Raven's Progressive Matrices plus several variations on the problems. In the variations, the concrete dimensions (shape, size, color) of the problem are changed, but the cognitive operations or type of reasoning represented by the problem is maintained. A child's initial performance is indicative of the child's ability to transfer operations across dimensions.

The training aspect of the LPAD Matrices Test is focused on teaching how to recognize and organize the relevant dimensions (input), the principles of reasoning (for example, analogy, permutation, logical multiplication), and inhibiting impulsive responding (output). The goal of the assessment is not classification with respect to level of ability, but rather an analysis of the individual's functioning and information about the degree of modifiability of the individual.

The final instrument in the LPAD battery is the Representational Stencil Design Test (RSDT) developed by Arthur (1930). The instrument consists of twenty stencils, each of which has a unique design characteristic. The basic task is to view a model design, constructed by superimposing two or more stencils, and indicate the stencils and order of position that produced that design. In the traditional method of presentation (Arthur, 1930) the subject is allowed to manipulate the stencils using a trial-and-error approach until the solution has been found or the time limit reached.

Feuerstein and others (1972) have found that, because of the deficient functioning of the cultural-familially mentally retarded child, a trial-and-error approach to problem solving invariably produced failure. For use as a measure of modifiability, the RSDT had to be changed. The LPAD Stencil Design Test is administered in a manner that promotes an internal, reflective approach to processing and does not allow the child actually to manipulate the stencils. This is done by displaying the stencils on a wall posted a few feet in front of the subject. The child must indicate verbally the stencils needed to construct the design and their order of placement.

The cognitive functions involved in this task can be divided among the three phases described before (input, elaboration, and output). At the input stage the subject must be able to discriminate color, form, size, and orientation in order to relate the model design to the various design characteristics found among the stencils. At the elaborational level the child must create a mental representation of the various stencils and imagine the design that would result from superimposing one stencil upon another. The output operation is a systematic comparison of possible combinations of stencils with the model design and self-correction based on feedback about the congruity of their proposed solution with the actual model design. Thus the LPAD Stencil Design Test clearly requires complex transformations of the concrete stimuli using internalized cognitive processes that, almost by definition, are usually inaccessible to the retarded performer.

The training process used with the Stencil Design Test begins with some simple tasks that help the individual become familiar with the design characteristics of the stencils and their location on the chart. A verbal interactive approach is used to describe the way stencils may be combined and the figure-ground principles involved. When the examiner has ascertained that the child understands the nature of the task, he is presented with twenty model designs and asked to write down (or to say aloud) the number of the stencils required and the order of assembly.

Since the development and preliminary application of the LPAD with retarded individuals, the Israeli researchers have developed a test battery for group administration which has shown very good results despite the limited opportunity for intervention and feedback. Feuerstein (personal communication, May 1974) feels that the major reason for the observed success with groups of retarded performers is that the group battery maintains the basic LPAD test-teach-test model for assessing modifiability.

The assessment of learning potential would be of little value if it did not lead to a program of intervention based on the information obtained by using it. The Israeli group has developed such a program called instrumental enrichment (Feuerstein and Hamburger, 1965) and defined as "a direct and focused attack on those intellective functions diagnostically determined as being responsible, because of their weakness or nonexistence, for poor intellectual performance" (Feuerstein, 1970, p. 363). Instrumental enrichment consists of about 200 hours of exercises, which can be administered during one school year. The exercises are largely content-free and focus on the operations and information-processing strategies identified as deficient by the LPAD. They include perceptual and cognitive functions, general learning sets, verbal skills, and motivational factors. The goal of instrumental enrichment is to enable the retarded performer to make efficient use of the content presented in academic, vocational, and personal environments within which the individual wants to function.

So far, the learning potential approach has been shown to be useful only with persons whose retardation is of mild or moderate degree, and largely with those whose retardation is associated with cultural deprivation. It is possible that the unique utility of this approach is confined to that group, although this has not been demonstrated. Extension of the theoretical bases upon which learning potential assessment has been constructed reveals no such limiting condition, but the necessary empirical observations simply have not been provided for use of the learning potential assessment methods with severely and profoundly retarded persons.

By contrast, the next section of the chapter is devoted to an approach that has been used fairly extensively for assessment and modification of the behavior of severely and profoundly retarded persons (as well as those whose behavioral maladaptation may be associated with emotional disturbance, learning disorders of organic origin, and such other less-well-defined conditions as oppositional behavior).

The Functional Analysis of Behavior

During the past ten years, there has been an increasing tendency to employ principles of operant conditioning for purposes of evaluation and diagnosis of behavioral deficiencies. Such terms as stimulus control, positive and negative reinforcement, schedules of reinforcement, and past reinforcement history previously heard only in reference to the experimental analysis of behavior (Skinner, 1966) are beginning to appear in discussions of alternatives to the traditional psychometric model of assessment (Filler, Robinson, Smith, Vincent-Smith, Bricker, and Bricker, in press). Clearly, both the importance that has been placed upon the habilitation of retarded persons and the realization that traditional psychometric techniques contribute little information that can be used to structure individual educational programs have added to the growing popularity of what Gardner (1971) and others have termed the functional analysis approach. Although functional analysis has been described before, there is confusion concerning both the underlying assumptions and the procedures, perhaps because they have been stated frequently in the context of broader discussions of the applied analysis of behavior and behavior modification. In this section of our chapter, we shall present briefly what appear to be some of the more important characteristics. For a more detailed discussion, the reader should consult Baer, Wolf, and Risley (1968), Bricker (1970), D. Bricker and W. Bricker (1973), Ferster (1965), Skinner (1953) and an excellent description by Gardner (1971).

Assumptions. Functional analysis approaches to assessment began, in large part, in reaction to the predominant tendency to view behavioral deficiencies as observable manifestations of deficiencies in the latent variable intelligence. Although, as we have indicated earlier, there are ample data to indicate that IQ tests do a good job of predicting academic achievement, it is apparent that they do not provide a very good basis for specific treatment decisions. To say that an individual is functioning within the retarded range is of little clinical value unless specific recommendations can be made for the remediation of observed deficits. In order to achieve the goal of treatment recommendations, factors that act to determine both quality and quantity of defined aspects of behavior must be isolated and their functional significance demonstrated. While there does not seem to be complete agreement as to the most efficient methods for obtaining such information, the following more general assumptions are implicit in a functional analysis approach.

The foremost goal of a functional analysis is the modification of deficient or unacceptable behavior. Unlike traditional psychometric procedures, the emphasis clearly is upon the delineation of conditions necessary to produce positive changes in criterion forms of behavior rather than upon the prediction of subsequent performance as measured by standardized tests. Thus the validity of the analysis is indicated by the extent to which behavior changes systematically as recommendations derived from the evaluation are implemented. In this characteristic, at least, the functional analysis of behavior is quite similar to the assessment of learning potential described earlier in this chapter.

Individual variations in competency are assumed to result

from diversity in organismic and environmental factors rather than from deficiencies in mediating processes. As Bijou (1963) has stated, "a retarded individual is viewed as one who has a limited repertoire of behavior evolving from interactions of the individual with his environmental contacts which constitute his history" (p. 101). Similarly, Bricker (1970) has described the retarded person as a person who "behaves in a retarded manner either because he has been taught to do so or because he has not been taught to behave in a more intelligent manner" (p. 16). While the role of genetic factors is not denied, the emphasis here is clearly upon the identification of current aspects of the environment. Biogenetic conditions are important only if they have been demonstrated to be related causally to the particular form of behavior that is the focus of concern. For example, surviving Trisomy 17–18 children often have mouth deformities including cleft palate. Such information is obviously important to a functional analysis of speech impediment.

The quality and quantity of present behavior is assumed to be related directly to the interaction of a finite number of environmental events that either immediately precede (antecedent events) or immediately follow (consequent events) behavior. As Gardner (1971) has pointed out, the focus of concern in a functional analysis is the determination of the nature of apparent relationships between antecedent and consequent events and behavior. Thus it becomes necessary to manipulate various aspects of the environmental context in which behavior occurs as part of the assessment process. Once functionality has been determined, controlling events assume a different status and, in effect, become explanations of behavior. Antecedent events are termed discriminative stimuli if a particular form of behavior is more likely to occur in their presence than in their absence and consequent events are reinforcers if it can be shown that the probability of occurrence of the behavior in which one is interested is increased once they are made contingent upon that behavior. Since functional analysis involves both description (through determination of correlative antecedent-behavior-consequences) and explanation (through determination of functionality) the traditional distinction between diagnosis and treatment is lessened.

Antecedent and consequent events are assumed to gain relevance as a result of how they have functioned in the past. Consider, for example, the case of a child who exhibits a certain form of disruptive behavior only while in the presence of a particular person. Such a situation could result from the fact that that individual has in the past inadvertently provided reinforcing consequences for the child, and by so doing has come to be a discriminative stimulus for disruptive behavior. Since cue properties of various aspects of the environment, including other people, occur as the result of a complex interaction of both past and present events, it is important to attempt to understand the ontogeny of behavior as part of the analysis.

Functional analysis is a continuing process, ending only when the desired change in behavior has been effected and is being maintained by the natural environment. Thus, parents or primary caretakers and other individuals who are likely to have contact with the client are integral to a functional analysis. As D. Bricker and W. Bricker (1973) have demonstrated, they often provide information critical to the identification of problem areas and, with support, can develop appropriate intervention strategies and implement procedures to assess program effectiveness.

Implementation. Both Lindsley (1964) and Gardner (1971) have provided detailed descriptions of procedures involved in a functional analysis of behavior. Gardner's Specific Behavior Analysis Report includes eight specific kinds of information and is intended to provide initial data relevant to the construction of educational programs. As Gardner has pointed out, Lindsley's procedures are most applicable to the evaluation of programs once they have been constructed. Both, however, exemplify at least three critical stages of functional analysis.

First, the behavior of concern must be described so that it is possible to measure reliably the frequency or rate of occurrence of the behavior. Often, natural language statements are too vague to allow quantification and it thus becomes necessary to translate them into specifications of observable patterns of responses. Presenting problems may involve deficiencies in self-help, social, academic or other critical skill areas or may result from the occurrence of unacceptable asocial forms of behavior. Before analysis can proceed, a decision must be made concerning the nature of the dependent variable. In this sense, functional analysis is not different from any other scientific investigation.

Once the behavior of interest has been isolated, the conditions under which it occurs must be specified as closely as possible prior to intervention. Since behavior is assumed to occur as the result of a complex interaction of a number of environmental events, observations should be made a number of times in a variety of natural settings; however, selection of particular settings depends to a large extent upon the nature of the behavior of interest as well as upon a number of practical considerations.

Each baseline observation should include careful descriptions of the antecedent and consequent events that may function as discriminative stimuli or serve as reinforcers. In addition, time, place, people present and, when appropriate, nature of the task should be specified for each observation period. There are some data to suggest that these contextual variables may affect both the behavior of interest and the manner in which other people in the environment arrange particular antecedent and consequent events. For example, Rheingold (1960) compared the frequencies of a number of forms of caretaking behavior as they occurred in the home and in an institution during a single eight-hour observation period and found that caretaking behavior (for example, looks at, plays with, feeds) occurred more often in the home than in the institution. Other studies have demonstrated that the behavior of trainers as well as that of children covaries with task differences (Lanzetta and Hannah, 1969) and preexisting relationships between trainer and child (Landauer, Carlsmith, and Leeper, 1970; Halverson and Waldrop, 1970). The latter finding emphasizes the importance of carefully specifying historical factors.

The third stage of functional analysis involves the testing of hypotheses of functionality that are generated from data obtained during the premanipulation baseline phase. Antecedent and consequent events that appear to be reliably associated with specific instances of the behavior of interest are systematically manipulated and careful observations are made of subsequent changes in the quality or quantity of behavior. Manipulations of consequent events could involve increasing or decreasing the amount and variety of positive feedback or altering the schedule of reinforcement that appears to be operative. Similarly, the discriminative function of stimuli which precede responding may be determined by varying the salience of relevant dimensions of task materials. However, establishing that particular events act as reinforcers or discriminative cues in one setting does not necessarily mean that they will have the same effect upon behavior in other settings. Ideally, measures of the effects of varying defined aspects of the environment should be obtained in a variety of relevant settings (for example, at home, at work, and at school)'.

Consistent with the operant orientation, functional analysis approaches to assessment have tended to emphasize the importance of identifying and modifying stimulus events that occur as consequences of behavior. Such an orientation often can be problematic when the goal is to strengthen forms of behavior that occur infrequently or to establish patterns of behavior not currently in the repertoire of the individual. In such situations, the tendency has been to look for responses that constitute components of the desired form of behavior. Unfortunately, however, operant technology does not specify the criteria by which one is to determine either the nature or number of components. Skinner (1953) has argued that common sense should be applied. Yet common sense does not seem to be of much help when more advanced cognitive, linguistic, and academic skills are involved. As W. Bricker and D. Bricker (1973) pointed out, functional analysis, to be successful, must include specification of the ways in which specific forms of behavior operate as prerequisites to the acquisition of more complex skills.

Summary

We have presented here, in summary form, two quite promising alternatives to the traditional practice of assessing only or chiefly the products of prior learning, and have suggested some applications of these methods to direct behavioral assessment of mentally retarded persons. The two approaches, characterized as assessment of learning potential and direct behavioral assessment by functional analysis of behavior, share a common goal: to specify, as a necessary part of the assessment procedure, the particular cognitive (in the one case) and behavioral (in the other case)' areas that can be modified, and the procedures for achieving appropriate modifications in those areas. Both methods reflect an individualized clinical approach as opposed to the more traditional normative approach; thus, their focus is much more clearly on prescriptive assessment and program development than on classification and labeling.

References

ARTHUR, G. A. *A Point Scale of Performance Tests*. Vol. 1. *Clinical Manual*. New York: Commonwealth Fund, 1930.

BAER, D. M., WOLF, M. M., AND RISLEY, T. R. "Some Current Dimensions of Applied Behavior Analysis." *Journal of Applied Behavior Analysis*, 1968, *1*, 91–97.

BELMONT, J. M. "Long-Term Memory in Mental Retardation." In N. R. Ellis (Ed.), *International Review of Research in Mental Retardation*. Vol. 1. New York: Academic Press, 1966.

BERNSTEIN, B. "Language and Social Class." *British Journal of Sociology*, 1960, *11*, 271–276.

BIJOU, S. W. "Theory and Research in Mental (Developmental) Retardation." *Psychological Record*, 1963, *13*, 95–110.

BLAUFARB, H. "A Demonstration of Verbal Abstracting Ability in Chronic Schizophrenics under Enriched Stimulus and Instructional Conditions." *Journal of Consulting Psychology*, 1962, *26*, 471–475.

BRICKER, D. D. AND BRICKER, W. A. "Infant, Toddler, and Preschool Research and Intervention Project Report: Year III." *IMRID Behavioral Science Monograph No. 23*. Nashville: George Peabody College, 1973.

BRICKER, W. A. "Identifying and Modifying Behavioral Deficits." *American Journal of Mental Deficiency*, 1970, *75*, 16–21.

BRICKER, W. A. AND BRICKER, D. D. "Early Language Intervention." Invited Address, NICHD Conference on Language Intervention with the Mentally Retarded, Wisconsin Dells, June, 1973.

BRUNER, J. S. "On Cognitive Growth: I and II." In J. S. Bruner, R. R. Olver, P. M. Greenfield, and others, *Studies in Cognitive Growth*. New York: Wiley, 1966.

BUDOFF, M. "Learning Potential among Institutionalized Young Adult Retardates." *American Journal of Mental Deficiency*, 1967, *72*, 404–411.

BUDOFF, M. "Learning Potential: A Supplementary Procedure for Assessing the Ability to Reason." *Seminars in Psychiatry,* August, 1969, *1* (3).

BUDOFF, M. *Learning Potential and Educability among the Educable Mentally Retarded.* (Progress report, Grant No. OEG-0-8-080506-4597 from National Institute of Education, HEW). Cambridge, Mass.: Research Institute for Educational Problems, 1973.

BUDOFF, M. AND CORMAN, L. "Demographic and Psychometric Factors Related to Improved Performance on the Kohs Learning Potential Procedure." *Studies in Learning Potential.* Cambridge, Mass.: Research Institute for Educational Problems, 1972.

BUDOFF, M. AND HUTTEN, L. "The Development of a Learning Potential Measure Based on Raven's Progressive Matrices." *Studies in Learning Potential.* Cambridge, Mass.: Research Institute for Educational Problems, 1971.

CALL, R. "Verbal Abstracting Performance of Low-SES Children: An Exploration of Jensen's Theory of Mental Retardation." Unpublished doctoral dissertation, George Peabody College, 1973.

CLARKE, A. M., CLARKE, A. D. B., AND COOPER, G. M. "The Development of a Set to Perceive Categorical Relations." In H. C. Haywood (Ed.), *Social-cultural Aspects of Mental Retardation.* New York: Appleton-Century-Crofts, 1970.

CORMAN, L. "Series Learning Potential Test Standardization: A Standardization of the Test, and Study of the Effects of Training." *Studies in Learning Potential.* Cambridge, Mass.: Research Institute for Educational Problems, 1973.

FERSTER, C. B. "Classification of Behavior Pathology." In L. Krasner and L. P. Ullmann (Eds.), *Research in Behavior Modification.* New York: Holt, Rinehart, and Winston, 1965.

FEUERSTEIN, R. "Learning Potential Assessment Device." In B. W. Richards (Ed.), *Proceedings of the First Congress of the International Association for the Scientific Study of Mental Deficiency.* Reigate, Surrey (England): Michael Jackson, 1968.

FEUERSTEIN, R. "A Dynamic Approach to the Causation, Prevention, and Alleviation of Retarded Performance." In H. C. Haywood (Ed.), *Social-cultural Aspects of Mental Retardation.* New York: Appleton-Century-Crofts, 1970.

FEUERSTEIN, R. AND HAMBURGER, M. "A Proposal to Study the Process of Redevelopment in Several Groups of Deprived Early Adolescents in Both Residential and Nonresidential Settings." Unpublished report for the Research Unit of the Hadassah-Wizo-

Canada Child Guidance Clinic, the Youth Aliyah Department of the Jewish Agency, Jerusalem, November, 1965.

FEUERSTEIN, R., HOFFMAN, M., SHALOM, H., KIRAM, L., NARROL, H., SCHACHTER, E., KATZ, D., AND RAND, Y. "The Dynamic Assessment of Retarded Performers: The Learning Potential Assessment Device, Theory, Instruments, and Techniques." *Studies in Cognitive Modifiability* (Report No. 1, Vol. I). Jerusalem: Hadassah-Wizo-Canada Research Institute, 1972.

FILLER, J. W., JR., ROBINSON, C. C., SMITH, R. A., VINCENT-SMITH, L., BRICKER, D. D., AND BRICKER, W. A. "Evaluation and Programming in Mental Retardation." In N. Hobbs (Ed.), *Issues in the Classification of Children.* San Francisco: Jossey-Bass, in press.

FLAVELL, J. *The Developmental Psychology of Jean Piaget.* New York: Litton, 1963.

FOSTER, M. "The Effects of Different Levels of Enriched Stimulus Input on the Abstracting Ability of Slow Learning Children." Unpublished master's thesis, George Peabody College, 1970.

FRANK, L. "The Effects of a Subject-Controlled Learning Procedure on Performance on the Enlarged Kohs' Block Designs." Unpublished report, 1970. Cited by M. Budoff, *Learning Potential and Educability among the Educable Mentally Retarded* (Project report, Grant No. OEG-0-8-080506-4597 from National Institute of Education, HEW). Cambridge, Mass.: Research Institute for Educational Problems, 1973.

GARDNER, W. I. *Behavior Modification in Mental Retardation.* Chicago: Aldine-Atherton, 1971.

GORDON, E. W. "Characteristics of Socially Disadvantaged Children." *Review of Educational Research,* 1965, *35,* 377–388.

GORDON, J. E. AND HAYWOOD, H. C. "Input Deficit in Cultural-Familial Retardation: Effect of Stimulus Enrichment." *American Journal of Mental Deficiency,* 1969, *73,* 604–610.

HAEUSSERMANN, E. *Developmental Potential of Preschool Children.* New York: Grune & Stratton, 1958.

HALVERSON, C. F. AND WALDROP, M. F. "Maternal Behavior Toward Own and Other Preschool Children: The Problem of Owners." *Child Development,* 1970, *41,* 839–845.

HAMLIN, R. M., HAYWOOD, H. C., AND FOLSOM, A. T. "Effect of Enriched Input on Schizophrenic Abstraction." *Journal of Abnormal Psychology,* 1965, *70,* 390–394.

HAYWOOD, H. C. (Ed.). *Social-Cultural Aspects of Mental Retardation.* New York: Appleton-Century-Crofts, 1970.

HAYWOOD, H. C. "Individual Differences in Motivational Orientation: A Trait Approach." In H. I. Day, D. E. Berlyne, and D. E. Hunt (Eds.), *Intrinsic Motivation: A New Direction in Education.* Toronto: Holt, Rinehart and Winston, 1971.

HAYWOOD, H. C. AND HEAL, L. W. "Retention of Learned Visual Associations as a Function of IQ and Learning Levels." *American Journal of Mental Deficiency,* 1968, *72,* 828–838.

HAYWOOD, H. C., HEAL, L. W., LUCKER, W. G., MANKINEN, R. L., AND HAYWOOD, N. P. "Learning and Retention of Visual Associations Under PassiveVisual and Visual-Motor Presentations." Unpublished manuscript, George Peabody College, 1970.

HAYWOOD, H. C. AND SWITZKY, H. N. "Children's Verbal Abstracting: Effects of Enriched Input, Age, and IQ." *American Journal of Mental Deficiency,* 1974, *78,* 556–565.

HUNT, J. MC V. *Intelligence and Experience.* New York: Ronald Press, 1961.

INHELDER, B. AND PIAGET, J. *The Growth of Logical Thinking from Childhood to Adolescence.* New York: Basic Books, 1958.

INHELDER, B. AND PIAGET, J. *The Early Growth of Logic in the Child.* New York: Humanities Press, 1964.

JENSEN, A. R. "How Much Can We Boost I.Q. and Scholastic Achievement?" *Harvard Educational Review,* 1969, *39,* 1–123.

JENSEN, A. R. "A Theory of Primary and Secondary Familial Mental Retardation." In N. R. Ellis (Ed.), *International Review of Research in Mental Retardation.* Vol. 4. New York: Academic Press, 1970.

LANDAUER, T. K., CARLSMITH, J. M., AND LEEPER, M. "Experimental Analysis of the Factors Determining Obedience of Four-year-old Children to Adult Females." *Child Development,* 1970, *41,* 601–611.

LANZETTA, J. T. AND HANNAH, T. E. "Reinforcing Behavior of 'Naive' Trainers." *Journal of Personality and Social Psychology,* 1969, *11,* 245–252.

LINDSLEY, O. R. "Direct Measurement and Prosthesis of Retarded Behavior." *Journal of Education,* 1964, *147,* 62–81.

MERCER, J. R. "Sociocultural Factors in Labeling Mental Retardates." *Peabody Journal of Education,* 1971, *48,* 188–203.

PIAGET, J. *The Construction of Reality in the Child.* New York: Basic Books, 1954.

PIAGET, J. *The Child's Conception of the World.* Totowa, N.J.: Little-field, Adams, 1960.

PIAGET, J. *The Origins of Intelligence in Children.* New York: W. W. Norton, 1963.

PIAGET, J. *The Mechanisms of Perception.* New York: Basic Books, 1969.

PIAGET, J. AND INHELDER, B. *Memory and Intelligence.* New York: Basic Books, 1972.

RAVEN, J. C. *Coloured Progressive Matrices: Sets A, AB, B.* London: H. K. Lewis, 1956.

RAVEN, J. C. *Standard Progressive Matrices: Sets A, B, C, D, E.* London, H. K. Lewis, 1958.

REY, A. "D'un Procédé pour Évaluer l'éducabilité (Quelques Applications en Psychopathologie)." *Archives de Psychologie,* 1934, *24,* 297–337.

REY, A. *Monographies de Psychologie Clinique.* Neuchâtel (Switzerland): Delachaux & Niestlé, 1952.

REY, A. AND DUPONT, J. B. "Organization de Groupes de points en Figures géométriques Simples." *Monographies de Psychologie Appliquée,* 1953, No. 3.

RHEINGOLD, H. "The Measurement of Maternal Care." *Child Development,* 1960, *31,* 565–575.

RIESSMAN, F. *The Culturally Deprived Child.* New York: Harper, 1962.

ROHWER, W. D., JR. "Learning, Race, and School Success." *Review of Educational Research,* 1971, *41,* 191–210.

SCHUCMAN, H. "The Development of an Educability Index for the Training Child." In B. W. Richards (Ed.), *Proceedings of the First Congress of the International Association for the Scientific Study of Mental Deficiency.* Reigate, Surrey (England): Michael Jackson, 1968.

SKINNER, B. F. *Science and Human Behavior.* New York: Macmillan, 1953.

SKINNER, B. F. "What Is the Experimental Analysis of Behavior?" *Journal of the Experimental Analysis of Behavior,* 1966, *9,* 213–218.

SWITZKY, H. N. AND HAYWOOD, H. C. "Motivational Orientation and the Relative Efficacy of Self-Monitored and Externally Imposed Reinforcement Systems in Children." *Journal of Personality and Social Psychology,* 1974, *30,* 360–366.

TYMCHUK, A. J. "Effects of Concept Familiarization vs. Stimulus Enhancement on Verbal Abstracting in Institutionalized Retarded Delinquent Boys." *American Journal of Mental Deficiency,* 1973, *77,* 551–555.

VYGOTSKY, L. S. *Thought and Language.* Tr. by E. Hanfmann and G. Vakar. Boston: MIT Press, 1962.

IV

Assessment of Infants

RAYMOND K. YANG, RICHARD Q. BELL

I nfancy is commonly conceptualized as the period between birth and the acquisition of language. Although the latter is not an abrupt occurrence, it is generally felt to occur at about two years of age—approximately the time at which communication with adults by spoken words is functional and burgeoning.

The purpose of this chapter is to describe and evaluate standardized techniques for assessment during infancy. Included here will be the scales pioneered by Arnold Gesell, as well as the ensuing scales developed by Psyche Cattell and Nancy Bayley. The second section contains two scales developed specifically for the neonate. In a third section, two recently developed scales based on the cognitive-developmental approach of Jean Piaget will be presented.

The human infant has never been consistently cooperative. This well-established fact, when juxtaposed with the infant's ability to manipulate adult behavior with little more than a smile, has posed no small problem for researchers trying to develop objective scales of assessment. Trained as the researcher might be, he or she remains responsive as a part of the measurement situation. Thus,

We would like to thank Charles F. Halverson, Jr., for his comments on this chapter, which was prepared at the National Institute for Mental Health and is in the public domain.

rapport and attention have been factors that psychometricians have had to confront directly in infant testing. Problems of maintaining infants' attention and keeping them focused on the task at hand have been handled, not always successfully, by trying to make test items interesting, brief, and direct. Problems of rapport have been met in part, by the interest level of the items and the guile of the tester. While stereotypic characteristics of the tester (race, for example) may not influence test performance here as at later ages, interpersonal skills may wield equally large effects. A unique challenge is often presented the tester when an anxious infant is allowed to sit on a familiar caretaker's lap (perhaps that of the mother) during testing. Here, the tester must not only establish rapport with the infant, but also with the caretaker. Certainly, special cognizance needs to be taken by the tester of the effect of the caretaker's anxiety on the infant if the caretaker perceives the infant to be overly upset or not performing well.

More serious problems relate to the rapidly developing characteristics of the young infant. For example, it is presumed that the infant is linguistically incompetent. Therefore, infant tests are largely composed of nonlanguage items. An increasing number of linguistically-referenced items (object recognition and naming, instruction comprehension), however, are used to assess and index the continuing development of the infant. And it is not until these types of items begin to predominate that substantial correlations begin to appear between early and later tests of development. This is not to suggest that simply placing linguistically-referenced items in the early tests will improve their predictivity. Characteristics of the infant delimit the types of items that can be used; linguistically-referenced items are of little relevance to an eight-month-old infant.

So the psychometrician specializing in infancy is in a paradoxical position: many of the behaviors defended as measures of individual developmental differences at one age do not correlate with behaviors similarly defended at later ages. For example, during the first months of life, gross motor behavior is an important factor in distinguishing differences among infants on a continuum of immobility to mobility. Items assessing gross motor ability are in abundance in early developmental tests. Yet at later ages infants are differentiated on a continuum of social and communicative behaviors, and items assessing these behaviors supersede gross motor items. Indeed, gross motor behavior not only disappears from the test format, but at times becomes a nuisance requiring subtle control by the tester. And so the life of the psychometrician specializing in infancy is complicated by the rapid passage of his subject through stages of behavior, all of which seem worth measuring and none of which has yet been shown to bear substantial quantitative relationships with one another.

As a substantive topic of research, intelligence more and more has come to reflect the value and virtue it has been accorded in western culture. As a result, there can no longer be brief discussions of the nature and development of intelligence. Rather there are extended statements summarizing research from one or another vantage point (Hunt, 1961; Jensen, 1969). An extensive discussion of intelligence as a research topic is not within the scope of this chapter. Interested readers are directed to other sources for complete discussions; Hunt (1961) and Stott and Ball (1965) provided historical information and carefully reasoned approaches to this subject.

When intelligence is viewed from a developmental perspective several issues are emphasized. The most prominent issue is that of dealing with the development of intelligence as a cumulative accretion of information (judged, perhaps by a vocabulary test), versus its development as a progression from stage to qualitatively different stage. Some tests yield indications of whether a certain stage has already been reached, but there is no general "developmental quotient." A related issue concerns the relationship between what has come to be called the development quotient and intelligence. A third issue deals with mature intelligence as a product of interacting genetic and environmental factors, the relative balance of which is deemed of some political import. Test performance is used to evaluate the effects of efforts to change the environment (for example, "early enrichment"). Generally, conclusions and recommendations are directed at factors other than the tests. An issue related to the interplay of genetic and environmental factors in affecting intelligence concerns the extent to which intelligence remains stable throughout the lifespan. As was the case with intelligence, this chapter cannot adequately confront each of these issues. They are too numerous and extended discussions already are available (Bayley,

1970). As the purpose of the chapter is to describe and evaluate tests directly related to these discussions, however, the extent to which specific tests relate to an issue or issues will be discussed.

Pioneering Work of Gesell

More than any other individual, Gesell defined the field of infant assessment. Not only was he one of the earliest protagonists of the importance of infancy as a period of rapid development, he was also the prime mover in establishing the field as a substantive one. His commitment to infancy was singular (Gesell, 1925, pp. 10–11): "The preschool period of development . . . holds an unambiguous and undisputed preeminence in the dynamic series. *It comes first.* This priority confers upon it a dominating influence. It is the most consequential period of development for the simple but decisive reason that it comes first. . . . The infant learns to see, to hear, handle, walk, comprehend, and talk. He acquires an unaccountable number of habits fundamental to the complex art of living. Never again will his mind, his character, his spirit advance as rapidly as in this formative preschool period of growth."

Although, as a field, infant assessment was nonexistent before Gesell, his intentions did not appear to be directed at establishing an open-ended research area, directed at developing issues and testing hypotheses. Rather his intentions were focused on pragmatic goals. "Infant welfare" and "infant hygiene" were the foci of Gesell's efforts, and the diagnostic scales he developed were intended to distinguish among infants for whom "welfare" and "hygiene" would become important. Certainly Gesell felt that the need to develop diagnostic capability in this area had been signaled by the (then) recent establishment of the Federal Children's Bureau, state level departments of child hygiene, and various Congressional acts promulgating mother and infant hygiene.

Gesell's model was taken from the work of Wilheim His, who published a definitive description of human embryonic development in 1885. Gesell (1925, p. 25) commented:

This fundamental contribution rested, in no small measure, upon an extraordinary number of microcrosssection views of the embryo which were assembled into contiguous series both transverse and longitudinally. By relating these sections serially and comparatively he built up an outline of morphogenesis. Must not genetic psychology build its foundation in a similar manner?

His answer and degree of commitment were clear (1925, p. 26):

> Just as the embryologist gets his basic conceptions of morphogenesis by building up indefatigably, step by step, detailed sectional views of growing organisms or of a growing organ, so may genetic psychology build up a continuing series of sections corresponding to the stages and moments of development. Even the cinema-film is a series of static pictures. When reproduced in close succession, this series restores the original motion. The analogy does not altogether break down in the domain of mental development.
>
> Mental development is dynamic and elusive but it is essentially no more elusive than physical development and, just as the science of embryology is clarifying the phenomena of physical growth through countless sectional studies, so may genetic psychology attain an insight into the obscure developmental mechanics of the growth of behavior. Genetic psychology has depended too much upon philosophical approaches to the problems of origin, unfoldment, and recapitulation.
>
> The securest basis for a developmental psychology is a vast amount of descriptive data which will delineate what the generic human individual is in the ascending stages of maturity. Interpretation of the behavior of this individual will be simple and certainly less speculative if rested upon such foundation. Statistical method will elucidate these observed data but will not contribute to the data themselves. These can come only through incessantly observing and recording. First of all, developmental psychology is descriptive; second, it is comparative, and finally, interpretative.

Although Gesell provided very perceptive descriptions of

neonatal behavior, he chose not to begin his normative efforts at that early an age. Rather, his initial starting point was at three months and included five other assessment points before two years: six, nine, twelve, eighteen, and twenty-four months of age. (Gesell also developed assessment procedures for children up to six years of age but these are not covered in this chapter.) The purpose of these scales was broad and more clinical than nonclinical; the inclusion of specific items was based more on normative and descriptive utility than on any particular conception of intelligence. Nevertheless, Gesell contended that the scales were of significant use in interpreting "capacity and personality."

The initial total scale, published in 1925, consisted of 144 items divided into four general fields. *Motor behavior* included postural control, locomotion, prehension, drawing and hand control. Items in this field were designed to assess coordination and motor capacity. *Language behavior* was assessed by means of vocabulary, word comprehension, conversation, and reproduction. *Adaptive behavior* was comprised of eye-hand coordination, imitation, object recovery, comprehension, discriminative performance, apperception and completion, and number conception. Items in this field were designed to assess responsivity to environmental change. *Personal and social behavior* included reactions to persons, personal habits, initiative and independence, play responses, and acquired information. These items were presumed to assess personality traits and were based on information gained in maternal interviews. While Gesell cautiously noted that these four fields were ". . . simply a codification . . . not to be applied in an artificial manner," he added that, ". . . the classification followed psychological lines as far as (this) was possible" (p. 60).

Each of the six infant schedules contained an average of thirty-two items, with some items appearing on more than one schedule. While motor items comprised 45 percent of the four-month schedule, language items comprised only 3 percent of that schedule. By the twenty-four-month schedule, however, motor items were reduced to only 11 percent of the schedule, while language items comprised 21 percent of the schedule; that is, while motor items were quartered, language items had been increased by sevenfold. The percentage of adaptive behavior items remained relatively unchanged throughout the six schedules, ranging between 25 and 34 percent of the total number of items. The personal-social items increased from 28 percent of the four-month schedule to 43 percent of the twenty-four-month schedule. This meant that there was a slight increase in the number of items assessed by interview as the infant grew, which at the same time may have introduced increasing amounts of social desirability into the assessment.

Although Gesell's intention was to select a ". . . representative, unselective sample of the prepublic school population . . . ," the composition of his longitudinal sample was difficult to ascertain. The population of infants was initially drawn from public county records. While subject attrition rates were not given for the infant sample, attrition rates of 72 percent and 61 percent were noted for the two-year-old and three-year-old children. The sample was generally balanced between males and females, and was composed of infants from "American homes." While infants from homes of professional classes were not excluded, the largest source of infants appeared to be from "baby welfare stations," attended by mothers from middle class homes. Markedly retarded children were excluded from the sample, as were markedly superior children.

Many of the specific items Gesell developed were adopted unchanged by later researchers. Although some have noted the need to revise the norms for certain items, none has questioned the appropriateness of the items for use with infants. Table 1 presents a sampling of some of Gesell's initial items and their average age of appearance (fiftieth percentile).

There have been no basic changes in the scale since 1925. The classification of items into motor, adaptive, language, and personal-social categories still is used. For fifteen years, the major efforts of Gesell and his co-workers were directed at making finer gradations in the schedules and in restandardization. In 1938, Gesell presented normative distinctions for four, six, eight, twelve, sixteen, twenty, twenty-four, twenty-eight, thirty-two, thirty-six, forty, forty-four, forty-eight, fifty-two, and fifty-six weeks; fifteen, eighteen, and twenty-one months; and two-year-old infants (Gesell and Thompson, 1938; Gesell, 1940). These distinctions were achieved not by changing specific items on the schedules, but by distinguishing finer gradations of response. For example, the response to the sound of

Table 1.

REPRESENTATIVE ITEMS FROM THE FIFTIETH PERCENTILE FOR
EACH MONTH FROM GESELL'S INITIAL SCALE (1925)

FOUR MONTHS

Turns head toward sound of bell
Complete thumb apposition
Defensive hand motions to paper
placed lightly on face

SIX MONTHS

Exploratory manipulation of spoon
Looks for fallen object
Reacts to mirror image

NINE MONTHS

Lifts inverted cup and secures cube
placed under it
Releases cube in cup
Holding two cubes, accepts a third
(without dropping any)

TWELVE MONTHS

Builds tower of three cubes
Spontaneously scribbles when given
paper and pencil
Walks unsupported

EIGHTEEN MONTHS

Builds tower of four cubes
Points to two or more parts of body
Asks for things by words

TWENTY-FOUR MONTHS

Imitatively builds a three-block
bridge
Uses color names
Gives full name and sex

the bell, once only head turning, was changed to distinguish degrees of postural orientation as well as cessation of body movement.

The normative samples on which these schedules were based were inadequate. One hundred and seven infants comprised the normative longitudinal sample, with about thirty-five infants seen at each age to fifty-six weeks. The infants were full term normal infants. The parents averaged twenty-nine years of age and were primarily middle class and of Northern European ancestry. The fifteen- and twenty-one-month schedules were based on another normative sample (twenty to thirty infants) that Gesell described as "clinical cases . . . less homogeneous than normative cases . . . but relatively normal children" (Gesell, 1940, p. 321). The composition of the eighteen-month and twenty-four-month normative samples is not clear.

It should be noted, however, that Gesell did defend his selection of subjects, writing, "Our problem was *not* the construction of a scale for the evaluation of a child's behavior in terms of *all* infants of his age. We desired instead to investigate the patterning of growth," but he added, enigmatically, "to plot the course of development of a statistically average individual" (Gesell and Thompson, 1938).

The maturational level of an infant is the highest normative level at which more items are passed than failed. This level, with consideration for factors the tester feels are important but unassessed by the schedule, represents the infant's developmental quotient.

Information essential to the prospective tester is in three volumes: *The Psychology of Early Growth* (Gesell and Thompson, 1938), *The First Five Years of Life* (Gesell, 1940), and *Developmental Diagnosis* (Gesell and Amatruda, 1947, 2nd edition). Of these three, *Developmental Diagnosis* is the best single source of information, as it contains the most detailed synopses of the major normative points.

Several attempts to examine the predictive validity of the Gesell schedules have been conducted since 1925, with not particularly encouraging results. Wittenborn and others (1956) attempted to assess the predictive validity of the schedules in groups of infants examined in Gesell's Yale Clinic. Wittenborn's sample was drawn from the population of the clinic and consisted largely of an adoptive sample, some tested before, and others after placement (total $N = 226$). In addition to the Gesell schedules, a number of assessments were made to cover areas possibly missed by the schedules, but still important in describing children. Most of the infants were assessed with the Gesell schedules before forty weeks of age and in no cases were tested after fourteen months of age. Some infants were tested twice if the tester was not confident of the infant's performance on the first test. Between five and nine years of age the Stanford-Binet was given and a number of selective assessments were made: scholastic achievement, physical development, and personal-social development. The correlations between the General Maturity Quotient of the Gesell and Stanford-Binet scores were uniformly low, ranging from $-.14$ to $.55$. Excluding infants placed with families after testing and for whom Wittenborn had demonstrated related selective placement, the average correlation between the Gesell and Stanford-Binet was $.09$. Although some additional correlations were obtained between other assessments made at both ages (that is, adaptive sub-scale of the Gesell and hand dynamometer grip strength, $r = .45$), their importance was minimized by the authors. Regarding the relationships between the Gesell schedules and the Stanford-Binet, Wittenborn concluded that the correlations they obtained "were not only unreliable, but . . . too small to be of any practical interest." The other correlations "were so infrequent as to possibly have occurred by chance" (p. 87).

Another attempt to assess the predictive validity of the Gesell schedules was made by Knobloch and Pasamanick (1960). They compared the scores of slightly under a thousand full-term and premature infants on the Gesell schedules for forty weeks of age and the Stanford-Binet for three years of age. In what appears to be a sharp contrast to Wittenborn and others, Knobloch and Pasamanick reported a correlation of .48 between the forty-week Gesell schedule and the three-year Stanford-Binet. This was not much different from the correlation between the forty-week and three-year Gesell schedules ($r = .51$).[1] However, Knobloch and Pasamanick were predicting over a much shorter time span in this study.

Apart from the time factor, another possible explanation of the large differences between the correlations of Wittenborn and those of Knobloch and Pasamanick may involve the rater reliability of the initial assessment. The procedure used by Wittenborn included reassessment with the Gesell if the examiner was not confident about an initial assessment during infancy. Rater agreement data was not presented but one might suspect that if the reassessment had been a part of the procedure, it may have been low. Knobloch and Pasamanick reported rater agreement correlations of over .98 between the training examiner and three trainees.

In a later study, Knobloch and Pasamanick (1966, cited in Thomas, 1970, p. 184) reported some of the highest correlations obtained with the Gesell scales. In a heterogeneous sample of normal and clinical infants seen before one year of age and tested seven years later with a Stanford-Binet, the authors obtained a correlation of .70 (N = 123) between the Gesell and the Stanford-Binet. However it appears likely that the size of the correlation was augmented by the heterogeneity of the sample.

[1] The three-year Gesell schedule and Stanford-Binet were correlated $r = .87$ in their data.

Knobloch and Pasamanick also recommended that the norms for many of the items on the thirty-six to fifty-six-week Gesell schedules be readjusted. They suggested that ten items, mostly involving adaptive behavior, be moved to adjacent later points in the schedule, and that thirty-two items, mostly involving personal-social and language items, be moved to an earlier point in the schedules. To our knowledge, these recommended changes have not been generally incorporated by researchers using Gesell's schedules, in spite of the fact that the recommendations were based on larger and probably more adequate normative groups than the original samples of Gesell.

Drillien (1961) also used a sample of heterogeneous infants in a longitudinal study of the effects of prematurity. As had Knobloch and Pasamanick (1966), Drillien obtained high correlations between Gesell schedules administered during infancy and tests administered several years later. Based on samples of more than 200 at each age, Drillien obtained correlations of .54, .57, and .66 between the Gesell schedules administered at six, twelve, and twenty-four months and the Terman-Miles which was administered at five years.

Aware of the variability in magnitude of predictive coefficients obtained by various investigators, Ames defended the use of infancy scales as a form of assessment (1967). She correctly noted that Gesell had not intended his scale to be an intelligence test. Therefore, attempts to minimize its utility by demonstrating low correlations with later intelligence tests were misdirected. Furthermore, the use of homogeneous samples of infants, excluding neurologically-damaged infants for whom the Gesell scales were also intended, artificially depressed test-retest correlations. In support of her contentions, Ames tested thirty-three infants between twenty-four weeks and one year of age, retesting them at ten years with the Wechsler Intelligence Scale for Children (WISC). Twenty-one of those infants retested at ten years had scores on both tests within ten points of one another. Sixteen of the twenty-one had scores differing by five points or less. She concluded that, "infant and preschool tests yield scores which are highly predictive of . . . ten-year-old performance on the WISC" (p. 235).

In objecting to the use of later intelligence tests as a measure of validity, it is not clear why Ames used the WISC rather than a broader form of assessment at ten years (as had Wittenborn). In addition, the majority of the Ames sample were children of Yale faculty members; not necessarily a heterogeneous group. And, although the presentation of percentages of infants maintaining scores within a given range at retesting is informative, the relation to other studies using the correlation coefficient as the index of predictive power is unclear. Nonetheless, our computation of correlation coefficients from Table Two of Ames' report (p. 226) yielded two significant correlations (of eight) between the infant scale and the WISC: at twenty-four weeks, $r = .58$ ($p < .05$, N = 11); and at twenty-eight weeks, $r = .82$ ($p < .02$, N = 7). These were the earliest testings in infancy. Why the later, more reliable infant testings did not yield significant correlations is unclear.

Three-factor analyses have been performed on selected Gesell scales. Richards and Nelson (1938) contended that the six-month Gesell scale could be broken into three factors: an "alertness" factor (items assessing attentiveness more than motor performance); a "motor ability" factor (items dealing with reaching, grasping, and manipulation); and a "testability" or "halo effect" factor common to all items except those assessed by the mother's report. The testability factor presumably reflected both the tester's rapport with the infant as well as the infant's predispositional set to testing on that particular day. However, in a later analysis of the six-, twelve-, and eighteen-month Gesell schedules, Richards and Nelson (1939) reported that the testability factor did not emerge, and they could only replicate the alertness and motor factors. Furthermore, the alertness factor was described as containing items dealing with "distance reception" and "playfulness." The motor factor was present in all items "because of the obvious fact that all behavior at this early level is . . . motor" (p. 317).

More recently, Stott and Ball (1965) performed varimax and biquartimin analyses on six-month and twelve-month Gesell scales, with clearest results on the six-month scale which yielded eight factors dealing with manual closure and generalized manipulation, memory, directed reaching and purposeful manipulation, locomotion, reflexes, manual production of sound, visually instigated action, and body control. Factors from the twelve-month scale involving responses to general social communication, responses to verbal communication, gross psychomotor control, memory of demonstrations, and deductive reasoning were less clear. Stott and Ball attributed the contrast between the number and types of factors in these analyses and those of Richards and Nelson, in part, to recent developments in computer technology.

The results of these studies are not impressive, particularly if the Gesell Scales are presumed to be compatible with the Stanford-Binet in assessing intelligence, a presumption Gesell never intended. He distinguished between psychometric intelligence and developmental status, which referred to a complete description of the child; his adaptive, linguistic, and personal-social behaviors. Gesell's interest was in assessing developmental status from a comparative perspective, feeling as he did that a moderately positive relationship between his scales and intelligence would have been theoretically appropriate.

Scales of Cattell and Bayley

Cattell Infant Intelligence Scale. Unlike Gesell, Cattell was less concerned with an enveloping, clinical assessment than with producing a standardized assessment of mental ability. Cattell found the Gesell Scales, as well as several others available during the 1930s, wanting in objectivity, standardization, appeal to young infants, and amenability to numerical ratings rather than descriptions. Cattell was particularly dissatisfied with the proliferation of motor performance items in the scale as they were "probably only indirectly related to mental development" (Cattell, 1940, pp. 15–21).

Cattell directed her efforts toward developing an assessment procedure free of these shortcomings. The degree to which she was successful is best reflected in her own words (1940, p. 23):

> The Gesell tests were used as a point from which to build. The items of the Gesell tests were first arranged in an age scale similar to that of the Stanford-Binet tests. In order to make the scale as much an intelligence scale as possible, over 100 items, the responses to which were thought to be unduly influenced by home training or to depend mainly on large muscular control, were eliminated. Other items collected from various sources

were added to fill the gaps. All the directions for giving
and scoring items have been written in a detailed and
in as objective a manner as possible. A large majority of
the items taken from the Gesell tests were modified,
more or less, in order to make the giving or scoring more
objective or to increase or decrease the difficulty for the
purpose of attaining an equal number of items at each
of the age levels covered. A total of 1346 examinations
were used in connection with the standardization, but,
unfortunately, those items which were added later were
not given to as many children as were those used from
the beginning.

The scale was designed to be compatible with the Stanford-
Binet. An inspection of the specific items in the scale indicates that,
by and large, they are similar to those in the Gesell Scales.

Cattell's normative sample consisted of 274 infants participating in a longitudinal study conducted at the Harvard School of
Public Health. The infants were seen at three, six, nine, twelve,
eighteen, twenty-four, thirty, and thirty-six months of age. They
were from normal deliveries and from families of Northern European ancestry in which the father was apparently gainfully employed. Their occupational descriptions indicated that the families
were largely of middle class status. A fifty-dollar fee covering pre-
natal, delivery, and postnatal care probably excluded lower class
families from participating. Subject attrition was 24 percent over a
seven-year period.

The scale consists of five items for each age level, with one or
two alternates. Each item is scored as pass or fail, and is proportion-
ately weighted in determining an infant's level of performance. The
split-half reliability of the three-month scale was poor ($r = .56$,
Spearman-Brown corrected); scales for later ages reached acceptable levels of reliability (Spearman-Brown correlations ranging from
.86 to .90). Notwithstanding, correlations with the Stanford-Binet
at three years of age were poor: $r = .10$ from three months; $r = .34$
from six months; $r = .18$ from nine months; $r = .56$ from twelve
months; $r = .67$ from eighteen months; and $r = .71$ from twenty-
four months (all samples ranging from 42 to 57). Given that her
scale was intended to be a downward extension of the Stanford-

Binet, Cattell did not appear to be appropriately circumspect in her general instructions regarding its use; her recommendations emphasized predictive power without respect to age. However, she did suggest that close attention be paid to clinical and other subjective impressions of the infant not specifically related to the test or testing situation. These, she admitted, could be of value in revealing areas of dysfunction which had distorted performance on a particular scale or item (Cattell, 1940, pp. 85–92).

A factor analysis of the three-month and six-month Cattell scales performed by Stott and Ball (1965) yielded four factors at each age. At three months, three of the factors had visual components: visual attention, hand and arm responses to visual stimuli, and visual anticipation. The fourth factor involved activity with the fingers. At six months the factors remained somewhat the same: direct reaching, manipulative evaluation, persistent goal-directed behavior, and exploratory manipulation.

Escalona examined the potential effects of "non-test" considerations on the Cattell Scales. Using a six-category classification of development (retarded to superior) based on either the Cattell or Gesell Scales, Escalona examined the relationship of test reliability to subjective judgments of maximal performance. The subjective judgments were based on the judges' "impression as to whether the subject had performed in as mature a manner as was possible for this particular infant" (Escalona, 1950, p. 122). In a sample of seventy-two adoptive children, Escalona found that thirty-eight infants had not been tested at their optimal level. Retesting the thirty-eight placed 80 percent of them in a developmental category different from their original placement. In contrast, slightly less than one-third of the thirty-four infants initially tested under optimal circumstances were placed in another category at retesting. Unfortunately, Escalona did not describe the time interval between test and retest beyond saying that it ranged from one-half to several years.

In a similar study Gallagher (1953) retested four- to twenty-four-month-old adopted infants on the basis of whether or not they were judged as having done their best on initial testing with the Cattell Scales. The infants were divided into two groups, one from deprived families and exhibiting poor performance at initial testing, the other, a control group of normals. Gallagher found that while one-third of the normal infants changed categories upon retesting, 42 percent of the deprived infants changed categories upon retesting. Gallagher also reported test-retest stabilities for both groups: for the deprived group a correlation of .77 at an interval of 7.9 months; for the nondeprived group a correlation of .83 at an interval of 7.2 months. Interestingly, while the deprived group significantly increased its average performance by nine points at retesting, the normal group did not change. Clearly, consideration of such factors is important in obtaining accurate assessments of infants. To administer routinely test items to an infant ignoring condition and qualitative aspects of the infant's performance runs the risk of obtaining distorted results.

Cavanaugh, Cohen, Dunphy, Ringwall, and Goldberg (1957) compared premature, term, and post-mature infants on the Cattell Scales and the Stanford-Binet. Assessment with the Cattell occurred at six, twelve, eighteen, and twenty-four months. Assessment with the Stanford-Binet occurred at thirty-six, forty-eight, and sixty months of age. The higher correlations between tests at different ages occurred in a subsample of term infants ($N = 34$) for whom longitudinal data from six to forty-eight months was complete and from whom it was thought that generally valid test scores had been obtained. The correlations generally increased in magnitude as the infant matured and the test-retest interval decreased (that is, the six- and twelve-month correlation was .32; the six-month and sixty-month correlation was .21; the forty-eight and sixty-month correlation was .69). These trends also characterized the correlations from the whole sample (premature, term, postmature). Changes in mean scores between the ages generally tended to be significant; differences existed between the means of the Cattell scores and those of the Stanford-Binet scores. The authors then questioned whether functions tapped by the Stanford-Binet and Cattell scales were similar, suggesting that the Cattell could not be empirically defended as a downward extension of the Stanford-Binet.

Escalona and Moriarity (1961) compared the Cattell and Gesell scales with the WISC, assessing infants from one to eight months with both scales and retesting them between seven and eight-and-a-half years of age with the WISC. The correlations between the Cattell and WISC scores, and the Gesell and WISC scores were −.05

and .08, respectively. Dividing the WISC scores into four categories, ranging from low-average to superior, yielded a slight, but still unimpressive, relationship between the infant assessments and later testing. The addition of clinical appraisal data collected during the infancy assessments provided some predictive ability and appeared more useful than the scales themselves in predicting the gross categorical distinctions based on the WISC. Escalona and Moriarity concluded that "for children in this age range, a clinical appraisal based on total test performance on two test instruments is a more accurate predictor of later intelligence range than are scores obtained from either the Cattell or Gesell tests alone" (pp. 604–605).

California Infant Scales. Bayley's reasons for developing her own scale appeared to be related to her dissatisfaction with currently available scales and the manner in which they had been standardized. She was particularly critical of small institutionalized samples in developing normative scales (1933, pp. 5–10). Although Bayley also relied heavily on Gesell's work in developing her own scale, she has continued more than anyone else, to improve her scales over the more than forty years since she developed them. Her efforts have been directed primarily toward strengthening the scales by revising them on larger normative samples. Because of these efforts, Bayley's scales are psychometrically the most adequate of the frequently-used scales.

Bayley's scales are divided into two broad areas: mental and motor. Among the mental test items are "tests of adaptability or learning and tests of sensory acuity and fine motor (manual) co-ordinations" (1933, p. 24). Motor items deal with "gross body co-ordinations" (p. 24). Although most of the specific test items were drawn from the Gesell Scales, Bayley omitted those that did not elicit differentiating behavior at successive ages or were not observed in sufficiently large numbers.

The California First Year Mental Scale (1933) was Bayley's first formal test. It contained 115 items, which were judged on a "pass-fail" basis. Items were not considered passed until consecutive successes had occurred to the same item on two adjacent tests. The scale started at one month and continued at monthly intervals until fifteen months of age was reached. Following that, three-month intervals separated the tests. Thus, before an item was considered as having been successfully passed at one month, it must also have been passed at two months. Rather than meaning that a test score could not be computed until an infant had been tested twice, this meant that a score was tentative and modifiable dependent on an ensuing test. An infant's score was cumulative from month to month, and consisted of all the previous items passed on preceding tests.

Bayley's original normative sample consisted of sixty-one normal infants born to upper middle class families in the Berkeley, California area. The infants were longitudinally tested over the duration of data collection. Subject attrition reduced the sample to fifty-three by the second year. Split-half reliabilities (Spearman-Brown corrected) computed on this initial sample were superior to those obtained by other infant scales, averaging $r = .63$ for the first three months, $r = .92$ for the fourth through the eighth month, and $r = .82$ thereafter until reaching two years of age. Concomitantly, test-retest reliabilities between successive tests averaged $r = .63$ for the first three months and $r = .80$ thereafter until two years of age.

Bayley's motor scale was published initially two years after her mental scale (1935) and was similar to the earlier scale, for it was drawn largely from the Gesell. The normative sample for it was the same as for the mental scale. Testing intervals were also identical to those used in the development of the mental scale. The scale contained seventy-six items and was scored in a cumulative fashion identical to the scoring procedure for the mental scale. Split-half reliabilities for the motor scale were not so high as for the mental scales during the early months; an average correlation of $r = .58$ for the first three months, .74 for months four through eight. Following eight months, the average correlation was as high as that of the mental scale. The test-retest correlations among consecutive tests ranging from one month through fifteen months yielded correlations comparable to those obtained for the mental scale; they were low for the early months but reached acceptable levels by the fifth month ($r = .75$). Unlike the mental scales, however, the test-retest correlations were very poor for the scales from fifteen to twenty-four months. Here, where tests occurred at three-month rather than one-month intervals, correlations averaged $r = .33$. Correlations between the initial mental and motor scales for months one through twenty-four were variable, averaging $r = .47$.

These initial mental and motor scales have undergone both major and minor revisions in the forty years that Bayley has worked with them. Samples from the Collaborative Study of the National Institute of Neurological Diseases and Blindness have provided additional bases for modifications, culminating in Bayley's test manual (1969), which contains a brief history of the development of the scales, standardization and reliability information, and complete instructions for administering and scoring tests. Performance on the mental scale is expressed in the form of a "mental development index"; performance on the motor scale is expressed on a "psychomotor development index." The mental scale contains 163 items and is normed at one-half month intervals from two to five months, and at one-month intervals from six to thirty months. The motor scale, containing eighty-one items, is normed at identical-age intervals. The Infant Behavior Record is described in the manual, and contains a set of ratings which provides quantitative and qualitative information regarding the infant's social, emotional, and stylistic behavior during administration of the mental and motor scales and which could possibly contribute considerably to an accurate assessment in light of the importance of "non-test" factors discussed earlier (Escalona, 1950; Gallagher, 1953).

The sample, comprised of 1262 term and normal infants, was stratified by sex, color ("white," "nonwhite"), rural-urban residence, and education of head of household. The only difference Bayley found between these stratifications was for color; nonwhite infants scored significantly higher than white infants on the Motor Scale between the third and fourteenth month. The corrected split-half reliabilities for the 1969 mental and motor scales were impressive, averaging .86. But these corrected split-half reliabilities did not include the one-half month intervals from two to five months and the one-month intervals from six to thirty months shown in the normative tables in the manual. Rather, one-month intervals were used between two and six months, two-month intervals between six and twelve months, and three-month intervals between twelve and thirty months.

The only observer-agreement (simultaneous observation) data available are for a preliminary version of the scale (Werner and Bayley, 1966). Summarizing their analyses based on a sample of ninety, Bayley reported 89 percent agreement for fifty-nine items on the eight-month mental scale, and 93 percent agreement for twenty items on the motor scale (Bayley, 1969). A subsample of this group ($N = 28$) tested at a one-week interval with the eight-month scale yielded test-retest observer agreement percentages of 76 percent for the mental scale and 75 percent for the motor scale (Bayley, 1969). The correlation between the mental and motor scales ranged from $r = .24$ to $r = .78$; the higher correlations occurring at the younger ages.

Correlations between the Bayley Mental Scale and the Stanford-Binet have ranged from minimal to moderate. Based on her 1933 sample Bayley reported low correlations (range: $-.13$ to $.02$) between the initial mental scale administered before two years of age and the Stanford-Binet from five to thirteen years of age (Bayley, 1949). She reported a correlation of $r = .53$ between the 24-month mental scale and Stanford-Binet on another sample of infants ($N = 120$).

Several attempts at *a priori* classifications of her 1933 and 1935 scales, provided Bayley with only one categorization of the mental scale that she thought was successful. That was separating sensorimotor from predominantly adaptive behaviors (1933). She was unable to make more specific categorizations such as visual behavior, eye-hand coordination, reaction to sound, and so on. The Initial Motor Scale (1935) was divided into "anti-gravity" and "gross body motion" categories. Anti-gravity behaviors were typified by head raising, maintaining erect posture while sitting or standing. Gross body motions, however, were represented by body turning, arm and leg thrusting, and lateral head movements.

Stott and Ball (1965) examined the factor groupings of a subset of Bayley's items at the six-month and twelve-month levels. At six months responses to external stimuli emerged which fell into affective evaluative, exploratory, cognitive, and motoric factors. At twelve months the factors were more reflective of self-initiating behaviors: understanding of relationships, linguistic communication, cognitively-adaptive behavior, and memory.

Ramey, Campbell, and Nicholson (1973) have reported high-magnitude correlations of the Bayley mental and motor scores with Stanford-Binet scores, stating that in situations where natural environmental variation was reduced, predictive power of the scales should be high, ostensibly reflecting the genetic composition of intelligence. Their sample consisted of twenty-four infants attending a day-care project over a three-year period. The average age of the infants entering the project was three months. Socio-economic status varied from poverty levels to upper middle class. Correlating performance on the motor scale at six to eight, nine to twelve, thirteen to sixteen months with Stanford-Binet scores at thirty-six months yielded rs of decreasing magnitude (.77, .56, and .43 respectively). Correlating performance on the mental scale at the same ages yielded rs of increasing magnitude (.49, .71, .90 respectively), all of which may be a reflection of the increasing differentiation between mental and motor abilities in the infant. Ramey and others attributed the magnitude of these correlations to the homogeneity of environmental conditions created by the day care. However, it is equally likely that the magnitude of the correlations was caused, at least in part, by chance fluctuations due to the small sample on which these correlations were based ($N = 11$). As noted earlier, Bayley has reported a correlation of .53 ($N = 120$) between her early scores and later Stanford-Binet scores.

Hofstaetter (1954) conducted a factor analysis of Bayley scale performance. He examined Bayley's published correlation matrices for performance on selected standardized tests between two months and eighteen years and described three orthogonal factors, each of which was impressively associated with a particular age. His first factor was similar to one described by Bayley and dealt with "sensorimotor alertness" at approximately twelve months of age. The second factor dealt with "persistence . . . , a tendency to act in accordance with an established set rather than upon interfering stimulation" (pp. 161–162). This factor peaked at about three years of age. The third factor became asymtotic at slightly over seven years. This factor appeared to deal with the manipulation of "symbols" and resembled Spearman's "g." This rather dramatic analysis was severely criticized thirteen years later by Cronbach (1967). Cronbach maintained that the matrices Hofstaetter used conformed to a simplex pattern, that is, one in which initially high correlations between adjacent measurements progressively decreased as the measurements became separated in time. Cronbach argued that Hofstaetter's factors were inherent in the simplex structure of the matrices, supporting his argument by replicating Hofstaetter's analysis and then demonstrating that a principle-components analysis and varimax rotation did not yield similar factors. Cronbach concluded that "students of child development should drop the Hofstaetter analysis from further consideration. It was an interesting exploration, nothing more" (p. 289).

Two efforts have been made to link the Bayley scales with earlier neonatal behavior. Honzik, Hutchings, and Burnip (1965) compared a four-category classification of birth status with performance on the Bayley mental and motor scales at eight months of age. The lowest classification, "definitely suspect," included infants who had experienced difficult deliveries and required resuscitation. These infants exhibited poor behavioral reflexes and evidence of neurological dysfunction at birth. The "suspect" and "possibly suspect" groups consisted of infants for whom some difficulties in delivery had occurred but who had exhibited rapid and spontaneous recovery. Honzik and others (1965) concluded that "definitely suspect" neonates were clearly distinguishable from "suspect," "possibly suspect," and "not suspect" groups in terms of their performances on both mental and motor scales. While their analyses of variance indicated such to be the case, inspection of their frequency distributions indicated considerable overlap between all classifications (their Figures 1 and 2, pp. 419–420).

Butler and Engel (1969) found that significant, but low magnitude positive relationships existed between neonatal photic latency (latency to the beginning of the first potential change of visual evoked potential, an averaged EEG response to visual stimulation) and performance on eighth-month mental, fine motor, and gross motor items from a modified version of the Bayley scales. However, they also found gestational age to be similarly related to performance on the Bayley items. When gestational age was partialled out, photic latency was negatively related to success on the mental items. Thus, it appears that there are areas of neonatal behavior that may bear some longitudinal relationships to later infant behaviors when assessed with a reliable instrument. Furthermore, the mediating effects of gestational age indicate that assessment soon after birth cannot be presumed to be taking place at a discrete point of origin; birth is but one significant landmark on an already established continuum of development.

A Perspective: Gesell, Cattell, Bayley

The efforts of Gesell, Cattell, and Bayley span a period of nearly seventy years. During that time American psychology has moved from its embryological beginnings to an impressive diversity of approaches. Interestingly, it has been both a shortcoming and a strength that the cumulative efforts of Gesell, Cattell, and Bayley have reflected only a limited part of that diversity. The press to move from behavioristic descriptions of molecular phenomena toward more abstract psychological processes was least felt by those studying infancy. While thus able to focus their efforts on behavior change and the intricacies of its assessment, they were also somewhat unappreciative of cognitively based approaches relating early sensorimotor skills to conceptual development. Nevertheless, each of their unique efforts was coordinated by their substantive focus on developmental measurements in infancy and their commitments to eliminating the shortcomings of earlier scales.

Although all three investigators focused on the assessment of developmental changes in infancy, each had somewhat different views regarding what their scales actually measured. Gesell eschewed the concept of intelligence, choosing instead to deal with developmental status. This was a holistic descriptor representing the totality of an infant's effective functioning, and was composed of motor, adaptive, personal-social, and language behaviors. And, although Gesell was very much aware of the necessary interplay of genetic and environmental influences, he saw development to be primarily a result of a maturational unfolding process generally unaffected by external influences. In contrast, Cattell's specific intent was to measure "intelligence." Her scales were to be a downward extension of the Stanford-Binet. The exclusion from her scale of Gesell items that she felt were unduly reflective of home influence or large muscle control, however, suggested that she was also sympathetic to a view of intelligence that was relatively unencumbered by environmental influence. Bayley was not as averse to restricting the role of developmental tests to the measurement of intelligence as was Gesell. She noted very early, however, that intelligence was an emergent function, taking different forms at different periods of development. Thus, from her view one would not have expected correlations to appear between what were disparate forms of intelligence at different ages.

Underlying all three approaches was the presumption that the motive force of development was provided by genetic factors. Ignoring the press of environmental over constitutional interpretations of phenotypic variation, these approaches have been cast (at least tacitly) as supporting a hereditary conception of intelligence.

The factor analytic studies of these scales produced some interesting findings. Most often cited is Hofstaetter's (1954) contention that three orthogonal factors described performance at three ages, those factors and ages having a surprising correspondence with Piaget's cognitive-developmental approach to intellectual functioning. Hofstaetter's first factor, "sensorimotor alertness," peaks at one year and corresponds to Piaget's "sensorimotor period." Hofstaetter's second factor, "persistence," peaks at three years and is somewhat compatible with Piaget's "preoperational period," a stage during which the child is beginning to establish rules of logical relationship. Hofstaetter's third factor, "planning," becomes asymtotic at about eight years. This factor is compatible with Piaget's period of "concrete operations," a stage during which the logical relationships between numbers and objects in time and space are established. The present writers have not encountered any studies attempting to replicate Hofstaetter's work with adjustments to accommodate Cronbach's (1967) telling criticism of the methodology used. Nevertheless, some communality has appeared in other kinds of factor analyses of the various scales (Stott and Ball, 1965): the early scales (six months) yield sensorimotor factors (exploration of the proximal environment and demonstration of minimal temporal integration in the form of short memory and goal-directed behavior). Factors for later ages (twelve months) entail primitive social awareness and communication. It therefore is likely that the Gesell, Cattell, and Bayley scales are tapping similar facets of infant behavior. This communality appears suggestive of the type of factor that Hofstaetter described for the earliest period, Cronbach's critique notwithstanding.

Two Neonatal Scales

Graham Test. In part, the same motivation that led Gesell, Cattell, and Bayley to develop assessment procedures for infants where there had been none previously, has led other researchers to develop procedures for assessing neonates. When standardized assessment procedures were available only to four years of age, early assessment referred to some period prior to four years. When assessment procedures were then developed for the third year, early assessment referred to the period prior to three years. It is this progressive redefinition that brought the neonatal period within its scope of assessment. It is doubtful that any methodological basis existed for extending early assessment into the neonatal period. The predominance of studies demonstrating that neither reliability nor predictive power could be easily obtained with the scales for the younger ages indicated the contrary.

However, there were reasons for developing scales for neonates beyond the need for extending boundaries to an earlier period. An impetus was also provided by a convergence of obstetric, pediatric, and psychological interests. In 1956, Graham, Matarazzo, and Caldwell described an assessment procedure designed to distinguish "normal" from "traumatized" newborns. Their intent was to develop a prognostic index that would locate those newborns, brain injured at birth, who might continue to develop abnormally as a result of their injuries. The procedure included five scales: a pain threshold scale using electric shock as the aversive stimulus; a maturation scale measuring motor behavior, auditory reactions and responses to obstruction of the nasal passages; a visual scale measuring fixation and horizontal pursuit; an irritability rating; and a muscle tension rating. The scale was standardized on a group of 265 normal and eighty-one brain-damaged newborns. Although complete data were not presented, interscorer agreement and reliabilities appeared sufficiently high. Corrected split-half reliabilities for the pain scale were $r = .87$ for normal newborns and $r = .97$ for the traumatized newborns. Twenty-four hour test-retest stabilities for all the scales were at or beyond $r = .62$ for normal newborns. These levels of reliability have been essentially replicated in two other studies of normal newborns (Rosenblith and Lipsitt, 1959; Bench and Parker, 1970).

Comparing the performance of the group of traumatized newborns with normal newborns yielded statistically significant differences for all five scales. Graham and others also found that by using the lower 1 percent of their sample distributions as a cutoff point, 51 percent of the traumatized infants could be correctly diagnosed by their low test performance, while 4 percent of the normal newborns were incorrectly diagnosed as traumatized. In another sample of newborns who had experienced perinatal anoxia, Graham found that severity of anoxia was positively related to her test scores (Graham, Pennoyer, Caldwell, Greenman, and Hartmann, 1957). With a sample of sixty infants, all evidencing varying amounts of fetal anoxia, perinatal anoxia, or postnatal central nervous system damage (and independently rated as to severity of condition) Graham and others found that performance on all of their scales decreased as severity of condition increased. The correlation between total test performance and severity of condition (higher scores indicating better condition) was $r = .46$. Adding a sample of sixty normal newborns (severity ratings of 0) to the sample increased the correlation to $r = .59$.

Two studies have examined the longterm predictive power of the Graham tests (Graham, Ernhart, Thurston, and Craft, 1962; Corah, Anthony, Painter, Stern, and Thurston, 1965). Graham and others (1962) were able to follow a group of 159 normal and 116 anoxic newborns over a three-year period. At three years of age the infants were assessed in three areas: cognitive performance with the Stanford-Binet or Cattell intelligence scale, perceptual-motor performance, and ratings of behavior based on parent questionnaires and observation. A standard neurological examination and anthropometric measurements were also included at three years. The correlations between the newborn and three year assessments generally were not impressive. For the anoxic sample, there were no statistically significant correlations between the Graham test score and any of the three-year variables. Only two correlations reached statistical significance, for the normal sample, enigmatically linking low performance on the Graham test with high performance on the perceptual motor tests. More reassuring and interpretable were statistically significant correlations for the group of newborns with miscellaneous complications other than anoxia, linking high performance on the Graham tests with high performance on cognitive tests, and the relation, for the combined normal, anoxic, and miscellaneous samples of a clinical rating of newborn condition, with favorable status on the three-year behavioral ratings obtained from parental questionnaires and observation. In this respect, the clinical prognosis was a better predictor of status at three years than the Graham newborn test score.

Corah and others (1965) retested the sample four years later at seven years of age. They essentially repeated and extended the Graham and others (1962) followup procedures, using cognitive assessments (WISC), perceptual motor assessments, ratings of behavior based on observation and parent ratings, anthropometric measurements, and a standard neurological examination. As in the previous followup, the relationships between the Graham newborn scales and later assessments were sparse. The authors noted that, "the very few correlations with the individual newborn behavior test scores which were significant were again too small to be of any interpretative value." Generally, Corah and others found that mean comparisons between anoxic and normal samples yielded some statistically significant differences, occurring primarily on the vocabulary subscale of the WISC, on behavioral ratings of distractability and impulsivity, and on the Vineland social maturity scale score. These differences were in the expected direction, the anoxic cases scoring lower than normals. And, as in the Graham and others analysis, the newborn clinical prognosis yielded statistically significant correlations supporting the mean differences between anoxic and normal groups.

Findings from the two followups are reasonably consistent. Generally, they suggest that while statistically significant, low magnitude relationships exist between perinatal trauma and later behavior, predictive validity exists (if at all) only for those infants evidencing massive and accumulative trauma during the newborn period. For the larger number of newborns evidencing moderate trauma, some statistical relationships can be found, but these are of magnitudes clearly insufficient for useful prediction. Nonetheless, the Graham scales were technically satisfactory. Thus, while it has been demonstrated that the ultimate downward extension in age of infant assessment need not result in psychometrically inadequate scales, predictive value has followed the general rule of decreasing value with earlier age of assessment. The research of Bell, Weller, and Waldrop (1971) indicates that the level of prediction from the newborn period can be higher than in the two followups discussed, possibly because they carried out separate analyses for the sexes, and studied the cases for a month on later followup. Nonetheless, the general level of prediction is still much lower than in the case of assessment carried out in later infancy.

A modification of the Graham test has been developed by Rosenblith (1961). Her modifications include the omission of the pain threshold scale, reorganization of the maturation scale into three categories containing the same items but with expanded response options: a motor-strength category, a tactile-adaptive category, and a sensory functioning category. The motor-strength category deals with general performance (that is, crawling). The tactile-adaptive category contains items dealing specifically with responses to respiratory obstruction. The items of the sensory functioning scale index visual and auditory perception. Aside from recategorizing Graham's maturation scale, Rosenblith's major change was to rescore the items, thereby allowing more variation in response. Rosenblith also expanded Graham's muscle tension and irritability ratings to allow for more variation in responses.

Rosenblith and Lipsitt (1959) have reported data on the Graham test "with slight modifications," but organized into categories identical to Graham's. Generally, the reliabilities reported for the vision and maturation scale were as good or better than Graham's, although those for the muscle tension and irritability ratings were much lower. Rosenblith's interscorer agreement and twenty-four-hour reliability were near 60 percent agreement for the muscle tension rating and slightly over 50 percent for the irritability rating. Mean scale scores for days one through five were generally at variance with those obtained by Graham. These differences may have been attributable to expansion of scores in Rosenblith's scale, or to her use of the best, rather than average score, as representative of the infant, as well as differences in hospital populations.

Rosenblith's modified tests revealed little predictive ability to eight months (1973). Using infants obtained in the Collaborative Perinatal Research Project of the National Institute of Neurological Diseases and Stroke, Rosenblith related performance on her modified tests to ratings at eight months of age on the Infant Behavior Profile Diagnosis (IBR, a part of the Bayley scales) covering mental, physical, socioemotional, gross and fine motor development, plus a rating of activity level. Four samples comprising a total of 1245 infants were tested, the first sample serving as a source of hypotheses, the last three serving as replication samples. The infants were randomly sampled from the hospital population, except for the exclusion of those exhibiting postnatal difficulty. The motor-strength and tactile-adaptive scales and, to a limited extent, general maturation, showed predictive ability. When trichotomized (upper quartile, two middle quartiles, lower quartile), the scales provided some discriminability between normal versus suspect and/or abnormal classifications on the total IBR score at eight months in two of the three replication samples (p range .02 to .20). However, no scales yielded statistically significant differences over the four samples.

The newborn scales were combined for predictions, but the most accurate individual predictors of suspect and/or abnormal behavior at eight months of age were the motor-strength and general maturation scores. In the combined samples, those scoring in the lowest quartile comprised 39 percent of those eventually classified as suspect and/or abnormal at eight months. However, 25 percent of those classified in the highest quartile were eventually classified as suspect and/or abnormal at eight months, thus, the lowest quartile contained only 14 percent more suspect or abnormal eight-month-old infants than the highest quartile.

A second modification of the Graham test has been reported by Bench and Parker (1970). As was true of Rosenblith, Bench and Parker were concerned primarily with improving the reliability of the test. And, again, as was the case in Rosenblith's work, Bench and Parker's major changes were to expand response scores for selected items to allow for more variation in response, and to standardize stimulus conditions more stringently. Tested on a sample of normal English newborns, the reliability of the scale was generally compatible with the Graham and Rosenblith versions. Observer agreement levels did not fall below $r = .77$ or 65 percent perfect agreement. Test-retest stability at a four-hour interval was better than that obtained by Graham or Rosenblith at twenty-four-hour intervals. Bench and Parker felt that their modification of the test did not yield any meaningful improvements in observer agreement or short-term stability over Graham's or Rosenblith's version.

All three versions of this test appear quite compatible. Administration of all can be readily learned from the procedural manuals, although Rosenblith's is still available only in unpublished form. The objective of both Graham and Rosenblith was to distinguish between normal and abnormal, traumatized and/or neurologically impaired infants. Both based their normative data in large part on essentially normal samples. Bench and Parker did not indicate whether they intended their modification to serve similar ends, but their normative data was based entirely on a normal sample. And, although Bench and Parker's modification has not yet been examined with regard to predictive ability, results from both Graham's and Rosenblith's versions suggest that there is not much likelihood of substantial improvement. Graham's version was not independently useful as a predictor to three and seven years of age, nor was Rosenblith's modification useful as a predictor to eight months; these statements are true even when the criterion was the gross one of normal versus abnormal status. But again, this should not be surprising. In the case of the Gesell, Cattell, and Bayley tests also, predictive power was poorest for the earliest periods of infancy.

Brazelton Neonatal Behavioral Assessment Scale. A newborn assessment recently developed by Brazelton (1973) is quite different from those developed by Graham, Rosenblith, and Bench and Parker. Graham's assessment was developed from the perspective of academic psychology. The revisions were carried out by investigators with extensive backgrounds in methodology who were interested in improving the psychometric qualities of the scales. Brazelton's assessment was based on extensive clinical pediatric practice, and he was also influenced by the pediatric neurological research of Prechtl and Beintema (1964). The Brazelton scales were designed not only to assess organismic variables as they might independently characterize the infant, but also to index behaviors that are potentially and concurrently relevant to social interaction. There are forty-seven items in the scale, twenty-seven of which involve nine-point ratings. The remaining twenty are measured with three-point ratings. These latter items involve elicited reflexes and movements, and are based directly on Prechtl and Beintema (1964). Also included are general ratings representing the examiner's judgment of the responses of the infant across a number of items.

Generally, the items of Brazelton's assessment appear to fall into several broad, overlapping categories: items concerning orientation toward, and response decrement (habituation) in response to external stimulation, that is, the neonate's progressive interaction with unchanging external stimuli; items concerning motor behavior, as assessed by ratings of tremulousness, hand-mouth coordination, spontaneous startles, and general motor activity; items concerning general arousal, including ratings of irritability, lability, peak arousal level, and rapidity of arousal, and; items assessing reflexive smiling, cuddliness, and consolability. The latter are most interesting with respect to social interaction. While these behaviors are inferred to a considerable extent from the reaction of the examiner to the infant, the inferences, if correct, could yield very important information concerning eliciting stimuli in interaction situations with a caregiver.

The first twenty-seven items comprise the major portion of the scale. The rating of response to each item should indicate only the infant's "best" behavior. The middle of the nine-point rating, Brazelton contends, is "related to expected behavior in an 'average' seven plus pound full term (forty weeks gestation), normal Caucasian infant whose mother has had not more than 100 milligrams of barbituates, fifty milligrams of other sedative drugs as premedication in the four hours prior to delivery, whose Apgars were no lower than seven-eight-eight one, five, and fifteen minutes after delivery, who needed no special care after delivery, and who had an apparently normal intrauterine experience . . . the behavior of the third day may be taken as the expected mean" (1973, p. 4).

In spite of Brazelton's focus on comprehensive coverage rather than on rigorous standardization of procedures, the scale is reported to have high reliability in one study (Horowitz, Self,

Paden, Culp, Laub, Boyd, and Mann, 1971) of sixty normal infants, tested at three and twenty-eight days of age. Horowitz and others used an early form of the Brazelton containing twenty-eight items with nine- and five-point rating scales. Defining agreement as identical or adjacent rating points recorded by two observers, it was found that concurrent rater agreement ranged between 90 and 100 percent for all items at both three and twenty-eight days of age. Based on the same criteria test-retest stability varied considerably. Agreement between three and twenty-eight days ranged from 24 to 79 percent for males (mean: 59 percent), and 42 to 85 percent for females (mean: 65 percent). Stability for specific items in the scale over the test-retest period also varied considerably. Ratings of passive movement, tremulousness, startles, and vigor yielded over 90 percent agreement. The rating of head movements in the prone position yielded only 29 percent agreement. Average stability across all twenty-eight items was 59 percent.

Two studies have examined the relationships between performance on the Brazelton scale and mother-infant interaction. Osofsky and Danzger (1974) attempted to relate the performance of fifty-one infants of poor, nonwhite mothers to their interaction with their mothers during the third or fourth day of the infant's life. Interaction was assessed during a fifteen-minute feeding period during which six maternal and nine infant behaviors were rated. Infant state, eye contact with the mother, and responsiveness to auditory stimulation from the mother were positively correlated with the Brazelton items. These behaviors from the observed interaction period involved the state of the infant, eye contact (with face and eyes of the mother) and responsiveness to auditory stimulation from the mother throughout the fifteen minutes. Unfortunately, Osofsky and Danzger did not examine the direct relationships between the Brazelton scale and maternal behaviors.

Bakow, Sameroff, Kelly, and Zax (1973) related the Brazelton performance from a heterogeneous sample of 144 infants to mother-infant interaction at four months of age. Rather than relating single measures between the Brazelton and the observation (as Osofsky and Danzger did), Bakow and others related two rotated factors obtained from the Brazelton scale items with five clusters of maternal behavior. They found that of the two large Brazelton factors, alertness and irritability, only alertness yielded significant (but low magnitude) correlations with maternal behaviors. The alertness factor was later associated with activity, stimulation, and responsiveness in the mother. Consistent with the latter finding, the only one of five infant behavior clusters at four months of age to be predicted from the Brazelton was that of responsiveness to the mother. With regard to the factor analysis of the Brazelton scale items, Bakow and others noted that the scales sampled a large variety of independent behaviors. Alertness and irritability, the two largest factors, were followed, in order of amount of variance explained, by five smaller factors.

Both of the studies just reviewed indicate that the Brazelton is assessing areas of neonatal behavior that are related to behaviors exhibited in mother-infant interaction, both early in life and later when interactive patterns may be more established. Both studies used infants not meeting all of Brazelton's operational criteria for normality. Other studies have demonstrated the scale's utility in cross-cultural situations (Horowitz, Aleksandrowicz, and Ashton, 1973) and in a clinical setting (Soule, Standley, Copans, and Davis, 1974) as well.

Influence of Piaget: Two Ordinal Scales

The onset of Piaget's great influence on American developmental psychology was dependent not so much on the original publication of his work, but rather on its translation into English. Thus, it was not until the 1950s that Piaget began to gain any sizeable readership among psychologists in America (Baldwin, 1967). Attempts to develop infant assessment procedures had long been underway and to the extent that Piaget had introduced a new theoretical approach to developmental psychology, traditional infant assessment procedures were devoid of that approach. From a Piagetian perspective, the assumptions implicit in the traditional tests were major and largely in error (Uzgiris and Hunt, 1974). Developmental progress was summative and nonhierarchical; progress was not dependent upon magnitude of achievement at one particular level, but only on the occurrence of a behavior (as assessed by a test item) within an array of other contemporaneous behaviors.

Piaget's approach was not so much psychologically oriented as it was epistemologically oriented. His concern was not with the developmental psychology of the child, but with the process of the child's coming to view the basic elements of existence. As Gesell was the prime mover in characterizing the maturational unfolding of the child, Piaget was the prime mover in describing the child as the prototypical epistemic philosopher. They were both different from one another in one other important aspect: the pragmatic Gesell took development to be primarily an accretion of increasingly complex behavioral units, relatively unaffected by environmental contingencies, whereas Piaget undertook to describe development as a series of hierarchical, qualitatively different stages, containing horizontal and vertical movement, and inextricably bound to environmental exchange. The initial stages were seen as primarily reflexive; the later stages represented the progressive integration of developing internal processes and physical coordination, neither of which could develop independently. (A review of Piaget's work is not within the purview of this chapter; excellent reviews of Piaget's theory are available: Baldwin, 1967; Flavell, 1963; Ginsburg and Opper, 1970). In one respect Piaget and Gesell were similar: they both undertook to describe the totality of the child's functioning, not a circumscribed area of behavior.

Two assessment procedures based on Piaget's theory have been developed recently (Corman and Escalona, 1969; Uzgiris and Hunt, 1974). The Einstein Scales of sensorimotor intelligence (Escalona and Corman, undated) are designed for infants between one month and two years of age. The procedure consists of three scales totaling fifty-four items. The Prehension Scale covers the development of adaptive reflexes (primary circular responses) and early systematic behavior (secondary circular responses) in the lowest age range. This scale includes spontaneous exploratory behavior, as well as items such as object-grasping that are identical to those developed by Gesell. The Object Permanence Scale focuses on the growing awareness of the infant that objects in the environment exist permanently and independently of his behavior. Items on the scale index the infant's ability to follow the trajectory of objects to the limits of his visual field, as well as his ability to continue behaviors initiated prior to visual obstruction. The Space Scale involves the infant's ability to function effectively in three-dimensional space. Included here are items assessing goal-directed behavior in the face of physical obstruction, and items eliciting object manipulation indicative of a three-dimensional perspective.

Corman and Escalona (1969) examined properties of the scales in an unselected sample of approximately 300 infants, ranging in age from slightly under a month to slightly over two years. Performance on the Prehension, Object Permanence, and Spatial Relationships Scales showed correlations with age ranging from .83 to .85 (rho). An appropriate indication of the adequacy of the scales was gained by determining the age at which a child entered a particular stage of performance. The scales defined four Piagetian stages and two substages. According to Piagetian theory, all of the stages should be passed in sequential order. The average age at entering into each stage was found to be sequential, beginning at 2.8 months for the first substage of Piagetian stage two and ending with entry into stage six at 10.1 months. Although some individual infants entered adjacent stages simultaneously, no infant was found to skip a stage or enter a later stage before an earlier stage. This supported the contention that the stages were invariant in sequence. Corman and Escalona correctly noted that their scales, rather than assessing "intelligence," generally defined as "the relative ability for successful problem-solving," measured the "methods and means employed in problem-solving." The scales should therefore be moderately, but not highly, correlated with standardized intelligence tests.

The assessment procedure developed by Uzgiris and Hunt (1974) is similar to the Einstein Scales in coverage, but is divided into six rather than three scales. The first scale, Visual Pursuit and Permanence of Objects, is concerned with the infant's increasing awareness of the existence of objects outside of the immediate perceptual field. Visual pursuit and behaviors indicating search for a hidden object are presumed to index this ability. This scale is comparable to the Einstein Object Permanence Scale. The second scale, Development of Means for Obtaining Desired Environmental Events, covers actions initiated by the infant to achieve a particular outcome. Included are sustained hand watching and the use of implements to obtain objects out of reach. This scale subsumes the Einstein Prehension Scale. The third scale, Development of Imitation, is divided into two subscales. The Vocal subscale begins with differentiation of distress and pleasure by crying and cooing, and ends with the repetition of words. Included are vocal behaviors apparently imitative, but also adaptive; these might be construed as externally-elicited circular reactions. The Gestural subscale is concerned with imitative responses requiring body action. The fourth scale is the Development of Operational Causality, and anticipatory behavior is the earliest behavior relevant to this scale; systematic behaviors (circular reactions included) directed toward establishing antecedent-consequent relationships are also included, whether or not the attribution of causality is internal or external. The fifth scale, Construction of Object Relations in Space, involves the infant's increasing capacity to appreciate three-dimensional space. Assessed here is the infant's ability to track and/or locate objects for which visual cues have been somehow interrupted. This scale is comparable to the Einstein Space Scale. The sixth scale is the Development of Schemes for Relating to Objects. It is generally directed at assessing the changing role of toys in the infant's environment and is not generally related to any particular stage. Progressive use of toys as extensions of the infant, as objects of curiosity and as functional units, are noted with this scale.

The scales were tested and revised on three samples, the first two of which totaled sixty-five. The infants were drawn exclusively from metropolitan middle-class families. The final sample consisted of eighty-four infants, also from middle-class families. Observer agreement and forty-eight-hour test-retest stability indices were high, ranging between 92 and 97 percent, and 70 and 85 percent stability by individual items in each scale. All of the scales were highly correlated with age; no pair of scales had a correlation of less than $r = .88$. Concomitantly, the intercorrelations of the scales were high, none falling below $r = .80$. However, with the effects of age partialled out, the intercorrelations decreased dramatically, only two of them yielding rs above .50. Mean ages for the achievement of each scale stage were presented, but Uzgiris and Hunt noted that their samples had not been selected with the intention of providing representative normative data for each age.

Comparisons of performance on the Uzgiris-Hunt Scales

and the Bayley Scales were made by King and Seegmiller (1973) on a group of unselected Harlem infants. The infants were assessed with both scales at fourteen, eighteen, and twenty-four months of age. Although King and Seegmiller were able to find mean differences in their sample supporting the ordinality of the Uzgiris-Hunt scales, they could not produce evidence of useful prediction to the Bayley. Between fourteen and eighteen months of age, only one of the six Piagetian scales yielded a significant correlation. Between eighteen and twenty-four months only two scales yielded significant correlations, neither of which demonstrated predictive ability between fourteen and eighteen months. The authors also noted that performance variation dropped sharply between fourteen and twenty-two months; in some cases these standard deviations were so low as to preclude valid correlational computations.

Overall, eight of fourteen correlations between the Uzgiris-Hunt Scales and Bayley's Mental and Motor Scales were significant, but of low order, ranging from $r = .23$ to $r = .44$. The correlation also decreased with increasing age, a result that is also partially attributable to the decreasing variance. King and Seegmiller suggested that the response categories should be expanded to allow for greater variation in response, and that procedures be more rigorously standardized. King and Seegmiller also suggested that the poor predictive power of the Uzgiris-Hunt scales was attributable to "uneven cognitive growth" (p. 325). It should be noted that the poor predictive power of the scales, as indexed by between-age correlations, does not detract from their validity, as indexed by the sequential entrance of stages. The latter may be a more appropriate criterion by Piagetian as well as statistical standards. In this respect, uneven cognitive growth might even be predicted.

Unfortunately neither the Einstein Scales nor the Uzgiris-Hunt Scales have been widely reported in recent research literature. The increasing popularity of Piagetian theory, however, suggests that both sets of scales will gain increasing approval. However, current use of the scales is not confined to evaluation of Piagetian theory; Wachs (1970) has used the Uzgiris-Hunt Scales in comparisons of mental retardates and normal children, and also in examining the long-term effects of early stimulation (Wachs and Cucinotta, 1971). Goldberg (1975, in press) has used the Einstein Scales in a

Zambian sample, relating infants' behavior to aspects of mother-infant interaction.

Discussion and Summary

Gesell's research began in the early 1920s. Since that time, there have been numerous efforts to develop assessment techniques for use with infants that would yield the power to predict future outcomes. The period of infancy, seen perhaps as of fundamental importance, was particularly enticing, for the ability to predict performance from this early age would have great practical value and social significance.

Seven major efforts to develop early assessment procedures have been reviewed in this chapter. The efforts of Gesell, Cattell, and Bayley were grouped together because of their substantive similarity and their common emphasis on nonenvironmental influences. The scales developed by Escalona and Corman, and Uzgiris and Hunt are based on Piagetian theory. While many items in these scales are similar to those originated by Gesell, their scoring and interpretation are quite different. Qualitative rather than quantitative changes are the units of measure; progress is ordinal rather than ratio-based.

Of the two scales assessing neonates, Brazelton's seems to offer more than Graham's, even though Brazelton's has not been as extensively evaluated. Brazelton's scale covers a broad range of behaviors presumably relevant to interaction situations. In contrast, Graham's scale is directed primarily at making diagnostic distinctions between normal and traumatized infants and, in the Rosenblith revision, taps general maturation.

Generally, all of the scales perform at psychometrically acceptable levels. They display adequate internal consistency, concurrent interrater agreement, and at least short-term test-retest stability. These facts alone reflect a considerable accomplishment, considering the unique problems encountered in working with infants. Although there is a tendency toward poorer psychometric performance with the scales for younger infants, even those scales reach minimally acceptable psychometric standards. The major shortcomings of the scales involve their normative samples. Unfortunately, only the Bayley scales have been based on large and varied samples. Bayley's samples, unlike the others, included nonwhite and rural born infants from geographically diverse areas of the United States.

In spite of the acceptable psychometric properties of all the scales, they have proved to be systematically poor predictors of later performance: the earlier in infancy the initial test, and the greater the time between initial and final testing, the poorer the predictive relationship. Thus, the loss of predictive power occurs precisely in the range for which there had been the most hope for strong relations: long range prediction from a point early in life. The evidence for the lack of early predictive power is most convincing for the Gesell, Cattell, and Bayley scales, but of course, these are the scales that have been most extensively used and studied. The others are too recent to have accumulated an extensive literature.

The scales of Gesell, Cattell, and Bayley comprise the traditional scales. These traditional scales had been described earlier as supporting—directly, in Gesell's case, and tacitly, in Bayley's case—a maturationally and genotypically controlled conception of development. While Bayley's conception of development did not preclude an *ex post facto* determination that intelligence is composed of emergent factors rather than of one general, fixed factor, it was clearly in line with a general factor orientation. Not until Bayley had collected her data was she drawn to a conception of intelligence as emergent and functionally unique at different periods (Bayley, 1933). By comparison, the Piaget-based scales (Uzgiris and Hunt, Escalona and Corman) were constructed from the viewpoint that qualitative changes in intelligence characterize growth. It remains to be seen whether the Piagetian scales will make long term growth processes more understandable. The question of whether they will lead to better prediction is one imposed on the approach by the advocates of an entirely different theoretical framework. If long-term predictive ability is to be achieved with the Piagetian scales, it will have to be done in a different way than for the traditional scales.

Reflecting the increasing appreciation of Piagetian theory, and a cognitive-developmental approach, McCall, Hogarty, and Hurlburt (1972) reanalyzed the data from the Fels Longitudinal

Study. They related early performance on the Gesell scales to later performance on the Stanford-Binet, WISC, or Wechsler-Bellevue. The Gesell scales had been administered at six, twelve, eighteen, and twenty-four months. The Stanford-Binet, WISC, or Wechsler-Bellevue had been administered between three and a half and thirteen years of age. The total sample was composed of approximately 150 children. Rather than correlating total scores, as had studies in the past, McCall and others performed principal components analyses at each infant testing age, relating those components to later performance.

Reduction of the Gesell data to principal components yielded a major component that was correlated between all ages (six, twelve, eighteen, and twenty-four months). While this might have been described as a general factor in intelligence ("g"), McCall and others suggested the contrary. This factor accounted for no more than 19 percent of the total test variance and, up to twelve months of age, showed no relationship to any of the later tests.

Although most principal components appeared similar for males and females within each age, the pattern of cross-age correlations between the components differed. Females tended to display cross-age continuity in the form of correlations between homologous components. Males, on the other hand, tended to exhibit cross-age continuity between nonhomologous components. Thus, by applying methods of analysis appropriate to a concept of intelligence as an emergent phenomenon, showing functionally different properties at different ages, this study was able to distinguish two pathways of cognitive development in the sexes.

Correlations between the major infancy component and later performance on the Stanford-Binet, WISC, or Wechsler-Bellevue, reached statistical significance at twelve months of age for females and eighteen months of age for males. The correlations for the females, ranging between .41 and .69, were impressive, particularly those with the Stanford-Binet. No major increase in predictive power occurred between twelve and twenty-four months of age, nor did any major loss of predictive power occur in predicting performance at three-and-a-half or ten years. This surprising retention of predictive power was not exhibited for males, for whom the results conformed to results from earlier studies: predictive power increased later in infancy, and decreased as the testing interval lengthened.

Since there were several components in the infancy tests, and only one of these showed substantial continuity, and that on only one sex, McCall and others concluded (1972, p. 746): "A simple conception of a constant and pervasive g factor is probably not tenable as a model for 'mental' development, especially for the infancy period. . . . The term 'mental' as applied to infant behavior or tests should be abandoned in favor of some conceptually more neutral label, perhaps Piaget's 'sensorimotor', 'perceptual motor', or even more specific classes of behaviors (for example, exploration of perceptual contingencies, imitation, language). The network of transitions between scales at one age and another is likely more specific and complex than once thought, and not accurately subsumed under one general concept."

The reexamination of the Gesell Scales from a cognitive developmental perspective is significant in that it is part of a larger and major redirection of the critical foci of early development toward inferences about internal processes. Observable behaviors are only of significance in the light of their assumed relevance to the internal processes. This redirection is suggestive of a paradigmatic shift (Kuhn, 1962). In such a shift, preexisting data are not necessarily cast aside, but may be treated differently in terms of new formulations. Emmerich's classification (1968) of developmental approaches into "classical," "differential," and "ipsative" orientations help to clarify this shift. The efforts of McCall and others, as well as the scales developed by Uzgiris and Hunt, and Escalona and Corman, represent "classical" orientations to development (Emmerich, 1968). This approach, which includes psychoanalytic theory, postulates a developmental progression through qualitatively different stages. Appropriate measurement is accorded through nominal classifications. Gesell's infant scales, in contrast, exemplify a differential orientation. Emmerich describes this orientation as the traditional area in which the study of dimensions of individual differences are pursued. This rubric subsumes testing, measurement, and other psychometric concerns. Each of the orientations—classical and differential—have traditionally maintained distinctive emphases in basic assumptions, methodology, and interpretation. The formulation of classical theory in differential terms, for the purposes of discussing test validation in this chapter, runs at cross purposes to the classical orientation. We need a reformulation of the means of specifying individual progress through Piaget's hierarchical stages which would be a basis for diagnosis and differential prediction. Whether this can be achieved remains to be seen.

Granting that a paradigmatic shift may be occurring, it remains interesting that the raw data for infant assessment have not changed. There is a general communality in items used in the infant scales, although this is less true for the neonatal scales. Despite the lesser communality in items for the neonatal scales, there is a continuity in the type of behaviors considered important. Evidence of this continuity comes from Gesell (1925). Although he did not develop a neonatal scale, the description of neonatal behaviors he considered important included quieting when picked up, visual fixation, adaptive modification of reflexes, and motor movements (Piagetian primary circular responses), as well as other reflexive behaviors more commonly known to be in the newborn's behavioral repertoire. Items such as these are contained in the Graham and Brazelton scales.

That the pool of items serving infant assessment procedures has not varied may be indicative of two overriding concerns. Achieving and maintaining psychometric stability may have introduced a conservatism on the part of most scale developers that was constructive only in the shortrun. While they would have achieved test stability, a sure prerequisite of statistical prediction, much may have been lost in the way of broad ranging, valid assessment. The relative novelty of the Brazelton items indicates the value of constructing the initial data base out of long and intensive observation, before turning to psychometric concerns. It also has been noted (Bell, 1965) that physicians have achieved higher predictive results than psychologists when using standardized assessment procedures with infants. Presuming psychologists to be, on the average, more concerned with maintaining procedural rigor than keeping subjective considerations from affecting their judgments, physicians may have been more appreciative of their subjective responses to the infants. Thus, physicians may have allowed these more important, but unstandardized factors to affect their judgments, the result being more accurate prediction (Bell, 1965).

One other possible explanaton for the communality of items in various infant scales relates to the presumption that the infant, by comparison with the adult, is a relatively simple organism. In this view, the infant's behavioral repertoire is inherently more limited and, therefore, more easily assessed. There may have been over-confidence that the infant is easily assessed when in fact it is not. It is possible that the behavioral repertoire of the infant has, in part, been limited by the assessment situation. These limitations might be based on the need for direct, unencumbered visibility of behavior. Sophisticated electronic equipment, long periods of testing, and extensive training are not conducive to expeditious assessment. Whatever limitations are inherent in infants, such as their rapid transition between different levels of physiological arousal, may have been further exacerbated by the need for efficiency in the assessment situation.

Recent years have seen the field of psychophysiology burgeon, with considerable effort being directed toward infancy. Developments in this area are occurring rapidly. The work of Butler and Engel (1969), cited earlier, relating neonatal photic responses to Bayley scores at eight months, is an example of a potentially useful area of further exploration. Lewis (1970) has reviewed evidence suggesting that decelerative heart rate responses to certain types of stimuli in infancy may be related to intellectual performance at four years of age. Graham and Jackson (1970) have extensively reviewed evidence concerning the relationships between infant heart rate responses and later behavior. Recent work with contingent negative variation, a specific response pattern of the electroencephalogram, suggests that the exploration of the parameters of this response in infants may provide interesting leads for assessment procedures (Gullickson, 1970). Tecce (1972) has reviewed research conducted on contingent negative variation since its first description in 1964, suggesting that it is related to cognitive, attentional, and motivational processes. All of these areas deserve further attention.

These studies, each reporting relationships between physiological variables and behaviors associated with cognitive processing, are not examples of specific leads for those in infant assessment. Indeed, those who conducted the studies may have had little of psychometric relevance in mind, in part, because delicate, sophisticated, and sometimes bulky equipment is required. Factors such as these, however, should not be of direct concern in developing reliable indices of behavior. While it remains far from obvious that exploration in these psychophysiological areas will provide psychometricians with new and useful tools, enough evidence has already accumulated to suggest that the exploration should occur.

References

AMES, L. B. "Predictive Value of Infant Behavior Examinations." In J. Hellmuth, ed., *Exceptional Infant,* Vol. I. Seattle: Straub and Hellmuth, 1967. Pp. 207–241.

BAKOW, H., SAMEROFF, A., KELLY, P., AND ZAX, M. "Relation Between Newborn Behavior and Mother-child Interaction at Four Months." Paper presented at the meeting of the Society for Research in Child Development, Philadelphia, 1973.

BALDWIN, A. L. *Theories of Child Development.* New York: Wiley and Sons, 1967.

BAYLEY, N. "Mental Growth During the First Three Years." *Genetic Psychology Monographs,* 1933, *14,* 1–92.

BAYLEY, N. "The Development of Motor Abilities During the First Three Years." *Monographs of the Society for Research in Child Development,* 1935, *1* (serial no. 1).

BAYLEY, N. "Consistency and Variability in the Growth of Intelligence from Birth to Eighteen Years." *Journal of Genetic Psychology,* 1949, *75,* 165–196.

BAYLEY, N. *Bayley Scales of Infant Development.* New York: Psychological Corporation, 1969.

BAYLEY, N. "Development of Mental Abilities." In P. H. Mussen, ed., *Carmichael's Manual of Child Psychology 1,* New York: Wiley and Sons, 1970.

BELL, R. Q. "Developmental Psychology." *Annual Review of Psychology,* 1965, *16.*

BELL, R. Q., WELLER, G. M., AND WALDROP, M. F. "Newborn and Preschooler: Organization of Behavior and Relations Between Periods." *Monographs of the Society for Research in Child Development,* 1971, *36* (1–2, serial no. 142).

BENCH, J., AND PARKER, A. "On the Reliability of the Graham/Rosenblith Behaviour Test for Neonates." *Journal of Child Psychology and Psychiatry,* 1970, *11,* 121–131.

BRAZELTON, T. B. *Neonatal Behavioral Assessment Scale.* (Clinics in Developmental Medicine, No. 50.) Spastics International Medical Publication. Prepublication testing manual. Philadelphia: Lippincott, 1973.

BUROS, O. K. *The Sixth Mental Measurements Yearbook.* Highland Park, New Jersey: Gryphon Press, 1965 (6).

BUTLER, B. V., AND ENGEL, R. "Mental and Motor Scores at Eight Months in Relation to Neonatal Photic Responses." *Developmental Medicine and Child Neurology,* 1969, *11,* 77–82.

CATTELL, P. *The Measurement of Intelligence of Infants and Young Children.* New York: Psychological Corporation, 1940.

CAVANAUGH, M. C., COHEN, I., DUNPHY, D., RINGWALL, E. A., AND GOLDBERG, I. D. "Prediction from the Cattell Infant Intelligence Scale." *Journal of Consulting Psychology,* 1957, *21,* 33–37.

CORAH, N. L., ANTHONY, E. J., PAINTER, P., STERN, J. A., AND THURSTON, D. L. "Effects of Perinatal Anoxia after Seven Years." *Psychological Monographs,* 1965, *79* (3, whole no. 596).

CORMAN, H. H., AND ESCALONA, S. K. "Stages of Sensorimotor Development: A Replication Study." *Merrill-Palmer Quarterly,* 1969, *15,* 351–361.

CRONBACH, L. J. "Year-to-Year Correlations of Mental Tests: a Review of the Hofstaetter Analysis." *Child Development,* 1967, *38,* 283–290.

DRILLIEN, C. M. "A Longitudinal Study of the Growth and Development of Prematurely and Maturely Born Children. Part VII: Mental Development Two–five Years." *Archives of Disease in Childhood,* 1961, *36,* 233–240.

EMMERICH, W. "Personality Development and Concepts of Structure." *Child Development,* 1968, *39,* 671–690.

ESCALONA, S. "The Use of Infant Tests for Predictive Purposes." *Bulletin of the Menninger Clinic,* 1950, *14,* 117–128.

ESCALONA, S., AND CORMAN, H. H. "Albert Einstein Scales of Sensorimotor Development." Department of Psychiatry, Albert Einstein College of Medicine, New York, 1969 (unpublished manual).

ESCALONA, S., AND MORIARTY, A. "Prediction of Schoolage Intelligence from Infant Tests." *Child Development,* 1961, *32,* 597–605.

FLAVELL, J. *The Developmental Psychology of Jean Piaget.* Princeton, New Jersey: Van Nostrand, 1963.

GALLAGHER, J. J. "Clinical Judgment and the Cattell Infant Intelligence Scale." *Journal of Consulting Psychology*, 1953, *17*, 303–305.

GESELL, A. *The Mental Growth of the Preschool Child.* New York: Macmillan, 1925.

GESELL, A. *The First Five Years of Life.* New York: Harper, 1940.

GESELL, A., AND AMATRUDA, C. S. *Developmental Diagnosis.* (2nd ed.) New York: Hoeber, 1947.

GESELL, A. AND THOMPSON, H. *The Psychology of Early Growth.* New York: Macmillan, 1938.

GINSBERG, H. AND OPPER, S. *Piaget's Theory of Intellectual Development.* New Jersey: Prentice-Hall, 1970.

GOLDBERG, S. "Infant Development and Mother-Infant Interaction in Urban Zambia." In S. R. Tulkin and P. H. Leiderman, eds., *Cultural and Social Influences in Infancy and Early Childhood.* Stanford, California: Stanford University Press (in press, 1975).

GRAHAM, F. K., ERNHART, C. B., THURSTON, D., AND CRAFT, M. "Development Three Years after Perinatal Anoxia and other Potentiality Damaging Newborn Experiences." *Psychological Monographs,* 1962, *76* (3, Whole No. 522).

GRAHAM, F. K., AND JACKSON, J. C. "Arousal Systems and Infant Heart Rate Responses." In L. P. Lipsitt and M. W. Reese, eds., Vol. 5. *Advances in Child Development and Behavior.* New York: Academic Press, 1970. Pp. 59–117.

GRAHAM, F. K., MATARAZZO, R. G., AND CALDWELL, B. M. "Behavioral Differences Between Normal and Traumatized Newborns: II. Standardization, Reliability, and Validity." *Psychological Monographs,* 1956, *70* (21, whole no. 428).

GRAHAM, F. K., PENNOYER, M. M., CALDWELL, B. M., GREENMAN, M., AND HARTMANN, A. F. "Relationship Between Clinical Status and Behavior Test Performance in a Newborn Group with Histories Suggesting Anoxia." *The Journal of Pediatrics,* 1957, *50*, 177–189.

GULLICKSON, G. R. "Contingent Negative Variation in the Preschool Child." *Dissertation Abstracts,* 1970, *31*, 3022B.

HOFSTAETTER, P. R. "The Changing Composition of 'Intelligence': A Study in t-Technique." *The Journal of Genetic Psychology,* 1954, *85*, 159–164.

HONZIK, M. P., HUTCHINGS, J. J., AND BURNIP, S. R. "Birth Record Assessments and Test Performance at Eight Months." *American Journal of Diseases of Children,* 1965, *109*, 416–426.

HOROWITZ, F. D., ALEKSANDROWICZ, M., AND ASHTON, J. "American and Uruguayan Infants: Reliabilities, Maternal Drug Histories, and Population Differences." Society for Research in Child Development meetings in Philadelphia, 1973.

HOROWITZ, F. D., SELF, P. A., PADEN, L. Y., CULP, R., LAUB, K., BOYD, E., AND MANN, M. E. "Newborn and Four-week Retest on a Normative Population using the Brazelton Newborn Assessment Procedure." Society for Research in Child Development meetings in Minneapolis, 1971.

HUNT, J. MC V. *Intelligence and Experience*. New York: Ronald Press, 1961.

JENSEN, A. R. "How Much Can We Boost IQ and School Achievement?" *Harvard Educational Review*, 1969, *39*, 1–123.

KING, W. L. AND SEEGMILLER, B. "Performance of Fourteen- to Twenty-two-month-old Black, Firstborn Male Infants on Two Tests of Cognitive Development: the Bayley Scales and the Infant Psychological Development Scale." *Developmental Psychology*, 1973, *8*, 317–326.

KNOBLOCH, H. AND PASAMANICK, B. "An Evaluation of the Consistency and Predictive Value of the Forty-week Gesell Developmental Schedule." *Psychiatric Research Reports*, 1960, *13*, 10–31.

KNOBLOCH, H. AND PASAMANICK, B. "Predicting from Assessment of Neuromotor and Intellectual Status in Infancy." Paper presented at the American Psychopathological Association Meeting, 1966. Cited in H. Thomas, "Psychological Assessment Instruments for Use with Human Infants." *Merrill-Palmer Quarterly*, 1970, *16*, 179–223.

KUHN, T. S. *The Structure of Scientific Revolutions*. University of Chicago Press, 1962.

LEWIS, M. "Individual Differences in the Measurement of Early Cognitive Growth." In J. Hellmuth, ed., *Exceptional Infant*, Vol. 2. Bainbridge Island, Wash.: Brunner, Mazel, Inc., 1970.

MCCALL, R. B., HOGARTY, P. S., AND HURLBURT, N. "Transitions in Infant Sensorimotor Development and the Prediction of Childhood IQ." *American Psychologist*, 1972, 728–748.

OSOFSKY, J. AND DANZGER, B. "Relationships Between Neonatal Characteristics and Mother-infant Interaction." *Developmental Psychology*, 1974, *10*, 124–130.

PRECHTL, H. F. R. AND BEINTEMA, D. *The Neurological Examination of the Full-term Newborn Infant*. Little Club Clinics in Developmental Medicine No. 12, London: Heinemann, 1964.

RAMEY, C. T., CAMPBELL, F. A., AND NICHOLSON, J. E. "The Predictive Power of the Bayley Scales of Infant Development and the Stanford-Binet Intelligence Test in a Relatively Constant Environment." *Child Development,* 1973, *44,* 790–795.

RICHARDS, T. W. AND NELSON, V. L. "Studies in Mental Development: II. Analysis of Abilities Tested at the Age of Six Months by the Gesell Schedules." *Journal of Genetic Psychology,* 1938, *52,* 327–331.

RICHARDS, T. W. AND NELSON, V. L. "Abilities of Infants During the First Eighteen Months." *Journal of Genetic Psychology,* 1939, *55,* 299–318.

ROSENBLITH, J. F. "Manual for Behavioral Examination of the Neonate as Modified by Rosenblith from Graham." Unpublished manuscript. Providence, R. I. Institute for Health Sciences, Brown University, 1961.

ROSENBLITH, J. F. "Relations Between Neonatal Behaviors and Those at Eight Months." Unpublished manuscript. Brown University and Wheaton College, 1973.

ROSENBLITH, J. F. AND LIPSITT, L. P. "Interscorer Agreement for the Graham Behavior Test for Neonates." *Journal of Pediatrics,* 1959, *54,* 200–205.

STOTT, L. H. AND BALL, R. S. "Infant and Preschool Mental Tests: Review and Evaluation." *Monographs of the Society for Research in Child Development,* 1965, *30,* 3.

SOULE, A. B., III, STANDLEY, K., COPANS, S., AND DAVIS, M. "Clinical Uses of the Brazelton Neonatal Scale." Unpublished manuscript. Social and Behavioral Sciences Branch, National Institute of Child Health and Human Development, Bethesda, Maryland, 1974.

TECCE, J. J. "Contingent Negative Variation (CNV) and Psychological Processes in Man." *Psychological Bulletin,* 1972, *77,* 73–108.

UZGIRIS, I. C. AND HUNT, J. MCV. *Toward Ordinal Scales of Psychological Development in Infancy.* University of Illinois Press, 1974.

WACHS, T. D. "Report on the Utility of a Piaget-based Infant Scale with Older Retarded Children." *Developmental Psychology,* 1970, *2,* 448.

WACHS, T. D. AND CUCINOTTA, P. "The Effects of Enriched Neonatal Experiences upon Later Cognitive Functioning." *Developmental Psychology,* 1971, *5,* 542.

WERNER, E. E. AND BAYLEY, N. "The Reliability of Bayley's Revised

Scale of Mental and Motor Development during the First Year of Life." *Child Development,* 1966, *37,* 39–50.

WITTENBORN, J. R., ASTRACHAN, M. A., DEGOOYER, M. W., GRANT, W. W., JANOFF, I. Z., KUGEL, R. B., MYERS, B. J., RIESS, A., AND RUSSELL, E. C. "A Study of Adoptive Children: II. The Predictive Validity of the Yale Developmental Examination of Infant Behavior." *Psychological Monographs,* 1956, *70* (2, whole no. 409).

V

Assessment of Brain-Behavior Relationships

RALPH M. REITAN

Formal assessment techniques in clinical psychology concerning evaluation of the status of brain functions in individual persons have a rather recent history, dating back only about forty years. Of course, interest in brain-behavior relationships, from both experimental and clinical points of view, goes back much further. It is not the purpose of this chapter to review the historical background of animal research nor of physiological or clinical neurological studies of brain functions or brain lesions, although the reader should be aware of this rich and important material (Boring, 1942; Halstead, 1947; Riese, 1959). Our purpose is to consider approaches and methods within the broad field of clinical psychology that were developed for the assessment of individual subjects.

As in other areas of psychological assessment, developments over the past thirty years have been very rapid. Before we begin

ski proposed that a number of "signs" could be identified that would classify the subject as having or not having a brain lesion. Aita, Reitan, and Ruth (1947), Hughes (1948), Reitan (1955d) and others attempted to validate Piotrowski's signs and to add additional signs based on their own observations. The sign approach, of course, has a long history in clinical medicine, being oriented particularly toward identifying abnormality or pathology in contrast with establishing a scaled score that falls somewhere in the normal probability distribution. This approach is still used in many aspects of clinical psychology, perhaps most frequently in assessing results of the Bender-Gestalt Test. The approach also has been used in many other areas. For example, clinical interpretation of electroencephalographic tracings is based principally upon identification of abnormalities in the tracings. Investigators have attempted to quantify ratings of the Bender-Gestalt as well as EEG tracings but it is important to recognize that such attempts, in effect, translate the results into continuous scaled distributions and complicate the problem of identifying a specific abnormality or pathological manifestation. The sign approach alone, however, obviously is not adequate because of the large number of false-negative classifications that it generates (Reitan, 1967c). The problem with this approach is that if a sign is defined so stringently that it includes only abnormality or pathology, the definition necessarily is so stringent that it will rule out many members of the pathological group who do not happen to show that particular manifestation. Thus, people with brain injuries who do not show the particular sign in question will be classified as normals.

The basic problem with earlier approaches to assessment of brain-behavior relationships stemmed from a failure to recognize the complexity of the problem, either from a behavioral or neurological point of view. While it is probably true that certain types of brain damage tend to affect certain abilities less than others, it is difficult to be confident of such judgments in any particular case. While language functions, for example, often have been identified as resistant to the effects of brain damage, the neurological literature makes it equally clear that severe organic language deficits in the form of aphasia are quite characteristic of damage to the left cerebral hemisphere (Weisenburg and McBride, 1935). It is perfectly obvious that the brain is the critical organ with respect to production of language and symbolic communication, just as it is of critical significance with respect to other behavioral manifestations. A question still facing us concerns the most systematic and efficient way to develop a set of measures that represent the behavioral manifestations of brain functions.

Equally complicating with respect to the development of assessment procedures in this area has been the tendency of psychologists to think of "brain damage" as a meaningful term. Brief reference to textbooks of neurology or neuropathology makes it quite clear that there are a tremendous number of adverse conditions (disease and injury) that may damage the brain. I recall a conversation with a neuropathologist, for example, in which we were considering the interindividual variability in a particular type of brain tumor. After studying a series of slides, and being duly impressed by the differences among subjects in this particular lesion, I commented that the lesions must show almost as much variability as did the individuals themselves. The neuropathologist gave me a rather cold look and responded, "Oh, much more so—they were only people."

Contributions from Experimental Psychology

Many contributions have been made to clinical assessment of human brain-behavior relationships from the area of experimental psychology. Perhaps the outstanding example was represented by the contributions of Halstead (1947). Halstead was trained as a physiological and experimental psychologist and, in fact, his doctoral dissertation was based upon evaluation of the influence of cerebellar lesions in pigeons on postrotational nystagmus. Nevertheless, he was interested more in human brains than in animal brains and he turned his attention to developing methods for assessing normal and impaired brain functions. Halstead began by performing a naturalistic observational experiment. In order to obtain firsthand information regarding the effects of cerebral damage, he associated with persons who had brain lesions; he visited them in their homes, went to work with them, engaged in recreational events with them and, in short, lived with them. On the basis of his observations he developed many experimental procedures from which he selected a series of laboratory experiments that showed validity in differentiating persons with and without cerebral lesions, and that also seemed to complement each other in terms of the range of functions measured. A number of these procedures reflected Halstead's prior training and experience in experimental and physiological psychology and, in fact, rather than representing the usual kinds of psychometric tests, could better be described as standardized experiments. A substantial learning element, for example, was apparent in some of the tasks. In one sense the experiments did not inquire so much as to what the subject might know as to how he might be able to adapt to the problem presented and solve it.

Methods of experimental psychology still are applied with definite advantages in the study of human brain-behavior relationships (Teuber, 1964) and some investigators are pointedly trying to adapt approaches and methods of human experimental psychology to practical procedures in clinical assessment (Klove and Matthews, 1966; Meier, 1970). Historically it is easy to see that experimental approaches have had a very broadening and valuable influence in the development of assessment procedures in this area, and that continued complementation between experimental and clinical psychology should be sought. However, there still continues to exist an experimentally (and physiologically) oriented approach as contrasted with the clinical approach in the area of human brain-behavior relationships. The experimental approach often emphasizes the research model derived from animal work and focuses on abstract problems of content rather than upon predictions or conclusions regarding the individual subject. The clinical approach emphasizes the psychometric model of assessment and focuses on classification (or diagnosis) of the individual subject, sometimes to the neglect of more basic conceptualizations (Meier, 1974; Reitan, 1966b, 1974a).

Coalescence of Experimental and Clinical Approaches

Certain principles regarding the structure and organization of the brain, even in a rather gross sense, and assessment procedures used in the clinical neurological sciences and/or clinical psychology have permitted the development of a conceptual framework for neuropsychological assessment. In American clinical psychology there is a strong tradition for quantification of measurements and development of normative distributions and tables. Without doubt, it is useful to know how well any particular subject has performed in comparison with a reference group. An approach based upon the subject's level of performance considered by itself is inadequate with respect to clinical neuropsychological assessment.

Clinical neurological evaluation has been heavily dependent upon examination procedures that identify specific signs of abnormality as mentioned above. Certain approaches in clinical psychological evaluation also have followed this procedure. The sign approach alone is inadequate but nevertheless can have an important complementary effect when used in conjunction with evaluation of level of performance.

The differential score approach, or evaluation of patterns or relationships among test results for individual subjects, is also inadequate when used in an inflexible and stereotyped way that presumes that all "brain damage" is alike and invariably has the same effect, from one individual to another, on ability relationships. Investigations in experimental psychology have made it quite clear that the brain, as the organ of adaptive behavior, subserves a great range of behaviors; and different lesions, of different types and in different locations, may have strikingly different behavioral correlates from one individual to another. Nevertheless, comparison of intraindividual ability patterns represents a very powerful method for drawing inferences about the condition of various parts of the brain (Reitan, 1964a; Wheeler and Reitan, 1962). Application of the method depends upon experimental investigations which have generated enough information to identify patterns of particular meaning for individual subjects. While much work has been done in this area, obviously much more remains to be done.

Finally, the structural anatomy of the brain with respect to contralaterality of control permits use of another important inferential method. The physical neurological examination takes advantage of knowledge of the structure of the nervous system in this regard, recognizing that impairment on one side of the body generally is associated with damage to the opposite side of the brain. Even a cursory review of pathways within the nervous system makes this quite clear. Thus, development of assessment procedures that permit comparison of the functional efficiency of the two sides of the body for an individual subject often provides very significant information with regard to the comparative status of the two cerebral hemispheres. If a subject consistently shows motor and sensory-perceptual deficits on the left side of the body, it is likely that his right cerebral hemisphere may be impaired. If he shows such lateralized deficits and, in addition, shows a pattern of test scores that reveals deficits in higher-level functions that relate to the right cerebral hemisphere, the overall picture becomes more convincing. If the subject also shows specific signs of abnormality that relate to right as contrasted with left cerebral damage (Wheeler and Reitan, 1962), the possibility for confident clinical judgments regarding the individual are even more improved. Finally, if the subject performs poorly, on tests that have been shown to have definite validity with respect to level of performance (such as the Halstead Impairment Index), the clinician can draw conclusions with strong confidence. The important point to mention here is that a coalescence of experimental and clinical approaches permits application of assessment procedures to individual subjects in describing the uniqueness of their higher-level brain functions.

Neuropsychological Tests

What we have been able to learn from critical evaluation of historical efforts in this area, together with the conceptual considerations mentioned above, has permitted the development of a battery of psychological tests for clinical assessment of brain-behavior relationships which has sometimes been called the Halstead-Reitan Neuropsychological Test Battery. It is important to recognize the individual contributions of these two investigators. Halstead developed a series of tests (1947) that showed definite promise in terms of assessment of human brain functions. Reitan felt that it was necessary to add additional tests in order to fill out the conceptual framework mentioned above and to obtain measurements across a broader range of psychological functions. Both Halstead and Reitan continuously assessed the adequacy of data they were collecting for making predictions with respect to individual subjects by making "blind" neurological predictions about individuals on the basis of the test results alone. This technique has been extremely valuable in terms of checking the actual clinical usefulness of the test results. For example, Reitan found in his early clinical investigations that it was very important to use a more complete assessment of general intelligence than Halstead was using. Reitan introduced the Wechsler-Bellevue Scale in his assessment whereas Halstead had used only the Henmon-Nelson Intelligence Test. Reitan also felt that comparisons of adequacy of motor functions on the two sides of the body, as well as a number of sensory-perceptual determinations, were important in terms of completing a subbattery for evaluation of the functional efficiency of the two sides of the body. Thus, Reitan added a considerable number of tests to Halstead's Neuropsychological Test Battery, as has been previously described (Reitan and Davison, 1974). Other investigators have developed additional subbatteries in accordance with their special interests or for particular investigative purposes (Klove and Matthews, 1966). The basic test battery, however, has been subjected to a great deal of validational research which, in turn, has established its clinical usefulness.

Halstead's research approach initially was oriented toward developing standardized experimental procedures, or psychological tests that would shed light on the types of psychological deficits associated with cerebral lesions. After developing a series of such procedures, he turned his attention quite abruptly to the localization question. Undoubtedly the general interest in specific deficits associated with frontal lobe lesions was a contributing factor in this regard (Dikmen, 1973). Halstead found that frontal lesions had a considerably more impairing effect on his measures than was true for lesions in nonfrontal locations (Halstead, 1947). These findings have never been validated. In fact, the consensus is that nonfrontal lesions often are associated with specific kinds of disorders, whereas the psychological correlates of frontal lesions are more general in nature and more difficult to specify (Reitan, 1964a). Another possible problem in the validation of Halstead's frontal findings relates to the type of material he used. Many of his patients, for example, had excisions of frontal lobe tissue in association with surgical extirpation of olfactory groove meningiomas. Patients with such lesions have not been studied in much detail by other investigators and the specificity of lesion types, as they differ from one investigation to another, could very possibly be of significance. It has been well demonstrated, for example, that different types of lesions have variable psychological correlates (Reitan, 1964a; Reitan and Fitzhugh, 1971). Nevertheless, Halstead's excellent insights into the types of testing situations that are directly relevant to brain functions have made a great impact on the field.

Reitan's approach in generating research information regarding the validity of psychological tests for assessment of brain lesions was oriented essentially toward systematic subdivision of the term *brain damage*. As mentioned above, *brain damage* represents a great host of specific kinds of disorders of the brain and one of the deficiencies in early clinical research was the failure to take into account the great diversity of conditions included under this general term. The research approach first inquired with respect to the general condition of *brain damage,* as contrasted with careful composition of control or comparison groups in whom no type of brain damage could be identified. Reitan's first study of this type compared the results obtained with Halstead's Tests in a group of fifty subjects having proved cerebral damage or dysfunction with a group of fifty subjects who showed no past or present signs or symptoms of cerebral damage or dysfunction (1955a). The results in comparing these two groups showed striking differences. In fact, few if any studies previously reported in the literature had achieved such a pronounced statistical differentiation of two such groups. Undoubtedly this result was due in part to careful selection of subjects according to predetermined criteria regarding the presence or absence of brain damage, and there has been something of a tendency to criticize such care in research procedure on the grounds that it does not simulate the realistic circumstances of clinical application (Brown, Casey, Fisch, and Neuringer, 1958). The obvious rejoinder is that when establishing basic principles it is clearly advisable to meet carefully the conditions of the research, and to lay the groundwork for generalization of conclusions, as contrasted with adopting a procedure which might replicate the "messy" circumstances of clinical practice. The latter course, in turn, would leave one in a completely insecure position with respect to valid generalization.

However, if an investigator wished to modify his independent variables in order to meet the particular clinical question that he was proposing, such a procedure would be entirely defensible provided he was able to define his independent variables in such a way that they could be similarly used by others. Ideally, after initial studies had been done in which clearcut and definitive differentiation between brain-damaged and nonbrain-damaged groups had been met, an investigator might wish to compose groups representing particular types of clinical problems.

Exactly such a study was carried out by Klove (1963); in this study he investigated the neuropsychological correlates of patients having proved brain lesions but who, in one group, had positive neurological findings and, in the other group, had no positive findings on physical neurological examination. This study was oriented toward providing information regarding the potential of neuropsychological assessment for identification cf deficit even in those patients who did not show positive findings on physical neurological examination. The results were quite clearcut, indicating that both groups were clearly impaired on neuropsychological measurements. An extensive series of studies of this kind could be done in a systematic manner, emphasizing one aspect or another of relevant clinical questions or problems.

In pursuing additional questions, one study after another has provided validational information regarding the general comparison by Reitan (1955a) of groups with and without cerebral damage. Reports in the literature have somewhat neglected the fact that these studies consistently have found strikingly significant differences between groups of subjects with and without cerebral lesions, even though the particular point of individual studies may have been oriented toward more specific questions. Positive cross-validation for tests proposed by Halstead and Reitan has been entered into the literature by Boll, Heaton, and Reitan (1974); Chapman and Wolff (1959); Doehring and Reitan (1961a, 1961b); Fitzhugh, K. B., Fitzhugh, L. C., and Reitan (1961, 1962a); Fitzhugh, L. C., Fitzhugh, K. B., and Reitan (1960, 1965); Heimburger, DeMyer, and Reitan (1964); Heimburger and Reitan (1961); Matthews, Shaw, and Klove (1966); Reed and Reitan (1962, 1963a, 1963b); Reitan (1955a, 1955b, 1958, 1959a, 1959b, 1960, 1964a, 1970a,

1970b); Reitan and Boll (1971); Reitan and Fitzhugh (1971); Reitan, Reed, and Dyken (1971); Ross and Reitan (1955); Shure and Halstead (1958); Vega and Parsons (1967); Wheeler, Burke, and Reitan (1963); and Wheeler and Reitan (1962, 1963). Each of these studies has shown strongly positive validational findings with respect to differentiation of groups with and without cerebral damage.

Occasional negative findings have been reported by those who compared brain-damaged subjects with persons in other pathological groups. For example, Watson, Thomas, Anderson, and Felling (1968) reported a failure to find differences between brain-damaged and schizophrenic groups. Both of their groups, according to previously published normative data, performed very poorly. However, the fact that the subjects with brain lesions did no worse than the schizophrenic subjects was interpreted as an indication of failure of the tests to be specifically sensitive to brain damage. This interpretation should be evaluated in terms of two points: in the context of the great number of consistently positive findings cited above, obtained under conditions of careful and exacting differentiation of subjects into groups with and without cerebral damage, and the fact that the brain-damaged subjects in the study by Watson and others (1968) performed poorly, just as brain-damaged subjects had done in all of the previous studies. In terms of uniqueness of the results, it is rather clear that the schizophrenic subjects, for whatever reason, performed poorly on the tests and that additional research was needed in order to determine whether impaired brain functions in the schizophrenics or other reasons were responsible. Klove (1974) has considered issues in additional detail regarding this study by Watson and his coworkers, and Davison (1974) has reviewed additional material concerned with assessment of brain damage and schizophrenia.

Similar research also has been done with the Wechsler-Bellevue Scale, first inquiring into the general effects of cerebral damage and proceeding to more detailed questions. These studies have recently been very capably reviewed by Matarazzo (1972). In fact, the major part of his review concerned work done on the Wechsler-Bellevue Scale in the same context as the references reported above. Research findings have indicated consistently that the

Wechsler-Bellevue Scale is sensitive to the condition of the cerebral hemispheres (Andersen, 1950; Doehring, Reitan, and Klove, 1961; Fitzhugh, Fitzhugh, and Reitan, 1962b; Klove, 1959a, 1959b; Klove and Reitan, 1958; Matthews, Guertin, and Reitan, 1962; Matthews and Reitan, 1964; Reed and Reitan, 1963b; Reitan, 1955c, 1960, 1964a, 1970a; Reitan and Fitzhugh, 1971; Wheeler, Burke, and Reitan, 1963; Wheeler and Reitan, 1963). However, a direct comparison of the sensitivity of the Halstead Impairment Index and various summary variables from the Wechsler-Bellevue Scale clearly and consistently indicated that the Impairment Index was significantly more sensitive to the effects of cerebral damage than were variables from the Wechsler Scales (Reitan, 1959a).

Following detailed investigations of the sensitivity of the various tests to the general effects of cerebral damage, pointed efforts have been made to learn about differential effects of damage to the right and left cerebral hemispheres. It has been known for many years (Weisenburg and McBride, 1935) that the left cerebral hemisphere generally plays a very significant role in speech and the use of language symbols for communication. We had observed early in the course of our investigations (Reitan, 1955c) that lesions of the right cerebral hemisphere often had a devastating effect with respect to the ability of the subject to deal with visuospatial configurations. Recognition of the significance of the right cerebral hemisphere in this respect, however, was gradual in coming. Even in the mid-1960s well-known neuropsychologists were raising a question as to whether the right cerebral hemisphere might have some specific function in this regard, but concluding that only a question and not any kind of answer was justified. Long before that time we had observed the effects of surgical damage to the right cerebral hemisphere, having tested subjects in advance of and following such damage. In one instance the subject's Performance IQ prior to surgical damage to the right cerebral hemisphere (in the course of removal of a meningioma) had been 136 but after the damage had occurred the patient's Performance IQ had been reduced to 79 (Reitan, 1967b). In addition, the patient's ability to copy simple spatial configurations had been essentially obliterated. Such direct observations of the effects of cerebral damage in single individuals comes about only when a psychologist is in the right location to make the appropriate observations, which is of critical importance with regard to learning some of the fundamentals. While other psychologists were questioning whether or not such things might be possible, we had actually seen them in specific cases. As Homer B. C. Reed, a neuropsychologist at Tufts-New England Medical Center, is fond of saying, "How many two-headed cows do you have to see before you believe they exist?" The significant point, however, is that psychologists often, in their daily work, have not been in settings that permit them to study patients with brain lesions of various types and in varying locations.

Evaluation of effects of lateralized cerebral lesions focused not only on differential performances on the Wechsler-Bellevue Scale, but also on aphasic versus nonaphasic manifestations and comparative performances on the two sides of the body. Specific language (aphasic) and nonlanguage disorders were examined in a series of studies and the results consistently showed the lateralizing value of the findings (Doehring and Reitan, 1961b; Heimburger and Reitan, 1961; Heimburger and others, 1964; Klove and Reitan, 1958; Reitan, 1959b, 1960, 1964b; Wheeler, 1964; Wheeler and Reitan, 1962). In brief, these various studies indicated that when specific discrete language functions were investigated, especially ones that did not relate to accumulated past experience and stored information as a basis for the immediate response, left cerebral lesions had an impairing effect, whereas right cerebral damage consistently impaired the subject's ability to deal with visuo-spatial and manipulatory problems. Further, the results indicated that recent acute destructive damage to one cerebral hemisphere or the other had a principal effect, whereas older, organized, and more stable lesions showed a lesser relationship to specific deficits. This latter finding suggested that normal brain functions, when precipitously disrupted, showed highly selective and severe losses as contrasted with the effects of chronic and longstanding lesions in adult subjects.

Let us discuss validation of a method of drawing inferences regarding cerebral functions that has proved to be very powerful. This method concerns comparison of motor and sensory-perceptual functions on the two sides of the body. Considering the organization of the nervous system, the right cerebral hemisphere is principally involved with functions on the left side of the body and the left cerebral hemisphere, conversely, relates to right-sided functions. This general principle, together with differential functions of the two cerebral hemispheres, has recently been "rediscovered" in human split-brain preparations, although similar information regarding the differential function of the two cerebral hemispheres had previously been published in some detail (Wheeler and Reitan, 1962). In fact, Andersen had indicated the differential relationship of the two cerebral hemispheres to Verbal and Performance intellectual functions long before that (1950). Comparison of sensory-perceptual and motor functions on the two sides of the body, as a basis for comparing the adequacy of the two cerebral hemispheres, has been validated in a number of research studies (Klove, 1959b; Reed, 1967; Reitan, 1959b, 1964a). While handedness must be taken into consideration with respect to expected differences on skilled tasks, handedness seems to make little difference with regard to sensory-perceptual functions. Semmes, Weinstein, Ghent, and Teuber (1960) and Semmes (1968) have postulated that sensory functions are differentially organized in the two cerebral hemispheres, and more recent evidence indicates that the right cerebral hemisphere may be more sensitive (as it relates to the left side of the body) than the left cerebral hemisphere is to the right side of the body (Boll, 1974b). The general principle, however, is one of contralaterality—poor performances occur on the side contralateral to the damaged cerebral hemisphere.

Many other questions have been investigated concerning the effects of cerebral damage on adaptive abilities of adult subjects. A more extensive review of this research has been presented previously (Reitan, 1966a) and will not be repeated here. It will be more useful to present an illustration of how these research findings may be applied in the assessment of individual adult subjects.

Clinical Applications to Adults

Clinical neuropsychological assessment may be done for many purposes, depending upon the individual problem. In some cases the question may concern neurological diagnosis, or whether the patient has a cerebral lesion, perhaps of a certain type or in a certain location. In other instances a lesion may have been identified but a question may exist as to whether the hemisphere involved subserves language or other functions. Emotional problems of adjustment frequently are present in persons who seek neurological evaluation, and assessment of the emotional component of the patient's complaints and symptoms, as compared with the neurological disorder, including interaction of neurological deficits and emotional problems, often gives significant information about approaches to treatment and management. Finally, it is important to remember that neuropsychological assessment is based on behavioral data related to brain functions, as contrasted with physical sources of evidence such as X-rays, electroencephalographic tracings, tissue sections, and similar neurological diagnostic evidence. Neuropsychological evidence, therefore, is relevant not only for brain inferences but also for assessment of behavioral consequences of brain lesions. These consequences vary from one individual to another, and raise many clinical questions regarding the interface between the patient's psychological deficits and his environment. With respect to rehabilitation efforts, for example, it takes no special insight to realize that it is of great advantage to know fully the deficits or needs of the patient in designing an appropriate rehabilitational program for him. Some patients, especially those with insults to the brain (such as traumatic injuries or sudden bleeding from a vascular anomaly), may later appear to show good recovery even though significant deficits still may be revealed by neuropsychological assessment. Unnecessary failure in vocational or academic pursuits can be avoided by identifying these neuropsychological deficits and helping the patient to adapt to them either by counseling, redirection of activities, delay of acceptance of formal responsibilities until spontaneous recovery can occur, or by initiation of a specific program of retraining and rehabilitation.

The validity of neuropsychological assessment for these purposes, however, depends on the validity with which inferences can be made regarding the brain. Further, such evidence of validity cannot be referred to statements regarding statistical probability levels of group differences, but must be valid for the individual subject in question (Reitan, 1974a). The best way to accrue evidence that validity standards of this type can be met is to put neuro-

psychological data to the test of individual prediction in the form
of "blind" assessments.

Case 1. The example which follows represents a completely
"blind" assessment, based on neuropsychological data alone, followed by a summary of neurological information independently obtained on the same patient. The analysis of the data may be somewhat difficult for the noninformed reader to follow; it will, however,
be meaningful to more advanced students and will help to give be-
ginners an introductory understanding of the procedure. Descriptions of the tests and basic principles of interpretation have been
presented elsewhere (Reitan, 1959b; Reitan and Davison, 1974).
In the Tables which present test results, blank spaces represent instances in which tests were not given. On the forms for the aphasia
examination, entries were made only when the subject had difficulty
with the task or made an error. In the Figures, which represent the
subject's figure drawings, writing, and calculating, the subject was
permitted to draw a second figure when he thought he could improve on his first drawing.

The patient was a fifty-eight-year-old woman who had nine
years of education and who was right-handed.

Psychologically, this patient showed evidence of severe general impairment and specific impairment in the area of language
functions (Tables 1 and 2 and Figure 1). She earned a Verbal IQ
that fell in the borderline range, approximately one and one-half
standard deviations below the mean. She performed very poorly on
the Similarities subtest, a finding that probably is more significant
for involvement of the left cerebral hemisphere than the low score
on Digit Span. The reason for this is that a considerable number of
hospitalized persons have low scores on Digit Span but, in the context of this patient's scores on Information, Comprehension, and
Vocabulary, the Similarities score was unusual and probably indicative of specific deficit in understanding the general meaning of
words. However, considering some of the better scores on the Performance subtests, we would postulate that the verbal intelligence
of this patient was generally depressed.

The aphasia examination yielded more specific information
regarding the difficulties of this patient in using language symbols
for communicational purposes. She showed typical manifestations

Table 1.

RESULTS OF NEUROPSYCHOLOGICAL EXAMINATION

Patient: #1   Age: 58   Sex: F   Education: 9   Handedness: R

WECHSLER-BELLEVUE SCALE (FORM 1)

VIQ	77
PIQ	119
FS IQ	94
VWS	19
PWS	46
Total WS	65
Information	6
Comprehension	4
Digit Span	2
Arithmetic	6
Similarities	1
Vocabulary	4
Picture Arrangement	4
Picture Completion	7
Block Design	13
Object Assembly	12
Digit Symbol	10

TRAIL MAKING TEST

Part A: 95 seconds, 1 errors
Part B: 214 seconds, ... errors

STRENGTH OF GRIP

Dominant hand: 20.0 kilograms
Non-dominant hand: 18.5 kilograms

MILES ABC TEST OF OCULAR DOMINANCE

Right: 0   Left: 10

REITAN-KLOVE TACTILE FORM RECOGNITION TEST

Dominant hand: .... errors, ... seconds

Non-dominant hand: .... errors, ... seconds

HALSTEAD'S NEURO-PSYCHOLOGICAL TEST BATTERY

Category Test	133

Tactual Performance Test

Dominant hand:	10.0 (2 in)
Non-dominant hand:	6.8 (all)
Both hands:	5.0 (all)
Total Time	21.8
Memory	4
Localization	1

Seashore Rhythm Test

Raw Score: ....   Disc.

Speech-sounds Perception Test   23

Finger Oscillation Test   36

Dominant hand: 36
Non-dominant hand: 36

Time Sense Test

Visual ....   Memory ....

Impairment Index: 1.0

MINNESOTA MULTIPHASIC PERSONALITY INVENTORY

?	....	Pd	....
L	....	Mf	....
F	....	Pa	....
K	....	Pt	....
Hs	....	Sc	....
D	....	Ma	....
Hy	....		

Table 2.
REITAN-INDIANA APHASIA SCREENING TEST

PATIENT: #1

Copy SQUARE	Repeat TRIANGLE
Name SQUARE "I know but I can't say" then OK.	Repeat MASSACHUSETTS "Massachusett"
Spell SQUARE "S-q, S-q-u" then OK.	Repeat METHODIST EPISCOPAL "Methodis" Episcopal
Copy CROSS	Write SQUARE
Name CROSS "Some kind of a square—I can't think"	Read SEVEN
Spell CROSS "Didn't I just spell cross?" "S-q-u-a-r-e" then OK.	Repeat SEVEN
Copy TRIANGLE	Repeat/Explain HE SHOUTED THE WARNING. Repeated several times. "He shotted the warmick."
Name TRIANGLE "I know but I can't say" then OK.	Write HE SHOUTED THE WARNING. Examiner had to repeat sentence.
Spell TRIANGLE "T-r-i, T-r-i" Much thought then OK.	Compute $85 - 27 =$
Name BABY	Compute $17 \times 3 =$ "1703" Pt. had difficulty understanding what to do.
Write CLOCK Patient drew clock. Said "Write it?"	Name KEY
Name FORK "I know what it is" then OK.	Demonstrate use of KEY. Excessive verbalization "I don't have anything like that at home."
Read 7 SIX 2	Draw KEY
Read MGW	Read PLACE LEFT HAND TO RIGHT EAR.
Reading I	Place LEFT HAND TO RIGHT EAR OK. Hesitation
Reading II	Place LEFT HAND TO LEFT ELBOW Patient was puzzled at first, but OK.

REITAN-KLOVE SENSORY-PERCEPTUAL EXAMINATION

(Instance indicated where stimulus was not perceived or was incorrectly perceived.)

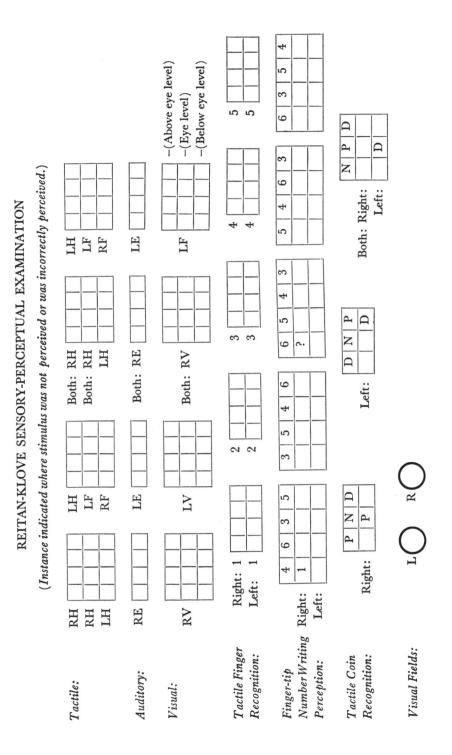

Tactile:

RH		LH		Both: RH		LH	
RH		LF		Both: RH		LF	
LH		RF		Both: LH		RF	

Auditory:

| RE | | LE | | Both: RE | | LE | |

Visual:

| RV | | LV | | Both: RV | | LV | |

- (Above eye level)
- (Eye level)
- (Below eye level)

Tactile Finger Recognition:

Right: 1   2   3   4   5
Left: 1   2   3   4   5

Finger-tip Number Writing Perception:

Right: 4 6 3 5   3 5 4 6   6 5 4 3   5 4 6 3   6 3 5 4
   1   ?
Left:

Tactile Coin Recognition:

Right: P N D / P   Left: D N P / D   Both: Right: N P D / D   Left:

Visual Fields:

L ◯   R ◯

FIGURE 1. Figure drawings, writing, and calculating performed by
patient 1 as part of the examination for aphasia and related deficits.

of dysnomia, having difficulty thinking of common names and, in addition, showed a very perseverative use of words and letters. When asked to name the cross, after having previously been asked to name a square, she perseverated with the word "square." She made the same kinds of mistakes in spelling. Thus, even in instances in which the patient did not make actual mistakes in spelling of simple words, her difficulty in accomplishing the task and the perseverative tendency identified her deficit. The patient also demonstrated clear deficiencies in calculating ability. Although she appeared to have solved the problem, "85 − 27" without difficulty, she answered "1703" to the problem "17 × 3." Thus, in spite of the fact that she was able to perform some problems, the types of mistakes that she made on others clearly identified her loss. A very significant aspect of the patient's difficulty with language related to auditory-verbal perception. When the patient was shown a picture of a clock and asked to write the name of the object, she drew a picture of the clock; apparently failing to understand the examiner's verbal directions (see Figure 1). When she finally did write a response, she still demonstrated a degree of confusion by writing "oclock." Her writing difficulties were more clearly demonstrated when she was asked to write from dictation the sentence, "He shouted the warning." The style of the patient's writing showed a degree of sophistication and previously-learned skill but her difficulty with the words "shouted" and "warning" were entirely inconsistent with the writing style. Another error of a lesser nature but also worth noting is that the patient printed rather than wrote the stimulus figure "SQUARE," again failing to be as alert to the examiner's instructions as is true for most subjects. Thus, the findings from the aphasia examination clearly indicated impairment of this subject's ability to deal efficiently with language symbols for communicational purposes, in spite of the fact that some of her performances showed an adequate prior level of skill.

Additional test results revealed that the patient was very seriously impaired in most areas of adaptive function. She was scarcely able to make any progress on the Category Test except for the first two subtests. The time required on both Parts A and B of the Trail Making Test were indicative of severe impairment. She made a very considerable number of errors on the Speech-sounds

Perception Test, another finding pointing toward impairment in the area of processing language symbols through the auditory and visual avenues. Her strongest functions related to motor, sensory-perceptual, and psychomotor skills, especially on the left (nonpreferred) side of the body. Finger-tapping speed appeared to be depressed to some extent with the right hand although strength of grip was essentially within normal limits and the relationship between the two hands was approximately as expected. The patient performed particularly well on the second (left hand) and third (both hands) trials on the Tactual Performance Test, although the results indicated that she was seriously impaired in this task with the right hand (first trial).

The overall results implied that this patient had experienced severe deterioration of many aspects of adaptive skills, but with special difficulties in the area of verbal intelligence and in processing of verbal information. A marked component of auditory receptive difficulty was present although the patient did not appear to have corresponding difficulty in visual perceptual functions related to language stimuli. She did have an element of expressive difficulty as manifested in her problems in naming common objects and in simple spelling. Her only significant strengths related to manipulatory skills with the left upper extremity and in problems that involved visuo-spatial configurations. It is difficult to understand the relatively good performance of this subject on the Digit Symbol subtest of the Wechsler Scale since one would have presumed the symbolic nature of the task to have represented a limiting factor in her performance. However, in practical terms related to aspects of everyday adjustment, the deficits and limitations of this patient preclude the possibility of a satisfactory outcome. She was very seriously impaired and would not be capable of handling everyday problems independently.

Translation of the test results into a corresponding neurological condition required consideration of the nature of the psychological deficit described above, together with evaluation of the motor and sensory-perceptual functions shown by this patient. First, she showed profound general impairment and specific difficulties involving language functions. The aphasic deficits, for example, certainly implicate the left cerebral hemisphere and the prominent auditory-verbal dysgnosia implies involvement more specifically of the posterior temporal area. In this context it is important to note that the patient had no difficulty on either hand in tactile finger localization and only minimal difficulty on the right hand in fingertip number writing perception. These tactile functions relate to the condition of the parietal area and it would appear that evidence of specific involvement of the left parietal area was rather minimal. Motor functions tended to be relatively spared as well. While the patient's finger-tapping speed was mildly reduced with the right hand, we cannot be confident that strength of grip in the right upper extremity was at all reduced. Nevertheless, the patient showed serious impairment in coordinated psychomotor skills with the right upper extremity as manifested by her difficulty on the first trial on the Tactual Performance Test. These results have implications both for the type of lesion and for its location. Mild impairment of motor speed and more serious impairment of coordinated functions of the right upper extremity could be accounted for by postulating a lesion in the left temporal lobe. An intrinsic tumor would be much less likely to cause profound motor and sensory-perceptual deficits than would be a vascular lesion in the same area. No evidence was recorded for this patient with respect to limitation of the visual fields, and she was able to respond to double simultaneous sensory stimulation correctly in every trial. Thus, the overall results would be compatible with a postulate of a glioma in the posterior part of the left cerebral hemisphere, probably involving the posterior left temporal area principally. Minor indications of right cerebral dysfunction were also present in the test results. The patient performed poorly on the Picture Arrangement subtest of the Wechsler Scale in comparison with results on the other Performance subtests. Secondly, when drawing the key, in one instance, she made notches in the same direction instead of representing them as mirror images. However, the overall drawings of the key and other figures were within acceptable limits. It would appear that the deficiencies possibly attributable to right cerebral dysfunction were not enough to form a basis for postulating a specific lesion of the right cerebral hemisphere either in terms of the number or severity of deficits. Thus, all of the results could be accounted for by postulating the presence of a single lesion in the left cerebral hemisphere. Other types of lesions possibly could be responsible for the set of test results shown by this patient. In some patients with single and fairly large abscesses, for example, results of this type could be expected. However, the overall findings, considered on a probability basis, would more likely be associated with an intrinsic cerebral neoplasm. The summary of this patient's neurological findings are found in Table 3.

Table 3.

NEUROLOGICAL SUMMARY

PATIENT: #1

Female, fifty-eight years of age. Neuropsychological examination done one day before hospital admission and seven days before craniotomy.

Symptoms:

About seven weeks prior to admission the patient noted occasional episodes of confusion and memory problems. Tinnitus of left ear and hypersensitivity and pain in left face followed shortly thereafter. About two weeks prior to admission the patient developed speech difficulties, episodes of dizziness and nausea, and offensive sensations of smell and taste, all of which seemed to be getting progressively worse. She also tended to drag her right foot while walking.

Signs:

Hypersensitivity of left face.
Hesitant gait.
Marked aphasia.

Diagnostic Tests:

EEG: Delta waves, Grade II, left parietal area.
Left carotid angiogram: Upward and medial displacement of the left middle cerebral artery suggestive of a left temporal mass.

Treatment:

Craniotomy and left temporal lobectomy with partial removal of a large tumor.

Diagnosis:

Left temporal glioblastoma multiforme.

Case 2. The second example of individual assessment is procedurally quite different from the first. While the first example was done "blindly," the following evaluation was performed in the usual clinical manner and was intended to help in understanding the patient's problems. The neuropsychological report gives a brief statement of the history.

This fifty-nine-year-old man, who had sixteen years of education and was right-handed, was referred by an internist who gave us some information regarding the patient's problems. He indicated that the patient had been a very capable salesman for his company, but recently had been having some difficulty with memory and judgment. The purpose of our examination was to determine whether or not there had been any significant intellectual impairment that might be associated with deterioration of brain functions.

We questioned the patient about his difficulties and he said that he tended to be forgetful, repeated himself unintentionally, and sometimes found himself mumbling words to himself. The patient indicated that the difficulties he experienced were noticed by other persons in his company before he noticed them himself. He felt that these problems started within the last three weeks, although he brought with him a copy of a report of a prior physical examination which showed these problems to have been of concern sixteen months previously.

This patient appeared to put forth a substantial effort on the various tests that were administered and we believe that we obtained valid results. He had a noticeable tremor of both upper extremities.

An extensive battery of psychological tests was administered in order to evaluate his past ability levels as well as his current skills in immediate problem-solving kinds of tasks. The orientation of our examination was directed toward evaluation of general intelligence, adaptive abilities dependent upon the condition of the brain, and the emotional status of the subject. The tests administered included the Wechsler-Bellevue Scale (Form 1), Halstead's Neuropsychological Test Battery, tests of lateral dominance, an aphasia examination, various measures of sensory-perceptual and motor functions, and the Minnesota Multiphasic Personality Inventory and Cornell Medical Index Health Questionnaire.

The principal generalization from our findings is that this patient showed evidence of having had relatively high ability levels in the past but the current findings reflect striking deterioration on complex problem-solving tests for which his background is not immediately relevant (Tables 4 and 5 and Figure 2). The Wechsler-

Table 4

RESULTS OF NEUROPSYCHOLOGICAL EXAMINATION

Patient: #2   Age: 59   Sex: M   Education: 16   Handedness: R

WECHSLER-BELLEVUE
SCALE (FORM I)

VIQ	106
PIQ	119
FS IQ	110
VWS	47
PWS	45
Total WS	92
Information	13
Comprehension	12
Digit Span	7
Arithmetic	9
Similarities	6
Vocabulary	14
Picture Arrangement	7
Picture Completion	13
Block Design	9
Object Assembly	9
Digit Symbol	7

TRAIL MAKING TEST

Part A: 37 seconds, 0 errors
Part B: 109 seconds, 0 errors

STRENGTH OF GRIP

Dominant hand: 29.5 kgs
Non-dominant hand: 26.5 kgs

MILES ABC TEST OF
OCULAR DOMINANCE

Right: 10   Left: 0

REITAN-KLOVE TACTILE
FORM RECOGNITION TEST

Dominant hand:
   0 errors, 18 seconds

Non-dominant hand:
   0 errors, 12 seconds

HALSTEAD'S NEUROPSY-
CHOLOGICAL TEST
BATTERY

Category Test   115

Tactual Performance Test

Dominant hand:	11.7
Non-dominant hand:	9.1
Both hands:	5.2
Total Time	25.9
Memory	7
Localization	5

Seashore Rhythm Test

Raw Score: 8

*Speech-sounds Perception
Test*   5

Finger Oscillation Test   40
   Dominant hand: 40
   Non-dominant hand: 40

Time Sense Test

Visual .... Memory ....

Impairment Index: 0.6

MINNESOTA MULTIPHASIC
PERSONALITY INVENTORY

?	50	Pd	60
L	66	Mf	61
F	50	Pa	50
K	57	Pt	50
Hs	54	Sc	44
D	56	Ma	48
Hy	60		

Table 5.

REITAN-INDIANA APHASIA SCREENING TEST

PATIENT: #2

Copy SQUARE	Repeat TRIANGLE
Name SQUARE	Repeat MASSACHUSETTS
Spell SQUARE	Repeat METHODIST EPISCOPAL
Copy CROSS	Write SQUARE
Name CROSS	Read SEVEN
Spell CROSS	Repeat SEVEN
Copy TRIANGLE	Repeat/Explain HE SHOUTED THE WARNING.
Name TRIANGLE	Write HE SHOUTED THE WARNING.
Spell TRIANGLE	Compute $85 - 27 =$
Name BABY	Compute $17 \times 3 =$
Write CLOCK	Name KEY
Name FORK	Demonstrate use of KEY Patient verbalized while demonstrating.
Read 7 SIX 2	Draw KEY
Read MGW	Read PLACE LEFT HAND TO RIGHT EAR.
Reading I	Place LEFT HAND TO RIGHT EAR
Reading II "He is friendly animal, a famous winner of dog shows."	Place LEFT HAND TO LEFT ELBOW "no," but patient seemed confused & tried.

continued on next page

REITAN-KLOVE SENSORY-PERCEPTUAL EXAMINATION

(Instance indicated where stimulus was not perceived or was incorrectly perceived.)

Tactile: RH   RH   LH   Both: RH   LH   LF   RF
Both: RH

Auditory: RE   Both: RE   LE

Visual: RV   Both: RV   LV   LF
—(Above eye level)
—(Eye level)
—(Below eye level)

Tactile Finger Recognition: Right: 1   2   3   4   5
Left: 1   2   3   4   5

Finger-tip Number Writing Perception:
Right: 4   6   3   5   3   5   4   6   6   5   4   3   5   4   6   3   6   3   5   4
Left: 6   5   4   3   3   6   3

Tactile Coin Recognition:
Right: P   N   D
Left: D   N   P
Both: Right: N   P   D
          Left:

Visual Fields: L   R

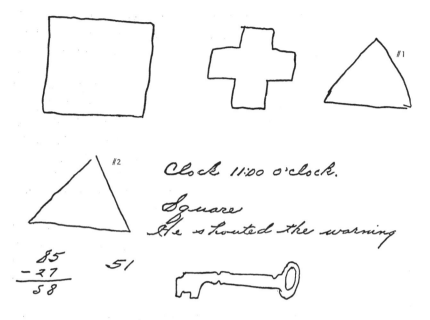

FIGURE 2.   Figure drawings, writing, and calculating performed by patient 2 as part of the examination for aphasia and related deficits.

Bellevue Scale (Form I) yielded a Verbal IQ that fell in the upper part of the normal distribution whereas the Performance IQ of this subject was in the upper part of the bright-normal range. The striking finding, however, related to the variability shown by the patient on individual tests of this Scale. His scores ranged from well above average, probably reflecting his past abilities to scores that exceeded only about 15 percent of the general population, probably due to his present impairment. The patient showed relatively good scores on tests such as Vocabulary and Information, which measured his stored background. He did much more poorly on Verbal tests that required insight and understanding with regard to the generalization and categorization of meaning of words, and he also did poorly on tests that required immediate attention and memory as well as tasks that required insightful organization and speed and efficiency.

The patient also showed considerable variation in level of performance on the tests in Halstead's Neuropsychological Test Battery. He performed best on tasks that were explicit in terms of their stimulus material and in terms of their requirements from him. When he understood exactly the task at hand and the test did not require definition of the nature of the problem, he performed relatively well. However, on tests requiring analytical judgment and reasoning ability, the patient performed very poorly. He had great difficulty forming hypotheses that might relate to the stimulus material that he observed, analyzing the nature of the material as the various elements of the problem were exposed, and organizing stimulus material in a meaningful way. It was clear from these results that this patient was seriously impaired in his ability to understand the essential nature of complex problem situations, to comprehend the subtleties that often are present, and to exercise good judgment in tasks requiring comparative analysis and understanding of the various elements. Further, it is clear that this patient will have great difficulty in dealing with problems that require careful assessment and analysis as the nature of the overall situation unfolds. In brief, the results indicated that this subject was seriously impaired in his ability to deal with new kinds of problem situations and that his best abilities related to performance of tasks with which he had a great deal of experience. This is exactly the type of change that customarily is shown in terms of the aging process. But this patient showed a much more pronounced and striking change in this direction than is true for most persons of his age. Our results indicated that the referring questions were quite valid and that the patient did have serious deterioration of his ability in the areas of analytical reasoning, judgment, and capability for solving new types of problems.

The Minnesota Multiphasic Personality Inventory and Cornell Medical Index were administered to obtain information regarding the emotional adjustment of the subject. Sometimes difficulties in thought processes can be attributed to serious emotional strain or, conversely, deterioration of adaptive skills related to brain functions can elicit various emotional stresses. Such possibilities did not seem to be the case for this patient. The results indicated that his general adjustment in the emotional area was within the range of normal variation. The Cornell Medical Index represents a rather straightforward question-and-answer procedure and the responses of the patient indicate that he has no special complaints in the area of somatic, psychophysiologic, or emotional aspects of his adjustment. The MMPI is a considerably more subtle technique, but the results on this instrument also were within the normal range. Thus, it would appear that the patient's adjustment was not complicated by any significant or striking emotional stresses or deviations from normality.

Results of the kind shown by this patient imply bilateral and generalized cerebral dysfunction that goes beyond expectation for persons in his age range. Certain of the findings implicated the left cerebral hemisphere but others pointed toward involvement of the right cerebral hemisphere. However, the lateralizing indications were not sufficiently strong to suggest that this patient had experienced any significant focal or localized damage in either cerebral hemisphere. We estimated that he had undergone some deterioration of Verbal intelligence, judging from the coincidence of low scores on certain of the Verbal subtests and corresponding indications from certain of our other examinations. The patient did not show any evidence of aphasia, but several of his responses on our aphasia test indicated that he was not quite so quick and alert in processing of verbal and language stimuli as would be expected. In addition, he showed evidence of some impairment of finger-tapping speed on his right side, in spite of the fact that our measures of lateral dominance indicated that he was strongly right-handed, right-footed, and right-eyed. He also had more difficulty in finger-tip number writing perception on the right hand than the left hand and was a little slower in tactile form recognition on his right hand than his left hand. While all of these findings would implicate the left cerebral hemisphere, the patient also showed evidence of mild constructional dyspraxia in his attempts to copy simple spatial configurations. He also did not do as well with his left hand as compared with his right hand on the Tactual Performance Test. All of these findings would be consistent with suggesting that this patient has experienced some generalized deterioration of cerebral functions. While we could not be positive with regard to an etiological basis for findings of this kind, similar results have been seen in patients with some type of generalized cerebrovascular dysfunction. We should also point out, however, that the results could be considered to be compatible with expected findings in instances of primary neuronal degenerative disease. Finally, similar results have been seen in alcoholic subjects. It is entirely possible that a combination of factors may have applied to this patient, but these various conditions tended to fall in the same general category of slowly progressive conditions of cerebral dysfunction and we would expect that the patient would show gradual deterioration of a continuing nature in the future.

It is sometimes helpful in instances of this kind to think of the results as implying that the patient is older than his actual chronological age. Although only fifty-nine years of age, he showed enough deterioration of immediate adaptive skills to indicate that he should avoid responsibility for any new types of tasks, should look to others for help in analyzing complex situations that involve critical judgment, and should begin to depend increasingly on his past experiences to guide him with respect to the contributions that he makes in his work. This patient should be able to continue to do routine tasks with which he is thoroughly familiar, but he should be alert to the possibility of having serious difficulties in analyzing complex situations or in dealing with new types of problems. Thus, a gradual disengagement from online responsibilities would be indicated for him. We see no evidence in our test results to imply the presence of a focal cerebral lesion, but the patient does seem to have a condition of generalized deterioration of brain functions that goes beyond expectation for persons of his age. Thus, it would be helpful for this man to be given assistance in order to avoid heavy pressures of work or especially stressful situations or circumstances. If he can begin a gradual withdrawal from his responsibilities, it would probably be helpful to him in his overall adjustment.

Limitations of Neuropsychological Assessment. It is important to recognize that neuropsychological assessment should be used in conjunction with the usual clinical assessment techniques. In fact, the usual clinical evaluation may serve as an excellent screening method for identifying candidates for neuropsychological evaluation. Conventional clinical tests such as the Wechsler Scale and the Minnesota Multiphasic Personality Inventory, in fact, complement the neuropsychological battery and form an integral part of the evaluation. Including these procedures, we customarily need about five hours of testing time to complete the battery. While some psychologists view this time requirement with concern, it is important to recognize that the information gained, as compared with many aspects of medical evaluation that require hospitalization, yields quite a high information-to-time ratio.

The major practical limitation concerns the fact that most psychologists, in their formal training, get little exposure to recent developments and techniques in current clinical neuropsychology. Many factors are responsible for this, including the fact that most faculty members of psychology departments have little access to, or practical experience with patients who have neurological problems. A gradual change seems to be taking place in this respect, however, as increasing numbers of psychologists are recognizing the importance of neuropsychological assessment and preparing themselves, through independent study, attendance at training sessions, and in other ways to undertake the responsibilities inherent in clinical work in this area. The promise of improved clinical skills, even with only a little additional training, is clearly highlighted by a recent article by Goldstein, Deysach, and Kleinknecht (1973). These authors demonstrated that inexperienced psychologists, using data collected with tests described earlier in this chapter and after having had a fifteen-hour course of didactic training, drew much better neurological inferences than did experienced clinical psychologists using traditional batteries.

Clinical Applications to Children

When Reitan founded his Neuropsychology Laboratory at the Indiana University Medical Center in 1951, very little systematic study of the psychological correlates of brain lesions in children had been done. Investigations of brain-injured adults, particularly in connection with World Wars I and II, had produced a substantial amount of information, but only scattered reports were available on children. Werner and Strauss had performed some investigations and Bender had published on difficulties in copying designs. Reitan felt that systematic development of a battery of tests, using the principles of inference described above with adults, would make a useful contribution for children. The first step was to administer the adult battery to children of progressively lesser age beginning at fourteen years. The purpose was to identify difficulties that these children had with the adult tests and to determine what modifications were necessary. In 1953 the necessary revisions and adaptations of Halstead's Tests, as well as others, were completed and systematized for use with children aged nine through fourteen years. After two years of data collection with this battery, and apparent evidence that the battery provided useful and valid information, Reitan undertook the development of still another related battery for younger children. In 1958 this battery was completed, standardized instructions for administration and scoring had been entirely worked out, and clinical and research evaluations begun with children in the five through eight-year age range. At present a tremendous amount of data has been collected on children. The battery for children aged nine through fourteen years is basically quite similar to the adult battery but a considerable number of revisions and new types of tests were necessary for children in the five through eight year age range. In discussion with Ward Halstead, a decision was made to call the battery for older children the Halstead Neuropsychological Test Battery for Children, recognizing that the revision of his adult tests utilized much of the content of the tests and many of the insights with regard to areas of measurement. The battery for younger children, while still utilizing many of Halstead's original ideas, was considerably more diversified in content and, since Reitan had done the adaptations for both age groups, the latter battery was called the Reitan-Indiana Neuropsychological Test Battery. Both of these batteries for children were developed using the same methodological and theoretical orientation that was employed in the adult battery and maintained the same orientation toward producing data that would be of value in understanding brain-behavior relationships not only generally but also with respect to the individual subject.

With respect to research strategy, we have continued to feel that it is important first to establish the validity of the various tests with respect to the effects of cerebral damage, as well as to learn the types of deficits shown by children with brain damage, before attempting to use the tests for research and clinical purposes in evaluation of conditions that may, or may not, be a result of impaired brain functions. Thus, before studying conditions such as reading and academic deficiencies, mental retardation, emotional and behavioral problems, and "minimal brain dysfunction," we have expended considerable effort in studying children in whom cerebral tissue damage has been verified by independent neurological evaluation. This approach was taken in recognition of the fact that it is necessary, in making research progress, to have a firm and definitive identification of certain variables that are to be related to others. If both sets of variables (neurological and psychological) represent unknowns, there is little if any chance to develop meaningful relationships between them.

Although our research efforts in development of tests and data collection had been going on for many years, the first formal comparison of children with and without cerebral lesions, using our test battery, was published in 1965 (Reed, Reitan, and Klove). The data indicated very striking and consistent differences between brain-damaged and nonbrain-damaged children who were of equivalent age. Investigation of the validity of tests for brain damage, and the nature of impairment of persons with brain damage, obviously are closely interrelated. A number of studies now have been performed in this area (Boll, 1972, 1974a, 1974b; Reed and Reitan, 1969; Reitan, 1967a, 1971a, 1971b, 1971c, 1974b). These studies include the effects of brain damage in younger children (Reitan, 1974b) and older children (Boll, 1974a) across an extensive range of tests, studies of results obtained with specific tests (Reitan, 1971c), and presentation of results of children with various types and durations of cerebral damage (Reitan, 1967a). Investigation of the nature of impairment in particular areas included sensory-motor functions (Reitan, 1971a; Boll, 1974b), complex motor functions (Reitan, 1971b), and comparative deficits of brain-damaged children as compared with control children in several areas (Boll, 1972). In this latter study Boll evaluated the degree of deficit in concept formation, tactile-perception, and motor functions in brain-damaged as compared with control children. While brain-damaged children are sometimes called "perceptually handicapped," it is interesting to note that Boll found that the conceptual losses of brain-damaged children were more pronounced than losses in the area of tactile perception. Of course, comparative studies of this kind need to be extended to include the area of visual perception and, very possibly, concept formation of different types. The important point, as was learned years ago in study of adult brain-damaged subjects, is that brain-behavior relationships are immensely complex, that the effects of cerebral damage may vary considerably from one child to another in spite of the fact that there are certain common deficits, and that a great deal of investigative work is necessary to obtain a fuller understanding of the significance of the brain for behavioral manifestations in children.

Enough groundwork has been done in studying children with known brain lesions, using our battery of tests, to have a good general idea of the types of deficits seen when brain damage is present. This condition has made it possible to begin investigations in other areas where brain damage might be a significant factor or where environmental influences might play a significant role in producing the deficit. Investigations have been made in the area of mental retardation (Reitan, 1967c), of children with reading and academic deficiencies (Reitan, 1964b), of children with an interaction of emotional and neurological problems (Reitan & Heineman, 1968), and of children classified as having minimal brain dysfunction (Reitan & Boll, 1973). In the latter study Reitan and Boll found that children who met criteria for classification as having minimal brain dysfunction resembled control children more closely than they did children with known structural cerebral lesions in terms of level of performance. However, when the results for each child were considered individually, and evaluated with respect to patterns and relationships among test scores that deviated from normality, nearly all of the children with minimal brain dysfunction could be differentiated from the control children. The results suggested that some kind of alteration or deviation of brain functions was present among children with minimal brain dysfunction, in spite of the fact that their ability levels were fairly good and they were essentially negative in terms of conventional neurological evaluations.

Our research with children has shown that neuropsychological evaluation may have very definite clinical significance, within the context of brain-behavior relationships, even when physical neurological examination and EEG are negative or noncontributory. In fact, probably the greatest number of children who present clinical problems are those in whom neurological evaluation is noncontributory even though there may be reason to believe that impaired or deviant brain function is of significance with respect to the child's problems. We should not deemphasize the importance of neuropsychological evaluation of children with known cerebral lesions, because it may be extremely important, in the interest of the child, to understand the psychological and behavioral correlates of the damage. However, children with known cerebral damage seem to be much less frequent in number than those with some type of learning or behavioral problem which *might* be due to either neurological or environmental factors. We continue to believe that an answer to the question of the organic versus environmental basis of the child's problem (or more importantly, the interaction of the two) may be of great significance in developing an appropriate habilitational program.

It is not possible, within the space limitations of this chapter, to present the many cases that would be necessary in order to do some kind of justice to the diversity of psychological deficits associated with brain damage and/or dysfunction. Thus, the following case must be considered strictly as an illustration.

Case 3. Examination of this seven-year, eleven-month-old boy (with 1.5 years of education and right-handed) was done for clinical purposes at the request of a child psychiatrist who had been treating the child at a child guidance clinic. The report to us was that the child's history and physical examination revealed no basis for brain damage or dysfunction. Nevertheless, the psychiatrist who had been working with the child had a "feeling" that some type of deviant brain functioning might be a factor. Interestingly, the frequency with which a postulate of this kind is raised is definitely increasing. It no longer seems necessary to presume that a child has actual structural tissue damage of the brain in order to raise a question as to whether or not some type of impairment of brain functions may be a contributing factor to his difficulties. Of course, the frequency with which such a postulate will occur to the professional person is variable, and depends upon his past training. Still, too often, the presumption is made that if a child has behavioral problems, and his physical neurological examination and EEG are not abnormal, that the difficulties must necessarily be "emotional" in nature and stem from environmental influences. We find, in fact, that deviant brain functions, according to neuropsychological assessment, are not uncommon and as a result some children are much more at risk in terms of developing adjustmental or academic problems as a result of adverse environmental factors. The following case represents such an instance. It would have been possible to have predicted the behavior problems of this child from the test results alone and this fact substantiates the additional insight and understanding of the child's behavior provided by the test results.

The mother of this seven-year, eleven-month-old boy indicated that the child's problems centered particularly around the classroom and school situation. He had been a difficult behavior problem in school and, in addition, was not making satisfactory academic progress, particularly in development of reading skills. The mother said that the teacher told the parents that the child was immature and undisciplined and, on this basis, she said that she decided to seek the help of a physician. The mother also indicated that the child tolerated frustration very poorly and had a "terrible temper." The patient did not like to be hurried in anything that he did. The mother said that the patient "tunes out" whenever he doesn't want to hear what is being said to him, frequently pays insufficient attention to circumstances and events in his environment, and is easily distracted. She reported that he had recently been tested to determine whether or not he was retarded and the results indicated that he was not, and, in fact, was above average in his intelligence. It was apparent that the patient had taken at least part of the WISC before, because during the testing he clearly remembered part of the test.

We questioned the mother with respect to possible other illnesses or conditions, including seizures or blackouts, head trauma, headaches, and so on that might possibly be associated with the child's difficulties, but the responses to this questioning were consistently negative.

This patient seemed to be very much interested in the tests and was attentive throughout the day-long examination. He seemed to do his best and it appeared that we were able to obtain valid results.

An extensive battery of psychological tests was administered in order to evaluate a broad range of adaptive abilities. The WISC was given to evaluate general intelligence, the Reitan-Indiana

Neuropsychological Test Battery was used to assess brain-behavior relationships, tests were given to determine lateral dominance, academic progress, sensory-perceptual and motor skills, and an aphasia examination was also administered.

The test results are presented in Tables 6 and 7 and Figure 3. The WISC yielded a Verbal IQ which was almost exactly at the average level, whereas the Performance IQ of this child was toward the upper end of the bright-normal range. It is difficult to know whether these scores were influenced by previous administration of the WISC, but we can be certain that the general intelligence of this child is at least within the average range. Inspection of the Scaled Scores for individual subtests indicates that this child performed at the average level or above on all of the subtests except for Comprehension and Digit Span. It would appear from these results that this child may be somewhat behind his age level in terms of awareness and understanding of social situations and in terms of his ability to concentrate his attention on immediate verbal stimuli. The results from the WISC would suggest that this child may be a little socially immature and distractible. In this sense, the results of the WISC may be thought of as confirming the current complaint but the findings on the WISC do not do very much to explain the nature of the difficulty.

Neuropsychological examination indicated that this child had generally fairly good abilities. However, the Reitan-Indiana Neuropsychological Test Battery is constructed in such a manner that it reflects not only level of performance across a broad range of adaptive abilities, but also inquires about specific types of deficits that are sometimes shown by persons with impaired brain functions, permits a comparison of various abilities that relate to differential functioning of various parts of the cerebral hemispheres, and compares the functional efficiency of the two sides of the body as a basis for inferring the comparative status of the two sides of the brain. Thus, while this child did relatively well on a number of tests, the results in other respects were clearly deviant from normal. With respect to comparative levels of performance, he performed very well on tasks that involved visuo-spatial analysis, flexibility in thought processes, adaptability to new types of tasks, and the ability to recapitulate elements of problem situations to which he had been

Table 6.

RESULTS OF NEUROPSYCHOLOGICAL EXAMINATION

Patient: #3   Age: 7–11   Sex: M   Education: 2.5   Handedness: R

WECHSLER INTELLIGENCE
SCALE FOR CHILDREN

Verbal IQ	97
Performance IQ	118
Full-Scale IQ	108
Verbal WS	48
Performance WS	63
Total WS	111
Information	11
Comprehension	7
Arithmetic	10
Similarities	12
Vocabulary	11
Digit Span	7
Picture Completion	12
Picture Arrangement	11
Block Design	14
Object Assembly	14
Coding	14
Mazes	11

JASTAK WIDE RANGE
ACHIEVEMENT TEST

Reading	1.9
Spelling	2.3
Arithmetic	2.8

Strength of Grip
  Dominant: 5.5 kgs.
  Non-dominant: 5.5 kgs.

REITAN-INDIANA NEURO-
PSYCHOLOGICAL TEST
BATTERY

Category Test   Errors 33

Tactual Performance Test
  Right Hand 4.4   Time   7.9
  Left Hand 1.6   Memory 4
  Both Hands 1.9   Location 4

Finger Oscillation Test
  Right Hand 31
  Left Hand   30

Target Test   18

Matching Pictures Test   17

Individual Performance Test
  Matching
    Figures   19 sec (0) errors
  Star   23 sec
  Matching V's   36 sec (2) errors
  Concentric
    Squares   30 sec

Marching Test
  Right Hand   27 sec (0) errors
  Left Hand   35 sec (5) errors

Progressive Figures Test
                39 sec (0) errors

Color Form Test
                44 sec (0) errors

Table 7.

REITAN-INDIANA APHASIA SCREENING TEST FOR YOUNGER CHILDREN

PATIENT: #3

Write NAME	COUNT fingers
Copy SQUARE	COMPUTE 2 + 2 (Verbal)
Copy CROSS	COMPUTE 2 + 1 (Written)
Copy TRIANGLE	COMPUTE 4 + 3 (Verbal)
Name BABY	Name KEY
Name CLOCK	Put FINGER on NOSE
Name FORK	Show TONGUE
Read 7 SIX 2 "7–2"	Where is EYEBROW?
Read MGW "M-G-H. I mean, W"	Point to ELBOW
Read SEE THE BLACK DOG	Put RIGHT HAND on NOSE
Print SQUARE	Put LEFT HAND on HEAD

continued on next page

SENSORY-PERCEPTUAL EXAMINATION

Indicate instance in which stimulus is not perceived or is incorrectly perceived:

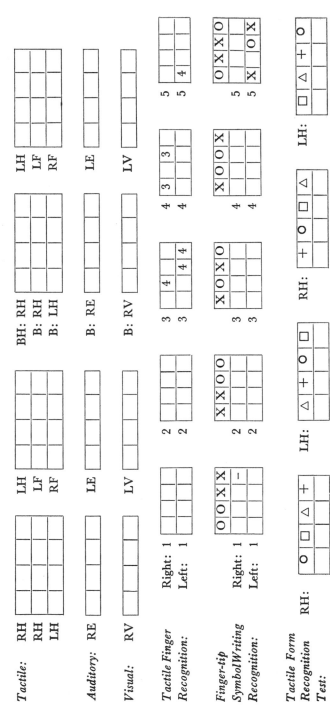

Tactile:	RH				BH: RH				LH		
	RH				B: RH				LF		
	LH				B: LH				RF		

Auditory:	RE			B: RE			LE	

Visual:	RV			B: RV			LV	

Tactile Finger	Right:	1		2		3	4	4	3	3	5	
Recognition:	Left:	1		2		3	4	4	4	3	5	4

Finger-tip	Right:	1	O	O	X	2	X	X	3	X	O	X	4	X	O	O	5	O	X	X	O
SymbolWriting Recognition:	Left:	1		-		2	X	O	3	X	O	X	4	X	O	O	5	X		O	X

Tactile Form Recognition Test:	RH:	O	□	△	+	LH:	△	+	O	□	RH:	+	O	□	△	LH:	□	△	+	O

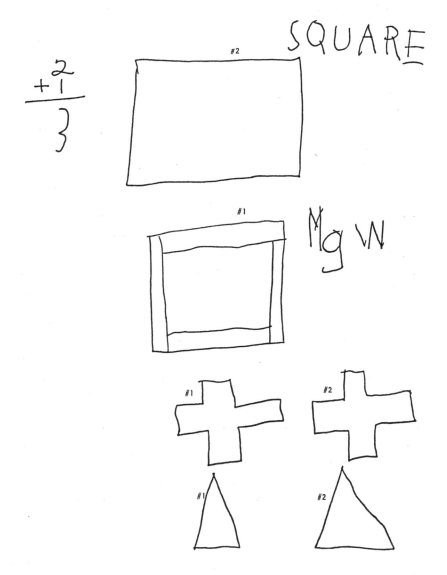

FIGURE 3. Figure drawings, writing, and calculating performed by patient 3 as part of the examination for aphasia and related deficits.

exposed. These are important capabilities with respect to effective adaptation to problems in everyday living. Conversely, the child performed poorly on tests that required processing of verbal information. In one respect the overall results confirm the differential levels of ability shown on measures of Verbal intelligence as compared with Performance intelligence as noted above. Comparison of performances on the two sides of the body, however, consistently indicated that this child performed relatively poorly on his *right* side. Measures of lateral dominance indicated that the child is strongly right-handed, right-footed, and right-eyed. Nevertheless, his finger-tapping speed was scarcely faster with his right hand than his left hand and his strength of grip was actually just a little less in his right upper extremity than his left. In addition, the child performed poorly on the Tactual Performance Test with his right hand as compared with his left hand, indicating that his proficiency in complex psychomotor performances, guided by haptic cues, was considerably less for his right hand than his left. The child also showed certain signs of deficiencies in performance in tactile-perceptual functions that are rarely found in children with perfectly normal brain functions. He had a little difficulty on both sides in tactile finger localization and also in fingertip symbol writing recognition. In a test of gross motor coordination, the Marching Test, his performances were somewhat poorer with his left hand than his right hand. Thus, the overall results tend to indicate that this right-handed child performed poorly on the right side of his body on most of the tests that offer a comparison of this type, although on a few tests he showed evidence of deficiencies on both sides. In any case, however, these results tend to deviate from normal findings.

The Wide Range Achievement Test was administered to evaluate academic progress. Our information indicated that this child was halfway through the second grade at the time. Therefore, average achievement scores would be approximately at a grade equivalent of 2.5. This child earned a Reading Grade Equivalent of 1.9; Spelling of 2.3; and Arithmetic of 2.8. It is apparent that he was not making as much progress in development of reading and spelling skills as might be hoped for, and the complaint of the school and the parents seemed to be documented by this finding. However, it was particularly important to notice that difficulties occurred on the right side of the body for this child, across from his left cerebral hemisphere, and that the left cerebral hemisphere, especially in right-handed persons, is the part of the brain involved in processing of verbal and numerical symbols. Thus, he seems to have some deficiency of functioning on the side of the brain that is particularly relevant with respect to academic progress.

The test findings, considered as a whole, certainly indicate that the left cerebral hemisphere of this child is not as efficient as the right. However, he did quite well on a number of tests. These good scores almost certainly ruled out the possibility of any significant structural cerebral damage and placed the findings for him in the category of some type of minimal dysfunction, possibly of the type that may be associated with developmental lag. From prior experience we would not postulate that actual damage of brain tissue was present, and correspondingly, from the current findings we would not postulate that the child's potential for developing higher-level abilities in the area of dealing with verbal symbols and academic subject matter was necessarily delimited. However, it is equally clear that this child needs to receive special help in developing left cerebral functions.

The results on this seven-year, eleven-month-old boy indicate that his general ability level was clearly at the average level or above. However, he definitely was not as proficient in dealing with verbal symbols and in measurements of verbal intelligence as he was in a number of other areas as noted above. Correspondingly, his development of academic skills was behind the level that would have been expected for a child of his general abilities. These findings are clearly related to evidence of impairment on the right side of the body in a number of types of tasks involving both motor and tactile-perceptual functions. These difficulties on the right side of the body, in this strongly right-handed child, almost certainly indicate that his left cerebral hemisphere is not as adequate in its function as the right cerebral hemisphere. This finding, in turn, offers a clear basis with respect to his limitation in development of verbal intelligence and academic skills. In addition, while this child showed fairly good ability in concept formation, abstract reasoning, and logical analysis on tasks in which the stimulus figure is clearly defined, he performed much more poorly on this type of task when the problem was one of discerning the missing element of the configuration as a basis for organizing his responses.

These various factors provided a basis for making some definite recommendations. First, he will need special help in terms of developing his academic skills. He urgently needed this kind of help when we saw him in order to keep him from falling farther and farther behind. He has a very good reason for his difficulties in developing academic proficiency (namely, mild impairment of function of the left cerebral hemisphere) and it is not surprising that he feels frustrated in the school situation. In addition, the selectivity of the area of deficiency makes it more difficult for him to tolerate the situation. His skills generally are at a higher level than those that he is able to command in the classroom situation, a kind of disparity which probably not only is a source of frustration for him but also may tend to create higher expectancies on the part of parents and of teachers than would otherwise be the case. In other words, they probably tend to judge the child and his potential in terms of his general abilities rather than the ones that relate specifically to his potential for academic progress. Thus, he needs much encouragement from those in his environment over and beyond the formal aspects of tutorial assistance for academic progress.

Second, he should receive tutorial help early in the day. It is difficult for him to face academic problems and he probably already has been "turned off" by the type of experiences he has had in school. Thus, it would be possible to work much more effectively with him on a tutorial basis early before the frustrations of the day have accumulated. In addition, the child will become less fatigued.

Thirdly, we would recommend that he be subjected to a rather routine and standardized type of environment, with the same type of things happening at the same time during the course of the day. He needs a well-organized environment in order to help him develop selective attention. When we saw him he was distractible, partly because he had something of a problem in identifying aspects of situations that are appropriate as compared with those that are not. Thus, he tended to respond to distracting stimuli in his environment more than the average child, who is able to be more selective with respect to appropriate types of stimuli as they relate to the purposes of the task at hand.

Our fourth recommendation would be that verbal communication to this child be deliberately slow, repetitive, concrete in nature, and redundant. It will be especially important for significant adults in his environment to address him in this slow, deliberate, and repetitive manner. He has difficulty processing language and verbal information and responding to it appropriately. It is not surprising that he "tunes out" anything that he does not want to hear, particularly if he has had nothing but frustration arising from his attempts to appreciate the information that is being communicated to him. Further, the patient does not like to be hurried because he needs time to process the information and solve the problem as he goes along.

Our results suggest that the complaints of the mother described reactions of the child to the frustration and difficulties that he encountered, which, in turn, related to the mild weakness of function of the left cerebral hemisphere that he showed. The basic corrective mechanism in this situation is to develop left hemisphere functions—namely, improved language skills in reception, comprehension, and expression of verbal, language, and numerical symbols. If the child is able to make improvement in this area, and thus relieve some of the strain and tension that his environment produces, it would seem likely that he would be able to show better progress. However, an approach recognizing his limitations in dealing with verbal and language material, either in everyday verbal communication or in the classroom situation, is imperative. Therefore, it would be quite important to remember the need for speaking slowly to him, using simple and concrete language, making a deliberate effort to be perfectly clear and straightforward, and repeating the same information in order to make sure that the child understands. The worst approach would be to overload him with verbal information that he is not able to comprehend and adequately process. In addition, a straightforward approach should be made in terms of trying to help the child understand the relevance of various circumstances and events in his environment to the activities presently at hand. If the child is able to develop an improved understanding of the point of the activities in which he engages, it is possible that his distractibility and lack of attention may become lessened. The prospects for his developing normal abilities seem to be good because he did so well on many of the tests that we administered. However, it would be important that the child receive help at once in order to be sure that the problem does not get worse.

Conclusions

This chapter has reviewed developments in the assessment of behavioral correlates of brain functions. Conceptual and methodological developments in clinical neuropsychology now permit valid inferences regarding the condition of the brain for individual subjects. In addition, these inferences are of considerable importance in the accurate and complete assessment of the adjustmental problems of many neurological patients. While there is a growing trend among psychologists to prepare themselves to perform responsible clinical neuropsychological assessments, it is important to remember that the area is rather different from the traditional areas of clinical psychology, human experimental psychology, or physiological psychology. Nevertheless, sufficient information now is available in the literature to permit psychologists from any of these areas to improve their skills in the area of human brain-behavior assessment.

References

AITA, J. A., ARMITAGE, S. G., REITAN, R. M., AND RABINOVITZ, A. "The Use of Certain Psychological Tests in the Evaluation of Brain Injury." *Journal of General Psychology*, 1947, *37*, 25–44.

AITA, J. A., REITAN, R. M., AND RUTH, J. M. "Rorschach's Test as a Diagnostic Aid in Brain Injury." *American Journal of Psychiatry*, 1947, *103*, 770–779.

ANDERSEN, A. L. "The Effect of Laterality Localization of Brain Damage on Wechsler-Bellevue Indices of Deterioration." *Journal of Clinical Psychology*, 1950, *6*, 191–194.

BABCOCK, H. "An Experiment in the Measurement of Mental Deterioration." *Archives of Psychology*, 1930, *18*, 5–105.

BOLL, T. J. "Correlation of WISC with Motor Speed and Strength for Brain-damaged and Normal Children." *Journal of Psychology*, 1971, *77*, 169–172.

BOLL, T. J. "Conceptual vs. Perceptual vs. Motor Deficits in Brain-damaged Children." *Journal of Clinical Psychology*, 1972, *28*, 157–159.

BOLL, T. J. "Behavioral Correlates of Cerebral Damage in Children Aged Nine through Fourteen." In R. M. Reitan and L. A. Davison (Eds.), *Clinical Neuropsychology: Current Status and Applications*, Washington, D.C.: V. H. Winston & Sons, 1974a.

BOLL, T. J. "Right and Left Cerebral Hemisphere Damage and Tactile Perception: Performance of the Ipsilateral and Contralateral Sides of the Body." *Neuropsychologia*, 1974b.

BOLL, T. J., HEATON, R. K., AND REITAN, R. M. "Neuropsychological and Emotional Correlates of Huntington's Chorea." *Journal of Nervous and Mental Disease*, 1974, *158*, 61–69.

BOLL, T. J. AND REITAN, R. M. "Comparative Ability Interrelationships in Brain-damaged and Normal Children." *Journal of Clinical Psychology*, 1972a, *28*, 152–156.

BOLL, T. J. AND REITAN, R. M. "Motor and Tactile Perceptual Deficits in Brain-damaged Children." *Perceptual and Motor Skills*, 1972b, *34*, 343–350.

BOLL, T. J. AND REITAN, R. M. "The Comparative Intercorrelations of Brain-damaged and Normal Children on the Trail Making Test and the Wechsler-Bellevue Scale." *Journal of Clinical Psychology*, 1972c, *28*, 491–493 (c).

BORING, E. G. *Sensation and Perception in the History of Experimental Psychology*. New York: Appleton-Century, 1942.

BROWN, E. C., CASEY, A., FISCH, R. I., AND NEURINGER, C. "Trail Making Test as a Screening Device for the Detection of Brain Damage." *Journal of Consulting Psychology*, 1958, *22*, 469–474.

CHAPMAN, L. F. AND WOLFF, H. G. "The Cerebral Hemispheres and the Highest Integrative Functions in Man." *AMA Archives of Neurology*, 1959, *1*, 357–424.

DAVISON, L. A. "Current Status of Clinical Neuropsychology." In R. M. Reitan and L. A. Davison (Eds.), *Clinical Neuropsychology: Current Status and Applications*. Washington, D.C.: V. H. Winston & Sons, Inc., 1974.

DIKMEN, S. "Minnesota Multiphasic Personality Inventory Correlates of Structural and Functional Cerebral Deficits in Patients with

Brain Lesions." Unpublished doctoral dissertation, University of Washington, 1973.

DOEHRING, D. G. AND REITAN, R. M. "Behavioral Consequences of Brain Damage Associated with Homonymous Visual Field Defects." *Journal of Comparative and Physiological Psychology*, 1961a, *54*, 489–492.

DOEHRING, D. G. AND REITAN, R. M. "Certain Language and Nonlanguage Disorders in Brain-damaged Patients with Homonymous Visual Field Defects." *AMA Archives of Neurology*, 1961b, *5*, 294–299.

DOEHRING, D. G., REITAN, R. M., AND KLOVE, H. "Changes in Patterns of Intelligence Test Performance Associated with Homonymous Visual Field Defects." *Journal of Nervous and Mental Disease,* 1961, *132*, 227–233.

FITZHUGH, K. B., FITZHUGH, L. C., AND REITAN, R. M. "Psychological Deficits in Relation to Acuteness of Brain Dysfunction." *Journal of Consulting Psychology*, 1961, *25*, 61–66.

FITZHUGH, K. B., FITZHUGH, L. C., AND REITAN, R. M. "The Relationship of Acuteness of Organic Brain Dysfunction to Trail Making Test Performances." *Perceptual and Motor Skills*, 1962a, *15*, 399–403.

FITZHUGH, K. B., FITZHUGH, L. C., AND REITAN, R. M. "Wechsler-Bellevue Comparisons in Groups of 'Chronic' and 'Current' Lateralized and Diffuse Brain Lesions." *Journal of Consulting Psychology*, 1962b, *26*, 306–310.

FITZHUGH, L. C., FITZHUGH, K. B., AND REITAN, R. M. "Adaptive Abilities and Intellectual Functioning in Hospitalized Alcoholics." *Quarterly Journal of Studies on Alcohol*, 1960, *21*, 414–423.

FITZHUGH, L. C., FITZHUGH, K. B., AND REITAN, R. M. "Adaptive Abilities and Intellectual Functioning in Hospitalized Alcoholics: Further Considerations." *Quarterly Journal of Studies on Alcohol*, 1965, *26*, 402–411.

GOLDSTEIN, S. G., DEYSACH, R. E., AND KLEINKNECHT, R. A. "Effect of Experience and Amount of Information on Identification of Cerebral Impairment." *Journal of Consulting and Clinical Psychology*, 1973, *41*, 30–34.

HALSTEAD, W. C. *Brain and Intelligence: A Quantitative Study of the Frontal Lobes.* Chicago: University of Chicago Press, 1947.

HALSTEAD, W. C. AND RENNICK, P. M. "Perceptual Cognitive Disorders in Children." In A. H. Kidd and J. L. Riviore (Eds.), *Percep-*

tual Development in Children. New York: International University Press, 1966.

HALSTEAD, W. C. AND SETTLAGE, P. H. "Grouping Behavior of Normal Persons and of Persons with Lesions of the Brain." *Archives of Neurology and Psychiatry,* 1943, *49,* 489–506.

HEIMBURGER, R. F., DE MYER, W., AND REITAN, R. M. "Implications of Gerstmann's Syndrome." *Journal of Neurology, Neurosurgery, and Psychiatry,* 1964, *27,* 52–57.

HEIMBURGER, R. F. AND REITAN, R. M. "Easily Administered Written Test for Lateralizing Brain Lesions." *Journal of Neurosurgery,* 1961, *18,* 301–312.

HEWSON, L. R. "The Wechsler-Bellevue Scale and the Substitution Test as Aids in Neuropsychiatric Diagnosis." *Journal of Nervous and Mental Disease,* 1949, *109,* 158–266.

HUGHES, R. M. "Rorschach Signs in the Diagnosis of Organic Pathology." *Rorschach Research Exchange,* 1948, *12,* 165–167.

HUNT, H. F. "A Practical Clinical Test for Organic Brain Damage." *Journal of Applied Psychology,* 1943, *27,* 375–386.

HUNT, H. F. "Diagnostic Methods: V. Psychological Testing." In A. B. Baker (Ed.), *Clinical Neurology I.* New York: Hoeber-Harper, 1955.

KLOVE, H. "Relationship of Differential Electroencephalographic Patterns to Distribution of Wechsler-Bellevue Scores." *Neurology,* 1959a, *9,* 871–876.

KLOVE, H. "The Relationship of Sensory Imperception to the Distribution of Wechsler-Bellevue Scores." Paper presented at the meetings of the Midwestern Psychological Association, Chicago, 1959b.

KLOVE, H. "The Relationship Between Neuropsychologic Test Performance and Neurologic Status." Paper presented at the meeting of the American Academy of Neurology, Minneapolis, 1963.

KLOVE, H. "Validation Studies in Adult Clinical Neuropsychology." In R. M. Reitan and L. A. Davison (Eds.), *Clinical Neuropsychology: Current Status and Applications.* Washington, D.C.: V. H. Winston & Sons, 1974.

KLOVE, H. AND MATTHEWS, C. G. "Psychometric and Adaptive Abilities in Epilepsy with Differential Etiology." *Epilepsia,* 1966, *7,* 330–338.

KLOVE, H. AND REITAN, R. M. "The Effect of Dysphasia and Spatial Distortion on Wechsler-Bellevue Results." *AMA Archives of Neurology and Psychiatry,* 1958, *80,* 708–713.

MATARAZZO, J. D. *Wechsler's Measurement and Appraisal of Adult Intelligence.* Baltimore: Williams & Wilkins, 1972.

MATTHEWS, C. G., GUERTIN, W. H., AND REITAN, R. M. "Wechsler-Bellevue Subtest Mean Rank Orders in Diverse Diagnostic Groups." *Psychological Reports,* 1962, *11,* 3–9.

MATTHEWS, C. G. AND REITAN, R. M. "Correlations of Wechsler-Bellevue Rank Orders of Subtest Means in Lateralized and Nonlateralized Brain-damaged Groups." *Perceptual and Motor Skills,* 1964, *19,* 391–399.

MATTHEWS, C. G., SHAW, D. J., AND KLOVE, H. "Psychological Test Performances in Neurologic and 'Pseudoneurologic' Subjects." *Cortex,* 1966, *2,* 244–253.

MEIER, M. J. "Effects of Focal Cerebral Lesions on Contralateral Visuomotor Adaptation to Reversal and Inversion of Visual Feedback." *Neuropsychologia,* 1970, *8,* 269–279.

MEIER, M. J. "Some Challenges for Clinical Neuropsychology." In R. M. Reitan and L. M. Davison (Eds.), *Clinical Neuropsychology: Current Status and Applications.* Washington, D.C.: V. H. Winston & Sons, 1974.

PIOTROWSKI, Z. "The Rorschach Ink-Blot Method in Organic Disturbances of the Central Nervous System." *Journal of Nervous and Mental Disease,* 1937, *86,* 525–537.

REED, H. B. C. AND REITAN, R. M. "The Significance of Age in the Performance of a Complex Psychomotor Task by Brain-damaged and Nonbrain-damaged Subjects." *Journal of Gerontology,* 1962, *17,* 193–196.

REED, H. B. C. AND REITAN, R. M. "A Comparison of the Effects of the Normal Aging Process with the Effects of Organic Brain Damage on Adaptive Abilities." *Journal of Gerontology,* 1963a, *18,* 177–179.

REED, H. B. C. AND REITAN, R. M. "Intelligence Test Performances of Brain-damaged Subjects with Lateralized Motor Deficits." *Journal of Consulting Psychology,* 1963b, *27,* 102–106.

REED, H. B. C., REITAN, R. M., AND KLOVE, H. "The Influence of Cerebral Lesions on Psychological Test Performances of Older Children." *Journal of Consulting Psychology,* 1965, *29,* 247–251.

REED, J. C. "Lateralized Finger Agnosia and Reading Achievement at Ages Six and Ten." *Child Development,* 1967, *38,* 213–220.

REED, J. C. AND REITAN, R. M. "Verbal and Performance Differences among Brain-injured Children with Lateralized Motor Deficits." *Perceptual and Motor Skills,* 1969, *29,* 747–752.

REITAN, R. M. "An Investigation of the Validity of Halstead's Measures of Biological Intelligence." *AMA Archives of Neurology and Psychiatry,* 1955a, *73,* 28–35.

REITAN, R. M. "The Relation of the Trail Making Test to Organic Brain Damage." *Journal of Consulting Psychology,* 1955b, *19,* 393–394.

REITAN, R. M. "Certain Differential Effects of Left and Right Cerebral Lesions in Human Adults." *Journal of Comparative and Physiological Psychology,* 1955c, *48,* 474–477.

REITAN, R. M. "Validity of Rorschach Test as Measure of Psychological Effects of Brain Damage." *AMA Archives of Neurology and Psychiatry,* 1955d, *73,* 445–451.

REITAN, R. M. "The Validity of the Trail Making Test as an Indicator of Organic Brain Damage." *Perceptual and Motor Skills,* 1958, *8,* 271–276.

REITAN, R. M. "The Comparative Effects of Brain Damage on the Halstead Impairment Index and the Wechsler-Bellevue Scale." *Journal of Clinical Psychology,* 1959a, *15,* 281–285.

REITAN, R. M. *The Effects of Brain Lesions on Adaptive Abilities in Human Beings.* Privately published mimeographed manuscript, 1959b.

REITAN, R. M. "The Significance of Dysphasia for Intelligence and Adaptive Abilities." *Journal of Psychology,* 1960, *50,* 355–376.

REITAN, R. M. "Psychological Deficits Resulting from Cerebral Lesions in Man." In J. M. Warren and K. Akert (Eds.), *The Frontal Granular Cortex and Behavior.* New York: McGraw-Hill, 1964a.

REITAN, R. M. "Relationships Between Neurological and Psychological Variables and Their Implications for Reading Instruction." In K. A. Robinson (Ed.), *Meeting Individual Differences in Reading.* Chicago: University of Chicago Press, 1964b.

REITAN, R. M. "A Research Program on the Psychological Effects of Brain Lesions in Human Beings." In N. R. Ellis (Ed.), *International Review of Research in Mental Retardation.* New York: Academic Press, 1966a.

REITAN, R. M. "Problems and Prospects in Studying the Psychological Correlates of Brain Lesions." *Cortex,* 1966b, *2,* 127–154.

REITAN, R. M. "The Needs of Teachers for Specialized Information in the Area of Neuropsychology." In W. Cruickshank (Ed.), *Syracuse University Special Education and Rehabilitation Series.* New York: Syracuse University Press, 1966c.

REITAN, R. M. *Psychological Effects of Brain Lesions in Children.* Privately published mimeographed manuscript, 1967a.

REITAN, R. M. "Problems and Prospects in Identifying the Effects of Brain Lesions with Psychological Tests." *Sinai Hospital Journal,* 1967b, *14,* 37–55.

REITAN, R. M. "Psychological Assessment of Deficits Associated with Brain Lesions in Subjects with Normal and Subnormal Intelligence." In J. L. Khanna (Ed.), *Brain Damage and Mental Retardation: A Psychological Evaluation.* Springfield, Illinois: Charles C. Thomas, 1967c.

REITAN, R. M. "Objective Behavioral Assessment in Diagnosis and Prediction." In A. L. Benton (Ed.), *Behavioral Change in Cerebrovascular Disease.* New York: Medical Department, Harper & Row, 1970a.

REITAN, R. M. "Sensorimotor Functions, Intelligence and Cognition, and Emotional Status in Subjects with Cerebral Lesions." *Perceptual and Motor Skills,* 1970b, *31,* 275–284.

REITAN, R. M. "Sensorimotor Functions in Brain-Damaged and Normal Children of Early School Age." *Perceptual and Motor Skills,* 1971a, *33,* 655–664.

REITAN, R. M. "Complex Motor Functions of the Preferred and Nonpreferred Hands in Brain-damaged and Normal Children." *Perceptual and Motor Skills,* 1971b, *33,* 671–675.

REITAN, R. M. "Trail Making Test Results for Normal and Brain-damaged Children." *Perceptual and Motor Skills,* 1971c, *33,* 575–581.

REITAN, R. M. "Methodological Problems in Clinical Neuropsychology." In R. M. Reitan and L. A. Davison (Eds.), *Clinical Neuropsychology: Current Status and Applications.* Washington, D.C.: V. H. Winston & Sons, 1974a.

REITAN, R. M. "Psychological Effects of Cerebral Lesions in Children of Early School Age." In R. M. Reitan and L. A. Davison (Eds.), *Clinical Neuropsychology: Current Status and Applications.* Washington, D.C.: V. H. Winston & Sons, Inc., 1974b.

REITAN, R. M. AND BOLL, T. J. "Intellectual and Cognitive Functions in Parkinson's Disease." *Journal of Consulting and Clinical Psychology,* 1971, *37,* 364–369.

REITAN, R. M. AND BOLL, T. J. "Neuropsychological Correlates of Minimal Brain Dysfunction." In Annals of the New York Academy of Sciences, *Conference on Minimal Brain Dysfunction,* New York: New York Academy of Sciences, 1973.

REITAN, R. M. AND DAVISON, L. A. (Eds.) *Clinical Neuropsychology: Current Status and Applications.* Washington, D.C.: Winston, 1974.

REITAN, R. M. AND FITZHUGH, K. B. "Behavioral Deficits in Groups with Cerebral Vascular Lesions." *Journal of Consulting and Clinical Psychology,* 1971, *37,* 215–223.

REITAN, R. M. AND HEINEMAN, C. E. "Interactions of Neurological Deficits and Emotional Disturbances in Children with Learning Disorders: Methods for their Differential Assessment." In J. Hellmuth (Ed.), *Learning Disorders, Vol. 3.* Seattle: Special Child Publications, 1968.

REITAN, R. M. AND REED, H. B. C. "Consistencies in Wechsler-Bellevue Mean Values in Brain-damaged Groups." *Perceptual and Motor Skills,* 1962, *15,* 119–121.

REITAN, R. M., REED, J. C., AND DYKEN, M. L. "Cognitive, Psychomotor, and Motor Correlates of Multiple Sclerosis." *Journal of Nervous and Mental Disease,* 1971, *153,* 218–224.

RIESE, W. *A History of Neurology.* New York: MD Publications, 1959.

ROSS, A. T. AND REITAN, R. M. "Intellectual and Affective Functions in Multiple Sclerosis: A Quantitative Study." *AMA Archives of Neurology and Psychiatry,* 1955, *73,* 663–677.

SEMMES, J. "Hemispheric Specialization: A Possible Clue to Mechanism." *Neuropsychologia,* 1968, *6,* 11–26.

SEMMES, J., WEINSTEIN, S., GHENT, L., AND TEUBER, H.-L. *Somatosensory Changes after Penetrating Brain Wounds in Man.* Cambridge, Mass.: Harvard University Press, 1960.

SHIPLEY, W. C. "A Self-administering Scale for Measuring Intellectual Impairment and Deterioration." *Journal of Psychology,* 1940, *9,* 371–377.

SHURE, G. H. AND HALSTEAD, W. C. "Cerebral Localization of Intellectual Processes." *Psychological Monographs,* 1958, *72* (12, Whole No. 465), 1–40.

TEUBER, H.-L. "The Riddle of Frontal Lobe Function in Man." In J. M. Warren and K. Akert (Eds.), *The Frontal Granular Cortex and Behavior.* New York: McGraw-Hill, 1964.

VEGA, A. AND PARSONS, O. A. "Cross-validation of the Halstead-Reitan Tests for Brain Damage." *Journal of Consulting Psychology,* 1967, *31,* 619–625.

WATSON, C. G., THOMAS, R. W., ANDERSON, D., AND FELLING, J. "Differentiation of Organics from Schizophrenics at Two Chronicity Levels by Use of the Reitan-Halstead Organic Test Battery."

Journal of Consulting and Clinical Psychology, 1968, *32,* 679–684.

WECHSLER, D. *The Measurement of Adult Intelligence.* Third edition. Baltimore: Williams & Wilkins, 1944.

WEISENBURG, T. AND MCBRIDE, K. E. *Aphasia: A Clinical and Psychological Study.* New York: The Commonwealth Fund, 1935.

WHEELER, L. "Complex Behavioral Indices Weighted by Linear Discriminant Functions for the Prediction of Cerebral Damage." *Perceptual and Motor Skills,* 1964, *19,* 907–923.

WHEELER, L., BURKE, C. J., AND REITAN, R. M. "An Application of Discriminant Functions to the Problem of Predicting Brain Damage using Behavioral Variables." *Perceptual and Motor Skills,* 1963, *16,* 417–440 (Monograph supplement).

WHEELER, L. AND REITAN, R. M. "The Presence and Laterality of Brain Damage Predicted from Responses to a Short Aphasia Screening Test." *Perceptual and Motor Skills,* 1962, *15,* 783–799.

WHEELER, L. AND REITAN, R. M. "Discriminant Functions Applied to the Problem of Predicting Cerebral Damage from Behavior Tests: A Cross-validation Study." *Perceptual and Motor Skills,* 1963, *16,* 681–701.

VI

New Developments in Holtzman Inkblot Technique

Wayne H. Holtzman

There was considerable speculation that the Holtzman Inkblot Technique (HIT) might supplant its highly popular predecessor, the Rorschach, within the next decade when it was first published in 1961. Twelve years have passed and the Rorschach continues to be the most widely used projective technique for the assessment of personality and differential diagnosis. At the same time, use of the HIT for a variety of purposes has increased steadily over the past twelve years. Over 300 articles on the HIT have been published in various journals, as well as several comprehensive reviews and books dealing with it. Our own work has moved forward along two general lines: cross-cultural longitudinal studies of personality development in children and technological extensions of methods for scoring and interpretation by computers. Before re-

243

viewing some of the newest developments on the HIT, we will discuss the salient characteristics of the technique.

Essential Features

The HIT consists of two parallel sets of inkblots, each containing forty-five test blots preceded by two trial blots, X and Y, that are identical in both Forms A and B.[1] Unlike the Rorschach, the subject is asked to give only one response per card and a simple standardized inquiry immediately follows in order to ascertain where the percept is seen and what qualities of the blot it suggested. Since the two parallel forms were constructed concurrently using psychometric methods of test development, they are truly equivalent forms that can be considered interchangeable for most purposes.

The ninety-two inkblots comprising the two parallel forms are the best of thousands of inkblots constructed over a period of four years with the help of a professional artist. Systematic variation in symmetry, form, color, and shading resulted in a much richer set of stimulus variables than those characterizing the ten Rorschach plates. The first thirty inkblots are carefully paired on both stimulus and response characteristics to enhance the equivalence of the two parallel forms. The last fifteen blots are balanced across the two forms although they are not precisely matched. With the possible exception of Space, a relatively rare variable measuring figure-ground reversals, no differences in the two forms have been discovered for the standardized set of scoring variables. Availability of genuine parallel forms is a decided advantage over the Rorschach since for the first time, studies of personality change or process variables through time can be properly carried out.

The final order of presentation for the inkblots in each form is arranged so that many of the best inkblots appear early in the series. After the two trial inkblots, two achromatic blots appear, followed by an inkblot that is predominantly black but has a splotch of bright red. Thereafter, the order of achromatic and chromatic

[1] Plates for Forms A and B, HIT *Administration and Scoring Guide,* individual and group Record Forms and Summary Sheets, and slide sets for group administration can be obtained from The Psychological Corporation, 304 East 45th Street, New York, New York 10017.

blots is sufficiently random to minimize undesirable sequential effects. The details of this early developmental work are described by Holtzman, Thorpe, Swartz, and Herron (1961).

Standardized inkblot protocols were obtained for over 1400 cases ranging from five-year-old normal children to superior adults; from mentally retarded individuals to chronic schizophrenic patients. Psychologists in universities and hospitals throughout the United States participated in the project by collecting test records and other relevant information from carefully defined populations. For example, psychologists in eleven different Veterans Administration hospitals cooperated in providing test data from depressed mental patients.

In the case of four samples of school children and young normal adults, it was possible to administer the HIT twice, using the alternate forms for the second administration. The time between test and retest sessions varied from one week to one year for the different samples, permitting rather broad generalizations about the equivalence of the two forms and the stability of inkblot scores over a period of time.

The scoring system developed for the HIT includes twenty-two different variables covering many aspects of an individual's response to an inkblot. These variables were defined by utilization of the more important systems for scoring the Rorschach so that most Rorschach scores could be derived easily from their basic elements. Several criteria played prominent roles in the formulation of variables for the scoring system. First, the variable had to be one which could be scored for any legitimate response, making it at least theoretically possible for a score to range from zero to forty-five when given unitary weight. Second, the variable had to be sufficiently objective to permit high scoring agreement among trained individuals. Third, the variable had to show some *a priori* promise of being pertinent to the study of personality through perception. And fourth, each variable had to be logically independent of the others wherever possible in order to code the maximum amount of information in the most flexible, efficient manner.

The name, abbreviation, brief definition, and scoring weights for each of the twenty-two variables when applied to a single response are given below.

Reaction Time (*RT*). The time in seconds from the presentation of the inkblot to the beginning of the primary response.

Rejection (*R*). Score 1 when S returns inkblot to E without giving a scorable response; otherwise score 0.

Location (*L*). Tendency to break down blot into smaller fragments. Score 0 for use of whole blot, 1 for large area, and 2 for smaller area.

Space (*S*). Score 1 for true figure-ground reversals; otherwise, score 0.

Form Definiteness (*FD*). The definiteness of the form of the concept reported, regardless of the goodness of fit to the inkblot. A five-point scale with 0 for very vague and 4 for highly specific.

Form Appropriateness (*FA*). The goodness of fit of the form of the precept to the form of the inkblot. Score 0 for poor, 1 for fair, and 2 for good.

Color (*C*). The apparent primacy of color (including black, gray, or white) as a response-determinant. Score 0 for no use of color, 1 for use secondary to form (like Rorschach FC), 2 when used as primary determinant but some form present (like CF), and 3 when used as a primary determinant with no form present (like C).

Shading (*Sh*). The apparent primacy of shading as response-determinant (texture, depth, or vista). Score 0 for no use of shading, 1 when used in secondary manner, and 2 when used as primary determinant with little or no form present.

Movement (*M*). The energy level of movement or potential movement ascribed to the percept, regardless of content. Score 0 for none, 1 for static potential, 2 for casual, 3 for dynamic, and 4 for violent movement.

Pathognomic Verbalization (*V*). Degree of autistic, bizarre thinking evident in the response as rated on a five-point scale. Score 0 where no pathology is present. The nine categories of V and the range of scoring weights for each is as follows: Fabulation, 1; Fabulized Combination, 2, 3, 4; Queer Response, 1, 2, 3; Incoherence, 4; Autistic Logic, 1, 2, 3, 4; Contamination, 2, 3, 4; Self Reference, 2, 3, 4; Deterioration Color, 2, 3, 4; Absurd Response, 3.

Integration (I). Score 1 for the organization of two or more adequately perceived blot elements into a larger whole; otherwise, score 0.

Human (H). Degree of human quality in the content of response. Score 0 for none, 1 for parts of humans, distortions, cartoons, and 2 for whole human beings or elaborated human faces.

Animal (A). Degree of animal quality in the content. Score 0 for none (including animal objects and microscopic life), 1 for animal parts, bugs, or insects, and 2 for whole animals.

Anatomy (At). Degree of "gutlike" quality in the content. Score 0 for none, 1 for bones, x-rays, or medical drawings, and 2 for visceral and crude anatomy.

Sex (Sx). Degree of sexual quality in the content. Score 0 for no sexual reference, 1 for socially-accepted sexual activity or expressions (buttocks, bust, kissing), and 2 for blatant sexual content (penis, vagina).

Abstract (Ab). Degree of abstract quality in the content. Score 0 for none, 1 for abstract elements along with other elements having form, and 2 for purely abstract content ("Bright colors remind me of gaiety").

Anxiety (Ax). Signs of anxiety in the fantasy content as indicated by emotions and attitudes, expressive behavior, symbolism, or cultural stereotypes of fear. Score 0 for none, 1 for questionable or indirect signs, and 2 for overt or clearcut evidence.

Hostility (Hs). Signs of hostility in the fantasy content. Scored on a four-point scale ranging from 0 for none to 3 for direct, violent, interpersonal destruction.

Barrier (Br). Score 1 for reference to any protective covering, membrane, shell, or skin that might be symbolically related to the perception of body-image boundaries; otherwise, score 0.

Penetration (Pn). Score 1 for concept which might be symbolic of an individual's feeling that his body exterior is of little protective value and can be easily penetrated; otherwise, score 0.

Balance (B). Score 1 where there is overt concern for the symmetry-asymmetry feature of the inkblot; otherwise, score 0.

Popular (P). Each form contains twenty-five inkblots in

which one or more popular percepts occur. "Popular" in the standardization studies means that a percept had to occur at least 14 percent of the time among normal subjects. Score 1 for popular core concepts (or their precision alternatives) as listed in the scoring manual; otherwise, score 0.

In all of our work with the HIT, scores on the twenty-two variables are punched on IBM cards for analysis; one card per response or a total of forty-five cards per protocol. Special computing routines have been developed for rapid data analysis using high-speed electronic computers. Handscoring and tabulation are used by investigators who do not have access to computers.

A major purpose of the initial standardization work on the HIT was to provide comprehensive information on interscorer agreement, internal consistency reliability, and test-retest stability using alternate forms and employing the twenty-two standardized inkblot variables. When highly trained scorers are employed interscorer agreement is exceptionally high for a projective technique. Only Penetration and Integration fall below reliabilities of .95, and in many cases the reliability approaches 1.00. The split-half reliabilities determined by computing the correlations between scores based on odd-numbered and even-numbered blots also are generally high. In the initial standardization work, median values for fifty different samples were generally in the .70s and .80s. Only Anxiety, Penetration, and Popular fell below this level, while Reaction Time, Rejection, and Location had average reliability coefficients above .90. These initial results for internal consistency have been repeatedly confirmed in more recent studies both in the United States and elsewhere.

Test-Retest Stability Across Time

Standardization studies for the HIT included four samples in which both forms were given, with intervals ranging from one week to one year between the two testing sessions. Test-retest correlations generally ranged from .36 for Popular to .81 for Location for normal adults.

As part of a larger investigation, test-retest stability coefficients recently have been computed for large numbers of children in the United States and Mexico over intervals ranging from one to five years. This cross-cultural longitudinal study of cognitive, perceptual, and personality development in children, initially described by Holtzman, Diaz-Guerrero, Swartz, and Lara Tapia (1968), now has been completed and will be published in a book in both Spanish and English in 1975. Repeated measures were obtained for the HIT and a variety of other tests on over 400 children in the United States and a similar number in Mexico who were tested once a year for six years. Three age groups of school children were tested in both cultures with initial ages for testing set at six years and eight months for the youngest group, nine years and eight months for the middle group, and twelve years and eight months for the oldest group of children. These particular ages were selected so that all testing could be done during the school years. Six years of repeated testing made correcting developmental trends for practice effects possible, yielding one continuous curve over the ages of six to seventeen for each variable studied in each culture.

The most stable of all the inkblot scores across repeated testing is Location. With the exception of the youngest children in the first year, the test-retest correlations for Location were high in both cultures, ranging into the .80s for the older children even after several years of testing. Close behind Location in stability are Reaction Time, Form Definiteness, Movement, and Human. All of these variables deal with the cognitive-perceptual aspects of the performance of the child rather than directly with his personality characteristics.

Rejection, Form Appropriateness, Shading, Pathognomic Verbalization, Barrier, and Penetration tended to have generally low stability coefficients, ranging from insignificant values into the .40s and .50s, with an occasional value into the .60s and .70s. Four variables—Space, Sex, Abstract and Balance—proved to be too infrequent in these samples of children to yield data amenable to treatment by product-moment correlation coefficients. The remainder had moderately high stability coefficients. As one would expect, test-retest stability increases with an increase in the age of the child. The oldest children in the study tended to have the highest degree of stability, and children in all three age groups showed higher test-retest stability in the later years of the project than in the initial years.

The degree of test-retest stability dropped off regularly as the length of intervals between tests grew. The average test-retest stability for all children over an interval of five years dropped to an insignificant level for Shading, Pathognomic Verbalization, Animal, and Penetration. Location, however, showed a higher degree of stability over the five-year period (.51) than was true of any of the subtests of the WISC. When three or four year intervals occurred between testing, all variables showed significant stability over time. When there was an interval of only one or two years, the level of stability was as high as in the earlier standardization studies using a one-year interval.

Most of the inkblot variables show a sufficiently high degree of stability across time to justify their use as predictors of later behavior. At the same time, the test-retest correlations are not so high as to suggest any kind of fixed traits that remain relatively invariant as the child grows older. Although the degree of test-retest stability was generally higher for the American children than for those in Mexico, regardless of age group, the absolute difference is small, indicating that the HIT has a satisfactory degree of test-retest stability for use in Mexico as well as in the United States.

The overlapping repeated-measures design employed in the six-year longitudinal study also provided some interesting information concerning practice and adaptation effects for HIT scores when the test is used repeatedly on the same individuals, alternating Forms A and B. While most of the scores revealed no major adaptation effects with repeated testing, there is some evidence of adaptation for Location which showed significant mean shifts that could not be explained on the basis of growth and development alone. Children of all ages in both cultures tended to use smaller detailed areas more frequently as the test was repeated. Most of this adaptation took place between the first and second year of testing. About five points on the Location scale could be attributed to adaptation even though the interval between testing was an entire year for the American children. The amount of adaptation was considerably greater, averaging about eleven points on the Location scale for the Mexican children. However, in spite of the noticeable adaptation of Location to repeated testing the stability of individual differences through time was very high.

Dimensions

In the initial developmental studies, intercorrelations were routinely computed among the twenty-two inkblot variables and factor analyses were carried out independently for each of the fifteen standardization samples to determine the common dimensions underlying inkblot perception and how they may differ in patterning from one population to the next. Almost invariably, five or six factors are necessary to explain the interrelationships among the twenty-two inkblot scores. The first three are the most important and have emerged repeatedly, regardless of the population studied. Defined primarily by Movement, Integration, Human, Barrier, and Popular, Factor I usually accounts for more variance than any other. Key variables in Factor II are Color and Shading, with Form Definiteness (reversed) also frequently present as a defining variable. Factor III is determined primarily by Pathognomic Verbalization, with Anxiety, Hostility, and Movement usually present. Although the pattern varies for the remaining three factors, the most common configuration involves Form Appropriateness and Location in Factor IV; Reaction Time, Rejection, and Animal (reversed) in Factor V; and Penetration, Anatomy, and Sex in Factor VI.

These factor groupings of the HIT variables have been used by Hill (1972) in developing a systematic procedure for clinical application of the HIT in personality assessment of individuals. Recent replications of these earlier factorial analyses in the cross-cultural longitudinal project on the children in the United States and Mexico verify the major factors reported earlier. However, some interesting departures from the standard patterns were noted for certain age levels in the two cultures, which have a bearing upon the manner in which the variables are interpreted. The highlights of these results and their significance follow.

Factor I. Movement, Integration and Human invariably have high loadings on Factor I for all samples of children in both cultures. The other two marker variables, Form Definiteness and

Popular, vary somewhat from one sample to the next. Location, Anxiety, Hostility, and Barrier are characteristically follower variables for Factor I, sometimes showing high loadings on this factor and at other times showing low loadings. Location appears to be more important as a variable identified with Factor I in the United States than in Mexico. Anxiety and Hostility, two marker variables for Factor III, are closely associated with Factor I, but only among the young adolescents in each culture. It is also interesting to note that Pathognomic Verbalization and Penetration have unusually high loadings on Factor I for the 14-year-olds in both cultures. On the basis of defining variables and earlier studies of their validity, a high amount of Factor I is generally interpreted as indicative of well organized ideational activity, good imaginative capacity, well differentiated ego boundaries, and awareness of conventional concepts. These most recent results, however, suggest that Factor I and Factor III may be closely intertwined for children in their early adolescence. A moderately high amount of Pathognomic Verbalization, Anxiety, and Hostility in these essentially normal young adolescents may not be indicative of psychopathology at all. It may well be that the turmoils of early adolescence result in a welling up of primary affective processes that break loose from ego control in an active fantasy life, thus accounting for the convergence of Factors I and III in this age group.

Factor II. As in the earlier work, Color, Shading, and Form Definiteness (reversed) generally have high loadings on Factor II in every sample. Occasional negative loadings for Location on Factor II are consistent with findings that high use of color and shading is associated with use of the whole inkblot rather than small areas. Unlike the earlier samples of children studied, five of the six samples in the current study reveal significant negative loadings on Factor II for Animal, which suggests that children use color and shading as stimulus determinants only when they cannot find a familiar animal form. The positive pole of this factor would indicate over-reactivity to color or shading, while the negative pole would indicate primary concern for form alone as a determinant.

Factor III. Generally defined by Pathognomic Verbalization, Movement, Anxiety and Hostility, Factor III tends to be correlated with Factor I for most of the samples of children, regardless of culture, making separation of the two factors in an orthogonal solution difficult. This interdependence of the two factors is particularly evident among the young teenagers. As in earlier studies, Penetration and Anatomy tend to be follower variables often associated with the three marker variables. Among normal children, moderately high scores on Factor III are indicative of affective expressivity and loose imagination in fantasy productions. Very high scores would be evidence of psychopathology and uncontrolled bizarreness (Holtzman and others, 1961; Conners, 1965; and Hill, 1972).

Factor IV. Location and Form Appropriateness served consistently as defining variables for this factor. The more an individual delves into small detail while responding to inkblots, the more likely he will be to find a percept for which the form of the blot is highly appropriate. Anatomy, Barrier, and Penetration also tend to have negative loadings on Factor IV in both cultures. In general, Factor IV is bipolar in nature, the positive pole tending to indicate perceptual differentiation coupled with a critical sense of good form, while the negative pole appears more indicative of immaturity, diffuse bodily preoccupation, and possibly psychopathology.

Factor V. Reaction Time and Rejection tend to be closely associated for obvious reasons. The longer a person takes to look at an inkblot before he gives a response, the more likely he is to reject the card without seeing anything in it. Of greater interest is the fact that Factor V emerges as a significant dimension orthogonal to the first four factors, indicating that an individual's performance on other inkblot scores is generally independent of his reaction time or the number of cards he rejects. The variable most commonly associated with Factor V other than Reaction Time and Rejection is Animal.

Factor VI. While usually defined by Anatomy, Sex, and Abstract, this residual factor is limited to Anatomy in the samples of normal children because Sex and Abstract occur too rarely for stable analysis. Factor VI can best be interpreted simply as an independent dimension dealing with inanimate content scores and unrelated to the other five factors among children.

Validity

Of all the studies on the HIT in the past twelve years, only a few have dealt directly with validity. Most of these studies were covered in earlier comprehensive reviews of the HIT (Holtzman, 1968, Gamble, 1972, Hill, 1972). Only the highlights of some recent results can be presented here.

Correlations between inkblot scores and scales in self-report personality inventories generally are low. High scores on Factor III variables—Pathognomic Verbalization, Anxiety, and Hostility—tend to be associated with high scores on Neuroticism from the Maudsley Personality Inventory (Megargee and Swartz, 1968), with Rigidity on the Sanford-Gough Test (Kidd and Kidd, 1971), and with the Guilt scale on the MMPI given to depressed patients (Moseley, Duffey, and Sherman, 1963). However, such scales as the Sarason Test Anxiety Scale for Children and Taylor's Manifest Anxiety Scale from the MMPI failed to show any correlation with inkblot scores of Anxiety and Hostility. It is quite evident that fantasy expressions of symbolic anxiety or hostility do not have a simple and direct relationship to observed anxiety in one's behavior or self-admission of such traits in personality inventories.

The most extensive study involving external correlates of inkblot variables is the recently completed cross-cultural longitudinal investigation involving children in Mexico and the United States mentioned earlier. The self-report inventories in this research consisted of Sarason's Test Anxiety Scale for Children and Jackson's Personality Research Form. While Anxiety and Hostility from the HIT failed to show any relationship to personality traits from the self-report inventories, interestingly, several other inkblot scores did prove to be significantly associated with certain scales in the Personality Research Form. High Color scores were significantly correlated (p < .01) with high scores on Exhibitionism, Impulsiveness, and Nurturance, all in the expected direction based on Rorschach theory concerning the meaning of Color. Integration proved to be positively correlated with the Understanding scale from the Personality Research Form, a finding also in the expected direction since Understanding relates to intellectual capacity. Anxiety and Hostility from the HIT do have some substantiation of their validity from other data collected in the longitudinal study of the American children. Using sociometric ratings it was found that children rejected by their classmates in the first and fourth grades gave significantly higher scores on Anxiety and Hostility six years later than did children who were accepted by their classmates initially. School counselors provided information about the emotional adjustment of forty-six of these children later. It was found that children with high scores on Pathognomic Verbalization, Anxiety, and Hostility indeed were those who later developed severe problems of emotional adjustment or behavior disorders (Currie, Holtzman and Swartz, 1974).

Many studies indicate Movement has a significant cognitive component, as one would anticipate from the earlier Rorschach studies. Repeatedly significant correlations ranging as high as .42 were obtained between Movement and wisc Vocabulary in all the age groups in both Mexico and the United States in the cross-cultural study. This bivariate relationship is about as high as the intercorrelation among certain of the wisc subtests. Several factor analyses using all of the wisc subtests, as well as several other cognitive variables and Movement from the hit, revealed a stable factor with high loadings on Movement, Vocabulary, Comprehension, and to some extent, Information and Similarities. This particular factor is orthogonal to a primary factor cutting across most of the wisc tests, indicating a second independent component of verbal ability characterized by a lively, active imagination and ability to project outward from one's fantasies. In this sense, Movement deals particularly with the expressive, imaginative aspects of verbal ability rather than with factual information, word meanings, and analytical problem-solving. Consistent with this interpretation is the earlier finding by Mueller and Abeles (1964) that Movement possibly is related to the degree of empathy in counselors. Further corroboration comes from Clark, Veldman and Thorpe (1965) who found that Movement is correlated with divergent thinking ability in talented adolescents. And finally, Movement rises markedly with increasing age until early adolescence (Thorpe and Swartz, 1965), a developmental change repeatedly found among normal children of different ages. The evidence is indeed strong that Movement is a valid measure of imaginative capacity and ideational maturity.

Barrier and Penetration have been studied extensively because of their direct relevance to body image and personality. Increased Barrier scores were found to result from body awareness training in schizophrenics (Darby, 1970). Low Barrier scores, together with high Color, were found to be predictive of poor performance in the Peace Corps (Holtzman, Santos, Bouquet, and Barth, 1966). Decreased Penetration scores were discovered after body awareness training in mental retardation (Chasey, Swartz, and Chasey, 1974). A review of Barrier and Penetration as measures of body image and personality has been published by Fisher (1970).

Even more striking results bearing upon the validity of the Holtzman Inkblot Technique have been obtained in studies of intergroup differences and differential diagnosis. The initial standardization studies included mental retardates, chronic schizophrenics and depressives, as well as normal individuals ranging in age from five-year-old children to middle-aged adults. Additional normative data have been published by Hill (1972) for emotionally disturbed children, emotionally disturbed adolescents, juvenile delinquents, neurotic adults, and alcoholics. Differences in means and standard deviations across these groups are striking and are in the direction to be expected from earlier Rorschach theory.

An interesting objective approach to differential diagnosis was done by Moseley (1963) using data from the initial standardization studies. Using linear discriminant functions to find the best linear combinations of 16 HIT variables, Moseley was able to classify accurately 82 percent of the normals from schizophrenics, 71 percent of the normals from depressives, and 78 percent of the depressives from schizophrenics. These results held up surprisingly well on cross-validation with independent samples. A two-stage model was used in which doubtful middle-range cases from the linear discriminant analysis were further classified solely on the basis of Pathognomic Verbalization, which improved the efficiency of the differential diagnosis even more. Hill (1972) has gone beyond these earlier studies of differential diagnosis in her handbook for clinical application of the Holtzman Inkblot Technique. A number of pattern scores and guidelines for clinical inference, many of them based upon empirical research as well as earlier Rorschach work, form the basis for her interpretive system.

Technological Advances and Variations in Standard Form

When we first developed the Holtzman Inkblot Technique, it was our hope that the great amount of empirical information on the ninety-two inkblots would help us to develop a variety of experimental forms for special purposes. The extensive item-analysis information available on each inkblot (Holtzman and others, 1961, for individual form, and Swartz, Witzke and Megargee, 1970, for group form) makes it a simple matter to establish experimental subsets for the study of unusual variables such as Space, Abstract, or Balance. Some investigators have used this information to establish smaller subsets of parallel forms. For example, Palmer (1963) constructed six sets of fifteen cards each for repeated measurement in the study of sleep deprivation over many days in a small number of subjects.

Two standardized, group-administered variations of the HIT have also been published. One involves the use of colored slides and a special booklet for a group administration (Swartz and Holtzman, 1963). A short form of this particular method using only thirty cards rather than all forty-five has been investigated and shows promise for many research purposes (Herron, 1963). The other standardized group method uses the same colored slides but utilizes a streamlined record form on which the subject merely writes a brief response and checks the amount of the blot used for the percept (Gorham, 1967). The group method of administration is particularly effective with the HIT because of the simple format involving only one response per card. It is also more economical since almost any number of individuals can be tested at once.

Split-half reliability and test-retest stability using parallel forms with a one-week interval essentially are as high for the group method as for the individual. A study comparing the individual and group methods given to the same subjects one week apart, found that only five of the eighteen inkblot scores analyzed showed any significant mean differences attributable to method of administration (Holtzman, Moseley, Reinehr, and Abbot, 1963). Location, Space, and Color scores were higher for the group method, and Barrier and Popular scores were higher for the individual method. Standard deviations of scores were the same for all variables except Anxiety which had a higher variance in the group method. Comparing the cross-method correlations in a multitrait-multimethod matrix revealed a striking degree of similarity across the two methods. These studies show that the group method can be safely substituted for the individual method in cases dealing with subjects who are competent to write out their own responses to the inkblots.

The method developed by Gorham, Moseley, and their associates (Moseley, Gorham, Hill, 1963; Gorham, 1967; Gorham, 1970) provided a system for scoring seventeen of the HIT variables by high-speed computer. An empirically derived dictionary containing about 4000 words was then compiled in English, Spanish and Portuguese to facilitate cross-cultural studies. Each word in the dictionary was assigned multiple scoring weights by an individual experienced in scoring HIT variables, which were checked and refined by independent expert review. Stored in the computer as a large table of scoring weights, the dictionary provides an automatic scoring system in any language for which words and weights have been compiled.[2] Agreement between hand and computed scoring of the same protocols is surprisingly high in spite of the fact that syntax is only taken into account by the computer program in a rudimentary way. Intercorrelations between the two methods of scoring are high (above .80) for seven variables—Rejection, Location, Movement, Human, Color, Form Definiteness, and Animal. Cross-method correlations for Hostility, Popular, Anxiety, Anatomy, Shading, Penetration, Abstract, Sex, Barrier, and Integration range from .50 to .75.

A logical extension of the computer-scored HIT is a computer-based system for personality interpretation using the extensive normative data and studies of group differences among psychiatric patients as a basis for the system. Evidence accumulated rapidly from Rorschach studies, and more recently with the HIT which support some personality interpretations while refuting others. The availability of objective norms for HIT scores based on large samples makes possible the codifying of complex patterns of scores to derive new configural scores that are close to those often used in clinical assessment of personality (Holtzman and Gorham, 1972).

Several hundred rules dealing with various aspects of personality that are purported to be revealed by patterns of inkblot scores were constructed, which (Hill, 1972) were refined by panels of experienced clinical psychologists and reduced to sixty care-

[2] Information on computer scoring services can be obtained from HIT Scoring Service, ARBEC, Inc., 3909G North I.H. 35, Austin, Texas, 78722.

fully defined patterns which were then coded and stored in a specially constructed computer program. An exploratory study of their validity was undertaken using fifty-eight normal men (Naval enlistees), seventy-eight neurotics, and 100 depressed patients as criterion samples. A large reference group of normals provided percentile norms for decision points on each score in a given pattern. Whenever the specific conditions for a given rule were met, the computer printed out the accompanying interpretive statement. A set of such statements constituted a "personality description" for a given individual.

Analysis of the frequency of occurrence of each rule among individuals in the three samples revealed highly significant differentiation for twenty-eight of the rules. Table 1 delineates the frequencies for each rule as distributed across the criterion samples in the direction hypothesized for the pattern of scores in each case.

The configural scoring patterns in Table 1 illustrate a wide range of possibilities, from a single score and its decision rule to a complex pattern containing several alternatives. In each case the percentile scores from a normative table for 205 U. S. Navy enlistees (Gorham, Moseley, and Holtzman, 1968) were used to define the configuration. The interpretive statement accompanying each configuration initially was prepared by Evelyn Hill on the basis of her own research (Hill, 1972) and then refined in conference with Donald Gorham and Jon Swartz, both of whom have had many years of experience in the interpretation of configural patterns in the HIT. The programming for the configural scoring and interpretation by computer was done by Donald Witzke, working closely with the other researchers. It is important to keep in mind that the interpretive statement and the accompanying pattern score were formulated initially without reference to the degree of differential diagnostic accuracy later attained. After an initial trial run of the interpretive program, some of the pattern scores were modified to tighten or relax the standards employed in choosing cutoff points for each variable. Initial guesses often proved to be too stringent, creating a pattern that rarely, if ever, was present in any of the cases. As illustrated in Table 1, MOD 2 of the program has a number of promising characteristics. A closer examination of each statement

Table 1.

Sample Statements, HIT Configural Patterns Associated With Them, and Differential Diagnostic Accuracy in Percent Frequencies for Fifty-eight Normals, Seventy-eight Neurotics, and 100 Depressed Patients

Statement	HIT Score Configuration*	Differential Diagnostic Accuracy		
		Normal	Neurotic	Depressed
A2. An integrative approach to life situations is revealed.	L < 21 +FD > 79 +I > 79	10	0	0
F2. Moderately high achievement motivation is indicated.	I > 49 +Br > 79 +L < 21 +R < 71	10	2	1
A7. This person is dull and stolid and seems to be making an inferior adjustment to life.	H < 6 +M < 6 +C < 21	0	0	7
B9. Little effort is made to organize experience beyond a diffuse perception.	L < 6 +FD < 6 +I < 6 +R > 79	0	0	3
C6. Emotional flatness and apathy are indicated in this record.	C < 6 +Sh < 11 +M < 6	0	0	4
G2. There is a lack of spontaneity and alertness to events in the environment.	C < 21 +Sh < 21 +P < 21 +L < 21	0	0	5
G6. There is a low capacity for active coping, structuring, integrating, and organizing.	C < 6 +L < 6 +I < 6 +FD < 21	0	0	3
E5. Neurotic constriction. Cannot acknowledge impulses through imaginal processes.	H < 6 +A < 6 +C < 21 +M < 21, H < 6 +A < 6 +C < 6 +M > 19, H > 6 +A < 6 +M < 6 +C < 19	2	0	7
A8. Lacks constitutional strength to carry out a program of self-development.	A < 6 +M < 11	2	4	9

Code	Description	Criteria			
D8.	Lowered ego control or non-adaptive preoccupation with original ideas indicated.	$A < 6$	5	7	10
B10.	Shows minor blocking of ideational activity.	$R > 89$	12	13	26
G3.	There is excess reliance on inner fantasy to the exclusion of reality.	$Ax > 94$ $\quad +H > 94$ $\quad +Pn > 94$ $\quad +I < 51$	0	6	0
E4.	Neurotic conflict and body concern is present to a greater degree than that found in normal somatic preoccupation.	$Ax > 94$ $\quad +Pn > 94$ $\quad +At > 94$	0	10	1
G4.	Record reveals emotional immaturity and body preoccupation.	$Ax > 79$ $\quad +H > 79$ $\quad +Pn > 79$ $\quad +At > 79$	2	17	0
C11.	Responses reveal an individual who has doubts, uncertainties and intense feelings of which he is only dimly aware. Overly sensitive, fearful, and vigilant.	$Sh > 98$ $\quad +Ax > 98$	0	25	2
C7.	Lack of conscious control over feelings and impulses. Inner unrest and lack of emotional stability revealed.	$H > 79$ $\quad +Sh > 79$ $\quad +C > 98$	2	18	6
E2.	This person is tense and alert as if facing an emergency.	$Ax > 94$ $\quad +M > 94$	2	13	4
E3.	There are feelings of personal inadequacy.	$Pn > 94$ $\quad +H < 21$	0	13	4
B4.	There is evidence of disturbed thought processes.	$At > 98$ $\quad +Pn > 98,$ $\quad R > 98,$ $\quad C > 79$ $\quad +M > 79$ $\quad +At > 79$ $\quad +Pn > 79$	0	24	12

Table 1. (cont.)

SAMPLE STATEMENTS, HIT CONFIGURAL PATTERNS ASSOCIATED WITH THEM, AND DIFFERENTIAL DIAGNOSTIC ACCURACY IN PERCENT FREQUENCIES FOR FIFTY-EIGHT NORMALS, SEVENTY-EIGHT NEUROTICS, AND 100 DEPRESSED PATIENTS

Statement	HIT Score Configuration*	Differential Diagnostic Accuracy		
		Normal	Neurotic	Depressed
B7. Restriction and reduction of intellectual drive is revealed.	At > 98	3	16	6
D5. Poor ego identity, poor sense of body boundary definiteness.	Pn > 94 +At > 79 I < 21	0	8	2
E7. Anxiety is apparent in the content of fantasy. Phobias may be present.	Ax > 98	2	35	3
E1. Fear and anxiety compel this person to cling to obvious and safe thoughts.	Ax > 79 +L > 79 +P > 79 +FD > 79	0	6	0
C9. Person is dominated by emotional reactivity.	C > 94 +FD < 21 +I < 6	0	8	3
A10. This person has problems in interpersonal relationships and fears people.	H > 94 +Ax > 94	0	7	0
A9. Lacks interest in other people and may have interpersonal problems.	H < 6	7	27	30
B5. There is a pedantic emphasis upon accuracy, correctness, and exactitude.	L > 79 +FD > 79	2	14	16
B8. This individual is interested in details for the sake of details rather than as part of a larger scheme of things.	L > 94	3	8	11

*Explanation of the symbols is as follows:

also reveals the subtle dynamics of configural pattern scoring for the interpretation of the HIT.

The twenty-eight items in Table 1 are arranged first in three clusters according to whether the statement is diagnostic of normality, neurotic trends, or depression. Diagnosing normality in a positive sense is the most difficult of the three tasks, as evidenced by the fact that only two statements (A2 and F2) are highly significant. Good Form Definiteness coupled with high Integration and whole responses (A2) cleanly differentiates 10 percent of the normals while yielding no false positives among the neurotics and depressed patients. A somewhat different pattern is F2 which focuses upon high achievement motivation. Above average Integration coupled with high Barrier, a predominance of whole responses, and low Rejection also correctly diagnoses 10 percent of the normals. Unlike A2, however, a small percentage of neurotic and depressed patients is included.

The second large cluster of statements contains pattern scores differentially diagnostic of depression. The first five patterns in this set contain no false positives of either normals or neurotics, although the percentage of depressed patients with the pattern is very low, ranging from only 3 to 7 percent. The remaining four statements in this set contain some normal or neurotic cases although there is a predominance of depressed patients. Examination of the statements in this cluster reveals a common theme of dullness, apathy, constriction, and blocking frequently associated with severe depression. Three of the patterns (C6, G6, and part of E5) involve very low scores on Color—at the fifth percentile or below among normals. Low Shading (C6 and G2) is also characteristic of several patterns. Movement is very low for four of the patterns (A7, C6, A8, and part of E5); and to some extent, the same can be said for Human and Integration. Low scores on Animal and Form Definiteness, as well as high scores on Rejection, complete the particular combinations characteristic of the pattern scores and statements diagnostic of depressed patients.

The third and largest set of pattern scores is differentially diagnostic of neurotics when compared with normals and depressed individuals. The fourteen statements from C3 to A10 contain significantly higher percentages of neurotics than either normals or depressed patients. Unlike the clusters of statements characterisic of normals and depressed individuals, the statements diagnostic of neurotic individuals are more heterogeneous and generally occur with higher frequency. Three statements, G3, E1, and A10, cleanly separate neurotics from the other two groups with no false positives. The pattern for G3 consists of very high Anxiety, Human, and Penetration coupled with below average Integration, resulting in an interpretive statement of excessive "reliance on inner fantasy to the exclusion of reality." The pattern for E1 contains moderately high Anxiety coupled with equally high Location (predominantly common detail areas) and Popular (obvious percepts) plus below average Integration, leading to the interpretation that "fear and anxiety compel this person to cling to obvious and safe thoughts." The pattern for A10 simply involves very high Human and Anxiety, indicating "person has problems in interpersonal relationships and fears people."

Most of the statements in this neurotic set involve some combination of Anxiety or Penetration with other inkblot scores. Exceptions are C7 and C9, both of which are characterized by very high scores on Color. Clearly, the statements characteristic of neurotic individuals tend to use such terms as anxiety, tension, emotional immaturity, and overreactivity, lack of impulse control, and excessive body preoccupation.

The fourth and last cluster contains three statements which are more commonly characteristic of both neurotic and depressed individuals as contrasted to normals. In one sense these statements are the reverse of the first small cluster that was positively diagnostic of normals (A2 and F2). They differ from all the other negatively-phrased statements by failing to differentiate between neurotic and depressed. One of them is a pattern score comprised of high Location (small detail) coupled with high specificity of form (B5). The other two are single scores rather than patterns. Lack of interest in other people and pedantic emphasis upon accuracy or details are more characteristic of both patient groups than of normals.

It is also apparent from an examination of Table 1 that some configurations are much more efficient in differential diagnosis than others. Indeed, in several instances, single scores are most efficient of all. For example, very high scores on Anxiety (E7) lead to the obvious interpretation that "anxiety is apparent in the content of fantasy," a statement characteristic of 35 percent of the neurotics as contrasted to only 2 percent and 3 percent of the normals and depressed patients. This rather dramatic differentiation provides strong evidence of the validity of very high Anxiety scores as indicative of neurotic anxiety or possibly phobias.

When other scores are added to Anxiety in order to increase the precision of the pattern, the few remaining "false positives" drop out of the picture, but at a cost of losing many neurotic cases as well. When compared to E7, E1 may be cleaner from the point of view of differential diagnosis, although its rarity makes it less useful. To some extent, the same can be said about several of the other pattern scores involving Anxiety, such as A10 or G3 where only neurotic cases are picked up by the pattern. These differences illustrate an important point to remember in establishing pattern scores and accompanying interpretive statements. Configurations occuring only rarely are of limited usefulness unless there are large numbers of such rare signs that operate somewhat independently of each other. Otherwise, the resulting interpretive system produces many more blank interpretations than positive statements when applied to a general population of protocols. It is probably better to relax the system enough to permit a substantial percentage of positive signs even at the risk of increasing the number of false positives.

The present computer-based interpretive system is still in its formative stages. In spite of very promising results with the current statements and decision rules, considerable refinement is essential before the system can be used for practical purposes in automated personality assessment. The low rate of occurrence for some statements in any of the three populations studied is a weakness that can be overcome in part by trial-and-error adjustment of cutting points in the pattern scores. Additional patterns can also be developed and some of those that did not prove significant in differentiating these particular three groups may still be useful in other situations.

The striking differential diagnostic accuracy of some configural patterns and their associated statements can be considered further validation of the HIT. In most instances, the statements associated with neurotic, depressed, or normal individuals are those one would hypothesize in advance.

The present system can employ either the hand-scored or computer-scored version of the HIT collected either by individual or group administration. Since the present interpretive system illustrated in Table 1 is built upon the computer-scored version of the HIT, a great deal of qualitative information in each protocol has been ignored. In addition, such important variables as Form Appropriateness and Pathognomic Verbalization are not scorable by computer and have, therefore, been omitted from the analysis. For this reason the results in this preliminary study are even more impressive.

Field studies are now underway in clinical settings to refine and validate the system of computer-based interpretation. Once the interpretive system has been fully developed in English on American populations, the system should be adaptable to a wide variety of other literate cultures. Local norms and changes in decision rules are easy to produce, given the availability of a high-speed computer for completing the adaptation.

Future Prospects

Twelve years after the appearance of a new technique for personality assessment is sufficient time to take stock of the strengths and weaknesses of the method, as well as its future prospects for further refinement and application. An annotated bibliography of the 300 articles, monographs, and books on HIT has been stored on magnetic tapes in computerized form where frequent updating and printout upon demand can be done economically (Swartz, Witzke and Holtzman, 1973). A handbook for clinical application (Hill, 1972), a workbook for the HIT (Hill and Peixotto, 1973), clinical interpretation forms (Megargee and Velez-Diaz, 1971, and Hill, 1972) and the computer scoring system have greatly augmented the original materials published in 1961. Translation of these aids into a number of other languages has led to a flurry of cross-cultural studies and applications. The original forty-five-card sets of inkblots and the twenty-two standardized variables have held up surprisingly well considering that most of the work bearing upon validation and application appeared after the initial developments. Before considering areas where additional research and development are needed, let us summarize the major accomplishments of the past decade.

The initial standardization and subsequent normative studies have been sufficiently comprehensive to demonstrate the precise equivalence of the parallel forms, A and B, the high degree of scoring reliability for the twenty-two standardized scores, the generally high degree of reliability of the scores, the comparability of the group and individual methods for most inkblot scores and most populations of subjects, and the richness of qualitative data for clinical interpretation in typical individually-administered protocols. The stability of inkblot scores over time up to intervals of five years between testing has been thoroughly documented by the large samples of Mexican and American children in a cross-cultural longitudinal study, as well as by the earlier standardization data on adults. Factor analytic studies of intercorrelations among the twenty-two variables have repeatedly yielded five or six factors regardless of age group, culture, or psychiatric classification. While the relative emphasis of different variables upon these factors and the degree of orthogonality among the major dimensions may vary somewhat from sample to sample, there is little doubt about the basic identity and meaning of the dimensions themselves. Large numbers of cases in dozens of samples from populations as diverse as mentally retarded children, schizophrenic adults, and superior college students have been transformed into normative tables for comparative purposes. Developmental norms from preschool children (Holtzman, and others, 1961) to old adults (Witzke, Swartz, and Drew, 1971) have repeatedly demonstrated sequences of perceptual development outlined by Werner (1957), progressing along a continuum of increasing differentiation and integration. Norms for the computer-scored HIT (Gorham, Moseley and Holtzman, 1968) based upon over 5000 cases have been presented for schizophrenics, depressives, psychoneurotics, alcoholics, and chronic brain-syndrome patients, as well as normal adults from the United States and sixteen different countries around the world. While additional well-defined norms are always welcome and useful, a strong basis already has been provided for the development of systems of differential diagnosis, such as the computer-based interpretive system described earlier. But as Gamble (1972) has urged in his comprehensive review of the HIT, little systematic work has been done on the issues of personality description versus diagnostic classification and test interpretation versus test score.

Still another area in which an impressive amount of information has accumulated in the past decade is the one bearing upon the external validity of the HIT. As indicated earlier, strong evidence has been amassed in support of some interpretations for such variables as Movement, Color, Pathognomic Verbalization, Integration, Human, Anatomy, Anxiety, Hostility, Barrier, and Penetration. At the same time, other interpretations have not been substantiated by the work to date. Only the highlights of such studies have been illustrated here. The reader is referred to such comprehensive reviews as those by Hill (1972), Gamble (1972), and Holtzman (1968). Different from reliability, stability through time, and standardization, the question of external validity can never be satisfactorily answered. Even with the accrual of information from scores of studies directly bearing upon validity, that which is still unknown is infinite. One can hardly scratch the surface of this topic, let alone exhaust its important possibilities.

Perhaps more fruitful than endless permutations of such correlational studies would be experiments aimed at clarifying and strengthening the theory underlying the technique. An example of this is the recent study by Holtzman, Swartz, and Thorpe (1971) which investigated the consequences of the projective hypothesis as revealed in three contrasting modes of visual experience—the perceptual styles of outstanding artists, architects, and engineers. The successful abstract artist has been trained to express feelings, emotion, and other nonverbal qualities in nonrepresentational visual forms. He draws heavily upon his own inner feelings, experiences, and thoughts in his creative productions. In contrast, the mechanical engineer who is highly successful as a draftsman has learned to follow rigid rules of geometric design which adhere closely to the structural-functional demands of reality. The successful architect embodies the characteristics of both the artist and the engineer. Concerned with harmony and proportion of visual designs as well as the strengths of materials and mechanical design, the architect should be more sensitive to the organization and the symmetry-asymmetry of the blots than either the artist or the engineer. Highly significant differences in the predicted direction were found in a comparison of HIT scores for artists, architects, and engineers. Artists obtained significantly lower scores on Location and Form Appropriateness and significantly higher scores on Pathognomic Verbalization, Anatomy and Sex than did the other two groups. Engineers obtained significantly lower scores on Human while architects obtained higher scores on Integration and Balance. Results for perceptual variables from other tests in the comprehensive battery strengthen the general conclusion still further.

While the qualitative differences in Pathognomic Verbalization have been studied among samples of normal, schizophrenic, depressed, and mentally retarded subjects by Swartz (1970), a great deal of additional work is necessary before the qualitatively different categories of disordered thinking are clearly understood. Fantasy productions in response to inkblots are rich with possibilities for the study of disordered thinking. Swartz found that normals tend to produce more fabulation and fabulized combinations while schizophrenics tend to give more contaminations, autistic logic and self-reference responses. Among normal children, fabulized responses increase with increasing age while autistic logic, contamination, and absurd responses drop significantly. With further study and refinement, it is quite possible that the Pathognomic Verbalization score could be divided into several new scores of greater validity than the original.

Four of the variables in the HIT—Space, Sex, Abstract, and Balance—generally have been overlooked in most of the research to date. While all four variables are relatively rare, they do occur with sufficient frequency in some populations to justify more systematic efforts aimed at improving the measures. It may well be that only by selecting subsets of inkblots from the entire pool in both forms, and by permitting two or three responses per card rather than one, will it be possible to develop reliable, useful measures of the concepts underlying these four variables. There is also no reason why additional variables cannot be derived from the inkblot protocols, particularly where there is a special interest in selected aspects of inkblot perception, such as Color (Hill, 1966). The content of inkblot responses is particularly well suited to such special treatment, as evidenced by Endicott's Suspiciousness score (1972) and "eye" responses (Coleman, 1966; Fernald and Stolurow, 1971). A great deal of fruitful work has been done with the body image scores, Barrier and Penetration, and there is no reason why other specialized content scores would not prove equally fruitful.

Technological extensions of the HIT have been successfully developed for group administration and computer-based scoring of seventeen HIT variables. Initial efforts in computer-based interpretation have been sufficiently promising to justify more extensive research in this area. Ideally, protocols should be obtained from large numbers of individuals for whom reliable personality assessments by independent judges are also available. Field studies now underway are aimed at achieving this goal. Looking even further to the future there is a possibility of automated testing, scoring, and interpretation, perhaps with the HIT in a battery of assessment techniques. The inkblots could easily be displayed in a standard console with keyboard entry of responses and immediate feedback of scores, reference norms, and interpretive statements. The hardware and software for such technology is already available (Holtzman, 1970) although costs are still prohibitive. More important than feasibility and cost, however, are the larger ethical issues in the promotion of obviously imperfect but completely automated systems for personality assessment and feedback.

In the foreseeable future it is unlikely that such technological extensions can replace the individually administered, scored, and interpreted HIT where a thorough, sensitive personality assessment is desired, especially in a clinical setting where decisions about the individual are paramount. Most of the qualitative nuances of the examiner-subject interaction, as well as the linguistic richness of verbal responses, are completely lost even in the group-administered version of the technique when hand-scored. Such important variables as Pathognomic Verbalization, Form Appropriateness, Abstract, Balance, and Reaction Time can only be properly measured by individual administration and scoring of the HIT.

The steadily growing acceptance of the HIT as an important assessment technique to be used in a wide variety of practical situations as well as research designs speaks well for its future. The basic stimuli are sufficiently rich; the standardized technique similar enough to its predecessor, yet the clear psychometric advantages over it combine to provide an attractive alternative. Whether the next decade will see such ascendancy of the Holtzman Inkblot Technique over the Rorschach, as optimistically predicted by Sundberg (1962), only time will tell.

References

CHASEY, W. C., SWARTZ, J. D., AND CHASEY, C. G. "Effect of Motor Development on Body Image Scores in Institutionalized Mentally Retarded Children." *American Journal of Mental Deficiency,* 1974, *78*(4), 440–445.

CLARK, C. M., VELDMAN, D. J., AND THORPE, J. S. "Convergent and Divergent Thinking Abilities of Talented Adolescents." *Journal of Educational Psychology,* 1965, *56,* 157–163.

COLEMAN, K. A. "The Significance of Eye Responses on the Holtzman Inkblot Technique as Measured by the Minnesota Counseling Inventory." *Springfield College Studies,* 1966, *1,* 41.

CONNERS, C. K. "Effects of Brief Psychotherapy, Drugs, and Type of Disturbance on Holtzman Inkblot Scores in Children." *Proceedings of the 73rd annual convention of the American Psychological Association,* 1965, 201–202.

CURRIE, S. F., HOLTZMAN, W. H., AND SWARTZ, J. D. "Early Indicators of Personality Traits Viewed Retrospectively." *Journal of School Psychology,* 1974, *12*(1), 51–59.

DARBY, J. A. "Alteration of Some Body Image Indexes in Schizophrenics." *Journal of Consulting and Clinical Psychology,* 1970, *35*(1), 116–121.

ENDICOTT, N. A. "The Holtzman Inkblot Technique Content Measures of Depression and Suspiciousness." *Journal of Personality Assessment,* 1972, *36*(5), 424–426.

FERNALD, P. S., AND STOLUROW, K. A. "Projected Eye Responses and Sensitivity to the Opinion of Others." *Journal of Clinical Psychology,* 1971, *27,* 258–259.

FISHER, S. *Body Experience in Fantasy and Behavior.* New York: Appleton-Century-Crofts, 1970.

GAMBLE, K. R. "The Holtzman Inkblot Technique: A Review." *Psychological Bulletin,* 1972, *77*(3), 172–194.

GORHAM, D. R. "Validity and Reliability Studies of a Computer-based Scoring System for Inkblot Responses." *Journal of Consulting Psychology,* 1967, *31,* 65–70.

GORHAM, D. R. "Cross-cultural Research Based on the Holtzman Inkblot Technique." *International Congress of the Rorschach and other Projective Techniques,* 1970, *7,* 158–164.

GORHAM, D. R., MOSELEY, E. C., AND HOLTZMAN, W. H. "Norms for the Computer Scored Holtzman Inkblot Technique." *Perceptual and Motor Skills Monograph Supplement,* 1968, *26,* 1279–1305.

HERRON, E. W. "Psychometric Characteristics of a Thirty-item Version of the Group Method of the Holtzman Inkblot Technique." *Journal of Clinical Psychology,* 1963, *19,* 450–453.

HILL, E. F. "Affect Aroused by Color, a Function of Stimulus Strength." *Journal of Projective Techniques and Personality Assessment,* 1966, *10,* 23–30.

HILL, E. F. *The Holtzman Inkblot Technique: A Handbook for Clinical Application.* San Francisco: Jossey-Bass, 1972.

HILL, E. F., AND PEIXOTTO, H. E. *Workbook for the Holtzman Inkblot Technique.* New York: The Psychological Corporation, 1973.

HOLTZMAN, W. H. "The Holtzman Inkblot Technique." In A. I. Rabin (Ed.), *Introduction to Modern Projective Techniques.* New York: Springer, 1968, 136–170.

HOLTZMAN, W. H. *Computer-Assisted Instruction, Testing and Guidance.* New York: Harper and Row, 1970.

HOLTZMAN, W. H., DIAZ-GUERRERO, R., SWARTZ, J. D., AND LARA TAPIA, L. "Cross-Cultural Longitudinal Research on Child Development: Studies of American and Mexican School Children." In J. Hill (Ed.), *Minnesota Symposia on Child Psychology,* Vol. II, Minneapolis: University of Minnesota Press, 1968, 125–159.

HOLTZMAN, W. H., AND GORHAM, D. R. "Automated Scoring and Interpretation of the Group-administered Holtzman Inkblot Technique by Computer." *Proceedings of the 80th annual convention of the American Psychological Association,* 1972.

HOLTZMAN, W. H., MOSELEY, E. C., REINEHR, R. C., AND ABBOTT, ELAINE. "Comparison of the Group Method and the Standard Individual Version of the Holtzman Technique." *Journal of Clinical Psychology,* 1963, *19,* 441–449.

HOLTZMAN, W. H., SANTOS, J. F., BOUQUET, S., AND BARTH, P. *The Peace Corps in Brazil: An Evaluation of the Sao Francisco Valley Project.* Austin: International Office, University of Texas, 1966.

HOLTZMAN, W. H., SWARTZ, J. D., AND THORPE, J. S. "Artists, Architects, and Engineers: Three Contrasting Modes of Visual Experience and Their Psychological Correlates." *Journal of Personality,* 1971, *39*(3), 432–449.

HOLTZMAN, W. H., THORPE, J. S., SWARTZ, J. D., AND HERRON, E. W. *Inkblot Perception and Personality*. Austin: The University of Texas Press, 1961.

KIDD, A. H. AND KIDD, R. A. "Relation of Holtzman Scores to Rigidity." *Perceptual and Motor Skills*, 1971, *32*(3), 1003–1010.

MEGARGEE, E. I. AND SWARTZ, J. D. "Extraversion, Neuroticism, and Scores on the Holtzman Inkblot Technique." *Journal of Projective Techniques and Personality Assessment*, 1968, *32*, 262–265.

MEGARGEE, E. I. AND VELEZ-DIAZ, A. "A Profile Sheet for the Clinical Interpretation of the Holtzman Inkblot Technique." *Journal of Personality Assessment*, 1971, *35*(6), 545–560.

MOSELEY, E. C. "Psychodiagnosis on the Basis of the Holtzman Inkblot Technique." *Journal of Projective Techniques and Personality Assessment*, 1963, *27*, 86–91.

MOSELEY, E. C., DUFFEY, R. F., AND SHERMAN, L. J. "An Extension of the Construct Validity of the Holtzman Inkblot Technique." *Journal of Clinical Psychology*, 1963, *19*, 186–192.

MOSELEY, E. C., GORHAM, D. R., AND HILL, E. "Computer Scoring of Inkblot Perceptions." *Perceptual and Motor Skills*, 1963, *17*, 498.

MUELLER, W. J. AND ABELES, N. "The Components of Empathy and their Relationship to the Projection of Human Movement Responses." *Journal of Projective Techniques and Personality Assessment*, 1964, *28*, 322–330.

PALMER, J. O. "Alterations in Rorschach's Experience Balance under Conditions of Food and Sleep Deprivation: a Construct Validation Study." *Journal of Projective Techniques and Personality Assessment*, 1963, *27*, 208–213.

SUNDBERG, N. D. "The Rorschach Americanized: Review of Inkblot Perception and Personality." *Contemporary Psychology*, 1962, *7*, 250–252.

SWARTZ, J. D. "Pathognomic Verbalizations in Normals, Psychotics, and Mental Retardates." *Dissertation Abstracts International*, 1970, *30*(12–8), 5703–5704.

SWARTZ, J. D. AND HOLTZMAN, W. H. "Group Method of Administration of the Holtzman Inkblot Technique." *Journal of Clinical Psychology*, 1963, *19*, 433–441.

SWARTZ, J. D., WITZKE, D. B., AND HOLTZMAN, W. H. *Holtzman Inkblot Technique Annotated Bibliography*. Austin, Texas: Hogg Foundation for Mental Health, 1973.

SWARTZ, J. D., WITZKE, D. B., AND MEGARGEE, E. I. "Normative Item

Statistics for the Group Form of the Holtzman Inkblot Technique." *Perceptual and Motor Skills,* 1970, *31*(1), 319–329.

THORPE, J. S. AND SWARTZ, J. D. "Level of Perceptual Development as Reflected in Responses to the Holtzman Inkblot Technique." *Journal of Projective Techniques and Personality Assessment,* 1965, *29,* 380–386.

WERNER, H. *Comparative Psychology of Mental Development.* (2nd ed.) New York: International Universities Press, 1957.

WITZKE, D. B., SWARTZ, J. D., AND DREW, C. J. "Level of Perceptual Development of Normal Adults as Measured by the Holtzman Inkblot Technique." *Proceedings of the Annual Convention of the American Psychological Association,* 1971, *6*(Pt. 2), 609–610.

VII

The Adjective Checklist Technique: A Review and Critique

SHARON MASTERSON

Ⓞne of the most pressing and persistent problems for researchers interested in personality has been the need for objective, quantifiable measures of personality variables which are simultaneously valid, yet pose minimal problems in terms of administration, scoring, and subject resistance. The adjective checklist approach to personality assessment is an attempt to answer this need. It is the purpose of this chapter to evaluate the checklist approach to personality measurement by presenting a limited review and critical evaluation of existing checklists, and by examining the implications of their use.

The adjective checklist approach to personality assessment is by no means a new one. Indeed, it goes back to the Hartshorne and May studies of the 1930s, in which teachers completed checklists to describe student conduct. Subsequent contributions to the approach were made by Allport and Odbert (1936), with their comprehensive list of trait names, by Cattell (1943), with his factorial studies of personality, and by Hathaway and Meehl in their background work with the Minnesota Multiphasic Personality Inventory (1951).

Today the literature on adjective checklists is voluminous and still growing. There are well over fifty different checklists represented in the current literature, reflecting a broad range of psychological variables. As an assessment technique the adjective checklist presents the subject with a list of descriptive terms covering the behavior or behaviors under consideration. The list is such that it can be filled in either by the subject himself or by an observer who records his reactions to the person (or stimulus) under consideration. Checking techniques and scoring procedures vary somewhat from one checklist to another, but the approach is usually typified by the simplicity of the response required such as a check placed beside any word characterizing the stimulus-person and by an uncomplicated scoring procedure. Emphasis is placed on obtaining a maximum amount of descriptive information with minimal emphasis on the mechanics of response. Proponents of the technique believe that the adjective checklist, as a psychometric instrument, has several advantages over the traditional personality inventory in that it is easy to administer and score, yet is sufficiently complex to cover a broad range of observed behavior. It also presents the subject with a task which is meaningful and nonthreatening, resulting in a minimal amount of test-taking resistance, and is typically structured so as to be amenable to both rational and empirical analysis while being almost limitless in its range of application.

Checklists in Use

The number of personality checklists available today is vast and growing, attesting to the widespread use of this technique as a method of personality measurement; however, the available instruments vary tremendously in psychometric characteristics. Several of the available checklists are standardized with ample information available in terms of purpose, techniques of development, standardization, cross-validation, validity and reliability, and scoring procedures. However, the literature also is replete with checklists for which none of this information is provided. Therefore in evaluating the merits of a given instrument, the reader should consider the features of that instrument, as well as the general characteristics of checklist approaches to assessment. This review is intended as a general survey and critique of checklist methods, within whose scope we will recognize that some instruments are better developed than others. (For other, more limited, reviews of particular checklists, see Goodstein, 1972; McNair, 1972; McReynolds, 1968; Rorer, 1972; Vance, 1972; Kelly, 1972; Megargee, 1972; Lykken, 1972.) The past and potential applications of the checklist technique are illustrated by the following selective review of studies employing checklist techniques.

Existent checklist techniques encompass a vast array of personality variables. Some (Gough and Heilbrun, 1965) represent attempts to quantify broad dimensions of the total personality; others are oriented toward the quantificaion of specific personality dimensions (Zuckerman and Lubin, 1965; Thayer, 1967). Following is a representative but by no means exhausting survey of the lists currently in use.

Perhaps the best known and most extensively used checklist is the Gough-Heilbrun Adjective Check List (ACL) (Gough and Heilbrun, 1965). It consists of 300 adjectives (for example, active, irritated, powerful) commonly used to describe individuals; it yields pertinent information in the form of twenty-four scale scores. Four of the scales are indices of test-taking variables: number of favorable adjectives checked, number of unfavorable adjectives checked, and defensiveness; four scales were empirically developed on the basis of relevant criteria: self-control, lability, self-confidence, and personal adjustment. An additional fifteen scales were developed, on a rational or theoretical basis, to measure the needs outlined by Murray (1938): dominance, endurance, order, achievement, intraception, nurturance, affiliation, heterosexuality, exhibition, autonomy, aggression, change, succorance, abasement, and deference. A final scale was included to measure counseling readiness. Individual scores on the ACL were converted to standard scores in accordance with score conversion tables presented in the ACL manual to control for the influence of the number of adjectives checked.

A somewhat different approach to checklist construction was

taken by Clarke (1956). He developed an adjective checklist, the Activity Vector Analysis Adjective Check List (AVA Check List) which is used largely in business and industry for personality measurement. The AVA Check List consists of eighty-one "nonderogatory" words (for example, appealing, open-minded, nervy) used to describe human behavior. Interpretation of the results is made through the ipsative integration of four basic unipolar factors: aggressiveness, sociability, emotional control, and social adaptability.

Checklists also have been adapted for use with children. Lipsitt (1958), for example, reports the use of a self-concept scale with children containing twenty-two trait descriptive adjectives (for example, brave, bashful, honest) each prefaced by "I am," followed by a five-point rating scale. In addition, adjective checklists have been developed for measuring affect and mood. The most widely used includes the Multiple Affect Adjective Check List (MAACL) (Zuckerman and Lubin, 1965). The MAACL consists of 132 adjectives (for example, fearful, hopeless, tender) with affective connotations. Scoring is based upon three scales for anxiety, depression, and hostility which were developed using an empirical item-selection approach. The selections for each scale were based upon the responses of patients rated as high on a particular affect, the responses of normals who were put into the particular affect state via hypnosis, or a combination of the two. The Affect Adjective Check List, AACL, was developed by Zuckerman in 1960 and has been included in the MAACL as the anxiety measure. The MAACL consists of a 130 or 145-word list of adjectives which apply to various mood states. Subjects are instructed to indicate their response to each adjective by marking a double check if the word is definitely applicable to their mood state at the moment; a single check if slightly applicable; a question mark if uncertain, and a "no" if the adjective definitely does not apply. Extensive factor analysis of the instrument has suggested six to twelve relevant mood factors for which results may be scored. Other mood-affect checklists include a 173-adjective checklist by Jacobs, Capek, and Meehan (1959), comprising four fourteen-adjective scales designed to measure the emotions of fear, danger, depression, and happiness; a 117-adjective list by Bahnson (Knapp and Bahnson, 1963), constructed around six bipolar a priori dimensions of emotion, a self-report measure of emotional

response by Radloff and Helmreich (1968), the Brentwood Mood
Scale, a seventy-two-item word list for the self description of present
emotional state (Crumpton, Grayson, and Keith-Lee, 1967), and
a sixty-two-item mood scale by Lorr and his associates (Lorr, Daston,
and Smith, 1967).

Additionally, Thayer (1967) has developed an Activation-
Deactivation Adjective Check List (ADACL) to measure transient
levels of activation; Sciortino (1968) has designed a Motivational
Adjective Check List (MACL), consisting of thirty items to be rated
on a five-point scale from least to most applicable; and Jackson and
Minton (1963) have constructed a forced-choice Adjective Preference Scale including adjectives related to cognitive complexity-
simplicity. Other scales include a checklist developed by Wendt and
his colleagues (Cameron, Specht, and Wendt, 1967; Wendt, Cameron, and Specht, 1962) to obtain repeated reports of mood in relation to specific drugs, and the Leary Interpersonal Check List (La-
Forge and Suczek, 1955) consisting of 128 items (eight for each
of sixteen dimensions) to measure interpersonal behavior as defined
by Leary's (1957) interpersonal theory of personality.

This sampling suggests the numerous and varied applications
of the checklist in personality research. Adjective checklists have
been used in an almost infinite variety of experimental paradigms,
and a tremendous amount of information has been accumulated on
the basis of checklist responses.

Representative Research

One of the outstanding features of the adjective checklist as
an instrument in personality research is the flexibility and adaptability of the technique to particular experimental designs. The following uses are representative of current research applications.

A number of studies have employed adjective checklists to
determine the self concept characteristics of a particular group. Mac-
Kinnon (1967), for example, found that creative adults tend to
score high on such Gough-Heilbrun ACL scales as autonomy and
aggression, with relatively lower scores on variables like deference,
abasement, and affiliation. Helson and Crutchfield (1970) similarly
identified the characteristics of the creative researcher in the field of

mathematics and several researchers—Nathan, Zare, Ferneau, and Lowenstein (1970), Vanderpool (1969), and Nathan, Titler, Lowenstein, Solomon, and Rossi (1970)—have applied adjective checklists to the assessment of self concepts of alcoholics. Hooke and Krauss (1971) in analyzing the ACL responses of successful police sergeant candidates, suggest that they tend to respond in a conventional and socially desirable fashion.

Adjective checklists have been used to determine parents' perceptions of their children (Brown, 1972; Scarr, 1966), patients' perceptions of their therapists (Reinehr, 1969), teachers' perceptions of their students (Kitchin, 1972), and employees' perceptions of their managers (Barron and Egan, 1968).

They also have been used in determine the degree of consensus in self concept within a particular group. Connor (in Reinehr, 1969), for example, found that nonhospitalized alcoholics were able to agree (70 percent agreement) on only eight adjectives out of the 300 on the Gough-Heilbrum ACL, whereas a sample of hospitalized alcoholics reached agreement on nineteen different adjectives (Reinehr, 1969) as being self descriptive.

One of the main advantages of the adjective check list is that it is infinitely repeatable and can be applied to almost any stimulus object. Therefore it is possible to use the technique as a basis of comparison between two concepts or between the same concept at two points in time. It is therefore feasible, as Gough and Heilbrun (1965) suggest, to use a checklist to describe a person when he is at his best, when he is at his worst, as he was five years ago, as his mother sees him, and so on. This fact contributes immeasurably to the flexibility and utility of the approach, and explains why adjective checklists have been used in a wide variety of comparison paradigms. Barron and Rosenberg (1968), for example, compared an actor's self-conception with his conception of himself in a role. In a study of the relationship between the assumed and real similarity of a subject to a stimulus person, Rodgers (1959) compared subjects' self perceptions to their perceptions of a person described to them. Heilbrun (1971) asked adolescents to describe themselves first as they saw themselves and secondly as they believed others saw them. Reinehr (1969) compared alcoholic patients' perceptions of themselves with their perceptions of their therapists, finding their perceptions of the therapist to be the more negative. Astin (1971) compared college protesters, nonprotest leaders, and random college students on the Gough-Heilbrun ACL, finding student activists and nonprotesters to be relatively similar in self concept. And Davis (1969) compared Gough-Heilbrun ACL descriptions of one's self, the personality characteristics needed to function effectively in the nursing role, and the personality characteristics needed to function effectively in social work, finding a significant correlation between students' self-concepts and their role expectations for their chosen occupations. Within this context, adjective checklists might be used to guess how another person would describe himself, to compare stereotypes with actual group characteristics, or to compare ideal with actual self concepts, and so on.

Because the adjective checklist approach is conducive to repetition, it has been used extensively to determine the effects of various experimental treatments. Zuckerman and his colleagues (Zuckerman, 1960; Zuckerman, Lubin, Vogel, and Valerius, 1964) have reported and replicated the finding that student anxiety, hostility, and depression scores on the MAACL rise (relative to baseline levels) with the threat of an examination. McGee and Williams (1971) used an unspecified checklist in conjunction with other measures to compare the outcomes of time-limited versus time-unlimited approaches to therapy. McGinnies (1968), using a list of nine bipolar adjectives to measure an audience's perception of a speaker, found audience perceptions to vary as a function of the position taken by the speaker on a political issue. Significant changes in volunteer workers' perceptions of mental patients have been reported from a pre-period to a post-period of volunteer work (Kulek, Martin, and Schiebe, 1969), and Datel and Lifrak (1969), using the MAACL, found that the level of distress (MAACL anxiety, depression, and hostility) experienced by military recruits during basic combat training was significantly less than the distress anticipated upon actually entering the training program. Bringman, Balance, and Krichev (1969) compared the effects of "hot" (movie) and "cool" (television) media presentations of a film on MAACL responses. And so on.

Not only have adjective checklists been used as indices of treatment outcomes, they also have been used to confirm that specific treatment effects have occurred. Nowlis (1965) suggested that adjective checklists may have a unique place as monitoring devices in studies involving other indices, and several researchers have used checklists in this capacity. Geer and Turteltaub (1967), for example, used the anxiety scale of the MAACL to determine if, in effect, a confederate acting either frightened or calm had communicated the desired affect. Helmreich and Hamilton (1968) also used a mood adjective checklist in an arousal manipulation to determine if a treatment had led to increases in fear. In relating the repression-sensitization scale to behavioral measures of repression and sensitization, Hoffman (1970) used the Gough-Heilbrun ACL to determine if his sample was atypical. And Wendt and his colleagues (Wendt, Cameron, and Specht, 1962), used an adjective checklist to keep track of the progress of drug experiments. Thus adjective checklists play a significant secondary role as well as a primary role in personality research.

Because adjective checklists can be simply and repeatedly administered to the same subjects, this technique has frequently been used to plot the development of and changes in various concepts over time. Lubin and Zuckerman (1967), for example, have used scores on the MAACL to study the occurrence of developmental trends in sensitivity training groups. The MAACL also has been used to determine patterns of emotional reaction among military recruits progressing through basic training, by plotting average changes in anxiety, depression, and hostility at various points in the training program (Datel, Gieseking, Engle, and Dougher, 1966; Datel and Lifrak, 1969). Wendt, Cameron and Specht (1962) used a 130-word mood adjective checklist to determine progressive changes in mood associated with increasing dosages of various drugs. And Williams (1966) has noted the progressive changes in ACL self concept occurring at various states of liquor consumption. Studies such as these suggest the utility of adjective checklists in measuring changes within a particular group as well as in measuring intergroup differences.

It is also true that the nature of the checklist procedure makes this approach to assessment amenable to the measurement of such things as ideas and subjects' concepts of inanimate objects.

Among other things, adjective checklist procedures have been applied to concepts of historical personages like Washington and Lincoln, and have been used in the description of cities (Gough and Heilbrun, 1965). They have been used in the assessment of occupational stereotypes (Hollander and Parker, 1969) and as indications of students' perceptions of various roles (Davis, 1969). The MAACL has been used as a "control" for checking behavior on another instrument (Cline and Chosy, 1972), and Knapp and Bahnson (1963) have developed an adjective checklist for use as a projective technique measuring latent or projected mood.

Uses of adjective checklists are obviously numerous and varied. As it is typically constructed the adjective checklist offers the researcher an opportunity to obtain a sizeable amount of information with a minimal amount of difficulty in administration, scoring, and test-taking resistance. The time factor is minimal, as even the lengthiest of the available lists can be administered in ten to fifteen minutes. This fact, together with the amount of information obtainable, has undoubtedly contributed substantially to the popularity and extensive use of the checklist method. In light of this extensive use, questions might properly be raised concerning the adequacy of checklist techniques as methods of assessment. Are these extensive and varied uses in keeping with the characteristics and limitations of the technique?

A general overview of the characteristics and shortcomings of checklists in general follows. As previously indicated, checklists vary tremendously in methods of construction, scoring procedures, length, validity, and reliability. The reader is again advised to apply what follows selectively, with a view to the particular characteristics of the instrument under consideration. This review will focus primarily on the two most widely used instruments, the Gough-Heilbrun ACL and the MAACL by Zuckerman and Lubin, using information on other checklists where applicable. Both have been thoroughly researched and offer extensive manuals describing characteristics of the instrument under consideration. They are generally representative of the strengths and shortcomings of checklist methods of assessment, and they reflect checklists in general in that the Gough-Heilbrun ACL is a broad and encompassing measure of personality variables, whereas the MAACL is concerned with a more limited dimension, specifically affect.

Reliability

In discussing the values and significance of adjective check-list measures, an immediate concern is whether or not they are reliable measures of personality. Yet in considering the adequacy of reliability coefficients associated with particular checklists, one immediately confronts the issue of whether or not a high test-retest coefficient is a necessary or even a desirable attribute for checklist methods of assessment. The question is a particularly significant one since several of the major checklists report only modest test-retest coefficients. Gough and Heilbrun (1965), for example, reported that for a sample of men tested twice at six-month intervals test-retest reliability coefficients ranged from a low of +.01 to a high of +.86 with a mean of +.54. They suggest that the mean figure indicates that the self-image as projected in ACL responses is perhaps not as stable as the data from self-report inventories using items and questions. Nowlis (1965), using the MAACL, asked college men to report their momentary moods at the same time daily for from twenty-five to sixty days. Test-retest coefficients ranged from .50 (for aggression) to .75 (for depression). Thayer (1967), included several variables a second time among the words in the Activation-Deactivation Adjective Check List, and found the median coefficient for adjectives repeated in the list a second time to be .75. These coefficients are typical of those reported for other currently available lists.

The nature of several existing checklists together with coefficients like these, suggests two alternatives: that moderate rather than high coefficients are an artifact of test construction, and thus a general characteristic of checklist methods; that low reliability coefficients accurately reflect the variable under consideration, and do not reflect inadequacies in the checklist technique.

It should be noted that several checklist measures (for example, the ACL and the MAACL-General) are concerned with the measurement of general and presumably enduring facets of personality. Yet a number of checklist techniques are designed to reflect the current status of variables which are subject to change. The

Nowlis MACL (Nowlis, 1965), for example, was designed to provide a measure of mood change, and Zuckerman and Lubin (1965) have developed a "Today" (subjects are instructed to check adjectives describing how they feel today, now) form of the MAACL to reflect changing rather than enduring dimensions of affect. The implications of low test-retest coefficients would thus seem to vary with the nature of the checklist approach. A reasonably high coefficient would seem imperative for an instrument purporting to measure enduring dimensions of personality. Yet a too-high test-retest correlation would actually suggest the insensitivity of an instrument intended to detect changes in personality dimensions. That it is possible to develop instruments for both purposes has been suggested by the work of Zuckerman and Lubin (1966). They developed the general form of the MAACL in which subjects are instructed to check adjectives which describe how they *generally* feel, with retest reliabilities ranging from .54 for hostility to .70 for anxiety. Using the same list of adjectives with altered instructions they also constructed the Today form of the MAACL with test-retest reliabilities of the order of .30.

The measurement of transitory states does not, of course, excuse checklist measures from reliability considerations. In measuring variables which are subject to change, the adequacy of the measure is still dependent on the reliability of scores in measuring the variable at any given time. Zuckerman and Lubin (1965) thus suggest that any instrument purporting to measure transitory states should report low test-retest reliabilities but high coefficients of internal consistency. Pankratz, Glaudin, and Goodmonson (1972), recognizing the need for reliability estimates even in instruments measuring fluctuating states, devised a procedure for estimating the reliability of the MAACL-Today. Correlating alternate forms of the MAACL administered within the same hour, they were able to determine that the MAACL-Today is a reliable instrument reflecting temporary state scores. (In dealing with state measures, one could always argue that the variable under consideration is so transitory in nature that one cannot expect significant correlations even across extremely short periods of time. But it would seem that the utility of so transient a variable in personality research is extremely limited and open to question.) Thus moderate-to-low reliability coefficients may, at least in some instances, be due to the nature of the measured variable.

An alternate approach to the question of low reliability coefficients has been suggested by Gough and Heilbrun (1965) and Parker (1971). Noting the low average reliability coefficients for the ACL, they suggest that stability vs. instability of self image on the ACL may reflect a meaningful personological disposition rather than statistical error. Gough and Heilbrun (1965) were able to identify adjectives which significantly differentiated between subjects with high stability coefficients and those with low stability coefficients. Parker (1971) developed a stability scale further suggesting that reliability or unreliability of ACL scores may be a valid individual difference variable that will prove useful in predicting and understanding behavior.

Regardless of whether low test-retest reliability coefficients are to be seen as error factors or individual difference variables, the literature suggests the need for internal reliability checks in using checklist measures. In approaching an adjective checklist, subjects are typically instructed to work quickly as they progress through a list of adjectives, often without concern for duplication or contradiction. Frequently the lists include antonyms and words which are theoretical, if not conceptual opposites. Yet almost none of the available checklists considers the eventuality that subjects may be simultaneously checking antonyms or words which are incompatible within the theoretical framework of the inventory. That this in fact may be a problem in the evaluation of check list protocols has been suggested by Yagi and Berkun (1961). Using the Nowlis MACL with enlisted military personnel, these authors concluded that 62 percent of their test records would have to be eliminated because of inconsistencies in checking antonyms, low internal reliability, that is, inconsistency in checking ten words which had been repeated in the long list, or inconsistency in checking words on a factor (activation-deactivation) which was considered to be bipolar. Parker (1969) reported marked inconsistencies in self-descriptions on the ACL and Plutchik, Platman, and Fieve (1971) suggested that the lack of methods to check on internal reliability and the consistency of antonym choices is a drawback of the MAACL. The problem, however, would seem to apply to any free-response checklist. In spite of the voluminous research using checklists, there is a paucity of research addressed to these questions. One would suspect that the issue of internal consistency would be less of a problem in checklists requiring a forced choice (for example, Nowlis, 1965; McGinnies, 1968) than in check lists with a free response format. But the literature has not addressed itself to this problem and until studies on this issue are forthcoming, the reliability and utility of existing checklists must be considered questionable.

Administration and Scoring

Not only do adjective checklists differ radically in scope and area of application, but also the procedures by which they are administered and scored vary from checklist to checklist and often from one administration to another. Basic checklist technique requires that subjects respond to a list of adjectives by checking those words applying to the stimulus person or variable under consideration. Within this framework the following variations are typical of the checklist formats in current use.

The Gough-Heilbrun ACL follows the traditional format. In one variation however it has been altered to require subjects to check a specific number of adjectives, rather than the unspecified and unlimited number possible in the traditional administration. Kaplan (1968) and Gough and Heilbrun (1965), for instance, have asked subjects to predict the responses of targets on adjective checklists by indicating, with a number of adjectives equal to the number checked by the target, the responses the target would use in describing himself. The standard format has also been changed to permit true-false responses to a list of adjectives. Rodgers (1959) employed this procedure to study real versus assumed similarities, and Siller and Chipman (1963) have adapted both the ACL and the MAACL to the true-false format. Warr and Knapper (1967) have further altered the traditional procedure requiring subjects to mark "yes" to any adjectives they feel apply, "no" to all words which do not apply, and to leave blank any adjective which has no relevance to the stimulus being considered. In addition, several authors have structured checklists to require forced-choice responses. Nowlis (1965) as noted earlier, requires that subjects responding to the

MACL circle a double check if the adjective definitely applies, a single check if it applies somewhat, a question mark if the subject is uncertain, and a "no" if the word does not apply. The Bahnson check list (Knapp and Bahnson, 1963) requires subjects to respond with one of four forced-choice replies to each adjective from strong presence to complete absence, and McGinnies (1968) has developed a nine-item bipolar adjective checklist requiring subjects to check one adjective in each pair.

The fact that the same sets of adjective stimuli are often used under such varied instructional sets raises questions concerning the equivalence of the information obtained via the above procedures. Research with the traditional response format has consistently shown, for example, that there are vast individual differences in the number of adjectives checked (Gough and Heilbrun, 1965). This suggests that the amount and kind of information obtained from any particular subject under free-response conditions will vary considerably from that obtained in a true-false or forced-choice administration, or under instructions to check a specified number of words. The question of the equivalence of obtained information is further confounded by the fact that scoring procedures used to tabulate adjective checklist responses are as varied as the instructional sets under which they are administered.

Typically, analysis of results has focused on specific scales, factors, or individual adjectives. The Gough-Heilbrun ACL, for example, is scored on twenty-four separate scales. Each scale is scored by subtracting the number of contraindicative adjectives checked on that scale from the number of indicative adjectives checked for the scale. Zuckerman and Lubin's MAACL is scored for three scales, anxiety, depression, and hostility, with each scale being scored by counting the number of plus items which are checked for the scale and the number of minus adjectives which are not checked. The Nowlis MACL is scored by adding the total ratings (based on a four-point rating scale) for all the mood adjectives representing a given factor. Jacobs, Capek, and Meehan's (1959) checklist of mood is scored by adding the number of adjectives checked which are indicative of the four measured dimensions of fear, anger, depression, and happiness. Finally, Carpenter (1968) used an adjective checklist which is scored by counting the number of positive items and the number of negative items and subtracting the smaller sum from the larger.

In light of such differences, a review of the literature suggests that an evaluation of the utility of each of these instruments and the value of a particular scoring system should consider the following points.

1. Several studies (for example, Goldman and Mendelsohn, 1969; Hooke and Krauss, 1971) have based their analyses of experimental results on group differences in responses to specific adjectives. While such differences may be highly informative, it also should be noted that they are based, in effect, on tests consisting of a single item, and the reliability of the obtained results may therefore be suspect.

2. Goldman and Mendelsohn (1969) have suggested that in examining a list of adjectives it is as important to note those which are not checked as to note those which are. Yet several of the current scoring systems leave open several questions as to the meaning of an unchecked adjective. As Warr and Knapper (1967) point out, an adjective which remains unchecked may be regarded by the subject as irrelevant to the stimulus person or object, or it may be considered definitely not descriptive; further, the possibility always exists that the item was simply overlooked. And yet, unchecked adjectives are being used in some scoring systems as contraindications and in others as indications of variables under consideration. In some cases they are simply not considered.

3. In a similar vein, checklists which offer subjects the option to check or not to check are in all likelihood equating judgments of "extremely applicable," "applicable," and possibly "questionable" under a single checking response. Various check lists differ in the degree to which responses are quantifiable. The "all or none" checking response, for example, provides a minimum of quantifiable information in comparison to procedures in which a subject is, say, required to respond to each adjective, on a four or five-point scale, from highly applicable to totally inapplicable. An adjective checklist which requires an "all or none" response to each adjective is distinctly different quantitatively from one which imposes a quantitative dimension in the form of a rating scale for each adjective. Consequently, checklists demanding such varied responses should not be

treated equivalently even though the stimuli may be the same for both.

4. As indicated previously, several of the scoring systems for existing checklists involve two-part scores, for example, the ACL, which is scored on the basis of indicative minus contraindicative checks, and the MAACL, which is scored on the basis of plus items checked and minus adjectives not checked. Where such two-part scores are used, a question arises as to the relative contribution of each part to experimental outcomes. For example, in a checklist where a highly favorable score is determined by a combination of the number of favorable and unfavorable adjectives checked, one could question whether a favorable outcome was the result of checking many favorable adjectives or of checking a high number of unfavorable ones. This is aptly illustrated in a study by Rodgers, Ziegler, and Levy (1967) comparing attitudes toward birth control pills and vasectomy as methods of contraception. Faced with the outcome that the pill was viewed as the more favorable alternative, they were then confronted with the question of whether the significant difference obtained was due to favorable attitudes toward the pill or to unfavorable attitudes toward vasectomy. Similarly Whittaker and Watts (1971), in comparing student activists with passively alienated nonstudents and with a general population of college students on ACL responses, found that alienated students checked significantly fewer adjectives as self-descriptive than did the nonstudents. The difference in this instance was largely attributable, however, to the fact that fewer unfavorable adjectives were checked by the student activists, since their mean was almost identical to the means of the other two groups in number of favorable adjectives checked.

In scoring systems involving two-part scores, the relationship of part scores to each other and their relative contribution to the total score also bear consideration. For example, it is possible to construct a two-part score with contraindicative or unchecked adjectives contributing disproportionately to the outcome. Herron (1969), for example, found that if subjects had turned in a blank MAACL protocol under two different experimental conditions they would have received scores above the mean on all three MAACL scales because of the disproportionate contribution of adjectives which are scored when not checked. That the relationship between part scores also bears investigation is illustrated in a study by Plutchik, Platman, and Fieve (1971) wherein the hypothesized negative relationship between the plus and minus "scales" of the MAACL was only partially upheld. In a study of the effects of examination stress on medical students Nichols and Spielberger (1967) have further illustrated the complexities involved in adjective checklists using two part scores, finding that the anxiety minus component of the MAACL-Today anxiety scale was at a higher level in the post-examination period than in the pre-exam period, whereas the anxiety plus component was lower in the post-examination phase than in the pre-examination period.

All of this is not to say that two-part scoring systems should be abandoned. In spite of their criticisms of the two-part score Plutchik, Platman, and Fieve (1971) concluded that it does have some redeeming qualities. They found with depressed patients, for example, that as patients became more clinically depressed there was no change in the frequency of checks for depression plus words on the MAACL, but there was a decrease in the frequency with which depression minus words were checked. The two-part score thus provided valuable information that might not otherwise have been obtained. Nonetheless two-part systems do present special problems of interpretation.

5. It is possible that the amount of error variance associated with a particular checklist fluctuates as the instructions and/or scoring systems are altered. That an alteration in instructions may influence the test-retest reliability of an instrument has been illustrated by Zuckerman and Lubin (1965) in the development of the Today form of the MAACL. An alteration in the instructions on this checklist was reflected, for example, in a change in the test-retest reliability scale for the Anxiety scale from an r of .68 for the General form to an r of .21 for the MAACL-Today. Although such an altered reliability coefficient is in keeping with the purposes of the Today form, which is intended to be a state rather than a trait measure, the fact that a simple alteration in instructions can substantially influence reliability suggests that the effects of such alterations in other instruments should be considered. Validity and reliability coefficients for the standard checklists are typically reported

for standard instructional sets and scoring procedures. Yet the instructions and scoring approaches are frequently altered to be in accord with experimental procedures. The literature generally is lacking in studies demonstrating the psychometric equivalence of these altered instruments with the original lists from which they were derived. Until proved to the contrary, we must consider the possibility that the reliability, the susceptibility to response set, and perhaps even the validity of certain checklists may vary with administrational procedures.

Validity

A comprehensive examination of studies bearing on the validity of various adjective checklist techniques is beyond the scope of this chapter. In terms of construct validity, the more thoroughly developed checklists do compare favorably as measurement techniques with other inventory methods of assessment. (The interested reader is referred to the ACL and MAACL manuals for thorough summaries of validational studies on these instruments.)

Nevertheless, several comments on the topic of validity seem to be in order. While the manuals for these two widely used check lists offer encouraging evidence of the concurrent and construct validities of the ACL and MAACL, one is simultaneously struck by the problems of discriminant validity associated with both instruments.

The ACL manual suggests that most of the scale intercorrelations are low enough to indicate an adequate degree of independence, though some scale intercorrelations are "rather high." Gough and Heilbrun (1965) suggest that such correlations are in large measure attributable to the fact that several scales overlap, having an appreciable number of items in common. They further indicate that it has not been possible to reduce overlap without simultaneously impairing validity. Nevertheless one of the most telling criticisms directed at the ACL has been that of low discriminant validity. Evans (1971) found a number of correlations between ACL scales which were "disturbingly high." Of 253 interscale correlations computed 211 were significant with thirty-three of these between .70 and .88, accounting for 49 percent to 77 percent of the total variance. These coefficients are considerably higher than those reported in the manual and Evans consequently concluded that the independence of some scales must be questioned. He suggests that if the ACL is to be maximally useful, overlapping items and interscale correlations should be reduced even at the expense of combining some scales. Several factor analyses of the ACL have been performed (Parker and Megargee, 1967; Scarr, 1966; McLaughlin, 1971; and Scott and Day, 1972) each yielding three or four factors which might be used in analyzing ACL responses. Scarr (1966) similarly reports thirty-one intercorrelations of a magnitude $r \geq .70$, accounting for half or more of the total variance. The convergent and discriminant validity of the ACL has further been investigated by Bouchard (1968) using the Dominance, Endurance and Order scales of the ACL. He concludes that all three variables meet the criteria of convergent validity but that the three scales meet the criteria of discriminant validity minimally or not at all. Bouchard, too, concluded that item overlap should be reduced and all scales subjected to further refinement.

Interscale correlations on the MAACL are comparably high. The MAACL manual reports correlations among the three scales ranging from .50 for anxiety and hostility to .86 for anxiety and depression. The sizeable interrelationships have been substantiated by other authors, including Datel, Gieseking, Engle, and Dougher (1966) who report MAACL interscale correlations ranging from .51 to .75 and Pankratz, Glaudin, and Goodmonson (1972) whose lowest scale intercorrelations ranged from .59 to .89. Commenting on the scale intercorrelations, Zuckerman, Lubin, Vogel, and Valerius (1964) suggest that the scales may be measuring a general "affect arousal," and Pankratz, Glaudin, and Goodmonson (1972) conclude that the three affect scales are in fact one score which might best be represented by sum scores.

The fact that problems of discriminant validity plague both of these instruments raises some interesting questions.

Are interscale correlations such as those reported to be expected on theoretical grounds? Perhaps there are no independent negative affects, as some authors have suggested. Thus anxiety, depression, and hostility may actually be substantially related, and the reported scale intercorrelations may simply reflect this "true" relationship. Similarly, ACL scale intercorrelations may reflect an "actual" relationship between Murray's needs to a greater extent than they reflect method variance.

Is low discriminant validity a characteristic of checklists in general? The fact that two of the most thoroughly developed and frequently used checklists simultaneously face the problem of poor discriminant validity in spite of differences in scope, focus, and methods of construction (the MAACL was developed empirically; the ACL rationally) suggests the possibility that substantial scale inter-correlations may characterize checklist measures. Whether or not poor discriminant validity is indeed a general characteristic of check-list tests remains to be seen. Differences in scoring procedures, meth-ods of construction, and the lack of reliability statistics for many available instruments make definitive conclusions difficult. Nonethe-less, there is evidence suggesting that checklist instruments may not be so discriminating as other personality measures.

Regardless of the interpretation chosen to account for such intercorrelations, the low discriminant validity of these instruments does pose problems of interpretation in evaluating experimental out-comes. An experiment, for example, which determines that several significant differences exist between groups on the basis of scores on a checklist with intercorrelated scales might suggest that these groups differ in several important respects, as indicated by signifi-cantly different scale scores. And yet, these significantly different scale scores might, because of scale intercorrelations, reflect only one or two substantial differences between groups. Intercorrelations thus muddy the interpretation of test results, and checklists of this nature may consequently be less appealing for specific research purposes than factorially pure instruments.

Correlates and Determinants of Responses

In spite of the vast research that has been undertaken using the checklist technique, relatively little attention has been given to factors determining or influencing responses on these inventories. Such research is vital, however, to a thorough understanding of checklist responses. A survey of available studies bearing on this topic tentatively suggests several factors that should be taken into consideration in interpreting responses obtained via checklist procedures.

Suggested Influences on Outcomes. Several studies have addressed themselves to the question of whether or not checking responses are at least partially determined by personal and situational variables. Herron (1969), using the MAACL, reported a significant relationship between the condition of high versus low anxiety and the total number of adjectives checked. Jacobs, Capek, and Meehan (1959), using a different checklist, have also noted the influence of situational variables on checking behavior, reporting that exposure to a "happiness" condition led to increases in the total number of adjectives checked, whereas exposure to conditions intended to arouse fear or depression led to a drop in the number of adjective responses.

That the instructional set associated with a checklist may influence the number of responses has been suggested by Johnson (1970). Hypothesizing that the instructions for the Today form of the MAACL would limit the number of active feelings which could be experienced and reported in comparison to the General form, Johnson found that significantly fewer words were checked on the MAACL-Today than on the General form of this test.

It has also been suggested that checklist responding may be an individual difference variable which cuts across the content of a particular checklist, Jacobs, Capek, and Meehan (1959), for example, report that individuals who report being most depressed by a depression stimulus are also likely to report being most fearful and most angry. And Gardner and Schoen (1962) report significant correlations between the number of adjectives checked on the ACL for description of self, a heroine, mother, father, a bullfighter, and a diplomat. Such studies suggest that there may indeed be general checking tendencies which cut across content areas.

The relationship between intelligence, education, and checklist responses has also come under scrutiny. The ACL manual suggests that the twenty-four scales on this instrument "are not very strongly related" to measures of intellectual functioning and the MAACL manual reports low and generally insignificant correlations between education, intelligence, and checklist scores. Hess and Bradshaw

(1970), however, report significant correlations between education and the number of adjectives checked on all ACL scales indicating that the ACL may be partially dependent on a person's vocabulary. (Standard score conversions have been adopted for this instrument to eliminate the effect of differences in the number of adjectives checked. Thus in all probability the scoring system largely eliminates this influence.) The relationship of ACL scores to educational level has also been investigated by Ivanoff, Layman, and Von Singer (1970), who compared ACL responses of beginning undergraduates in education, student teachers, and graduate students in education. Scores on only three of the nine ACL scales which differentiated between groups (Achievement, Endurance, and Order) increased with educational level. A relationship to IQ has been reported by Joesting and Joesting (1969) with a sample of Negro college students. Using the ACL these authors found that of five groups differing in IQ level, the group with the highest IQs (120 or above) checked the most adjectives. However, the lowest number of checks was associated with the next to highest IQ group (IQ level 110–119). The weight of the evidence is thus against a significant linear relationship between intelligence, education, and checklist scores.

Jenkins and Vroegh (1969), using an adjective checklist to investigate concepts of masculinity and femininity, suggest that an additional factor may be involved. They reported that subjects seem to be more willing to use extreme adjectives in the description of ideal concepts than in describing real ones and that more adjectives are endorsed when imagined rather than real concepts are being described.

The typical checklist procedure, which requires that all subjects respond to a specified list of adjectives by either checking or not checking each adjective, and which scores checklist protocols on a comparable basis, raises several additional possibilities for consideration. Checklist methodology is largely founded on the assumption that a common meaning is associated with each stimulus word. Yet, one could ask whether dictionary meanings convey similar semantic connotations across subjects, and could question the extent to which such different meanings contribute to checklist responses.

Reported contradictions and inconsistencies in subject response also raise important questions concerning the role of subjective interpretations of particular stimuli. Parker (1969), in developing a femininity scale for the ACL, found what seemed to be gross inconsistencies in the ACL self descriptions of his subjects. A significant proportion of his sample, for example, were able to see themselves as moody *and* pleasant or sentimental *and* hardheaded. He concluded that a sizeable segment of his sample (female) were able to report several pairs of logically inconsistent or even mutually exclusive characteristics within a single self-concept framework. The issue of internal consistency raised by such mutual contradictions already has been pointed out as a problem. However, Parker and Veldman (1969) also have reported that a number of words on the ACL are used in dissimilar contexts by male and female subjects. In the light of such results one might speculate about the causes of response inconsistencies both within and across subjects. It is possible, as the Parker and Veldman (1969) study suggests, that the context within which adjectives are judged is an individual difference variable which differs from subject to subject. It is also possible that the structure of a particular checklist defines and delineates a concept, by the nature of the adjectives in the list, in greater detail or in a way which is inconsistent with the subject's definition and delineation of the concept in question. In defining a concept within the particular framework set down by the checklist the subject may not recognize or may not be concerned with the inconsistencies in his responses. An alternate possibility is that the context or frame of reference within which an adjective is evaluated shifts as the subject moves from one adjective to another. Thus, not only may the meaning of an adjective vary somewhat from subject to subject but a subject, in checking inconsistent or contradictory adjectives, may be looking at himself and evaluating his behavior from two or more different points of view. By and large the literature has not addressed itself to these questions and additional research is needed to determine the degree of consensus concerning word meanings, the reasons for response inconsistencies, the subject's frame or frames of reference in responding, and the degree to which these factors influence responses.

A further issue is raised by the possibility that different subjects may approach checklist inventories with different self-instructions concerning checking (Wendt, Cameron, and Specht, 1962).

A pertinent question in this regard concerns individual differences in the threshold of response, particularly on free response checklists. It would seem reasonable to assume that subjects will respond to stimuli which apply within predetermined and individually set limits, and will not respond to those which do not reach this threshold. However, the threshold for checking may vary from subject to subject, and might fluctuate within the same individual with the adjective under consideration. Hence two subjects with equally negative self concepts might vary considerably in their responses to a particular list, with one subject checking almost any word with negative connotations, and another checking only those with the most extreme implications.

Subjects may similarly vary in the degree to which they judge a particular adjective applicable to the concept under consideration. Few studies are available in the current literature investigating the degree to which certain adjectives apply to various concepts, and one can only speculate about the degree to which individual differences in judged applicability of adjectives might influence checklist scores.

Influence of Response Sets. In examining the correlates and determinants of checking behavior, individual differences in the number of adjectives checked is a matter of considerable concern. The fact that wide individual differences have been observed in the number of adjectives checked suggests the possibility that response sets may be operating to influence checklist outcomes. In past years the validity and utility of personality measures have sometimes been questioned on the basis that extraneous response tendencies may serve to contaminate personality inventory responses. Assuming that the concern with the influence of response sets is a valid one, a pertinent question arises concerning the influence of these tendencies on adjective check lists. Individual differences in the number of adjectives checked clearly causes concerns about acquiescence tendencies. But a legitimate question might also be raised concerning the influence of social desirability and other systematic response factors.

Acquiescence. That acquiescence may be a problem for checklists is certainly suggested by the fact that individual differences do exist in the number of adjectives checked. And the possible problem is further confounded by the fact that uncorrected scale scores on checklists like the ACL often are substantially correlated with the number of words checked. If checklists like this are to be useful, some control for the number of adjectives checked obviously is essential. A checklist with thirty responses clearly is not comparable to one with 300 checks in terms of the amount and possibly the kind of information provided.

The problems posed by differences in checking frequency are aptly represented in a study by Herron, Bernstein, and Rosen (1968) on the effect of response set on MAACL-Today scores. Significant negative correlations were found in this study between the total number of checks for the instrument and scores for anxiety (−.56), depression (−.57), and hostility (−.66). A further result indicated that the total number of adjectives checked was much more highly related to scores that are "scored when not checked" (blank) than to scores based on adjectives which are "scored when checked." The total number of checks correlates, for example, −.84 with anxiety adjectives which are scored when not checked, but only .21 with anxiety adjectives which are scored when checked, suggesting that the blank component of the scale is very much a function of the total number of adjectives indicated. Finally the authors suggest that the influence of the response set may elevate reported internal reliability coefficients, since "scored when checked" and "scored when not checked" adjectives are included in each split half. This study thus suggests that a "checking set" may influence scale scores, the relative influence of part scores, and reliability estimates.

Still, a question should be raised concerning the extent to which differences in checking frequency reflect error variance, that is, a response set contaminating the obtained results, and the extent to which the differences reflect valid personality dimensions. Herron (1969) has partially illustrated the complexities involved in disentangling response sets as error variance from the variable under consideration. In a study exposing subjects to an anxiety-arousing situation, results indicated that anxiety scores on the MAACL increased with treatment, but so did the total number of adjectives checked, suggesting that factors which influence the variable under consideration may simultaneously influence the checking response. While the tendency to respond or not to respond may be intimately related to some personality factors, the problems of determining how much of the contribution of the tendency is valid and how much is error are obviously immense.

In spite of these problems, the use of the total number of checks as an index of acquiescence response tendency may bypass the possibility that the number of checks does reflect a valid and meaningful personality dimension. It is possible, for example, that subjects differ in the degree of development and differentiation of self concept and that this difference may be reflected in the number of adjectives checked. Thus, a distinction might be made between acquiescence and what might be termed inclusiveness or complexity, defined as the number of distinct variables or elements included in a particular concept. A pertinent question would thus seem to be whether there is a relationship between inclusiveness or cognitive complexity and checking behavior. Do individuals who check more adjectives have more highly developed and differentiated concepts than persons who check fewer adjectives?

The available literature offers only suggestive answers to this question. Pettigrew (1958), relating ACL responses to category width, found self-concept span, that is, the number of adjectives checked as self-descriptive, to be positively related to category width. Gardner and Schoen (1962) were unable to replicate Pettigrew's results, finding an insignificant relationship between category width and the number of adjectives checked. Stinson (1968), using the number of adjectives checked on the ACL as a measure of structural differentiation, hypothesized that a factor analysis with a battery of measures of self concept, divergent thinking, intelligence, and measures of structural differentiation of descriptive trait systems would reveal several factors including a structural differentiation factor. Results suggested, however, that the number of adjectives checked on the ACL had no relation to structural differentiation as factorially defined, and Stinson concluded that the number of adjectives checked should not be considered an operational definition of the number of attributes a person perceives in himself. What evidence there is thus suggests that the free checking of provided adjectives probably is more closely related to stylistic response tendencies than to cognitive differentiation of concepts. However, it should be noted that the conclusion is based on an extremely limited amount of data, and further research is badly needed before any definitive conclusions can be drawn concerning the relative contribution of acquiescence and cognitive differentiation to the number of adjectives checked.

In evaluating the contribution of acquiescence tendencies to checklist results it should also be noted that acquiescence may not apply to free response checklists in the same sense that it applies to inventories requiring a specific yes-no or agree-disagree response. The free response checklist instructs the subject to check those adjectives which reflect the characteristics of the person under consideration. The subject is not so much required to agree or disagree as to determine with which of the adjectives presented he agrees. In such inventories a yes or no decision is not being forced to the same extent as in other inventories and, as a consequence, the number of adjectives checked may reflect more than the strength of the tendency to agree. One can, of course, maintain that each individual adjective is a stimulus requiring a yes or no decision, but the yes "pull" would seem to be less in these than in other inventories. That a simple yes-no decision may not accurately represent the process taking place is suggested by Warr and Knapper (1967), who indicate that subjects may be responding to checklist items by agreeing, disagreeing, or deciding that the item is inapplicable. Joesting and Joesting (1969) also question the use of total number of checks as a measure of acquiescence, suggesting that a true-false format presents a more accurate picture of the influence of acquiescence on checklist responses.

Social Desirability and Other Tendencies. In discussing the relative contribution of response sets to checklist scores, the authors of both the ACL and MAACL manuals point to substantial results indicating that checklists are no more susceptible, if not less susceptible, to social desirability responding than are most personality measures currently in use. The research literature does, however, suggest some interesting considerations with regard to social desirability. Several studies (for example, Green, 1964) suggest that subjects are able to agree with remarkable consistency on the social desirability of checklist adjectives. While such results do not indicate that checklist responses reflect social desirability responding they do suggest the susceptibility of these instruments to "faking good." Several studies suggest that the endorsement of adjectives is, at least under some circumstances, related to judged social desirability. Bates (1970), for instance, found endorsement of individual adjectives on the MAACL to be highly correlated with the rated social desirability of the same items. He further found significant differences in MAACL responses on both the Today and General forms of the MAACL between subjects who were high and low on social desirability response tendencies. The evidence in the ACL and MAACL manuals against a substantial social desirability factor is nonetheless convincing. The simple fact that the adjective checklist presents the subject with a task which is understandable, meaningful, nonthreatening, and ostensibly removed from any connection with psychopathology may mitigate against the activation of social desirability responding under most circumstances; the fact remains, however, that checklists appear to be quite susceptible to socially desirable responding by any subject who chooses to respond in this way. Other factors also may be systematically operative in checklist measurement.

The fact that adjective checklists can be repeatedly administered raises the question of a potential carryover effect from one administration to another. It is possible that subjects exposed to the same checklist repeatedly, often within a short period of time, will find it difficult to respond sensitively and to report changes as measurement continues. Response stereotype consequently is a possibility in repeatedly administering any check list. Datel and Lifrak (1969) tested the contaminating effects of prior administrations of the MAACL by comparing the mean MAACL responses of military recruits in training who had undergone several testing sessions with the mean for a group of recruits also in training who were taking the MAACL for the first time. These authors conclude that carryover effects do not distort the results of repeated MAACL measurements. Somewhat different results are reported by Green (1964), however. In this study college men reported their momentary moods on the MAACL at the same time daily for periods of from twenty-five to sixty days. When scores within each factor on this test (for days two, three, five, seven, nine, sixteen, twenty-nine, and thirty) were intercorrelated, there was a tendency for day-to-day correlations to increase with repeated use of the test. Further studies such as these are needed to determine the effects of repeated administrations on checklist outcomes.

A question also has been raised concerning the contribution of serial position effects to checklist scores. Warr and Knapper (1967) suggested that the constant order of presentation of items in a lengthy checklist like the ACL might result in systematic changes in response tendencies. They tested serial position effects by comparing the number of responses made at various stages by two groups given ACLs with the words in different sequential order. Results indicated a slight primacy effect with the first thirty items receiving more positive responses than the last thirty. No effect was observed, however, for items in more central positions.

Conclusion

It is the author's opinion that adjective checklist measures occupy a unique place and serve a definite function in personality assessment. Having reviewed the characteristics and shortcomings of these instruments it might be well to reiterate the advantages of the technique listed earlier.

In many ways the adjective checklist is unparalleled as a personality technique. These measures are easy to administer and score yet they can be complex enough to cover a broad range of behaviors; they typically present subjects with a meaningful and non-threatening task which meets with a minimum of subject resistance; they can be analyzed in a variety of ways, both rationally and empirically, and they are almost limitless in range of application.

Nonetheless, as an assessment technique, the adjective checklist is not without limitations. The current appeal of the method seems to lie largely in its simplicity. The checklist is undoubtedly quick to administer and score and provides a wealth of easily-obtainable information. Yet in a very real sense these strengths may also function as the greatest weaknesses of the technique. There is evidence that suggests, for example, that what it gains in an ease of administration and scoring it may lose in sensitivity. Dichotomous responses such as those required on many checklists, for example, are less precise than those which can be quantified. It has been suggested (Wendt, Cameron, and Specht, 1962) that the possibility of measuring change is more restricted with checklists than with other methods of assessment. On an all-or-no response checklist, a subject may not increase his response to an adjective which has already been checked nor decrease his response to one left blank. And the issue of sensitivity has been raised with the question of discriminant validity. Additionally, problems arise with the reliability coefficients for many checklists, and there are open questions concerning the determinants of responses or changes in responses on checklist inventories. Nowlis (1965) has also suggested that the MAACL, because of its limitations, should not be used as the sole index of a dependent variable, and the point might be well taken in relation to other checklists.

In the author's opinion, however, the greatest shortcomings of this method of assessment lie, not with the checklist itself, but with its application. In evaluating the overall method, it must be said that the validity of many of the criticisms voiced is largely dependent upon the particular application of the technique, as well as upon the characteristics of the instrument itself. A review of the literature suggests, however, that too many researchers have yielded to the temptation of a large amount of data easily obtained and have failed to consider the specific limitations of the checklist relative to their specific purposes. With this in mind, the reader is advised to weigh the strengths and limitations of checklist methods of assessment against other available methodologies. He is also advised to examine carefully the characteristics of any particular checklist and the psychometric data available on it before accepting a checklist at face value. Perhaps because there is a great deal of face validity associated with most checklist measures, the literature reveals far too many instances of checklists employed for experimental purposes with virtually no information provided on such vital concerns as method of test construction and word choice, validity, reliability, and scoring procedures. Further, where such information is provided, consideration frequently is not given to the potential influence of such factors as variations in standard instructions or administrative procedures or to the influence of specific scoring procedures on test results. Attention to these considerations is vital if the checklist is to remain a useful instrument in personality assessment.

The hidden strength of the checklist method of assessment

lies, not in its speed and ease of administration, but in its flexibility and potential breadth of application. When the characteristics of the technique are duly considered, the adjective checklist has limitless value, particularly in probing uncharted areas, and pointing the way to further research. Appropriately used, the adjective checklist can be a quick, easily-administered, and yet valid source of information in personality assessment.

References

ALLPORT, G. W. AND ODBERT, H. "Trait Names: A Psycho-Lexical Study." *Psychological Monographs,* 1936, *47* (1, Whole No. 211).

ASTIN, H. S. "Self-perceptions of Student Activists." *Journal of College Student Personnel,* 1971, *12,* 263–271.

BARRON, F. AND EGAN, D. "Leaders and Innovators in Irish Management." *Journal of Management Studies,* 1968, *5,* 41–61.

BARRON, F. AND ROSENBERG, M. "King Lear and His Fool: A Study of the Conception and Enactment of Dramatic Role in Relation to Self-conception." *Proceeding of the 76th Annual Convention of the American Psychological Association,* 1968, 369–370.

BATES, H. O. "Frequency of Affect Adjective Check List Endorsements of a Function of Item Social Desirability." *Newsletter for Research in Psychology,* 1970, *12,* 4–5.

BOUCHARD, T. J. "Convergent and Discriminant Validity of the Adjective Check List and Edwards Personal Preference Schedule." *Educational and Psychological Measurement,* 1968, *28,* 1165–1171.

BRINGMAN, W., BALANCE, W., AND KRICHEV, A. "Experimental Investigation of McLuhan's Ideas Concerning Effects of 'Hot' and 'Cool' Communications Media." *Psychological Reports,* 1969, *25,* 447–451.

BROWN, R. D. "The Relationship of Parental Perceptions of University Life and Their Characterizations of Their College Sons and Daughters." *Educational and Psychological Measurement,* 1972, *32,* 365–375.

CAMERON, J., SPECHT, P., AND WENDT, G. R. "Effects of Meprobamate on Moods, Emotions, and Motivation." *Journal of Psychology,* 1967, *65,* 209–221.

CARPENTER, J. C. "Two Related Studies on Mood and Precognition

Run-score Variance." *Journal of Parapsychology,* 1968, *32,* 75–89.

CATTELL, R. B. "The Description of Personality: 2. Basic Traits Resolved into Clusters." *Journal of Abnormal and Social Psychology,* 1943, *38,* 476–507.

CLARKE, W. U. "The Construction of an Industrial Selection Personality Test." *Journal of Psychology,* 1956, *41,* 374–394.

CLINE, D. W. AND CHOSY, J. J. "A Prospective Study of Life Changes and Subsequent Health Changes." *Archives of General Psychiatry,* 1972, *27,* 51–53.

CRUMPTON, E., GRAYSON, H. M., AND KEITH-LEE, P. "What Kinds of Anxiety Does the Taylor MA Measure?" *Journal of Consulting Psychology,* 1967, *31,* 324–326.

DATEL, W. E., GIESEKING, C. F., ENGLE, E. O., AND DOUGHER, M. J. "Affect Levels in a Platoon of Basic Trainees." *Psychological Reports,* 1966, *18,* 271–285.

DATEL, W. E. AND LIFRAK, S. T. "Expectations, Affect Change, and Military Performance in the Army Recruit." *Psychological Report,* 1969, *18,* 271–285.

DAVIS, A. J. "Self-concept, Occupational Role Expectations and Occupational Choice in Nursing and Social Work." *Nursing Research,* 1969, *18,* 55–59.

EVANS, R. B. "Adjective Check List Scores of Homosexual Men." *Journal of Personality Assessment,* 1971, *35,* 344–349.

GARDNER, R. W. AND SCHOEN, R. A. "Differentiation and Abstraction in Concept Formation." *Psychological Monographs,* 1962, *76.* Whole No. 41, 1–21.

GEER, J. H. AND TURTELTAUB, A. "Fear Reduction Following Observation of a Model." *Journal of Personality and Social Psychology,* 1967, *6,* 327–331.

GOLDMAN, R. AND MENDELSOHN, G. "Psychotherapeutic Change and Social Adjustment: A Report of a National Survey of Psychotherapists." *Journal of Abnormal Psychology,* 1969, *74,* 164–172.

GOODSTEIN, L. D. "The Depression Adjective Check Lists." In O. K. Buros (Ed.), *The Mental Measurements Yearbook.* Highland Park, N.J.: Gryphon Press, 1972. Pp. 132–133.

GOUGH, H. G. AND HEILBRUN, A. B. *The Adjective Check List Manual.* Palo Alto: Consulting Psychologists Press, 1965.

GREEN, R. F. "The Measurement of Mood." Technical Report, Office of Naval Research. Contract No. Nonr 668 (*12*), 1964.

HARTSHORNE, H. AND MAY, M. A. *Studies in the Nature of Character.* III: *Studies in the Organization of Character.* New York: Macmillan, 1930.

HATHAWAY, S. R. AND MEEHL, P. E. "The Minnesota Multiphasic Personality Inventory." In *Military Clinical Psychology.* Department of the Army Technical Manual 8-242; Department of the Air Force Manual 160-45. Washington, D.C.: Government Printing Office, 1951.

HEILBRUN, A. B. "Maternal Child Rearing and Creativity in Sons." *Journal of Genetic Psychology,* 1971, *119,* 175–179.

HELMREICH, R. AND HAMILTON, J. "Effects of Stress, Communication Relevance, and Birth Order on Opinion Change." *Psychonomic Science,* 1968, *11,* 297–298.

HELSON, R. AND CRUTCHFIELD, R. S. "Creative Types in Mathematics." *Journal of Personality,* 1970, *38,* 177–197.

HERRON, E. W. "The Multiple Affect Adjective Check List: A Critical Analysis." *Journal of Clinical Psychology,* 1969, *25,* 46–53.

HERRON, E. W., BERNSTEIN, L., AND ROSEN, H. "Psychometric Analysis of the Multiple Affect Adjective Check List: MAACL-Today." *Journal of Clinical Psychology,* 1968, *24,* 448–450.

HESS, A. L. AND BRADSHAW, H. L. "Positiveness of Self-concept and Ideal Self as a Function of Age." *Journal of Genetic Psychology,* 1970, *117,* 57–67.

HOFFMAN, H. E. "Use of Avoidance and Vigilance by Repressors and Sensitizers." *Journal of Consulting and Clinical Psychology,* 1970, *34,* 91–96.

HOLLANDER, M. A. AND PARKER, H. J. "Occupational Stereotypes and Self-descriptions: Their Relationship to Vocational Choice." *Journal of Vocational Behavior,* 1969, *2,* 57–65.

HOOKE, J. F. AND KRAUSS, H. H. "Personality Characteristics of Successful Police Sergeant Candidates." *Journal of Criminal Law, Criminology, and Police Science,* 1971, *62,* 104–106.

IVANOFF, J. M., LAYMAN, J. A., AND VON SINGER, R. "Changes in Adjective Checklist Scales Corresponding to Changes in Educational Levels." *Psychological Reports,* 1970, *27,* 359–363.

JACKSON, D. AND MINTON, H. "A Forced-choice Adjective Preference Scale for Personality Assessment." *Psychological Reports,* 1963, *12,* 515–520.

JACOBS, A., CAPEK, L., AND MEEHAN, J. P. "The Development of an Adjective Checklist to Measure Affective States." *Psychological Newsletter,* 1959, *12,* 515–520.

JENKINS, N. AND VROEGH, K. "Contemporary Concepts of Masculinity and Femininity." *Psychological Reports,* 1969, *25,* 679–697.

JOESTING, J. AND JOESTING, R. "Differences Among Self-descriptions of Gifted Black College Students and Their Less Intelligent Counterparts." *Gifted Child Quarterly,* 1969, *13,* 175–179.

JOHNSON, D. T. "Response Set and an Adjective Checklist: A Second Look." *Journal of Clinical Psychology,* 1970, *26,* 88–90.

KAPLAN, M. F. "Repression-sensitization and Prediction of Self-descriptive Behavior: Response vs. Situational Cue Variables." *Journal of Abnormal Psychology,* 1967, *72,* 354–361.

KAPLAN, M. F. "Elicitation of Information and Response Biases of Repressors, Sensitizers, and Neutrals in Behavior Prediction." *Journal of Personality,* 1968, *36,* 84–91.

KELLY, E. L. "The Multiple Affect Adjective Check List." In O. K. Buros (Ed.), *The Mental Measurements Yearbook.* Highland Park, N.J.: Gryphon Press, 1972. Pp. 271–272.

KITCHIN, W. "Teachers View Students: an Attitude Assessment Through Personality Profiles." *Adult Education,* 1972, *22,* 136–149.

KNAPP, P. H. AND BAHNSON, C. B. "The Emotional Field: A Sequential Study of Mood and Fantasy in Two Asthmatic Patients." *Psychosomatic Medicine,* 1963, *25,* 460–483.

KULEK, J. A., MARTIN, R. A., AND SCHIEBE, K. E. "Effects of Mental Hospital Volunteer Work on Students, Conceptions of Mental Illness." *Journal of Clinical Psychology,* 1969, *25,* 326–329.

LAFORGE, R. AND SUCZEK, R. "The Interpersonal Dimension of Personality: III. An Interpersonal Checklist." *Journal of Personality,* 1955, *24,* 94–112.

LEARY, T. F. *Interpersonal Diagnosis of Personality: A Functional Theory and Methodology for Personality Evaluation.* New York: Ronald Press, 1957.

LIPSITT, L. P. "A Self-concept Scale for Children and Its Relationship to the Children's Form of the Manifest Anxiety Scale." *Child Development,* 1958, *29,* 463–472.

LORR, M., DASTON, P., AND SMITH, I. R. "An Analysis of Mood States." *Educational and Psychological Measurement,* 1967, *27,* 89–96.

LUBIN, B. AND ZUCKERMAN, M. "Affective and Perceptual-cognitive Patterns in Sensitivity-training Groups." *Psychological Reports,* 1967, *21,* 365–376.

LYKKEN, D. T. "The Clyde Mood Scale." In O. K. Buros (Ed.), *The*

Mental Measurements Yearbook. Highland Park, N.J.: Gryphon Press, 1972. Pp. 55–56.

MACKINNON, D. W. "Creativity and Images of the Self." In R. W. White (Ed.), *The Study of Lives: Essays on Personality in Honor of Henry A. Murray.* New York: Atherton Press, 1963.

MACKINNON, D. W. "Assessing Creative Persons." *Journal of Creative Behavior,* 1967, *1,* 291–304.

MC GEE, T. F. AND WILLIAMS, M. "Time-limited and Time-unlimited Psychotherapy: A Comparison with Schizophrenic Patients." *Comparative Group Studies,* 1971, *2,* 71–84.

MC GINNIES, E. "Studies in Persuasion: v. Perception of a Speaker as Related to Communication Content." *Journal of Social Psychology,* 1968, *75,* 21–33.

MC LAUGHLIN, F. E. "Personality Changes Through Alternate Group Leadership." *Nursing Research,* 1971, *20,* 123–130.

MC NAIR, D. M. "The Depression Adjective Check Lists." In O. K. Buros (Ed.), *The Mental Measurements Yearbook.* Highland Park, N.J.: Gryphon Press, 1972. Pp. 133–134.

MC REYNOLDS, P. "The Assessment of Anxiety: A Survey of Available Techniques." In P. McReynolds (Ed.), *Advances in Psychological Assessment, Vol. I.* Palo Alto: Science and Behavior Books, 1968.

MEGARGEE, E. I. "The Multiple Affect Adjective Check List." In O. K. Buros (Ed.), *The Mental Measurements Yearbook.* Highland Park, N.J.: Gryphon Press, 1972. Pp. 272–274.

MURRAY, H. *Explorations in Personality: A Clinical and Experimental Study of Fifty Men of College Age.* New York: Oxford, 1938.

NATHAN, P. E., TITLER, N. A., LOWENSTEIN, L. H., SOLOMON, P., AND ROSSI, A. M. "Behavioral Analysis of Chronic Alcoholism: Interaction of Alcohol and Human Contact." *Archives of General Psychiatry,* 1970, *22,* 419–430.

NATHAN, P. E., ZARE, N. C., FERNEAU, E. W., AND LOWENSTEIN, L. M. "Effects of Congener Differences in Alcoholic Beverages on the Behavior of Alcoholics." *Quarterly Journal of Studies on Alcoholism,* 1970, Supplement No. *5,* 87–100.

NICHOLS, E. V. AND SPIELBERGER, C. D. "Effects of Medical Education on Anxiety in Medical Students." *Mental Hygiene,* 1967, *51,* 74–79.

NOWLIS, V. "Research with the Mood Adjective Check List." In S. Tompkins and C. Izard (Eds.), *Affect, Cognition, and Personality.* New York, Springer, 1965.

PANKRATZ, L., GLAUDIN, V., AND GOODMONSON, C. "Reliability of the Multiple Affect Adjective Check List." *Journal of Personality Assessment,* 1972, *36,* 371–373.

PARKER, G. V. C. "Sex Differences in Self-description on the Adjective Check List." *Educational and Psychological Measurement,* 1969, *29,* 99–113.

PARKER, G. V. C. "Prediction of Individual Stability." *Educational and Psychological Measurement,* 1971, *31,* 875–886.

PARKER, G. V. C. AND MEGARGEE, E. I. "Factor Analytic Studies of the Adjective Check List." In *Proceedings of the 75th Annual Convention.* Washington, D.C.: American Psychological Association, 1967.

PARKER, G. V. C. AND VELDMAN, D. J. "Item Factor Structure of the Adjective Check List." *Educational and Psychological Measurement,* 1969, *29,* 605–613.

PETTIGREW, T. F. "The Measurement and Correlates of Category Width as a Cognitive Variable." *Journal of Personality,* 1958, *26,* 532–544.

PLUTCHIK, R., PLATMAN, S. R., AND FIEVE, R. R. "Evaluation of Manic-depressive States with an Affect Adjective Checklist." *Journal of Clinical Psychology,* 1971, *27,* 310–314.

RADLOFF, R. AND HELMREICH, R. *Groups under Stress: Psychological Research in SEALAB II.* New York: Appleton-Century-Crofts, Inc., 1968.

REINEHR, R. C. "Therapist and Patient Perceptions of Hospitalized Alcoholics." *Journal of Clinical Psychology,* 1969, *25,* 443–445.

RODGERS, D. A. "Relationship Between Real Similarity and Assumed Similarity with Favorability Controlled." *Journal of Abnormal and Social Psychology,* 1959, *59,* 431–433.

RODGERS, D. A., ZIEGLER, F. J., AND LEVY, N. "Prevailing Cultural Attitudes Toward Vasectomy: a Possible Explanation of Postoperative Psychological Response." *Psychosomatic Medicine,* 1967, *29,* 367–375.

RORER, L. G. "The Adjective Check List." In O. K. Buros (Ed.), *The Mental Measurements Yearbook.* Highland Park, N.J.: Gryphon Press, 1972.

SCARR, S. "The Adjective Checklist Personality Assessment Technique with Children: Validity of the Scales." *Journal of Consulting Psychology,* 1966, *30,* 122–128.

SCIORTINO, R. "Analysis of Factor Variance of Motivational Self-ratings by Male and Female Subjects." *Journal of Psychology,* 1968, *69,* 169–174.

SCOTT, W. E. AND DAY, G. J. "Personality Dimensions and Vocational Interests among Graduate Business Students." *Journal of Counseling Psychology,* 1972, *19,* 30–36.

SILLER, J. AND CHIPMAN, A. "Response Set Paralysis: Implications for Measurement and Control." *Journal of Consulting Psychology,* 1963, *27,* 432–438.

STINSON, R. C. "Factor Analytic Approach to the Structural Differentiation of Description." *Journal of Counseling Psychology,* 1968, *15,* 301–307.

THAYER, R. F. "Measurement of Activation through Self-report." *Psychological Reports,* 1967, *20,* 663–678.

VANCE, F. L. "The Adjective Check List." In O. K. Buros (Ed.), *The Mental Measurements Yearbook.* Highland Park, N.J.: Gryphon Press, 1972.

VANDERPOOL, J. A. "Alcoholism and the Self-concept." *Quarterly Journal of Studies on Alcoholism,* 1969, *30A,* 59–77.

WARR, P. B. AND KNAPPER, C. "Negative Responses and Serial Position Effects on the Adjective Check List." *Journal of Social Psychology,* 1967, *73,* 191–197.

WENDT, G. R., CAMERON, J. S., AND SPECHT, P. P. "Chemical Studies of Behavior VI: Placebo and Dramamine as Methodological Controls and Effects on Mood, Emotion, and Motivation." *Journal of Psychology,* 1962, *53,* 257–279.

WHITTAKER, D. AND WATTS, W. A. "Personality Characteristics Associated with Activism and Disaffiliation in Today's College Age Youth." *Journal of Counseling Psychology,* 1971, *18,* 200–206.

WILLIAMS, A. F. "Social Drinking Anxiety, and Depression." *Journal of Personality and Social Psychology,* 1966, *3,* 689–693.

YAGI, K. AND BERKUN, M. "Some Problems in the Reliability of the Adjective Checklist." Paper read at Western Psychological Association, June, 1961.

ZUCKERMAN, M. "The Development of an Affect Adjective Check List for the Measurement of Anxiety." *Journal of Consulting Psychology,* 1960, *24,* 457–462.

ZUCKERMAN, M. AND LUBIN, B. *Manual for the Multiple Affect Adjective Check List.* San Diego: Educational and Industrial Testing Service, 1965.

ZUCKERMAN, M. AND LUBIN, B. *Addendum to the Manual for the Multiple Affect Adjective Check List.* Unpublished manuscript, 1966.

ZUCKERMAN, M., LUBIN, B., VOGEL, L., AND VALERIUS, E. "Measurement of Experimentally Induced Affects." *Journal of Consulting Psychology,* 1964, *28,* 418–425.

VIII

Use of Group Tests in Clinical Settings

A. Jack Jernigan

As far as is known, this is the first attempt to summarize the development of group testing in clinical settings. When one considers the vast amount of assessment literature and then finds the paucity of documentation on group psychological testing, this, in itself, becomes a topic worthy of review. Most psychological writers neglect the treatment of group assessment in their discussions of clinical procedures, and, in general, leave the reader with the impression that all clinical assessment is individual.

An operational definition of clinical group assessment is necessary: group testing is considered to be the product of the administration of a battery of psychological techniques to a group of individuals at one time by one examiner. Some psychologists have considered the term *group test* a misnomer and have suggested that another designation be sought (Sharma, 1954). But while it is true

I wish to thank Verl Childers and Kathy Meyer for their assistance in library research, article translation, and preparation of tables; Walter Penk for his critical review; and Susan Gallo for her encouragement and the preparation of the manuscript. The influence of my colleagues in the Veterans Administration is evident throughout this chapter.

313

that all so-called group testing is essentially individual testing, and while it is true that clinicians do not actually test the groups as such, nevertheless the title *group testing* is quite proper and fitting as a designation for a unique and useful psychological method. In the course of this discussion, more will be said on the subject of the uniqueness of group testing as contrasted with individual testing.

Specifically, the aim of this chapter is to provide something of the historical background of the group testing movement, to discuss where the group testing movement falls within the conceptual model of assessment, to describe and give examples of styles of group testing in medical settings, to review the current batteries and note their relationship with the trend toward automation, to discuss current research, and to set forth some personal opinions about where group testing will move in the future. Hopefully, this chapter will demonstrate the importance and usefulness of group tests in clinical assessment.

Historical Background

The infrequent reference to *group tests, group assessment, group battery,* and like terms in prominent psychological texts, reviews, and journals, coupled with the apparent actual widespread use of the group test approach, emphasizes the need for a review of this subject. For example, the report of the American Psychological Association Committee on Test Standards (1966) fails to mention group test criteria in its Standards for Educational and Psychological Tests and Manuals. Buros (1972), in his Seventh Mental Measurements Yearbook, has a single section entitled Group Intelligence. His reviewers frequently neglect the question of whether given tests are intended for individual or group administration. Textbooks on assessment typically have limited their discussion of group testing to the administration of intelligence and achievement tests, and have given little or no coverage to the clinical use of group tests.

In attempting to fix in time the beginnings of group testing, DuBois (1970) identified the pioneer study of Ebbinghaus as the first group test of intelligence in 1896 with a completion test using a selection from the German version of *Gulliver's Travels,* with words and parts of words omitted from the text. This was the forerunner of a number of later, similar tests. For some reason, most psychologists have not regarded devices such as these as proper tools for clinicians, and perhaps herein lies one reason why clinical group testing has been ignored in the literature. For example, Anastasi states that "while individual scales such as the Stanford-Binet find their principal application in the clinic, group tests are used primarily in the educational system, in industry, and in the Armed Services" (1970, p. 213). And Cronbach writes that "group tests have their own content, often selected to predict school or work performance rather than for psychological meaningfulness" (1970, p. 268).

Several other psychologists, in addition to Ebbinghaus, also are important in the early evolution of clinical group testing. DuBois summarizes the early development of group testing as follows: "Pyle (1913) published age norms for a battery of group mental tests which had been described in Whipple's Manual, including several association tests from the Woodworth-Wells Series. The battery was intended to be used diagnostically. Memory was tested in two ways: by a logical memory test in which ideas were counted in the child's written reproduction of a story, and by memory span for words. Quickness of learning was tested by two substitution tests, digit-symbol and symbol-digit. Tests intended to measure inventiveness, imagination, and speed of assocation, were also included" (1970, p. 59). Stenquist is given credit for developing an early technique for the measurement of mechanical ability; his procedure involved testing large groups of children (twenty-four at a time), including clinical subjects composed of dependent and delinquent children (DuBois, 1970). It is interesting to note at this point that clinical group testing follows a pattern similar to clinical individual testing, in that the earlier development of both individual and group procedures began with children.

This leads us to World War I, when the next important phase of group testing took place, and which frequently has been described as the springboard for large-scale testing. This involved the widespread application of the Army Program with its important influence on the standardization of new tests. Hunt and Stevenson (1946), writing about the revolutionary testing programs in World War II, answered "no" to the hypothetical question of whether psychological testing made the same advances in World War II by reminding us of the immature state of group testing at the outbreak of World War I and its tremendous growth during that original conflict. Following World War I, group testing of normal individuals mushroomed, mainly in industrial and academic settings, and it has grown to the point where today most school children become familiar with standardized group tests in their first year of school.

However, by sheer numbers, nothing can compare with the massive group testing which took place during the war years of the forties. For example, at the San Antonio Aviation Cadet Center where the author served as a psychomotor test examiner, each day 500 cadets were given group paper and pencil tests in groups of 250, and psychomotor tests in groups of four, with this testing pace extending for months on end, seven days a week. And this is only a sample of what was taking place in one branch at one Center; thus, the example given was multiplied throughout the U.S. Armed Services.

When the early trickle of the fourteen million returning veterans began in 1943–1944, psychologists with clinical backgrounds immediately came into great demand, although their numbers were few. Meyer Williams, reassigned from the Air Force pilot selection program to the Army Air Force Psychiatric Convalescent Hospital at Fort Logan, Colorado, as a clinical psychologist, reports that five psychologists began processing up to sixty people a day (personal communication, 1973). The birth of group testing in rehabilitation centers probably occurred about this time as Army hospitals began group assessment programs out of sheer necessity, in the sense that there were too many veterans to deal with on an exclusively individual testing basis.

At the close of World War II, the Veterans Administration began the monumental task of guiding the reentry of the discharged veterans into civilian life, and of rehabilitating millions of men and women. Psychology was given a major responsibility in this endeavor, and the resulting VA-University sponsored Clinical Psychology Training Program had a significant influence on the field of psychology. On the occasion of the twentieth anniversary of the Veterans Administration Psychology Training Program, Ash identified the following joint goals of the University-Veterans Administration Co-operative Plan: first, to help meet the patient care needs of veterans returning from World War II, as well as veterans from other wars; and second, to further the development of the nation's manpower in the mental health field (1968). The results of the joint venture helped to mold a unique training program and greatly influenced the development of the profession of clinical psychology.

Individual assessment was the primary focus of both training and work for the graduate student who entered the expanding field of clinical psychology in post-World War II days. Certainly, at most VA hospitals the assessment of veteran patients was a one-to-one procedure, emphasizing individual psychodiagnostic procedures such as the Wechsler-Bellevue, the Thematic Apperception Test, and the Rorschach. The earliest documented clinical group assessment program began at the VA Hospital in Los Angeles on July 5, 1947, under the leadership of Harry Grayson. On republishing his Psychological Admissions Testing Program and Manual, Grayson wrote: "The first issue of the Manual (June, 1950) has been completely exhausted as a result of requests from a variety of agencies, mostly Veterans Administration and State neuropsychiatric hospitals and mental hygiene clinics. It has pleased me to learn that this Manual is also being used by a number of university training programs in Clinical Psychology and by several Army and Navy hospitals where it has served as a guide in inaugurating similar service programs" (1951).

For the past twenty years, the entire field of psychological testing has undergone revolutionary changes, and group testing has been both a cause and effect in this fast moving current called "assessment." The remainder of this chapter will be devoted to documenting a portion of this growing tide as seen from the viewpoint of group testing. To summarize the historical antecedents of clinical group testing: many psychological pioneers laid the foundation for the development of the large-scale testing program developed during World War I, and following this period group testing moved primarily in the direction of meeting needs in schools and industry. With the advent of World War II, the science of assessment had advanced to the degree that psychologists were in the forefront of determining whether men should be placed in service assignments, and what methods should be used in their rehabilitation. At this point, the demand for improvements in clinical technology reemphasized the trend toward group testing as another dimension in the assessment of clinical subjects.

Theoretical Background

In locating clinical group testing within the theoretical framework of psychological assessment, the question of why clinical group testing evolved needs to be further explored. The most obvious answer is expediency, that is, the demand for psychological services, with insufficient numbers of trained clinicians available to meet these demands through individual testing (Harrower-Erickson, 1945; Meyer Williams, personal communication, 1973). Therefore, in emergency, ways had to be found to overcome deficiencies of trained personnel through crash training programs so that it would be possible, at least in principle, to meet clinical needs solely through individual testing. Perhaps another answer to the question of the use of group testing, an answer which also is part of the American psychological scene, is the restless search of psychologists for new methods, their motivation for change, and their propensity toward experimentation.

The fact cannot be overlooked that many clinical and counseling psychologists resist doing psychological assessment for such reasons as: testing is time consuming, is believed to be of questionable value, or because they feel their time can be devoted to more relevant service functions. Psychology trainees are driven by the urge "to heal," and many of them, after a handful of individual assessment experiences, must be encouraged in order to recognize that psychological assessment can be a never-ending learning process. Group testing has helped bridge the void created by this level of low interest or motivation in trainees, and this fact in part explains its existence and continued growth.

A less obvious explanation for the continuing evolution of clinical group testing may lie somewhere within the treatment framework that brought about the group psychotherapeutic movement. As Slavson observes, "The phenomenon of grouping is ever present all around us. . . . When we deal with groups we deal with the very essence of life and the persistent oversight of group attitudes and group pressures in education and therapy has retarded our understanding of man and his motives" (1947, p. 24). In group testing, as in group psychotherapy, it is an error to speak of "the group" as an entity, since in assessment it is the individual, and not the group, who remains the center of the psychologist's attention.

This conclusion leads to an additional possible theoretical explanation for the vitality of clinical group testing, namely, that clinical group testing can be considered a new and unique resource in assessment, and not simply a dilution of or a substitute for the individual assessment process (Jernigan, 1972). To date, this viewpoint remains a hypothesis which no one has attempted to confirm in a rigorous way, though there are several relevant studies on the differences and similarities between group and individual administrations of particular techniques (McQuary and Truax, 1952; Swartz and Holtzman, 1963; Nelson, 1963). The fact that centralized group assessment has continued to grow in clinical settings which are no longer faced with shortages of psychological personnel suggests that group testing is serving a unique and significant role in its own right (Buttiglieri, 1971).

Concerning the question of just where clinical group testing falls within the theoretical framework of assessment, one can say that as a strict data-gathering procedure, group testing can meet the requirements of any conceptual model of assessment. This point is clearly evident in the conclusions of the task force on group and centralized assessment of the VA Conference on Automation, based upon its review of the variety of group assessment patterns in VA hospitals across the nation (Veterans Administration, 1971). The criteria for successful group testing programs established by the task force can be adapted straightforwardly to each of the three conceptual models of assessment outlined by McReynolds: the attribute model (prediction of traits); the decision model (whom to assign to what therapy); and the analytic model (behavior identification, distribution, determinants, and consequences) (1971). The examples of applied and research group test programs to follow in this chapter will further elucidate the theoretical orientation of clinical group testing.

Styles of Group Assessment

Since there are few published descriptions of clinical group testing programs, the information in this section necessarily comes from a variety of sources, including journal articles, conference reports, personal experiences, and interviews with psychologists who use group test procedures. An extensive survey of group test practice was conducted by Buttiglieri at the request of the Veterans Administration (Buttiglieri, 1971). While preparing a research protocol on group assessment, I made an additional survey (somewhat less extensive than Buttiglieri's) of a number of psychologists reported to have an interest in group testing (Jernigan, Penk, and Tucker, 1969). Further, considerable anecdotal information has come to my attention following participation in the 1966 Texas State Survey of Psychiatric Patients (Pokorny and Frazier, 1967); this information collectively indicates deep interest in and wide use of group testing procedures in clinical settings.

Strict attention to appropriate test administration procedures has always been considered an important variable in the science of testing, and was one of the six different aspects in the classification of projective techniques utilized by Lindzey in his proposed taxonomy. Lindzey conceived this classification as involving "a set of categories that are concerned with 'differences in the administration of the test,' for example, group technique as opposed to individual technique, or self-administered versus examiner-administered" (1959, p. 162). To explore styles in test administration further, we recently conducted a limited survey of journal articles reporting studies involving psychological tests administered to children or adults in a clinical setting over a four-year period. The fifty-eight articles meeting the criteria were distributed by method of test administration as follows: group, seven (12 percent); individual, eighteen (31 percent); both group and individual, six (10 percent); and not identified as either group or individual, twenty-nine (50 percent). The finding that only half of the studies gave sufficient information to identify method of test administration has multiple interpretations but, for this discussion, points out a possible relaxation by investigators in their reports of methods of test administration (Meyer and Jernigan, 1973).

The question of self-administered versus examiner-administered tests is a subtopic within this area; clearly, a variety of test administration patterns are permissible with tests such as the MMPI. It is my contention that well-defined group test procedures can help eliminate weaknesses inherent in the frequently relaxed administration of self-administered tests in the typical individual test setting.

Almost all known individual clinical-type tests have been administered at one time or another in clinical group settings, sometimes with modifications, and many of the group designed interest, aptitude, achievement, and industrial tests have found their way into clinical group testing programs. Buttiglieri found seventy VA hospitals to be employing some level of group testing, and further, that all the hospitals combined were using some 270 different techniques (1971). Reviewing eighteen tests which he found in use in several different countries of the world, Groffman concluded that the tests which lend themselves most readily to group application are those which are visually or auditorially administered, and which require written or drawn responses (1957). Although many others, including Harrower-Erickson (1945), Lindzey (1959), and Penk (1972) have attempted to detect techniques most suitable for group administration, there has been no known systematic study of the criteria which characterize the "best" group battery.

Early clinical group batteries such as the World War II assessment battery seem to have been selected on the basis of good clinical judgment. The test battery selected by Williams and his fellow Army psychologists in 1943 at the Army Air Force Psychiatric Convalescent Hospital at Fort Logan, Colorado, consisted of the following tests: Minnesota Multiphasic Personality Inventory, a Self-Rating Inventory, preliminary forms of Rotter Sentence Completion Test, Cornell Medical Index, Human Figure Drawings, Harrower-Erickson Group Rorschach, and a seventeen-minute interview (personal communication, 1973). Administered to as many as sixty patients at a time, they provided the clinicians with sufficient information for diagnostic and treatment recommendations for most subjects.

Grayson's initial admissions testing battery, originally developed in 1947 for the VA, underwent several revisions before it reached the standard battery outlined in Table 1 (1951)'.

Table 1.

Test	Overall Time	Area of Appraisal
Shipley-Hartford Scale	25 Min.	Intelligence level and impairment
Grayson-Perceptualization	5 Min.	Encephalopathy
Draw-A-Person	10 Min.	Personality dynamics
Sentence Completion	25 Min.	Attitudes and conflicts
Minnesota Multiphasic Personality Inventory	60–90 Min.	Personality disturbance

This battery was administered twice weekly to groups ranging in size from six to fifteen patients. A brief statement designed to establish rapport and to provide an explanation of the purpose of testing preceded the administration of the tests by psychology trainees. As a part of the procedure, the trainees were directed to record behavioral observations as well as other informational data elicited from the patients. Trainees were responsible for a written report of findings, with copies being forwarded to the patient's physician, the clinical record of the patient, and the Psychology Department file.

Grayson cited a number of advantages derived from the group testing program which can be summarized as follows: the patients' perceptions of treatment were enhanced; psychiatrists and ward physicians improved their treatment program through early diagnosis and accelerated therapy decisions; administration of veteran clinical records and rating requests were improved; trainees were afforded broader and more valuable training experiences; more patients received psychological services; and the psychologists were freed to render other significant service in areas of psychotherapy and research.

Following the pattern outlined by Grayson, the Psychology

staff of the Waco Veterans Administration Hospital surveyed the group test experiences of Grayson and others and, following a series of Psychology staff conferences, designed a battery "which would give maximum understanding of the patient," which was put into effect in May, 1952 (Baugh and Robinowitz, 1962). The following areas of appraisal were selected: behavioral observation; intellectual functioning, and personality dynamics including attitudes and conflicts. Findings were summarized so as to give diagnostic impression and recommendations for treatment. The test battery consisted of the following:

Test	Area of Appraisal
Kent E-G-Y Oral Emergency	Mental functioning
Picture Completion Test (Baugh)	Measure of reality testing
Visual Motor Gestalt (Bender)	Personality integration
Draw-A-Person	Personality dynamics
Sentence Completion	Defensive modes of adjustment

This group battery was administered to groups of six to fifteen patients by an experienced staff psychologist, assisted by a second staff member or trainee for the larger groups. Seriously disturbed, physically ill, or illiterate patients were excluded, although many of the latter were able to participate in part. A Spanish interpreter was assigned to help those patients unable to communicate well in English. The psychologists did not consider the group test battery a substitute for individual psychological evaluation, but rather as an aid in making a significant contribution toward diagnostic understanding and planning for large groups of patients. This battery and/or a modified version of it has now been in use for twenty years.

An innovative group screening technique, with complete reliance on the interview, was developed by Salzberg and his staff associates at the VA Hospital, Augusta, Georgia (Salzberg and Heckel, 1963; Salzberg and Bidus, 1966). These psychologists developed a systematic group interview, relying upon their clinical experience as observers in group psychotherapy, and upon their earlier experience with a group evaluation battery that they had found time-consuming and not adequate to treatment program demands. In early experimentation with the procedure, it was decided to limit the groups to six patients, with each patient, in turn, invited to give his ideas regarding why he was in the hospital, followed by the psychologist's facilitation of interaction among the group members regarding their opinions of each other's problems.

A formalized five-point ten-item scale evolved from empirical data accumulated over several months' use of this group screening technique (Salzberg and Bidus, 1966, p. 479). The Group Screening Scale covered the following areas: Marital Status; Education-Intelligence; Chronicity, last five years NP Hospital; Work History, last five years; Level of Work, highest ever achieved; Somatic (Complaints); Motivation for Psychotherapy; Interaction, Spontaneity, and Psychic Energy; Reality Contact; and Extrapunitive. Most of the items were rated on a five-point scale, ranging from very low to very high, with vague items such as marital status indicated on a continuum from single to married with step intervals of divorced, remarried, or widowed. The first five items of the scale consisted of self-reported demographic data, while the last five items were more judgmental, being based on observations made during the group interview. Salzberg found an acceptable level of interrater reliability (rho = .86) and a factor analysis yielded four meaningful factors: intellectual achievement, social adaptability, acceptance of responsibility, and psychological mindedness in attitude toward treatment (Salzberg and Bidus, 1966).

A personal letter from Donald Bidus describes the application of the group interview screening technique in the following words: "On the basis of this interview, a brief report is immediately dictated for each patient after each session covering the information in the ten areas and whatever else might be garnered, the primary purpose being to answer three questions: (1) can the patient handle privileges? (2) is the patient amenable to any particular kind of therapeutic intervention, especially group psychotherapy? and (3) is further formal psychological evaluation necessary? Frequently, additional statements concerning intellectual functioning, personality parameters, precipitating and maintaining factors, diagnostic impressions, and recommendations for other evaluative procedures can also be made" (1969).

The technique has merit in that it relies upon the patient's perception of his illness and, to some extent, on his evaluation of his adjustment needs as rated by a trained observer. The technique is limited in that the observer must be unusually alert and skilled in group dynamics, and must have an advanced background in clinical test techniques.

A still different style in group assessment has been developed by L'Abate, emphasizing a laboratory method in the psychological testing of a family. For many years, L'Abate has been a vocal advocate of a laboratory approach in the testing of children, emphasizing three major advantages of this method: division of labor; standardized test batteries; and "blind" interpretation of test protocols and results (1967). It is his contention that laboratory technique should be uniformly directed toward the evaluation of four major heterogeneously dependent classes of variables, namely: intellectual functioning, cerebral dysfunctioning, psychopathology, and vocational maladjustment.

L'Abate began to search for ways to extend his laboratory method with children in order to include the entire family, limiting the assessment to a single family as a unit. Taking into account Satir's (1972) framework of family dysfunctions, he began with a particular theory, and from this developed a systematic methodology for assessment. He asked such questions as "How is the self asserted in the family and how can we assess it?" (L'Abate, 1972).

The tasks designed by L'Abate and his associates to assess family groups are:

1. Family Symbol Test—using a series of fifty-two symbols (anger, hate, livelihood, etc.), each member is asked to assign the symbols to self and every family member.

2. Drawing of Pictures of Family—pictures of the family (father, mother, male adolescent, female adolescent, male child, and female child) and each drawn to represent four major feelings: anger, sadness, action, and distance. Each member is asked to select pictures which represent feelings of self and each member of the family and the subject records his choice on an individual answer sheet.

3. Animal Picture Sorting—each member is invited to sort pictures of ninety animals into four sortings, using a semantic differential approach.

4. An Adjective Checklist—this checklist is composed of items selected directly from family therapy content and is optional in the group test battery. For example, families with children under age six are excluded.

5. Analysis of Relationships Within Family—this task is organized around the description of four dysfunctions: blaming, placating, distracting, and computing (Satir, 1972). A series of 260 pictures representative of a family unit of six is used as a stimulus in the selection task.

This laboratory assessment method has been designed so that the results for a family unit can be administered and scored within an hour. The method has been shown to be a reliable and useful approach in family assessment, and has the advantage over other group methods of reviewing the family as a dynamic functioning unit (L'Abate, 1972).

Two of the preceding five-group assessment procedures were included in the programs surveyed by Buttiglieri in 1970. This Veterans Administration survey was designed to identify the scope, variety, and manpower associated with group testing in the VA system. Its long-range goals were the evaluation of the methods employed and a determination of the most workable, reliable, and effective group assessment procedures.

Almost all of the seventy-two identified group test programs were located in hospitals and domiciliaries, with a majority, sixty-four of the seventy-two, having been in existence for more than two years. As noted earlier, these combined programs included the use, at the time of survey, of some 246 different tests, many of which probably were designed to tap assessment problems at the local hospital level; nevertheless, this variety allowed for an average unique test battery of 3.4 tests per station (Buttiglieri, 1971).

A modal test battery for the seventy-two stations would consist of the tests listed at the top of the next page.

The survey highlighted the breadth and scope of centralized group assessment by disclosing that approximately 900 patients were group-assessed each week within the VA system. In most hospitals,

Test	Number Stations Using
Minnesota Multiphasic Personality Inventory	58
Sentence Completion Test	39
Shipley-Hartford Scale	36
Bender-Gestalt	29
Kuder Vocational Inventory	29
General Aptitude Test Battery	21

group assessment was employed as an intake screening device, but it also was used in a variety of other ways with a variety of patient populations. This survey, along with the other program examples cited, indicated that group assessment permits a rapid appraisal of large numbers of patients early in their treatment programs.

Research and Clinical Group Testing

Most research related to clinical group testing involves the development and standardization of individual instruments which have been found, through subsequent research, to have significant group test application (Swartz and Holtzman, 1963; Moran, 1966). In many innovative programs such as the human resources training laboratory experiments, group assessment has been an integral part of the total program (Rothaus, Morton, Johnson, Cleveland, and Lyle, 1963); and many clinical research studies use group testing as an expedient method for data collection.

An opportunity was afforded in 1966 to test out the feasibility of using large-scale group testing in psychiatric settings and to determine the testability of chronic, regressed patients under group conditions. The Texas Commissioner of Mental Health undertook a comprehensive evaluation of a 10 percent sample, stratified for age, sex, ethnicity, and length of stay, of the 15,000 patients in Texas mental hospitals (Pokorny and Frazier, 1967).

The initial plan of the psychological phase of the survey was drawn up by a committee of psychologists who suggested a tentative group battery for the assessment of 200 patients daily by five teams of psychologists, with each team consisting of an examiner and two proctors. Eighteen psychological tests were reviewed in a series of pilot studies designed to test the appropriateness of each psychological task for the population, its ease of administration, the time required to administer it, and its potential contribution to the objectives of the testing program (Jernigan, 1967b). The criteria of selection consisted of the extent to which a test contributed to an adequate estimate of a patient's present level of functioning and degree of impairment in the area of intelligence, personality integration, educational achievement, and self-perception. The pilot studies were recorded so that the tapes could be reviewed to improve instructions, timing, and sequence, and as an aid in the evaluation of an empirically-derived scale for rating patient behavior in a group test situation. The third pilot study attempted to simulate the anticipated testing environment as closely as possible. The fourth and final pilot was a demonstration of the group test procedure at one of the three state hospitals to be used in the survey, in order to insure uniformity of data collection by the five examiners and their proctors. The test battery used in the survey is summarized in Table 2.

In an eleven-day period, 1475 psychiatric patients were tested, with approximately 70 percent of the stratified sample participating in the group assessment procedure and 30 percent tested individually, or observed. The special utility of a group test approach in assessing large numbers of patients was demonstrated inasmuch as there was no known precedent for mass group testing of a state psychiatric patient population.

Ten weeks after the end of the psychological testing, a committee composed of two psychiatrists and two social workers began a review of all summarized data for the purpose of deciding the most appropriate diagnosis, rehabilitation plan, and placement for each patient. During the interval between the end of testing and the final review, the psychological data were scored, summarized, and made available for rating by a panel of fifteen psychologists who, during a two-day period, rated the 1475 protocols. A committee of psychologists, psychiatrists and statisticians, chaired by Wayne Holtzman, designed a nine-item, eight-point scale rating form that was then used in the individual review of each protocol (see Figure 1). A summary of the mean psychological ratings for each variable (Jernigan, 1967a) is reported graphically in Figure 1.

Table 2.

GROUP PSYCHOLOGICAL TEST BATTERY, TEXAS STATE SURVEY (1966)

Test Order	*Method*	*Response*	*Test Source*
Kent E-G-Y Scale D	Dictated	Written	Adapted
Logical Memory (Story A of Wechsler Memory, Form I)	Dictated	Written	Adapted
Holtzman Inkblot Technique, Form A	Slides	Written	Adapted (30 slides)
Benton Visual Retention Test, Form E	Slides	Drawn	Adapted
Otis Arithmetic Reasoning Test, Form A	Test Form	Written	Standard
Word Association (Moran 66-Item Word List)	Dictated	Written	Standard
Bender-Gestalt	Cards	Drawn	Standard
Human Figure Drawings	Dictated	Drawn	Adapted
Cornell Medical Index	Test Form	Written	Standard
Description of Condition	Test Form	Written	Developed
Behavior Observation Record	Test Form		Developed

It is interesting to note that the ratings from the group psychological test findings support the Pokorny review committee ratings which are based on decisions from a vast pool of data.

The participation of patients in clinical group testing was explored further in a study derived from a multipurpose group test research project (Jernigan, Penk, and Tucker, 1969). Many of the tests and procedures designed for the 1966 Texas Survey were in-

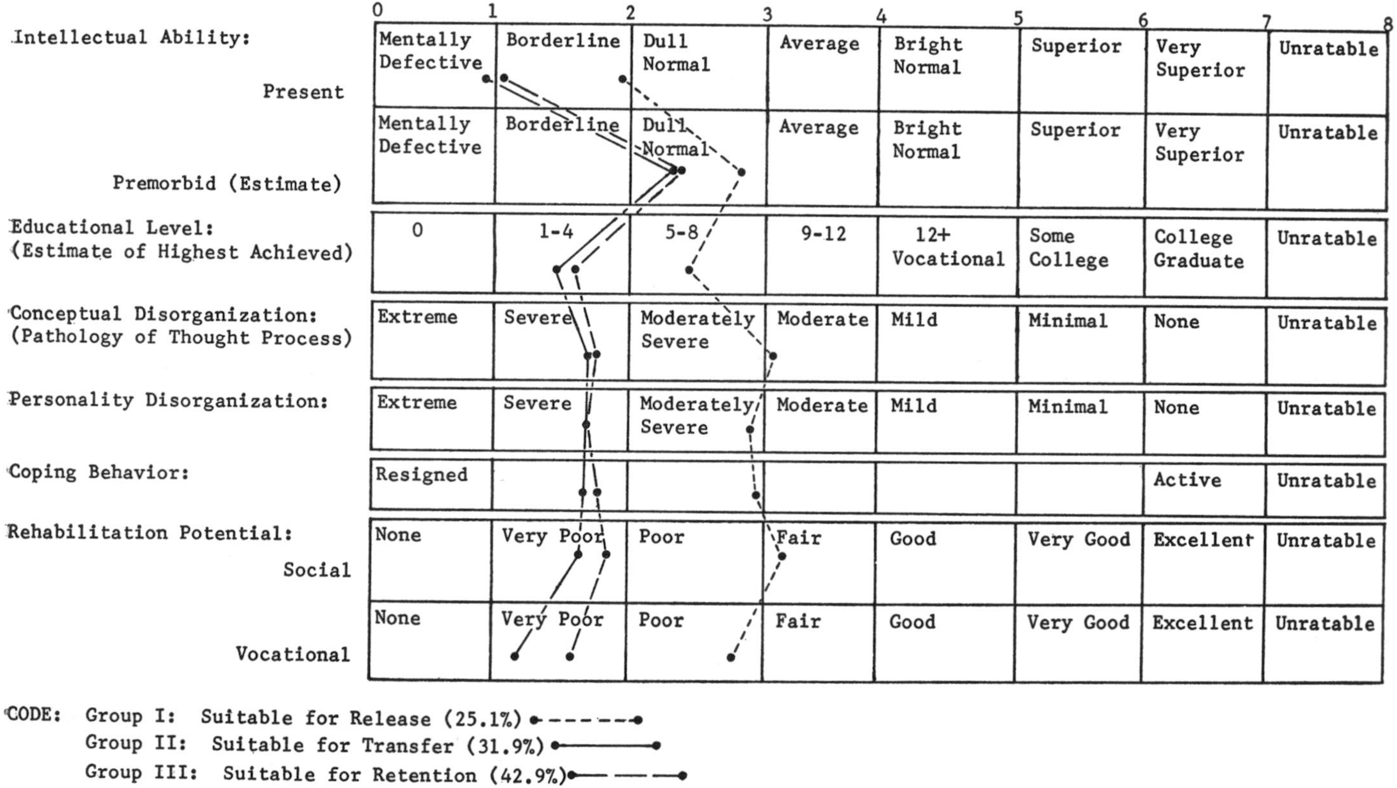

FIGURE 1. Summary of psychological ratings in survey of Texas state mental hospitals, 1966.

cluded in the group test battery that was used to assess all admissions to an acute psychiatric ward in a Veterans Administration hospital. Findings of the first six months of the program were compared with the State Survey data. For the state population, 70 percent of the sample were group testable, with an average completion of battery index of 58 percent; for the veteran population (N-146), 88 percent were group testable, with an average completion of battery index of 80 percent. Even though there were a number of dissimilar characteristics in the two populations, such as unequal distribution of sex, race, length of stay in hospital, and educational background, these percentages serve as a guide to the differences in group testability of two psychiatric populations.

Perhaps the most comprehensive research currently underway concerning group test issues is that of Penk (1972). This investigator revised the Object Sorting Test, and developed equivalent forms for use in group assessment. His work has resulted in a series of well-designed group assessment projects which have demonstrated ways to combine effectively research and clinical service. An example of the type of experimental group test battery designed by Penk is shown in his test outline for the comparison of a day hospital population with a matched inpatient psychiatric population, as shown in Table 3.

The need is great for further research into some of the fundamental questions about group assessment. For many years examiners frequently have been surprised by the unpredicted productivity of grossly psychotic individuals in the presence of other patients also undergoing similar testing; in other words, experience has indicated that even grossly psychotic patients typically are able to participate in group testing sessions. In a recent conference on group assessment approaches, Penk pointed out that "the idea of group assessment in clinical settings not only opens for review the entire spectrum of traditional concepts of assessment, but also forces consideration of new, unchartered elements—particularly the role of peer influence on an individual's test response" (1972). McReynolds expanded this idea further with the comment that "we need to do some systematic investigations on group procedures as such. We might find, for example, that some individuals do better under group procedures and some do better under individual procedures, and

Table 3.

EXPERIMENTAL GROUP TEST BATTERY FOR MEASURING
TWO DIFFERENT TREATMENT CONDITIONS (Penk, 1972)

PRE-GROUP TEST BATTERY	AREA OF APPRAISAL
Benton Visual Retention Test	Organic brain impairment
Moran Word Association Test	Idiodynamic sets
Shipley-Hartford Scale	Abstraction processes
Biographical Inventory	Demographic characteristics
Minnesota Multiphasic Personality Inventory (Mini-Mult)	Personality dimensions
Eysenck Personality Inventory	Personality dimensions
Ullman & Giovanni Process-Reactive Scale	Illness chronicity

EXPERIMENTAL BATTERY	MEASURES DERIVED FROM EACH STUDY
Listing, grouping objects	Cognitive dimensionality
Object rating (liking)	Attribute articulation
Describing objects	Attribute centrality
Listing objects common	Ambivalence
Rating objects I	Affective salience
Rating Treatment Activities	Treatment expectancy
Naming objects on attributes	Cognitive balance
Rating objects II	Objects commonality
Rating treatment activities I and II	Treatment expectancy

that some tests are more suited for individual administration and some more suited for group administration" (1972). Though many of us know that group assessment "works," it really never has had a theory of its own. We need now to investigate how and under what circumstances group testing is most effective.

A Look Ahead

In this section I wish to express certain observations and suggestions about the future of group assessment, and will discuss important issues concerning group assessment. First, I would like to refute the common misconception that clinical group testing requires less technical skill than individual testing does. This misconception may have emerged from observations of group assessment programs in education, Civil Service, industry, and the military services. In contrasting group testing with the extensive training required to administer the Stanford-Binet, Anastasi writes that "most group tests require only the ability to read simple instructions to subjects and to keep accurate time" (1970, p. 214). Buttiglieri noted that some centralized testing programs have used such diversified personnel as nurses, aides, volunteers, students, and secretaries, as well as patient assignees, as test administrators (1971). In my judgment, however, psychologists err by giving group test administration roles to non-psychologists in a clinic or hospital setting. DuBois quotes Binet and Simon on their rejection of a mechanistic view of intelligence testing and administration of the Binet: "Neither is it a routine operation, and we predict that the hurried physician who wants to have it applied by nurses will have his vexations" (1970, p. 39). The "hurried" psychologist should heed a similar warning and confine the administration of group psychological testing to psychologists, psychology trainees, or psychology aides or technicians.

Not all psychologists, trainees, or technicians make good group test administrators, however. Certainly, the criteria are more complex than simply requiring someone who can run a stop watch, read directions, and keep order. Harrower gives a sound definition for a group test administration in describing requirements for administering the group Rorschach technique; she writes: "To a large extent the successful presentation of the group method, as indeed of the individual method, depends upon a proper rapport between the experimenter and his subjects, between the psychologist and his patients. The handling of groups is different from the handling of an individual, and any administrator of the Group Technique should think primarily in terms of establishing a good group relationship" (1950, p. 147).

The selection of a clinical group battery can be an exciting step, and can serve as a stimulus to psychologists and others for the reappraisal of the assessment process. There is a host of questions which should be answered: Is assessment of this population indicated? What are the needs (and rights) of the subject? What benefits will accrue to the subject? What are the risks and how can they be reduced? What conceptual model will best fit the program requirements? Are adequate provisions made for the development of norms and for feedback through research design? What methods will be used to communicate clinical findings to the subject and to the program staff?

The selection, creation, and modification of techniques for clinical group assessment programs challenges the skills of clinicians. Lindzey attends to this problem in his classification of projective techniques: "Further, we might distinguish between the tests that are administered individually, as opposed to those that are capable of group administration. Actually, this is a difficult distinction to maintain, for as soon as someone develops an individual technique that seems to possess utility, there are certain to be a number of investigators eagerly seeking to adapt the technique for group administration. Nevertheless, at any given point in time, it is possible to distinguish between tests in terms of how readily they can be adapted to meet the demands of group administration. For example, the sentence completion test can be given in group settings very readily, while doll play or word association techniques are considerably more difficult to administer outside of the individual sessions" (1959, p. 161).

Ironically, soon after these remarks were made by Lindzey, Moran began a series of experiments with word association techniques which could be group administered to college students, and which later were adapted to patient populations (1966). Breger, in reviewing the use of tests for clinical and research purposes, counseled against the tendency toward dependence on single instruments, such as the Rorschach, and instead recommended the selection of methods in regard to specific goals (1968). A multidimensional battery is within the tradition of individual clinical assessment, and is even more necessary in assessing the individual from group test data.

The future of group testing is inextricably related to the contemporary trend toward automation in assessment, and if the two areas are properly integrated, this can reduce accusations that automation is too impersonal. Klett and Pumroy (1971) pointed out that the earliest efforts in the automation of objective testing were the development of mechanical methods for recording responses and then later came the preparation of computer programs for test scoring. Still later came the systems for scoring and interpreting test findings, the most notable being the series of computer printout interpretations of the MMPI. Recently, many of the complex clinical techniques, such as the Rorschach, the Holtzman Ink Blot Technique, the Thematic Apperception Test, and Wechsler Adult Intelligence Scale have been modified and have moved into the era of automation. However, some of the less complex, yet equally popular tests, such as the Bender-Gestalt, Draw-A-Person, or House-Tree-Person tests, have not yet reached even the earliest stages of automation. Most clinicians continue to evaluate such techniques with the time honored inspection method, but it is within the realm of possibility to bring these types of tests under the automation umbrella.

At any rate, developers of group test batteries should devise scoring systems for each task and procedure included in a battery, and should have a plan for processing and reporting the findings which, in time, could become the foundation for automation of the total procedure. It is interesting to note that in 1910 Thorndike developed a scale for the measurement of handwriting, yet over a half century later clinicians continue to overlook this important bit of data in the analyses of patient behavior (1910). The quantification of tests does not eliminate the clinician's privilege or need to scan data for intuitive interpretation, and when the goal of computer printout interpretation is achieved, the psychologist will be responsible for the total integration of the findings for the individual patient. Finally, to make the test battery viable there must be a plan for the continuous evaluation for the contribution of each test, with back-up plans for revision when the facts so indicate.

In closing, I should like to review some personal observations about clinical group testing. The usual expressed merits of group testing are that it permits mass testing, and insures uniformity of procedure, and that the role of the examiner is simplified. I agree with all of these points except the latter, a statement which is frequently expressed about group testing within the educational system or industry. Actually, as is true of group psychotherapy, clinical group testing can magnify the complexity of the examiner's role.

Uniformity of procedure usually is not considered a serious ingredient of individual assessment except that each psychologist is expected, in general, to follow standard instructions in the administration of projective and intelligence tests. In fact, many psychologists have relegated group testing to an inferior role because the examiner is perceived to be limited in his use of clinical skills in the group assessment process. A part of this misperception may stem from a reduction of the opportunity, on the part of the group tester, to follow the "voyeuristic, autocratic, oracular, and saintly" role of the individual tester as described by Schafer (Cronbach, 1956, p. 175). Even though, by definition, group testing can insure more uniformity of procedure, among the many merits of group assessment is the flexibility it offers the individual psychologist in the assessment of patients.

A sound group test program includes a manual of instructions in order to insure standardization of procedure; this is especially important when there are multiple examiners with various levels of training participating in the program. A rating form designed to summarize the observations of the examiner is necessary for rating the behavior of each subject during the total process. The test session should be limited to a maximum of three hours, and preferably two hours. This limitation necessarily requires careful preselection of the test battery. For most patient populations, only a single test session is necessary.

Size of the group is determined in part by the types of patients under review, but usually it is difficult for a single examiner to carefully assess a group larger than six to eight subjects. A group interview of ten to fifteen minutes establishes rapport, reduces anxiety, provides an opportunity for explaining the purposes of the testing, and thus adds greatly to the effectiveness of the assessment procedures. Of equal importance is the opportunity it gives the examiner to employ clinical observations, as well as to communicate to each person the examiner's interest in his welfare. A complete assessment program is obligated to give appropriate feedback to the subject, and to provide for followup, and through these to begin the evaluation of the reliability and utility of the testing program.

The psychologist in a clinical setting can find group assessment an efficient, time-saving method which produces results comparable to the one-to-one individual test approach. Consistent test administration is more accurately maintained, and data are more likely to be used in the development of local norms than is ordinarily the case in individual testing. The examination of patients in groups constitutes a situation that begins to approach a naturalistic observation of the individual, in the sense that peer, social, and cultural influences can be evaluated by the psychologist. Finally, through group testing psychologists are more likely to establish and achieve goals for automation of the assessment process.

Summary

Group assessment of medical and psychiatric patients can be as meaningful psychologically as is individual assessment of such patients; at the same time, group assessment preserves the psychologist's degree of flexibility without loss of clinical judgment. Some fundamental guidelines are necessary in conducting group clinical assessment; accordingly, an effort has been made in this chapter to outline clinical group test principles along with examples of some useful group batteries. Emphasis has been placed upon the need to carefully select and train individuals in the administration of group clinical tests, and the profession is exhorted to confine group test administration to psychology personnel. A significant merit of group assessment is that it permits a multi-dimensional approach in the testing of subjects and it is readily adaptable to a research orientation in the everyday world of clinical psychology.

So far, only the surface has been scratched in research capitalizing upon the opportunities made possible by using the group test approach in the clinic. However, of more urgency at this time is the need for research into clinical group testing itself, which should explore such areas as: What techniques are best suited for group administration? What is the role of peer influence on an individual's test performance, and what is the role of the examiner in group testing? Further, research should be addressed to the study of methods of data evaluation and of follow-up. In this era of automation, the group assessment approach can play a significant role in revealing new insights into human behavior.

References

AMERICAN PSYCHOLOGICAL ASSOCIATION. *Standards for Educational and Psychological Tests and Manuals,* Washington, D.C.: APA, 1966.

ANASTASI, ANNE. *Psychological Testing* (3rd ed.), Toronto, Ontario: Macmillan Corporation, 1970.

ASH, E. "The Veterans Administration Psychology Training Program." *The Clinical Psychologist,* Vol. XXI, Winter, 1968, pp. 67–69.

BAUGH, V. S. AND ROBINOWITZ, R. "Admission Testing Program." *The Journal of Genetic Psychology,* 1962, *100,* 309–312.

BREGER, L. "Psychological Testing: Treatment and Research Implications." *Journal of Consulting and Clinical Psychology, 32*(2), pp. 176–181, 1968.

BUROS, O. (Ed.) *The Seventh Mental Measurements Yearbook,* Highland Park, New Jersey: Gryphon Press, 1972.

BUTTIGLIERI, M. W. "Survey of Centralized Testing Program in the Veterans Administration." *Newsletter for Research in Psychology, 13*(2), 1971, pp. 29–34, Veterans Administration Hospital, Bay Pines, Florida.

CRONBACH, L. J. "Assessment of Individual Differences." In Farnsworth, P. R. and McNemar, Q. (Eds.) *Annual Review of Psychology,* 7, pp. 173–196, 1956.

CRONBACH, L. J. *Essentials of Psychological Testing* (3rd ed.) New York: Harper and Row, 1970.

DUBOIS, P. H. *A History of Psychological Testing,* Boston: Allyn and Bacon, 1970.

GRAYSON, HARRY M. *Psychological Admissions Testing Program and Manual.* Los Angeles, California, 1951.

GROFFMAN, V. K. J. "Personlichkeitsdiagnostik im Gruppenverfohren." *Journal of Diagnostic Psychology,* 1957, *5,* 314–331.

HARROWER, M. R. "Group Techniques for the Rorschach Test." In Abt, L. E. and Bellak, L. (Eds.), *Projective Psychology,* 1950, pp. 146–184. New York: Alfred A. Knopf.

HARROWER-ERICKSON, M. R. *Large Scale Rorschach Techniques.* Springfield: Charles C. Thomas, 1945.

HUNT, WILLIAM A. AND STEVENSON, IRIS. "Psychological Testing in Military Psychology: II. Personality Testing." *Psychological Review, 53*(2), 1946, pp. 107–115.

JERNIGAN, A. J. "Assessment of Hospitalized Patients." *Proceedings of Seventeenth Conference of Psychological Directors and Consultants in State, Federal and Territorial Mental Health Programs,* Sheraton-Park Hotel, Washington, D.C., August 30–31, 1967a, pp. 15–22.

JERNIGAN, A. J. "Large Scale Assessment of State Mental Patients." *Journal of Clinical Psychology, 23,* 1967b, pp. 504–506.

JERNIGAN, A. J. Remarks to Symposium: "Group Assessment Approaches." *Proceedings 80th Annual Convention American Psychological Association, 7*(2), 1972, p. 921, Honolulu, Hawaii, September 1–8.

JERNIGAN, A. J., PENK, W., AND TUCKER, R. B. "An Empirically Derived Group Assessment Approach." *Highlights of the Fourteenth Annual Conference, Veterans Administration Cooperative Studies in Psychiatry,* Houston, Texas, 1969, p. 69.

KLETT, C. JAMES AND PUMROY, DONALD K. "Automated Procedures in Assessment." In McReynolds, P. (Ed.), *Advances in Psychological Assessment,* Vol. III, 1971, pp. 14–39. Palto Alto, California: Science and Behavior Books.

L'ABATE, L. "The Laboratory Method of Evaluation." *American Psychologist* (abstract), *22,* 1967, p. 503.

L'ABATE, L. "Laboratory Assessment of Families." Abstract from "Symposium: Group Assessment Approaches." *Proceedings 80th Annual Convention American Psychological Association, 7*(2), 1972, p. 921.

LINDZEY, G. "On the Classification of Projective Techniques." *Psychological Bulletin, 56*(2), 1959, pp. 158–168.

MC QUARY, J. P. AND TRUAX, W. E., JR. "A Comparison of the Group and Individual Forms of the Minnesota Multiphasic Personality Inventory." *Journal of Educational Research, 45,* 1952, pp. 609–614.

MC REYNOLDS, P. "Introduction." In McReynolds, P. (Ed.), *Advances in Psychological Assessment,* Vol. II, 1971, pp. 1–13. Palo Alto, California: Science and Behavior Books.

MC REYNOLDS, P. W. Discussant, Symposium: "Group Assessment Approaches." *Proceedings 80th Annual Convention American Psychological Association, 7*(2), 1972, p. 921.

MEYER, K. AND JERNIGAN, A. J. "Incidence of Group Test Administration over Four-year Period as Reported by *Journal of Consulting and Clinical Psychology.*" Unpublished paper, Veterans Administration Hospital, Dallas, Texas, 1973.

MORAN, L. "The Generality of Word-association Response Sets." *Psychological Monographs,* 80, 1966.

NELSON, DON A. "Group vs. Individual Administration of the Kent-E-G-Y." *Newsletter for Research in Psychology,* 2(1), 1963, p. 12, Veterans Administration Hospital, Kecoaghton, Virginia.

PENK, W. "Problems Encountered in Revising the Object Sorting Test for a Group Assessment Format." Abstract from "Symposium: Group Assessment Approaches." *Proceedings 80th Annual Convention American Psychological Association,* 7(2), 1972, p. 921.

POKORNY, A. D. AND FRAZIER, S. H. *Report of the Administrative Survey of Texas State Mental Hospitals,* 1966. Austin, Texas: Texas Foundation for Mental Health Research, 1967.

ROTHAUS, PAUL, MORTON, R. B., JOHNSON, D. L., CLEVELAND, S. E., AND LYLE, F. A. "Human Relations Training for Psychiatric Patients." *Archives of General Psychiatry,* 8, 1963, pp. 68–77.

SALZBERG, HERMAN C. AND BIDUS, D. R. "Development of a Group Psychotherapy Screening Scale: An Attempt to Select Suitable Candidates and Predict Successful Outcome." *Journal of Psychology,* 22(4), 1966, pp. 478–481.

SALZBERG, H. C. AND HECKEL, R. V. "Psychological Screening Utilizing the Group Approach." *The International Journal of Group Psychotherapy,* 13(2), 1963, pp. 214–215.

SATIR, V. M. *People Making.* Palo Alto, Calif.: Science and Behavior Books, 1972.

SHARMA, S. L. "Group Testing—A Misnomer." *Education and Psychology,* 1954, *1,* 129–130.

SLAVSON, S. R. (Ed.) *The Practice of Group Therapy.* New York: International Universities Press, 1947.

SWARTZ, J. D. AND HOLTZMAN, W. H. "Group Method of Administration for the Holtzman Inkblot Technique." *Journal of Clinical Psychology,* 19, 1963, pp. 433–441.

THORNDIKE, E. L. "Handwriting." *Teachers College Record,* 1910, *11*(2).

VETERANS ADMINISTRATION CONFERENCE. "Automation: Psychological Assessment." *Newsletter for Research in Psychology,* 1971, *13*(2), 20–60.

IX

Role of Assessment in Behavior Therapy

CHARLES R. DICKSON

Within the past two decades, the translation of learning theory into behavioral therapeutic interventions has mushroomed from a few scattered experiments in reciprocal inhibition and operant conditioning into common practice in almost every mental health or mental retardation agency. Despite this tremendous growth in the number and variety of applied behavioral techniques, however, the development of specific indicators to determine when behavior therapy should be applied, what forms of behavioral intervention might be utilized, and what units of behavior should be the therapeutic targets has been proceeding slowly. This chapter will trace the development of the more prominent measurement instruments which have been designed to be useful in the application of behavior modification procedures.

Nature and Variety of Interventions

In discussing various areas that have been neglected within the literature on behavior therapy, Goodkin suggests that the problem of behavioral diagnosis has not received proper attention. He defines diagnosis as the selection of behaviors to be dealt with, and the subsequent determination of a treatment procedure. Goodkin suggests that clients are inclined to talk about general uneasiness, rather than about specific behaviors during initial interviews (1967). This may, of course, be a function of the questions asked by the clinician. There does not appear to be a behavioral assessment technique that dictates definitively the units of behavior that should be shaped or altered. Similarly, there does not seem to be a behavioral assessment technique that dictates the style of behavioral intervention.

Within behavioral assessment philosophy, there is a growing trend to conceive of assessment procedures as including the target behaviors and their field of reference. Goldfried and Pomeranz believe that it is necessary to include a broad spectrum of relevant factors in the assessment process. They agree with Goodkin that two of the aspects in which assessment within the behavior modification framework is most inadequate are: the identification of the most crucial targets, behavioral as well as environmental, for modification; and the selection of the most appropriate and effective behavior modification techniques. In defining the process of selecting the target behaviors in need of modification, Goldfried and Pomeranz would include appropriate attention to antecedent situational events, mediational responses, the maladaptive behavior, and the consequent changes in the environment (1968).

Cautela defines assessment in a broader conceptual framework than Goodkin or Goldfried and Pomeranz. He suggests that assessment is usually made up of three stages, "During stage one a behaviorist determines which behavior or behaviors are maladaptive. Stage two consists of developing and applying treatment strategy in three different phases: phase one: determination of treatment procedures; phase two: evaluation of on-going treatment procedures; phase three: decision on termination of treatment. In stage three, the therapist conducts a follow-up on treatment outcome" (1968, p. 175). Cautela includes the treatment and follow-up aspects of intervention as part of the broad assessment procedure.

While there is some debate as to whether traditional assessment can be useful to behavioral therapies, there is a general consensus that a behavioral form of assessment can be more beneficial.

Techniques of assessment in this chapter will be limited primarily to those utilized prior to or during therapeutic interventions. The chapter will not include the many outcome studies that have followed behavior modification therapeutic interventions. My approach will be to focus on a few primary tests in which there has been considerable work toward standardization. This choice, however, means that many aspects of assessment within the behavioral model have had to be excluded. In particular, the recent work in observation reliability (Jones, 1973; Skindrud, 1973; Johnson and Bolstad, 1973; Romanczyk, Kent, Diament, and O'Leary, 1973; Fixsen, Phillips, and Wolf, 1973; Patterson, 1971; Chapter Two in this present volume) is omitted. Furthermore, the considerable work employing psychophysiological measures in the assessment and modification of sexual behavior, in particular the works of Bancroft (1973); Bancroft, Jones, and Pullan (1966); Bancroft and Mathews (1971); Freund, Sedlacek, and Knob (1965); Bentler (1968); Barlow, Becker, Leitenberg, and Agras (1970); Freund (1971); Zuckerman (1971); and McCullough and Montgomery (1972), is not summarized in this chapter. Finally, this review will not encompass the many emerging electrical physiological measures and their potential uses within a behavioral model (Lader, Gelder and Marks, 1967; Lang, 1971; Yonovitz and Kuman, 1972; Borkovec, 1973a; and Borkovec, 1973b).

Within the clinical field, assessment is theoretically utilized to gather information necessary for decision-making. These decisions are related to potential therapeutic strategies, educational or vocational programming, and/or admissions to programs or facilities. In actual practice, the assessment information often leads to labeling without further significant utilization of the information. Behaviorists would contend that assessment findings can best be integrated within the ongoing therapeutic intervention process.

In a brief history of the role of psychological testing from the behavioral viewpoint, Greenspoon and Gersten (1967) point out that the original purposes of assessment were intellectual evaluation and diagnostic labeling. They contend that in the former, intelligence tests were used to make predictions about how well an individual would do in school, and that these predictions often were rather negative in the sense that the psychologist could predict much more successfully that an individual would do poorly, rather than do well. Greenspoon and Gersten point to the development of the therapeutic community and the emergence of behavior therapies as significant factors in a reevaluation of the purposes of psychological testing. In general, they believe that material previously revealed by psychological testing is not particularly useful for the broad range of practitioners within the therapeutic community. They also contend that the behavior therapist has not found information from traditional testing particularly useful to the nature of behavioral interventions.

Mischel (1968) suggests that the most important purpose of assessment is to design treatments implicitly required by the client's problems. In defining the process of behavioral assessment within a social behavioral theory, Mischel suggests that there are four phases that must be covered, which are defining the problem behaviors, assessing the maintaining conditions, implementing the necessary behavior change operations, and evaluating the treatments.

Kanfer and Phillips (1970) hold that the purposes of assessment within a behavioristic framework are to locate the problem to be exposed to therapeutic attention and to translate the initial complaint about the patient into a language and a set of questions that can be fruitfully pursued by available behavioral technology. They do not believe, however, that behaviorists typically are very rigorous in following these purposes.

While behavior therapists have been diligent in adhering to a scientific model and in utilizing the findings of that model to alter their interventions, a similar statement cannot be made so strongly for the design of behavioral assessment techniques. The lengthy standardization procedures of a major intelligence scale, or of a major projective test, are not to be found among the available behavioral assessment tools. This may reflect an inherent difference in the approach of behavioral interventions versus other forms of interventions. It is possible that a behavioral intervention represents a single experiment in which the practitioner applies the principles of scientific investigation in a flexible manner, rather than the application of a standardized testing approach to the client.

Behavioral assessment can be contrasted with traditional clinical assessment in terms of the various assumptions made for each approach and in terms of the personality trait theory versus the behavioral personality theory.

Goldfried and Kent (1972) describe many of the assumptions underlying the traditional and behavioral assessment techniques. They note that the traditional conception of personality functioning includes the assumption that consistencies in behavior, such as traits, exist independently of situational variables. They suggest that available research fails to confirm this assumption. Their second assumption within the traditional model is that the protocol for interpretation provides a sufficient sample of the individual's personality characteristics. In contrast to this approach, the behavioral assessment procedure uses as its basic unit of consideration the individual's response to specific aspects of his environment. A crucial requirement of behavioral tests is that stimulus situations be adequately represented in the testing process. Goldfried and Kent suggest that in a Fear Survey Schedule, for example, it is necessary to obtain measures of fear in situations which representatively sample the population of potentially anxiety-producing situations. They observe that behaviorists typically approach test interpretation from a sampling orientation—that is, with the assumption that this behavior constitutes a subset of the actual behaviors of interest—whereas the traditional personality tests have typically taken the sign approach to interpretation.

Greenspoon and Gersten (1967) give a number of necessary assumptions if assessment materials are to be useful in applying behavior modification. Specifically, they refer to the assumption that behavior is lawful; that test behavior is related to behavior exhibited by the test-taker outside the testing situation; and that behavior is learned.

Goodkin (1967) points out a basic difference between traditional assessment and behavioral assessment models by noting that there is no clear model of normality within the behavioral therapy approach. According to Goodkin, all behavior is seen as normal in terms of stimuli and behavioral consequences. One of the consequences of not having a model of maladaptive behavior is the inability of the behavioral analyst to fully describe what might be ideal adaptive behaviors to serve as a model. The options that Goodkin describes are societal standards, personal standards, and those of the therapist.

Fiske and Pearson (1970) hold that personality phenomena are multi-determined, believing that no one can isolate and describe all of the kinds of relevant variances in measurements. They further suggest that steps should be directed toward the use of simple and accessible variables in order to ascertain success in measurement of these variables. Fiske and Pearson believe that several personality aspects could be construed in such a manner that a close coordination between conceptualization and measurement operations would exist in each domain. The relationships among the conceptualizations of the several domains could then be determined at a later stage in the development of the science of personality. A Fear Survey Schedule is an example of a limited measurement within the limited conceptualization of behavioral theory, research, and practice.

Behavioral assessment is unique in the sense that it focuses as much attention on maintenance conditions as on initial change conditions. Traditional assessment focuses primarily on the condition of a single organism which might reflect a need for therapeutic intervention. In general, it does not assess the conditions necessary for the successful maintenance of therapeutic changes by an organism. Behavioral theory would suggest that the arrangement of the elements necessary for behavioral change may be quite different from the arrangement of elements necessary for the maintenance of a particular change.

Many authorities believe that one of the primary differences between behavioral and traditional assessment is in the distinction between trait versus behavioral models of personality. This distinction is frequently characterized in terms of personality predispositions versus specific behaviors; of broad personality assessment procedures versus the assessment of observable, here-and-now behaviors; and of the measurements of indices from which one can make inferences versus attempts to measure more directly observable behavioral antecedents associated with behavioral performances.

Kanfer and Phillips (1970) argue that behavior assessment does not attempt to describe the total personality, but instead narrows its focus to those variables particularly relevant for treatment. They stress that the behavioral assessment approach collects data that are direct samples of behavior in specific situations, instead of indirect and generalized indicants of behavioral predispositions. Similarly, Franks and Wilson (1973) suggest that conventional diagnosis in clinical psychology focuses on variables that are particularly pertinent to the problem. Mischel (1968) points out that trait-oriented psychometric assessment investigates either the accuracy of the client's statements, as indices of his non-test behavior, or treats his verbalizations as signs of his relative position on a personality dimension or on a criterion variable. He states that behavioral analyses seek the current variables and conditions controlling the behaviors of interest, without as much focus on historical roots in developmental etiology as in conventional assessment.

The following section covers Fear Survey Schedules, behavioral analyses within an operant model, imagery assessment procedures, and measures of assertiveness.

Fear Survey Schedules

In the past ten years, Fear Survey Schedules (FSS) have emerged to partially fill the need for pretherapy assessment for selected behavior modification interventions. The FSS is a Likert-type scale with a graded response to each item, and is scored on a point-per-item of zero to four, one to five, or one to seven, depending on the form used. The sum of the item credits represents the individual's total score.

Refinement of the FSS has begun to reach a high level of test sophistication, as will be readily demonstrated. The limited scope of the FSS allows one to see the difficulties in origin, growth, and maturity of an assessment technique.

While there are numerous questionnaires for assessing anxiety, there are very few for the measurement of fear (McReynolds, 1968). McReynolds suggests that inventory scales can be subdivided in terms of whether they are intended to assess characteristic levels of existent anxiety or the proneness to become anxious under given conditions. He further states that scales can be subdivided with respect to whether they focus primarily on antecedent or consequent aspects of anxiety. These he equates with stimulus or response aspects of anxiety. With these differentiations, McReynolds describes the FSS under the heading, "Stimulus Oriented Measures of Existent Anxieties" (1968, p. 251). Since a FSS has been designed to assess one's fear relative to a particular phobic object, and since fear is reduced by avoiding that object, the description of the FSS as assessing characteristic levels of existent anxiety is open to different interpretations. McReynolds acknowledges this when he implies that the FSS could also be interpreted as a measure of anxiety proneness.

The review of literature concerning the FSS is extremely confusing since the label "Fear Survey Schedule" covers a wide variety of approaches to standardize an assessment procedure for fears within clients and experimental subjects. Over a dozen different versions of the test exist, resulting from additions or deletions of items relative to standardization or factor analysis. Wolpe and Lang (1964) labeled as a "Fear Survey Schedule I" the Lang and Lazovik (1963) version of the scale. The Fear Survey Schedule II is a series of items factor-analyzed by Geer which was reported to Wolpe and Lang in a personal communication in 1963 and later standardized in an extensive study by Geer (1965). Fear Survey Schedule III consists of seventy-two items, based on a need for a schedule in assessing the nature of phobias within a clinical population (Wolpe and Lang, 1964). The following ten items which were taken from the Fear Survey Schedule III represent typical Fear Survey Schedule questions, with each subject being instructed to indicate how much the item disturbs him on a five-point scale, ranging from "not at all" to "very much": (1) noise of vacuum cleaners; (2) open wounds; (3) being alone; (4) being in a strange place; (5) loud voices; (6) dead people; (7) speaking in public; (8) crossing streets; (9) people who seem insane; (10) falling. The labels "Fear Survey Schedule I," "II," and "III," have lost their meaning relative to the most recent schedules now available.

Lang and Lazovik (1963) used a FSS (FSS-I) in their classic study of "Experimental Desensitization of a Phobia". They used the schedule as a pre-, post-, and follow-up measure, describing the schedule as a list of fifty phobias, each of which is rated by the subjects on a seven-point scale. Their primary interest in the experimental desensitization was with a snake phobia. They utilized Walk's (1956) "Fear Thermometer," which is a ten-point, self-rating fear scale, used in this situation to measure fear while the subject was holding a snake. This type of measure seems to be a forerunner of the FSS. Although Lang and Lazovik do not give credit to Akutagawa (1956) for the development of the basic FSS, both Wolpe and Lang (1964) and Geer (1965) acknowledge that Akutagawa constructed the first inventory.

Geer published the first definitive work on the FSS (FSS-II). He defined fear as a negative emotional response evoked by a relatively specific stimulus. Geer saw the difference between fear and anxiety as being in the specificity of eliciting a stimulus. In general, he considered fear to be a response to a specific stimulus and anxiety a response to a more general or pervasive stimulus.

Geer's subjects consisted of 783 students in Introductory Psychology courses at the State University of New York at Buffalo. Geer selected his items on an empirical basis, requesting subjects to report fears. He then grouped the most frequent fears reported. Geer had seven intensities for each of the fear items rated by the subjects, ranging from none through much to terror. Geer's test refinements resulted in fifty-one items. He indicated that the FSS-II appeared to be a scale with high internal consistency reliability.

The rationale for developing an FSS (FSS-III), according to Wolpe and Lang (1964), was a need for a description of the stimulus antecedents of neurotic reactions. Wolpe and Geer worked on the FSS independently, yet had the common denominator of basing their work on that of Akutagawa.

The Wolpe-Lang (1964) FSS-III consists of seventy-two items. Wolpe feels that these items include the most frequent neurotic anxiety stimuli that he has encountered in patients in fifteen years of practice. The items listed cause very much fear, much, a fair amount, a little, or none at all. Wolpe and Lang suggest that the stimulus situations forming the content of the inventory are situations to which it is maladaptive for a person to have anything more than mild anxiety. Wolpe and Lang's seventy-two items are grouped into six subcategories which are animal, social or interpersonal, tissue damage, noises, other classical phobias, and miscellaneous.

Scherer and Nakamura (1968) constructed an FSS for children (FSS-FC). The eighty items for the FSS-FC were selected on a conceptual basis similar to that of the Wolpe-Lang Scale. Many of the items overlap with the adult scale, however other items were developed in consultation with graduate students and school personnel familiar with children's fears. The items were divided into the following categories: school, home, social, physical, animal, travel, classical phobia, and miscellaneous.

One of the difficulties in arriving at a reasonably standard FSS has been the inclusion or deletion of various items prior to factor analysis by a number of authors. Rubin, Katkin, Weiss, and Efran (1968) completed the first of a series of factor analyses on the FSS. Their work was based on Geer's FSS-II (1965). Rubin and others concluded that the responses of subjects to the FSS-II items can be divided into four major areas. Two of these four major areas, "water" and "death-and-illness," remained relatively constant over two samples which were factor-analyzed for each sex. The other two areas, interpersonal events and discrete objects, showed some slight variability in the females of one sample. On the basis of this factor analysis, Rubin and others, assumed that the fifty-one items on the FSS-II were drawn largely from the above-mentioned four areas.

Rubin and his colleagues believe that the total score or number of items checked as being extremely fearful may, in itself, be a very misleading criterion. They point out that based on this factor analysis, there are only five items which can potentially contribute to the "fear of water" factor on the FSS-II, while there are fourteen items which can contribute to the "interpersonal events" factor. Rubin concluded that an FSS, in order to differentiate successfully between high and low fear groups, must take into account the areas of fear from which the individual items are drawn.

Scherer and Nakamura (1968) factor analyzed the eighty items of the FSS-FC and thirty-five items from the Children's Manifest Anxiety Scale (CMAS) (Castaneda, McCandless and Palermo, 1956). Through an intercorrelation matrix of the Children's Factor Scores on each subscale, it was learned that the subscales of "failure," "medical," and "miscellaneous fears" are somewhat interrelated. Most of the anxiety items from the CMAS fell into two separate groups which were labeled "anxiety neurosis" and "anxiety worry". There was a low positive correlation between these two subscales ($r = .30$). Scherer and Nakamura concluded that a factor analyzed FSS-FC could be used in the assessment of fear relative to particular cues, as pre and post measures of therapeutic effects, as a means of specifying individual differences in research arousal studies, and as a means of selecting subjects for desensitization studies.

In 1969 three studies were made on factor analysis of the FSS. Rubin, Lawlis, Tasto, and Namanek (1969) factor-analyzed a 122 item FSS originally based on Lang and Lazovik's (1963) work. The purpose of the Rubin factor analysis was to measure the generalization of a fear element. The method of factor-analysis involved rotation to an oblique structure with the result that five conceptually pure factors emerged, accounting for 90 percent of the variance, which were fears relating to small animals, fears of the precipitators and manifestations of hostility, moralistically related fears and sexual fears, fears of isolation and loneliness, and fears of anatomical destruction and physical pain.

Rubin and his coauthors concluded that forty of the 122 items could be divided among the five distinct factors. They felt these forty items could be combined into a new FSS which could be utilized for a quick diagnosis of areas of phobic reaction, and they suggested that after a particular desensitization hierarchy had been accomplished, the new FSS could be employed to measure generalization of the elimination of fear towards stimuli similar to those already desensitized. In this way a therapist could decide when it was no longer necessary to go through an additional hierarchy.

Braun and Reynolds (1969) constructed a 100-item FSS inventory based on previously published FSSs. They factor-analyzed the 100-item inventory and found twenty-one interpretable factors within each sex. They titled the inventory "The Temple Fear Survey Inventory" (TFSI). Braun and Reynolds contrast their results with those of Rubin and others (1968). They readily admitted that the number of factors in an analysis is a function of the number of input items, and saw this as the primary reason for the difference between their findings and other factor analysis results.

The final factor analysis in 1969 on the FSS was done by Bernstein and Allen (1969). They utilized Geer's FSS-II with 946 males and 868 females in Introductory Psychology courses at the University of Illinois. Factor analysis of the total sample data resulted in six factors which accounted for 45.5 percent of the total variance: "live organisms," "social interaction," "negative social evaluation," "personal illness or death," "water," and "illness or death of others." They pointed out the fallacy of assuming that paper-and-pencil expressed fear is consistent with actual situational fear, and conceived that verbal report and physiological overt motor measures represent relatively independent aspects of fear. They cautioned that subjects should not be chosen or evaluated on the basis of total scores of the FSS-II, but rather on the basis of individual item or factor scores.

Landy and Gaupp (1971) factor-analyzed responses to the Wolpe-Lang (1964) FSS-III. They repeated the analysis of factors emerging on an initial sample, which consisted of 319 Introductory Psychology students, both men and women, with a second sample consisting of 175 similar students. The emergent factors were labeled as: fear of animate nonhuman organisms, interpersonal events, the unknown, noise, and medical surgical procedures.

Following the factor analysis, Landy and Gaupp gave the FSS-III to twenty-six subjects who described themselves as roach phobics and twenty-six subjects randomly selected from a normal population. They then computed factor scores for both groups on factor one, "fear of animate nonhuman organisms," and found that the phobic subjects manifested significantly greater mean factor scores than the normal subjects.

Lawlis (1971) completed the first factor analysis utilizing a clinical patient population. A 122-item fear survey schedule (Rubin and others, 1969) was administered to 185 patients, seventy-one psychotic clients, forty-seven neurotic clients, and fifty-nine clients classified as having behavior disorders. There were 109 female subjects and seventy-six male subjects in the research. Lawlis found three factors, of which the first accounted for 87.3 percent of the variance. These were fear of losing status and fear of social inadequacy, such as losing control, being rejected by others, feeling angry, failing, looking foolish, hurting others, being ignored, being dominated by others, and so on. The second factor accounted for 2.1 percent of the variance and was related to fear of small animals, such as spiders and insects. The third factor, accounting for 1.4 percent of the variance, was interpreted as primarily a general fear of disease and wounds.

Rothstein, Holmes and Boblitt (1972) factor-analyzed the Wolpe-Lazarus (1966) Fear Survey Schedule on 100 inpatients, including fifty males and fifty females of a psychiatric institute. They found six factors, each of which accounted for 5 percent or more of the variance, which they then contrasted with the postulated sub-classifications of the Wolpe-Lang (1964) FSS-III. Factors one, "fear of being socially unacceptable," and three, "fear of exposure to suffering," accounted for 25 percent of the variance and, accord-ing to the authors, seemed comparable to two of the Wolpe-Lang subclassifications, that is, "social or interpersonal" and "tissue dam-age." The authors did not feel that the four other subclassifications of Wolpe and Lang (animals, noises, other classical phobias, and miscellaneous) were directly comparable to the statistically-deter-mined factors in their study, namely, "fear of destructive agents," "fear of repulsive phenomena," "fear of vast expanses," and "fear of authority."

One of the consistent findings within the standardized pro-cess for the Fear Survey Schedule is the relatively higher scores for females than males on the various versions of the test. This was one of the primary findings on a normative study by Manosevitz and Lanyon (1965), utilizing the Wolpe-Lang FSS-III. Additional items were added, making a total of ninety-eight. Sixty-four male and forty-nine female college students were used as subjects. Within the range of total scores from ninety-eight to 490, it was found that the males had a mean FSS score of 188.6 while females had a mean of 207.8; the difference between these was significant. The authors proposed two explanations concerning this difference. The first is the possibility that the females actually were more upset and disturbed by the situations assessed in the FSS. The second explanation is the possibility that the females were more honest in reporting their feel-ings. There was a significant difference between males and females on thirty of the 98 items. In only two of these did the males average higher. These two were, "noise of vacuum cleaners" and "being an adopted child." The highest average score by either females or males on any item was 3.89, out of a potential of five, for the item, "feeling rejected by others," given by the female sample.

Geer's study (1965) also found considerable difference in the total scores of men and women, as well as on individual items between men and women, with women consistently checking items at a greater intensity of fear than men. Hannah, Storm, and Caird,

(1965) offered three possible explanations for their similar findings of higher scores for women. One, sex differences in response to the FSS may be a reflection of genuine temperamental differences between the sexes in susceptibility to fear, genetic in origin; two, there may be general differences in susceptibility to fear arising from differential environmental pressures to suppress or control fear; and three, the differences may indicate greater female willingness to admit fear.

Consistent with the findings on the FSS, Scherer and Nakamura (1968) collected data on the FSS-FC suggesting that girls indicate more readiness to acknowledge fears, or greater potential reactivity to fear stimuli.

In a study by Rothstein and Boblitt (1970) relating to the Wolpe-Lazarus (1966) FSS, with fifty male and fifty female psychiatric inpatients, sex and age differences were found to be significant, with females obtaining higher fear scores than males and with younger people obtaining higher fear scores than older people. Both males and females rated the item "losing control" as the one with the highest mean scores. In offering basically the same explanation for his finding, Lawlis (1971) suggests that women were more willing to express their fears than men, were more fearful than men, or the items were culturally biased so as to elicit fear responses of women. Hersen (1971) found females to report experiencing significantly higher degrees of fear intensities than their male counterparts on both the Geer (1965) FSS-II and the Wolpe-Lang Fear Survey Schedule III (1964). Hersen's findings, as would be expected, revealed that inpatients were significantly more fearful than the original college standardization sample as utilized by Geer. In addition, Hersen reports that both the FSS-II and the FSS-III have exceptionally high internal consistency in addition to being highly correlated. Bernstein and Allen (1969), in utilizing the Geer FSS-II, also found a significant difference between males and females in terms of reported fear, with the females reporting the higher intensities.

Suinn (1969) attempted to measure change over time, or test-retest reliability, on the FSS and the Test Anxiety Scale (TAS) (Sarason, 1957). He omitted the item "feeling rejected by others," and included twenty-three new items. Suinn gave the FSS and TAS to eighty-two students enrolled in a state university, and reexamined the same students five weeks later. The mean scores for the FSS were 222.54 for the first testing (S.D. = 56.8) and 212.40 for the second testing (S.D. = 56.1). The test-retest reliability of the FSS was .72, and the analogous reliability of the TAS was .78. In a later study, Tasto and Suinn (1972), using a 122-item FSS, measured changes on total scale score and factor scale scores over a ten week period for nontreated subjects. The subjects consisted of approximately 100 students at Colorado State University. The authors found that while the scale factors and total scores were relatively stable over time, mean differences on some factors did occur without therapeutic intervention. They caution that such differences should be accounted for when using the FSS as a measure of therapeutic effectiveness, and noted that all of the statistically significant changes represent decreases in factor or total scores.

The various reported correlations of the Fear Survey Schedule to other tests of anxiety do not present a clear discrimination between anxiety as measured by standardized tests and fear as measured by the various versions of the Fear Survey Schedule. Geer (1965) found that the FSS-II correlated positively with the Taylor (1953) Manifest Anxiety Scale (MAS) and the Welsh (1965) A Scale. He also found a low negative correlation with social desirability. Manosevitz and Lanyon (1965), using males as subjects, found a correlation of .27 between the Fear Survey Scale and Taylor Manifest Anxiety Scale. Grossberg and Wilson (1965) found that the Wolpe-Lang FSS-III and the Taylor Manifest Anxiety Scale had a correlation of .46, based on administration to 203 male and 302 female undergraduate students. Grossberg and Wilson suggested that both tests are measuring some of the common aspects of behavior to a limited degree, but that the tests definitely are not interchangeable. Suinn (1969) found a correlation of .49 between the Test Anxiety Scale (TAS) (Sarason, 1957) and a modified version of the FSS. This particular version had ninety-eight items, most of which came from the Wolpe-Lang FSS-III. In a second study, they found a correlation of .38 between the two scales. Utilizing the Wolpe-Lazarus FSS (1966), Bates (1971) found after factor-analyzing the results that the largest factor, "tissue damage-medical," was uncorrelated with either the MAS or the Minnesota Multiphasic Personality Inventory (MMPI) scales. Bates' study utilized 100 male subjects who were classified as neurotic. He found that total fear survey schedule scores and factor two, "interpersonal," showed a similar pattern of significant positive associations with both the MAS and MMPI. Bates concluded that reports of fears in specified areas may be unrelated to reports of general fearfulness and trait anxiety and also that factors accounting for most of the variance of the FSS may be tapping dimensions independent of those measured by scales of the MMPI.

In correlating the Children's Manifest Anxiety Scale (Castaneda, McCandless and Palermo, 1956) with the Fear Survey Schedule for Children, Scherer and Nakamura (1968) found a correlation of .55. The authors suggest that the FSS-FC theoretically measures the type and effectiveness of fear stimuli which evoke emotional arousal. In contrast, they believe the Children's Manifest Anxiety Scale measures the predisposition for anxiety or drive level. They recommend using the two scales in conjunction with one another.

Tasto and Hickson (1970) were the first to attempt to standardize and scale the FSS. They utilized original work by Lang and Lazovik (1963) as their format (this was not the original fifty-item list as published by Lang and Lazovik; rather, it was an unpublished 122-item pool). These investigations attempted to standardize, analyze, and scale each item on the 122-item FSS. They hold that it is more valuable to know how a subject rates a given item relative to the population than it is to know the absolute score he gives the item. Further, they suggest that this approach handles the problem of "social desirability" (Tasto and Hickson, 1970, p. 483), arguing that if an individual has a high degree of anxiety over a specific stimulus, but perhaps rates only a three rather than a five on that item because it is socially undesirable to have such a fear, this information would not be apparent from looking solely at his raw score, whereas if the average rating on that item were low, for example 1.5, due to social desirability affecting the "average" person, the individual's above-average fear rating in that item would become apparent in the scale score which would be weighted well above average. Tasto and Hickson indicate that their research should not be generalized beyond the college population and that standardization and scaling should also take place with other populations.

Tasto, Hickson and Rubin (1971), utilizing the factor analysis completed by Rubin and others (1969) and the standardization item analysis and scaling completed by Tasto and Hickson (1970), attempted to develop a profile analysis in T-score terms for the five factors that were factor-analyzed from the 122-item FSS. The authors first found the mean scale score for each factor, with the factors being: fears relating to small animals, fears of the precipitators and manifestations of hostility, primitive moralistically-related fears and sexual fears, fears of isolation and loneliness, and fears of anatomical destruction and physical pain. They then converted these values to T scores of fifty, with standard deviations of ten.

A study by Levis (1969) exemplifies one usage of the FSS in research. Levis was concerned with the measurement of distance from a phobic test object as used in analogue studies. He suggested that latency of movement toward the phobic test object would be an additional meaningful measure of fear, and accordingly designed an apparatus containing the phobic test object, which in this case was a snake or a rat that could be moved toward the subject in one foot increments when the subject pressed a button. The FSS-II was used as a pretest measure. In addition, the items "fear of snakes" and "fear of rats" were used as measured when the snake or rat was at its greatest distance from the subject and at the closest approach that the subject would allow. The initial usage of the FSS was as a screening device to recruit subjects who rated high on fear of snakes or rats. It was found that when these particular items were given immediately before the subject was to press the button, bringing the snake or rat closer, the scores on the scales discriminated subjects who would contact the phobic object from those who would not.

Borkovec and Craighead (1971) contrasted measurements obtained when a subject approaches a feared object, such as a snake or a rat, in a traditional manner (that is, by walking toward the rat, eventually touching it, and picking it up) with measurements obtained by the phobic test apparatus measurement system as described by Levis. They found equally reliable measurements in four groups of subjects on approach, on pulse-rate scores, and on discrimination of touch and no-touch subjects on the basis of response latency in both test methods. They concluded that the two test methods may be reliably used either alone or in combination to assess fear, as defined by physical approach to the phobic object or by pulse rate indices. They further concluded that repeated testing with either method, or a combination of methods, results in similar change (decrease) in fear behavior as measured by approach distance and self-reported fear, and that such testing also results in similar lack of change in fear behavior as measured by pulse rate.

Utilizing the phobic test apparatus format, Mac and Fazio (1972) hypothesized that adding the dimension of time in the measurement of approaches to a phobic object (in this case, cockroaches) would increase the sensitivity of the attitudinal-behavioral evaluation. Through a series of timed and untimed approaches to the aversive stimulus, Mac and Fazio were able to demonstrate support for their hypothesis; that is, that the addition of the time variable produced a more sensitive measure of approach-avoidance behavior. They believe that by adding the time dimension it may be possible to reduce some of the attitude-behavior inconsistencies in the measurement of fear and/or anxiety.

Geer (1965) completed a series of validity studies on the FSS-II. He differentiated subjects into high fear, medium fear, and low fear groups on the basis of FSS-II scores. Subjects were asked to approach a fear stimulus such as a dog or a rat. Measures included latency in seconds from the end of the instructions until the subject either touched the fear stimulus or was at his point of closest proximity to it; distance in inches at which the subject stopped from the fear stimulus, if he did not touch it; subjects' self-rating of fear on the seven-point scale; ratings of a subject by an experimenter; and lastly, Zuckerman's (1960) Multiple Affect Adjective Check List. In general, Geer found the measures were consistent with the differentiations made on the basis of original FSS scores.

The second study by Geer (1965) involved introducing a time delay between instructions and execution of the experimental task. In general, it was found that high fear subjects were more resistant to change than low fear subjects in terms of the time delay.

In a followup study, Geer (1966), using the FSS-II, rated thirty-two female undergraduates as high fear or low fear on spiders. Experimental subjects also checked "no fear" for snakes. Subjects were then shown several pictures, some of which were of spiders and snakes. Geer had appropriate control groups for the experimental condition. The results were higher and longer durations of GSR intensities for experimental subjects. Geer concluded that subjects were either reflecting an increased emotional response relative to pictures of FSS-II high-fear items, or they were responding with increased attention to these particular pictures.

Weiss, Katkin and Rubin (1969) attempted to test the utility of one of the derived factors, "fear of death and illness," from the Rubin and others (1968) factor analysis of the FSS-II. Subjects who scored differentially on the "fear of death and illness" factor were shown a film which stressed the deleterious and even fatal effects of a specific disease. It was postulated that following the presentation of such a film, subjects scoring high on the "fear of death and illness" factor would perform less efficiently on a complex task than would subjects scoring low on the factor. The dependent variable was motor errors and perceptual errors on a modified version of a Digit Symbol subtest of the Wechsler-Bellevue Intelligence Scale. In general, response disruption on the task took place for those subjects who scored high on the factor in question and did not exist for those subjects scoring low in the factor.

Lawlis (1971) found indications that subjects in different diagnostic categories differ in their responses to fear items. Neurotic and psychotic subjects in his study had significantly higher overall scores on the fear schedule than did subjects diagnosed as having behavior disorders.

Adams and Rothstein (1971) found that by utilizing the Wolpe-Lazarus (1966) version of the FSS, they could differentiate adult psychiatric outpatients from parents of child psychiatric patients. The adult psychiatric outpatients demonstrate higher fear factor scores than the parents of child psychiatric patients. The authors believe that these results are particularly impressive in view of the fact that parents of child outpatients often have been regarded as being in a quasi-patient category themselves. Adams and Roth-

stein presented their study as another indication of the clinical utilization of the fear survey schedule.

In general, the FSS has been utilized to assess changes in
reported fear when the method of therapeutic intervention has been
designed to reduce fear as measured by the FSS. Going beyond this
usage, Adams hypothesized that the fear survey scores of psychiatric
inpatients would be smaller at the end than at the beginning of a
period of "milieu therapy" (1971, p. 533). He used male and female experimental groups and twenty-five male prisoners for a control group. He found that both of the experimental psychiatric
groups did change to a less fearful response on the FSS, although
not as a function of sex, while the male inmate group showed no
change.

In an excellent survey of FSSs, Hersen (1973) points up
several areas in the literature that are in need of further exploration.
He concludes that the absence of long-term test-retest studies of a
longitudinal nature make it difficult to estimate the possibility of
naturally-occurring decrements of fear over time. He further indicates that reliability of the FSS has not been established with as
great a range of population samples as would be necessary for its
most effective use within the clinical area.

In discussing the tendency for females to score higher than
males on the test, Hersen suggests that it might be useful to compare
high-fear male and high-fear female subjects under different conditions of social pressure. This procedure might reveal additional information concerning the effects of social desirability. Hersen notes
the considerable overlap of scales with redundant items, resulting in
needless duplication of measurement. He believes that additional
factor analyses would help solve this problem. An additional area in
need of further study is the relationship between psychological indices and self-reported high levels of fear. Hersen's final remarks
concerning further research with the FSS are related to the attitudinal lag in desensitization; his concern here is with the frequently
noted phenomenon of overt behavioral change preceding attitudinal
(self-report) change.

The FSS represents the most sophisticated assessment instrument in the conventional test format that has yet been developed

within the behavioral model. The assessment techniques reviewed in the remainder of this chapter have not been subjected to lengthy test construction procedures.

Operant Conditioning

While various terms, such as functional analysis and behavioral analysis are frequently used to refer to particular assessment procedures in the operant conditioning approach to behavior modification, there are few systematic schedules in this area which have demonstrated reliability and which have been factor-analyzed and standardized. Interestingly, there is a notable similarity between many of the techniques in the operant paradigm for assessment and those techniques which have existed within the general field of psychiatric social work for several decades. For example, the psychiatric social work case history is similar to some of the techniques that are now evolving to assess reinforcement histories, learning patterns within the family, communication patterns, and so on. In a similar vein, some of the observational techniques are closely related to what was typified as process recording within the psychiatric social work field. Perhaps the greatest distinction between the behavioral approach and the psychiatric social work approach in assessment is the reliance of the former on a behavioral theory, rather than on a psychodynamic model for therapeutic interventions.

A second distinction concerns the developing, recording, precision, coding, reliability,and validity techniques now being utilized in naturalistic observation procedures (Chapter Two in the present volume).

According to Mischel (1968), there are six major steps in utilizing assessment relating to the change of social behavior. These are: definition of the problem behaviors and clarification of their behavioral referents; definition of the desired objectives and clarification of their behavioral referents; description of the exact circumstances provoking the problem behaviors; identification of the conditions maintaining the problem behaviors; selection of the particular behavior-change operations most likely to produce the desired objectives; and evaluation of the treatment. In recent discussions of functional analysis, considerable detail is given which could be summed under the general major steps as outlined by Mischel.

In establishing criteria for assessment within the operant conditioning area, Peterson (1968) believes that if one accepts behavior therapy as a psychoeducational task, then a type of assessment which includes more than simply a study of the individual is required. In order to successfully perform behavioral assessment, one should know the reinforcing consequences which sustain the maladaptive behavior, and one should know of stimulus changes which might elicit and sustain a more acceptable pattern of activity. Peterson indicates that designations of diseases are useless. He does not believe that a profile of traits can be helpful, nor that knowledge of dynamics is sufficient.

Kanfer and Saslow (1969) have described an elaborate assessment technique within the operant model which offers an alternative to the standard psychiatric classification system. Their approach, which is labeled behavioral analysis, attempts to answer the following three questions: "Which specific behavior patterns require change in their frequency of occurrence, their intensity, their duration or in the conditions under which they occur? What are the conditions under which this behavior was acquired, and what factors are currently maintaining it? What are the best practical means which can produce the desired changes in this individual (manipulation of the environment, the behavior, or the self-attitudes of the patient)?" (Kanfer and Saslow, 1969, p. 419).

A functional analysis stresses that the unit of analysis is a relationship between the environment and behavior, with attention not only to antecedent variables but also to the impact of behavioral acts on the patient's environment. The patient is considered to be a member of several social systems. It is assumed that his behavior contributes to the maintenance or disruption of these social systems, just as the group norms of these systems affect his behavior. In addition to the typical elements stressed within a functional analysis (such as stimulus, response, contingencies, consequences, and organism specific variables), Kanfer and Saslow also stress the need for attention to biological, economic, and social variables, to the consequences of the patient's behavior on the environment, to the patient's history, to the limit of his capacities, and to the norms of his membership and reference groups. They emphasize the importance of continued analysis, rather than simply a preliminary diagnostic analysis, and suggest that intervention may take place either with the organism proper or with his social environment exclusively or with some combination of both.

The format of the behavioral analysis proposed by Kanfer and Saslow is divided into seven major categories. The first category is the initial analysis of the problem situation. Within that category, Kanfer and Saslow suggest that the behavioral excesses should be recorded in terms of frequency, intensity, duration, and occurrence under inappropriate conditions. They suggest classifying the behavioral deficits and assets in a similar fashion. The second major category, clarification of the problem situation, involves designating the person(s) who object(s) to the specified behaviors, who support those behaviors, what consequences the behaviors have for the client or others, and under what conditions the behaviors occur. The third category is titled motivational analysis, and involves probing for the reinforcers which maintain the specified client's behaviors. Kanfer and Saslow divide the next category, developmental analysis, into three areas: biological changes, sociological changes, and behavioral changes, again posing a series of questions to gather data in each area. The fifth category, analysis of self-control, requires defining the situations in which the client can control his behavior, and in what manner he is able to control his behavior. The sixth category, analysis of social relationships, attempts to define the significant others within the patient's environments, along with their specific roles relative to the patient. The final category is analysis of the social-cultural-physical environment. Within this area, there are questions relating to the client's social milieu, such as the behaviors about which there are complaints, cultural norms within the client's social milieu, limitations, and assets of the client's environment, and so on. Implied within the outline by Kanfer and Saslow is the need for a thorough, detailed accounting of the client's behavioral patterns prior to the events which led to a clinical referral. Many of the recent examples of functional analysis are indebted to the detailed and elaborate description of behavioral analysis by Kanfer and Saslow.

A frequent utilization of assessment techniques within an operant paradigm is the assessment of the antecedents and consequences of behavior. Nurnberger and Zimmerman (1970) have presented two examples of this approach, one concerning weight reduction and the second concerning the assessment and structuring of thesis-writing avoidance behavior. In the latter case, the authors stress that the typical analytic motivational approach was unsuccessfully attempted through fourteen ninety-minute psychotherapy sessions. By providing consequences for the client's writing behavior, the case was successfully treated. The article by Nurnberger and Zimmerman represents an approach in which behaviors are assessed, contingencies are arranged on the basis of that assessment, and a contract is made with a client which leads to the modification of his behavior. This approach represents an assessment technique rather than a test. The technique is based on principles of learning, and is readily adaptable to the particular deviant behavior in question.

In applying the functional analysis procedure to a target group of children, Bijou and Peterson (1971) suggest that assessment may be viewed as consisting of four parts. The first involves an analysis of the particular difficulty that brings the youngster to the attention of a professional person. In analyzing the presenting problem, they suggest that data should be collected concerning behavioral excesses, behavioral deficits, and should include problems which involve behaviors under inappropriate stimulus control. As can readily be seen from the description by Bijou and Peterson, their format very carefully follows the behavioral analysis format as presented earlier by Kanfer and Saslow (1969). Continuing with the assessment model of Bijou and Peterson, the second part involves an evaluation of the child's behavioral repertoires. The authors would include within this area motivational assessment; that is, the assessment of potential reinforcers and discriminations between various environmental situations relating to the behavioral repertoire. Bijou and Peterson suggest that the behavioral assessor may have to visit the home, the school, or other environments in order to accurately assess the behavioral repertoires. They further state that age norms for specified behaviors are necessary in order to assess the appropriateness of specific behaviors. The third phase of behavioral assessment deals with evaluation of progress in the treatment program.

The authors stress that assessments in the form of running accounts of how a child is reacting to the contingencies which constitute his treatment program are necessary. The final part of the assessment procedure concerns assessment of behavior after the completion of treatment. The authors do not rule out the need for follow-up studies but suggest that these measures will indicate whether the behaviors assessed at the end of treatment have been maintained, extinguished, or weakened by the contingencies in the natural environment.

While the Kanfer and Saslow (1969) format for functional analysis provides the behavior therapist with a systematic procedure for gathering data, it does not allow a scientific approach in interpreting the data collected. Thus, the behavioral assessor still is very much an artist in selecting those behaviors for intervention, in deciding what frequencies define excesses or deficits, and in discriminating whether to intervene within the environment containing the controlling stimuli, or within the organism.

Yates and Poole (1972) provide a logical extension of the behavioral analysis approach in their description of a case of excessive frequency of micturition. Prior to behavioral therapeutic intervention, the authors needed to determine what constituted excessive micturition. The patient's micturition frequency was assessed and then compared with control data obtained from three samples of students. These three samples of students consisted of a total of 118 males and seventy-four females within an age range of eighteen to twenty-five years. They found that within the control group, 90 percent of both males and females had daily waking frequencies of approximately six or less, while 97 to 98 percent had frequencies of eight or less. They found a high degree of consistency in frequency from day to day, especially for very low and very high frequency subjects. The average frequency for both males and females at night was less than one per two nights. They learned that there was no tendency for a high waking frequency to be accompanied by a high sleeping frequency. The authors concluded that excessive frequency of micturition may be statistically defined as a rate exceeding eight times per day during the waking period, if this is manifested regularly over a period of time, and that a persistent frequency greater than one per night would appear to be statistically abnormal. The experimental subject within this behavioral analysis had a frequency of micturition during the waking period for one week of 234. It was obvious that the patient could be labeled as suffering from excessive frequency of micturition.

The detailed and elaborate manner in which Yates and Poole performed their research affords a good example of the general task of establishing norms for use in evaluating particular behavioral excesses, deficits, or assets in order to elevate the behavioral engineer from the status of artist to scientist.

Reinforcement Survey Schedule. As mentioned earlier in this chapter, one of the seven major headings in the format for behavioral analysis by Kanfer and Saslow (1969) was motivational analysis. This represents one area of functional analysis in which there has been a systematic attempt to structure an assessment procedure. Cautela and Kastenbaum (1967)' presented the Reinforcement Survey Schedule (RSS)' as a method for listing those stimuli which can be used to evoke adaptive responses, in contrast to stimuli which tend to evoke maladaptive responses. Within this broad definition, the authors believe that the RSS can be used by persons who engage in classical conditioning, operant conditioning or other forms of therapeutic interventions. The RSS is divided into four major sections. In the first three sections, the respondent is asked to rate items on a five-point scale, representing the degree to which the stimuli give joy or other pleasurable feelings. In section four, the respondent is asked to list things which he does, or thinks about more than five times, more than ten times, more than fifteen times, and more than twenty times per day.

Section one of the RSS consists of thirty-three items divided into ten general categories. Some of the categories, such as "beautiful women," have only one item, while some categories, such as "listening to music," have as many as eight items. The respondent is presented with an item, such as "jazz," and asked to rate whether the stimulus gives him pleasurable feelings or joy, on a scale ranging from (1)' not at all, to (5) very much. Section one consists of items that can be presented to a subject or client in conventional settings. Section two has 106 items, subheaded under forty-four categories. Cautela and Kastenbaum indicate that this section consists of items which for most practical purposes can be presented only through facsimile or imagination. Section three differs from the preceding sections in that it presents situations, rather than discrete objects and activities. A typical example of one of the six items for section three is, "You have just led your team to victory. An old friend comes over and says, 'You played a terrific game; let me treat you to dinner and drinks,' " (Cautela and Kastenbaum, 1967, p. 1121).

In an initial stage of standardization, Cautela and Kastenbaum presented the RSS to 111 male undergraduates and fifty-four female undergraduates. A chi-square analysis of the frequency of choice for each response category showed no significant differences, that is, there was no tendency to pick any one category, such as "a fair amount," over any other category. However, comparisons of male and female responses from this study, for each category, indicated that females tended to choose a greater percentage of "very much" responses for each of the three sections. Cautela and Kastenbaum pointed out the need for additional research within these areas of standardization.

Research on test-retest coefficients of the RSS was performed by Kleinknecht, McCormick, and Thorndike (1973). The initial subject group was 313 undergraduate students, of which 111 were males and 202 were females. One hundred eighteen subjects were retested after one week, fifty-four after three weeks, and 141 after five weeks. The authors found that the median correlations for the 140 items from sections one and two, across subjects, were .73, .66, and .71 for one, three, and five week intervals, respectively. Median correlations for subjects across items for the same intervals were .83, .77, and .80. Kleinknecht, and others (1973) concluded that these reliability coefficients are of sufficient magnitude to render the scale useful as a clinical and research instrument. They called for validity studies, which might include testing the effects of satiation and deprivation of certain stimuli that are alleged to be reinforcing.

Marital Relations. The terms deviance, behavioral excesses, behavioral assets, and behavioral deficits are cultural and societal terms that have ever-changing meanings. Behavioral assessment techniques can become extremely sophisticated in their technologies, reliabilities, and even validities, yet their worth is related to the values of the particular reference norms within society. Examples of this are seen in the various attempts to alter behavior patterns within marital relationships. Thomas, Carter, Gambrill, and Butterfield (1970) devised a special signaling system referred to as SAM after its acronym, SSAMB (Signal System for the Assessment and Modification of Behavior). This device is basically an electromechanical system consisting of client button boxes to transmit signals, client light boxes to receive signals, and a therapist control box to regulate the system. The rationale of the system is to offer an alternative to language communications through communication by light signals which have certain distinct meanings attached to the various lights.

In a later publication, Carter and Thomas (1973) present two examples of this signaling system within the framework of marital counseling. The authors indicate that after initial exploratory interviews with a couple, it was determined that a central feature of a couple's communication difficulties involved verbal conversational control. There was considerable interruption, with the husband tending to dominate the conversation. In order to gain further assessment of these hunches, the signal system was applied while the couple was instructed to discuss specific topics. Each partner was supplied with a signal button box and light box and the couple was told that the red signal was to mean, "stop, I wish to talk now," and the green meant, "you talk." The recorded data revealed that the husband was indeed dominant in conversation. The system provided considerable instruction to the couple in order to help them arrive at parity in the control of the signaling system and, therefore, to the eventual control of communications. The implied assumption is that the marital relationship would be better if there was parity. In a second experiment, the couple was able to speak with greater specificity in describing money problems through the use of the light signal as reinforcement for language specificity. These experiments and this technology represent an attempt to attain a more reliable baseline, a better description of baseline communications, and a system for continually monitoring the activities or behaviors to be altered.

An example of an overall behavioral assessment technique related to marital problems is presented in the form of a Marital Pre-Counseling Inventory, by Stuart and Stuart (1972). This inventory, eleven pages long, is designed to be filled out by each marital partner independently. Areas covered within the inventory are:

goals for behavior change relating to shared behaviors, behaviors of others, and one's own behavior; assessment of the resources for change within the marriage and each of the partners; assessment of the degree of mutual understanding of power distribution; evaluation of congruence of priorities; assessment of communication effectiveness; assessment of sexual satisfaction; and of congruence in child management; and measures of general satisfaction. An example of assessment of the resources for change would be a question which asks the respondent to "list ten things which your spouse does which please you" (Stuart and Stuart, 1972, p. 3). Within this questionnaire much information is contained which could very easily provide the tools for reciprocity counseling.

Token Economies. As this sampling of assessment procedures within an operant behavioral model will indicate, there is movement from the assessment of a unit of one to the assessment of marital interactions, family interactions, total hospital ward behavior, interactions in an open community and finally, assessment of the environment.

Milby, Willicutt, Hawk, MacDonald and Whitfield (1973) present a system used to record and summarize individual behavior data in a token economy program which stresses ongoing assessment, in contrast to the traditional preintervention assessment models. The data sheets described within the system of Milby and his colleagues consist of an individual patient's card, which he carries with him at all times, and a master data matrix, which contains summarized portions of the individual patient data card. The individual token cards are used to record events only where tokens are exchanged. A staff member collects or delivers tokens for the observed event, records the time, the number of tokens exchanged, and signs his initials. This information is then transferred to the master data matrix which is divided into five main sections. The first section provides space for the patient's name and his job assignment. The second section permits recording all earnings for the day. The third section provides for recording all spendings for the day. The fourth section of the master data matrix includes space for calculating the new balance for the next day. Space is also provided for recording total earnings and spendings. The difference between these two entries is then added to or subtracted from the previous balance, and the result is entered as the new balance. The final section provides for recording time sample data for the day. These data are used in establishing baselines and assessing treatment procedures. A column is provided for the reliability of these time samples. The authors indicate that the average time spent in daily preparation of the master matrix for twenty patients during a three-week period was one hour and twenty-seven minutes. In general, this format provides the staff with an accountability system relative to specified target behaviors, to how the clients utilize and spend their token privileges, and to their abilities in self-management, and which reflects any inconsistencies within the economic accounting system. The staff is able to monitor total ward progress and to know areas of deficits or excesses in particular patient performances. While the general concepts of this format have been available for a number of years, the particular program described represents increased sophistication in recording systems which are necessary within the operant paradigm.

It frequently has been observed that when rats find their way into research laboratories, they develop the skills necessary to control the feeding behavior of experimenters. Colman and Boren (1969) took advantage of these data in utilizing hospital ward recording sheets to manipulate staff behavior. Their purpose was to put the staff under the control of a data system so that the staff could evaluate their effects on the patients and devise more effective procedures for modifying patient behaviors. The primary recording matrix consisted of a description of earnings and spendings for each patient, cumulative totals for wages, total spendings, and a daily balance. These data were kept in a matrix which was clearly visible to staff and patients at all times. The procedure represented the typical token economy process, in this instance utilized with a psychiatric ward of delinquent adult patients. By collecting the assessment data, the researchers were able to learn what portions of the recorded behaviors were attended to by staff. They were able to manipulate these data so that staff would view the behaviors in a positive light and therefore increase positive attention to patients. The staff rather systematically began to attend more and more to the data matrix, and less and less to typical case notes. In essence, the assessment procedure was used as a shaping technique for staff behaviors.

Community Clinic. In the field of behavioral modification, numerous treatment techniques have been developed which, when applied to properly assessed problems, can be expected to lead to a reasonable amount of success. The great variety of techniques now available, and the large number of behavioral problems that are typically brought to a community mental health clinic and community family service clinic present the practitioner with a great host of possible combinations of treatments and problems. In an attempt to offer procedural steps that could be utilized within an open treatment situation, Thomas and Walter (1973) designed a procedure for the assessment and modification of behavior in open settings (PAMBOS)'. By examining the authors' fifteen sequential steps, one can see the similarities between this procedure and the behavioral analysis as described by Kanfer and Saslow (1969)'. Step number one consists of an inventory of problem areas, which involves client and therapist descriptions of problem areas. The same information could be derived from Kanfer and Saslow's labels, behavioral excesses, and behavioral deficits. Step number two, within PAMBOS, concerns problem selection and contracting, which basically is an agreement between client and therapist on which problem is in need of attention first. Step number three is titled commitment to cooperate, and requires some commitment from the client to a potential modification program. Step number four requires the specification of problem behaviors. Samples of behavioral components of the designated problem areas and positive alternatives are indicated. Within the Kanfer and Saslow framework, this would be a comparison of behavioral excesses and behavioral deficits with the client's behavioral assets. Step number five is a plan for collecting baseline data of focal behavior. In general, the authors are talking here about the frequency, intensity, magnitude, duration, and latency of behaviors. Step number six is the identification of probable controlling conditions. Thomas and Walter are interested in events occurring before, during, or after particular problem behaviors. In the Kanfer-Saslow scheme, this step would be labeled occurrence under inappropriate conditions (who objects to these behaviors, who supports these behaviors, consequences of particular behaviors for self or others, under what conditions the behaviors occur, and so on)'. Step number seven is an assessment of environment and behavioral resources with particular emphasis on the potential mediators, such as friend and family members, potential reinforcers, and potential aversive conditions. Step number eight is a specification of behavioral objectives, involving the elaboration of the terminal behavioral repertoires desired with those successive approximations necessary to reach the terminal behaviors. Step number nine is a formulation of a behavior modification plan, with the assumption that the therapist will be familiar with the various modification techniques. Step number ten is simply the execution of the modification plan, and step number eleven is the monitoring of the outcomes of the modification plan. During the monitoring it is important that the same measures are used that were used to establish the baseline. Step number twelve concerns the formulation of a maintenance plan, thirteen is the execution of the maintenance plan, and fourteen the monitoring of the outcomes of the maintenance plan. Again, it is important that the same measures are used in the monitoring that were used in the baseline and in modification procedures. The final step refers to a follow-up at some future designated time. As can be seen from the description, many of the steps follow the sequence of the format that was described by Kanfer and Saslow in their behavioral assessment description (1969). Thomas and Walter presented examples of the application of their plan and evaluate its utilization with thirty-two cases within two family treatment centers. They concluded that it represents a favorable approach in the utilization of behavior modification techniques within an open community setting.

Additional Techniques

Imagery. A variety of clinical treatment techniques rely upon the individual's ability to imagine various scenes or situations. In systematic desensitization (Wolpe, 1958, 1969), a person is required to report states or levels of subjective anxiety in connection with clear visual images. Covert reinforcement and covert sensitization are two clinical techniques discussed by Cautela (1968, 1970) which require visual images. In covert reinforcement, the client imagines himself obtaining a reinforcer for the performance of a desired behavior; and in covert sensitization, he imagines punishment for an undesirable behavior. Aversive techniques, as noted by

Marks and Gelder (1967), and implosion therapy (Stampfl and Levis, 1967) also require the ability to vividly imagine situations. As interest increases in these various clinical treatment techniques, methods are sought to determine the ability of the client to produce and determine the clarity or vividness of the desired imagery.

Sheehan (1967a) used Betts' Questionnaire Upon Mental Imagery (Betts, 1909) to measure the vividness of imagery. The Questionnaire Upon Mental Imagery measures seven different sensory modalities: visual, auditory, cutaneous, kinaesthetic, gustatory, olefactory, and organic. The individual is asked to imagine an object that is suggested in the questionnaire (for example, "the sun is sinking below the horizon"), and then to rate the vividness of the particular image. The vividness of the image is rated on a scale ranging from one (image is clear and vivid) to seven (no image present at all). The scale items can be rated to give a sensory modality score and a total imagery score. Sheehan (1967a) constructed a thirty-five-item test of imagery from Betts' 150-item questionnaire using Australian college students as subjects. In a subsequent study, the Sheehan short form version of the Betts Questionnaire was standardized on sixty-two male American college students. The American and Australian samples were relatively similar (Sheehan, 1967b).

Another technique for measuring the clarity of imagery is presented by McCullough and Powell (1972). No attempt is made to relate this measure with other vividness scales. First, the client imagines the clearest scene possible and raises his index finger when the image is clear. Second, he relates the scene to the therapist and it is given a unit value of ten. Third, the subject is requested to imagine an unclear or hazy scene and fourth, relate it to the therapist who tells the client it will have a value of zero. This four-step procedure establishes the client's own subjective unit of imagery scale from zero to ten, which can be helpful in assessing clarity of imagery during treatment.

Danaher and Thoresen (1972) suggest that not only should work continue to find a visual-behavioral correlate of the self-reporting of visualization, but that investigators should also include procedures to assess and train both somatic and visual sensory awareness.

Assertiveness Measures. Assertive training is an important contribution to the field of behavior therapy (Galassi, DeLo, Galassi and Bastien, 1974). Assertion has been defined by Wolpe (1958) as the outward expression of feelings other than anxiety, and these may include friendly and affectionate actions as well as resentment and anger.

Early research in assertion relied upon nonspecific or unstandardized measures (Hedquist and Weinhold, 1970; Lazarus, 1966). However, a number of researchers have recognized the value of a standardized measure to assess client assertive needs, specification of problem areas, and change following treatment (Bates and Zimmerman, 1971; Rathus, 1973; and Galassi and others, 1974). The review of the following three scales provides a sample of some of the work in the assertive measurement area.

Bates and Zimmerman (1971) drew a distinction between assertive behavior which is appropriate and adaptive and that which is negative. The authors used the term constriction to denote nonassertion in which covert responses in an interpersonal context interferes with appropriate expression. The Screening Scale for Assertive Training (Bates and Zimmerman, 1971) is defined as a constrictive scale. Items for this scale were conceptualized from a behavioral analysis framework (Kanfer and Saslow, 1965) and contain three elements: stimulus person, situation, and subject's response.

The subjects for the development of the test included 600 middle class college freshmen, with a mean age of eighteen years. The initial item pool of 200 was shortened to twenty-three items. A forced yes-no answer required the subjects to identify whether they reacted in the manner described. The total test score reflects responses in the constricted direction. A correlation of the test with the Eysenck Personality Inventory (Eysenck and Eysenck, 1968) suggests that the long form of the constriction test is linked to the neuroticism, fear, and introversion scales. High scores on the constriction test, which suggest yielding and socially compliant behavior, are correlated with higher grade point averages. Bates and Zimmerman suggest that cross-validation and additional normative data are required before the test's utility can be assessed. The authors caution that any clinical application should also consider age, sex, and social class norms.

The Rathus Assertiveness Schedule (RAS) (Rathus, 1973) is a thirty-item test based on the work of Wolpe (1969), Wolpe and Lazarus (1966), Allport (1928), Guilford and Zimmerman (1956), and college student diaries. The subjects were sixty-eight male and female college students, aged seventeen to twenty-seven years. Test-retest over eight weeks was moderate to high with moderate to high split-half homogeneity. Scores on the RAS were validated on a seventeen-item schedule constructed according to the semantic differential technique (Osgood, Suci, and Tannenbaum, 1957). The Rathus Assertiveness Schedule correlated significantly with five of the scales: boldness, outspokenness, assertiveness, aggressiveness, and confidence, and covaried negatively with a niceness scale. Rathus (1973) suggests the RAS is a reliable and valid assessment of social boldness and may be useful in research and in treatment.

The College Self-Expression Scale (CSES) by Galassi, DeLo, Galassi, and Bastien (1974) is a fifty-item self-report inventory measuring positive assertiveness, negative assertiveness, and self denial within several situational contexts including family, strangers, business relations, authority figures, and like and opposite sex peers. Items are from materials by Wolpe and Lazarus (1966), Wolpe (1969) and Lazarus (1971).

The CSES was found to correlate positively with appropriate scales of the Adjective Check List (Gough and Heilbrun, 1965), suggesting characteristics which the authors (Galassi and others, 1974) typified as assertive: expressive, spontaneous, well defended, confident, and able to influence and lead others. The College Self-Expression Scale correlated negatively with scales reflecting non-assertiveness. A nonsignificant correlation between aggression and CSES was considered especially significant since these concepts are often confused. Galassi and his associates suggest that the CSES can be useful for research, for example, in assisting in the selection of research subjects, and also as a clinical tool, for example, to assess client needs for assertive training and as a way of identifying specific interpersonal situations in which training in assertion is appropriate.

These three scales represent an optimistic beginning for utilization of measures of assertiveness in treatment and research. Additional work is needed to develop test norms, to elaborate socio-

economic and age differences, and to assess the actual sensitivity of
the instruments in measuring treatment changes.

Projective Techniques. Lazarus (1971) gives examples of
unstructured assessment techniques which he labels as verbal assessment procedures. One of these tests is labeled "the desert island
fantasy" (Lazarus, 1971, p. 66). In this situation, the therapist in-
vites a female client to describe the activities that she and the therapist might participate in were they to be magically transformed to
a desert island without the distractions of work, television, or other
people. Lazarus suggests that this structured projective technique
rapidly yields important behavioral data. He indicates that the technique is more difficult to use if the therapist is female and the client
male.

Within this structured projective technique, the client is
given the option of going to the island alone versus going with a
therapist. Lazarus suggests that if the client chooses to go alone that
two or three things may be going on within her; for example, she
may be extremely afraid of relating to men in general or anxious
about sexual relations in particular. Lazarus points out that schizophrenic patients often choose to go alone to the desert island. Interpretations from the test are similar to the following: "Some patients
are unable to suspend their aggression, hostility or depression, even
in fantasy, and talk of committing murder or suicide on the island,
or else they predict entering into six months of continuous withdrawal or melancholy preoccupations. These reactions should
prompt most therapists to look into the threatening properties of
close relationships per se, in addition to the more obvious aspects of
their psychopathology" (Lazarus, 1971, p. 75). Lazarus states that
the purpose of this test is to examine the patient's capacity for close,
meaningful relationships.

Future Directions

The final analysis of the role of behavioral assessment within
the behavior modification framework is an evaluation of the usefulness of this style of assessment. At the present time, assessment in terms
of pretherapeutic intervention evaluation has a rather minor role
within the behavioral framework. This is partly a function of the im-

maturity of behavioral assessment techniques and partly a function of the nature of behavior therapy as a model. If one considers the Fear Survey Schedule as exemplifying the movement toward structured behavioral assessment measures, then it is apparent that there has been an enormous amount of work in test construction, reliability studies, factor analyses, and steps toward standardization. It may be that this trend toward standardization of behavioral assessment techniques, which is also exemplified by assertiveness and imagery schedules, is contradicted by the essence of behavioral theory. If one assumes that each target for assessment represents a single experiment, then what is needed is the scientific method of experimentation and research, rather than a formalized schedule for assessment. Whether the target represents a unit of behavior for a single organism or for a total community, the experimenter can apply the rules of experimental evaluation to that target with great flexibility. Within this framework, each situation is seen as unique, and the reliability of the approach is not a function of standardization techniques or of test-retest techniques, but rather is a function of following the experimental method in evaluation.

The experimental approach to behavioral assessment is clearly represented in the work by Thomas and Walter (1973) on the procedure for the assessment and modification of behavior in open settings (PAMBOS). If a behavioral therapist were to utilize a single assessment technique, his time would be well spent by beginning with PAMBOS, which represents the most comprehensive behavioral assessment technique available and the greatest integration of assessment and therapy of any approach reported within this survey. The system does not exclude the utilization of other behavioral assessment techniques. Rather, it provides the assessor with information that defines the most effective use of other behavioral assessment approaches.

Most of the remaining issues concerning behavioral assessment schedules are related to controlling the confounding variables of social desirability, tester bias, and demand characteristics of the test; reliability of self-report measures; generalization to the naturalistic environment; and of course predictiveness. The development of the FSS suggests the natural emergence from both the laboratory and the clinic of an instrument which would have predictive validity for clinical populations, as well as college populations, concerning fear. Most persons, particularly clinical clients, who are fearful of fairly specific stimulus objects within their environment can readily describe the objects that they fear without utilizing schedules. Thus, the elaborate standardization techniques for the Fear Survey Schedule may not have, as yet, provided a system for gaining information more effectively than can be obtained simply by asking a client or a student the nature of his specific fear. But while it is probable that persons within the general population can describe fear stimulus objects with considerable specificity, there is less certainty in the meaning of their descriptions. For example, the relationship of a particularly high rating to a stimulus fear object question and immobilization or ineffectiveness within a client is still unclear. This fact would suggest that more work is needed in validity studies relating to the FSS, and certainly more work is needed on scaling and standardization with various populations. At the present time, the work by Tasto, Hickson, and Rubin (1971) is the most sophisticated in terms of providing a clinician with information that might be useful relative to therapeutic interventions. Their development of a profile analysis which would allow a clinician to determine the relationship of a particular score on an item to a norm can be valuable in determining the meaning of such a score. With additional standardizations, such as that begun by Tasto and his colleagues (1971), a test could result which would be extremely valuable in behavioral assessment of potential problems for therapeutic intervention. Its use in the clinical field should take place within the framework of PAMBOS or of a general behavioral analysis (Kanfer and Saslow, 1969) system.

Behavioral assessment approaches within the general area of the operant model remain as techniques rather than as tests. The behavioral analysis approach suggested by Kanfer and Saslow (1969) is the basis for most of the techniques that have evolved within the operant model. The approach, in effect, suggests that before a person can apply a behavioral assessment technique, he must be extremely well trained and knowledgeable in learning theory. The approach assumes that behavior is a function of learning and that the assessment is simply a matter of pointing up the development of particular behavioral habits and patterns. There is a need for scaling and standardization of various aspects of the model presented by Kanfer and Saslow. The Cautela and Kastenbaum (1967) Reinforcement Survey Schedule is an approach for assessing motivational factors. Similar approaches need to be developed in evaluating behavioral excesses, deficits, and behavioral assets. The need for norms within the functional analysis approach cannot be stressed too much. What are the acceptable standards for behaviors within today's society? What constitutes aggressive acting-out behavior within a particular classroom? What frequency of communication can be labeled a behavioral deficit? The logical extension of the Kanfer-Saslow (1969) model of behavioral analysis is the establishment of norms for particular environments. Before a functional analysis can have meaning, the behavior in question must be related to client baselines, situational expectations, and peer performances. Only after this information is gathered should intervention take place.

Many of the instruments now being developed within the operant model could provide considerable efficiency to the clinician who is in the problem-solving business. One outstanding example surveyed in this chapter is the marital precounseling inventory by Stuart and Stuart (1972). This approach represents an ideal way to group data, both in terms of kinds and intensities of problems, which lead naturally into therapeutic interventions. The data grouped could very well be utilized as reinforcers within the marital interaction. This particular scale represents one of the most positive systematic approaches to marital counseling that can be found in the literature. It is possible that many areas of this test could profit from standardization techniques; however, even in its present form, the information can be applied very effectively, both from the point of view of the time efficiency of the therapist and therapy cost reduction for the clients.

Development of schedules within the areas of imagery assessment and assertion measures are in their embryonic stages. The whole question of the necessity for imagery in desensitization is not yet resolved (for example, imagery versus photographic slides). The growth and differentiation of behavioral therapies dictate the need for assessment techniques that evaluate the client-environmental situation and correlate indices from assessment procedures with intervention strategies. The imagery assessment techniques and assertion measures have not yet reached this level of development.

In summary, it appears that a fairly sophisticated Fear Survey Schedule (Tasto and others, 1971), which has considerable utility for clinicians, is now available. Other behavioral assessment techniques, notably functional analysis and ongoing assessment techniques within token economy programs, are in the process of development. Methods for evaluating learning histories are becoming slightly more systematic. Naturalistic observation has reached a sophisticated level now in terms of measurement theory (see Chapter Two in this present volume). In the United States, behavioral modification is used consistently with mentally retarded populations. There now are emerging creative applications of behavioral assessments with mentally retarded populations (see Chapter Three in this present volume). And within the field of behavioral assessment, there is a growing consensus that assessment includes the total behavioral field of the organism or organisms. This consensus can be expected to lead to considerable research in the future on issues and ethics of behavioral intervention.

References

ADAMS, J. "Change on the Fear Survey Schedule during Psychiatric Hospitalization." *Journal of Clinical Psychology,* 1971, *27,* 533–535.

ADAMS, J. AND ROTHSTEIN, W. "The Relationship Between Sixteen Fear Factors and Psychiatric Status." *Behaviour Research and Therapy,* 1971, *9,* 361–365.

AKUTAGAWA, D. "A Study in Construct Validity of the Psychoanalytic Concept of Latent Anxiety and Test of a Projection Distance Hypothesis." Unpublished Doctoral Dissertation, 1956, University of Pittsburgh.

ALLPORT, G. *A-S Reaction Study.* Boston: Houghton-Mifflin, 1928.

BANCROFT, J. H. J. "The Application of Psychophysiological Measures to the Assessment and Modification of Sexual Behavior." In C. M. Franks and G. T. Wilson (Eds.), *Annual Review of Behavior Therapy, Theory & Practice 1973*. New York: Brunner/Mazel, 1973.

BANCROFT, J. H. J., JONES, H. G., AND PULLAN, B. R. "A Simple Transducer for Measuring Penile Erection, with Comments on its Use in the Treatment of Sexual Disorders." *Behaviour Research and Therapy*, 1966, *4*, 239–241.

BANCROFT, J. H. J. AND MATHEWS, A. M. "Autonomic Correlates of Penile Erection." *Journal of Psychosomatic Research*, 1971, *15*, 159–167.

BARLOW, D. H., BECKER, R., LEITENBERG, H., AND AGRAS, W. S. "Technical Note. A Mechanical Strain Gauge for Recording Penile Circumference Change." *Journal of Applied Behavior Analysis*, 1970, *3*, 73–76.

BATES, H. D. "Factorial Structure and MMPI Correlates of a Fear Survey Schedule in a Clinical Population." *Behaviour Research and Therapy*, 1971, *9*, 355–360.

BATES, H. D. AND ZIMMERMAN, S. F. "Toward the Development of a Screening Scale for Assertive Training." *Psychological Reports*, 1971, *28*, 99–107.

BENTLER, P. M. "Heterosexual Behavior Assessment, I: Males." *Behaviour Research and Therapy*, 1968, *6*, 21–25.

BERNSTEIN, D. A. AND ALLEN, G. J. "Fear Survey Schedule (II) Normative Data and Factor Analysis Based upon a Large College Sample." *Behavior Therapy Research*, 1969, *I*, 403.

BETTS, G. H. "The Distribution and Functions of Mental Imagery." *Columbia University Contributions to Education*, 1909, *26*, 1–99.

BIJOU, S. W. AND PETERSON, R. F. "Functional Analysis in the Assessment of Children." In P. McReynolds (Ed.), *Advances in Psychological Assessment, Volume II*. Palo Alto: Science and Behavior Books, Inc., 1971.

BORKOVEC, T. D. "The Effects of Instructional Suggestion and Physiological Cues on Analogue Fear." *Behavior Therapy*, 1973a, *4*, 185–192.

BORKOVEC, T. D. "The Role of Expectancy and Physiological Feedback in Fear Research: a Review with Special Reference to Subject Characteristics." *Behavior Therapy*, 1973b, *4*, 491–505.

BORKOVEC, T. D. AND CRAIGHEAD, W. E. "The Comparison of Two

Methods of Assessing Fear and Avoidance Behavior." *Behaviour Research and Therapy,* 1971, *9,* 285–291.

BRAUN, P. R. AND REYNOLDS, D. J. "A Factor Analysis of a 100-Item Fear Survey Inventory." *Behaviour Research and Therapy,* 1969, *7,* 399–402.

CARTER, R. D. AND THOMAS, E. J. "A Case Application of a Signaling System (SAM) to the Assessment and Modification of Selected Problems of Marital Communication." *Behavior Therapy,* 1973, *4,* 629–645.

CASTANEDA, A., MC CANDLESS, B. R., AND PALERMO, D. C. "The Children's Form of the Manifest-Anxiety Scale." *Child Development,* 1956, *27,* 317–326.

CAUTELA, J. R. "Behavior Therapy and the Need for Behavioral Assessment." *Psychotherapy, Theory, Research and Practice,* 1968, *5,* 175–179.

CAUTELA, J. R. "Covert Reinforcement." *Behavior Therapy,* 1970, *1,* 35–40.

CAUTELA, J. R. AND KASTENBAUM, R. "A Reinforcement Survey Schedule for use in Therapy, Training, and Research." *Psychological Reports,* 1967, *20,* 1115–1130.

COLMAN, A. D. AND BOREN, J. J. "An Information System for Measuring Patient Behavior and Its Use by Staff." *Journal of Applied Behavior Analysis,* 1969, *2,* 207–214.

DANAHER, B. G. AND THORESEN, C. E. "Imagery Assessment by Self-report and Behavioral Measures." *Behaviour Research and Therapy,* 1972, *10,* 131–138.

EYSENCK, H. J. AND EYSENCK, S. B. *Manual for the Eysenck Personality Inventory.* San Diego: Educational and Industrial Testing Service, 1968.

FISKE, D. W. AND PEARSON, P. H. "Theory and Technique of Personality Measurement." In P. H. Mussen and M. R. Rosenzweig (Eds.), *Annual Review of Psychology.* Palo Alto: Annual Reviews, Inc., 1970.

FIXSEN, D. L., PHILLIPS, E. L., AND WOLF, M. M. "Achievement Place: the Reliability of Self-reporting and Peer-reporting and their Effects on Behavior." In C. M. Franks and G. T. Wilson (Eds.), *Annual Review of Behavior Therapy Theory and Practice 1973.* New York: Brunner/Mazel, 1973.

FRANKS, C. M. AND WILSON, G. T. "Commentary: Assessment Measurement." In C. M. Franks and G. T. Wilson (Eds.), *Annual Re-*

view of Behavior Therapy Theory and Practice 1973. New York: Brunner/Mazel, 1973.

FREUND, K. "A Note on the Use of the Phallometric Method of Measuring Mild Sexual Arousal in the Male." *Behavior Therapy,* 1971, *2,* 223–228.

FREUND, K., SEDLACEK, F., AND KNOB, K. "A Simple Transducer for Mechanical Plethysmography of the Male Genital." *Journal of Experimental Analysis of Behavior,* 1965, *8,* 169–170.

GALASSI, J. P., DE LO, J. S., GALASSI, M. D., AND BASTIEN, S. "The College Self-Expression Scale: A Measure of Assertiveness." *Behavior Therapy,* 1974, *5,* 165–171.

GEER, J. H. "The Development of a Scale to Measure Fear." *Behaviour Research and Therapy,* 1965, *13,* 45–53.

GEER, J. H. "Fear and Automatic Arousal." *Journal of Abnormal Psychology,* 1966, *71,* 253–255.

GOLDFRIED, M. R. AND KENT, R. N. "Traditional versus Behavioral Personality Assessment: a Comparison of Methodological and Theoretical Assumptions." *Psychological Bulletin,* 1972, *77,* 409–420.

GOLDFRIED, M. R. AND POMERANZ, D. M. "Role of Assessment in Behavior Modification." *Psychological Reports,* 1968, *23,* 75–87.

GOODKIN, R. "Some Neglected Issues in the Literature on Behavior Therapy." *Psychological Reports,* 1967, *20,* 415–420.

GOUGH, H. G. AND HEILBRUN, A. B. *Adjective Check List Manual.* Palo Alto: Consulting Psychologists Press, 1965.

GREENSPOON, J. AND GERSTEN, C. D. "A New Look at Psychological Testing: Psychological Testing from the Standpoint of a Behaviorist." *American Psychologist,* 1967, *22,* 848–853.

GROSSBERG, J. M. AND WILSON, H. R. "A Correlation Comparison of the Wolpe-Lang Fear Survey Schedule and the Taylor Manifest Anxiety Scale." *Behaviour Research and Therapy,* 1965, *3.*

GUILFORD, J. P. AND ZIMMERMAN, W. S. *The Guilford-Zimmerman Temperament Survey.* Beverly Hills: Sheridan Psychological Services, 1956.

HANNAH, F., STORM, T., AND CAIRD, W. K. "Sex Differences and Relationships among Neuroticism, Extroversion, and Expressed Fears." *Perceptual and Motor Skills,* 1965, *20,* 1214–1216.

HEDQUIST, F. J. AND WEINHOLD, B. K. "Behavioral Counseling with Socially Anxious and Unassertive College Students." *Journal of Counseling Psychology,* 1970, *17,* 237–242.

HERSEN, M. "Fear Scale Norms for an Inpatient Population." *Journal of Clinical Psychology,* 1971, *27,* 375–378.

HERSEN, M. "Self-assessment of Fear." *Behavior Therapy,* 1973, *4,* 241–257.

JOHNSON, S. M. AND BOLSTAD, O. "Methodological Issues in Naturalistic Observation: Some Problems and Solutions for Field Research." In L. Hamerlynck, L. Handy, and E. Mash (Eds.), *Behavior Change-Methodology Concepts and Practice.* Champaign, Illinois: Research Press, 1973.

JONES, R. R. "Behavioral Observation and Frequency Data: Problems in Scoring, Analysis, and Interpretation." In L. Hamerlynck, L. Handy, and E. Mash (Eds.), *Behavior Change—Methodology Concepts and Practice.* Champaign, Illinois: Research Press, 1973.

KANFER, F. H. AND PHILLIPS, J. S. *Learning Foundations of Behavior Therapy.* New York: Wiley, 1970.

KANFER, F. H. AND SASLOW, G. "Behavioral Analysis: an Alternative to Diagnostic Classification." *Archives of General Psychiatry,* 1965, *12,* 529–538.

KANFER, F. H. AND SASLOW, G. "Behavioral Diagnosis." In C. M. Franks (Ed.), *Behavior Therapy: Appraisal and Status.* New York: McGraw Hill, 1969.

KLEINKNECHT, R. A., MC CORMICK, C. E., AND THORNDIKE, R. M. "Stability of Stated Reinforcers as Measured by the Reinforcement Survey Schedule." *Behavior Therapy,* 1973, *4,* 407–413.

LADER, M. H., GELDER, M. G., AND MARKS, I. M. "Palmar Skin Conductance Measures as Predictors of Response to Desensitization." *Journal of Psychosomatic Research,* 1967, *11,* 283–290.

LANDY, F. J. AND GAUPP, L. A. "A Factor Analysis of the Fear Survey Schedule-III." *Behaviour Research and Therapy,* 1971, *9,* 89–93.

LANG, P. J. "The Application of Psychophysiological Methods to the Study of Psychotherapy and Behavior Modification." In A. E. Bergin and S. L. Garfield (Eds.), *Handbook of Psychotherapy and Behavior Change.* New York: Wiley & Sons, Inc., 1971.

LANG, P. J. AND LAZOVIK, A. D. "Experimental Desensitization of a Phobia." *Journal of Abnormal (and Social) Psychology,* 1963, *66,* 519–525.

LAWLIS, G. F. "Response Styles of a Patient Population on the Fear Survey Schedule." *Behaviour Research and Therapy,* 1971, *9,* 95–102.

LAZARUS, A. A. "Behavioral Rehearsal versus Nondirective Therapy Versus Advice in Effecting Behavior Change." *Behaviour Research and Therapy*, 1966, *4*, 209–212.

LAZARUS, A. A. *Behavior Therapy and Beyond*. New York: McGraw-Hill, 1971.

LEVIS, D. J. "The Phobic Test Apparatus: an Objective Measure of Human Avoidance Behavior to Small Objects." *Behaviour Research and Therapy*, 1969, *7*, 309–315.

MC CULLOUGH, J. P. AND MONTGOMERY, L. E. "A Technique for Measuring Subjective Arousal in Therapy Clients." *Behavior Therapy*, 1972, *3*, 627–628.

MC CULLOUGH, J. P. AND POWELL, P. O. "A Technique for Measuring Clarity of Imagery in Therapy Clients." *Behavior Therapy*, 1972, *3*, 447–448.

MC REYNOLDS, P. "The Assessment of Anxiety: a Survey of Available Techniques." In P. McReynolds (Ed.), *Advances in Psychological Assessment*. Vol. 1. Palo Alto: Science and Behavior Books, 1968.

MAC, R. AND FAZIO, A. F. "Self-report Overt Behavioral Measures of Fear with Changes in Aversive Stimuli." *Behaviour Research and Therapy*, 1972, *10*, 283–285.

MANOSEVITZ, M. AND LANYON, R. I. "Fear Survey Schedule: a Normative Study." *Psychological Reports*, 1965, *17*, 699–703.

MARKS, I. M. AND GELDER, M. G. "Transvestism and Fetishism: Clinical and Psychological Changes during Faradic Aversion." *British Journal of Psychiatry*, 1967, *113*, 711–729.

MILBY, J. B., JR., WILLICUTT, H. C., HAWK, J. W., JR., MAC DONALD, M., AND WHITFIELD, K. "A System for Recording Individualized Behavioral Data in a Token Program." *Journal of Applied Behavior Analysis*, 1973, *6*, 333–338.

MISCHEL, W. *Personality and Assessment*. New York: Wiley, 1968.

NURNBERGER, J. I. AND ZIMMERMAN, J. "Applied Analysis of Human Behavior: an Alternative to Conventional Motivational Inferences and Unconscious Determination in Therapeutic Programming." *Behavior Therapy*, 1970, *1*, 59–69.

OSGOOD, C. E., SUCI, G. J., AND TANNENBAUM, P. H. *The Measurement of Meaning*. Urbana, Illinois: University of Illinois Press, 1957.

PATTERSON, G. R. "Behavioral Intervention Procedures in the Classroom and in the Home." In A. E. Bergin and S. L. Garfield

(Eds.), *Handbook of Psychotherapy and Behavior Change*. New York: Wiley & Sons, Inc., 1971.

PETERSON, D. R. *The Clinical Study of Social Behavior*. New York: Appleton-Century-Crofts, 1968.

RATHUS, S. A. "A Thirty-item Schedule for Assessing Assertive Behavior." *Behavior Therapy*, 1973, *4*, 398–406.

ROMANCZYK, R. G., KENT, R. N., DIAMENT, C., AND O'LEARY, K. D. "Measuring the Reliability of Observational Data: a Reactive Process." *Journal of Applied Behavior Analysis*, 1973, *6*, 173–184.

ROTHSTEIN, W. AND BOBLITT, W. E. "Expressed Fears of Psychiatric Patients." *Journal of Clinical Psychology*, 1970, *26*, 277–279.

ROTHSTEIN, W., HOLMES, G. R., AND BOBLITT, W. E. "A Factor Analysis of the Fear Survey Schedule with a Psychiatric Population." *Journal of Clinical Psychology*, 1972, *28*, 78–80.

RUBIN, B. M., KATKIN, E. S., WEISS, B. W., AND EFRAN, J. S. "Factor Analysis of Fear Survey Schedule." *Behaviour Research and Therapy*, 1968, *6*, 65–75.

RUBIN, S. E., LAWLIS, G. F., TASTO, D. L., AND NAMANEK, T. "Factor Analysis of the 122-item Fear Survey Schedule." *Behaviour Research and Therapy*, 1969, *7*, 381–386.

SARASON, I. "Test Anxiety, General Anxiety, and Intellectual Performance." *Journal of Consulting Psychology*, 1957, *21*, 485–490.

SCHERER, M. AND NAKAMURA, C. Y. "A Fear Survey Schedule for Children (FSS-FC): A Factor Analytic Comparison with Manifest Anxiety (CMAS)." *Behaviour Research and Therapy*, 1968, *6*, 173–182.

SHEEHAN, P. W. "A Shortened Form of Betts' Questionnaire upon Mental Imagery." *Journal of Clinical Psychology*, 1967a, *23*, 386–389.

SHEEHAN, P. W. "Reliability of a Short Test of Imagery." *Perceptual and Motor Skills*, 1967b, *25*, 744.

SKINDRUD, K. "Field Evaluation of Observer Bias under Overt and Covert Monitoring." In L. Hamerlynck, L. Handy and E. Mash (Eds.), *Behavior Change-Methodology Concepts and Practice*. Champaign, Illinois: Research Press, 1973.

STAMPFL, T. G. AND LEVIS, D. J. "Essentials of Implosion Therapy: a Learning-Theory-Based Psychodynamic Behavioral Therapy." *Journal of Abnormal Psychology*, 1967, *72*, 496–503.

STUART, R. B. AND STUART, F. *Marital Precounseling Inventory Counselors Guide*. Champaign, Illinois: Research Press, 1972.

SUINN, R. M. "Changes in Nontreated Subjects over Time: Data on a

Fear Survey Schedule and the Test Anxiety Scale." *Behaviour Research and Therapy*, 1969, *7*, 205–206.

TASTO, D. L. AND HICKSON, R. "Standardization Item Analysis and Scaling of the 122-item Fear Survey Schedule." *Behavior Therapy*, 1970, *1*, 473–484.

TASTO, D. L., HICKSON, R., AND RUBIN, S. E. "Scaled Profile Analysis of Fear Survey Schedule Factors." *Behavior Therapy*, 1971, *2*, 543–549.

TASTO, D. L. AND SUINN, R. M. "Fear Survey Schedule Changes on Total and Factor Scores Due to Nontreatment Effects." *Behavior Therapy*, 1972, *3*, 275–278.

TAYLOR, J. A. "A Personality Scale of Manifest Anxiety." *Journal of Abnormal (and Social) Psychology*, 1953, *48*, 285–290.

THOMAS, E. J., CARTER, R. D., GAMBRILL, E. D., AND BUTTERFIELD, W. H. "A Signal System for the Assessment and Modification of Behavior (SAM)." *Behavior Therapy*, 1970, *1*, 252–259.

THOMAS, E. J. AND WALTER, C. L. "Guidelines for Behavioral Practice in the Open Community Agency: Procedure and Evaluation." *Behaviour Research and Therapy*, 1973, *11*, 193–205.

WALK, R. D. "Self-ratings of Fear in a Fear Invoking Situation." *Journal of Abnormal (and Social) Psychology*, 1956, *52*, 171–178.

WEISS, B. W., KATKIN, E. S., AND RUBIN, B. M. "Relationship Between a Factor Analytically Derived Measure of a Specific Fear and Performance after Related Fear Induction." *Journal of Abnormal Psychology*, 1969, *73*, 461–463.

WELSH, G. S. "MMPI Profiles and Factor Scales A and R." *Journal of Clinical Psychology*, 1965, *XXI*, 43–47.

WOLPE, J. *Psychotherapy by Reciprocal Inhibition*. Palo Alto: Stanford University Press, 1958.

WOLPE, J. *The Practice of Behavior Therapy*. New York: Pergamon Press, 1969.

WOLPE, J. AND LANG, P. J. "A Fear Survey Schedule for Use in Behavior Therapy." *Behaviour Research and Therapy*, 1964, *2*, 27–30.

WOLPE, J. AND LAZARUS, A. A. *Behavior Therapy Techniques: A Guide to the Treatment of Neuroses*. New York: Pergamon Press, 1966.

YATES, A. J. AND POOLE, A. D. "Case Studies. Behavioral Analysis in a Case of Excessive Frequency of Micturition." *Behavior Therapy*, 1972, *3*, 449–453.

YONOVITZ, A. AND KUMAN, A. "An Economical, Easily Recordable Galvanic Skin Response Apparatus." *Behavior Therapy,* 1972, *3,* 629–630.

ZUCKERMAN, M. "The Development of an Affect Adjective Checklist for the Measurement of Anxiety." *Journal of Consulting Psychology,* 1960, *24,* 457–462.

ZUCKERMAN, M. "Physiological Measures of Sexual Arousal in the Human." *Psychological Bulletin,* 1971, *75,* 347–356.

X

Evaluation in
Community Mental Health

JAMES K. MIKAWA

In recent years the personnel of community mental health centers have become increasingly concerned about evaluation and assessment. The general trend toward community-oriented mental health services has highlighted the importance of knowing what particular needs are prevalent in a community, what community services are required, and how these services can best be provided. Additionally, and in contrast to an earlier emphasis on isolated one-to-one therapeutic interactions, community mental health services have emphasized the development of broad programs oriented toward the community as a whole. The evaluation of community mental health to determine whether the objectives of the health service are being met has become a focus of increasing interest as larger areas of service have been defined.

A major pressure toward evaluation and assessment has come from governmental and other funding sources stressing the need for program accountability. Federal policies, in particular, now demand accountability and justification of resource allocation for service programs (Mushkin, 1973). Consequently, substantial federal funds have been expended in developing evaluation models and demonstration projects. As a result of this trend the professional evaluator—an individual responsible for the evaluation process in

larger community mental health centers—has become a new and
distinct entity in the mental health staffing mosaic. Clinical service
staff have often viewed these individuals, who are primarily from
nonclinical backgrounds, with alarm, threat, and suspicion (Weiss,
1972). Demand for accountability, however, has forced the clinician
to recognize more clearly than ever before that evaluation may be a
necessary component of his program, if his program is to exist at
all. Some clinicians, of course, have welcomed the trend toward
accountability, seeing it as a positive force in the provision of more
effective services. The process and outcome of evaluation are seen by
them as tools in determining how they can be most effective.

A central issue for both clinicians and evaluators is the adequacy of evaluation methodology and the validity of techniques used
in evaluation. Efforts in past evaluations of individual psychotherapy have been particularly discouraging, with conflicting results
being a common occurrence (Rubinstein and Parloff, 1959; Stieper
and Wiener, 1965; Strupp, 1973). The development of valid evaluation methodology for community mental health programs has been
a challenge resulting in a variety of approaches and directions in
recent years. The focus of the present chapter is to describe and
critically examine some of the major practices and methodological
bases currently used in the evaluation and assessment of community
mental health services. I will also discuss some of the more important
issues relating to evaluative practices and their implementation.

The presentation will be oriented around the concerns of the
practitioner as he works in the field. I will begin with an assessment
of needs in the community; then turn to the measurement of outcome as a gauge of program effectiveness; then shift to the relation
of management information systems to decision-making and planning; and finally, I will examine certain crucial issues in evaluation.
The explosive rate of development in the arena of the evaluation of
community mental health services makes it impossible to present
a comprehensive account in the space available; this review, therefore, will necessarily be in the nature of a selective survey.

Assessment of Needs

The assessment of needs in the community should be one of
the first and most important steps in a mental health center's evalu-

ative procedure. To obtain accurate and reliable estimates of the needs in the community is an extremely difficult and complicated task. However, without knowledge of these needs, the evaluation of services is seriously hampered. Knowledge of needs in the community must therefore be the foundation from which services develop and change.

Schulberg and Wechsler (1967) have urged recognition of the need-assessment procedures stipulated by the 1964 Federal Regulations for the Community Mental Health Centers Act. These regulations require each state seeking construction funds to specifically indicate the steps that have been taken to assess the community's mental health needs. The guidelines indicate that need should be defined on the basis of the extent of mental illness and mental disorder for both the population directly involved and for those persons affected by it. Other related indices involved are the extent of low income per capita, chronic unemployment, substandard housing, alcoholism, drug abuse, crime, delinquency, and other problems related to mental health. The special mental health needs of particular groups, such as the aged, the handicapped, and children should also be considered.

Techniques employed in assessing mental health needs in the community have varied through the years, with the tendency to use easier methods, such as a quick survey of client usage of particular services, rather than to expend considerable energy and effort in carrying out a comprehensive assessment of needs. Consequently, most community mental health centers actually have very little knowledge of the extent and the particular characteristics of the mental health needs in their communities. Some approaches for the assessment of needs which have been used are discussed in this section; these include such approaches as true prevalence studies, census tract analyses, the development of statistical indicators of related problems, case register studies, and surveys of client utilization patterns and problems.

True Prevalence Studies. Estimates of pathology in a community frequently are based on the findings of true prevalence survey studies done in selected communities. The term *true prevalence studies* refers to attempts to identify the prevalence and distribution of psychiatric disorders in the general population by obtaining a sample of both untreated and treated disorders for a specific period of time. Ratios or percentages of expected psychiatric disorders obtained in these studies are often extrapolated for use by individual mental health centers to indicate need for services.

The measurement of pathology in various communities through the employment of true prevalence studies has been carried out for many years, with an emphasis on their use in the 50s and 60s. Bruce and Barbara Dohrenwend reported on forty-four such community studies, including one done as early as 1917 (1972). Some of the studies utilized quite large samples reflecting massive efforts (Srole, Langner, Michael, Opler, and Rennie, 1962; Leighton, Harding, Macklin, Macmillan, and Leighton, 1963).

The studies have varied considerably in design, making it difficult to compare results. Methodological differences can be noted in directness of contact with subjects; use of records or informants; size and qualitative characteristics of communities; urban versus rural; socioeconomic definitions and levels; use and variation of interviews; use and variation of questions asked; use of diagnostic categories; use and variation of psychiatric ratings; criteria used to define sick and well; age ranges; sample size; and length of time period that the pathology has existed.

Notable differences have appeared in the results of these studies, with the overall rates of psychiatric disorders reported to range from less than 1 percent to more than 60 percent (Dohrenwend and Dohrenwend, 1969). In rural settings in the United States, the following rates have been reported: 6.9 percent (Roth and Luton, 1943), 18.0 percent (Trussel, Elinson, and Levin, 1956), and 27.5 percent (Phillips, 1966). The following rates have been reported in urban settings: 3.4 percent (Manis, Brawer, Hunt, and Kercher, 1964), 10.9 percent (Pasamanick, Roberts, Lemkau, and Krueger, 1957), 23.4 percent (Srole and others, 1962), and 32.0 percent (Cole, Branch, and Orla, 1957).

Questions have been raised about the validity of the measures of disorders used in these various studies. Dohrenwend and Dohrenwend (1969) have pointed out a number of methodological problems. In almost all of these studies, clinical judgement was used as the basis for determining whether a case should be defined as pathological or not. In many instances, the determination was based on psychiatric diagnoses described in terms of the categories found in the *Diagnostic and Statistical Manual* of the American Psychiatric Association (1952). The unreliability of psychiatric diagnoses based on these categories, however, has been well documented (Schmidt and Fonda, 1956; Zigler and Phillips, 1961; Ward, Beck, Mendelson, Mock, and Erbaugh, 1962).

Some of the more sophisticated studies have avoided using diagnostic categories as a basis of judgement, and have rated information in more general terms, such as the degree of severity of the disorder, on a continuum ranging from "well" to "incapacitated" (Srole and others, 1962). Structured questionnaires also have been used in hopes of increasing the reliability of data (Srole and others, 1962; Leighton and others, 1963). Dohrenwend and Dohrenwend note, however, that in these studies, item selection procedures were not used in the development of the questionnaires (1969).

A critical issue is the question of what constitutes an adequate and reliable definition of psychopathology. Some attempts have been made to cross-validate questionnaires used on surveys, particularly the Midtown Questionnaire (Srole and others, 1962). Two studies (Leighton, Leighton, and Danley, 1966; Fabrega and McBee, 1970) independently examined individuals using both the survey technique and clinical evaluations. Leighton, Leighton, and Danley found considerable agreement between the two methods, whereas Fabrega and McBee found that the various items of the Midtown questionnaire correlated to differing degrees with the professional estimates of psychiatric disability. In originally developing the Midtown questionnaire, concurrent validity was obtained for the items, using groups of individuals identified as well or not well (Srole and others, 1962). However, since clinical judgments were used in both of the methods that were compared, the question can be raised as to the independence of the different criteria and methods.

Underlying many of the problems uncovered by true prevalence studies is the fact that no agreed-upon definition of psychological well being and disorder exists. Until reliable definitions are specified and indices reflecting these definitions are delineated, findings can be expected to vary considerably.

Census Tract Analysis. Census tract analysis is a means by which census data are used to locate high risk geographical areas with respect to mental health problems. High risk is defined in terms of conditions which have been found to be associated with mental health problems in various research studies. For example, poverty has been found to be associated with greater incidence of mental health problems (Hollingshead and Redlich, 1958; Srole and others, 1962; Mishler and Scotch, 1965). In analyzing census tract characteristics in a large city, Bloom also identified certain community characteristics which were significantly related to socially deviant behavior (1966). The National Institute of Mental Health (NIMH) recently has developed a model for the selection and analysis of census data which also identifies these conditions according to census tract locations (Goldsmith and Unger, 1970).

In their development of the NIMH model, Goldsmith and Unger attempted to identify "the key social, and economic and demographic axes and associated behaviors that differentiate residential suburbs" which can be measured by census data (1970, p. 2). As a part of the social area analysis, three key dimensions which could be related to the available census data were selected; they were social rank, life style, and ethnicity. Social rank refers to factors such as social class, education, occupation, and income. Life style indicates the way of life chosen, such as a working couple living in a single family dwelling versus living in an apartment complex. Ethnicity refers to the differentiating racial and cultural backgrounds.

Goldsmith and Unger suggest that the economic, social, and educational components of social rank should be treated separately since empirically these components do not vary together in an area, in that low correlations are frequently found among them. Census measures which can be used as indicators of economic status are median house value, median rent, median income of families and unrelated individuals, percent of families below poverty level, employment level, and labor force participation. Census indicators for social status include the percentage of males in low status occupations, middle occupational status and in high status occupations. The census measure for education is the median school years completed among persons twenty-five and over.

Likewise, four components of life style are identified: family status, family life cycle, residential style of life, and familism. The concept of family status refers to whether an orientation toward living in a family situation is present or not. The census measure of family status is percent of husband-wife households. The concept of residential style of life refers to the day-to-day activities that are conducted in the immediate vicinity of the residence, which is directly related to the kind and condition of housing units available. Census measures indicating residential style of life are percentage of one-unit structures, percentage of persons in overcrowded households, percentage of standard housing units, percentage of single dwelling units, and percentage of highrise apartments. The concept of familism refers to the value placed on family living, such as in a tendency toward child centeredness. Census measures for this component have not been defined.

Ethnicity was not broken down into separate components. The census measures indicating ethnicity are what percentage Negro, what percentage other nonwhite race, and what percentage foreign stock.

Community instability also was identified as having social area relevance. The census measures indicating this factor are percentage of recent movers, percentage of mobile persons, and percentage of migrants.

In addition to the census measures presented for the above dimensions, other relevant census indicators are available and provide additional information for analysis (Goldsmith and Unger, 1970). For example, subpopulations with a high potential for mental health and related problems can be identified. Census measures suggested were the percentage of teenagers not in school, the percentage of Negro teenagers not in school, the percentage of working mothers with children, the percentage of working mothers with preschool children, the percentage of aged persons living alone, the percentage of aged persons in poverty, the percentage of female heads of households with own children, the percentage of large families in poverty, the percentage of disabled population, the percentage of disabled population unable to work, and the percentage of poverty children.

The NIMH census tract analysis has been tested and demonstrated in various communities (Redick, Goldsmith, and Unger,

1971; Goldsmith and Unger, 1972; Harakal and Silver, 1973). A Mental Health Small-Area Demographic Profile System (MHDP) has also been developed to handle the unique characteristics of the inner city (Goldsmith and Unger, 1972).

Census tract analysis seems to have considerable promise as a way of locating conditions in a community which have been correlated with poor mental health. Census tract data, however, refer to gross demographic factors. Consequently, they may not be a sensitive indicator of mental health states, although they can provide an estimate of areas of need. A major advantage of this type of analysis is that it can be used in every American community. It also can be employed as a vehicle for comparison studies across communities.

As previously stated, use of census tract analysis is based on the theoretical foundation, supported by numerous studies, that various conditions, such as poverty, broken homes, and mobility of residents contribute to poor mental health. Validation studies directly relating specific census indicators to mental health states, however, have not been reported. Until such studies have been done and unless they indicate significant degrees of relationship among specific census tract indicators and mental health states, it appears that estimates of areas of need based on census data remain at a crude level and are subject to many questions regarding validity.

Official Statistics of Related Problems. Official statistics of related problems such as suicide and crime are used by many people to indicate mental health needs and to justify mental health services. The statistics used are typically gathered by official governmental bodies, such as the police and the coroner's office. Most localities in the United States report these statistics on a regular basis, which leads to their accessibility and attractiveness for assessing needs. However, there are many issues connected with the use of official statistics as a reliable means of assessing mental health needs.

For example, it is extremely difficult to get an accurate recording of suicides, suicide attempts, or suicide threats (Farberow and Shneidman, 1965; Litman, Curphey, Shneidman, Farberow, and Tabachnik, 1963). One of the major difficulties encountered in attempting to define suicide reliably is the lack of agreed-upon criteria for determining when a death should be classified as a suicide. Farberow and Shneidmen (1965) have noted the variety of evidence used by public officials to certify if death by suicide has occurred. Some coroners will certify death by suicide only if a suicide note is present. In one study, these authors found that only 35 percent of their sample identified as suicides wrote notes. Douglas (1967) notes that laws specify intention as necessary for legal categorization of suicide as the cause of death, but that intention with regard to suicide has socially ambiguous connotations. Public officials differ on what evidence they consider as indicating intention to die.

Strong social pressures exist to classify suicides in certain ways. The social disapprobation connected with self-destruction has led to laws forbidding suicide, and to the insistence from family members that a suicide did not occur, even hiding the fact from public officials. Recently, studies have pointed out the suicidal implications of one-car fatalities normally classified as accidents (Tabachnik, Litman, Osman, Jones, Cohn, Kasper, and Moffat, 1966; MacDonald, 1964). In addition, deaths classified as accidental in the United States generally result in a double indemnity payment by the insurance company, while suicides do not.

Similar problems are encountered in the accuracy and reliability of crime statistics. Cressey (1970) presents several concerns about official statistics of crime. First, it is impossible to determine the extent of crime in an area, since many are not discovered, not reported, or not officially recorded. Second, conditions vary so much from year to year, and from jurisdiction to jurisdiction, that it is difficult to compare crime rates. Third, indices of crime are not representative of true crime rate, since the index items are only partially representative of the whole picture. Fourth, variations in recorded rates of some crimes, such as white-collar crimes, are not compiled. Fifth, delinquency, in particular, is not well defined, and inconsistencies in recording instances of delinquent behavior are common. And sixth, the amount of statistical error is unknown, since data on crime rates are not developed with research as the primary reason for compilation.

Social pressures, public opinion, politics, and the interpretation of laws and police practices all affect statements of crime rates. Whether individuals report criminal activities or not depends to some extent on the social climate in which these activities occur.

Official statistics on crime and suicide should be used with caution in assessing the mental health needs in a community. Unfortunately, there is a general tendency to use these statistics without much reservation or qualification, possibly because of their official nature. Despite their limitations we can expect that these statistics will continue to be used for assessment of mental health needs, because of their availability.

Preliminary attempts to form a multiple index of need by combining official statistics with other social indicators have been initiated (Fowler and Pullan, 1972; Schulberg and Wechsler, 1967). This task probably is more complicated and complex than it seems on the surface.

Case Register. The psychiatric case register has been used to determine both rates of pathology and mental health needs in the community. The case register method collects information on individuals in a cumulative manner over time. Clinical data are usually collected. Information for the system normally is drawn from a defined population of individuals, such as the residents of a particular geographical area. The size of the geographical area covered by one case register has varied from counties to states (Bahn, 1965). Other characteristics of this method are that data collection is systematic, standardized data are collected, the data are prospective rather than retrospective, and longitudinal rather than cross-sectional (Baldwin, 1972).

Information contained in a case register usually includes an identification number; a contact summary, such as initial contact with the program; diagnoses; treatment decisions; previous and current medical, psychological, and psychiatric history; test results; sociocultural factors; emergency contacts; patient movement data; and discharge or transfer summaries. A case register often reflects massive efforts to collect information and a computer system is almost always required in order to deal with it effectively. The Monroe County, New York register, which began in 1960, added an average of 4900 people a year (Bahn, 1965).

Gorwitz, Bahn, Chandler, and Martin (1963) note several advantages of the case register method. The use of broader case findings than otherwise available is one of the main advantages. The extensive records also allow the possibility of studying the overlap of the clients of particular psychiatric and nonpsychiatric agencies.

Cumulative records, in addition, lend themselves to follow-up studies. Research on the onset of mental disorders and their subsequent patterns can be accomplished because of the lifetime data characteristics of case registers. They also facilitate a variety of clinical and epidemiological research possibilities and sometimes have been used to determine the incidence of pathology in a community. Incidence rates have been calculated by counting the new cases of mental disorder occurring over a specified period of time. Large case registers have been able to record all the first admissions of a sizable geographical area, such as a state, in order to provide a tally of new cases.

Bahn, Gardner, Alltop, Knalterud, and Solomon (1966) studied three case register areas to compare rates of first admissions over a period of a year. Rates per 100,000 population were as follows: Hawaii, 353; Maryland, 556; and Monroe County, New York, 807. Incidence rates were all below 1 percent, or .35, .55 and .80, respectively for the above areas.

Prevalence rates also have been estimated on the basis of case register data. Prevalence rates are the number of cases of mental disorder present in a population group as of a specified interval of time. Bahn and others, (1966) found prevalence rates of 839 per 100,000 for a year period in Hawaii, 1057 in Maryland, and 1347 in Monroe County, New York.

A mass of other information can be obtained through the use of a case register. Information regarding such phenomena as client utilization of services and diagnostic patterns can be easily obtained and analysed. The fact that information can be combined in a variety of ways is an attractive feature of the case register.

It is desirable in utilizing this case register approach to have a clearly stated goal. A mass of information collected without any previously specified purpose would be an expensive and cumbersome endeavor. It would be expected that data gathered for a specific purpose, such as a management decision or a research hypothesis, could be gathered more economically and with greater relevance to the question asked. Research questions necessarily have to be limited to the kinds of data available in the case register, if no prior goals are specified.

As with any large information gathering system, considerable difficulties are associated with the data gathering process in the case register approach. Data often are not reported or are distorted. Clinical staff often do not see the relevance of the data gathered and are not cooperative. Certain kinds of data, such as diagnosis, are dependent upon clinical judgment, and the usefulness of such information is limited to the reliability of these judgments. In general, the reliability and validity of the original data input into the register are of critical concern.

Survey of Client Utilization Patterns and Problems. Mental health needs in the community also can be estimated by surveying a sample of the population. Most mental health centers do informally survey client utilization patterns, primarily for budget justification reasons. Much effort has been expended by staffs of community mental health programs in order to obtain client utilization data, because of the demands of governmental bodies and granting agencies. Indeed, Attkisson, McIntyre, Hargreaves, Harris, and Ochberg (1973) found that community centers tend to exhaust their evaluation efforts carrying out utilization surveys at the expense of other evaluation activities which would provide more meaningful returns, such as management data. Others have indicated that the collection of traditional information regarding patients receiving care has led to the neglect of attempts to define broad community mental health needs (Moore, Bloom, Gaylin, Pepper, Pettus, Willis, and Bahn, 1967).

Formal surveys of samples of the population for need assessment purposes, however, have generally been limited to prevalence studies of pathology. Surveys to determine the nature and extent of specific psychological problems in the community rarely have been attempted. The tendency has been to focus on gross categories of impairment, rather than on specific problems, such as marital conflicts, depression, anxiety, and crisis situations.

Outcome Evaluation of Programs

The determination of the effectiveness of community mental health programs is of critical importance to all those connected with evaluation, development and planning of programs, and implementation of services. This task, however, is probably one of the most difficult in the entire area of mental health evaluation. The methodological problems are many, complex, and diverse. They range from difficulties in determining which criteria are to be considered as clinically meaningful to problems in the development of reliable measuring instruments.

Recent trends in community mental health program outcome evaluation have been directed toward the development of community-oriented measures, individualized goal attainment models, the assessment of indirect services, such as consultation, and the evaluation of psychosocial systems. The influence of business and management is seen in the emphasis on goals and objectives, and on systems analysis. It appears that the challenge of mental health program evaluation has moved evaluators closer to established applied evaluation models and further away from strict experimental designs.

Goal Attainment Models. Goal attainment models are procedures for evaluating the effectiveness of programs by determining if the goals of individual clients have been met. In contrast to earlier scales which measured general adjustment, goal attainment instruments are individualized (Davis, 1973), in that standardization of the particular instruments or development of norms is not necessary.

Goal attainment models have caught the imagination of a number of investigators and several different approaches have been developed (Bonstedt, 1973; Stelmachers, Lund, and Meade, 1972; Ellis and Wilson, 1973; Honigfeld and Klein, 1973; Kiresuk, 1973). I will now briefly describe two models (GAS and ATGON) as examples of this approach.

The technique known as Goal Attainment Scaling (GAS) is a product of several years of development (Kiresuk & Sherman, 1968). The application of this procedure involves three steps: goal selection and scaling, assignment of the patient to one of the treatment modalities, and a follow-up of each patient to evaluate his or her progress with respect to the goals and scale values chosen at intake.

Initially, the patient goals selected in intake interviews are evaluated by intake workers with respect to probable outcome as assessed on a follow-up date according to the question, "Given this patient with her background, her environment, her abilities and liabilities, and hopes for the future, and given the capabilities of our treatment staff to treat such cases, as well as the current state of knowledge, what can we expect her to be doing, to be like, at the time of follow-up?" (Kiresuk and Sherman, 1968). Using the Goal Attainment Follow-up Guide, the intake worker marks the probable outcome on a grid with precise and objective descriptions to enable others to determine whether the patient lies above or below that point. Numerical values are assigned to these points, with the value of zero representing the outcome expected, +2 standing for a most favorable outcome, and −2 reflecting a most unfavorable outcome. The continuum of obtained probable outcome data approximates a bell-shaped curve, allowing aggregate scores to be converted into standard scores. Roughly 68 percent of scores should fall within the +1, 0, −1 range.

Weights for the goals can be assigned to indicate the relative value of each goal. Key problem areas are assigned higher weights.

Reliability coefficients of .70 have been established between goal attainment guides constructed independently by different staff at different times. Repeat scoring of the same guides with an average of twenty-six days between scoring also has resulted in reliability coefficients of about .70.

The Automated Tri-informant Goal Oriented Progress Note (ATGON) was developed at the Fort Logan Mental Health Center (Wilson, Ellis, Booth and Mumpower, 1973). ATGON is an evaluation system which uses IBM optical-scan forms for an automated recording of selection of goals and treatment methods, and of the importance of each goal to the patient and patient movement toward or away from the goals.

In contrast to the GAS, which is individually tailored to the needs of each client, ATGON uses a general goal list of 703 items, developed by staff consensus. This list includes six dimensions: medical; symptom alleviation; self-concept; patient-initiated interaction; other initiated interaction; and disposition. A staff interviewer, using a semistructured approach, interviews the patient and a close community informant to determine the selection of goals. Community informants are included in order to select goals from a source close to but separate from the patient. The tri-informants, then, include the patient, the clinician and a close relative or friend, all of whom select goals for the patient. A summary of the goals and treatment methods selected are then printed in a narrative computer language, NOVEL. Concurrently, a second printout (Response Rating Scale) lists the goals selected, along wth two scales indicating the importance of the goal for the patient (five point scale), and the patient's movement toward or away from a goal (six point scale). A staff version of the form includes the treatment methods chosen for each goal, and a scale for evaluating their helpfulness (five point scale). Goals are evaluated by the tri-informants on a monthly basis for the first three months, every three months thereafter, and at termination. Goal success scores are computed using the following formula: goal importance (actual) × goal attainment (actual) + 10/goal importance (maximum) × goal attainment (maximum) + 10.

The range of the success score is from 0.00 to 1.00, with .40 seen as indicating essentially no change and lesser scores reflecting failure. The way the scores are computed allows comparisons between patients and patient aggregates.

The structured approach tends to increase reliability. Coefficients of .94 were obtained for inter-interviewer reliability, and .93 and .96 for test-retest reliabilities for the two interviewers over a three-month interval.

The system is set up to provide continuous feedback to staff and administrators. In this sense, it is seen as part of the total evaluative and planning picture.

At large facilities, ATGON will require the support of a computer, although it can be run by clerical personnel with smaller patient loads. The data processing costs at Fort Logan are estimated at fifteen cents for one complete goal-method cycle from each informant. The average census is 300–350 patients, with an average admission rate of forty patients per month. There are also time savings in the completion of automated versus handwritten treatment notes.

Whether goal attainment models are seen as beneficial from the clinicians' point of view depends largely on one's orientation toward therapy. The approach is based upon the definition of specific goals and objectives typically early in the work with the patient. Bonstedt (1973) suggests that the attainment approach can be seen as behavioristic, since it focuses upon behavioral output. He also views the approach as clashing with the values of certain traditional treatment orientations which do not specify goals during therapy. For some clinicians the goals may not be individualized or idiosyncratic enough, and can be seen as forcing individuals to accept obvious goals because the procedures require them to do so. For others, the lack of standardization and norms may seem to represent a loss of objectivity and an increase of the possibility of bias.

Davis (1973) notes that the utilization of goal attainment models has received little attention so far, and points out that the question of whether the time and effort that it requires from staff will be offset by the benefits it yields has not yet been adequately defined. Questions can also be raised as to what the possible benefits of this approach are, and who will perceive them as benefits. Considerable time, effort, and expense appear to be inevitable corollaries of the goal attainment approach, especially if every goal of each patient is evaluated. Attkisson and others (1973), however, emphasize that much more time and effort than has been customary must be expended if evaluations are to be truly effective, noting that only 2.2 to 2.7 percent of all mental health center staff time is currently being devoted to research and evaluation.

In general, goal attainment models of assessment show a great deal of promise, but their effectiveness and validity as a means of evaluation must still be demonstrated. Utilization and comparison studies would be helpful. The individualized input that this approach can provide to an overall system of evaluation may be its greatest asset.

Psychosocial Environments. Community mental health programs depend upon halfway houses, day care centers, and community care homes to provide transitional care for those unable to function autonomously in the community. Assessment of these environments with respect to treatment has been an important concern (Fairweather, Sanders, Cressler, and Maynard, 1969; Raush and Raush, 1968; Glasscote, Gudeman and Elpers, 1971; Moos, 1972). Moos has developed a scale, the Community-Oriented Programs Environment Scale (copes), which can be used to systematically assess the psychosocial environments of community-oriented treatment programs such as halfway houses (1972).

copes is a 102-item schedule which involves ten subscales: program involvement; support; spontaneity; autonomy; practical orientation; personal problem orientation; anger, and aggression; order and organization; program clarity; and staff control. The first three subscales are intended to measure relationship variables such as the involvement of members in the program, their motivation to improve, the support of staff and members for each other, encouragement to act openly and express feelings openly, and encouragement to express themselves openly to staff and to show feelings. The next four subscales measure treatment program variables, such as the extent to which the staff acts on member suggestion, the extent to which the environment orients the members toward preparing themselves for release from the program, the program's encouragement of member's planning for the future, the extent to which the program involves sharing of personal problems, the degree of staff interest in learning about member's feelings, the extent to which members are allowed and encouraged to display aggressive behavior, and whether the staff believes that it is sometimes healthy to argue, and whether they permit the members to gripe. The last three subscales are designed to measure administrative structure variables, such as the importance and implementation of activity planning, neatness in the program, clarity of goal expectation and rules, member knowledge of consequences of rule breaking, staff determination of rules, requirements of members to follow schedules, and member's knowledge of who is in charge.

COPES presently consists of two forms: Form C and Form I, which differ from one another only in the instructions. Form C instructs the person to answer according to how he presently views the treatment program, whereas Form I asks him to respond according to how he ideally would like to see the program function. Discrepancies between the two scores are evaluated and used as feedback for program planning and change. Both forms utilize a true-false response format.

Internal consistency correlations of items with their respective subscales were above .30 for most items. Average correlation among subscales were .23 and .24 for member and staff samples respectively (Moos, 1972).

Moos cites several possible benefits to be gained from use of the scale (1971). First, it can provide data on relevant and important dimensions on which programs can be systematically assessed.

Second, the nature of COPES allows it to be used as an analytic tool to evaluate whether the perceived environment is related to the program's purposes and goals. Third, it can furnish information concerning the similarities and discrepancies between member and staff perceptions of both the real and an ideal program. And fourth, it allows comparison with the Ward Atmosphere Scale (WAS) which was developed by Moos and Houts (1968) to evaluate psychiatric ward environments (the subscales on the two instruments are directly parallel). Also, the use of the COPES for repeated or period measurements over time can be useful as a way of providing feedback and monitoring capability, which can then be used to bring about desired changes in the environment.

The idea of evaluating programs by assessing the psychosocial atmospheres of halfway houses, day care centers, and community care houses, appears to be an interesting and promising one. One wonders, however, whether a self-report inventory represents the most accurate, reliable, and valid way to do the job. It is, to be sure, a relatively inexpensive and quick way, which may, for these reasons, be advantageous. Systems assessment, however, in other settings is found to be a complicated, difficult process which usually involves a variety of assessment techniques, including self-reports (Schmuck and Miles, 1971).

The COPES scale is currently in an experimental stage of development and needs to be validated in a variety of settings. Construct validity studies would also be helpful.

Consultation. Mental health consultation has been identified as one of the significant approaches of the community mental health movement. It is a form of indirect service which is particularly attractive, since the primary goal is to "affect many people by working through key care-givers" (Altrocchi, 1972, p. 479). Consultation is provided to such key care-givers as policemen, teachers, clergymen, and others who are in continual contact with people throughout the community, and are in a position to provide useful psychological services.

Outcome studies on consultation have concentrated on two major topics. First, the goal of providing the key care-giver or consultee with greater knowledge and more proficient skills in providing psychological services, and second, the objective of effecting eventual changes in the client group through the consultation process. A third topic which has been much less involved in evaluation activity is that of implementing change in the system, or organizational and institutional structure toward the direction of improved mental health climate (Mannino and Shore, 1972).

Outcome measures in consultation studies have tended to lack goal specificity and, instead, have been oriented toward assessing general characteristics of the consultee or the client population. The main focus has been on large-scale studies with broad measuring instruments (Mannino and Shore, 1972).

For example, in several studies, measures of attitude changes of consultees toward greater appreciation of psychological practices, positive attitudes toward clients, concerns about prevention, and increased confidence in their abilities have been utilized in the evaluation of outcome (Dorsey, Matsunaga, and Bauman, 1964; Mariner, Brandt, Stone, and Mirmow, 1961; Pierce-Jones, Iscoe, and Cunningham, 1968; Zacker, Rutter, and Bard, 1971). Behavioral ratings of such variables as professional growth, increased communication, and problem solving ability also have been used (Dorsey and others, 1964; Deloughery, Neuman and Gebbie, 1972; Tobiessen and Shai, 1971).

Measurement of the effects of consultation on the client is extremely difficult because the effects can only be assessed indirectly, through changes in the client who is affected by the consultee who, in turn, is influenced by the consultant. To relate changes in the client to the behavior of the consultant obviously involves the consideration of a number of contributing variables and complicating factors. Studies on consultation with respect to the application of behavioral changes in clients as a result of a consultant's intervention have been made (Walder, Cohen, Breiter, Warman, Orme-Johnson, and Pavey, 1972).

As in other mental health evaluation efforts, studies on the effects of consultation have made minimal use of control or contrasting groups. Further, critical comparisons of results across studies is difficult due to differences in methodology and varying definitions. Replication of studies has been almost nonexistent (Mannino & Shore, 1972).

Multi-Dimensional Measures. Several instruments have been

developed which attempt to measure program outcome by evaluating client adjustment and performance in the community (Burnes and Roen, 1967; Ciarlo, Lin, Bigelow, and Biggerstaff, 1972; Ellsworth, 1973). These include the Community Adaptation Scale (Burnes & Roen, 1967), the Personal Adjustment and Role Skill Scale (Ellsworth, 1973), and the Denver Community Mental Health Outcome Questionnaire (Ciarlo and others, 1972). All of these instruments are characterized by their community-oriented, multidimensional quality, and all reflect the view that the adjustment of clients in the community is an important measure of the effectiveness of a mental health program.

The Denver Community Mental Health Outcome Questionnaire (DCMHQ) (Ciarlo and others, 1972) was developed primarily in order to monitor program outcome levels related to changes in programs over time. Information gained would then be fed back to management for further decisions about programs.

The seventy-one item questionnaire is grouped into seven separate dimensions: Psychological Distress, Interpersonal Isolation, Nonproductivity, Substance Abuse, Trouble With the Law, System Dependency, and Client Satisfaction. Psychological Distress measures a subjective sense of distress, upset, malaise or discomfort, often expressed in somatic terms. Interpersonal Isolation refers to the amount of personal involvement, primarily by initiative of the person himself, that the client has with family and friends. Nonproductivity measures the extent to which an individual fails to engage in constructive, socially approved instrumental activity or self-development in areas such as employment, functioning in the home, and education. Substance Abuse assesses the individual's characteristic frequency of usage of intoxicating substances of various kinds, and the troublesome or negative consequences related to the use of these substances. Trouble With the Law refers to legal difficulties in connection with traffic violations, drug abuse, loitering, and vagrancy. System Dependency measures the amount of dependence upon public resources such as welfare, rehabilitation, medical, and mental health services. Client Satisfaction refers to attitudes of service recipients. Internal consistency correlations of items in each dimension range from .34 to .81. Scale intercorrelations range from .05 to .24.

In the administration of the form, both self-report ratings

and interviewer ratings can be obtained. Most of the dimensions, with the exception of system dependency, are scored on a 0–3 range for each item. The instrument is designed for the assessment of adults between eighteen and sixty-five.

The questionnaire appears to be in the early stages of development, with validity studies currently restricted to comparisons of clients' self-reports with the judgments of the interviewers; and to comparisons of self-reports of clients to judgments of collaterals who know the persons well. Its usefulness as an outcome measure and its psychometric solidness as an instrument still need to be tested.

The Personal Adjustment and Role Skill Scale. Three forms of the Personal Adjustment and Role Skill Scale (PARS) have been developed (Ellsworth, 1973). The PARS-I Scale, which includes thirty-nine items, was developed for use by relatives of hospitalized veterans with a diagnosis of schizophrenia. PARS-II was an expanded eighty-nine items version of the original scale for use with all veterans with psychiatric problems. PARS-III was developed in conjunction with work in community clinics and included nonhospitalized community clients. The male form consists of 118 items and the female form has 120 items.

PARS-III was designed to measure the adjustment of patients in the community, using ratings by significant others of the patient. It is used to assess program effectiveness and to allow comparisons between programs. Adjustment dimensions measured by the items were obtained through a factor analytic process.

Seven factors have been defined for the male form of PARS-III. These include interpersonal involvement, confusion, anxiety, agitation-depression, alcohol/drug abuse, outside social, and employment. Interpersonal involvement measures the consideration for, and interest in significant others, and the willingness to listen and talk about important matters and angry feelings. Confusion refers to losing track of time, forgetting important things, difficulty in making decisions, need for supervision, and appearance of being in a daze. The anxiety factor assesses difficulty in eating and sleeping plus feelings of nervousness, restlessness, tension, and guilt. Agitation-depression refers to statements that people don't care about him, are unfair to him, and push him around, that something terrible will happen, that things look hopeless, and that life is not worth living.

Alcohol/drug abuse refers to drinking or using drugs to excess, letting it interfere with family and job, and spending his money unwisely. Outside social assesses attendance at, and participation in activities and recreation outside the home. Employment refers to holding a job and satisfaction with the job and fellow workers.

Six factors were obtained for the female form of PARS-III. These are interpersonal involvement, confusion, agitation, alcohol/drug abuse, household management, and outside social. The definition of these dimensions are very similar to those on the male form, except for agitation and household management. Agitation refers to acting upset, suspicious, restless, and nervous, along with talk of being afraid and of things appearing hopeless. Household management refers to shopping, preparing dinner, cleaning, doing the laundry, and other chores. The employment area is added for females who work outside the home. The parenthood skills dimension can also be included on both forms if appropriate.

Reported internal consistency correlations for each of the factors range from .79 to .93 for the male form, and .65 to .92 for the female form. Test-retest correlations of a one-week interval on the male form range from .80 to .95. Interrater correlations range from .70 to .90, including relatives of patient ratings. Intercorrelations of ratings by relatives were found to be as high as those obtained by staff, a finding which supports the view that relatives can be used in an effective manner in assessment.

The PARS has successfully differentiated clinic clients from nonclients (Ellsworth, 1973). Further validation studies of the scale would be helpful.

Community Adaptation Schedule. The Community Adaptation Schedule (CAS) is a 217 item self-report adjustment questionnaire designed to measure adjustment of clients in the community. It assays behavioral, affective, and cognitive behaviors (Burnes & Roen, 1967). Several scores can be obtained, including a score for Total Adaptation, Common Question Total, Consistency, Affect, Behavior, Cognition and six chapter scores, as follows: Work Community, Family Community, Social Community, Larger Community, Commercial Community, and Professional Community.

Each of the chapter sections have from four to eight subsections reflecting items tapping various aspects. For example, the

Commercial Community chapter has finances, shopping, transportation, modern technology, and housing as subsections.

The scale still is in its early stages of development and needs further validation studies. Cook, Looney, & Pine (1973) were unable to replicate an earlier validation study (Burnes & Roen, 1967) in using the scale to differentiate between hospital and nonhospital groups.

Management Information Systems

Management information systems (Elpers, 1972; Hargreaves, & Attkisson, 1974) are one of the most recent innovations in the mental health program evaluation field. Management information systems refer to a form of systematic information gathering and analysis primarily for management purposes. The system may take many forms depending upon the requirements of the users. It promises to be a difficult, albeit exciting, prospect since it directly attempts to tie whatever is being evaluated into the management decision-making and planning process. In order to do this effectively, the system should implement functions which allow decisions to be based on continual feedback of information and knowledge regarding the following areas: priority and distribution of existing needs, nature and extent of service utilization, data generation for various uses, allocation of manpower and financial resources, effectiveness of different service programs, movement of clients, specific weaknesses, trouble spots and strengths in programs, community attitudes and reactions to the mental health center's policies and programs, changes or impact of programs in the community, and impact of management decisions and policies. When working effectively, a management information system should provide quickly accessible, up-to-date, accurate, and relevant information on a daily basis. Integration of the critical functions is important in setting up the system. The focus in evaluation is on process rather than outcome.

The specific characteristics of a management information system are somewhat varied since we are describing a system rather than a single fixed entity. In fact, an effective management information system would probably include elements of or that relate to most of the evaluation procedures described previously in this chapter. Elpers (1972) indicates that structures and procedures should be set up which will allow planning, implementation, and feedback on five major requirements: a definition of how current resources are being spent, a determination of the structure of the service system, the provision of monitoring aids for program managers, the provision of data for multiple reporting requirements of funding agencies, and the generation of necessary data for planning purposes. For purposes of this chapter, management information systems will be described with respect to information relating to continuity of care, cost-benefit analysis, monitoring information capability, management support information networks, planning, and decision-making.

A danger in the use of management information systems is the possible development of a top-heavy administrative and recording system which creates a bureaucracy against which staff and clients have to struggle. To offset this tendency, the system should facilitate communication across levels, should allow relevant input from various levels to affect decisions and planning, and determine the effectiveness of programs. The gap between evaluation efforts and decision-making should be reduced so that staff members can see direct evidence, in terms of changes in decisions and planning, for the effectiveness of their involvement in the evaluation process.

The modification of evaluation efforts in ways which would include value judgments and preferences of the decision-maker in the data-gathering process has been suggested (Cobb, 1971; Guttentag, 1973). The value judgments of the decision-maker are among the critical elements to be examined in considering what evaluation data would be gathered. Guttentag (1973) suggests that Edwards' multi-attribute utilities method could be used as a way of measuring the values or utilities of various potential action alternatives (Edwards, 1971). In this method, quantifiable values are placed on broad programs or administrative strategies and on their potential outcomes, including their costs. Once values are determined with respect to decision-making, the hypotheses can be developed, and the investigator can have a clear idea of what he must investigate. The advantages in this process are that important values would be linked to data gathered by the researcher, the researcher would be forced out of narrow operationalism to gathering multiple measures on a variety of levels, the data gathered would have significance to the group which originally placed a value on the action alternatives related to the data, and values could be quantified and explicit. The method, however, may be difficult to carry out in practice.

In the Community Mental Health Centers Act of 1963, continuity of care was conceived as one of the most important functions to be developed by mental health centers. The concept of continuity of care implies that an individual should be able to receive a continuation of care, without getting lost or dropped, depending on his particular need for services. Typically, a person has difficulty moving from one service component to another, or from agency to agency, because of gaps in the referral process. Duplication and fragmentation of procedures and treatment also sometimes occur because of deficiencies in the transmittal of key information.

Bloom (1972) described an automated system of human accountability which gathered and disseminated information on contacts, or transactions with clients for the Westside Community Mental Health Center. This organization is a consortium of mental health agencies in San Francisco. Client transactions included in this system are: put client on waiting list (accepted for future service), remove client from waiting list, brief contact with client (no continued clinical responsibility), admission of client (accepted for current care), refer client to another Westside agency, refer client outside the consortium, discharge client by mutual agreement, discharge client by dropout or against professional advice, discharge client by other means (moved, died, etc.), discharge and transfer client to another Westside agency (by prior arrangement), discharge and transfer client outside of the consortium, and arrange for concomitant care of client. A transaction report on an individual client is a simple, single form which can be filled out in thirty seconds by the staff member. Daily pickups of transaction reports and delivery of computer outputs to agencies occurs routinely.

Computer outputs include a master list that lists identifying data and printouts of all transactions of each individual client. Another part of the computer output can provide accountability information about patient movement within the system such as the capacity of each unit to provide service, lists of clients currently being served by the agency, lists of clients being served in other agencies, and indications of concomitant care. The computer output also provides group data along four client parameters: age, sex, ethnic group, and census tract location. The output data make it possible to analyze client parameters with respect to such dimensions as the frequency of occurrence of any specified transaction during any specified time period.

This accountability system allows for the monitoring of patient movement, and potentially provides for the generation of a wide range of data for evaluation purposes. However, it is relatively expensive to set up and run for small centers, although automation would not be necessary to monitor small caseloads. The possibility of the maintenance of a system of comprehensive records of patient movement seems attractive from an evaluative viewpoint. In their study of the continuity of care in a community mental health center, Bass and Windle found that the sparseness of data in the records was a major obstacle (1972). Recently, they have developed a Continuity of Care Inventory for use in measuring the continuity of care in mental health centers (1972). The inventory was developed with a prospective orientation to offset dependence on past records.

In most mental health centers, monitoring of programs occurs through case conferences, reviews of client utilization rates, and individual supervision. The management information system, however, presents the possibility of more effectively monitoring both the process and the outcomes of programs and capabilities of the mental health center. The information and recording system is supplemental to more traditional ways of monitoring particular programs. Monitoring, in this sense, is a way of quickly detecting strengths, weaknesses, and trouble spots. Hargreaves and Attkisson (1974) indicate that information monitored may point out situations which have a greater than average probability of a problem needing intervention. Management decisions of whether to take any action are then based on the comparison of present monitoring measurements with previous ones.

Hargreaves and Attkisson conceive that the purpose of monitoring program outcome is to increase the quality of programs to a maximum relative to program costs. The idea is to present the most effective programs in the most efficient manner, and thereby to achieve proper balance in the relation of outcome to cost. In order to provide a minimum amount of routine outcome monitoring, these authors suggest three types of outcome measures: a standardized judgment of global functioning, a measure of client satisfaction, and the evaluation of the individual goals of clients. These three kinds of measures help to provide bases for determining the cost-effectiveness of programs. Cost-effectiveness refers to the quality of a program, related to its cost at a given time. The accurate determination of the cost-effectiveness of a program is extremely difficult, because of the lack of comparison norms or standards.

The implementation of huge information networks which can be readily accessible to management has occurred along with the development of sophisticated computer technology. Data banks of information can be gathered on a variety of individual and group characteristics, all available for quick retrieval. In many ways, these systems are similar to the case register, but with extended capabilities. Primarily, they serve as reservoirs for computer processable information which can be available for a variety of purposes.

The possibility of having masses of information readily available is highly attractive. As with case registers, however, the collection of information without prior specific purpose or plan for usage is somewhat wasteful. Initial determination of what data will be gathered, and in what form, may not be relevant to the questions asked at a later date. On the other hand, the general availability of information permits data to be combined in a variety of ways. Data input on nonreplicated clinical judgments, such as diagnostic categories, also presents problems of reliability which may limit usage. The cost of computer based information systems may require that information collected be related in a systematic way to planning and decision-making functions.

The advantage of management support information networks is that large amounts of current information about clients can be made available to the management and treatment staffs. The data gathered can be used to monitor and evaluate specific programs, and comparisons across facilities can be made if more than one facility is included in the network. Further, information can be quickly retrieved for decision and planning purposes, and data can be used for specific studies of the mental health system.

Several versions of management support information networks have been developed (Sheehan and Reinehr, 1973; Lipton, Lawton, Kleban, McGuire, deRivas, and Cowell, 1971; Vanhoudnos, 1971; Laska, Logemann, Honigfield, Weinstein, and Bank, 1972). The largest computer-based psychiatric information network, Multi-State Information System (msis) is briefly described below (Laska and others, 1972).

The msis is a large information network that serves agencies in Connecticut, Hawaii, Maine, Massachusetts, New York, Rhode Island, Vermont, and the District of Columbia, with a total of approximately 300,000 admissions per year. Over 700 psychiatric facilities are represented. Multiple-choice lists on preprinted questionnaires are used to allow collection of clinical data in checklisted form. The data then are read by machine, or are key-punched for transmittal to central computers. Regular output reports are provided, as well as outputs for special requests for information.

The msis has been developed in modular form so that participant members can select only those modular portions which are relevant to their needs. Five general areas of information are included: demographic, administrative, patient progress, treatment, and services rendered (Laska and others, 1972). The demographic area includes data such as sex, birthdate, address, marital status, income, ethnic group, religion, and household composition. Examples of the administrative area are legal status, physical location of patient or name of treating unit, type of treating unit, prior psychiatric service, and sources of referral and disposition. Patient progress information includes clinical judgments of the patient's psychiatric condition, such as mental status examinations, progress reports, diagnoses, appraisals of problems, and case history. The treatment area includes a general system for recording all treatment contacts and a detailed system of recording drug treatment. Examples of information related to the services rendered area are direct services, indirect service and auxiliary services, such as dental tests.

The ready availability of information makes possible studies of treatment patterns, patient characteristics, and multi-facility comparisons. One of the advantages of the msis is the uniform data procedures used across a variety of geographical and philosophical approaches, which permit the investigation to make interesting comparisons. Information also can be used for budget justification purposes, and for reallocating mental health resources. The MSIS appears to be a useful aid to management decisions and planning.

The most important component of the management information system for those in management or associated with funding bodies probably is the statistical and accounting subsystems associated with cost-benefit or cost-effectiveness analysis. This component, however, cannot work in isolation from other evaluation subsystems, since adequate data regarding other elements must be available for cost-finding to be possible (Sorensen and Phipps, 1972). In fact, most of the difficulties associated with determining cost-effectiveness are due to inadequate data regarding program effectiveness.

Some authorities have differentiated between the terms cost-benefit and cost-effectiveness, with the former referring to the assessment of costs in terms of resources expended, and the latter relating such costs to perceived effectiveness of programs. In this section, however, these terms will be used interchangeably as referring to costs expended and benefits accrued and the distinction will be ignored.

The initial step in cost-benefit analysis, and probably the easiest one, is to determine the nature and amount of resources expended by a program. This task, however, is actually a complex one since a considerable diversity of costs, such as indirect and direct services, administrative overhead, and research and development have to be weighed and assessed. Some variation is present from one agency to another in how costs are determined, depending upon the number of factors included, the specificity of the breakdown, the distribution of administrative costs over programs, and the use of modifying weighting values. The greatest emphasis generally is on staff service time and costs, since this factor constitutes the largest bulk of the resource expenditures in mental health centers.

In order to determine the costs of programs, records of staff activity must be carefully kept so that time can be accurately allocated to various aspects of the program and to individual clients. In most cases, hourly dollar rates are computed for the time spent in each activity. Costs per individual client or person affected by the program also can be calculated.

In a study at Ft. Logan base rates for utilization of staff

resources by clients were calculated in order to determine heavy and light users of resources (Weeks, 1969). This information was then available for use in predicting utilization in the future. Excess users of resources also could be identified. The relative cost per day for each treatment modality was computed and weighted in order to allow comparison across modalities.

The ratio of the costs of the program to the perceived effectiveness or value of the program is in principle, of critical importance in cost-benefit analysis. Once this ratio is determined for various alternatives concerning programs, management can have a rational basis for decision-making. At the present time, however, the actual use of such a ratio in cost-benefit analysis is not particularly feasible. The greatest obstacle is that methods for determining the effectiveness of programs have not progressed to a satisfactory level for reliable use in such analyses. Methods for accurately comparing programs in this respect have also not yet been developed. Regardless of the problems in making cost-benefit analyses, however, it appears that this ratio has been in fact used for policy decisions. Rossi (1972) notes in his discussion of a conference on poverty that cost-benefit analysis has affected federal policies.

A function of cost-benefit analysis is rate-setting for services. If accurate cost-finding is available, then fair rates can be determined, even for individual clients. Equitable rates also can be determined for third party payers and intergovernmental transfers of funds (Sorensen and Phipps, 1972).

Issues in Evaluation

The history of efforts to develop techniques for carrying out evaluations in mental health and in other social areas has been disappointing in several respects. These include, first, the resistance toward and lack of involvement of clinical staff in systematic evaluation efforts; second, the uncontrolled, complex, and vague nature of clinical practice and its naturalistic setting; third, the poor quality of evaluation efforts, particularly with respect to controls; and fourth, the frequent misuse of the results of evaluation.

Staff Resistance. In most evaluative efforts, the evaluator is dependent upon clinical staff for accurate data, maintenance of systematic procedures of evaluation, accessibility to records, and other important functions. However, staff resistance to evaluation requirements is a common problem (Weiss, 1972). Clinical staff are often reluctant to spend much effort or time in evaluative procedures, when their primary concern is providing services. When evaluative requirements are demanded of clinical staff, they may react through some form of sabotage, such as providing data in a careless and inaccurate way. In addition, evaluations are often conceived as judgmental in a perjorative sense, which may have dire consequences in terms of jobs or the elimination of programs. Change, in and of itself, is frequently resisted, and when the staff also perceives the possibility of negative consequences of their evaluations, their resistance and uncooperativeness are understandable. The problems of obtaining accurate data from a client and staff may be magnified if the evaluator is an outsider and is seen as a threat.

Suchman (1972) suggests that clinical staff should be involved as much as possible in the original selection of the goals for evaluators, and in the development of measurement procedures. In this way, the possibility of staff cooperativeness can be enhanced. Involvement of clinical staff in this way, however, increases the possibility of bias and subjectivity in the data-gathering process. Suchman believes that an evaluator cannot maintain complete detachment anyway, and is biased to a degree toward the system he is evaluating. Since the clinic staff will be an important determinant of whether the evaluation is effective or not, and also of whether the evaluation recommendations will be followed, however, it appears that the better alternative is to involve them in the evaluation process from the very beginning.

Another possibility is to reduce the impact of negative results of evaluation. One suggestion is to view all programs as experimental prior to evaluation, so that their staffs will have less commitment and involvement regarding positive evaluation outcomes, and can readily shift to another experimental program if the results are negative (Campbell, 1972). The focus of evaluation also can be directed toward the improvement of the program, rather than simply in conveying a pass-fail judgment. An awareness and appreciation of the problems faced by the clinician, as a part of an organizational analysis by the evaluator prior to the implementation of evaluation procedures, is also helpful.

Problems of Naturalistic Evaluation. Several problems are faced by the evaluator of mental health programs in natural settings. One of the problems is that the goals of programs are often expressed by the staff in vague, abstract, and nonmeasurable terms. The multiplicity and complexity of goals also results in a lack of consensus among staff regarding the priority and relevance of particular goals. Consequently, the evaluator may produce goals from his own analysis, or select goals which he can measure and then later find that the goals are seen as irrelevant by the staff. Weiss (1972) recognizes the importance of the evaluator working closely with the staff in order to define resource allocations, values, and priorities with respect to goals, and in order to render a consensus on the specific, concrete definitions of the goals for evaluation prior to proceeding in the implementation of the study.

Since top priority is necessarily given to the optimal functioning of programs, and specifically to service needs, the demands of evaluation are usually compromised whenever a conflict occurs between service and evaluation needs. Ethical and confidential matters involved in working with clients also may intrude in preventing the use of optimum evaluation strategies. Manipulations of conditions which are not seen as valuable from a service viewpoint may be resisted. Conditions such as when the program begins or the length of time it continues often are not subject to manipulation by the evaluator, which frequently results in difficulties in the control and relevance of the evaluation with respect to the planning of, and the decisions regarding, the program.

Another problem is defining and measuring stable, influential components of a complex mental health program (Weiss, 1972). Considerable variation occurs in how staff function, in the kinds of clients served, theoretical orientations, definition of concepts, and decisions about what should be accomplished. In addition, considerable movement in clients, and in staff leaving or being added to the program, normally occurs in a program's history. At times, the basic thrust of the program may drastically change as administrative policies or leaders change. These influences, plus the general complexity of mental health practice, makes the evaluation task an arduous one.

Poor Quality. After studying 181 evaluations studies of efforts to produce changes of broad social significance, Mann decided that the quality of evaluation research is "remarkably poor" (1972, p. 278). After studying a number of National Institute of Mental Health community projects, Weiss concluded that organizational constraints on the researcher's ability to apply what he knows rather than lack of research expertise are the main reasons for evaluation research falling short of expectations (1973). Alternative experimental designs are needed since organizational and other constraints probably will remain, and the evaluator must do what he can within the limits of the situation.

Campbell (1972) has suggested (at least) two quasi-experimental designs which are particularly appropriate for dealing with the limitations found in social research. The interrupted time-series design is used when no control group is available, and measures taken over periodic intervals, before and after treatment begins, are used as a background for the possible treatment effects evaluated. It is superior to the simple pretest-posttest design. The control series design requires a nonequivalent control group in which pretest and posttest measures are taken on both treatment and control groups. Matching on pretest scores is avoided in order to reduce regression artifacts. Some control over history, maturation, and test-retest is provided in this design.

Some evaluators have suggested that experimental designs may not be appropriate in practice (Weiss and Rein, 1972; Glaser and Backer, 1972; Guba, 1972). They cite the difficulty of selecting satisfactory criteria, the uncontrolled nature of the situation, the lack of standardization of treatment, the limitedness of information produced by experimental designs, conflict over control over program development, dependence on uncommitted record keepers, and the fact that operationalisms may become leading goals and the research staff may be ignorant of what is happening to the action program in the field (Weiss and Rein, 1972). Other alternatives have been suggested, such as a clinical approach to program evaluation (Glaser and Backer, 1972), goal-attainment models (Davis, 1973), process-oriented qualitative research (Weiss and Rein, 1972), system approaches (Elpers, 1972), and assessment of the value of decisions (Guttentag, 1973).

Use and Misuse of Results. There seems to be general agreement that evaluation results have often remained unused, or have been misused (Suchman, 1972; Weiss, 1972; Larsen and Nichols, 1972; Mushkin, 1973). A large number of evaluators have felt frustrated in the past because evaluation findings were often ignored when decisions were made regarding programs. A major contributing influence appeared to be that most outcome findings have tended to be negative with respect to programs. Staff have been reluctant to accept these findings, citing methodological discrepancies or other reasons for not agreeing with the results. Decision-makers are often more concerned about factors such as political pressure, loss of funding, ideological commitments, and unknown consequences of change (Weiss, 1972).

Evaluation has tended to become increasingly political in recent years (Weiss, 1972). Large scale evaluations, such as studies of the Headstart and Job Corps programs, have gained national attention and have affected federal policies. Allocations of resources may be dependent upon evaluation results. Consequently, increased pressures of various sorts, depending upon the interests of their sources have been brought to bear on evaluations and on the evaluators.

Mushkin (1973) believes that evaluation is being used as a decision-making tool more than the present state of methodology warrants. She also believes that the public and its officials misunderstand the nature of evaluation and have unrealistic expectations of its value. She suggests that evaluations be used with "extreme caution" (p. 31). It is unlikely, however, that her sensible suggestion will be heeded as the bandwagon builds for evaluations of mental health programs.

Neglected Areas

Certain areas have been neglected in community mental health evaluation. These areas, to some extent, reflect the priorities of professionals in community mental health and the interests of those involved in evaluation. Methodological difficulties in evaluating these areas also are indicated.

One of the areas neglected by evaluation procedures, and, indeed, by community mental health procedures in general, is that of consumer involvement and participation in decision-making and planning. In response to federal regulations, most community mental health centers do have citizen's advisory boards, but these rarely are representative, nor do they typically have a significant voice in critical decisions regarding programs (Chu and Trotter, 1972). In fact, consumer's ideas about what services are needed, or how services should be provided, are rarely sought by center staffs. The people being served have very little direct control or influence on community mental health services, except in those instances in which they have revolted against the system (Holden, 1971). The bureaucratic and political orientations of community mental health duties may be a significant factor to evaluate in considering the disappointing record of mental health programs (Atthowe, 1973).

Preventive programs usually have low priority in community mental health programming. They are difficult to implement and are seen as less urgent by staff. Budgeting for preventive programs is another problem. Preventive programs have not been well supported by budgetary committees. The intangibility of prevention efforts has contributed to the lack of support. In contrast, large buildings—which probably have the least value to effective community mental health programs—have proved to be one of the easiest items to justify (Chu and Trotter, 1972).

The focus of evaluation also indicates the low priority of preventive programs. Few preventive programs have been evaluated except for consultation efforts; similarly, few studies have been done on the effects of mental health practices on the problems of mental health in the total community (Edgerton, 1971). The problems and paucity of models for evaluating preventive programs also may be a factor. Generally speaking systematic methodologies for evaluating preventive programs have not yet been well worked out. Kelly (1971) however offers three tentative models for evaluating preventive programs in natural settings in terms of their effects on changes in community social systems.

Evaluations of the effects of evaluations of mental health programs and of the consequences of such evaluations on programs are greatly needed. With the increasing influence of evaluation on whether a program will continue to exist or not, and on the nature of services provided, it is important to know exactly the effects of evaluation. Studies on psychotherapy have shown the significant influence on therapy of the criteria used to evaluate outcome (Luborsky, Chandler, Auerbach, Cohen, and Bachrach, 1971). The tendency in evaluation is to focus on measurable aspects of a criteria and to ignore the rest. In many ways the available methodology has determined the factors which are considered to be important in experimental studies, with the result that relevant variables are sometimes ignored (Deese, 1969). The result is that mental health services may be oriented toward measurable outcome factors, in a manner similar to what has happened with the use of achievement scores in public schools. Consequently, the kinds of mental health services provided may depend heavily on the state of advancement in the methodology of evaluation. Outcome criteria and factors which are not easily measurable may be ignored and neglected by both evaluators and clinical staff as service priorities are determined. A dreary prospect indeed for community mental health services!

In addition to studying effects of evaluation on outcome, the influence of evaluation on the clinical process should also be assessed. To what extent will the activities and attitudes of the clinical staff change as evaluation becomes a dominant force? Will innovative practices increase or decrease? What values and positions regarding mental health will be promoted or discarded, depending on the focus of evaluation? How will clinical staff react to evaluation in their daily activities? Will two sets of clinical activity develop, one for evaluation purposes, and the other for what the clinician considers to be really important? These and other questions regarding the process of how services are provided should be assessed as evaluation proceeds. The ultimate value of evaluation as an influence in promoting better community mental health may be at stake.

Finally, it must be recognized that the methods and approaches used in evaluation are not value free. Among the contributing value-laden factors are the philosophical biases of evaluation approaches; current trends and fads in the mental health field; pressures from the scientific community; client privacy and confidentiality rights; the political realities of the moment; the beliefs of evaluators, administrators, and those in charge of funding regarding the value of certain outcome criteria; and the feasibility of the implementation of evaluation procedures in view of the costs involved and the prevailing social climate. Examiner biases and other factors influencing the results of evaluation also must be recognized. The context of evaluation and its influences should be measured, and the relative contribution of its effects on the direction of evaluation results should be noted. Hopefully, the value biases of particular evaluation approaches could be clearly stated and described, indicating the limitations imposed as a consequence. In other words, evaluators must become more responsible with respect to their own values and beliefs as their influence increases in community mental health practices.

References

ALTROCCHI, J. "Mental Health Consultation." In S. Golann and C. Eisdorfer (Eds.), *Handbook of Community Mental Health.* New York: Appleton-Century-Crofts, 1972, pp. 477–508.

AMERICAN PSYCHIATRIC ASSOCIATION. "Committee on Nomenclature and Statistics." *Mental Disorders: Diagnostic and Statistical Manual.* Washington, D.C.: American Psychiatric Association Hospital Service, 1952.

ATTHOWE, J. "Behavior Innovation and Persistence." *American Psychologist,* 1973, *28,* 34–41.

ATTKISSON, C., MC INTYRE, M., HARGREAVES, W., HARRIS, M., AND OCHBERG, F. "Toward a Working Model for Mental Health Program Evaluation." Unpublished manuscript, 1973.

BAHN, A. *Psychiatric Case Register Conference, 1965.* Washington, D.C.: Outpatient Studies Section, Office of Biometry, National Institute of Mental Health, 1965.

BAHN, A., GARDNER, E., ALLTOP, L., KNALTERUD, G., AND SOLOMON, M. "Admission and Prevalence Rates for Psychiatric Facilities in Four Register Areas." *American Journal of Public Health,* 1966, *56,* 2033–2051.

BALDWIN, J. "Community Mental Health Information Systems: The Psychiatric Case Register as a Data Blank." In S. Golann and C. Eisdorfer (Eds.), *Handbook of Community Mental Health.* New York: Appleton-Century-Crofts, 1972, pp. 779–818.

BASS, R. AND WINDLE, C. "Continuity of Care: An Approach to Measurement." *American Journal of Psychiatry,* 1972, *129,* 196–201.

BLOOM, B. "A Census Trait Analysis of Socially Deviant Behaviors." *Multivariate Behavioral Research,* 1966, *1,* 307–320.

BLOOM, B. "Human Accountability in a Community Mental Health Center: Report on an Automated System." *Community Mental Health Journal,* 1972, *8,* 251–260.

BONSTEDT, T. "Concrete Goal-setting for Patients in a Day Hospital." *Evaluation,* Special Monograph Number 1, 1973, 3–5.

BURNES, A. AND ROEN, S. "Social Roles and Adaptation to the Community." *Community Mental Health Journal,* 1967, *3,* 153–158.

CAMPBELL, D. "Reforms as Experiments." In C. Weiss (Ed.) *Evaluating action programs.* Boston: Allyn & Bacon, 1972, pp. 187–223.

CHU, F., AND TROTTER, S. "The Mental Health Complex, Part I: The Community Mental Health Centers." Washington, D.C.: Center For Study of Responsible Law. Unpublished manuscript, 1972.

CIARLO, J., LIN, S., BIGELOW, D., AND BIGGERSTAFF, M. "A Multi-Dimensional Outcome Measure for Evaluating Community Mental Health Programs." Evaluation Project of the Denver General Hospital Mental Health Center, Denver, Colorado. Unpublished manuscript, 1972.

COBB, C. "A Management Information System for Mental Health Planning and Program Evaluation." *Community Mental Health Journal,* 1971, *7,* 280–287.

COLE, N., BRANCH, C., AND ORLA, M. "Mental Illness." *American Medical Association Archives of Neurology and Psychiatry,* 1957, *77,* 393–398.

COOK, P., LOONEY, M., AND PINE, L. "The Community Adaptation Schedule and the Adjective Check List: A Validational Study with Psychiatric Inpatients and Outpatients." *Community Mental Health Journal,* 1973, *9,* 11–17.

CRESSEY, D. "Measuring Crime Rates." In A. Guenther (Ed.), *Criminal Behavior and Social Systems.* Chicago: Rand McNally and Company, 1970, pp. 55–59.

DAVIS, H. "Four Ways to Goal Attainment." *Evaluation,* 1973, *1,* 43–48.

DEESE, J. "Behavior and Fact." *American Psychologist,* 1969, *24,* 515–522.

DELOUGHERY, G., NEUMAN, B., AND GEBBIE, K. "Mental Health Consultation as a Means for Improving Problem Solving Ability in Work Groups: A Pilot Study." *Comparative Group Studies,* 1972, *3,* 89–97.

DOHRENWEND, B. P. AND DOHRENWEND, B. S. *Social Status and Psycho-*

logical Disorder: A Causal Inquiry. New York: John Wiley and Sons, 1969.

DOHRENWEND, B. P. AND DOHRENWEND, B. S. "Psychiatric Epidemiology: An Analysis of 'True Prevalence' Studies." In S. Golann and C. Eisdorfer (Eds.), *Handbook of Community Mental Health.* New York: Appleton-Century-Crofts, 1972, pp. 283–302.

DORSEY, J., MATSUNAGA, G., AND BAUMAN, G. "Training Public Health Nurses in Mental Health." *Archives of General Psychiatry,* 1964, *11,* 214–222.

DOUGLAS, J. *The Social Meanings of Suicide.* Princeton, New Jersey: Princeton University Press, 1967.

EDGERTON, J. "Evaluation in Community Mental Health." In G. Rosenblaum (Ed.), *Issues in Community Psychology and Preventive Mental Health.* New York: Behavioral Publications, Inc., 1971, pp. 89–108.

EDWARDS, W. "Social Utilities." *The Engineering Economist,* Summer Symposium Series, *VI,* 1971.

ELLIS, R., AND WILSON, N. "Evaluating Treatment Effectiveness Using a Goal-Oriented Automated Progress Note." *Evaluation,* Special Monographs Number 1, 1973, 6–11.

ELLSWORTH, R. "Consumer Feedback in Measuring the Effectiveness of Mental Health Programs." Unpublished manuscript, 1973.

ELPERS, J. "Management Information Systems: Tools for Integrating Human Services." Paper presented at the Twenty-Fourth Institute on Hospital and Community Psychiatry, St. Louis, Missouri, 1972.

FABREGA, H. AND MC BEE, G. "Validity Features of a Mental Health Questionnaire." *Social Science and Medicine,* 1970, *4,* 669–673.

FAIRWEATHER, G., SANDERS, D., CRESSLER, D., AND MAYNARD, H. *Community Life for the Mentally Ill: An Alternative to Institutional Care.* Chicago: Aldine Publishing Company, 1969.

FARBEROW, N., AND SHNEIDMAN, E. *The Cry for Help.* New York: McGraw-Hill, 1965.

FOWLER, G., AND PULLAN, E. "1972 Index of Needs for Mental Health Services." Unpublished manuscript, 1972.

GLASER, E. AND BACKER, T. "A Clinical Approach to Program Evaluation." *Evaluation,* 1972, *1,* 54–55.

GLASSCOTE, R., GUDEMAN, J., AND ELPERS, R. *Halfway Houses for the Mentally Ill.* Washington, D.C.: The Joint Information Service of the American Psychiatric Association, 1971.

GOLDSMITH, H., AND UNGER, E. "Differentiation of Urban Subareas: A Reexamination of Social Area Dimensions." Laboratory Paper No. 35, Washington, D.C.: Mental Health Study Center, National Institute of Mental Health, 1970.

GOLDSMITH, H., AND UNGER, E. "Social Areas: Identification Procedures Using 1970 Census Data." Laboratory Paper No. 37, Mental Health Study Center, National Institute of Mental Health, 1972a.

GOLDSMITH, H., AND UNGER, E. "Social Area Analysis: Procedures and Illustrative Applications Based on the Mental Health Demographic Profile System." Paper presented at the American Statistical Association, 1972b.

GORWITZ, K., BAHN, A., CHANDLER, C., AND MARTIN, W. "Planned Use of a Statewide Psychiatric Register for Aiding Mental Health in the Community." *American Journal of Orthopsychiatry,* 1963, *33,* 494–500.

GUBA, E. "The Failure of Educational Evaluation." In C. Weiss (Ed.) *Evaluating Action Programs.* Boston: Allyn and Bacon, 1972, pp. 250–266.

GUTTENTAG, M. "Subjectivity and Its Use in Evaluation in Research." *Evaluation,* 1973, *1,* 60–65.

HARAKAL, C., AND SILVER, M. "Identifying High Risk Populations for Mental Health Services Using 1970 Census Data." Unpublished manuscript, 1973.

HARGREAVES, W. AND ATTKISSON, C. "On the Horizon: Outcome Evaluation." In T. Smith & J. Sorensen (Eds.) *Integrated Management Information Systems for Community Mental Health Centers.* Rockville, Maryland: National Institute of Mental Health, 1974.

HOLDEN, C. "Community Mental Health Centers: Growing Movement Seeks Identity." *Science,* 1971, *174,* 1110–1113.

HOLLINGSHEAD, A. AND REDLICH, F. *Social Class and Mental Illness.* New York: Wiley, 1958.

HONIGFELD, G. AND KLEIN, D. "The Hillside Hospital Patient Progress Record: Explorations in Clinical Management by Objective and Exception." *Evaluation,* Special Monograph Number 1, 1973, 19–22.

KELLY, J. "The Quest for Valid Preventive Interventions." In G. Rosenblaum (Ed.), *Issues in Community Psychology and Preventive Mental Health.* New York: Behavioral Publications, Inc., 1971, pp. 109–140.

KIRESUK, T. "Goal Attainment Scaling at a County Mental Health Service." *Evaluation,* Special Monograph Number 1, 1973, 12–18.

KIRESUK, T. AND SHERMAN, R. "Goal Attainment Scaling: A General Method for Evaluating Comprehensive Community Mental Health Programs." *Community Mental Health Journal,* 1968, *4,* 443–453.

LARSEN, J. AND NICHOLS, D. "If Nobody Knows You've Done it, Have You?" *Evaluation,* 1972, *1,* 39–44.

LASKA, E., LOGEMANN, G., HONIGFIELD, G., WEINSTEIN, A., AND BANK, R. "The Multi-State Information System." *Evaluation,* 1972, *1,* 66–71.

LEIGHTON, D., HARDING, J., MACKLIN, D., MACMILLAN, A., AND LEIGHTON, A. *The Character of Danger.* New York: Basic Books, 1963.

LEIGHTON, A., LEIGHTON, D., AND DANLEY, R. "Validity in Mental Health Surveys." *Canadian Psychiatric Association Journal,* 1966, *11,* 167–178.

LIPTON, M., LAWTON, M., KLEBAN, M., MC GUIRE, M., DE RIVAS, C., AND COWELL, L. "Mental Health Program Evaluation, Record Automation, and Self-regulatory Feedback in a Large Mental Health Service Agency." Unpublished manuscript, 1971.

LITMAN, R., CURPHEY, T., SHNEIDMAN, E., FARBEROW, N., AND TABACHNIK, N. "Investigation of Equivocal Suicides." *Journal of American Medical Association,* 1963, *184,* 924–929.

LUBORSKY, L., CHANDLER, M., AUERBACH, A., COHEN, J., AND BACHRACH, H. "Factors Influencing the Outcome of Psychotherapy: A Review of Quantitative Research." *Psychological Bulletin,* 1971, *75,* 145–185.

MAC DONALD, J. "Suicide and Homocide by Automobile." *American Journal of Psychiatry,* 1964, *121,* 336–370.

MANIS, J., BRAWER, M., HUNT, C., AND KERCHER, L. "Estimating the Prevalence of Mental Illness." *American Sociological Review,* 1964, *29,* 84–89.

MANN, J. "The Outcome of Evaluative Research." In C. Weiss (Ed.) *Evaluating Action Programs.* Boston: Allyn and Bacon, Inc., 1972, pp. 267–282.

MANNINO, F. AND SHORE, M. "Research in Mental Health Consultation." In S. Golann and C. Eisdorfer (Eds.), *Handbook of Community Mental Health.* New York: Appleton-Century-Crofts, 1972, pp. 755–778.

MARINER, A., BRANDT, E., STONE, E., AND MIRMOW, E. "Group Psychiatric Consultation with Public School Personnel: A Two Year Study." *Personnel and Guidance Journal*, 1961, *40*, 254–258.

MISHLER, E., AND SCOTCH, N. "Sociocultural Factors in the Epidemiology of Schizophrenia: A Review." *International Journal of Psychiatry*, 1965, *1*, 258–293.

MOORE, D., BLOOM, B., GAYLIN, S., PEPPER, M., PETTUS, C., WILLIS, E., AND BAHN, A. "Data Utilization for Local Mental Health Program Development." *Community Mental Health Journal*, 1967, *3*, 30–32.

MOOS, R. "The Community-Oriented Programs Environment Scales (COPES)." Technical Report, Social Ecology Laboratory, Palo Alto, California: Department of Psychiatry, Stanford University, 1971.

MOOS, R. "Assessment of the Psychosocial Environments of Community-oriented Psychiatric Treatment Programs." *Journal of Abnormal Psychology*, 1972, *79*, 9–18.

MOOS, R. AND HOUTS, P. "Assessment of the Social Atmospheres of Psychiatric Wards." *Journal of Abnormal Psychology*, 1968, *73*, 595–604.

MUSHKIN, S. "Evaluations: Use with Caution." *Evaluation*, 1973, *1*, 30–35.

PASAMANICK, B., ROBERTS, D., LEMKAU, P., AND KRUEGER, D. "A Survey of Mental Disease in an Urban Population: Prevalence by Age, Sex, and Severity of Impairment." *American Journal of Public Health*, 1957, *47*, 923–929.

PHILLIPS, D. "The 'True Prevalence' of Mental Illness in a New England State." *Community Mental Health Journal*, 1966, *2*, 35–40.

PIERCE-JONES, J., ISCOE, I., AND CUNNINGHAM, G. *Child Behavior Consultation in Elementary Schools: A Demonstration and Research Program.* Austin, Texas: University of Texas Press, 1968.

RAUSH, H. AND RAUSH, C. *The Halfway House Movement: A Search for Sanity.* New York: Appleton-Century-Crofts, 1968.

REDICK, R., GOLDSMITH, H., AND UNGER, E. "1970 Census Data Used to Indicate Areas with Different Potentials for Mental Health and Related Problems." (DHEW Publication No. HSM-72-9051) Washington, D.C..: United States Government Printing Office, 1971.

ROSSI, P. "Testing for Success and Failure in Social Action." In

P. Rossi and W. Williams (Eds.), *Evaluating Social Programs.*
New York: Seminar Press, 1972, pp. 11–49.

ROTH, W. AND LUTON, F. "The Mental Hygiene Program in Tennessee."
American Journal of Psychiatry, 1943, *99,* 662–675.

RUBINSTEIN, E. AND PARLOFF, M. *Research in Psychotherapy.* Washington, D.C.: American Psychological Association, 1959.

SCHAEFER, C. "Statistics System of the Denver General Hospital Community Mental Health Center." Unpublished manuscript, 1973.

SCHMIDT, H. AND FONDA, C. "The Reliability of Psychiatric Diagnosis: A New Look." *Journal of Abnormal and Social Psychology,* 1956, *52,* 262–267.

SCHMUCK, R. AND MILES, M. *Organizational Development in Schools.* Palo Alto, California: National Press Books, 1971.

SCHULBERG, H. AND WECHSLER, A. "The Uses and Misuses of Data in Assessing Mental Health Needs." *Community Mental Health Journal,* 1967, *3,* 389–395.

SHEEHAN, D. AND REINEHR, R. "Computer-Assisted Program Administration in Texas Psychiatric Hospitals." *Hospital and Community Psychiatry,* 1973, *24,* 27–29.

SORENSEN, J., AND PHIPPS, D. "Cost Finding: A Tool for Managing Your Community Mental Health Center." *Administration in Mental Health,* 1972, 68–73.

SROLE, L., LANGNER, T., MICHAEL, S., OPLER, M., AND RENNIE, T. *Mental Health in the Metropolis: The Midtown Manhattan Study.* New York: McGraw-Hill, 1962.

STELMACHERS, Z., LUND, S., AND MEADE, C. "Hennepin County Crisis Intervention Center: Evaluation of its Effectiveness." *Evaluation,* 1972, *1,* 61–65.

STIEPER, D. AND WIENER, D. *Dimensions of Psychotherapy.* Chicago: Aldine Publishing Company, 1965.

STRUPP, H. *Psychotherapy: Clinical, Research, and Theoretical Issues.* New York: Jason Aronson, Inc., 1973.

SUCHMAN, E. "Actions for What? A Critique of Evaluative Research." In C. Weiss (Ed.), *Evaluating Action Programs.* Boston: Allyn & Bacon, 1972, pp. 52–84.

TABACHNIK, N., LITMAN, R., OSMAN, M., JONES, W., COHN, S., KASPER, A., AND MOFFAT, J. "Comparative Psychiatric Study of Accidental and Suicidal Death." *Archives of General Psychiatry,* 1966, *14,* 60–68.

TOBIESSEN, J. AND SHAI, A. "A Comparison of Individual and Group

Mental Health Consultation with Teachers." *Community Mental Health Journal,* 1971, *7,* 218–226.

TRUSSELL, R., ELINSON, J., AND LEVIN, M. "Comparisons of Various Methods of Estimating the Prevalence of Chronic Disease in a Community—the Hunterdon County Study." *American Journal of Public Health,* 1956, *46,* 173–182.

VANHOUDNOS, H. "An Automated Community Mental Health Information System." Unpublished manuscript, 1971.

WALDER, L., COHEN, S., BREITER, D., WARMAN, F., ORME-JOHNSON, D., AND PAVEY, S. "Parents as Agents of Behavior Change." In S. Golann & C. Eisdorfer (Eds.), *Handbook of Community Mental Health.* New York: Appleton-Century-Crofts, 1972.

WARD, C., BECK, A., MENDELSON, M., MOCK, J., AND ERBAUGH, J. "The Psychiatric Nomenclature." *Archives of General Psychiatry,* 1962, *7,* 198–205.

WEEKS, L. "Resource Use of Base Rates." In Western Interstate Commission for Higher Education. (Ed.), *A Demonstration of Statistical Techniques in a Mental Health Program.* Boulder, Colorado, 1969, pp. 80–91.

WEISS, C. "Evaluating Educational and Social Action Programs: A Treeful of Owls." In C. Weiss (Ed.), *Evaluating Action Programs.* Boston: Allyn and Bacon, 1972, pp. 3–27.

WEISS, C. "Between the Cup and the Lip." *Evaluation,* 1973, *1,* 49–55.

WEISS, R. AND REIN, M. "The Evaluation of Broad-Aim Programs: Difficulties in Experimental Design and an Alternative." In C. Weiss (Ed.), *Evaluating Action Programs.* Boston: Allyn and Bacon, 1972, pp. 236–249.

WILSON, N., ELLIS, R., BOOTH, R., AND MUMPOWER, J. "The Automated Tri-informant Goal Oriented Progress Note: Overview." A Publication of ATGON. Fort Logan Mental Health Center, Denver, Colorado, 1973.

ZACKER, J., RUTTER, E., AND BARD, M. "Evaluation of Attitudinal Changes in a Program of Community Consultation." *Community Mental Health Journal,* 1971, *7,* 236–241.

ZIGLER, E., AND PHILLIPS, L. "Psychiatric Diagnosis and Symptomatology." *Journal of Abnormal and Social Psychology,* 1961, *63,* 69–75.

XI

Scalp-Recorded Potential Correlates of Psychological Phenomena in Man

BERT S. KOPELL, MARGARET J. ROSENBLOOM

Ever since Berger (1929) described the electrical activity of the cortex recorded from the intact human scalp, many attempts have been made to study higher brain functioning by analyzing the electroencephalogram (EEG) (Glaser, 1963; Wilson, 1965). For a long while such attempts have been disappointing and the main value of the EEG has lain in its clinical applications (Hill and Parr, 1963). However, the development of techniques for summing or averaging the responses to specific stimuli has yielded new measures which have been found to be sensitive to a number of psychological processes (Callaway, 1966; Regan, 1972; Shagass, 1972a). This chapter will mainly deal with the relationship between psychological phenomena and averaged EEG measures. Studies of the effects of physical features of stimuli on averaged EEG measures (Regan, 1972, 31–132); animal studies; and studies investigating basic neurological origins of the EEG (Regan, 1972; McSherry, 1973) will not be included in this chapter.

433

Among the psychological phenomena which have been correlated with averaged EEG measures are: forms of attention (Callaway, 1966; Tecce, 1970); motivation (Knott, 1972); expectation (Walter, Cooper, Aldridge, McCallum, and Winter, 1964); decision making (Sutton, Tueting, Zubin, and John, 1967; Roth, Kopell, Tinklenberg, Darley, Sikora, and Vesecky, 1974); certainty and uncertainty (Sutton, Braren, Zubin, and John, 1965); learning (Jenness, 1972); memory processes (Weinberg, Walter, and Crow, 1970); the effect of set on perception (Begleiter, Porjesz, Yerre, and Kissin, 1973); and the assigning of semantic content to stimuli (Buchsbaum and Fedio, 1969). While most research has proceeded on the assumption that individual differences in these processes are of normal distribution, some recent work has indicated averaged EEG differences which correlate with individual differences such as personality (Knott and Irwin, 1973), perceptual style (Silverman, 1970; Buchsbaum and Pfefferbaum, 1971); sex (Silverman, Buchsbaum, and Stierlin, 1973; Knott and Peters, 1974); IQ (Callaway, 1973); and psychopathology (Shagass, 1972a, 1972b).

This chapter contains first a description of the most important averaged EEG measures; second, a brief survey of the main methodological problems associated with research using these measures; third, a summary and assessment of the EP (evoked potential) and CNV (contingent negative variation) as objective indicators of psychological processes; fourth, a summary and assessment of the use of the EP and CNV indicators to measure psychological individual differences; and fifth, a discussion of the use of averaged EEG techniques in the assessment of psychological changes induced by drugs.

Averaged EEG Measures

The unaveraged EEG as recorded from the scalp is a representation of the enormously complex electrical activity of the brain. The response of the brain to any particular stimuli or events usually cannot be seen in the unaveraged EEG since these potentials are of lower amplitude than the background EEG. For example, the scalp-recorded electrical potential evoked by a single stimulus may only be a few millionths of a volt (μV), while alpha waves, the dominant frequency in the EEG, can be as great as fifty or 100 microvolts

(Callaway, 1966). However, since the EP to any particular stimulus is reproducible, a technique of averaging or summing repeated responses to repeated presentations of the same stimulus enables those potentials specifically time-locked to the particular stimulus to be summed, while the other random activity, or noise (that is, non-time-locked potentials) cancel themselves out.

The EP and the CNV are two characteristic responses revealed by this averaging technique. The EP consists of a distinctive series of positive and negative peaks which are believed to represent the sequence of neural events by which the stimulus is perceived and processed by the brain (Mackworth, 1969). The CNV is a slow negative potential shift which develops in a foreperiod reaction time (RT) format when a subject knows that the first stimulus (S_1) is a warning that the second stimulus (S_2), an event of importance, will follow (Walter and others, 1964). While the EP in part reflects the physical properties of the stimulus (Regan, 1972), the CNV is a phenomenon almost entirely dependent on a psychological association developing between stimuli and is independent of the physical qualities of the stimuli per se (Walter, 1964a), though the psychological effect of varying stimulus features certainly modulates CNV amplitude (Picton and Low, 1971).

The EP can be elicited by stimuli of all sensory modalities. While each modality yields EPs of distinct topographic and structural features (Goff, 1969), and while EPs do vary between individuals, it is possible both to identify homologous peaks in responses evoked in different modalities and a standard sequence of components in the EPs of different individuals. This is because variations in EP between subjects tend to be in the amplitude rather than in the latency of components (Vaughan and Ritter, 1973). An individual's EP tends to be quite stable over time (Dustman and Beck, 1963).

The different components of the EP can be identified on the basis of their poststimulus latency and their amplitude. There are several different conventions used for identifying and labelling the component peaks of the EP, though order of appearance and positivity and negativity are usually indicated (Goff, Matsumiya, Allison, and Goff, 1969). Since the different equipment and techniques used in different laboratories also affect structural features of the EPS recorded there (Bergamini and Bergamasco, 1967), comparisons between EPS recorded in different laboratories should be made with caution. See Figure 1 for an EP recorded in our laboratory to an unexpected tone.

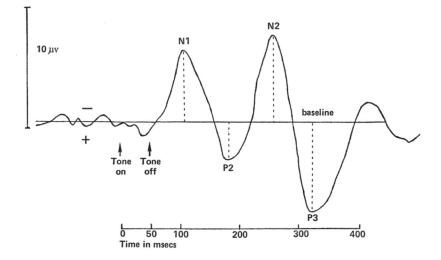

FIGURE 1. Evoked potential to unexpected stimulus, average of thirty-two responses.

Because it is conceptually convenient, the EP is often broken down into early and late components (Callaway, 1966). A great deal of evidence indicates that the early components of the EP (occurring less than 80 msec after the stimulus) reflect simple sensory processing of the stimulus, and are insensitive to psychological and drug-induced changes in human subjects. The late components reflect higher processing of stimuli, and do reflect psychological and drug-induced changes. The neurological basis for distinguishing between early and late components of the EP is not above dispute (Walter, 1964a; Goff, 1969), and the psychologist using EP measures should be aware of the significance of physical differences in stimuli used, and keep this element of his paradigm constant. Of the later components of the EP, a positive component occurring at between 250 and 400 msec poststimulus appears to be most sensitive to psychological phenomena. It is usually the third positive component and has been variously referred to as P_3, P_{300}, or Late Positive Component.

The most commonly used measures of the EP are latency and amplitude of specified peaks. Amplitude is generally measured from a prestimulus baseline to the peak of the component, though peak-to-peak measures of adjacent components are also used. Other measures derived from the data presented by the EP include measures of replicability (Donchin, 1969a, 1969b), variability (Callaway and Halliday, 1973) and frequency, determined by Fourier analysis (Shucard and Callaway, 1973).

Discovery of the CNV was made possible only with the development of techniques for DC recording (Walter and others, 1964). It was initially called the E or expectancy wave. Its apparent reflection of such psychological processes as motivation, expectation, attention and preparedness has led to a great deal of interest in this phenomenon. Since 1964, studies focusing on the CNV can be numbered in the hundreds. Recent reviews of this phenomenon are available (Tecce, 1971, 1972; McCallum and Knott, 1973). Its presence or absence and variations in its rise time (Cohen, 1969), amplitude area (Rebert and Sperry, 1973), and resolution (Wilkinson and Spence, 1973; Roth and others, 1974) are believed to be sensitive indicators of psychological factors. CNV negativity begins to develop at about 400 msec after the first stimulus (Rebert and Knott, 1970). The amplitude of the CNV is calculated by measuring the height of the slope above a prestimulus baseline at certain points. Laboratories differ in the exact details of technique (Tecce, 1972). At its maximal point this amplitude averages around 20 μV (Tecce, 1972). See Figure 2 for a diagram of a CNV with paradigm and measuring points used in our laboratory. The subject is instructed to press the button which turns off the tone as soon as the tone is heard. He is told that the tone (S_2) is preceded by one second by the appearance of a star (S_1).

The CNV is a relatively small potential change on a standing or baseline DC potential. This DC baseline is subject to quite large fluctuations due to electrode polarization, spontaneous autonomic changes and so on. Such fluctuations can take the EEG signal beyond the range of amplifiers. In order to obtain consistent, reliable, re-

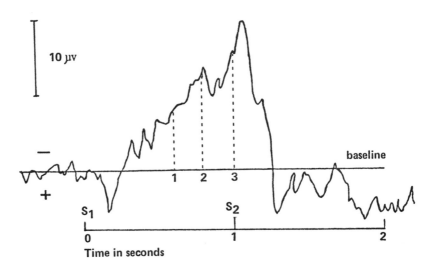

FIGURE 2. Contingent Negative Variation (CNV area equals the
sum of amplitude at points 1, 2, and 3), average of
thirty-two responses.

peated measures of the CNV, we utilize a device to zero-set the signal before the recording of each trial or segment to be averaged
(Macpherson and Kopell, 1972).

Methodological Problems

A study of the psychological correlates of averaged EEG measures involves a variety of methodological problems. Certain technical problems relating to the methods of stimuli presentation, EEG
recording, and averaging have been reviewed by Regan (1972,
196–258) and Shagass (1972a, 7–48), and will not be discussed
here. Problems more specific to the study of psychological correlates
of averaged EEG measures are presented below.

A prevailing problem in EEG research is the gratuitous recording of noncortical electrical signals along with cortical signals.
When such noncortical potentials derive from autonomic changes
which correlate with psychological processes (Lang, 1971), the
validity of EEG measures is threatened. Muscular potentials, particu-

larly from neck and facial muscles, Galvanic Skin Response (GSR), and eye movements and blinks contaminate the scalp-recorded EEG (Callaway, 1966). In averaged EEG measures, these contaminants are especially troublesome, since frequently they are responses to the repeated stimuli, become enhanced by the procedure of summing, and so produce gross distortions of the cortical potentials being studied. Because of its long latency the CNV is particularly susceptible to distortions by eye-movements and the Cephalic Skin Potential. Methods for correcting or controlling for these distortions have been developed and significantly improve the validity of EP and CNV measures (Hillyard and Galambos, 1970; Corby and Kopell, 1972; Picton and Hillyard, 1972; Corby, Roth and Kopell, 1974).

Pupil size is another example of a physiological variable which correlates with psychological state. However, studies linking pupil-size with psychological variables are not unanimous in their results; and the effect of differences in pupil-size on the averaged EEG measures appears to be limited (Schechter and Buchsbaum, 1973).

Various biological rhythms such as the cardiac and respiratory cycles, and features of background EEG, such as the alpha cycle and alpha synchronization and desynchronization, have been found to affect features of the EP and CNV (Callaway and Layne, 1964; Callaway, 1966; Ciganek, 1969; Tecce, 1970, 1972; Gullickson and Darrow, 1973; and Lacey and Lacey, 1973). While such changes cannot easily be controlled, it is important that the investigator be aware of the possible effects of these additional variables on his data.

The general level of subject alertness or arousal affects the resting DC level of the EEG (Jasper, 1936; Knott, 1972). Changes in phasic arousal have been associated with significant slow negative shifts (Karrer, Kohn, and Ivins, 1973). Heightened phasic arousal has also been found to enhance both the EP (Eason and Dudley, 1971) and the CNV (Tecce, 1972), though apparently CNV enhancement bears an inverted U relationship to increases in behavioral arousal. However, available evidence suggests that the relationship between the CNV and independent autonomic measures of arousal such as GSR is not simple or direct (Low, Coats, Rettig and McSherry, 1967; Knott, 1972; Papakostopoulos, 1973). Paradigms requiring subjects to respond at designated times, even without the use of aversive stimuli, are likely to produce fluctuations in alertness as an intrinsic part of task-performance (Karlin, 1970). The concurrent recording of independent autonomic measures of arousal such as GSR, as well as the monitoring of baseline DC changes throughout recording sessions (Corby and Kopell, 1973) are valuable techniques for assessing the effects of arousal fluctuations on averaged EEG measures. The effect of baseline DC changes on the CNV and EP, and their relationships to psychological phenomena such as attention are extremely complex. Further discussions of this problem can be found in the discussion of the relationship between CNV and P_3 on pages 450–452.

CNV and EP paradigms necessitate repetition of stimuli in order to sum responses. This procedure introduces the problem both of neurophysiological habituation of the orienting response (a marked decrement of response to a monotonously repeated stimulus) (Thompson and Spencer, 1966), and more general decline in subject alertness. Where possible, separate averages for successive segments of a recording session provide valuable information about fluctuations in alertness associated with fatigue (Roth, 1973; Ford, Roth, and Kopell, 1974). In experiments in which subjects are given a variety of tests, it is essential to balance the order of presenting the tests across subjects to avoid the possibility that the last test effect or fatigue may contaminate results.

As stated earlier, intersubject differences are greater than intrasubject differences. This makes it necessary to run a considerable number of subjects in order to demonstrate differences between groups. It is preferable to use subjects as their own control, particularly in research involving different treatments such as psychological manipulations or drug administration (Kopell, Tinklenberg, and Hollister, 1972). Each subject comes to the experimental situation with his particular history, aptitudes, and expectations. Whether paradigms which employ some form of explicit instructions and tasks for subjects provide a greater degree of control over subjects' idiosyncratic mental activities than those which merely record EPs to stimuli in undefined situations is a moot point (Roth, 1973), and the techniques adopted reflect the personal confidence of the investigator in the trustworthiness of the subject. While it is obviously impossible to obtain complete control over the subjects' hearts and minds during the experiment (Sutton, 1969), it is possible and highly desirable to conduct debriefing interviews to assess gross variations in subjects' attitudes toward the experience (Rebert and Sperry, 1973).

The use of averaged EEG measures to study psychological phenomena represents a challenging feat of interdisciplinary tightrope walking. Each discipline has distinct foci of interest, methodological values, and conceptual and substantive shortcomings. Problems which trouble neurophysiologists may be of little concern per se to psychologists, for example, the effect of volume conduction in confounding magnitude with spatial distribution of cortical responses (Vaughan and Ritter, 1973). Problems which fascinate psychologists, but which they are poorly able to define and control, such as motivational and attentional variables, are so much interference to neurophysiologists in their study of intercellular and intracellular events. The psychologist's concern with problems of validity and reliability is not generally shared by neurophysiologists and electroencephalographers (Ellingson, 1966). In spite of these difficulties, however, there appear to be some consistent correlations between neurophysiological and psychological phenomena, and these must provide the impetus to establishing a clearer understanding of their mutual relationships.

The focus of this chapter will be on averaged EEG measures and how they reflect differences in experimentally manipulated psychological conditions. Essentially, we are reporting on studies in which paradigms have been devised to manipulate subjects' psychological states while EEG recordings were taken. At this point, it is essential to stress that the psychological phenomena can only be defined in terms of the paradigms eliciting them, and are not necessarily of broader applicability. Listening to a constant series of tones to detect an occasional change, which must be signalled (Ford and others, 1974), can be cited as a form of attention involving recognition and decision-making processes. However, the extrapolation from this specific manifestation of attention to a more global concept can only be made with caution. Conflicting findings regarding EP correlates of attention can only result (Callaway, 1966). Twice over is faith demanded in this kind of research: first, that subjects have indeed followed instructions, and have been psychologically affected in the manner intended; and secondly, that the recording procedures and equipment employed also have provided an accurate and reliable reflection of cortical electrical activity.

Averaged EEG Measures and Psychological Processes

In this section some psychological correlates of the EP, and particularly the P_3 component will be examined. EPS have been elicited by paradigms which have been interpreted as activating a whole range of psychological variables (Sutton, 1969). While recognizing the limitations stated above, regarding the generalizability from an experimental paradigm to a broad psychological concept, let us examine the relationship between these measures and psychological variables.

The concept of attention has fascinated neurophysiologists and psychologists, has generated considerable controversy and confusion, and has been the topic of several conferences and symposia (Sanders, 1967, 1970; Evans and Mulholland, 1969; Koster, 1969; Mostofsky, 1970; Kornblum, 1973). Berlyne (1969) traced the vicissitudes of the concept since the mid-18th century, noting its suppression during the behaviorist revolution and its recent revival as a legitimate area of study for psychologists now that other disciplines are providing objective indicators of its operation. Attention can be paid generally, relating to the external environment as a whole, or selectively, allocated among competing stimuli in that environment. Attention can also be sustained over time, that is, consciously directed toward an anticipated event; or it can be involuntarily demanded of one, as in the orienting response to an unexpected event. Averaged EEG measures, elicited in paradigms which can be said to activate these forms of attention, have been shown to change with paradigm changes.

A great deal of evidence indicates that attended stimuli evoke larger EPS, usually with marked P_3, than ignored or irrelevant stimuli. Not all investigators have been able to demonstrate a selective attention effect (Callaway, 1966); however, such failure is probably due to the use of inappropriate stimuli (Kopell, Wittner, and Warrick, 1969; Hillyard, 1973a), rather than to the actual absence of the selective attention phenomenon. The validity of changes in the EP as indicators of attentional changes has been criticized on the grounds that other variables are responsible for these apparent effects. Among the principal confounding variables are the following.

The attention effect is due to physical characteristics of the attended versus nonattended stimuli. This possibility, however, can be neutralized by alternating the identity of the relevant and irrelevant stimuli between runs (Kopell and others, 1969; Corby and Kopell, 1973).

Selective attention is operating at a (modality specific) peripheral level rather than at a central level. This criticism is particularly relevant on studies using stimuli of different modalities to demonstrate selective attention (Spong, Haider, and Lindsley, 1965). Co-occurring randomized stimuli of the same modality minimize the strength of this criticism (Donchin and Cohen, 1967).

The selective attention effect is due to DC baseline changes reflecting increases in arousal before and release from tension after the relevant stimulus, or in other words, resolution of the CNV which develops before a predictable relevant stimulus (Naatanen, 1967, 1969a, 1969b; Karlin, 1970; Wilkinson and Lee, 1972). This criticism has provoked a great deal of interest and is discussed in greater detail in the discussion of the relationship between CNV and P_3 on pages 450–452.

Recent studies by Ford and others (1973) and Hillyard (1973a) have demonstrated not only EP evidence for selective attention but also that latency differences reflect the stage of discrimination involved in identifying target stimuli. Ford and others (1973) presented four different stimuli in two modalities (a click and a change in background noise level, a flash and a change in background light intensity) with instructions to attend to each one separately on different runs. They found that amplitude differences at N_2 reflected selective attention between modalities while P_3 amplitude differences reflected the selective attention operating within a modality. Hillyard (1973a) found a similar latency effect with binaurally-presented stimuli. In both of these experiments, it appears that the earlier negative component reflects the initial broad discrimination necessary to identify the target stimulus, while P_3 reflects a finer subsequent discrimination.

The sensitivity of the late positive component, or P_3 of the EP to psychological manipulations probably was first systematically investigated by Sutton, Braren, Zubin, and John (1965). They asked subjects to guess the modality (light or sound) of an upcoming stimulus. Prior to their guess and the test stimuli, subjects were presented with one of two types of cueing stimuli. One type of cue directly informed subjects of the identity of the upcoming stimulus; the other provided no reliable information. EPs to the stimuli about which subjects experienced uncertainty exhibited significantly higher P_3s than EPs to stimuli about which subjects experienced no uncertainty, or which they expected on the basis of the cue stimulus.

Following up the implications of this pioneer study, most investigators have interpreted P_3 as a reflection of cognitive, integrative responses to, or processing of a stimulus. Enhanced P_3s have been obtained in the following situations: To a signal which confirms or disconfirms a prior guess (Sutton, Braren, Zubin, and John, 1965; Sutton, Tueting, Zubin, and John, 1967; Tueting, Sutton, and Zubin, 1971; Poon, Thompson, Williams, and Marsh, 1974); on the detection of a low intensity stimulus (Hillyard, Squires, Bauer, and Lindsay, 1971; Paul and Sutton, 1972; Squires, Hillyard, and Lindsay, 1973); on attending barely distinguishable tones to perform discrimination tasks (Ritter and Vaughan, 1969; Jenness, 1972); to a signal for a simple choice reaction (Donchin and Cohen, 1967; Kopell and others, 1969; Corby and Kopell, 1973); to an occasional stimulus change (Ritter, Vaughan, and Costa, 1968; Roth, 1973; Roth and Kopell, 1973); to a gap in a sequence of regular stimuli (Klinke, Fruhstorfer, and Finkenzeller, 1968; Barlow, 1969; Picton, Hillyard, and Galambos, 1973; Ford and others, 1974); to a signal to shift sensory-motor set (Donald and Goff, 1971); to a letter which completes a word (Shelburne, 1972, 1973); and while reading meaningful material, in contrast to optokinetic nystagmus (Barlow, 1971).

Squires and others (1973) have suggested two necessary, but not sufficient conditions for P_3 development: The subject must be paying attention to task-relevant stimuli, and there must be uncertainty about some aspect of signal scheduling. He postulates a model of information processing such that a template of the target signal (the task-relevant one) is created, against which incoming stimuli are matched. P_3 amplitude varies directly with the closeness of the template match and inversely with the degree of expectancy of that signal (1973, 29). When something is quite unexpected, or when its exact time of occurrence is difficult to predict, it evokes a larger P_3 than when it occurs predictably. This has been found true for task-relevant stimuli (Tueting and others, 1971; Corby and Kopell, 1973) and for task-irrelevant stimuli (Roth, 1973; Ritter and others, 1968). EPs to feedback stimuli which confirm a correct response differ from those which disconfirm an incorrect response. The finding that a disconfirming feedback stimulus produces a larger P_3 than a confirming stimulus has been interpreted to reflect both the unexpectedness of such stimuli (Sutton and others, 1965; Paul and Sutton, 1972), and the informational and emotional value for future performance of a disconfirming stimulus (Squires and others, 1973).

The EP also has been shown to be sensitive to learning and memory. The EP evidence for learning is in the form of before-after differences in potentials evoked by identical stimuli about which subjects learn something during the experiment (Jenness, 1972; Poon and others, 1974), and results are inconsistent. Poon and others (1974) report amplitude diminution of P_3s to stimuli whose pattern of alternation has been learned. Jenness (1972) reports amplitude enhancement of P_3s to stimuli which subjects had learned to discriminate from each other. Both experiments contain a variety of other manipulations of subjects' interests and motivation, so comparisons should be made with caution. Jenness also reports that there was much more variability of EP response during early low accuracy trials than during the later high accuracy trials and concludes that these results imply that EPs are "not just correlates of perceptual activity, but represent, reflect, or provide for a processing or coding mechanism that may in part determine which response is emitted" (1972, p. 88). Jenness further states that his data provide compelling evidence that "evoked responses differentiated gradually during the course of instrumental learning," and demonstrate "the formation of information-carrying mechanisms that are not trivially associated with the occurrence of differentiated responses to which tangible consequences are attached" (1972, p. 89).

Direct studies of EP correlates of memory in humans are limited. Some investigators have inferred the representation of memory from studies in which EPs corresponded not to the actual stimuli presented but to previously experienced stimuli which the subject expected (Begleiter and others, 1973; Weinberg and others, 1970). The argument here is that some representation of the previously experienced stimulus is held in memory and emitted when that stimulus is expected, regardless of the actual stimulus (John, Bartlett, Shimokochi, and Kleinman, 1973). Studies which demonstrate EPS to unexpected gaps in sequences of attended stimuli (Rusinov, 1960; Klinke and others, 1968; Barlow, 1969; Picton and others, 1973; Ford and others, 1974) could be interpreted in the same way. However, Picton and others (1973) have pointed out that:

1. A missing-stimulus EP has common features across modalities, while EPs elicited by actual stimuli in various modalities differ;

2. The topology of the missing-stimulus EP is different from the topology of the actual stimulus EP;

3. The amplitude of missing-stimulus EP is enhanced by decreasing interstimulus intervals, whereas the amplitude of an actual stimulus EP is decreased by decreasing interstimulus interval, because of the reduction in the recovery period.

They argue that EP to a gap reflects cerebral events involved in making an active perceptual decision, and note its similarity to potentials evoked by a changed click when subjects are required to attend to a sequence of clicks of which occasional ones are of lowered intensity. In other words, they are saying that potentials evoked by missing expected stimuli in attend conditions reflect no more than processes of selective attention. However, such potentials provide a methodological bonus in that the decision complex reflected in them is uncontaminated by stimulus characteristics.

A recent experiment (Roth and others, 1974) analyzed the EPS produced during the performance of a version of a memory retrieval task of Sternberg (1969). On each trial, subjects were presented visually with a series of target digits to hold in memory, then a warning tone was delivered, and 1.5 seconds later a probe digit appeared. The CNV returned to baseline after the probe more slowly in trials in which there were more targets, reflecting the slower decision process when more memory items had to be scanned. This effect was present whether a button press response was required or not, and back-averaging of the press responses indicated that the decision occurred on the average of 200 msec or more before the button press was made. Differences in CNV amplitude dependent on target set size were also obtained before the probe was presented. This implies that current models of data processing in memory retrieval that are restricted to events occurring after the probe are incomplete. In this study averaged EEG measures have provided objective evidence of psychological processes which previously could only be hypothesized.

The semantic content of stimuli is reflected both in the amplitude and hemispheric location of EPs. Buchsbaum and Fedio (1969) compared Visual Evoked Potentials (VEPs) to slides, matched for physical characteristics, but containing either verbal or nonverbal material. VEPs recorded from the left hemisphere to verbal and nonverbal stimuli showed greater differences in amplitude than VEPs recorded to these different stimuli from the right hemisphere. Hemispheric asymmetry has also been demonstrated using auditory stimuli with and without semantic content (McAdam and Whitaker, 1971; Wood, Goff, and Day, 1971; Matsumiya, Tagliasco, Lombroso, and Goodlass, 1972).

As stated above, the CNV is a slow negative potential which is contingent upon a psychological association between two stimuli. Other slow response-related potential shifts have been reported, particularly shifts preceding voluntary movement (Kornhuber and Deecke, 1965). In a review McAdam refers to such shifts as "close relatives of the CNV" (1973, p. 79). Weinberg (1973) cautions against thinking of the CNV as a unitary phenomenon. There appears to be sufficient evidence to establish the existence of negative potential shifts in situations not contingent on a motor response (Donchin, Gerbrandt, Leifer, and Tucker, 1972); and also in situations not dependent on a purely temporal conditioned response (Blowers, Ongley, and Shaw, 1973). The CNV is most commonly recorded from the vertex (Tecce, 1972). However, it has been identified both in depth recordings (McCallum, Papakostopoulos, Gombi, Winter, Cooper, and Griffith, 1973), and at other scalp locations in humans (Jarvilehto and Fruhstorfer, 1970). Investigations are currently under way on the functional differentiation of topographically distinct CNVs (Hillyard, 1973b; Poon and others, 1974).

The CNV amplitude provides an index of prestimulus attention (Tecce, 1972); interest, motivation (Irwin, Knott, McAdam, and Rebert, 1966); expectancy (Walter and others, 1964); and preparedness to respond (Roth and others, 1974). Distraction during the S_1-S_2 interval reduces amplitude of the CNV (McCallum and Walter, 1968; Tecce and Scheff, 1969; Delse, Marsh, and Thompson, 1972). CNVs preceding correctly identified test stimuli are reliably higher than those preceding incorrectly identified stimuli (Hillyard and others, 1971). However, there have been contrary findings (Paul and Sutton, 1972; Jenness, 1972; Poon and others, 1974). Higher CNVs also are generally associated with shorter RTs, but again, there are exceptions (Rebert and Tecce, 1973). Therefore, whether the CNV represents some kind of cortical priming and as such facilitates the response to S_2 (Walter and others, 1964) is currently a moot point. The identification of the CNV as a direct measure of any specific psychological process encounters the same constraints that exist in interpretation of the EP. Hillyard (1973b) has classified the paradigms in which CNVs have been generated as follows: holding a motor response in readiness; preparing for a perceptual judgment; anticipation of positive or negative reinforcement; preparing for a cognitive decision. The CNV can only be said to index those forms of attention and preparedness that are activated by specific paradigms. Apparently conflicting results may be due both to experimental differences and more basic deficiencies in existing knowledge of the sources and kinds of CNVs (McSherry, 1973; Hillyard, 1973b).

The CNV has been interpreted as providing indirect evidence for learning. McAdam (1966) demonstrated an inverted U shaped relationship between CNV amplitude and increasing accuracy in a time production task. After fifty trials each with corrective feedback, there was a marked improvement in time production accuracy (interpreted as evidence of learning), but during the session CNV amplitude initially increased and then declined. McAdam talks about how this experiment shows CNV is not simply related to expectancy, since expectancy becomes very precise toward the end of the experiment, while CNV amplitude declines. It can be added that the task becomes less interesting, less able to hold the subjects' attention as their accuracy increases and reaches a plateau, and this is possibly what the CNV inverted U process reflects. Picton and Low (1971) and Low, Klonoff, and Marcus (1973) found a relationship between difficulty of a discrimination task, and the extent to which CNV was sustained after performance of this task until presentation of a feedback signal which informed subjects whether they had been right or wrong. They suggest that a decline in amplitude of pre-feedback CNV over a series of trials would indicate that subjects have learned the discrimination, are more sure they are right, and so are less interested in the feedback signal.

In another study utilizing a double-CNV paradigm, Wilkinson and Spence (1973) compared CNV resolution in continued expectancy and noncontinued expectancy conditions. They found that resolution of the CNV is arrested by the development of a second CNV in continued expectancy conditions. In noncontinued expectancy conditions CNV resolution continues to baseline. The latency of this second CNV was found to correlate positively with intersubject differences in RT. The authors utilize a successive discriminations model to explain their results, similar to that utilized by Ford and others (1973) and Hillyard (1973a). They postulate that the peaking over of the CNV is the first coarse identification of the imperative stimulus as a relevant stimulus. The subsequent development of a second CNV in continued expectancy conditions at an average latency of 316 msec indicates completion of a finer discrimination or recognition of that stimulus as a high tone signaling a subsequent task. The positive relationship between RTs and upturn of second CNV indicates that it is differences in speed of information processing, rather than overt motor activity, which underlie individual differences in RT.

Costell, Lunde, Kopell, and Wittner (1972) provide further evidence that the CNV yields a measure of subject interest in specific classes of stimuli. In this study, male and female subjects were presented with randomly ordered slides depicting male nudes, female nudes, and a sexually neutral silhouette, all matched for such physical properties as brightness and contrast. Each presentation, lasting 2000 msec, was preceded at a constant interval by a 500 msec flash of the same slide. This informed the subject of the sexual content of the upcoming slide. The authors found that subjects exhibited higher amplitude cnvs before presentation of a slide depicting an opposite sex nude.

Donchin and Smith (1970) noted a possible relationship between the cnv and the P_3, and raised the question of whether enhancement of P_3 in a selective attention paradigm could be the post-stimulus stage or resolution of the cnv. Both phenomena are elicited in situations in which subjects expect, or are waiting to detect a stimulus to which they are required to respond. The main difference is that the classic cnv paradigm contains an explicit warning stimulus (S_1) preceding the imperative stimulus (S_2) by a fixed period, while P_3 paradigms do not explicitly provide subjects with warning for the relevant (imperative) stimulus. However, the nature of such paradigms, particularly the ones that use a constant interstimulus interval, is that one relevant stimulus serves as warning for the next one. Even in paradigms with irregular interstimulus intervals, it can be argued that provided the interstimulus interval is not too long, one stimulus still serves to warn that the next will follow (Wilkinson and Lee, 1972).

Karlin (1970), in a review of work relating eps to attention, noted that when a subject is waiting to detect the stimulus to which he must respond, he is in a state of increasing preparation or arousal. Once the relevant stimulus has occurred, the subject knows that another one will not follow immediately, and relaxes briefly on completing his task. Karlin's argument includes three significant points.

Increased arousal produces increased dc baseline negativity (analogous to the cnv) which is resolved or goes positive on presentation of task relevant stimuli; the enhanced ep, therefore, is due not to selective attention but to variations in general arousal resulting from the predictability of the relevant stimuli; even if relevant stimuli are unpredictable, such that dc baseline negativity does not increase in a regular way prior to them, it is still possible that whatever standing negativity there might be prior to relevant stimulus is resolved when this is present—another possible mechanism for EP enhancement.

Corby and Kopell (1973) designed an experiment explicitly to investigate these points. In this study predictable and unpredictable stimuli presentations were compared, and DC baselines prior to presentation of relevant stimuli were examined. This study showed that indeed there is greater baseline DC negativity prior to predictable than unpredictable stimuli, but that EP enhancement occurs to relevant stimuli in both predictable and unpredictable conditions.

In other words, though differential prior arousal does occur, it does not account for the selective attention effect. Corby and Kopell thus answer the first two points raised by Karlin and have ruled out the necessity of the third as an explanation for selective attention EP enhancement. They have not ruled out the possibility that this is an explanation.

Roth and others (1974) found that in their variation of Sternberg's (1969) memory retrieval task no reliably definable P_3 appeared following the presentation of the probe digit. This was contrary to initial expectations and it was not until the CNV developing prior to the probe digit was examined that a meaningful pattern of events became apparent. CNVs following a single target digit are higher than those following multiple target digits, indicating the distracting effect of remembering several digits to perform the task (Delse and others, 1972). Amplitude of the EP (measured from the peak of the CNV) at 300 msec after the probe varies indirectly with the number of target digits which had been presented.

In other words, the CNV resolved itself and became positive more quickly when there was a single target digit to scan than when there were many. Combined with RT evidence this suggests that resolution of CNV provides a measure of the decision complex involved in the performance of this task.

Several other studies have examined prestimulus and poststimulus potentials and found a dissociation between experimentally induced changes in the CNV and P_3 (Donald and Goff, 1971; Friedman, 1971; Paul and Sutton, 1972; Jenness, 1972). Tueting and Sutton (1973) review the available data and note that while in some cases prestimulus negative shifts are indeed associated with positive enhancement of the P_3, there is sufficient evidence of dissociation to indicate this as an area needing considerable further investigation.

Averaged EEG Measures and Individual Differences

Instead of assuming or hoping that individual differences do not seriously bias results, some investigators have explicitly investigated this topic. There have been many attempts to relate variously defined personality differences to various unaveraged EEG phenomena (Wilson, 1965; Hill, 1963; Ellingson, 1956; Lindsley, 1944). In general, these investigations have been disappointing as much due to poorly conceptualized personality variables, as because of uncritical use of EEG data. Recently, more rigorous investigations of EEG correlates of Eysenck's (1967, 1970) Introvert/Extrovert personality dimension still have failed to demonstrate significant relationships between the EEG and the psychological variable (Gale, Coles, Kline and Penfold, 1971).

Since averaged EEG measures provide objective correlates of perceptual and attentive processes, they should also provide measures of individual differences in these areas. Averaged EEG correlates of individual differences in perceptual styles will be reviewed below. Two topics, intelligence and psychopathology, have been recently reviewed (Callaway, 1973; Shagass, 1972a, 1972b; Dongier, 1973), and so we will discuss them briefly here. CNV correlates of anxiety states and traits will also be presented.

Some correlations have been established between IQ as measured by standard IQ tests and certain averaged EEG measures. For example, latency of EP components is shorter in intelligent subjects; hemispheric asymmetry is greater; variability of response from trial to trial is less in intelligent subjects on tests requiring stable responses, but in situations requiring different responses, EP amplitudes are more variable. CNV is absent or attenuated in retarded subjects. Callaway (1973) points out that these findings provide objective evidence to support some common-sense notions about intelligence. For example, bright subjects lose interest in repetitive stimuli more rapidly than dull subjects; bright subjects have a greater propensity to think in verbal or propositional terms than dull subjects; bright subjects are more able to deal with repetitive stimuli (when required) in a stable fashion than dull subjects; and bright subjects are more capable of plasticity of response than dull subjects.

Shagass (1972a, 220) identifies two separate points of view for interpreting averaged EEG differences between various patient populations and normals. He adopts the pathophysiological position which holds that averaged EEG differences between patients and normals reflect underlying disturbances of Central Nervous System activity, and a direct one-to-one correspondence between averaged EEG phenomena and behavior should not be expected. In contrast, the psychophysiological position holds that patients exhibit different averaged EEG responses than normals because they behave differently; for example, they are less capable of focusing attention and are more distractible.

Some averaged EEG correlates of psychopathology will be listed below. The Recovery Function is a measure of the extent to which the EP to the second of two closely paired stimuli shows equivalent amplitude to the EP to the first stimulus. The degree of recovery is a function of the interval between stimuli and is believed to reflect cortical excitability. Patients show diminished amplitude recovery compared to normals, and this could indicate some underlying Central Nervous System disturbances (Shagass, 1972). Schizophrenics are characterized by greater EP variability than normals; that is, their responses vary more from trial to trial (Callaway, Jones, and Donchin, 1970). CNV variability has also been noted. Walter (1964b) has claimed that the CNV of psychopaths is generally absent or of small amplitude. It is particularly susceptible to reduction by distractions (McCallum and Abraham, 1973). These responses could be related to a limited capacity to sustain attention over time, and limited condition ability in psychopaths (McCallum, 1973). In some circumstances, the CNV is prolonged after the second stimulus instead of returning to baseline (Dongier, Timsit-Berthier, Koninckx, and Delaunoy, 1973). The authors suggest that disturbance of the feedback effect, due to Central Nervous System disturbance, may be a possible explanation for this phenomenon.

The CNV appears to be a response in which there is considerable individual variability. The work of Irwin and others on motivational determinants of the CNV (1966) demonstrated that paradigms requiring an actual response to S_2 elicit higher CNVs than those only requiring attention, and paradigms using an avoidable (by speedy response) noxious S_2 elicit higher CNVs than those utilizing an innocuous S_2. This enhanced motivation could also be interpreted as enhanced situational anxiety, raising the question, If the CNV is indicative of situational anxiety, can it also discriminate between persons with relatively permanent differences in anxiety-proneness? It was hypothesized that anxiety-prone subjects would exhibit higher CNVs than nonanxious subjects (Knott and Irwin, 1968, 1973).

However, it was found that while there was very little difference in the CNV amplitudes of both groups in relatively unstressful paradigms, in the stressful situation, anxiety-prone subjects had lower CNVs than nonanxious subjects. Thus, it seemed that while situational anxiety did enhance CNVs among subjects not already given to anxiety, this was not the case for subjects with a relatively permanent predisposition to anxiety. Knott and Irwin explain this seemingly paradoxical data by postulating a hypothetical ceiling for cortical negativity. Since anxious persons operate under a higher baseline cortical negativity than nonanxious ones, the anxiety induced by the stressful paradigm takes them close to their ceiling, and so little further negativity is possible. Results reported by Low and Swift (1971) substantiate Knott and Irwin's finding that in stressful situations, high-anxiety subjects develop smaller amplitude CNVs than low-anxiety subjects. They also found that CNV magnitudes for both high and low-anxiety subjects progressively decrease as the stress/anxiety content of the paradigms increases. Knott and Peters (1974) have found that females show greater sensitivity in CNV response to stressful situations than males.

The recent demonstration of corresponding individual differences in both perceptual style tests and averaged EEG measures has greatly enhanced the confidence which can be placed in both. The perceptual style differences discussed below include Rod and Frame Test performance and Stimulus Intensity Modulation. The EP components which reflect individual differences in perceptual style are primarily in the 80–140 msec latency range (Buchsbaum and

Pfefferbaum, 1971). Little is known about individual differences in the P_3 phenomenon, discussed in the previous section. The recent demonstration that P_3 is sensitive to Rotter's Internal-External Scale (Rotter, 1966) (which measures the extent to which a person thinks himself capable of influencing external events) will probably stimulate further investigation in this area (Poon and others, 1974). The Rod and Frame Test yields a measure of perceptual style (field-dependence versus field-independence) which has been related to a number of other psychological variables (Witkin, Dyk, Faterson, Goodenough, and Karp, 1962). Buchsbaum and Silverman (1970) recorded EPS to the rod stimuli while subjects were performing the Rod and Frame Test. The EPS of field-independent subjects to four different degrees of tilt were significantly different, while the EPS of field-dependent subjects to these different stimuli were not. These results were replicated in a later study (Silverman and others, 1973).

CNV correlates of Rod and Frame Test performance have been investigated as part of a broader study of CNV correlates of anxiety (Knott, 1972; Knott, Van Veen, Miller, Peters, and Cohen, 1973). While some relationship seems to exist between Rod and Frame Test performance and CNV performance under conditions of varying stress, results have not been entirely consistent; and the effect of such long-term subject variables as anxiety-proneness and sex need to be further investigated.

People differ in their perception of the intensity of stimulation. Petrie (1967) was able to measure this perception-personality dimension by means of a kinesthetic figural aftereffect test and to divide people into three categories: augmenters, reducers, and moderates. Augmenters tend to overestimate the intensity of strong stimuli, while reducers are hypersensitive individuals who tend to underestimate the intensity of such stimuli.

Increasing the physical intensity of stimulation generally produces increases in the amplitude of the EP (Regan, 1972) but considerable variability has been noted between subjects in their responses to stimuli of different intensities. This has been demonstrated for auditory (Henry and Teas, 1968), visual (Vaughan and Hull, 1965) and somatosensory (Shagass and Schwartz, 1963) stimuli. Taking their cue from Petrie's conceptualization of augmenters and reducers, several investigators have examined these interindividual differences for consistent patterns of response to stimuli of differing intensity, under normal and various drug-induced changes in receptivity to stimulation (Buschbaum and Silverman, 1968; Blacker, Jones, Stone, and Pfefferbaum, 1968; Spilker and Callaway, 1969a, 1969b; Buchsbaum and Pfefferbaum, 1971; Schechter and Buchsbaum, 1973).

Buchsbaum and Silverman (1968) developed a measure of stimulus intensity modulation derived from the slope of a line representing the changes in amplitude in EPs elicited by stimuli of differing intensity. Augmenters (as defined by performance on kinesthetic figural aftereffect test) show increased EP amplitude to increased stimulus intensity; while reducers reduce amplitude with intensified stimuli. These results, examined, with greater control for alternative explanations, were later replicated (Buchsbaum and Pfefferbaum, 1971). However, augmenters and reducers show equal amplitudes and equal slopes at the lowest intensity ranges of stimulation. The augmenting-reducing difference was seen only at the highest levels of stimulus intensity, which contradicts Silverman's (1970) suggestion that reducers would be likely not only to reduce high-intensity sensory input, but also to respond strongly to low-intensity stimulation.

Silverman and others (1973) take stimulus-intensity modulation and perceptual differentiation measures a step further by attempting to correlate them with more broadly defined personality categories such as neuroticism and anxiety. An interesting pattern of sex-based differences emerges. Among males, high anxiety and high neuroticism tend to be associated with undifferentiated perceptual responsiveness (as measured by the Rod and Frame Test) and stimulus intensity augmentation; while among females, these same personality features are associated with differentiated perceptual responsiveness and stimulus intensity reduction.

Schechter and Buchsbaum (1973) examined the effect of attentional changes on stimulus intensity modulation in the auditory and visual modalities. They found that instructions designed to create a range of attentional conditions do not alter group differences between augmenters and reducers; and that, for visual stimuli, attentional differences have greater effect at low intensities. For auditory stimuli, attentional changes have equal effects across all intensities. A no instruction attentional condition yielded amplitude-intensity slopes which correlated highest with a distraction condition. This led to the supposition that subjects in the earlier above-cited studies, who were given no instructions, probably ignored the stimuli. Schechter and Buchsbaum conclude that "differences in amplitude-intensity slopes may therefore reflect not only underlying biological mechanisms but habitual deployment of attention as well" (1973, p. 399).

Spilker and Callaway (1969b) used drugs to manipulate levels of arousal and investigate the effect of this variable on the augmenting-reducing phenomenon. They found that sodium pentobarbital and ethyl alcohol (both depressants) reduced the stimulus intensity modulation slope. This suggests that arousal fluctuation is one factor contributing to the augmenting-reducing phenomenon.

In our laboratory we are currently using the EP measure of stimulus intensity modulation to test the hypothesis that opiate addicts are augmenters who develop a susceptibility to this particular drug because it helps them reduce.

Assessment of Psychological Changes Induced by Drugs

We have found that studying psychological effects of drug administration is an extremely valuable application of averaged EEG techniques. In the first place, the use of a subject as his own control for testing different drug treatments takes advantage of the considerable intraindividual stability of averaged EEG responses, and avoids the hazards posed by individual differences in these measures. Secondly, drug dosage provides a highly controllable independent variable with more reliable behavioral and psychological effects than those yielded by paradigmatic manipulations.

The rest of this section will be devoted to examples drawn primarily from our own laboratory of the use of averaged EEG techniques to measure the effects of various drugs. We use three different paradigms: the CNV paradigm, a selective attention paradigm, and a passive attention paradigm. The CNV provides a measure of attention and motivation. The selective attention test provides an EP measure of capacity to focus attention on a relevant stimulus and screen out irrelevant stimuli. The passive attention test provides an

EP measure of the extent to which freefloating attention is attracted by extraneous irrelevant stimuli. Standardized procedures for testing drug effects include the following: using subjects as their own controls; separation of placebo and drug days by sufficiently long intervals to minimize drug interactions; randomization of order of drug and placebo administration across subjects; double-blind administration of drugs; standardizing food and other drug consumption for the duration of the experiment.

Hyperthyroidism is a condition characterized by hyperexcitability and exaggerated responses to extraneous stimuli. The administration of triiodothyronine to normal subjects eliminates the selective attention effect found under placebo conditions. The drug increases EPs to the irrelevant stimulus to the same level as those to the relevant stimulus. This objective corroboration of clinical descriptions of hyperthyroidism (patients often complain of being disturbed by stimuli which normally they would ignore) was obtained at doses of the drug which neither produced subjective feelings of intoxication, nor affected behavior in a way amenable to measurement by standard psychological tests (Kopell, Wittner, Lunde, Warrick, and Edwards, 1970b).

Behavioral abnormalities have been found to accompany both Cushing's Disease (brought on by elevated steroid levels) and the exogenous administration of corticosteroids. The possibility that such mental disturbances could result from an individual's inability to filter out irrelevant stimuli and process only meaningful stimuli brought about by the excess cortisol levels accompanying these syndromes was investigated by using the selective attention test. Cortisol or placebo saline were intravenously administered to normal subjects who performed the selective attention test. Cortisol was found to reduce the amplitude of EPs to relevant stimuli. It is interesting to compare this effect, that of a reduction in the processing of significant information, with the effect obtained from triiodothyronine, an increase in the processing of irrelevant information. The relationship between these findings and underlying neurologic effects of these hormones remains to be investigated (Kopell, Wittner, Lunde, Warrick, and Edwards, 1970a).

Amphetamine is a drug known to increase attention and motivation, as measured by standard psychological tests (Talland

and Quarton, 1966; Day and Thomas, 1967) and is believed to increase arousal through its effect on the reticular formation (Bradley, 1958). Our finding that amphetamine enhances the amplitude of the CNV (Kopell, Wittner, Lunde, Woolcott, and Tinklenberg, 1974a) corroborates this evidence. Walter (1964b) reports that subjects deprived of caffeine for thirty-six hours exhibit an attenuated CNV, which is restored following consumption of caffeine, and that amphetamine enhances the CNV. Dalmane, a sedative, depresses the CNV, a result which parallels subjective reports of drowsiness and inattentiveness (Hablitz and Borda, 1973).

In contrast to amphetamine, alcohol has been found to reduce performance on a range of standard psychological tests, though the exact locus of its effect is unclear (Kleinknecht and Goldstein, 1972). We have found that alcohol reduces the CNV (Kopell and others, 1972).

In a more recent study in which we continued testing subjects for a period of four hours following alcohol administration, we found significant depressing effects on both the CNV and the EP (Kopell, Roth, and Tinklenberg, 1974b). However, while EP depression follows the time-action curve of various non-EEG measures of alcoholic intoxication, CNV depression follows an independent time-course: one of continuously increasing depression. Apparently, this effect represents a longterm reduction in arousal (hangover effect) which persists after other measures of intoxication have worn off. Our findings of reduced EP amplitude in the auditory modality are in accord with those of Gross, Begleiter, Tobin, and Kissin (1966). Lewis, Dustman, and Beck (1970) have demonstrated that alcohol depresses later components of the somatosensory and visual evoked potentials (SEP and VEP); and Salamy and Williams (1973) have also shown that alcohol's depressing effect on late vertex SEPs parallel the time course of other measures of intoxication and are independent of changes in EEG background rhythm.

Marijuana is a drug whose effects are notoriously elusive and unamenable to objective documentation by scientific methods. A marked feature of the marijuana experience is the capacity of experienced marijuana users to pull themselves together to a certain extent to meet particular situational demands (Crancer, Dille, Delay, Wallace, and Haykin, 1969). Yet, when at liberty to do so, mari-

juana users experience a withdrawal from the external environment
and an inner-directed focusing of attention (Anonymous, 1969).
This fluctuating drug effect means that many EEG paradigms, in
which subjects are not free to indulge in the delights of their intoxication, fail to demonstrate any significant drug effect (Rodin,
Domino, and Porzak, 1970; Jones and Stone, 1970).

Roth, Galanter, Weingartner, Vaughan, and Wyatt (1973)
used the passive attention test which elicits EPs to a regularly repeated tone, occasionally alternated with an irregular tone of another frequency while subjects are ignoring all tones. In such a
situation, no performance demands are being made on the subject.
Subjects underwent the passive attention test before smoking placebo,
marijuana or synthetic $\triangle^9$-tetrahydrocannabinol (THC) cigarettes
on separate days, one week apart. They then repeated the test at an
interval after smoking during which subjective drug effect was reported as being above 80 percent of peak intensity. The test lasted
eleven minutes. In this type of paradigm, the irregular tone usually
elicits an EP with a marked P_3 which has been interpreted as an
orienting response to an unexpected event (Roth, 1973). It was
found that marijuana reduced the amplitude of this P_3 to the irregular tone, and also the amplitude of the P_2 to the regular tones (no
P_3 was elicited by regular tones). However, this effect was apparent
only at the very beginning of the test run, and by the end of the
run there was no significant difference between placebo, THC or
marijuana treatment. These results can be interpreted to suggest
that marijuana enables subjects to follow the instructions to ignore
the tones better than they could without the drug. This rather subtle
effect is not apparent when EP amplitudes, averaged for the entire
run are examined. A more recent study (Kopell and others, 1974b)
found no marijuana effect on EP amplitude and did not substantiate
the recently reported slowing of EP latency produced by marijuana
(Lewis, Dustman, Peters, Straight, and Beck, 1973).

Kopell and others (1972) found that marijuana enhances
the CNV. This effect demonstrates the influence of this drug in en-
abling subjects to tune out the outside world, and be less distracted
while performing a CNV task. In a subsequent study, in which repeated measures were taken for four hours after drug administration, no significant marijuana effect on the CNV was found (Kopell

and others, 1974b). This failure to replicate the earlier finding illustrates the probable influence of wide individual differences in response to this particular drug and fluctuations in effect over time. Walter (1964b) reports an informal observation of an augmented-CNV effect from LSD, a drug in some respects similar to marijuana.

The use of averaged EEG measures to study drug effects is still new and yet to be fully proved but we feel that this method of obtaining information on psychological changes in humans is one of the most promising applications of averaged EEG techniques. Stoyva and Kamiya (1968) have illustrated the immense value to the study of sleep and dreaming of the convergency of physiological and psychological techniques. Berlyne (1969) noted the unfashionableness of the concept of attention to psychologists until neurophysiological techniques provided objective evidence of its existence. Averaged EEG measures of psychological processes similarly complement and enhance more standard psychological assessments and the establishment of common results by different methods increases the confidence which can be placed in both techniques. In some areas, particularly that of memory retrieval, averaged EEG measures are providing evidence which contradicts models developed on the basis of external responses alone (Roth and others, 1974).

General Conclusions

Averaged EEG techniques provide measures of brain functioning related to psychological processes which are both objective and reproducible. In addition, these measures are considerably more culturally and linguistically free than are most standard psychological tests. The technique can demonstrate changes in attention deployment and decision-making which are not always behaviorally apparent. Its sensitivity to drug effects, not otherwise measurable, is illustrated by our research on thyroid effects on attention (Kopell and others, 1970b). A disadvantage of the technique is the expense of the complicated equipment required. Certain conclusions may be more efficiently elicited by direct observation or questioning than by averaged EEG techniques. However, the kind of evidence available through these techniques strengthens certain psychological findings and also points the way to further investigation of old problems.

As an example let us consider briefly the relationship between RT and averaged EEG measures of attention. RT evidence is certainly a cheaper source of data on attentiveness than either the CNV or the EP. In many cases, speed of RT and amplitude of the CNV are positively related. However, dissociations have been noted (Rebert and Tecce, 1973) suggesting that the CNV must be measuring different aspects of attention than RT, and that in certain conditions they operate independently of each other. What these aspects are, and what are the conditions for the dissociation become new, and hopefully fruitful, topics for investigation.

As averaged EEG techniques become more sophisticated, and as more laboratories are capable of pursuing this kind of research, considerable advances can be expected. Recent detailed investigations of separate components of the EP are attempting to document a physiological reality for mental events which up till now have been considered only hypothetical constructs. Some of the most exciting psychological applications of averaged EEG measures are still in the experimental stage. Among these projects are such investigations as comparing the effect on long latency components of the EP of responses to different kinds of unexpected stimuli—ones which match an expected target and ones which do not; pinpointing physically, hypothesized stages of memorization such as encoding, placing in short-term and long-term store and retrieval; assessing the relative influence of stimulus set and response set on the process of selective attention and documenting neural correlates of decision criteria.

In all these most recent applications of averaged EEG measures, the same provisos and limitations mentioned above also hold equally true. Procedures to eliminate noncerebral artifacts are essential if the signal recorded from the scalp is to accurately represent what is going on in the brain beneath. A realistic, if not conservative, interpretation of the wider implication of experimental paradigms should be adopted. This and the recognition that the extent of the range and distribution of interpersonal differences in averaged EEG responses is scarcely known should limit the breadth of applicability of single studies.

As we mentioned above, techniques and instrumentation for averaged EEG research vary from laboratory to laboratory. This variability should be disappearing as the necessary equipment becomes commercially available in standardized form, and as communication between investigators in the field increases. Conceptualization of psychological variables also varies from theoretician to theoretician. The bridge between psychological and neurophysiological variables will be further strengthened as more investigators using averaged EEG measures also utilize a wider variety of paper and pencil psychological tests to provide independent measures of the psychological phenomena they are studying. As Stoyva and Kamiya (1968) have noted, the convergence of separate techniques on an area of study cannot but be beneficial. Perhaps such convergence poses more questions than it can provide answers for, creates smoke if not fire, but above all it generates more intellectual stimulation than either discipline produces alone.

Despite the expense and difficulty of recording these measures, and the present limitations on their interpretation, psychological application of averaged EEG measures is an exciting new frontier and one to which we hope this chapter will serve as an introduction.

References

ANONYMOUS. "The Effects of Marijuana on Consciousness." In C. T. Tart (Ed.), *Altered States of Consciousness,* New York: John Wiley, 1969, 335–356.

BARLOW, J. S. "Some Observations on the Electrophysiology of Timing in the Nervous System." *Electroencephalography and Clinical Neurophysiology,* 1969, *27,* 545.

BARLOW, J. S. "Brain Information Processing During Reading: Electrophysiological Correlates." *Diseases of the Nervous System,* 1971, *32,* 668–672.

BEGLEITER, H., PORJESZ, B., YERRE, C., AND KISSIN, B. "Evoked Potential Correlates of Expected Stimulus Intensity." *Science,* 1973, *179,* 814–816.

BERGAMINI, L. AND BERGAMASCO, B. *Cortical Evoked Potentials in Man.* Springfield, Ill.: Charles C. Thomas, 1967.

BERGER, H. "Uber das Elektrenkephalogramm des Menschen." *Archiv fur Psychiatrie,* 1929, *87,* 527–570.

BERLYNE, D. E. "The Development of the Concept of Attention in Psychology." In C. R. Evans and T. B. Mulholland (Eds.), *Attention in Neurophysiology,* New York: Appleton-Century-Crofts, 1969, 1–26.

BLACKER, K. H., JONES, R. T., STONE, G. C., AND PFEFFERBAUM, A. "Chronic Users of L.S.D.: 'The Acidheads'." *American Journal of Psychiatry*, 1968, *125*, 341–351.

BLOWERS, G., ONGLEY, C., AND SHAW, J. C. "The Effect of Reducing Temporal Expectancy on the Contingent Negative Variation." *Electroencephalography and Clinical Neurophysiology*, 1973, *34*, 259–264.

BRADLEY, P. B. "The Central Action of Certain Drugs in Relation to the Reticular Formation of the Brain." In H. Jasper, L. Proctor, R. Knighton, W. Nashoy, and R. Costello (Eds.), *Reticular Formation of the Brain*, Boston: Little, Brown, 1958, 123–149.

BUCHSBAUM, M. AND FEDIO, P. "Visual Information and Evoked Responses from the Left and Right Hemispheres." *Electroencephalography and Clinical Neurophysiology*, 1969, *26*, 266–272.

BUCHSBAUM, M. AND PFEFFERBAUM, A. "Individual Differences in Stimulus Intensity Response." *Psychophysiology*, 1971, *8*, 600–611.

BUCHSBAUM, M. AND SILVERMAN, J. "Stimulus Intensity Control and the Cortical Evoked Response." *Psychosomatic Medicine*, 1968, *30*, 12–22.

BUCHSBAUM, M. AND SILVERMAN, J. "Average Evoked Response and Perception of the Vertical." *Journal of Experimental Research in Personality*, 1970, *4*, 79–83.

CALLAWAY, E. "Averaged Evoked Responses in Psychiatry." *Journal of Nervous and Mental Diseases*, 1966, *143*, 80–94.

CALLAWAY, E. "Correlations Between Averaged Evoked Potentials and Measures of Intelligence." *Archives of General Psychiatry*, 1973, *29*, 553–558.

CALLAWAY, E. AND HALLIDAY, R. A. "Evoked Potential Variability: Effects of Age, Amplitude, and Methods of Measurement." *Electroencephalography and Clinical Neurophysiology*, 1973, *34*, 125–133.

CALLAWAY, E., JONES, R. T., AND DONCHIN, E. "Auditory Evoked Potential Variability in Schizophrenia." *Electroencephalography and Clinical Neurophysiology*, 1970, *29*, 421–428.

CALLAWAY, E. AND LAYNE, R. S. "Interaction Between the Visual Evoked Response and Two Spontaneous Biological Rhythms." *Annals of the New York Academy of Science*, 1964, *112*, 421–431.

CIGANEK, L. "Variability of the Human Visual Evoked Potential: Normative Data." *Electroencephalography and Clinical Neurophysiology*, 1969, *27*, 35–42.

COHEN, J. "Very Slow Brain Potentials Relating to Expectancy: The CNV." In E. Donchin and D. B. Lindsley (Eds.), *Average Evoked Potentials*, Washington, D.C.: NASA SP-191, 1969, 143–198.

CORBY, J. AND KOPELL, B. S. "Differential Contributions of Blinks and Vertical Eye Movements as Artifacts in EEG Recording." *Psychophysiology*, 1972, *9*, 640–644.

CORBY, J. AND KOPELL, B. S. "The Effect of Predictability on Evoked Response Enhancement in Intramodal Selective Attention." *Psychophysiology*, 1973, *10*, 335–346.

CORBY, J., ROTH, W. T., AND KOPELL, B. S. "Prevalence and Methods of Control of the Cephalic Skin Potential EEG Artifact." *Psychophysiology*, 1974, *11*, 350–360.

COSTELL, R. M., LUNDE, D. T., KOPELL, B. S., AND WITTNER, W. K. "Contingent Negative Variation as an Indicator of Sexual Object Preference." *Science*, 1972, *177*, 718–720.

CRANCER, A., JR., DILLE, J. M., DELAY, J. C., WALLACE, J. E., AND HAYKIN, M. D. "Comparison of the Effects of Marijuana and Alcohol on Simulated Driving Performance." *Science*, 1969, *164*, 851–854.

DAY, H. AND THOMAS, E. L. "Effects of Amphetamine on Selective Attention." *Perceptual and Motor Skills*, 1967, *24*, 1119–1125.

DELSE, F. C., MARSH, G. R., AND THOMPSON, L. W. "CNV Correlates of Task Difficulty and Accuracy of Pitch Discrimination." *Psychophysiology*, 1972, *9*, 53–62.

DONALD, M. W. AND GOFF, W. R. "Attention-Related Increases in Cortical Responsivity Dissociated from the Contingent Negative Variation." *Science*, 1971, *172*, 1163–1166.

DONCHIN, E. "Data Analysis Techniques in Average Evoked Potential Research." In E. Donchin and D. B. Lindsley (Eds.), *Average Evoked Potentials*, Washington, D.C.: NASA SP-191, 1969a, 199–236.

DONCHIN, E. "Discriminant Analysis in Average Evoked Response Studies: The Study of Single Trial Data." *Electroencephalography and Clinical Neurophysiology*, 1969b, *27*, 311–314.

DONCHIN, E. AND COHEN, L. "Averaged Evoked Potentials and Intramodality Selective Attention." *Electroencephalography and Clinical Neurophysiology*, 1967, *22*, 537–546.

DONCHIN, E., GERBRANDT, L. A., LEIFER, L., AND TUCKER, L. "Is the Contingent Negative Variation Contingent on a Motor Response?" *Psychophysiology*, 1972, *9*, 178–188.

DONCHIN, E. AND SMITH, D. B. D. "The Contingent Negative Variation and the Late Positive Wave of the Average Evoked Potential." *Electroencephalography and Clinical Neurophysiology*, 1970, *29*, 201–203.

DONGIER, M. "Clinical Application of the CNV: A Review." *Electroencephalography and Clinical Neurophysiology*, 1973, Supplement *33*, 309–316.

DONGIER, M., TIMSIT-BERTHIER, M., KONINCKX, N., AND DELAUNOY, J. "Compared Clinical Significance of CNV and Other Slow Potential Changes in Psychiatry." *Electroencephalography and Clinical Neurophysiology*, 1973, Supplement *33*, 321–326.

DUSTMAN, R. E. AND BECK, E. C. "Long-term Stability of Visually Evoked Potentials in Man." *Science*, 1963, *142*, 1480–1481.

EASON, R. G. AND DUDLEY, L. M. "Physiological and Behavioral Indicants of Activation." *Psychophysiology*, 1971, *7*, 223–232.

ELLINGSON, R. J. "Brain Waves and Problems of Psychology." *Psychological Bulletin*, 1956, *53*, 1–34.

ELLINGSON, R. J. "Relationship Between EEG and Test Intelligence: A Commentary." *Psychological Bulletin*, 1966, *65*, 91–98.

EVANS, C. R. AND MULHOLLAND, T. B. (Eds.). *Attention in Neurophysiology: An International Conference*. New York: Appleton-Century-Crofts, 1969.

EYSENCK, H. J. *The Biological Basis of Personality*. Springfield, Ill.: Charles C. Thomas, 1967.

EYSENCK, H. J. *The Structure of Human Personality*. London: Methuen, 1970.

FORD, J. M., ROTH, W. T., DIRKS, S. J., KOPELL, B. S. "Evoked Potential Correlates of Signal Recognition Between and Within Modalities." *Science*, 1973, 181, 465–466.

FORD, J. M., ROTH, W. T., AND KOPELL, B. S. "Attention Effects on Auditory Evoked Potentials to Infrequent Events." Submitted for publication, 1974.

FRIEDMAN, D. "The Effects of Stimulus Uncertainty on Pupillary Dilation Response and the Vertex Evoked Potential in Man." Unpublished doctoral dissertation, The City University of New York, 1971.

GALE, A., COLES, M., KLINE, P., AND PENFOLD, V. "Extraversion-Introversion, Neuroticism and the EEG: Basal and Response Measures During Habituation of the Orienting Response." *British Journal of Psychology,* 1971, *62,* 533–543.

GLASER, G. H. *EEG and Behavior.* New York: Basic Books, 1963.

GOFF, W. R. "Evoked Potential Correlates of Perceptual Organization in Man." In C. R. Evans and T. B. Mulholland (Eds.), *Attention in Neurophysiology,* New York: Appleton-Century-Crofts, 1969, 169–193.

GOFF, W. R., MATSUMIYA, Y., ALLISON, T., AND GOFF, G. D. "Cross-modality comparisons of Average Evoked Potentials." In E. Donchin and D. B. Lindsley (Eds.), *Average Evoked Potentials,* Washington, D.C., NASA SP-191, 1969, 95–142.

GROSS, M. M., BEGLEITER, H., TOBIN, M., AND KISSIN, G. "Changes in Auditory Evoked Response Induced by Alcohol." *Journal of Nervous and Mental Disease,* 1966, *143,* 152–156.

GULLICKSON, G. R., AND DARROW, C. W. "Contingent Negative Variation Modified by Respiratory Phase." *Electroencephalography and Clinical Neurophysiology,* 1973, Supplement *33,* 295–298.

HABLITZ, J. J., AND BORDA, R. P. "The Effects of Dalmane ® (flurazepam hydrochloride) on the Contingent Negative Variation." *Electroencephalography and Clinical Neurophysiology,* 1973, Supplement *33,* 317–320.

HENRY, G. AND TEAS, D. "AER and Loudness: Analysis of Response Estimates." *Journal of Speech and Hearing Research,* 1968, *11,* 334–342.

HILL, D. "The EEG in Psychiatry." In D. Hill and G. Parr (Eds.), *Electroencephalography: A Symposium on its Various Aspects,* 2nd Edition, 1963, New York: Macmillan, 368–428.

HILL, D., AND PARR, G. (Eds.). *Electroencephalography: A Symposium on its Various Aspects.* (2nd ed.) New York: Macmillan, 1963.

HILLYARD, S. A. "Electrical Signs of Selective Attention in the Human Brain." *Science,* 1973a, *182,* 177–179.

HILLYARD, S. A. "The CNV and Human Behavior: A Review." *Electroencephalography and Clinical Neurophysiology,* 1973b, Supplement *33,* 161–171.

HILLYARD, S. A. AND GALAMBOS, R. "Eye Movement Artifact in the CNV." *Electroencephalography and Clinical Neurophysiology,* 1970, *28,* 173–182.

HILLYARD, S. A., SQUIRES, K. C., BAUER, J. W., AND LINDSAY, P. H. "Evoked Potential Correlates of Auditory Signal Detection." *Science,* 1971, *172,* 1357–1360.

IRWIN, D. A., KNOTT, J. R., MC ADAM, D. W., AND REBERT, C. S. "Motivational Determinants of the 'Contingent Negative Variation'." *Electroencephalography and Clinical Neurophysiology,* 1966, *21,* 538–543.

JARVILEHTO, T. AND FRUHSTORFER, H. "Differentiation Between Slow Cortical Potentials Associated with Motor and Mental Acts in Man." *Experimental Brain Research,* 1970, *11,* 309–317.

JASPER, H. H. "Cortical Excitatory State and Synchronism in the Control of Bioelectric Autonomous Rhythms." *Cold Spring Harbor Symposia on Quantitative Biology,* 1936, *4,* 320–338.

JENNESS, D. "Auditory Evoked Response Differentiation with Discrimination Learning in Humans." *Journal of Comparative and Physiological Psychology,* 1972, *80,* 75–90.

JOHN, E. R., BARTLETT, F., SHIMOKOCHI, M., AND KLEINMAN, D. "Neural Readout from Memory." *Journal of Neurophysiology,* 1973, *36,* 893–924.

JONES, R. T. AND STONE, G. C. "Psychological Studies of Marijuana and Alcohol in Man." *Psychopharmacologia,* 1970, *18,* 108–117.

KARLIN, L. "Cognition, Preparation, and Sensory-evoked Potentials." *Psychological Bulletin,* 1970, *73,* 122–136.

KARRER, R., KOHN, H., AND IVINS, J. "Large Steady Potential Shifts Accompanying Phasic Arousal during CNV Recording in Man." *Electroencephalography and Clinical Neurophysiology,* 1973, Supplement *33,* 119–124.

KLEINKNECHT, R. A. AND GOLDSTEIN, S. G. "Neuropsychological Deficits Associated with Alcoholism." *Quarterly Journal of Studies in Alcoholism,* 1972, *33,* 999–1019.

KLINKE, R., FRUHSTORFER, H., AND FINKENZELLER, P. "Evoked Responses as a Function of External and Stored Information." *Electroencephalography and Clinical Neurophysiology,* 1968, *25,* 119–122.

KNOTT, J. R. "Central and Peripheral Measures of Motivational States." *Electroencephalography and Clinical Neurophysiology,* 1972, Supplement *31,* 131–137.

KNOTT, J. R. AND IRWIN, D. A. "Anxiety, Stress, and the Contingent Negative Variation (CNV)." *Electroencephalography and Clinical Neurophysiology,* 1968, *24,* 286.

KNOTT, J. R. AND IRWIN, D. A. "Anxiety, Stress, and the Contingent Negative Variation." *Archives of General Psychiatry,* 1973, *29,* 538–541.

KNOTT, J. R. AND PETERS, J. F. "Changes in CNV Amplitude with Progressive Induction of Stress as a Function of Sex." *Electroencephalography and Clinical Neurophysiology*, 1974, *36*, 47–51.

KNOTT, J. R., VAN VEEN, W. J., MILLER, L. H., PETERS, J. F., AND COHEN, S. I. "Perceptual Mode, Anxiety, Sex and the Contingent Negative Variation." *Biological Psychiatry*, 1973, *7*, 43–52.

KOPELL, B. S., ROTH, W. T., AND TINKLENBERG, J. R. "Time-course Effects of Alcohol and Marijuana on the Evoked Potential and the Contingent Negative Variation." 1974b, in preparation.

KOPELL, B. S., TINKLENBERG, J. R., AND HOLLISTER, L. E. "Contingent Negative Variation Amplitudes." *Archives of General Psychiatry*, 1972, *27*, 809–811.

KOPELL, B. S., WITTNER, W. K., LUNDE, D. T., WARRICK, G., AND EDWARDS, D. "Cortisol Effects on the Averaged Evoked Potential, Alpha Rhythm, Time Estimation, and the Two-Flash Threshold." *Psychosomatic Medicine*, 1970a, *32*, 39–49.

KOPELL, B. S., WITTNER, W. K., LUNDE, D., WARRICK, G., AND EDWARDS, D. "Influence of Triiodothyronine on Selective Attention as Measured by the Averaged Evoked Potential in Man." *Psychosomatic Medicine*, 1970b, *32*, 495–502.

KOPELL, B. S., WITTNER, W. K., LUNDE, D., WOOLCOTT, L., AND TINKLENBERG, J. R. "The Effects of Methamphetamine and Secobarbital on the Contingent Negative Variation Amplitude." *Psychopharmacologia*, 1974a, *34*, 55–62.

KOPELL, B. S., WITTNER, W. K., AND WARRICK, G. L. "The Effects of Stimulus Differences, Light Intensity, and Selective Attention on the Amplitude of the Visual Averaged Evoked Potential in Man." *Electroencephalography and Clinical Neurophysiology*, 1969, *26*, 619–622.

KORNBLUM, S. (Ed.). *Attention and Performance IV*, New York: Academic Press, 1973.

KORNHUBER, H. H. AND DEECKE, L. "Hirnpotentialanderungen bei Wilkurbewegungen und Passiven Bewegungen des Menschen: Bereitschaftspotential und Reafferente Potentiale." *Pflugers Archiv fur die gesamte Physiologie des Menschen und der Tiere*, 1965, *284*, 1–17.

KOSTER, W. G. "Attention and Performance II." *Acta Psychologica*, 1969, *30*.

LACEY, J. I. AND LACEY, B. C. "Experimental Association and Dissociation of Phasic Bradycardia and Vertex-negative Waves: A Psychophysiological Study of Attention and Response-intention."

Electroencephalography and Clinical Neurophysiology, 1973 Supplement *33,* 281–286.

LANG, P. J. "The Application of Psychophysiological Methods to the Study of Psychotherapy and Behavior Modification." In A. E. Bergin and S. L. Garfield (Eds.), *Handbook of Psychotherapy and Behavior Change,* New York: John Wiley, 1971.

LEWIS, E. G., DUSTMAN, R. E., AND BECK, E. C. "The Effects of Alcohol on Visual and Somatosensory Evoked Responses." *Electroencephalography and Clinical Neurophysiology,* 1970, *28,* 202–205.

LEWIS, E. G., DUSTMAN, R. E., PETERS, B. A., STRAIGHT, R. C., AND BECK, E. C. "The Effects of Varying Doses of $\triangle$-9-Tetrahydrocannabinol on the Human Visual and Somatosensory Evoked Response." *Electroencephalography and Clinical Neurophysiology,* 1973, *35,* 347–354.

LINDSLEY, D. B. "Electroencephalography." In J. McV. Hunt (Ed.), *Personality and the Behavior Disorders,* Vol. 2, New York: Ronald Press, 1944, 1033–1091.

LOW, M. D., COATS, A. C., RETTIG, G. M., AND MC SHERRY, J. W. "Anxiety, Attentiveness, Alertness: A Phenomenological Study of the CNV." *Neuropsychologia,* 1967, *5,* 379–384.

LOW, M., KLONOFF, H., AND MARCUS, A. "The Neurophysiological Basis of the Marijuana Experience." *Canadian Medical Association Journal,* 1973, *108,* 157–165.

LOW, M., AND SWIFT, S. J. "The Contingent Negative Variation and the 'Resting' D.C. Potential of the Human Brain: Effects of Situational Anxiety." *Neuropsychologia,* 1971, *9,* 203–208.

MC ADAM, D. W. "Slow Potential Changes Recorded from the Human Brain During Learning of a Temporal Interval." *Psychonomic Science,* 1966, *6,* 435–436.

MC ADAM, D. W. "Physiological Mechanisms of the CNV: A Review." *Electroencephalography and Clinical Neurophysiology,* 1973, Supplement *33,* 79–86.

MC ADAM, D. W. AND WHITAKER, H. A. "Language Production: Electroencephalographic Localization in the Normal Human Brain." *Science,* 1971, *172,* 499–502.

MC CALLUM, W. C. "The CNV and Conditionability in Psychopaths." *Electroencephalography and Clinical Neurophysiology,* 1973, Supplement *33,* 337–343.

MC CALLUM, W. C. AND ABRAHAM, P. "The Contingent Negative Variation in Psychosis." *Electroencephalography and Clinical Neurophysiology*, 1973, Supplement *33*, 329–335.

MC CALLUM, W. C. AND KNOTT, J. R. (Eds.). *Event-Related Potentials of the Brain*. Amsterdam: Elsevier, 1973. (*Electroencephalography and Clinical Neurophysiology*, Supplement 33.)

MC CALLUM, W. C., PAPAKOSTOPOULOS, D., GOMBI, R., WINTER, A. L., COOPER, R., AND GRIFFITH, H. B. "Event Related Slow Potential Changes in Human Brain Stem." *Nature*, 1973, *242*, 465–467.

MC CALLUM, W. C. AND WALTER, W. G. "The Effects of Attention and Distraction on the Contingent Negative Variation in Normal and Neurotic Subjects." *Electroencephalography and Clinical Neurophysiology*, 1968, *25*, 319–329.

MACKWORTH, J. F. *Vigilance and Habituation*, Baltimore: Penguin Books, 1969.

MACPHERSON, L., AND KOPELL, B. S. "A Zero-setter and Voltage Reference Unit for EEG Amplifier Systems." *Psychophysiology*, 1972, *9*, 262–265.

MC SHERRY, J. W. "Physiological Origins of the CNV: A Review." *Electroencephalography and Clinical Neurophysiology*, 1973, Supplement *33*, 53–61.

MATSUMIYA, Y., TAGLIASCO, V., LOMBROSO, C. T., AND GOODLASS, H. "Auditory Evoked Response: Meaningfulness of Stimuli and Interhemispheric Asymmetry." *Science*, 1972, *175*, 790–792.

MOSTOFSKY, D. (Ed.). *Attention: Contemporary Theory and Analysis*. New York: Appleton-Century-Crofts, 1970.

NAATANEN, R. "Selective Attention and Evoked Potentials." *Annals of the Finnish Academy of Science*, 1967, *151*, 1–226.

NAATANEN, R. "Anticipation of Relevant Stimuli and Evoked Potentials: A Comment on Donchin's and Cohen's 'Averaged Evoked Potentials and Intramodality Selective Attention'." *Perceptual and Motor Skills*, 1969a, *28*, 639–646.

NAATANEN, R. "Anticipation of Relevant Stimuli and Evoked Potentials: A Reply to Donchin and Cohen." *Perceptual and Motor Skills*, 1969b, *29*, 233–234.

PAPAKOSTOPOULOS, D. "CNV and Autonomic Function: A Review." *Electroencephalography and Clinical Neurophysiology*, 1973, Supplement *33*, 269–280.

PAUL, D. D. AND SUTTON, S. "Evoked Potential Correlates of Response Criterion in Auditory Signal Detection." *Science*, 1972, *177*.

PETRIE, A. *Individuality in Pain and Suffering*, Chicago: University of Chicago Press, 1967.

PICTON, T. W. AND HILLYARD, S. A. "Cephalic Skin Potentials in Electroencephalography." *Electroencephalography and Clinical Neurophysiology*, 1972, *33*, 419–424.

PICTON, T. W., HILLYARD, S. A., AND GALAMBOS, R. "Cortical Evoked Responses to Omitted Stimuli." In M. N. Livanov (Ed.), *Major Problems of Brain Electrophysiology*, USSR Academy of Sciences, 1973.

PICTON, T. W. AND LOW, M. D. "The CNV and Semantic Content of Stimuli in the Experimental Paradigm: Effects of Feedback." *Electroencephalography and Clinical Neurophysiology*, 1971, *31*, 451–456.

POON, L. W., THOMPSON, L. W., WILLIAMS, R. B., JR., AND MARSH, G. R. "Changes of Anteroposterior Distribution of CNV and Late Positive Component as a Function of Information Processing Demands." *Psychophysiology*, 1974, in press.

REBERT, C. S. AND KNOTT, J. R. "The Vertex Nonspecific Evoked Potential and Latency of Contingent Negative Variation." *Electroencephalography and Clinical Neurophysiology*, 1970, *28*.

REBERT, C. S. AND SPERRY, K. G. "Subjective and Response-Related Determinants of CNV Amplitude." *Psychophysiology*, 1973, *10*, 139–144.

REBERT, C. S. AND TECCE, J. J. "A Summary of CNV and Reaction Time." *Electroencephalography and Clinical Neurophysiology*, 1973, Supplement *33*, 173–178.

REGAN, D. *Evoked Potentials in Psychology, Sensory Physiology and Clinical Medicine*, London: Chapman and Hall, 1972.

RITTER, W. AND VAUGHAN, H. G., JR. "Averaged Evoked Responses in Vigilance and Discrimination: A Reassessment." *Science*, 1969, *164*, 326–328.

RITTER, W., VAUGHAN, H. G., JR., AND COSTA, L. D. "Orienting and Habituation to Auditory Stimuli: A Study of Short Term Changes in Average Evoked Responses." *Electroencephalography and Clinical Neurophysiology*, 1968, *25*, 550–556.

RODIN, E. A., DOMINO, E. F., AND PORZAK, J. P. "The Marijuana-Induced 'Social High'." *Journal of American Medical Association*, 1970, *213*, 1300–1302.

ROTH, W. T. "Auditory Evoked Responses to Unpredictable Stimuli." *Psychophysiology*, 1973, *10*, 125–138.

ROTH, W. T., GALANTER, M., WEINGARTNER, H., VAUGHAN, T. B., AND WYATT, R. J. "Marijuana and Synthetic Delta-9-trans-Tetrahydrocannabinol: Some Effects on the Auditory Evoked Response and Background EEG in Humans." *Biological Psychiatry*, 1973, *6*, 221–233.

ROTH, W. T. AND KOPELL, B. S. "P$_{300}$: An Orienting Reaction in the Human Auditory Evoked Response." *Perceptual and Motor Skills*, 1973, *36*, 219–225.

ROTH, W. T., KOPELL, B. S., TINKLENBERG, J. R., DARLEY, C. F., SIKORA, R., AND VESECKY, T. B. "Contingent Negative Variation During a Memory Retrieval Task." *Electroencephalography and Clinical Neurophysiology*, 1974, in press.

ROTTER, J. B. "Generalized Expectancies for Internal Versus External Control of Reinforcement." *Psychological Monographs*, 1966, *80* (1, whole no. 609).

RUSINOV, V. S. "General and Localized Alteration in the Electroencephalogram During the Formation of the Conditioned Reflexes in Man." *Electroencephalography and Clinical Neurophysiology*, 1960, Supplement *13*, 309–319.

SALAMY, A. AND WILLIAMS, H. L. "The Effects of Alcohol on Sensory Evoked and Spontaneous Cerebral Potentials in Man." *Electroencephalography and Clinical Neurophysiology*, 1973, *35*, 3–11.

SANDERS, A. F. (Ed.). "Attention and Performance." *Acta Psychologica*, 1967, *27*.

SANDERS, A. F. (Ed.). "Attention and Performance III." *Acta Psychologica*, 1970, *33*.

SCHECHTER, G. AND BUCHSBAUM, M. "The Effects of Attention, Stimulus Intensity and Individual Differences on the Average Evoked Response." *Psychophysiology*, 1973, *10*, 392–400.

SHAGASS, C. *Evoked Brain Potentials in Psychiatry*. New York: Plenum, 1972a.

SHAGASS, C. "Electrophysiological Studies of Psychiatric Problems." *Review of Canadian Biology*, 1972b, *31*, Supplement, 77–95.

SHAGASS, C. AND SCHWARTZ, M. "Cerebral Responsiveness in Psychiatric Patients." *Archives of General Psychiatry*, 1963, *8*, 87–99.

SHELBURNE, S. A., JR. "Visual Evoked Responses to Word and Nonsense Syllable Stimuli." *Electroencephalography and Clinical Neurophysiology*, 1972, *32*, 17–25.

SHELBURNE, S. A., JR. "Visual Evoked Responses to Language Stimuli in Normal Children." *Electroencephalography and Clinical Neurophysiology*, 1973, *34*, 135–143.

SHUCARD, D. W. AND CALLAWAY, E. "Relationship Between Human Intelligence and Frequency Analysis of Cortical Evoked Responses." *Perceptual and Motor Skills*, 1973, *36*, 147–151.

SILVERMAN, J. "Attentional Styles and the Study of Sex Differences." In D. I. Mostofsky (Ed.), *Attention: Contemporary Theory and Analysis,* New York: Appleton-Century-Crofts, 1970, 61–98.

SILVERMAN, J., BUCHSBAUM, M., AND STIERLIN, H. "Sex Differences in Perceptual Differentiation and Stimulus Intensity Control." *Journal of Personality and Social Psychology,* 1973, *25,* 309–318.

SILVERMAN, J. AND KING, C. "Pseudo-Perceptual Differentiation." *Journal of Consulting and Clinical Psychology,* 1970, *34,* 119–123.

SPILKER, B. AND CALLAWAY, E. " 'Augmenting' and 'Reducing' in Averaged Visual Evoked Responses to Sine-Wave Light." *Psychophysiology,* 1969a, *6,* 49–57.

SPILKER, B. AND CALLAWAY, E. "Effect of Drugs on 'Augmenting/Reducing' in Averaged Visual Evoked Responses in Man." *Psychopharmacologia,* 1969b, *15,* 116–124.

SPONG, P., HAIDER, M., AND LINDSLEY, D. B. "Selective Attentiveness and Cortical Evoked Responses to Visual and Auditory Stimuli." *Science,* 1965, *148,* 395–397.

SQUIRES, K. C., HILLYARD, S. A., AND LINDSAY, P. H. "Cortical Potentials Evoked by Confirming and Disconfirming Feedback Following an Auditory Discrimination." *Perception and Psychophysics,* 1973, *13,* 25–31.

STERNBERG, S. "Memory Scanning: Mental Processes Revealed by Reaction Time Experiments." *American Scientist,* 1969, *57,* 421–457.

STOYVA, J. AND KAMIYA, J. "Electrophysiological Studies of Dreaming as the Prototype of a New Strategy in the Study of Consciousness." *Psychological Review,* 1968, *75,* 192–205.

SUTTON, S. "The Specification of Psychological Variables in an Average Evoked Potential Experiment." In E. Donchin and D. B. Lindsley (Eds.), *Average Evoked Potentials,* Washington, D.C.: NASA SP-191, 1969, 237–298.

SUTTON, S., BRAREN, M., ZUBIN, J., AND JOHN, E. R. "Evoked-Potential Correlates of Stimulus Uncertainty." *Science,* 1965, *150,* 1187–1188.

SUTTON, S., TUETING, P., ZUBIN, J., AND JOHN, E. R. "Information Delivery and the Sensory Evoked Potential." *Science,* 1967, *155,* 1436–1439.

TALLAND, G. A. AND QUARTON, C. Q. "The Effects of Drugs and Familiarity on Performance in Continuous Visual Search." *Journal of Nervous and Mental Disease*, 1966, *143*, 266–274.

TECCE, J. J. "Attention and Evoked Potentials in Man." In D. I. Mostofsky (Ed.), *Attention: Contemporary Theory and Analysis*, New York: Appleton-Century-Crofts, 1970, 331–365.

TECCE, J. J. "Contingent Negative Variation and Individual Differences: A New Approach in Brain Research." *Archives of General Psychiatry*, 1971, *24*, 1–16.

TECCE, J. J. "Contingent Negative Variation (CNV) and Psychological Processes in Man." *Psychological Bulletin*, 1972, *77*, 73–108.

TECCE, J. J. AND SCHEFF, N. M. "Attention Reduction and Suppressed Direct-Current Potentials in the Human Brain." *Science*, 1969, *164*, 331–333.

THOMPSON, R. F. AND SPENCER, W. A. "Habituation: A Model Phenomenon for the Study of Neuronal Substrates of Behavior." *Psychological Review*, 1966, *73*, 16–43.

TUETING, P. AND SUTTON, S. "The Relationship Between Prestimulus Negative Shifts and Poststimulus Components of the Averaged Evoked Potential." In S. Kornblum (Ed.), *Attention and Performance IV*, New York: Academic Press, 1973, 185–207.

TUETING, P., SUTTON, S., AND ZUBIN, J. "Quantitative Evoked Potential Correlates of the Probability of Events." *Psychophysiology*, 1971, *7*, 385–394.

VAUGHAN, H. G., JR., AND HULL, R. "Functional Relation Between Stimulus Intensity and Photically Induced Cerebral Responses in Man." *Nature*, 1965, *206*, 720–722.

VAUGHAN, H. G., JR. AND RITTER, W. "Physiologic Approaches to the Analysis of Attention and Performance." In S. Kornblum (Ed.), *Attention and Performance IV*, New York: Academic Press, 1973, 129–154.

WALTER, W. G. "The Convergence and Interaction of Visual, Auditory, and Tactile Responses in Human Nonspecific Cortex." *Annals of the New York Academy of Sciences*, 1964a, *112*, 320–361.

WALTER, W. G. "Slow Potential Waves in the Human Brain Associated with Expectancy, Attention, and Decision." *Archiv fur Psychiatrie und Nervenkrankheiten* (Berlin), 1964b, *206*, 309–322.

WALTER, W. G., COOPER, R., ALDRIDGE, V. J., MC CALLUM, W. C., AND WINTER, A. L. "Contingent Negative Variation: An Electric Sign of Sensorimotor Association and Expectancy in the Human Brain." *Nature*, 1964, *203*, 380–384.

WEINBERG, H. "Physiological Mechanisms of the CNV: Interrelationship with Other Potentials." *Electroencephalography and Clinical Neurophysiology*, 1973, Supplement *33*, 77–78.

WEINBERG, H., WALTER, W. G., AND CROW, H. J. "Intracerebral Events in Humans Related to Real and Imaginary Stimuli." *Electroencephalography and Clinical Neurophysiology*, 1970, *29*, 1–9.

WILKINSON, R. T. AND LEE, M. V. "Auditory Evoked Potentials and Selective Attention." *Electroencephalography and Clinical Neurophysiology*, 1972, *33*, 411–418.

WILKINSON, R. T. AND SPENCE, M. T. "Determinants of the Poststimulus Resolution of Contingent Negative Variation (CNV)." *Electroencephalography and Clinical Neurophysiology*, 1973, *35*, 503–510.

WILSON, W. P. (Ed.). *Applications of Electroencephalography in Psychiatry*. Durham, N.C.: Duke University Press, 1965.

WITKIN, H. A., DYK, R. B., FATERSON, H. F., GOODENOUGH, D. R., AND KARP, S. A. *Psychological Differentiation*. New York: John Wiley, 1962.

WOOD, C. C., GOFF, W. R., AND DAY, R. S. "Auditory Evoked Potentials During Speech Perception." *Science*, 1971, *173*, 1248–1251.

XII

Historical Antecedents of Personality Assessment

PAUL McREYNOLDS

In the sense of objective, systematic, and standardized procedures for learning about the personal characteristics of human beings the study of personality assessment can be said to have gotten seriously underway by the latter part of the last century, particularly in the extensive studies of Galton (1907; originally published 1883) in England and Cattell (1890) in the United States. Because of the innovative empirical work done by these two men, especially by Galton, many writers on assessment assume that the idea of assessing men began with Galton, and that prior to this time no such notion existed. Such a view, however, as I trust this chapter will make clear, would be quite inaccurate. While it is true that the modern tradition of formal, examiner-subject oriented testing derives mainly from Galton, it is also true that this development did not originate out of a prior cultural vacuum. On the contrary, there is a history going back to antiquity of people's interests in understanding other persons, and of their attempts to develop and codify ways of so doing. Some of the approaches developed

477

lasted for thousands of years,and in some cases, are still used. All of these approaches are fascinating in their own right, and all tell us something about the relations among general cultural patterns and the kinds of cues that people use in judging their fellows. Further, and most important for our present interest, these earlier approaches constitute an essential aspect of the historical background that led directly to the intellectual climate of ideas in which later contributions, such as those of Galton and Cattell, could germinate and grow.

It will thus be our pleasant task to trace the historical antecedents of the current scene in psychological assessment, beginning with the ancient period and coming up to the latter part of the last century. Several major limitations should be indicated at the outset: the first is the restriction of space. Our topic could easily fill a book, and our examination of it must necessarily be in the nature of a selective survey. There will, however, be opportunity to note most of the highlights—the major persons, books, and trends—in the area, and to linger briefly with some of them. Despite the prominence of assessment in contemporary psychology, I believe this chapter to be the first attempt to delineate systematically its early historical roots. This, however, is not to say that the area has been totally neglected by previous writers. Indeed, several historians of psychology (Brett, 1921; Watson, 1968; Linden and Linden, 1968) have called attention to the importance of Juan Huarte, whose *Examen de Ingenios* (1575) occupies an epochal place in the history of assessment. None of these writers, however, has gone into this interesting volume in any detail. Another respect in which the early history of personality assessment has not been completely passed by is in the consideration of phrenology. But with certain exceptions (Bakan, 1966; Walsh, 1970) most of the critical literature on phrenology has been shallow and has focussed on its invalidity to the exclusion of its historical significance.

The second limitation of this chapter is in its coverage. I will focus on the historical precursors of ways of assessing the global, overall personalities of individuals, and will not deal with historical developments more directly related to the testing of knowledge and learned skills. This topic, which is quite interesting in its own right, has recently been treated elsewhere (Linden and Linden, 1968; DuBois, 1970; Doyle, 1974). It involves an elaborate system of Civil Service Examinations in ancient China,[1] going back as far as 2200 B.C.; a somewhat unsystematic, but widespread practice of evaluating physical achievement in ancient Greece; formal examinations in the medieval universities, perhaps beginning at the University of Bologna in 1219; and various legalistic procedures for attempting to determine a person's guilt or innocence of various charges, and whether or not he was mentally able to be responsible for the charges. Another large area that I will omit is the influence on the rise of assessment of the development of the foundations of experimental psychology in the 18th and 19th centuries. This movement had two relevant channels: First, the discussion by various philosopher-psychologists—for example, von Wolff (1738) and Bonnet (1781)—of the possibility of measurements of psychological attributes; this topic has been reviewed by Ramul (1960). And second, the development of the theory and practice of demographic (Quetelet, 1835) and psychophysical (DeJaager and Jacob, 1970; Boring, 1942) methods of measurement. Also, I will not be concerned in this chapter with the history of methods of diagnosing abnormal mental conditions (Alexander and Selesnick, 1966; Bondy, 1974) though this is obviously related to the notion of personality assessment. A final area of study which I believe to have certain implications for the history of assessment, but which I will not attempt to review in these pages, is early Chinese philosophy and

[1] The development of Civil Service examinations in ancient China is of outstanding importance in the history of assessment, yet as DuBois, who is responsible for bringing this background to our contemporary attention, notes, "The prolonged and intensive Chinese experience with testing seems to have been completely ignored by contemporary psychometricians" (1964, p. 29). According to DuBois, "The earliest development seems to have been a rudimentary form of proficiency testing. About the year 2200 B.C. the emperor of China is said to have examined his officials every third year. . . . A thousand years later in 1115 B.C., at the beginning of the Chan dynasty, formal examining procedures were established. Here the record is clear. Job sample tests were used requiring proficiency in the five basic arts: music, archery, horsemanship, writing, and arithmetic. . . . Knowledge of a sixth art was also required—skill in the rites and ceremonies of public and social life" (pp. 30–31). Other relevant sources are Martin (1870), Têng (1943), and Kracke (1953).

medicine. We will restrict ourselves, except for opening comments on Mesopotamia, to the Western cultural tradition.

Concept of Assessment

By assessment I mean the process whereby one person attempts to know, understand, or "size up" another person; I will further limit the term to the delineation of conscious, deliberate systems for assessing persons. We will be looking, then, at those instances in earlier history in which some savant developed, or contributed to a systematic way of evaluating men and women. I am using assessment in a fairly broad way, and am in no sense limiting it to the kinds of procedures professional psychologists employ: there were personality assessors long before there were psychologists. Now, any system of assessment is based upon two kinds of items: first, a conceptualization of what people are potentially like—what the relevant dimensions and features of personality are, what the language of personal description is to be; and second, a specification of the particular observable cues, signs, and behaviors that one is to look for in describing a given person. Because of our focus on assessment technology, we will be interested mainly in the second of these. But since it is impossible to think in terms of cues for assessment in a meaningful way without at the same time conceptualizing, at least implicitly, certain personality variables or characteristics that these cues imply, it will also be necessary for us to give considerable attention to historical conceptualizations of personality structure. For example, when we examine the various physiognomic systems that have been used for assessing persons, it will be necessary to look not only at the particular physiognomic signs that are considered significant, but also at the personality variables that these signs were held to reflect.

The idea of assessment, the function and the charm of it, and the charismatic appeal of those presumed able to do it, is that of being able to know things about another person—or about oneself—that are not readily apparent. The core idea of an assessment technique is a set of procedures, or way of interpreting information that affords a picture of what a person is like that is more detailed, or more accurate than one could gain without this special technique. This assumption is true whether the assessment technique is observing and properly interpreting the meaning of the way a person shifts his eyes in conversations; or of noting, and deriving the appropriate conclusions from the particular constellation of the planets at the time of his birth; or of recording, and drawing the proper inferences from the statements that a person gives in response to a series of pictures. There is a story from Diogenes Laertius (1966, Vol. 2, p. 279), the third century biographer of ancient philosophers, about Cleanthes, the Stoic, in which Cleanthes was able to detect that a youth is effeminate solely from the way he sneezed. The notion that by special techniques one can gain unique insights into character is clearly indicated again in the title of a book by Christian Thomasius (1691), which translates (Gardiner, Metcalf, and Beebe-Center, 1937, p. 144) *New Discovery of a Well-Grounded and for the Community Most Necessary Science of the Knowledge of the Secrets of the Heart of Other Men from Daily Conversation, Even Against Their Will*. Similarly, de La Chambre, writing earlier in the same century, stated that in interpreting a man's intentions, it is not necessary to depend upon his words since one may also see imprinted "on his forehead and in his eyes, the images of his thoughts; that if his speech *happened* to belye his heart, his face should give the lie to his speech. In effect how secret soever the motions of his soul are, what care soever he takes to hide them, they are no sooner formed but they appear in his face" (1650, p. 1). And in contemporary assessment, there is, of course, the aura of special, secretive routes to the knowledge of man that surrounds the use of techniques such as the Rorschach, the MMPI, and the polygraph.

It seems that societies develop characteristic ways of knowing people. Some of these ways, no doubt, are based on folk wisdom, such as cultural assumptions as to what men, women, and children are like, and so on, while others reflect common cultural patterns, such as which gestures connote greetings or feelings of friendliness. Still other ways are more special in that they represent highly technical ways of knowing others, and can be mastered only after careful study; thus they tend to require professional experts such as phrenologists, physiognomists or other specialists to carry them out. In this sense modern assessment psychology, with its armamentarium of standardized tests, observational techniques, and psychophysiological instrumentation, is the successor to such earlier specialized routes to personality analysis as astrology, chiromancy, physiognomy, humorology, and phrenology, and probably occupies a somewhat similar role in the view of the societies involved.

To say that contemporary psychological assessment is in these ways similar to such discredited systems as astrology and phrenology is, I should emphasize, not to derogate modern assessment, any more than it would be a derogation of modern medicine or of modern chemistry to examine their primitive forerunners in earlier societies, and to see the relations between them and the modern scene. On the contrary, such a historical approach can lead to a greater appreciation of the current state of a given discipline.

The essence of individual assessment, insofar as it is influenced by practical considerations, is in its ability to predict what a person will do or what will happen to him. Underlying such attempts at prediction are broad, basic, and generally implicit cultural assumptions. Thus, techniques for individual assessment are more likely to occur in individualistically-oriented societies like ancient Greece, Renaissance Italy, Enlightenment England, and contemporary America than in autocratic or repressive societies. A culture's interpretations of the underlying causes of events also is important: if it is assumed that individual persons significantly control what happens to them, then it makes sense to assay a given person in order to predict his future. On the other hand, if a culture assumes that man is a pawn in the hands of the gods or of fate, then there is less point in assessing the individual in order to predict what he will do. The individual assessment itself would be different in a society which attributes to the individual the capacity to influence his future by his own abilities and efforts than in a society which holds that the makeup of the individual is largely predetermined.

Until recently American psychological assessment has given almost exclusive attention to the evaluation of individuals as contrasted with situations. This approach, however, has not proved as successful as had been hoped, and in recent years a notable trend has developed in techniques for assessing situations in which persons behave as a way of increasing the validity of predictions about behavior. Nevertheless, contemporary assessment remains primarily a matter of the evaluation of individuals.

Antiquity

Turning now to a consideration of the origins of assessment in ancient times, we will see that there was a close interplay between the kinds of assessment employed and the world views of the cultures involved.

So far as prehistoric cultures are concerned, it is impossible even to speculate fruitfully about any personality assessment practices that may have been employed. Presumably men always have had an interest in knowing what other men are like, and it is perhaps not implausible to conjecture that in certain prehistoric groups the medicine man, shaman, or some other functionary might have attained, or claimed to have attained special expertise in this area. If so, this would have amounted, in effect, to the real beginnings of systematic personality assessment. But about this we can only conjecture. We turn, then, for a look at the earliest civilization: Mesopotamia. The breakthrough to civilization was made first by the Sumerians, in the third and fourth millenia B.C., and they were later succeeded in dominance by the Babylonians and Assyrians. The world view of the Sumerian and later Mesopotamian cultures conceived of men and events as being under the control of all-powerful gods; hence many of their activities were concerned with serving and propitiating the controlling divinities. Further, it clearly made sense to be able to predict—to divine—what the wishes and whims of the divinities were, and what events they would cause to occur. A wide variety of attempts, within the limits of their ingenuity and their conceptions of reality, were undertaken to obtain such information: these attempts consisted of various ways of looking for informative signs or omens.

One of the most prominent of these ways was hepatoscopy; this consisted of the minute examination of the liver of a sacrificed animal in order to ascertain the presence or absence of particular signs which, when properly interpreted, would give some clue to the future. To think of this procedure merely as a primitive, misdirected superstition misses the point: in terms of the overall conceptions of the Mesopotamian culture, we can assume that this procedure was based, in its inception, on a reasonable rationale. This rationale appears to have included the notion of the liver as the primary mental organ (somewhat in the way that we think of the brain), a general conception of the interrelatedness of all things, and the assumption that all processes and events were subject to the control of the gods. The reading of the liver amounted to a kind of assessment; it was not, to be sure, a psychological assessment of persons, yet like psychological assessment it was intended primarily as a way of predicting the likelihood of given events in the future. In the very nature of the Mesopotamian world view, which emphasized the power of the gods as contrasted with that of men, it made considerably more sense to attempt to understand the gods' wishes, in order to predict the future, than to examine the capacities and traits of persons.

Many early peoples, of course, devised systems of beliefs and procedures for the recognition and interpretation of significant omens. All these procedures came to be thought of as attempts to assess the controlling environment in order to predict the future. As with hepatoscopy, however, these procedures were not, as such, systematic assessments of individual persons. But as to when the first individual personality assessment, in the sense of a systematic, specialized procedure, occurred, there is no sure way of knowing. If we think of the earliest phase of man's attempts to understand and predict his environment as expressing itself in the utilization of cues, signs, and omens relevant to the entire range of his perceptual world, then the transition to a later phase in which he used particular techniques for understanding and predicting other persons' behaviors very probably developed gradually, over a period of centuries. It is quite possible, then, that there is no clear answer to the question: when did personality assessment begin?

Nevertheless, it is interesting to speculate on the origins of personality assessment, and in this context there are two early practices that suggest themselves: astrology and physiognomy. Both reached the stage of systematic applications to individuals several centuries before the Christian era.

Astrology. Although there is no way of knowing for sure, it is quite possible that the first personality assessment technique was astrology, and that the first psychological "test" was the individual horoscope. I will now briefly trace the origin of astrology in Babylonia, and its spread to and further development in ancient Egypt, Greece, Rome, India, and China, showing its relevance for the history of psychological assessment. In doing this, it is essential that we keep in mind two interrelated points. First, we must guard against rejecting a proper appreciation of the historical significance of early astrology by our own awareness of its scientific invalidity; and second, we should realize that in the cultural matrix in which it arose and first developed, the practice of interpreting reality through the positions of the stars was in no sense seen as something bizarre or farfetched. On the contrary, it seemed a natural approach to take. The Babylonians, like all ancient peoples, took for granted the great importance and significance of the heavenly bodies, which they believed in some sense to be alive, and either themselves deities or under the control of gods.

Unlike other peoples of their time, however, the Babylonians developed a highly sophisticated knowledge of the heavens (Sarton, 1952; Neugebauer, 1969; Lindsay, 1971). They constructed observatories, plotted the courses of the planets, and maintained detailed records of astronomical phenomena over hundreds of years. By 1000 B.C. a listing of some 7000 celestial omens had been recorded (Neugebauer, 1969). The idea of the zodiac—an imaginary belt in the heavens covering the apparent paths of the planets, and including twelve divisions called signs of the zodiac—was invented in the fourth century B.C., and thereafter the basic notions of astrology were developed relatively rapidly (Lindsay, 1971; McIntosh, 1969). From Babylonia astrological lore was disseminated to Egypt and Greece, as well as to India and China and later to Rome.

From the earliest times the relative positions of the planets were used to attempt to foretell important political and natural events, such as wars, floods, famines, and so on, but our interest here is in the personal horoscope, that is, in the application of astrology to individuals. This stage in the development of astrology began probably sometime in the fifth century B.C. The theory of horoscopal astrology was that the relative positions of the planets at the time of a person's birth determined, or at least influenced, the kind of person he would be and the kinds of things that would happen to him, so that by noting, through appropriate tables, what the planetary positions had been at the time of birth, it was possible both to describe an individual's personality, and to predict certain events of his life. It is the former of these that can be seen as a forerunner of psychological assessment. One might suppose that the idea of the personal horoscope would have arisen first in Greece, with its greater sensitivity to individuals, rather than in Mesopotamia. Indeed, it was the Greeks who were primarily responsible for the development and elaboration of horoscopal astrology, but its actual beginnings were definitely in Babylon (Sachs, 1952; Lindsay, 1971, p. 48).

The most prominent early work on astrology still extant is the *Tetrabiblos* (Robbins, 1940) generally—though not exclusively —attributed to Ptolemy (Claudius Ptolemaeus), the second century A.D. Greek astronomer, geographer, and mathematician. This is an exceedingly interesting work and is believed to have been compiled from a number of earlier astrological manuals. As its name implies, it consists of four books. Of these the most interesting for our present inquiry is Book III, which concerns the applications of astrology to the understanding of individuals, especially Chapter 13 which treats the relations of horoscopal signs to psychological traits. This book, and especially this chapter, was a kind of handbook for astrological assessors not unlike those used today, which, after all, are derived from it. For the student of assessment the most impressive feature of the work is the rather elaborate usage of descriptive adjectives in the delineations of personality types. For example, Ptolemy writes that "bicorporeal signs make souls complex, changeable, hard to apprehend, light, unstable, fickle, amorous, versatile, fond of music, lazy, easily acquisitive, prone to change their minds" (p. 335).

The main difficulty with astrology was a simple but crucial fact: it was invalid. Yet we must not judge it too harshly as it appeared in the ancient world; many other conceptions of thought of that period were also wrong, yet they contributed in some fashion to the onward progress of thought. From the perspective of our present interest in psychological assessment, three summary points can be made about astrology.

First, it was ancient astrology that brought about, in the form of the horoscope, possibly the earliest assessment—almost certainly the earliest written assessment—of individual personalities. This assessment was made not by an analyis of the individual himself but by an analysis of the factors—the positions of the planets at the time of his birth—held to be causal with respect to his personality. This assumption was wrong, but this does not alter the fact that the individual assessments were made. Along with the horoscopes as such, there was the birth, or at least the nurturing of the *idea* of individual assessment, with the attendant notions of the subject, the assessor, the protocol (chart), and its interpretation. While it would surely be an oversimplification to attribute this set of concepts solely to ancient astrology, it would be equally inappropriate to ignore the parallel.

Second, all systems of personality assessment necessarily imply an underlying theory of personality, and the basic premise of astrological assessment was a world view in which the psychological makeup of the individual is largely predetermined, and in which the efforts and learned skills of the person have relatively less influence on his personality. This is similar in effect to a strongly genetic hypothesis of personality traits, in that it deemphasizes the role of experience and individual growth on the development of personality traits. This was characteristic of assessment approaches in the ancient world.

Third, early horoscopal assessment contributed to the development of taxonomical categories in terms of which persons could be categorized. This legacy is witnessed by adjectives in our language, descriptive of persons, such as jovial, mercurial, saturnine, and the like.

Physiognomy. One of the characteristics of horoscopal assessment was that it did not involve any actual contact with the subject at all. This statement definitely cannot be made for the other pioneering approach to person assessment emphasized in antiquity: physiognomy, the art of interpreting one's character from his physique. The practice of physiognomics, as the recent monograph by Evans (1969) makes clear, was widespread throughout the ancient world, and reached a peak of interest in the second century A.D. (Evan's paper is the leading work in the field, and I have drawn heavily on it in this section.)

The basic assumption of physiognomics is that the inner, personal characteristics of a person are revealed in his outer, observable features and behaviors. This, on the face of it, is certainly a natural and plausible assumption. Physiognomy as a discipline includes one additional premise: the outer cues of inner traits are not necessarily obvious, but require a certain trained expertise for their interpretation. And whereas astrology was primarily Babylonian in origin, physiognomy was invented by the Greeks. Among the prominent Greek thinkers who accepted and contributed to the development of physiognomic principles were Hippocrates, Plato, Aristotle, and Galen. The development of physiognomy apparently derived, at least in part, from an earlier literary tradition, as illustrated by the following passage from the Iliad, in which Idomeneus compares the behavior of brave men and cowards (translation in Rieu, 1950, p. 241): "There is nothing like an ambush for bringing a man's worth to light and picking out the cowards from the brave. A coward changes colour all the time; he cannot sit still for nervousness, but squats down, first on one heel, then on the other; his heart thumps in his breast as he thinks of death in all its forms, and one can hear the chattering of his teeth. But the brave man never changes colour at all and is not unduly perturbed, from the moment when he takes his seat in ambush with the rest. All he prays for is to come to grips with the enemy as quickly as may be."

The later Greeks seem, for the most part, to have considered Pythagoras (sixth century B.C.) to have been the founder of physiognomy, though Galen gave this distinction to Hippocrates (fifth century B.C.). For the student of psychological assessment the role of Pythagoras is especially significant, since there is good evidence for believing that it was he who was responsible for the first personality assessment procedure.

Little is known definitely about the life of Pythagoras. Certainly he was a real person, he was active in the latter part of the sixth century, he developed, at least in part, an influential philosophical system built around the symbolism of numbers, and he was involved in some kind of brotherhood, school, or movement at Crotona, in southern Italy. Much of the ambiguity surrounding Pythagoras' life centers on the nature of this Pythagorean center (Sarton, 1952; Philip, 1966; Evans, 1969). It seems generally agreed, however, that it was some kind of live-in organization of a theological-philosophical-scientific nature, with strict rules, including various taboos and vows of secrecy for members, all built in some manner around the dominating and charismatic figure of Pythagoras.

Evans (1969) notes that according to several ancient authorities Pythagoras developed and utilized a special procedure for evaluating candidates for admission into his brotherhood. It is this procedure, which was based largely on physiognomic assumptions, that I am suggesting may have constituted the earliest personality assessment procedure. Apparently it antedated the first individual horoscopes by perhaps a century, though of course we cannot be sure of this. Our knowledge of Pythagoras' examining procedure is based primarily on the accounts of Aulus Gellius (second century A.D.) and Iamblichus (third century A.D.); the relevant passages are the following:

> It is said that the order and method followed by Pythagoras, and afterwards by his school and his successors in admitting and training their pupils were as follows: At the very outset he "physiognomized" the young men who presented themselves for instruction. That word means to inquire into the character and dispositions of men by an inference drawn from their facial appearance and expression, and from the form and bearing of their whole body. Then, when he had thus examined a man and found him suitable, he at once gave orders that he should be admitted to the school [Rolfe, 1946, pp. 45, 47].
>
> Pythagoras in making trial [of the aptitude of those that came to him] considered whether they could *echemuthein*, i.e., whether they were able to refrain from speaking (for this was the word which he used), and surveyed whether they could conceal in silence and presence what they had learnt and heard. In the next place, he observed whether they were modest. For he was much more anxious that they should be silent than that they should speak. He likewise directed his attention to every other particular; such as whether they were astonished by the energies of any immoderate passion or desire. Nor did he in a superficial manner consider how they were affected with respect to anger or desire, or whether

they were contentious or ambitious, or how they were disposed with reference to friendship or strife. And if on his surveying all these particulars accurately, they appeared to him to be endured with worthy manners, then he directed his attention to their facility in learning and their memory. And in the first place, indeed, he considered whether they were able to follow what was said, with rapidity and perspicuity; but in the next place, whether a certain love and temperance attended them towards the disciplines which they were taught. For he surveyed how they were naturally disposed with respect to gentleness. But he called this *catartysis,* i.e., *elegance of manners.* And he considered ferocity as hostile to such a mode of education. For impudence, shamelessness, intemperance, slothfulness, slowness in learning, unrestrained licentiousness, disgrace, and the like, are the attendants on savage manners; but the contraries on gentleness and mildness. He considered these things, therefore, in making trial of those that came to him, and in these he exercised the learners. And those that were adapted to receive the goods of the wisdom he possessed, he admitted to be his disciples, and thus endeavored to elevate them to scientific knowledge. But if he perceived that anyone of them was unadapted, he expelled him as one of another tribe, and a stranger [Iamblichus, 1818, pp. 69–70].

These accounts are, at the very least, fascinating, and one wishes it were possible to know more about the testing procedures of Pythagoras.[2] As to the authenticity of the accounts no really

---

[2] Robert Burton—the author of *The Anatomy of Melancholy* (1621) —also wrote a Latin play, titled *The Philosophaster* (Pack, 1935). One scene, as noted by Pack, is evidently based on Pythagoras' mode of examination. In Edward Schuré's (1971, pp. 54–58; originally published 1889) imaginative reconstruction of the Pythagorean assessment procedure, it resembles the live-in assessment procedures employed by the OSS (Office of Strategic Services in World War II) and the Institute for Personality Assessment and Research, in Berkeley. Schuré also suggests—on what evidence it is not clear —that part of the tests (not the physiognomic parts) were adapted from older Egyptian initiation rites (Schuré, 1971, pp. 54–58; originally published 1889).

definitive statement can be made. They were written some seven or eight centuries after Pythagoras, but presumably were based upon earlier sources, now lost. Iamblickus is generally considered to be rather fanciful and not wholly reliable, yet he and Gellius evidently utilized different earlier sources, and the fact that they both refer to some kind of entrance examination is clearly significant. Also, there are other authorities (Evans, 1969, note 106, p. 27) for the view that Pythagoras was considered by the latter classical writers as the founder of physiognomy. All in all, we may conclude that Pythagoras conducted some kind of systematic personality assessment involving, but probably not limited to, physiognomic interpretations. It is interesting to note that the date usually given for the founding of his center at Crotona is 529 B.C. Thus, we can plausibly conjecture that the first personality assessment battery is almost exactly 2500 years old!

Aristotle was one of the major contributors to ancient physiognomy. In the words of Evans, "with Aristotle we come to the first analytical treatment of physiognomics preserved in Greek literature" (1969, p. 22). Statements relevant to physiognomy are found in the *Rhetoric, Analytica Priora, De Partibus Animalium, Historia Animalium,* and *De Anima.* In *Analytica Priora* (Tredennick, 1967) Aristotle states that "it is possible to judge men's character from the physical appearance, if one grants that body and soul change together in all natural affections. . . . Supposing, then, this is granted, and also that there is one sign of one affection, and that we can recognize the affection and sign proper to each class of creatures, we shall be able to judge character from physical appearance" (II, 27, 70b, pp. 527–528). And in *Historia Animalium* (Peck, 1965) he concludes that "persons who have a large forehead are sluggish, those who have a small one are fickle; those who have a broad one are excitable, those who have a bulging one, quick-tempered" (I, VIII, 891b, p. 39).

Of the many early works that are believed to have been written on physiognomy, four are extant (Evans, 1969). The oldest and most important of these, *Physiognomica*[3] (Hett, 1936), was

---

[3] The three other early handbooks on physiognomy that have come down to us are those by Polermo Rhetor of Laodicea (Second century A.D.)

originally attributed to Aristotle—perhaps it is the one referred to
by Diogenes Laertius (1966, vol. 1, p. 471); it is now believed,
however, not to have been composed by Aristotle himself, but more
probably by several other authors belonging to, or sympathetic to
the Peripatetic school. The treatise is about the same length as the
present paper. It begins by summarizing the methods that previous
physiognomists have used. These are: (1) the examinations of
parallels between physiques in men and animals; (2) comparisons
of different ethnic groups; and (3) the study of the relations between bodily characteristics and particular dispositions. The author
then criticizes the dependence, in physiognomy, upon separate,
superficial characteristics. He notes, for example, that "some men
who are in no sense alike, have the same facial expressions (for instance the brave and the shameless man have the same expressions),
but are widely different in disposition . . ." (805b, p. 87). Further, he points out that bodily signs do not help "one to recognize
a doctor or a musician; for the man who studies some branch of
learning produces no change in the signs of which the physiognomist
makes use" (806a, p. 91).

The writer concludes, therefore, that physiognomics must
deal with a limited number of recognizable signs, including "movements, shapes and colours, and from habits as appearing in the
face, from the growth of hair, from the smoothness of the skin, from
voice, from the condition of the flesh, from parts of the body, and
from the general character of the body" (806a, p. 93). The book
then gives a number of specific signs that the physiognomist can
look for, for example, "Sluggish movements denote a soft disposition,
quick ones a fervent one . . . the deep and full voice denotes
courage, when high and slack it means cowardice" (806b, p. 95).
The author makes it clear, however, that "Generally speaking, it is

---

Adamantius (fourth century A.D.), and an anonymous Latin technical manual
(probably fourth century A.D.) (Evans, 1969, p. 5; for texts see Forster, 1893).
Polermo includes a detailed discussion of characterological likenesses between
men and animals, and examines some ninety-two animals in this context. The
last eighteen (of seventy) chapters delineate the physiognomic signs of given
psychological types, for example, of a robust, daring man; of a timid man; a
sad and downcast man; and so on. The work by Adamantius places great
emphasis upon the interpretation of personality from observation of the eyes
of the subject.

foolish to put one's faith in any one of the signs; but when one finds several of the signs in agreement in one individual, one would probably have more justification for believing the inference true" (807a, p. 95).

The ancient science of physiognomy, developed mainly in the Greek classical period and the early Roman world, must be counted as a notable achievement in the long endeavor to see through man's exterior into his inner self. Though largely misguided, it was hardly naive, as the above quotations make clear. Compared with horoscopal assessment, it was more plausible, more flexible, and more applicable to the uniquenesses of individuals. In its furthest advances it was not limited to the reading of physical features in the narrow sense, but took on something of the broader quality of what we today would call naturalisic observation.

Discussion. We must now bring another strand into our narrative. This is the Greek theory of the humors, developed over a period of several centuries, beginning with the physician Alcmaeon (sixth century B.C.) and culminating in the writings of Galen (second century A.D.). The general notion of humoral theory was that health and functioning of the body is dependent upon having the proper *krasis* or mixture among the four postulated humors—blood, phlegm, yellow bile, and black bile. Different temperaments were held to be related to the dominance of one or another of the humors, for example, a dominance of blood was conceived to lead to a sanguine temperament. Associated with the concept of humors were two pairs of opposites—hot and cold, and wet and dry; for example, blood was hot and moist, phlegm cold and moist, and so on. It is not necessary that we go into humoral psychology at length in this chapter, but it should be noted that physiognomic theory and humoral theory in many ways became fused in Hellenistic times. Galen, in particular, brought about an integration of these two theoretical traditions. In his *De Temperamentis* he maintained that, in the words of Evans (1969), "the best-tempered (or blended) person is one who represents the absolute mean between extremes, thinness and fatness, softness and hardness, warmth and cold" (p. 26). Evans concludes that "it is Galen who first of all skillfully combined the Aristotelian parallelisms of men and animals in the study of physiognomy with the theory of the humors circulating in the body, and thus laid the foundations for what have become commonplaces through the centuries in the interpretation of the character of a man from his physique" (p. 26).

A specific way in which humoral variables could affect physiognomy, and thus facilitate personality assessment, would be in the flushing in one's face when he is angry, brought about by the fact that the hot blood is stirred up in emotion of anger. Heat and cold, wetness and dryness in the environment also were conceived as important variables in humoral psychology. An important work by Hippocrates (fifth century B.C.; 1952) titled *On Air, Waters, and Places,* discusses the effects of these factors on health and temperament. This work, parenthetically, appears to be historically relevant to the current interest in ecological variables in assessment.

The study of physiognomy became intertwined not only with humoral psychology, but also with astrology, and all three of these vigorous currents of thought passed into the Roman world. (One other early portent of assessment should be at least mentioned: this is dream analysis, concerned mainly with the prediction of future events, and permeated with the superstitions of the time. Our best source of ancient dream interpretation is the second *Oneirocritica* of Artemidorus (second century A.D.; Artemidorus, 1606.)

So far I have implied that both of the major precursors of person assessment in the ancient world—horoscopal astrology and physiognomy—reflected the cultural assumptions of their particular places and times. This point of view merits further discussion. The main assumption appears to have been that a person's character was predetermined, either by the stars or his ancestors. Little allowance was made for an individual to develop or change: people were the way they were, and that was that. This assumption of the fixity of human nature was less conspicuous in the Greek-oriented physiognomy than in the more Babylonian-oriented astrology. Yet it was characteristic of both. All of this, of course, is not to say that there was no conception of individual differences in antiquity. On the contrary, it was because of the recognition that persons differ from one to another that some rudimentary form of assessment was recognized as desirable. The following lines spoken by Polydamas, in the Iliad, illustrate this awareness of significant individual differences: "People differ in their gifts. One man can fight, another dance, or play the lute and sing; and yet another is endowed by all-seeing Zeus with a good brain" (Rieu, 1950, pp. 253–254).

Medieval Period and the Renaissance

The main legacies from the ancient world concerning psychological assessment were horoscopal astrology and physiognomy, both of which became part of the ongoing stream of Western culture. During the interregnum in the progress of European civilization that lasted from the close of the classical era to the twelfth century, both conceptions lost something of their former influence. But in the recovery of the classical tradition that took place in the period of the Italian Renaissance, both staged a powerful revival. Indeed, though neither made any scientific or objective advances, viewed simply as social phenomena, both became stronger than they had ever been. With respect to astrology, both public and private decisions of all sorts were suited to the predictions of the planets, and "in all the better families," according to Burckhardt (1958), "the horoscope of the children was drawn as a matter of course, and it sometimes happened that for half a lifetime men were haunted by the idle expectation of events which never occurred" (vol. 2, p. 486). With respect to physiognomy, it appeared at this stage, according to Burckhardt, not "as the sister and ally of art and psychology, but as a view from the fatalistic superstition" (p. 508).

The persistence of a system as irrational as astrology into the height of the Renaissance, which is usually considered as the period of transition from the medieval to the modern world, may at first seem strange. We must remember, however, that this was a period in which the ancient world, newly recovered and revered, was perhaps overevaluated. Also, the religious faith of the prior centuries was less secure, creating a greater need for other kinds of certainty; and further, the ancient cosmology, in terms of which astrological theories had originally been constructed, was still accepted, and would be until after the Copernican breakthrough (1543). Finally, as Dresden (1968) has noted, it would be a mistake to draw too sharp a distinction between the Renaissance and the Middle Ages. All aspects considered, it is clear that so far as the development of psychological assessment is concerned, astrology by this time had nothing further to contribute. The significance of physiognomy for assessment, however, particularly in the wider, more behavioral interpretation of this term, had not yet run its course—indeed it still has not. We will be following it throughout the rest of this chapter. During the Renaissance period the acceptance of humoral psychology (Tillyard, 1944) and physiognomic methods of evaluating people was widespread, and a part of the general culture. These views were promulgated not only through learned treatises in Latin, but also by means of popular works in the vernacular, which appeared then as now. The following passage from James Yonge's popular translation (Matthews, 1963, pp. 211–212) from the *Secreta Secretorum*,[4] in 1422, is illustrative of such works: "Physiognomy is a science to deem the conditions or virtues and manners of people after the tokens or signs that appeareth in fashion or making of body, and namely [especially] of visage and of the voice and of the color. One light manner and general of physiognomy is to deem virtues and manners of men after the complexion. Complexions be four, for a man is sanguine or phlegmatic or choleric or melancholy. . . . He that hath a sharp nose and small, he is wrathful. And he that hath a long nose and somewhat stooping and stretching toward the mouth he is worthy and hardy. He that hath a crooked nose, he is hasty, malicious, and angry."

I must comment briefly on the conceptions of the individual person in this period. A serious interest in personality assessment in the systematic evaluation of individual persons would seem to depend upon the existence in a given culture of a recognition of the significance of individuals, and upon an interest in understanding them. Such a recognition and interest increased greatly during this period. That this is true of the fifteenth century Renaissance is universally acknowledged (Burckhardt, 1958, pp. 303–323). Recently, Morris (1972) and others have traced out a prior, relatively sudden spurt of interest in the individual, manifested in a concern with the sense of the inner self, and with biographies and portraits, in the

---

[4] The *Secreta Secretorum* has a fascinating history. Popularly, though probably incorrectly, attributed to Aristotle, it appeared in various languages and various editions in the medieval and Renaissance periods, and consisted of what was represented to be advice from Aristotle to Alexander on government and on ways of maintaining the health of the soul and the body.

twelfth century. One would expect this overall change in attitude toward the individual to have led eventually to a changed conception of psychological assessment, and later in this chapter I will attempt to show that this was indeed the case.

In order for the prediction I have just stated to make sense, it is necessary to assume a significant relationship between the pattern of a culture and the psychological assessment practices within it. It may seem that such a relationship is unlikely, that the kinds of assessments carried out are essentially determined by the few assessors who may happen to exist in a culture and that psychological assessment constitutes an altogether too trivial part of an overall society to affect, or be affected by, the larger culture. I believe, however, that there is good reason for believing that this is not the case, for believing, on the contrary, that there is characteristically a very close relationship between a society and the assessment practices carried on within it, whether by a professional group of assessors (astrologers, physiognomists or psychologists) or by laymen.

In our society, which is a highly organized, computer-linked technical system, assessment increasingly takes on similar characteristics. In societies whose world views attributed causal significance to the movements of the stars, assessment practices did the same. And in many societies professional assessors have been assigned positions of key importance, indicating the cultural significance of the assessment role. Thus, in ancient nations from Babylon to Rome, as well as in many Renaissance city-states, there were official astrologers who provided advice. de La Chambre, whom we will consider presently, was private counselor to Louis XIV. And in our own period, professional psychological assessment plays an increasingly important role in education, government, and business.

Age of Reason

In accord with general usage, I will use the term Age of Reason to cover the period approximately from the middle of the sixteenth century to the latter part of the eighteenth. It is, of course, an arbitrary division, but is useful as a way of referring roughly to a period having some degree of intellectual homogeneity. During this period a number of books appeared which were highly relevant to assessment, and which reflected the new interest in the individual and the optimistic orientation of the Enlightenment. We will begin our survey with an important work published in Spain.

The Tryal of Wits. In the year 1575, in Spain, Juan de Dios Huarte y Navarro (c. 1530–1589), a physician of possibly Basque origin, brought out at his own expense, in an edition of 1500 copies, a book titled *Examen de Ingenios para las Ciencas.* This work proved to be very popular, and went through some twenty-seven later editions in Spanish, as well as twenty-four in French, seven in Italian, five in English, three in Latin, two in German, and one in Dutch. The first English rendering, in 1594, was from an Italian edition.[5] My summary of the book below is based on a 1698 London edition; the full translation of the title is *The Tryal of Wits, Discovering The great Difference of Wits among Men, and what Sort of Learning suits best with each Genius.* A line suggests that the work may be "Useful to all Fathers, Masters, Tutors, etc."

This book is of great importance in the history of assessment, and we must examine it in some detail. Before doing this, however, let me briefly set the stage by alluding to the historical context in which the book appeared. In 1575, Spain, under Philip II, was at its strongest, most farreaching, and most civilized position. Elizabeth I was Queen of England. In France, Michel Montaigne had withdrawn to his beloved library and was writing his essays which he would publish in 1580. Galileo and Shakespeare each were eleven years old, and Hobbes and Descartes had not yet been born. Culturally, Europe was in a period of transition, with the thought patterns of the past still strong. Astrology and magic, though less firmly entrenched than formerly, were still widely accepted. The great retrogression was the widespread belief in and the persecution of witches.

Huarte's predecessor in Spain was the philosopher-psychologist Juan Luis Vives (1492–1540). Vives had been concerned, in particular, with improvements in education, and he had set a style

---

[5] The reference is Huarte de San Juan, Juan (1594). The Introduction, by Carmen Rogers, is a good source on the life of Huarte. Huarte's book was widely circulated in 17th century England, and presumably exercised considerable influence on both parents and schoolmasters (Craig, 1936).

for independent thinking. Though Huarte does not refer to Vives, we can assume that he was familiar with the latter's work.

I will begin with a general summary of the contents of *The Tryal of Wits,* and will then develop in more detail the points in the work that deal specifically with assessment. The book consists of a dedicatory letter to the king, a Proem and seventeen chapters, totaling some 542 pages. The main theme of the book is that individuals differ greatly from one to another, both in what we would term their intelligence ("wit") and in their specific talents; further, that different vocations require, for one's success in them, different patterns of abilities; and finally, that it would therefore make sense to determine the particular abilities of each person, in order that he might be guided into the appropriate type of education and profession. I would like here to emphasize the importance of this conception. Though commonplace today, it was essentially new in 1575, and it could have arisen seriously only in the changing cultural ethos which assigned a greater role to the significance of the individ- of a person's talents. In part this was because such a policy, he be- lieved, would effectively serve the state. Thus, the opening lines of his lieved would effectively serve the state. Thus, the opening lines of his dedicatory letter to the king read "SIR, To the end that the Works of all Artists may attain the utmost Pitch of Perfection, and be of the greatest use to the Common-Wealth." And here he goes on to explain his idea that "there should be *Triers* appointed by the State, Men of approved Sagacity and Knowledge, to search and found the Abilities of Youth, and after due Search, to oblige them to the Study of that Science their Heads leaned most to, instead of abandoning them to their own Choice" (the word "Science" was used in Huarte's time to mean a branch of knowledge).

But Huarte was thinking also of the individual welfare of the persons involved. This attitude is evident in the following passages: " 'Tis not to be denied, but that some Wits that are disposed for one, are not fit for another Science. And for that very reason, it is convenient before the Child be sent to School, to discover his In- clination, to find out what Study is most agreeable to his Capacity" (p. 37); and further, "which Difference of Wit each sort of Science in particular corresponds, to the end that every one may distinctly understand (after having first discovered his own Nature and Temperament) to which Art he is most inclined" (p. 183); and elsewhere, "were I my self a Master, before I received any Scholar to my School, I would sift him narrowly, to find out if I could, what kind of *Genius* he had; and if I discover'd in him a propensity for learning, I profess I should cheerfully receive him; for it is a great satisfaction to the Teacher to instruct a Man of Parts, otherwise I should advise him to apply himself to some Study fitter for him; but if I found he was not in the least capable of any Learning, I should address to him in such tender and endearing Words as these: Brother, there being no likelihood of your ever succeeding in what you have undertaken, for God's sake, waste no more Time, nor lose no more Pains, but seek out some other way to live, that requires not such Abilities as Learning" (p. 35) (by "Genius" one is understood to have a particular natural talent; "sift" meant to examine minutely)'.

The overall psychological theory underlying Huarte's proposal was relatively, though not entirely, orthodox. In accordance with the prevailing opinion of his day, he divided the cognitive portion of the mind into the Understanding, Memory, and Imagination, and he accepted, almost as a matter of course, the traditional theory of the four humors and the four qualities. Indeed, his book is one of the best sources on the humoral psychology of this period. Nevertheless, he did not hesitate to disagree with Hippocrates, Aristotle, and Galen when it suited his purpose.

I have indicated that Huarte placed great emphasis upon differences among individuals, and this fact is central to his importance in the history of assessment. Early in the book he suggests that "if a Thousand Persons meet together, to give their Opinion upon any Point, each will have his particular Sentiment, and not one Man's shall agree with anothers . . ." (unnumbered, first page of Supplement to Proem). Later, at various places throughout the book, he indicates some of the ways in which people differ—in terms of their humors, their passions, their inclinations, and so on. I will limit myself to one brief quotation: "If we pass to the Generative Faculty, we shall find therein . . . many Appetites and Varieties: for some Men there are who affect a Homely, and abhor a Handsom Woman; and others are better pleased with a Fool, than a Wise

Woman; some who love a Lean, and hate a Fat one; even Silks and a gay Dress displease those, who run mad for one in Rags" (p. 261).

The main dimensions of individual differences that Huarte is interested in, however, are those concerning the three cognitive functions: Understanding (wit), Memory, and Imagination (fancy). He uses these three functions essentially as variables, and develops, in effect, a psychogram in terms of them for the requirements of each of several major professions. His discussions of these topics are, to be sure, somewhat naive from our perspective. They are nevertheless extremely interesting in the context of modern factor-analytic attempts to break down the components of various skills. Huarte concludes that the field of School-Divinity pertains primarily to the Understanding, but that "Preaching (which is the Practice) is a Work of the Imagination. And accordingly as it is difficult to join in the same Brain a good Understanding with a great Imagination, so it cannot be that a Man should at the same time be a great School-Divine and a famous Preacher" (p. 215). The theory of law, he holds, pertains mainly to the Memory, whereas pleading and judging causes is related more to the Understanding function (Chapter 13). The theory of medicine (Physic) is based in part on the Memory, and in part on the Understanding, the practice of medicine is based primarily on the Imagination, and so on.

The next step in Huarte's analysis—after having specified the psychological requirements of the various professions—is that of assessing the individual to determine the degree to which he possesses the necessary traits. This is all very modern in principle, though Huarte's approach, based as it is largely in the terms of humoral psychology, will amaze the modern reader. First, a few words about his terminology are in order. The term for the procedure of evaluation is *Tryal*. At one point he does use the word *Test*. The persons conducting the Tryals are not examiners, but *Triers* (as noted in an earlier quotation, above, they should be persons of Sagacity and knowledge). The cues that the Triers are to look for in making their assessments, are referred to as *Signs, Marks* or *Tokens*. The term *Wit*, though sometimes used in that period as synonomous with Understanding (which in turn is fairly close to the modern intelligence, though it includes more of the notion of good judgment), here is used in a broader way, and is closer to what we would call mental abilities.

Now, what techniques of assessment does Huarte recommend? Here, unless he has the proper historical perspective, the modern reader is likely to be quite disappointed. Huarte's book is primarily programmatic, and his actual techniques are crude and nonsystematic. Still, it was a beginning, more global and practical than even the best prior approaches, such as physiognomy. And he avoided the errors of astrology and other forms of divination, which, after all, were a part of his culture. In general, one gets the impression that the Triers would gather data about a person whom they were assessing from whatever sources they could, and then would combine these sources into some kind of overall judgment. At one point, Huarte suggests that "There is no better Test to discover, if a Man wants Understanding, than to note if he be Haughty in Punctilios of Honour, Presumptuous, Elated, Ambitious, and Ceremonious." On the other hand, a man who is naturally humble "may justly pass for a Man of great Understanding, but of little Imagination or Memory" (p. 200).

In discussing the methods for carrying out a "Trial of the Wit" of those considering the law, Huarte offers a number of fairly straightforward suggestions. A good measure of Memory is how readily a child learns the letters and order of the alphabet. Further, "To Write a running fair Hand . . . discovers the Imagination; so much that the Child who in a few Days knows how to hold his Hand upon his Paper, to draw his Lines strait, and to put all his Letters even, and in good Form and Figure, gives Proof of a mean Understanding, because this is the Work of the Imagination, and these two Powers have a great Contrariety between them" (p. 275). A facility in learning Grammar is another indication of good Memory; good Memory, however, is rarely found in combination with good Understanding, so that "If a Child advance not much in Grammar, it is to be suspected that he has a good Understanding" (p. 277). A better measure of Understanding, however, is how the child performs in Logic; indeed, says Huarte, "This Science bears the same proportion with the Understanding, as the Touchstone does with Gold" (p. 277).

These examples will suffice, I think, to convey something of the diversity of Huarte's notions of assessment. Certain of his suggestions, for example, that "Hair Nut-brown, between fair and red" is a sign of "the well tempered Man" (p. 372–373), are more traditional and less related to actual behavior, and verge—from our perspective—on the fantastic. There is no point in pretending that his specific technical proposals were highly sophisticated. They weren't. Yet much more important than these specific procedures was the central idea that he set forth: that each person has certain useful talents. "There is no man," he asserted, "how gross and imperfect soever formed, but Nature has design'd him for something" (p. 26). And it is possible, through the use of appropriate Tryals, conducted by men of Sagacity and Knowledge, to determine for each individual what these talents are.

Bacon, Wright, and Bulwer. We go now to England, to Francis Bacon, and the year 1605. As a way of identifying this year, it was the time in which Shakespeare's King Lear was first performed, and two years before the founding of Jamestown in America. It was also the year in which Bacon's *Advancement of Learning* was published.

In this work, which he dedicated to King James, who had succeeded Queen Elizabeth only two years before, Bacon set out to review the various branches of knowledge, and to note areas in the sciences in which further progress was needed. He discussed at one point that branch of study "which is *the knowledge of ourselves*" (1605, p. 236). This knowledge, he said, can be divided into two branches, Discovery and Impression. The former concerns the ways in which one can learn about the mind through the medium of the body, and vice versa; and the second concerns how the body affects the mind, and the opposite. Our interest here is the first of these; according to Bacon, this approach "hath begotten two arts," about which he comments as follows (1869 edition, pp. 238–239):

> The first is Physiognomy, which discovereth the disposition of the mind by the lineaments of the body. The second is the Exposition of Natural Dreams, which discovereth the state of the body by the imaginations of the mind. In the former of these I note a deficience. For Aristotle hath very ingeniously and diligently handled the factures of the body, but not the gestures of the

body, which are no less comprehensible by art, and of greater use and advantage. For the Lineaments of the body do disclose the disposition and inclination of the mind in general; but the Motions of the countenance and parts do not only so, but do further disclose the present humour and state of the mind and will. For as your Majesty saith most aptly and elegantly, *As the tongue speaketh to the ear, so the gesture speaketh to the eye.*

With respect to the first of the arts noted by Bacon—dream analysis—he elsewhere (*De Augmentis;* Bacon, 1869 edit., Vol VI, p. 238) observes that the treatment this topic has received is full of follies, and is not yet solidly based. With respect to physiognomy Bacon's main complaint is that it has been too much based upon the static contours and features of the body and not sufficiently upon movements. In effect, he is calling for further research along this line.

The two books that we will next consider can best be considered in the context of Bacon's critique. Actually, the first one, by Thomas Wright, was published before *The Advancement of Learning,* in 1601; yet it fits clearly into the pattern delineated by Bacon, and came out of the same climate of ideas. The second one, by Bulwer (1644), directly acknowledges the inspiration of Bacon's work.

Wright's book, *The Passions of the Minde in Generall,* is, as its title suggests, primarily a contribution to the psychology of the passions as conceived in that era. Of particular interest to the historian of assessment, however, is the fact that it includes two chapters on how the passions may be "discovered." Since the concept of passion was broader then than it is today—it included essentially what we would mean by both motives and emotions—it is evident that this work is extremely relevant in the history of personality assessment.

Before examining the book, let us consider for a moment its author.[6] He appears to have been a highly intriguing man; certainly

---

[6] I am indebted to Thomas O. Sloan, author of the Introduction to the recent facsimile edition of *The Passions* (Wright, 1630), for most of my information on Wright.

his life had few dull episodes. Born in York in 1561, at a time of great religious unrest, he became a Jesuit priest, and was engaged, over most of the rest of his life, in various attempts, some open and some under cover, to advance the cause of religious tolerance in England. Much of his life was spent on the continent, and much of his time in England was spent in prisons. Indeed, *The Passions* was completed while he was confined in Bridewell. Wright was evidently a friend of Ben Jonson, as the 1604 edition included a commendatory sonnet by Jonson. This edition was notable, too, in that it was dedicated to the Earl of Southampton, who, it will be remembered, was Shakespeare's patron. Wright also was presumably well acquainted with Bacon. At one time they both were a part of the circle of the Earl of Essex. Later, when Essex was brought to trial for treason, Bacon was one of the prosecutors and Wright was a witness for the prosecution.

Turning now to the book itself, to the two chapters (Chapters 1, 2, pp. 104–144, Bk, 4, 1630 edit.) on assessment, we find the following opening lines (facsimile edition, pp. 104–105):

> As by experience men may discouer the inclinations of dogs and horses, and other beasts, euen so by certaine signes wise men may gather the inclinations whereunto other men are subject . . . I will briefly deliuer here some meanes, whereby in particular conuersation, euery one may discouer his fellowes naturall inclinations, not by philosophicall demonstrations, but onely by naturall coniectures and probabilities, because that wise men mortifie their passions, and craftie men dissemble: yet we may for the most part attaine vnto the knowledge of them, for that most men follow the instinct of Nature, and few, either the precepts of reason, or exquisite craftiness, by which two meanes passions are concealed.

Wright then states that since it is not possible to enter directly into a man's heart in order to determine his passions and inclinations, we must trace them out by their "effects and externall operations." There are two, and only two ways in which this can be done, namely, through the man's speech and through his actions.

Chapter 1, Book Four of *The Passions* is concerned with the ways
that one may use in understanding a person from his speech, and
Chapter 2 with "The discouery of Passions by externall Actions."
The rationale for the analysis of a person's inclinations through the
things that he says is as follows (facsimile edition, p. 106):

> Sometimes I haue enquired of sundry persons,
> what they thought of certaine mens inclinations; and I
> found that almost whatsoeuer they had noted in others,
> commonly to proceed from one sort of speech or
> other. Plainly you may perceiue, if mens words openly
> tend to their owne commendations, if they brag or boast
> of their valour in warres, learning, qualities giuen by
> nature, or purchased by labor, that they are of a proud
> disposition: if they discourse lasciuiously or shamlesly,
> questionlesse what the tongue speaketh the heart affect-
> eth: if men talke of meate and drinke, of gulling and
> feasting, wishing for this meat, lamenting of that meat,
> such persons, for most part, addict themselves to glut-
> tonie: if they rage with furious words, brawle or wrangle,
> such carie the conscience of cholericke.

Wright then discusses at some length six different patterns of
speaking, and indicates for each the kind of person that is to be inferred. These six patterns are: "Much talke," "Taciturnitie," "Slow-
nesse in speech," "Rashnesse in speech," "Affectation in speech,"
and "Scoffing speeches." He is aware, however, that some men do
not reveal themselves quite so openly, and that in these cases "wee
must looks into their demeanour more narrowly" (p. 114). In this
perspective he discusses other patterns of speech behavior, including
"Disputation aboue the speakers capacitie," the "Spirit of Contradiction," "Concealing and reuealing of Secrets," and "Sowers of
dissention."

In his discussion of how the passions that characterize a person may be identified by observation of his overt behaviors, Wright
focusses on eight classes of behavior: play, feasting, drinking, gestur-
ing, praising, the wearing of apparell, conversing, and writing. I will
comment briefly on Wright's treatment of two of these. In introducing his discussion of play, Wright states: "Play pregnantly proueth

passions: for pride, choller, and couetousness, commonly wait vpon great gamesters. Some, when they leese, are so inflamed with ire and choller, that you would take them rather for bedlams than reasonable creatures" (p. 125) . . . . Others, in play shew likewise their passions albeit they exceed not much the lawful quantity requisit to recreation, yet they carry a secret pride, and vehement desire to win, because they would not be inferiour to others, euen so much as in play" (p. 126). These, and Wright's succeeding observations of play, though quaintly worded by modern standards, must be counted as highly insightful by any standards. His discussion of gestures is broken down into a separate discussion of the eyes, the voice, the managing of the hands and body, and the "manner of going" (walking).

We must now leave Wright and move on. The third of the trio of English books reserved for this section is *Chirologia,* by John Bulwer (1644). This work, as we have already noted, was a followup of an implied suggestion in *The Advancement of Learning,* specifically, of the importance of gestures in understanding personality. Bulwer, a physician, was particularly interested in the psychological significance of movements of the hands and fingers.[7] At the beginning of his treatise he put the rationale of his approach in the following words (p. 2):

> For, as *Hand* being the *Substitute* and *Viceregent* of the Tongue, in a full, and majestique way of expression, presents the *signifing faculties* of the Soule, and the inward discourse of Reason; and as *another Tongue,* which we may justly call the *Spokesman* of the Body, it *speaks* for all the members thereof, denoting their *Suffrages,* and including their *Votes.* So that whatever thought can be delivered, or made *significantly manifest,* by the united motions and conative endeavors of all the other members: the same may be as evidently exhibited by the sole devoyre, and *discoursing gestures* of the *Hand.*

[7] Bulwer played a central role in the eventual development of a sign language for the deaf. His books, other than *Chirologia* include *Chiromania, or The Art of Manual Rhetoric,* published jointly with *Chirologia* (1644); *Philocophus; or the Deafe and Dumbe Man's Friend* (1648); and *Pathomyotomia, or a Dissection of the Significantive Muscles of the Affections of the Minde* (1649).

Bulwer considers the language of manual gestures to be a universal, and presumably innate language, "generally understood and known by all Nations" (p. 3). A major portion of his book is taken up with the detailed descriptions and interpretations of sixty-four different manual expressions. Thus, "To Wring the Hands is a naturall expression of excessive griefe, used by those who console, bewaile, and lament" (p. 24); "To Shew And Shake the Bended Fist At One, is their habit who are angry, threaten, would strike terror, menace, revenge, shew enmity . . ." (p. 57); and "To Extend and Offer Out the Right Hand Unto Any, is an expression of pity, and of an intention to afford comfort . . ." (p. 65).

The three English works that we have considered, especially that by Wright, represent a definite movement forward in the status of personality assessment. Bacon is easily the most learned, the most critical, and the most modern of the writers we have considered; unfortunately, he gave but little attention to the problem of assessment. Bulwer is full of enthusiasm, something of a zealot apparently, but naive in his tendency to exaggerate the universality of gestures. Wright is clearly the most impressive of the group. His approach to assessment seems on the whole to be straightforward, plausible, and wise. His emphasis on the direct observation of verbal and overt behavior is suggestive of current trends in behavioral assessment. One suspects that he was a good judge of men. From our perspective he seems—as does Bacon—to be in the same practical tradition as Huarte. How much, if anything, he owes to Huarte is not clear. We know, however, that he had read *The Tryal of Wits*, since he refers to it in his book (p. 67), though only briefly. Also, he emphasizes (p. 100), as did Huarte, the desirability of men being employed in occupations suitable to their natural inclinations.

The Art, or Science of Knowing Men. Later in the seventeenth century there were two continental philosophers, Marin Cureau de la Chambre (1594–1669) in France and Christian Thomasius (1655–1728) in Germany, who made contributions to the developing art of assessment and who next merit our examination here. We will turn our attention first to de La Chambre.

de La Chambre has been referred to by Diamond (1968) as the first person in history to play the part of psychologist in the full sense, even though the term *psychologist* was not in general use in his day. There is, indeed, reason to believe that he carried out regular functions as an assessor of men, and possibly as something of a psychotherapist as well. I would doubt, however, that he was the first to serve these dual duties. de La Chambre, in any event, was an eminent French physician, whose patients included Louis XIII, Louis XIV, Chancellor Siguier, Cardinal Richelieu, and Cardinal Mazarin. His services were more than purely medical, however, and it is said (Diamond, 1968, p. 40) that he advised Louis XIV on the qualifications of all candidates for high office. This seems quite probable, since de La Chambre was personally close to the king, and was intensely interested in methods of assessment.

de La Chambre's books which bear directly on assessment are *Les Characteres des passions* (five vols., 1640–1962); English edition, 1650, vol. 1 only), *L'art de Connoistre les Hommes* (1659; English edition, 1665); and *Discovrs svr les principes de la chiromance* (1653; English edition, 1658). In the first of these, *The Characters of the Passions* (1650), de La Chambre sets forth his general approach to assessment (the word *characters* here meant *signs* or *marks*). His general plan, which he never carried through to completion, was to write a series of seven volumes covering in its entirety "The Art to know Men."[8] This Art, he says, "contains Five general Rules," as follows (pp. a2, a3):

> The first is founded on the Characters of the Passions, of the Vertues and the Vices; and shews that those who naturally have the same air [that is, manner] which accompanies the Passions or Actions of Vertue or Vice, are also naturally inclined to the same Passions, and to the same Actions. The second is drawn from the resemblance Men have with other Creatures; and teacheth us, that those who have any part like to those of beasts, have also the inclinations they have. The third is grounded on the beauty of the Sex; and shews that men who have anything of a feminine beauty, are naturally effeminate; and that those women who have any touch of a manly beauty, participate also of manly incli-

[8] In 1665, in his last publication, de La Chambre confessed that his overall plan was beyond both his powers and his years (Gardiner, Metcalf, and Beebe-Center, 1937, p. 145).

nations. The fourth is drawn from the likeness which the men of one Climat have with that of another. So those who have short noses, thick lips, curl'd hair, and a tawny skin, as the Moors have, are subject to the same vices to which they are inclined. The fifth and last may be called Syllogistick, because that without using particular signes, which usually designe the Manners of persons, it discovers them by discourse and reasonings: which is done by two principal means: The First is the knowledge of Tempers: for without knowing the signes of the inclination a man hath to be angry, so as we know that he is cholerick, it will suffice to speak him to be inclined to that Passion. The second is the most ingenuous, and is drawn from the connexion and concatenation which the Passions and the Habits have amongst themselves. So when we know a man is fearful, we may assure our selves that he is inclined to Avarice, that he is cunning and dissembling, that he usually speaks softly and submissively, that he is suspicious, incredulous, an ill friend, and the like.

As can be gathered from this passage, de La Chambre's approach to personality assessment was primarily through physiognomic signs, though the fifth rule above, which is based on the alleged correlations of traits, makes him somewhat broader than the usual physiognomist of his time. In his discussion of the characters (signs) of love (1650, pp. 82–104), de La Chambre is perhaps at his best, or in event at his most interesting: he discusses in detail such presumed cues of love as the motions of the eyes, the inflections of the voice, the color of the lips (red and moist), and so on. One imagines that as a person de La Chambre was quite captivating, and as an assessor probably very insightful. Nevertheless, his approach to assessment was for the most part quite traditional,[9] and burdened

[9] De La Chambre was a strange compound of the old and the innovative; a link between two ages. In the words of Gardiner (Gardiner, Metcalf, and Beebe-Center, 1937), "de La Chambre's work is a most extraordinary mixture of medieval tradition and modern learning, of naive credulity combined with acute observation and critical independence of judgment" (p. 145). An illustration of de La Chambre's independence of thought is the fact that, as noted by Diamond (1968), he was evidently the second Frenchman

with innumerable superstitions of the past. This last point is particularly evident in his *Discours sur les principes de la chiromance* (1653) and *L'art de Connoistre les Hommes* (1660). For example, in the former of these treatises, on chiromancy (palmistry), de La Chambre attributes certain personality traits to internal organs such as the heart and the liver, and states that by secret channels the states of these organs are reflected in the fingers. Further, it is all tied in with planetary influences. Thus, the same planets which influence the internal organs also influence the corresponding fingers. There are also lunar effects on behavior: "The moon," de La Chambre wrote, "has a secret influence on the brain, and that makes it feel its power more than other planets. For the brain swells and lowers, increases or decreases depending on whether that planet is waxing or waning" (p. 124–125).

While de La Chambre's world view was not atypical of his time, it is interesting to contrast it with the more rationalistic portions of Hobbes and Descartes, who were his contemporaries. Further, at the time of his death in 1669, Newton's *Principia* and Locke's *Essay*, which would usher in the Enlightenment, were only a couple of decades away. The pace of change was becoming faster.

Christian Thomasius (1655–1728), who was an outstanding philosopher and jurist, was one of the inaugurators of the German Enlightenment. He helped to found the University of Halle, and became professor of law there in 1694. He believed that philosophy should be concerned with the practical affairs of men, and with the nature and directions of man's aspirations.

Two of Thomasius' works—a very small portion of his total output—concern personality assessment, and represent, at least in principle, a clear advance over previous writers. The first of these was published in 1691 and was titled (English translation) *New Discovery of a Well-Grounded and for the Community Most Necessary Science of the Knowledge of the Secrets of the Heart of Other Men from Daily Conversation, Even Against Their Will*. In March, 1692 this tract received a critical review, and in response Thomasius

---

to write a scientific treatise in the vernacular. This is a good place to note that Diamond's interesting paper is the most detailed available on de La Chambre's psychological system.

(1692) wrote a longer treatise titled (as translated) *Further Eluci-dation by Different Examples of the Recent Proposals for a New Science for Obtaining a Knowledge of Other Men's Minds.* The great significance of the two works for the history of psychological assessment is that here for the first time we come across the use of quantitative data and empirical analysis. Further, the notion of a psychogram, in the sense of numbers assigned to several personality variables and considered as a profile, makes its first appearance. These are striking advances, indeed, and the fact that they were hesitant, limited, and apparently not followed-up does not negate the credit due to Thomasius for having invented them.[10] This was, after all, nearly 300 years ago.

Thomasius began his *New Discovery* paper by comparing the state of the art of knowing men in Germany with its status in France, to the disadvantage of the latter; presumably he was refer-ring here, at least in part, to the works of de La Chambre. The tract is highly programmatic about specific methods of evaluating men, except that this is to be done on the basis of their conversation. Further, Thomasius cautioned that an observer must distinguish be-tween genuine and affected feelings, and against the tendency of persons to avoid the expression of their cruder emotions. He stated that he carried out practical tests of his techniques by writing down in advance the answers that he predicted people would give to cer-tain questions, and then asking them these questions, after short, indifferent conversations, as a way of checking up on his predictions.

Thomasius conceptualized personality in terms of four pro-visional dimensions: sensual pleasure; ambition; greed; and rational love (pure, selfless goodness). The strongest of these in a person was termed that person's dominating passion, and the overall nature of the person is determined by the *mix* of the four variables. In his *Further Elucidations* Thomasius reports a project carried out in a practical course that he taught on the science of knowing men. This

[10] Thomasius has been almost completely overlooked by historians of psychology. The only reference to him in a standard source of which I am aware is the brief one by Gardiner (Gardiner, Metcalf, and Beebe-Center, 1937), to which I am personally indebted. The two relevant works by Thomasius can be found in the library of the University of Halle, from which I obtained microfilms.

project is summarized by Steinitzer (1889) in the following way (p. 234):

> He had his students write short essays about individual persons. The definite "theme" of a person was given, in which each of the four major inclinations was designated with a number from five to sixty, and from which the different single external characteristics were now deduced: his behavior toward friends, in society, toward women, and so on. For example, someone might have a high degree of ambition; he may also be sensuous, yet not as strongly (about fifty-five), little inclined toward greed (ten), and have the usual quantity of rational love . . . Which behavior can we expect from him in this or that situation in life? Thomasius took the "themes" from people he knew, and his pupils formed pictures accordingly. The comparison of these pictures with reality was very satisfying to him.

Though this informal little study was evidently carried out in a rather casual and loose manner, by today's standards, it nevertheless involved what I believe to be the first use of rating scales in psychological assessment, and indeed, perhaps the first attempt at empirical research in all of psychology anywhere. Thomasius' course on the art of knowing men must also be counted as something of a first, though as a course on assessment it was preceded by the teaching of astrology and physiognomy in the late medieval and Renaissance universities.

With respect to the mainstream of scientific psychology, which in this period was just about to get underway, Thomasius can be seen as having had some influence on his younger contemporary at Halle, Christian Wolff (1679–1754), whose books, *Psychologia Empirica* (1732) and *Psychologia Rationalis* (1734) were epochal in the origins of psychology as a discipline; the philosophical orientations of Thomasius and Wolff were, however, quite different, with the former much more interested in the practical affairs of men.

Discussion. First, let me briefly mention several authors whom I had to omit in the discussion above in order to keep on the major course of the development of assessment, but who were, at least in some degree, relevant to the early history of assessment. Leonardo da Vinci (1452–1519), in his *Treatise on Painting* (Rigaud, 1877; originally published 1551), examined the relations between various emotions and their overt expressions, and the ways these should be represented in paintings. In 1586 John Baptista Porta published a work titled *De Humana Physiognomia* in Naples; derived from Aristotle's *Physiognomica*, it is built around the notion that a person's character may be read by the resemblance of his features to those of particular animals. It includes, as do many of the later works on physiognomy, a number of fascinating drawings. Porta himself was evidently a brilliant, if somewhat eccentric representative of an unconventional age. His most important book, highly significant in the history of science, was *Natural Magick* (1957; original version 1558; first English edition, 1658). This is a curious work, indeed, covering a variety of topics of popular concern in this prescientific era. It is additionally important in that it was written in part by other members of the first scientific society, the Otiosi (literally, men of leisure). Porta is also responsible for an even more amazing book, titled *Phytognomonica* (1588) which is an elucidation of vegetable physiognomy—the art of determining the nature of plants from their appearances.

The volume of Scipio Claramontius titled *De Conjectandis Cuisque Moribus et Habitantibus Animi Affectibus* (1665), on the nature of the emotions, is also relevant here: Claramontius, according to Gardiner (Gardiner, Metcalf, and Beebe-Center, 1937) was responsible for the view that pulse and respiration provide the most reliable physiological signs of emotion, a very modern-sounding notion.

In addition to these writers, there were a number of other prominent philosophers, including Vives, Comenius, Descartes, Hobbes, Shaftesbury, Hutcheson, and Bentham, whose contributions undoubtedly had certain implications for assessment—mainly in the sense of suggesting systems for conceptualizing human nature. But these contributions were less direct than those we have already considered, and we need not go into them here.

In this period, as always, there was a connection between the scholarly, learned "Art of knowing men," on the one hand, and the conceptions along this line of the uneducated majority, on the other. Literature served in part as the bridge and promulgator of ideas between these two subcultures, with the passage of ideas going, again as always, in both directions. Thus Montaigne (1533–1592), completing his *Essays* in 1587 or thereabouts, puts down these words on ways of knowing people: "The face is a weak guarantee: yet it deserves some consideration. . . . It seems as if some faces are lucky, others unlucky. And I think there is some art for distinguishing the kindly faces from the simple, the severe from the rough, the malicious from the gloomy, the disdainful from the melancholy, and other such adjacent qualities. . . . As for prognosticating future events from them, those are matters that I leave undecided" (Frame, 1965, p. 811). And playgoers to Shakespeare's *Julius Caesar* in 1599 would have heard and understood these lines of Caesar's (Act 1, ii, 192–195):

> Let me have men around me that are fat,
> Sleek-headed men, and such as sleep o'nights:
> Yond Cassius has a lean and hungry look;
> He thinks too much: such men are dangerous.

The main theme of the period we are discussing is individual differences; particularly in the most important works on assessment —Huarte's *Tryal of Wits,* Wright's *Passions of the Minde,* and Thomasius' *New Discovery.* The emphasis is on the fact that, and the various ways in which, people differ from one another. Further, there was an insistence that these differences can be measured, and that it was important for the happiness of individual persons that they be measured. It was an ambitious, exuberant, optimistic philosophy, tied to the newly-developing currents of science, and just what one would expect of the emerging age of the Enlightenment. Its importance for us here is that the concept of individual differences is basic to the theory of assessment.

From Thomasius to Galton

From what I have just suggested, one would have expected the period of the Enlightenment, roughly, the eighteenth century, to have seen the further, perhaps even the more rapid development of psychology oriented around the notion of individual differences. This is particularly true in view of the fact that the Enlightenment was a time of concern for the dignity of man. Nevertheless, such an expectation would have been wrong. One would have to go ahead to the time of phrenology, early in the nineteenth century, to find a renewed interest in individual differences. In the mainstream of psychology one would have to go even further—to the statistical analyses of Quetelet in 1835, in his *Sur L'Homme,* and the wide-ranging *Inquiries into Human Faculty,* by Galton, in 1883.

What was the reason for this apparent hiatus in progress? There are many possibilities: perhaps the lack of men with sufficient interest and talent to carry on the development; or the fact, possibly, that the earlier surge of interest in the assessment of individual differences had been premature, ahead of its time and beyond the technological capacities of the era. But the main reason, I suspect, was the towering influence of Isaac Newton. It is difficult to over-estimate the impact of the Newtonian revolution in science, which brought to a culmination the efforts of Galileo, Kepler and other scientific giants, and, more than any other single factor, ushered in the modern age. The essence of the Newtonian breakthrough was the apparent discovery of general, timeless, universal laws according to which the universe operates. The result was to shift the direction in psychology to a search for the general laws of behavior, to the attempt to determine how man-in-general functions, and thus away from the concern with differences among men. The Newtonian model became, as it were, the paradigm for psychology, as is evident, for example, in the works of Hume (1965), Hartley (1966), and Bentham (1789).

In any event, and for whatever reason, the leading figures in psychology in the eighteenth century—Wolff, Hutcheson, Berkeley, Hume, Hartley, and Bentham—were concerned primarily with man-in-general, rather than with individuals. The interest in assessment did not, of course, disappear entirely. In its philosophical bases there were, indeed, major advances. The writings of Rousseau contributed to an increased sense of the worth of individual persons. In America, where eventually the notion of assessment was to have its greatest vogue, Thomas Jefferson and Benjamin Rush, the physician-philosopher, emphasized the diversity of men, as Boorstin (1948) has made clear in an informative chapter titled "The Happy Variety of Minds." Boorstin quotes Rush as saying that "It is obvious [that] there is the same variety in the texture of the minds, that there is in the bodies of men." He adds that "Jefferson agreed and drew an important conclusion: 'As the Creator has made no two faces alike, so no two minds' " (p. 120).

In the realm of the practice of personality assessment there was a revival of physiognomy, stimulated by the publication by Johann Lavater of *Physiognomische Fragmente* (1775–78). In a sense, of course, physiognomy had never been dead, and this treatise was part of a direct line from the authors of antiquity, through Porta, and eventually to Wells (1894). Lavater's orientation was largely traditional, and whereas in its inception this approach had represented considerable originality, and even plausibility, by this period it could no longer be taken seriously.

Phrenology. The new assessment technique of the nineteenth century was phrenology. Though in some respects similar to, and perhaps in part derived from classical physiognomy, it was basically new. Its similarity with physiognomy lay in the fact that in both techniques inferences were made to personality variables from external bodily features—in physiognomy from facial (and other) characteristics, and in phrenology from the external formations of the skull. The theoretical rationales underlying the two approaches, however, were quite different. In physiognomy the underlying assumption was that a person's feelings and passions are reflected systematically in his facial features, voice, gait, and so on. No assumptions were made, however, as to the nature of the internal representations of the feelings and passions. In phrenology there were two fundamental assumptions: mental functions are based on specific processes localized in given areas in the brain; and the intensity of magnitude of these functions is reflected in the contours and external topography of the skull.

The history of phrenology and its significance in the development of psychology has recently been reviewed in an extremely readable paper by Bakan (1966; see also Walsh, 1970; Davies, 1955; and Stern, 1971), and I need not go into the subject in detail here. It is important, however, that we carefully evaluate the historical significance of phrenological theory. This is particularly true because most contemporary psychologists judge phrenology solely in terms of its validity, which was nil, and persist in underestimating its historical significance, which was considerable.

The theoretical basis of phrenology was developed around the beginning of the nineteenth century by Franz Joseph Gall (1758–1828), a highly able German neuroanatomist, in Vienna. One of Gall's first students was Johann Gasper Spurzheim (1776–1832). Presently the two began working closely together, and Spurzheim, except for the original conception, contributed perhaps as much to the eventual form of phrenology as did Gall. Indeed, Spurzheim, who was more of an organizer and propagandist than Gall, was considerably more responsible for the phrenological movement throughout western Europe and America. It was Spurzheim who coined the term "phrenology" (literally, study of the mind, from the Greek phren: mind). The major works of Gall were *Anatomie et physiologie du systeme nerveux en general, et du cerveau en particulier* (1810–19; with Spurzheim's collaboration in the first two volumes) and *On the functions of the cerebellum* (1838). Spurzheim's chief works were *The Physiognomical System of Drs. Gall and Spurzheim* (1815) and *Phrenology, or the Doctrine of Mental Phenomena* (1970; original edition 1834).

Prominent among the followers of the phrenological conception were the Combe brothers, George, a philosopher, and Andrew, a physician, both of Edinburgh. George Combe, in particular, wrote very extensively.[11] His *System of Phrenology* (1876; original edition 1825) is perhaps the best statement of the final phrenological position (Combe, 1837, 1841). Phrenology was brought to America by Charles Caldwell, a physician at Transylvania University, but it was not until the visit of Spurzheim to America in 1832 and the later

[11] An interesting historical sidelight in the early history of phrenology is the dispute between the Combes and Peter Mark Roget, who is best remembered as the author of the *Thesaurus of English Words and Phrases* (1852). Roget, who was a prominent physician, wrote an article on "Cranioscopy" for the 1818 Supplement to the *Encyclopaedia Britannica*, in which he severely criticized the theories of Gall and Spurzheim. There then followed an exchange of letters and articles, all in the most gentlemanly style, between the Combes and Roget. The entire correspondence, and the relevant articles, are contained as a supplement in *On the Function of the Cerebellum* (Gall, Vimont, and Broussais, 1838, pp. 195–240). The matter is also discussed at length in Emblen (1970, pp. 132–152).

American visits of the Combe brothers that phrenology became popular in America (Curti, 1943). The chief popularizers were the Fowler brothers (Fowler, Fowler, and Kirkham, 1839; Fowler, O. S., 1851), Samuel Wells (1894), and Silas Jones (1836). Of these, Wells (1894) attempted an integration of phrenology with classical physiognomy.

Before examining the implications of phrenology for the history of assessment it will be helpful to comment briefly on, first, its role in the history of general scientific psychology, and second, phrenology as a social movement in the last century. With respect to the former of these, the main contribution of Gall and Spurzheim—and it was a highly important one in the history of science—was to state the hypothesis of cerebral localization of function. While many writers, even as far back as Pythagoras, had considered the brain to be in some sense the seat of mental functions, Gall and Spurzheim were the first to take this position truly seriously. Further, whereas earlier thinkers had conceived the brain as the place where the immaterial soul interacted with the body, Gall and Spurzheim held that the operation of the brain *was* the mind, that is, they were complete materialists. Further, their laboratory work was of a very high order. Thus Krech (1962), who has evaluated this area in depth, concludes that "In reading Gall and Spurzheim one must be impressed with the soundness and sophistication of their philosophy of science and the reasonableness of their general argument" (p. 34). Krech also writes that Gall and Spurzheim "were responsible for many important and lasting discoveries in neuroanatomy and neurophysiology. Gall's neurological work was primarily responsible for the first modern views of the function of the cortex. Where formerly the cortex was considered an inert 'covering' of the brain (and hence its name), Gall realized that the cortex consisted of functioning neural cells" (p. 32). Boring's (1950) evaluation of the work of Gall is equally high.

Gall and Spurzheim believed that mental functions can be categorized into a number—most phrenological listings included thirty-five—of separate faculties, and that each of these is subserved by a given part of the brain. The cerebellum, for example, was held to be the organ of amativeness (Gall, 1838). In addition, it was maintained, as I have already implied, that the stronger a certain faculty the larger the involved part of the brain, and further, that resulting differences in the topography of the brain were represented, in turn, by alterations in the shape of the skull. Hence, it should be possible to identify an individual's major and minor faculties—in effect, to do a complete personality assessment—by an examination of the bumps on and the contours of his skull.

It was as an assessment technique that phrenology attained such an amazing degree of popular appeal in the last century (Curti, 1943; Bakan, 1966). All over the country lectures were attended, books and journals were read, and phrenological societies were founded. Practicing phrenologists, many of them unquestionably sincere, and others no doubt pure quacks, went about the country giving personality "readings." Curti (1943) summarizes the role of these readings as follows (p. 342):

> The vogue for phrenological "readings" among the common people can be in part explained by the prevailing social atmosphere. In a period when the common man began to feel within him the stir of power and ambition, phrenology had much to offer him. It was not merely that he could have, from a wandering "practicing phrenologist" or the "parlors" of Fowler and Wells on Broadway, a reading which would set him right regarding the mate that he, with his properties should choose; nor was it even that he might be told the vocation of business for which he was best adapted. These things, of course, were important. But as one of the critics of phrenology remarked, the common man seeks for something which will solve all his difficulties, something which will reveal nature's secrets and savor of a mystery or miracle.

All this should not be surprising. As I have tried to make clear in this chapter, ways of knowing oneself, and particular paths to the understanding of one's fellows, have always had a vogue in society, from the ancient days of Alexandrian physiognomy to the contemporary phase of computer assisted services designed to match men and women having similar personalities. Contemporary assessment psychologists are sometimes embarrassed by the phrenological episode in their history, but they need not be. The technique was, to be sure, totally invalid, but its popularity was not due as much to an overselling job by its practitioners as to a feeling of need on the part of its clients. As with the earliest hepatologists, horoscopal astrologers, and chiromancers, the early phrenologists were doing the best they could with what they had.

Let us turn now to the four positive contributions of phrenology in the historical development of assessment, which I feel are quite impressive.

(1) *Emphasis on individual differences.* The notion of individual differences is central to assessment psychology, and we have noted that this emphasis dropped out of the mainstream of psychology in the eighteenth century. It returned very strongly, however, in phrenology. I can illustrate this readily by two apt quotations. Krech, observing that Gall was impressed with individual differences, states that Gall sought a listing of faculties "the different proportions of which" —these are Gall's words— ". . . explain individual differences" (Krech, 1962, p. 34); the approach is the same as most of Thomasius, only more detailed. And George Combe, in a letter of criticism of the psychology of Reid, Stewart, and Brown at the time he was being considered for an appointment in logic at the University of Edinburgh, complained that "they give no account of the obvious fact of individuals possessing the faculties in different degrees of endowment which fit them for different pursuits" (Bakan, 1966, p. 210).

(2) *Assessment paradigm.* The phrenologists did much to set the pattern for the style and expectations of assessment practices which were to follow, and which are still employed. This includes the notions of assessor and subject, the systematic collections of data on an individual on the basis of a single session, and written reports, including quantitative profiles.

(3) *Objectivity.* Despite the fact that Gall and Spinoza were extremely loose in gathering evidence, mostly anecdotal, in order to attribute particular psychological functions to given parts of the brain, the phrenological movement greatly helped to advance the cause of objectivity in assessment. Though such a basic statistical device as the coefficient of correlation had yet to be invented, phrenological theorists were clearly groping for some systematic

means of assaying the degrees of concomitant variation between psychological traits and physical measurements. They used blind analyses, on occasion, as a way of testing their theories. And they developed, through the firm of Fowler and Wells, a form incorporating systematic seven-point rating scales for each of thirty-seven personality variables (Bakan, 1966).

(4) *Taxonomy of personality structure*. As I indicated near the beginning of this chapter, an adequate assessment technology is dependent upon a satisfactory taxonomy of the variables to be assessed. The major contribution of phrenology to assessment psychology was in the development of a primitive taxonomical system. I will now describe this system briefly, following Spurzheim (1834). There was a total of thirty-five faculties (different books included slightly different listings, with slightly different totals), as indicated in Table 1, divided into the affective and the intellectual faculties. The former, in turn, is divided into propensities—another word coined by Spurzheim—and sentiments, with the latter further subdivided into perceptive and reflective faculties. The propensities are more or less what we would think of as motives, and the sentiments are closer to our conception of personality traits. The history of conceptions of personality structure is a fascinating narrative in its own right, one which, unfortunately, we cannot go into in detail here. We may observe, however, first, that Gall depended very heavily upon the Scottish faculty psychologists (Thomas Reid, Dugald Stewart, and Thomas Brown) in devising his system of mental traits, and second, that the phrenological system in turn affected the later dimensional taxonomies of William James, William McDougall, and others (Bakan, 1966), which in their turn are the direct ancestors of today's classificatory systems of personality.

Quetelet and Psychological Statistics. Lambert Quetelet (1796–1874), a Belgian mathematician, was the founder of sociological and psychological statistics. In 1823 he was sent by the government—Belgium was then a part of the kingdom of the Netherlands—to Paris to study at the observatory there. While in Paris he met Laplace and Fourier, who were then developing the new theory of probability. Back in Brussels Quetelet began the development of a new field: the application of statistical procedures, mainly those concerned with norms and central tendencies, to vari-

Table 1.

PHRENOLOGICAL TAXONOMY OF MENTAL FUNCTIONS

Affective Faculties	Intellectual Faculties
PROPENSITIES	PERCEPTIVE
1. Destructiveness	22. Individuality
2. Amativeness	23. Configuration
3. Philoprogenitiveness	24. Size
4. Adhesiveness	25. Weight and
5. Inhabitiveness	Resistance
6. Combativeness	26. Coloring
7. Secretiveness	27. Locality
8. Acquisitiveness	28. Order
9. Constructiveness	29. Calculation
	30. Eventuality
SENTIMENTS	31. Time
10. Cautiousness	32. Tune
11. Approbativeness	33. Language
12. Self-Esteem	
13. Benevolence	REFLECTIVE
14. Reverence	34. Comparison
15. Firmness	35. Causality
16. Conscientiousness	
17. Hope	
18. Marvelousness	
19. Ideality	
20. Mirthfulness	
21. Imitation	

ous kinds of events which occur in the ongoing nature of society, such as suicides, births, marriages, murders, and the like. The new field was called moral statistics. In 1835 Quetelet published a book, *Sur L'Homme* (English: *A Treatise on Man*, 1842, reprinted 1969), which included a great wealth of demographic data, and became a classic in the area. Though Quetelet was not himself optimistic about the measurement of psychological variables (1969, p. 73), actually his book was an important step in the eventual development of just those statistical procedures which came to make such measurements possible.

Discussion. We have reached now essentially the end of our present narrative. With the work of the phrenologists and of Quetelet the stage is set for the emergence of Francis Galton and the beginnings of the modern era in assessment. Perhaps one additional factor that I should add here is the influence of Charles Darwin and the theory of evolution, with its renewed emphasis on individual differences. Galton, as we know from his pupil, Karl Pearson (1914, Vol. 1, p. 157), was influenced toward his early anthropometric investigations by his boyhood interest in phrenology.[12] He was indebted also, for his basic work in statistics—he developed the concept of the correlation coefficient—to the conception of Quetelet (Boring, 1950, p. 476). And to make the picture complete, he was the cousin of Charles Darwin.

Summing Up

It would be idle to attempt to summarize in a few paragraphs the amount of history that we have covered in this chapter. Instead, I will use these last few paragraphs to offer several personal observations on the long background of our field. The psychology of assessment grew out of man's interest in himself. As Boring (1950) put it, "The most important and greatest puzzle which every man faces is himself, and secondarily, other persons" (p. 56). The psychological assessor, when he carries out his tasks, is offering a service which man has sought since the earliest times. This is something for us to recognize not only with interest, but also with humility.

It is easy, but perhaps unwise, to disparage unkindly the assessment techniques of our predecessors. We know that such techniques as chiromancy, metoposcopy, and phrenology are in principle all totally invalid, yet I suspect that in the hands of insightful and discerning practitioners they may, at least on occasion, have been more valid than we suppose, even if for different reasons

[12] This is not to say that Galton came to support phrenology, since he did not. Thus, with respect to the particular conceptions of localization of brain functions championed by the phrenologists, Galton in 1906 wrote: "Why capable observers should have come to such strange conclusions [can] be accounted for . . . most easily on the supposition of unconscious bias in collecting data" (quoted in Pearson, 1930, Vol. IIIb, p. 577).

than their users, much less their clients, imagined. William James (1890, vol. 1) allowed that "there seems to be no doubt that phrenology, however little it satisfy our scientific curiosity about the functions of different parts of the brain, may still be, in the hands of intelligent practitioners, a useful help in the art of reading character" (p. 28). No doubt the assessors of the future will (let us hope!) look back at our own time, and marvel at the crudity of our methods, even as we do at those which preceded ours.

Until the Age of Reason the notion of assessment was for the most part intertwined with the art of divination. In that period men like Huarte, Bacon, and Wright began to distinguish scientific from supernatural attempts at prediction, and since that time progress in assessment has been relatively rapid. Perhaps as a culture, however, we are not so far removed from the dark past as we would like to think. It is well to remember that many procedures such as hepatoscopy, astrology, phrenology, and the like were not superstitions when they were first used, but became so only when they were continued long after evidence against their validity and rationality was overwhelming. Such persistence of the irrational is, indeed, a definition of superstition. Whether our present age is entering into a protracted period of such irrationality, or whether the apparent resurgence of discredited techniques such as astrology is only a passing fad remains to be seen.

The record for the longest continued assessment technique with a claim to rationality is that of physiognomy. Indeed, in its newer forms this approach is still with us, and rightly so, as I will indicate in a moment. Though it is often thought of simply in terms of such static features as height of forehead, slant of nose, and so on, actually from its earliest applications physiognomy, as I trust I have made clear in these pages, involved the careful observation of individuals in naturalistic and controlled environments. Seen in this broad context, it included what we today would refer to as the understanding and prediction of behavior from selected samples of behavior. In this perspective, contemporary empirical work such as that by Mahl (1956) and Gleser, Gottschalk, and Springer (1961) on speech patterns; by Hall (1959), Eibl-Eibesfeldt (1971) and Haas (1972) on ethology of movements; of Izard (1971) and

Ekman and others (Ekman, 1973; Ekman, Friesen, and Ellsworth, 1972) on emotions and facial expressions; and of Hess and others (Hess and Polt, 1960; Hess, Seltzer, and Schlien, 1965) on the relation of pupil size to affect, can all be related in a meaningful way to earlier physiognomic conceptions. So, for that matter, can such contemporary approaches as those of Sheldon (1940) and Lowen (1971). From a somewhat broader, but no less accurate perspective, the current work on behavioral assessment, as exemplified, for example, by the chapters by Moos, by Jones and others, and by Haywood and others in this volume, can be viewed as being only the latest in a long sequence of attempts to fathom the meaning of overt behaviors. Indeed, the quotation from Wright (1604), at the beginning of this book, can be read as almost a definition of behavioral assessment.

So things move on, in personality assessment as elsewhere, always new, yet ever the same. We are a part of the living past, and though we do not know it yet, a part of the future also. We should, then, look back to the past, not with a quality of disdain, but with a true willingness to learn from our predecessors. And of all that our scientific ancestors bequeathed to us, what could be more pertinent, more intrinsically fascinating than, in the words of Marin Cureau de La Chambre, "L'art de connoistre les Hommes," or, The Art of Knowing Men.[13]

[13] I am indebted to Daniele Vuylsteke for translations from de La Chambre, to Barbara Lide for translations from Steinitzer, to Klaus Ludwig for translations from Thomasius, and to Robert Gorrell for his helpfulness in research on the Elizabethan period.

References

ALEXANDER, F. G. AND SELESNICK, S. T. *The History of Psychiatry*. New York: Harper and Row, 1966.

ARTEMIDORUS. *The Judgment of Dreams*. Translated by Robert Wood. London: William Iones, 1606.

BACON, F. *The Advancement of Learning*. In J. Spedding, R. L. Ellis, and D. N. Heath (Eds.). *The Works of Francis Bacon*, Vol. VI, 1869, pp. 77–412 (originally published 1605).

BAKAN, D. "The Influence of Phrenology on American Psychology."

Journal of the History of the Behavioral Sciences, 1966, *2,* 200–220.

BENTHAM, J. *The Principles of Morals and Legislation.* New York: Hafner, 1948 (originally published 1789).

BONDY, M. "Psychiatric Antecedents of Psychological Testing (Before Binet)." *Journal of the History of the Behavioral Sciences,* 1974, X, 180–194.

BONNET, C. "Principes Philosophiques sur la Cause Premiére et sur son Effect." In C. Bonnet, *Collection Compléte des Oeuvres.* Vol. 17. Neuchatel, 1781. Chapter 5, Part 6.

BOORSTIN, D. *The Lost World of Thomas Jefferson.* Boston: Beacon Press, 1948.

BORING, E. G. *Sensation and Perception in the History of Experimental Psychology.* New York: D. Appleton-Century-Crofts, 1942.

BORING, E. G. *A History of Experimental Psychology.* 2nd Edit. New York: Appleton-Century-Crofts, 1950.

BRETT, G. S. *A History of Psychology.* London: George Allen and Unwin, 1921.

BULWER, JOHN. *Chirologia, or the Natural Language of the Hand.* Whereunto is Added, *Chiromania:* Or, the Art of Manuall *Rhetoricke.* London: Printed by Thomas Harper, 1644.

BULWER, JOHN. *Philocophus: Or, the Deafe and Dumbe Man's Friend.* London: Humphrey Moseley, 1648.

BULWER, JOHN. *Pathomyotomia, or a Dissection of the Significantive Muscles of the Affections of the Minde.* London: Humphrey Moseley, 1649.

BURCKHARDT, J. *The Civilization of the Renaissance in Italy.* Vol. 2. New York: Harper and Row, 1958 (originally published 1860).

BURTON, R. *The Anatomy of Melancholy.* Oxford: Lichfield and Short, 1621.

CATTELL, J. MCK. "Mental Tests and Measurements." *Mind,* 1890, *15,* 373–381.

CLARAMONTIUS, SCIPIO. *De Coniectandis Cvisque Moribus et Habitantibus Animi Affectibus.* Helmstadt, 1665.

COMBE, G. *The Constitution of Man.* 3rd Edit. Boston: Marsh, Capen, and Lyon, 1837.

COMBE, G. *Notes on the United States of America during a Phrenological Visit.* Philadelphia: Carey and Hart, 1841.

COMBE, G. *A System of Phrenology.* New York: S. R. Wells and Co., 1876.

CRAIG, H. *The Enchanted Glass.* New York: Oxford University Press, 1936.

CURTI, M. *The Growth of American Thought.* New York: Harper and Row, 1943.

DAVIES, J. *Phrenology, Fad and Science: A Nineteenth Century Crusade.* New Haven: Yale University Press, 1955.

DA VINCI LEONARDO. *A Treatise on Painting.* Trans. by J. F. Rigaud. London: George Bell & Sons, 1877.

DE JAAGER, J. AND JACOB, J. *Origins of Psychometry: A Review Article.* In J. Brozek & M. Sibing (Eds.) Nieuwkoop: B. De Graaf, 1970 (originally published 1865).

DIAMOND, S. "Marin Cureau de La Chambre." *Journal of the History of the Behavioral Sciences,* 1968, IV, 40–54.

DIOGENES LAERTIUS. *Lives of Eminent Philosophers.* Cambridge: Harvard University Press, 1966.

DOYLE, K. O. "Theory and Practice of Ability Testing in Ancient Greece." *Journal of the History of the Behavioral Sciences,* 1974, X, 202–212.

DRESDEN, S. *Humanism in the Renaissance.* New York: McGraw-Hill, 1968.

DUBOIS, P. "Testing in Ancient China." In A. Anastasi (Ed.) *Testing Problems in Perspective.* Princeton, N.J.: Educational Testing Service, 1966, pp. 29–36.

DUBOIS, P. H. *A History of Psychological Testing.* Boston: Allyn and Bacon, Inc., 1970.

EIBL-EIBESFELDT, I. *Love and Hate.* New York: Holt, Rinehart and Winston, 1971.

EKMAN, P. (Ed.) *Darwin and Facial Expression.* New York: Academic Press, 1973.

EKMAN, P., FRIESEN, W. V., AND ELLSWORTH, P. *Emotion in the Human Face.* New York: Pergamon Press, 1972.

EMBLEN, D. L. *Peter Mark Roget: The Word and the Man.* New York: Thomas Y. Crowell, 1970.

EVANS, E. C. "Physiognomics in the Ancient World." *Transactions of the American Philosophical Association,* 1969, Vol. 59, Part 5.

FORSTER, R. *Scriptores Physiognomonics.* 2 Vol. Leipzig, 1893.

FOWLER, L. N., FOWLER, O. S., AND KIRKHAM, S. *Phrenology Proved, Illustrated, and Applied, Accompanied by a Chart.* Philadelphia: Fowler and Brevoort, 1839.

FOWLER, O. S. *Practical Phrenology.* New York: Fowler and Wells, 1851.

FRAME, D. M. (Editor and Translator) *The Essays of Montaigne*. Stanford, Calif.: Stanford University Press, 1965.

GALEN. "De Temperamentis." In C. K. Kuhn (Ed.) *Claudii Galeni Opera Omnia*. Leipzig, 1821–1833.

GALL, F. *Anotomie et Physiologie du Systeme Nerveux en General, et du Curveau en Particulier*. Four vols., first two vols. in collaboration with G. Spurzheim. Paris: D'Hantel, 1810–1819.

GALL, F. *On the Functions of the Cerebellum*. With sections by J. Vimont and F. J. V. Broussais. Trans. by G. Combe. Edinburgh: Maclacklan and Stewart, 1838.

GALTON, F. *Inquiries into Human Faculty and Its Development*. London: Macmillan, 1883.

GARDINER, H. M., METCALF, R. C., AND BEEBE-CENTER, J. G. *Feeling and Emotion: A History of Theories*. New York: American Book Co., 1937.

GLESER, G., GOTTSCHALK, L. A., AND SPRINGER, K. J. "An Anxiety Scale Applicable to Verbal Samples." *Archives of General Psychiatry*, 1961, *5*, 593–604.

HAAS, H. *The Human Animal*. New York: Dell Publishing Co., 1972.

HALL, E. T. *The Silent Language*. New York: Doubleday, 1959.

HARTLEY, D. *Observations on Man, his Frame, his Duty, and his Expectations*. Gainesville, Fla.: Scholars Facsimiles and Reprints, 1966 (originally published 1789).

HESS, E. II. AND POLT, J. M. "Pupil Size as Related to Interest Value of Visual Stimuli." *Science*, 1960, *132*, 349–350.

HESS, E. H., SELTZER, A. L., AND SCHLIEN, J. M. "Pupil Response of Hetero- and Homosexual Males to Pictures of Men and Women: A Pilot Study." *Journal of Abnormal Psychology*, 1965, *70*, 165–168.

HETT, W. S. (Editor and translator) "Physiognomics." In *Aristotle: Minor Works*. Cambridge, Mass.: Harvard University Press, 1936.

HIPPOCRATES. "On Air, Waters, and Places." In R. Hutchins (Ed.) *Great Books of the Western World*. Vol. 10, pp. 9–19. Chicago: Encyclopaedia Britannica, 1952.

HUARTE, J. *Examen de Ingenios Para Las Ciencias*. Baeza, 1575.

HUARTE, J. *Examen de Ingenios: The Examination of Mens Wits*. Trans. to Italian by M. C. Camilli; to English by R. Carew (1594). Facsimile edition, with an Introduction by C. Rogers. Gainesville, Fla.: Scholars Facsimiles and Reprints, 1959.

HUARTE, J. *The Tryal of Wits.* Trans. by E. Bellamy. London: Richard Sare, at Grays-Inn Gate in Holborn, 1698.

HUME, D. *A Treatise of Human Nature.* Oxford: Clarendon Press, 1965 (originally published 1739, 1740).

IAMBLICHUS (JAMBLICHUS). *Life of Pythagoras.* Trans. by Thomas Taylor. London: A. J. Valpy, 1818.

IZARD, C. E. *The Face of Emotion.* New York: Appleton-Century-Crofts, 1971.

JAMES, W. *Principles of Psychology.* 2 vol. New York: Henry Holt, 1890.

JONES, S. *Practical Phrenology.* Boston: Russell, Shattuck, and Williams, 1836.

KRACKE, E. A., JR. *Civil Service in Early Sreng China, 906–1067.* Cambridge: Harvard University Press, 1953.

KRECH, D. "Cortical Localization of Function." In L. Postman (Ed.) *Psychology in the Making.* New York: Knopf, 1962, pp. 31–72.

LA CHAMBRE, M. C., DE. *Les Charactéres des passions.* Vol. 1–5. Paris, 1640 (I), 1645 (II), 1659 (III, IV), 1662 (V).

LA CHAMBRE, M. C., DE. *The Characters of the Passions.* Vol. 1. London, 1650.

LA CHAMBRE, M. C., DE. *Discours sur les principes de la chiromance.* Paris: P. Rocolet, 1653.

DE LA CHAMBRE, M. C. *A Discourse on the Principles of Chiromancy.* London: 1658.

LA CHAMBRE, M. C., DE. *L'art de Connoistre les Hommes.* Paris, 1659.

LA CHAMBRE, M. C., DE. *The Art How to Know Men.* London, 1665.

LAVATER, J. *Physiognomische Fragmente.* Leipzig und Winterthur, 1775–78.

LINDEN, K. W. AND LINDEN, J. D. *Modern Mental Measurement: A Historical Perspective.* Boston: Houghton Mifflin Co., 1968.

LINDSAY, J. *Origins of Astrology.* New York: Barnes and Noble, 1971.

LOWEN, A. *The Language of the Body.* New York: Macmillan, 1971.

MAHL, G. F. "Disturbances and Silences in the Patient's Speech in Psychotherapy." *Journal of Abnormal and Social Psychology,* 1956, *52,* 1–15.

MARTIN, W. A. P. "Competitive Examinations in China." *North American Review,* 1870, *111,* 62–77.

MATTHEWS, W. *Later Medieval English Prose.* New York: Appleton-Century-Crofts, 1963.

MC INTOSH, C. *The Astrologers and their Creed: An Historical Outline.* New York: Frederick A. Praeger, 1969.

MORRIS, C. *Discovery of the Individual.* New York: Harper and Row, 1972.

NEUGEBAUER, O. *The Exact Sciences in Antiquity.* 2nd edit. New York: Dover Publications, 1969.

PACK, R. A. "Physiognomical Entrance Examinations." *Classical Journal,* 1935, *31,* 42–43.

PEARSON, K. *The Life, Letters and Labours of Francis Galton.* 3 vols. Cambridge: University Press, 1914–1930.

PECK, A. L. (Ed. and Trans.) *Aristotle: Historia Animalium.* Cambridge, Mass.: Harvard University Press, 1965.

PHILIP, J. A. *Pythagoras and Early Pythagoreanism.* Toronto: University of Toronto Press, 1966.

PORTA, J. B. *De Humana Physiognomia.* Apud J. Cacchium: Vici Aequensis, 1586.

PORTA, J. B. *Phytognomica.* Neapoli: H. Saluianum, 1588.

PORTA, J. B. (Ed. by D. J. Price) *Natural Magick.* New York: Basic Books, 1957.

QUETELET, L. A. J. *Sur L'Homme et le Development de ses Faculties.* Paris, 1835.

QUETELET, L. A. J. (With an introduction by S. Diamond) *A Treatise on Man.* Gainesville, Fla.: Scholars Facsimiles and Reprints, 1969.

RAMUL, K. "The Problem of Measurement in the Psychology of the Eighteenth Century." *American Psychologist,* 1960, *15,* 256–265.

RIEU, E. V. (Translator) *Homer: The Iliad.* Hammondsworth, Middlesex: Penguin, 1950.

RIGAUD, F. E. (Editor and Translator) *A Treatise on Painting, by Leonardo Da Vinci.* London: George Bell and Sons, 1877.

ROBBINS, F. E. (Editor and Translator) *Ptolemy: Tetrabiblos.* Cambridge, Mass.: Harvard University Press, 1940.

ROGET, P. *Thesaurus of English Words and Phrases.* London: Longmen, Brown, Green, and Longmans, 1852.

ROLFE, J. C. *The Attic Nights of Aulus Gellius.* Vol. 1. Trans. by J. C. Rolfe. Cambridge, Mass.: Harvard Univ. Press, 1946.

SACHS, A. "Babylonian Horoscopes." *Journal of Cuneiform Studies,* 1952, *6,* 49–75.

SARTON, G. *A History of Science: Ancient Science Through the Golden Age of Greece.* New York: John Wiley, 1952.

SARTON, G. *A History of Science: Hellenistic Science and Culture in the Last Three Centuries B.C.* New York: John Wiley, 1959.

SCHURE, E. *The Ancient Mysteries of Delphi: Pythagoras.* New York: Rudolf Steiner Publications, 1971 (originally published 1889).

SHELDON, W. H., WITH STEVENS, S. S. AND TUCKER, W. B. *The Varieties of Human Physique: An Introduction to Constitutional Psychology.* New York: Harper and Row, 1940.

SPURZHEIM, G. *The Physiognomical System of Drs. Gall and Spurzheim.* London: Baldwin, Cradock and Joy, 1815.

SPURZHEIM, J. C. (Edited by A. A. Walsh) *Phrenology, or the Doctrine of Mental Phenomena.* Gainesville, Fla.: Scholars Facsimilies and Reprints, 1970 (original edition 1834).

STEINITZER, M. *Die Menschlichen und Tierischen Gemütsbewegungen als Gegenstand der Wissenschaft.* Munich, 1889.

STERN, M. B. *Heads and Headlines: The Phrenological Fowlers.* Norman, Okla.: University of Oklahoma Press, 1971.

TENG, SSU-YU. "Chinese Influence on the Western Examination System." *Harvard Journal of Asiatic Studies,* 1943, 7, 267–312.

THOMASIUS, C. *Das Verborgene des Herzens anderer Menschen auch wider ihren Willen laus der täglichen Conversation zuerkennen.* Christoph Salfeld, Halle, 1691.

THOMASIUS, C. *Weitere Erleuterung durch unterschiedene Exempel des ohnelangst gethanen Vorschlags wegen der neuen Wissenschaft Anderer Menschen Gemuther erkennenaulernen.* Christoph Salfeld, Halle, 1692.

TILLYARD, E. M. W. *The Elizabethan World Picture.* New York: Macmillan, 1944.

TREDENNICK, H. (Editor and Translator) *Aristotle's Prior Analytics.* Cambridge, Mass.: Harvard University Press, 1967.

WALSH, A. A. "Is Phrenology Foolish? A Rejoinder." *Journal of the History of the Behavioral Sciences,* 1970, 6, 358–361.

WATSON, R. I. *The Great Psychologists.* Philadelphia: J. B. Lippincott, 2nd edit., 1968.

WELLS, S. R. *New Physiognomy.* New York: Fowler and Wells, 1894.

WOLFF, C. *Psychologia Rationalis.* Frankfurti et Lipsiae, 1734.

WOLFF, C. *Psychologia Empirica* (2nd ed.) Frankfurti et Lipsiae, 1738 (1st edit., 1732).

WRIGHT, T. *The Passions of the Minds in Generall.* London: Miles Flesher, 1630 (Earlier editions 1601, 1604, 1620, 1621). Facsimile Edition, with an Introduction by T. O. Sloan. Urbana: University of Illinois Press, 1971.

Name Index

Subject Index

A

Accommodation, 102
Activation - Deactivation Adjective Check List, 279, 284
Activity Vector Analysis Check List, 278
Adaptation, 102
Adaptive behavior, 142, 147
Adjective check list: acquiescence and, 298-301; for children, 278; determinants of responses on, 294-302; methodology for, 296; as monitoring device, 282; reliability of, 284-287; self-concept scale of, 278; technique for, 275-312; validity of, 292-294. *See also* Gough-Heilbrun Adjective Chect List
Adjective Preference Scale, 279
Affect Adjective Check List (AACL), 278
Aggression, 11, 49; in children, 86-88
Aging, 216
Alcohol, 459
Alertness factor, 157, 160
Alpha wave, 434
American Psychological Association Committee on Test Standards, 314

Amphetamine, 458
ANOVA model, 60, 61, 62
Anoxia, 162, 163
Antecedent event, 127, 129
Anxiety proneness, 454, 455
Aphasia, 189, 204, 206, 217; test for, 204, 206, 207, 229
Approach-avoidance behavior, 358
Assertiveness measure, 374-376, 377, 379
Assimilation, 102
Astrology, 482, 484-487, 494, 498, 513, 525; horoscopal, 495
Attention, 442-443, 461; and EP, 450; selective, 446, 451, 462; thyroid and, 461
Autistic child, 35
Automated personality assessment, 265
Automated Tri-informant Goal Oriented Progress Note (ATGON), 402-403
Automation, 413, 414, 415
Averaged EEG measures, 433, 434-438, 441; and psychological processes, 442-452; and response time, 462
Aversive techniques, 372-373

B

Baugh Picture Completion Test, 323